T0111933

Cloud Security:

Concepts, Methodologies, Tools, and Applications

Information Resources Management Association
USA

Volume III

Published in the United States of America by
    IGI Global
    Engineering Science Reference (an imprint of IGI Global)
    701 E. Chocolate Avenue
    Hershey PA, USA 17033
    Tel: 717-533-8845
    Fax: 717-533-8661
    E-mail: cust@igi-global.com
    Web site: http://www.igi-global.com

Copyright © 2019 by IGI Global. All rights reserved. No part of this publication may be reproduced, stored or distributed in any form or by any means, electronic or mechanical, including photocopying, without written permission from the publisher. Product or company names used in this set are for identification purposes only. Inclusion of the names of the products or companies does not indicate a claim of ownership by IGI Global of the trademark or registered trademark.

Library of Congress Cataloging-in-Publication Data

Names: Information Resources Management Association, editor.
Title: Cloud security : concepts, methodologies, tools, and applications /
  Information Resources Management Association, editor.
Description: Hershey, PA : Engineering Science Reference, [2019] | Includes
  bibliographical references.
Identifiers: LCCN 2018048047| ISBN 9781522581765 (hardcover) | ISBN
  9781522581772 (ebook)
Subjects: LCSH: Cloud computing--Security measures.
Classification: LCC QA76.585 .C5864 2019 | DDC 004.67/82--dc23 LC record available at https://lccn.loc.gov/2018048047

British Cataloguing in Publication Data
A Cataloguing in Publication record for this book is available from the British Library.

The views expressed in this book are those of the authors, but not necessarily of the publisher.

For electronic access to this publication, please contact: eresources@igi-global.com.

Editor-in-Chief

Mehdi Khosrow-Pour, DBA
Information Resources Management Association, USA

Associate Editors

Steve Clarke, *University of Hull, UK*
Murray E. Jennex, *San Diego State University, USA*
Annie Becker, *Florida Institute of Technology, USA*
Ari-Veikko Anttiroiko, *University of Tampere, Finland*

Editorial Advisory Board

Sherif Kamel, *American University in Cairo, Egypt*
In Lee, *Western Illinois University, USA*
Jerzy Kisielnicki, *Warsaw University, Poland*
Amar Gupta, *Arizona University, USA*
Craig van Slyke, *University of Central Florida, USA*
John Wang, *Montclair State University, USA*
Vishanth Weerakkody, *Brunel University, UK*

List of Contributors

Table of Contents

Volume I

Section 1
Fundamental Concepts and Theories

Section 2
Development and Design Methodologies

Section 4
Utilization and Applications

Section 5
Organizational and Social Implications

Volume IV

Section 6
Managerial Impact

Section 7
Critical Issues and Challenges

Section 8
Emerging Trends

Preface

The constantly changing landscape of Cloud Security makes it challenging for experts and practitioners to stay informed of the field's most up-to-date research. That is why Engineering Science Reference is pleased to offer this four-volume reference collection that will empower students, researchers, and academicians with a strong understanding of critical issues within Cloud Security by providing both broad and detailed perspectives on cutting-edge theories and developments. This reference is designed to act as a single reference source on conceptual, methodological, technical, and managerial issues, as well as to provide insight into emerging trends and future opportunities within the discipline.

Cloud Security: Concepts, Methodologies, Tools, and Applications is organized into eight distinct sections that provide comprehensive coverage of important topics. The sections are:

1. Fundamental Concepts and Theories;
2. Development and Design Methodologies;
3. Tools and Technologies;
4. Utilization and Applications;
5. Organizational and Social Implications;
6. Managerial Impact;
7. Critical Issues and Challenges; and
8. Emerging Trends.

The following paragraphs provide a summary of what to expect from this invaluable reference tool.

Section 1, "Fundamental Concepts and Theories," serves as a foundation for this extensive reference tool by addressing crucial theories essential to the understanding of Cloud Security. Introducing the book is "Curtailing the Threats to Cloud Computing in the Fourth Industrial Revolution?" by John Gyang Chaka and Mudaray Marimuthu: a great foundation laying the groundwork for the basic concepts and theories that will be discussed throughout the rest of the book. Section 1 concludes and leads into the following portion of the book with a nice segue chapter, "Approaches to Cloud Computing in the Public Sector" by Jeffrey Chang and Mark Johnston.

Section 2, "Development and Design Methodologies," presents in-depth coverage of the conceptual design and architecture of Cloud Security. Opening the section is "A Multi-Dimensional Mean Failure Cost Model to Enhance Security of Cloud Computing Systems" by Mouna Jouini and Latifa Ben Arfa Rabai. Through case studies, this section lays excellent groundwork for later sections that will get into present and future applications for Cloud Security. The section concludes with an excellent work by Rekha Kashyap and Deo Prakash Vidyarthi, "A Secured Real Time Scheduling Model for Cloud Hypervisor."

Section 3, "Tools and Technologies," presents extensive coverage of the various tools and technologies used in the implementation of Cloud Security. The first chapter, "CCCE: Cryptographic Cloud Computing Environment Based on Quantum Computations" by Omer K. Jasim, Safia Abbas, El-Sayed M. El-Horbaty, and Abdel-Badeeh M. Salem, lays a framework for the types of works that can be found in this section. The section concludes with "Keystroke Dynamics Authentication in Cloud Computing" by Basma Mohammed Hassan, Khaled Mohammed Fouad, and Mahmoud Fathy Hassan. Where Section 3 described specific tools and technologies at the disposal of practitioners, Section 4 describes the use and applications of the tools and frameworks discussed in previous sections.

Section 4, "Utilization and Applications," describes how the broad range of Cloud Security efforts has been utilized and offers insight on and important lessons for their applications and impact. The first chapter in the section is "Cloud Computing and Cybersecurity Issues Facing Local Enterprises" written by Emre Erturk. This section includes the widest range of topics because it describes case studies, research, methodologies, frameworks, architectures, theory, analysis, and guides for implementation. The breadth of topics covered in the section is also reflected in the diversity of its authors, from countries all over the globe. The section concludes with "Necessity of Key Aggregation Cryptosystem for Data Sharing in Cloud Computing" by R. Deepthi Crestose Rebekah, Dhanaraj Cheelu, and M. Rajasekhara Babu, a great transition chapter into the next section.

Section 5, "Organizational and Social Implications," includes chapters discussing the organizational and social impact of Cloud Security. The section opens with "Impact of Technology Innovation: A Study on Cloud Risk Mitigation" by Niranjali Suresh and Manish Gupta. This section focuses exclusively on how these technologies affect human lives, either through the way they interact with each other or through how they affect behavioral/workplace situations. The section concludes with "Trust Management in Cloud Computing" by Vijay L. Hallappanavar and Mahantesh N. Birje.

Section 6, "Managerial Impact," presents focused coverage of Cloud Security in a managerial perspective. The section begins with "The Collaborative Use of Patients' Health-Related Information: Challenges and Research Problems in a Networked World" by Fadi Alhaddadin, Jairo A. Gutiérrez, and William Liu. This section serves as a vital resource for developers who want to utilize the latest research to bolster the capabilities and functionalities of their processes. The chapters in this section offer unmistakable value to managers looking to implement new strategies that work at larger bureaucratic levels. The section concludes with "Smart Healthcare Administration Over Cloud" by Govinda K. and S. Ramasubbareddy.

Section 7, "Critical Issues and Challenges," presents coverage of academic and research perspectives on Cloud Security tools and applications. The section begins with "A Comparative Study of Privacy Protection Practices in the US, Europe, and Asia" by Noushin Ashrafi and Jean-Pierre Kuilboer. Chapters in this section will look into theoretical approaches and offer alternatives to crucial questions on the subject of Cloud Security. The section concludes with "Privacy Preserving Public Auditing in Cloud: Literature Review" by Thangavel M., Varalakshmi P., Sridhar S., and Sindhuja R.

Section 8, "Emerging Trends," highlights areas for future research within the field of Cloud Security, opening with "Advances in Information, Security, Privacy, and Ethics: Use of Cloud Computing for Education" by Joseph M. Woodside. This section contains chapters that look at what might happen in the coming years that can extend the already staggering amount of applications for Cloud Security. The final chapter of the book looks at an emerging field within Cloud Security in the excellent contribution "Emerging Cloud Computing Services: A Brief Opinion Article" by Yulin Yao.

Although the primary organization of the contents in this multi-volume work is based on its eight sections, offering a progression of coverage of the important concepts, methodologies, technologies, applications, social issues, and emerging trends, the reader can also identify specific contents by utilizing the extensive indexing system listed at the end of each volume. As a comprehensive collection of research on the latest findings related to using technology to providing various services, *Cloud Security: Concepts, Methodologies, Tools, and Applications* provides researchers, administrators, and all audiences with a complete understanding of the development of applications and concepts in Cloud Security. Given the vast number of issues concerning usage, failure, success, policies, strategies, and applications of Cloud Security in countries around the world, *Cloud Security: Concepts, Methodologies, Tools, and Applications* addresses the demand for a resource that encompasses the most pertinent research in technologies being employed to globally bolster the knowledge and applications of Cloud Security.

Chapter 57
Secure Mobile Multi Cloud Architecture for Authentication and Data Storage

Karim Zkik
University of Mohammed V in Rabat, Morocco

Ghizlane Orhanou
University of Mohammed V in Rabat, Morocco

Said El Hajji
University of Mohammed V in Rabat, Morocco

ABSTRACT

The use of Cloud Computing in the mobile networks offer more advantages and possibilities to the mobile users such as storing, downloading and making calculation on data on demand and its offer more resources to these users such as the storage resources and calculation power. So, Mobile Cloud Computing allows users to fully utilize mobile technologies to store, to download, share and retrieve their personal data anywhere and anytime. As many recent researches show, the main problem of fully expansion and use of mobile cloud computing is security, and it's because the increasing flows and data circulation through internet that many security problems emerged and sparked the interest of the attackers. To face all this security problems, we propose in this paper an authentication and confidentiality scheme based on homomorphic encryption, and also a recovery mechanism to secure access for mobile users to the remote multi cloud servers. We also provide an implementation of our framework to demonstrate its robustness and efficiently, and a security analysis.

INTRODUCTION

The use of mobile technologies grew by a phenomenal way during the recent years. According to the annual report of Ericsson mobile traffic increased by 55% between 2013 and 2014, more than 4 billion smartphones available on the market in 2016, and 90% of the world population will have a smartphone by 2020. The use of cloud computing has contributed directly to increasing use of mobile services,

DOI: 10.4018/978-1-5225-8176-5.ch057

Copyright © 2019, IGI Global. Copying or distributing in print or electronic forms without written permission of IGI Global is prohibited.

because it allows users to freely access and use different platforms and applications, and it allows them to store their data in remote servers that they can access anytime and anywhere.

The major concern of the use of Cloud Mobile is security (Fernando, Seng, & Rahayu, 2013) because many attackers constantly try to take advantage of vulnerabilities in mobile networks to access data stored in the remote cloud servers. The use of multi Cloud Computing (Ardagna, 2015) instead of single cloud allowed to offer more possibility in terms of security and data management (Tebaa, & El Hajji, 2014; Aljawarneh, 2011). It allows among others to reduce the risk of data loss, it duplicates the resources and allows dividing the security tasks across multiple servers.

Despite the use of multi cloud services, there are still number of security concerns that are related to the limitation of mobile device resources, the possibility of connection through any network even if it is not secure and lack of authentication and encryption platforms in the majority of the existing mobile applications, in addition to the risk of infection by worms or other malicious codes (Aljawarneh & others, 2016).

The aim of our work is to develop a security platform that allows user authentication and data encryption. We will use for that the properties of homomorphic encryption to generate a robust electronic signature. Then we'll use the features of multi Cloud computing to enhance the authentication mechanism by dividing the verification tasks on different virtual machines so that an attacker will never be able to recover or intercept passwords or some other personal information of the concerned mobile user. We will also use a mechanism that classify the data according to their degree of sensitivity and generates a new password for each new connection to reduce the risk that an attacker can gain access to user's account. As high availability is one of the main aspects of security in Mobile Cloud Computing networks, we developed a recovery mechanism by adding a new backup server, which communicates with the storage server and can take over in case of infection and attacks or when the storage server is down.

The rest of paper is structured as follows. In section 2 we discuss some security notion that will be used in our framework, we enumerate some security issue of mobile networks in Cloud and Multi Cloud Computing and we present some related works. In section 3 we present our proposed framework, and we detail the generation of the homomorphic signature, the authentication and the confidentiality mechanism, and the recovery scheme. We present also a security analysis to prove the robustness of our framework. In section 4 we conclude the paper.

SECURITY CONCERN IN MOBILE CLOUD COMPUTING

Preliminaries

In this part, we will present some concepts that we used in designing our model, including the multi cloud computing, homomorphic encryption and security requirements in MCC, and we will present the main threats and attacks in a MCC environment.

Mobile Multi Cloud Computing

Mobile Cloud Computing is a model where applications and mobile data are downloaded stored and hosted using cloud computing technology. This technology allowed changing our lives because all data, applications and services that would be needed are now available anywhere and anytime. The mobile cloud computing is primarily used to deport our personal data from the mobile device to remote cloud servers.

Despite these advantages, the mobile cloud still suffers in terms of security because the data stored in the cloud are often personal and very sensitive. So, they are targeted by attackers who aim to exploit different vulnerabilities in computer networks in order to corrupt steal or delete this data.

To work around these problems Vukolic introduced the concept of multi cloud computing (Vukolic, 2010). So instead of deporting the data using a single cloud server, it is best done by using multi Cloud Servers to decrease the risk of losing data and making difficult corrupting or stealing the user identities. The use of multi-Cloud has opened several possibilities in terms of security and management of mobile networks. So, several studies have been based on the concept of multi Cloud Computing to build robust security architectures for mobile networks.

Homomorphic Encryption

The homomorphic encryption (Dagli, 2013) allows making calculations on encrypted data without decrypting it. The homomorphic cryptosystem used to perform calculations on the data stored on remote cloud servers without having to decrypt them. This mathematical concept has opened huge opportunities in terms of security and confidentiality of data, and it allows offering more privacy to users who use the services of Cloud Computing.

To mathematically explain the functioning of homomorphic encryption, we proceed as follows: Assume that we have two values a and b and E (a) and E (b) are their respective encrypted values so:

If $a \times b = c$ So $E(a) \times E(b) = E(c)$ (1)

Or if $a + b = c$ So $E(a) + E(b) = E(c)$ (2)

Several cryptosystems are homomorphic, for example RSA and Pailler. But this cryptosystem is very limited because they need so much time and calculation resources and they work only for addition or multiplication. Some studies try to find algorithms completely hommomophe (Gentry, 2009), but unfortunately, there are still not really applicable.

The homomorphic encryption seems to be the ideal solution for users of cloud computing, but its use poses some problems because its takes so much time to calculate the encrypted data and it consume so mush calculation resources. Some research (Johnson, Molnar, Song, & Wagner, 2002) trying to fully optimize the calculation time, but meanwhile to reach practical results, other studies use the homomorphic encryption to calculated very sensitive data with small size (Zkik, Tebaa, & El Hajji, 2015), or to calculate digital signatures (Zkik, Tebaa, & El Hajji, 2016).

Security Issues in MCC

The Mobile Cloud computing has become very popular and is increasingly used by different users. But there are several limitations that prevent its use. Despite the huge technological advances in manufacturing of mobile devices, they still suffer from limitations in terms of lifetimes of batteries, storage capacity and computational power. Various problems in terms of security also prevents the Mobile Cloud Computing to achieve a higher level of maturity, especially in relation to its use in banking transactions, the sharing of data and storing highly sensitive data. Several attackers try through these security vulnerabilities to recover the personal data of mobile users. So, several attacks have been developed, which primarily target the mobile cloud computing services:

- **Forgery Attack**: This attack allows attackers to forge validates digital signatures and tags during the exchanges of data between the different entities of the network, or when sending authentication or downloading requests.
- **Unauthorized Server Attack**: As the flow of data circulating between users and cloud servers is routed through internet, multiple attackers pass themselves as authentic cloud servers to retrieve all the flow of data. This type of attack is done through several ways, such as spoofing IP and MAC addresses.
- **Brute Force Attack**: Data encryption requires considerable computing power. The computing resource limitations in mobile require users to use small encryption keys, making them vulnerable to attacks by brute force.
- **Replay Attack**: Some attacks aimed at the listening of the network to gather fragments that constitute the personal data of users in order to generate valid identity, and later retrieve the data stored in the cloud server.

RELATED WORKS

Several security architectures have been constructed by using the Multi Cloud Computing. Mohammed A. AlZain and al. surveyed recent research related to single and multi-cloud security and addresses the existent solutions and their limitations (AlZain, Pardede, Soh, & Thom, 2012). Mojtaba Alizadeh discuss some recent research on authentication in mobile cloud computing, presents a comparison between all this authentication methods and architectures and they present their limitations (Alizadeh, Abolfazli, Zamani, Baharun, & Sakurai, 2015).

Several security frameworks in mobile network and mobile computing are made during the recent years that aim to ensure the authentication, the confidentiality and the privacy. Maya Louk and al. made an implementation and an evaluation of Homomorphic Encryption in Mobile Multi Cloud Computing (Louk, & Lim, 2015). Jeong et al. proposed a multi-factor authentication method for Mobile Cloud and it use different authentication features such as basic ID/password, mobile identification number, and various bio-information of user are combined to preserve security (Jeong, Park, & Park, 2015). Dey et al. proposed an authentication scheme using MDA that protect mobile user against different potential security attacks (Dey, & Sampalli, 2013). Omri et al. proposed to use user handwriting as an authentication factor to access the cloud securely (Omri, Hamil, Foufou, & Jarraya, 2012).

PROPOSED MOBILE MULTI CLOUD SECURITY SCHEME

The aim of our work is to build a security architecture for mobile networks that enables secure access to remote cloud servers. The proposed structure should be light to not overload mobile devices and offers a good level of integrity, authentication and security. In order to exploit the benefits of homomorphic encryption, we'll use it to build a mechanism that generates and verifies the validity of a digital signature instead of using the homomorphic encryption to encrypt data on the network which can overload the machine. We'll also build an authentication mechanism that is based on using multi Cloud Computing and then we will propose an encryption mechanism that fits with the degree of sensitivity of the transferred data.

Homomorphic Signature Scheme

To sign a message, we generally use a standards hash functions and the signature is often based on the ID number of the user. After that we encrypt the signature using a well-known crypto system. But, there are several deficiencies in this model:

- A key exchange is required between the mobile client and the server to encrypt the signature, so an attacker can easily sniff data on the network in order to collect the encryption keys.
- In most hash functions used it can be easily to find the text in clear. So an attacker can find the security settings used from a certain number of communications between the mobile client and the server, and then retrieve the user's ID.
- In the standards generation and signature verification scheme, there is usually just one parameter to check the validity of the signature. So the attacker can easily fool the server and forge a valid signature.

To bypass this problem, it is proposed to use a homomorphic signature based on several parameters including the user ID and the time t of generation of the signature. This scheme was introduced by Zhiwei Wang and al. and we have using it in earlier work in a cloud computing environment. It is proposed in this paper to use homomorphic signature to secure client-server communication in a mobile multi cloud environment, which will allow us to have more flexibility and data security.

For forging our homomorphic signatures, we proceed as shows in Figure 1. The mobile generates a private key SK and a public key PK, and then he will compute the signature using a hash function H, his ID attributes vi, the time of generation of the signature t and a chosen random elements ri, mi and u.

For every attribute of the identity vi we will calculate a part of the signature si:

$$S_i = ((r_i)^{v_i} \times u^{m_i})^{1/T} (\mathrm{mod}\, N) \tag{3}$$

The full signature is:

$$Sig = (Sig_1, ..., Sig_n) \text{ as } Sig_i = (S_i, m_i, T) \tag{4}$$

The mobile device sends the full signature to the distant cloud server. To verify this signature the server will compute a partial signature on a vector Ni that it made from one ID attribute and 0, and then it will compute a verification value x and it will compare it with the full signature received from the mobile device:

Figure 1. Homomorphic signature scheme

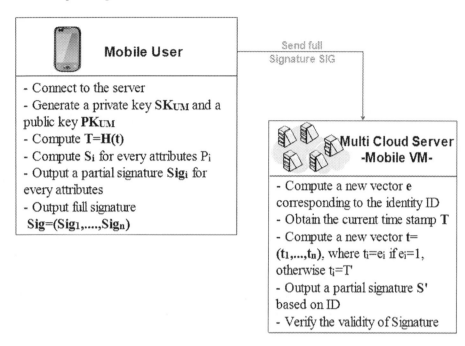

$$S'_i = \prod_{i=1}^{n} S_i^{N_i} \tag{5}$$

$$x = \prod_{i=1}^{n} r_i^{v_i} \times u^{v'} \text{ as } v' = \sum_{i=1}^{n} N_i \times v_i \tag{6}$$

if $Sig^T = x (\mathrm{mod}\, N)$ output 1, otherwise output 0. (7)

The homomorphic aspect of our mechanism appears in the fact that the signature verification is made without having to decipher it. The homomorphic scheme helps to forge a robust signature, very difficult to usurp by malicious persons, because the verification requires no key exchange and the verification is made from two parameters time and ID which increases the robustness and the efficiency of this mechanism.

We will use this signature scheme in our authentication mechanism to ensure confidentiality and integrity of all messages transiting through the network and to more secure communication between the mobile device and remote multi cloud servers.

Authentication and Confidentiality Scheme

The mobile devices are often the most vulnerable point in mobile network architecture, because they are relatively easy to infect, users usually have no knowledge in computer security, and it is very easy to

Figure 2. Secure communication between access plan and multi cloud server

recover mobile data at its loss or theft. Mobile devices can easily be infected by malware or other malicious programs because the several vulnerabilities in mobile's operating systems. According to a study conducted by the Alcatel-Lucent group, more than 16 million mobile devices were infected by a single virus in 2014. There are many attacks aiming to infect mobiles as the Spoofing attacks, malware infections and DoS and DDoS attacks, but generally the attacks on mobiles devices have two main goals. The first goal would be to infect the mobile in order to recover all kinds of data, passwords and confidential personal information of the user and the second goal is to infect the mobile in order to reach network and mobile Cloud equipment to which it is connected. The second scenario is more dangerous and more complex because it allows the attacker to infect other users, or to infect other equipment in the network architecture (Router, switches, servers, remote cloud servers and controller).

Our concern in this section is securing the communication and the flow between mobile users and remote cloud servers. For that we will propose an authentication and encryption mechanism. We'll use the one-time password at each login attempts to ensure more safety during client-server communications. As shown in Figure 2, we propose a client-server communication mechanism for authentication, integrity, confidentiality and privacy in a Mobile Cloud Computing environment. Our scheme works as follow:

Authentication

Authentication is considered as a critical aspect of security enforcement in Mobile Cloud Computing. The authentication process is essential to validate the identity of the mobile user and to protect users against existing security threats by preventing unauthorized access to the mobile cloud user information. Therefore, considering the limitation of the mobile Cloud Computing, authentication solutions are expected to be lightweight with the least possible computing, memory, and storage overheads.

The main goal of our authentication scheme is to offer a good level of security to the mobile user without overloading the mobile device without being complex using just a few parameters and steps. Our scheme works as follow:

Each user must authenticate to the cloud server to initiate the communication. The authentication request is constructed from the personal data of the user (ID, password PWD, Phone number PN), the international mobile equipment identity (IMEI) and International Mobile subscriber identity (IMSI). The authentication request must be encrypted using RSA to bypass impersonation attacks. The choice of this crypto system based on the fact that it is very robust, and that the request is not voluminous, allowing its use without risking to overload machine with calculations. To ensure the integrity of the request we will forge an electronic signature using robust hash functions:

$$\text{Re}\,q = E(ID, PWD, PN), E(IMEI, IMSI);$$
$$Sig = H(\text{Re}\,q); \tag{8}$$
$$Auth\_\text{Re}\,q = \text{Re}\,q, Sig;$$

Verification

In this step the cloud verify the authentication request and signature. For verification, we use the properties of multi Cloud to reduce the time of an authentication procedure. In this procedure each individual VMs process each factor of authentication simultaneously.

The Cloud server will decrypt the authentication request and verify the validity of the mobile user, and it will verify the validity of the homomorphic signature to ensure the integrity and verify the authenticity of these data.

One Time Password

One of the most dangerous attack on MCC is the replay attack, and it's occur when using the same password for a long time. To prevent this type of attack we propose the use of one-time password to reduce the risk of an external attack. To do this we precede as follow:

The Cloud sends a one-time password (OTP) to the user to open a secure communication channel. When the user quit the session, he must ask for another One Time Password for another connexion.

$$OTP = E(Session\_PWD), H(E(Session\_PWD)) \tag{9}$$

The use of this procedure gives more safety to users, and avoids the risk of loss sensitive data when losing password or the mobile device.

Data Encryption

To ensure privacy and confidentiality we will encrypt users' data before storing them in the cloud server. But as we know, the mobile devices cannot encrypt a big volume of data using a robust crypto system, because it will be overloaded.

To bypass this problem, the encryption will be done according to the sensitivity level of data. We will split our data into two main categories: Sensitive data that will be encrypted using a robust crypto system as RSA, and Public data that will be encrypted by using somehow weak crypto system, which does not need a lot off processing calculation power and using a small key size like 3DES to keep a minimum security level.

This process enables the encryption of data without overloading the mobile device with the calculations. The user generates a new electronic signature from the one-time password and then he sends this signature and the encrypted data in one package to the remote cloud server.

- *Input Data, OPT;*
- *Output Enc_Data; //Encrypted data*
    - *if data_type=1 //sensitive data*
    - *{Encryption with (ECC, RSA)*
    - *Sig= E(ID,OPT);*
    - *Enc_Data=E(OTP, DATA),Sig;*
    - *Export.Enc_Data;}*
    - *if data_type=0 //public data*
    - *{Encryption with (AES, 3DES);*
    - *Enc_Data=E(OTP, DATA),Sig;*
- *Export.Enc_Data;}*

Storing Data

Finally, the cloud server receives the encrypted data and verifies the validity of signatures and data before storing them.

We will also use a VM in the Multi cloud to register the activity logs, to better detect penetrations or infections attempts on our network.

Recovery Scheme

To better secure our platform and improve its quality of services, it is necessary to provide a mechanism that ensures high availability. For this we propose to use the various advantages of multi Cloud Computing and to build an efficient recovery mechanism.

Several attacks may damage the operation of cloud services especially DoS and DDoS attacks that can disable several remote cloud servers. Other problems can also cause a malfunction of cloud services like when an application enters into an infinite loop or when servers are overloaded.

Many researches propose recovery mechanism to protect networks and ensure the availability to their platform (Fonseca, Bennesby, Mota, & Passito, 2012). To secure our Mobile Cloud Servers we will also build a recovery mechanism that it adapted to our network. The purpose of this mechanism is to allow mobile users to recover their data at any time even after an attack or malfunction of the remote cloud server. For that we will develop a recovery mechanism that duplicate data and store them on a backup server. This mechanism will allow us to ensure the high availability of our network.

As shown in Figure 3 the backup server periodically receives updates from the central server and it takes over in case of rupture of connection from the central server.

We will describe the behavior of our servers during normal operation and during an external attack. Our mechanism in the first case is as follows:

1. The server receives the data from different mobile users to store them and then it verifies their authenticity by checking the validity of the received homomorphic signature.
2. The server duplicates received data and send a copy to the backup server.
3. The backup server sends a message confirming the reception of data.
4. In case of any modification on stored data, the central server informs immediately the backup server using the state update messages.

Figure 3. Recovery scheme

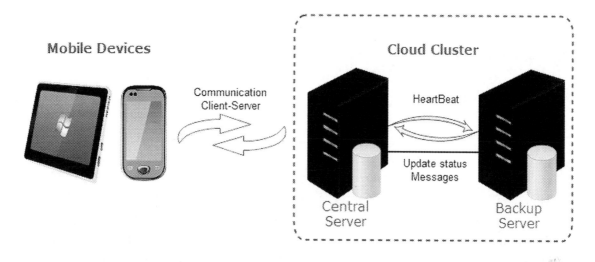

Communication between the central server and the back-up server is maintained by the heartbeat messages.

In case of inactivity or communications breaking during a period T, the back-up server assumes that the central server is down. Functioning of our mechanism in this case is as follows:

1. The packets are redirected to the backup server, which is now responsible for receiving data from mobile users.
2. The backup server to verify the authenticity and validity of the data before storing them
3. A Failure Report is sent to administrators to neutralize the attack. Once the problem solved the central server resumes those functions.

SIMULATION RESULTS

Environment

Practical simulation is performed in a personal computer, with the following characteristics:

- Intel(R) Core(TM) i7-2670QM CPU @ 2.20GHz (8 CPUs), ~2.2GHz.
- Memory 8192 MB RAM

We used a private Cloud to simulate the communication with the mobile device and the remote Cloud server.

For that we used a PC Server with the following characteristics:

- HP DL380G6 Xeon quad-core E5504 2.00GHz
- Memory 16000 MB RAM 4-core

- Memory 2To
- Open source virtualization platform XEN server

In our simulation, we used also a mobile device with the following characteristics:

- Processor dual-core 1.2GHz.
- Memory 2 Go

RESULTS

We will present in this section, the simulation results of the implementation of our framework. We'll start by generating an authentication request and a homomorphic signature from the mobile user parameters. After, we will initiate communication with the remote cloud server. Then we will encrypt mobile data before storing them in the remote server. Table 1 shows the results of the various steps of our model.

We have simulated a DoS attack to demonstrate the robustness is the effectiveness of our recovery scheme.

As shown in Figure 4, the attack can be initiated in two different ways. The attacker can directly launch a DoS attack on the server in order to saturate it or install a botnet network on mobile devices and then launch a DDoS attack on the server from these infected mobile devices.

Table 1. Test of use of our framework

Registration: (Mobile Device)	
Login:	Karim.zkik
Password:	LabMia2016
Authentication: (Mobile Device)	
Phone_Number	0668541985
ID	001
IMEI	353750060723890
N = p*q:	88407837176022112881193105375012785 1754
Time Digest	3881c655f1ff1de774005f8da13f4294
Homomorphic Signature	4733881961518405385573053642078479894671610504189158496210120369289787389236892576306852636422506666650118258540381433947290705423107441743566746108682776615620672394494686318186439230594326490208763699147561886053624304563561937095967680895926766398265137037501105960099781987233964086899293030752627032123 78168
Authentication Request	aab3238922bcc25a6f606eb525ffdc56
Verification: (Central Server)	
Partial Homomorphique Signature	178179480135440826416015625
Verifaction	1
Opening a Communication Canal: (Central Server)	
One Time Password	F52A23BD

Figure 4. Simulation of DoS attack

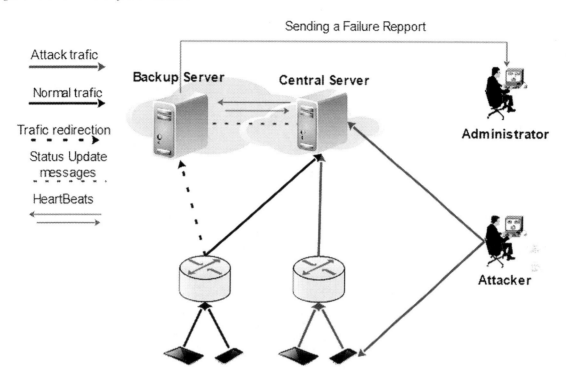

The second attack can be more dangerous because the attack is launched on several fronts, and it is more difficult to find the identity of the attacker in this case.

To avoid damage that can be caused due to such attacks, we have set up a backup server that takes over in case of infection on the central server. Administrators must be informed immediately by the attack and they will block any suspicious flows and put in place adequate security measures, in order to permit to the central server to regain its normal functions.

The results of our test conclude that our platform can store user data safely by ensuring its confidentiality, integrity, along with user privacy and ensure service availability.

Security Analysis

We will propose in this part a performance and security analysis of our model. We will discuss first performance and flexibility of our model, then we will discuss the different possible attacks in a sensor network, and the various countermeasures established in this direction.

Figure 5 shows the generation time of the encryption keys and the generation time of the homomorphic signature.

Figure 6 shows the consumption of CPU when generating the keys and the signature.

Despite the excessive need of homomorphic encryption for resources, it is clear that the use of this type of encryption for signature generation does not take much time, and it does not consume a lot of hardware resources of the mobile devices and in addition it offers a strength level of security especially in terms of integrity.

Figure 5. Key and signature generation

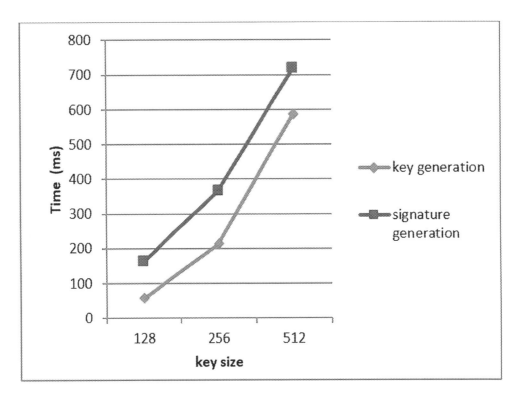

Figure 6. CPU consumption

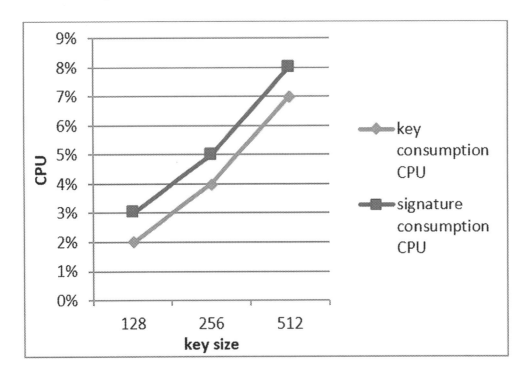

Using a recovery scheme allows ensuring resilience and high availability on our mobile cloud network.

Figure 7 shows the behavior of the central storage server and the backup server during a denial of service attack. In order to perform this attack, we use the software h3 ping and we made the attack on a private cloud in our laboratory using a HP DL380G6 Xeon server and many virtual machines.

Table 2 shows the various safety aspects of our architecture as offers data compared to other existing architecture.

Figure 7. Recovery scheme during a DoS attack

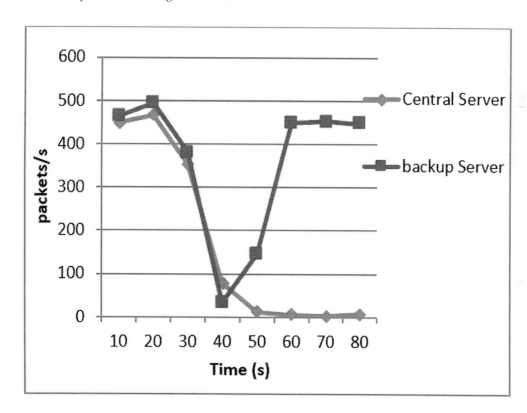

Table 2. Comparison of security frameworks in mcc

	M. Louk	**Y. S. Jeong**	**S. Dey**	**F. Omri**	**Our Architecture**
Authentication	No	Yes	Yes	Yes	Yes
Homomorphic encryption	Yes	No	No	No	Yes
Data Confidentiality	Yes	No	Yes	No	Yes
Secure password	No	No	No	Yes	Yes
Data Integrity	No	Yes	Yes	Yes	Yes
High-Availability	No	No	No	No	Yes
Privacy	Yes	No	No	No	Yes
Recovery Scheme	No	No	No	No	Yes

Our architecture has a light authentication mechanism based on the properties of multi Cloud Computing and uses the concept of the one-time password. This mechanism makes our architecture more secure and it ensures that users do not risk losing their sensitives data even if they lose their mobile devices.

In terms of confidentiality we have developed a system that classifies data of users according to their importance and their sensitivities. So we will not need to encrypt all mobile data to avoid overloading the device with additional calculations and we can encrypt the most sensitive data while providing more security to users.

CONCLUSION

Mobile Multi Cloud Computing is more and more used as it offers enormous facilities in terms of management of networks and it provides agility and flexibility. The use of Multi Cloud Computing in mobile networks offers huge benefits for mobile operators and cloud services concerning the management of flows, but there are several security problems that emerged and that disrupt its use and deployment.

We have developed a security architecture that can generate a homomorphic signature to ensure the integrity and which has an authentication scheme, a classification mechanism and a data encryption scheme. We developed a recovery mechanism to ensure the high availability and to prevent our network from distributing denial of services attack.

We made a security analysis to show the strength of our platform and we made a little comparison with existing work.

Regarding our future work, we would like to develop a fully homomorphic signing protocol to be more efficient, and it is expected to develop more suitable encryption system for Multi Mobile Cloud Computing environment.

REFERENCES

Alizadeh, M., Abolfazli, S., Zamani, M., Baharun, S., & Sakurai, K. (2015). Authentication in mobile cloud computing: A survey. *Journal of Network and Computer Applications, 61*, 59–80.

Aljawarneh, S. (2011). Cloud Security Engineering: Avoiding Security Threats the Right Way. *International Journal of Cloud Applications and Computing, 1*(2), 64–70. doi:10.4018/ijcac.2011040105

Aljawarneh, S. A., Moftah, R. A., & Maatuk, A. M. (2016). Investigations of automatic methods for detecting the polymorphic worms signatures. *Future Generation Computer Systems, 60*, 67–77. doi:10.1016/j.future.2016.01.020

AlZain, A. M., Pardede, E., Soh, B., & Thom, A. J. (2012). Cloud computing security: from single to multi-clouds. *Proceedings of the 45th Hawaii International Conference on System Science* (pp. 5491- 5499).

Ardagna, D. (2015). Cloud and Multi-Cloud Computing: Current Challenges and Future Applications. *Proceedings of the IEEE/ACM 7th International Workshop on Principles of Engineering Service-Oriented and Cloud Systems.*

Dagli, H. (2013). Homomorphic Encryption. *Procedia Computer Science*, *20*, 502–509. doi:10.1016/j.procs.2013.09.310

Dey, S., & Sampalli, S. (2013). Message digest as authentication entity for mobile cloud computing. *Proceedings of the 32nd international performance computing and communications conference*, San Diego, USA. IEEE.

Fernando, N., Seng, W. L., & Rahayu, W. (2013). Mobile cloud computing: A survey. *Future Generation Computer Systems*, *29*(1), 84–106. doi:10.1016/j.future.2012.05.023

Fonseca, P., Bennesby, R., Mota, E., & Passito, A. (2012). A Replication Component for Resilient OpenFlow-based Networking. *Proceedings of the IEEE Network Operations and Management Symposium (NOMS) Mini-Conference*. 10.1109/NOMS.2012.6212011

Gentry, C. (2009) Fully homomorphic encryption using ideal lattices. *Proceedings of the forty-first annual ACM symposium on Theory of computing STOC 09* (pp. 169-178).

Jeong, Y. S., Park, J. S., & Park, J. H. (2015). An efficient authentication system of smart device using multi factors in mobile cloud service architecture. *International Journal of Communication Systems*, *28*(4), 659–674. doi:10.1002/dac.2694

Johnson, R., Molnar, D., Song, D., & Wagner, D. (2002). Homomorphic signature schemes. In L. N. C. S. Springer (Ed.), *Topics in Cryptology CT-RSA 2002* (Vol. 2271, pp. 244–262). doi:10.1007/3-540-45760-7_17

Louk, M., & Lim, H. (2015). Homomorphic Encryption in Mobile Multi Cloud Computing. *Proceedings of IEEE ICOIN* (pp. 493-497).

Omri, F., Hamila, R., Foufou, S., & Jarraya, S. (2012). Cloud-ready biometric system for mobile security access. In R. Benlamri (Ed.), *Networked digital technologies, CCIS* (Vol. 294, pp. 192–200). Berlin: Springer.

Tebaa, M., & El Hajji, S. (2014). From Single to Multi-Clouds Computing Privacy and Fault Tolerance. *Proceedings of the International Conference on Future Information Engineering* (pp. 112-118). 10.1016/j.ieri.2014.09.099

Vukolic, M. (2010). The Byzantine empire in the intercloud. *ACM SIGACT News*, *41*(3), 105–111. doi:10.1145/1855118.1855137

Zkik, K., Tebaa, M., & El Hajji, S. (2015). New Homomorphic Platform for Authentication and Downloading Data. *Proceedings of The World Congress on Engineering '15* (pp. 508-514).

Zkik, K., Tebaa, M., & El Hajji S. (2016). A New Secure Framework in MCC Using Homomorphic Signature: Application in Banking Data. In *Transactions on Engineering Technologies* (pp. 413-427). Springer Singapore.

This research was previously published in the International Journal of Cloud Applications and Computing (IJCAC), 7(2); edited by B. B. Gupta and Dharma P. Agrawal, pages 62-76, copyright year 2017 by IGI Publishing (an imprint of IGI Global).

Chapter 58

Data Storage Security Service in Cloud Computing:
Challenges and Solutions

Alshaimaa Abo-alian
Ain Shams University, Egypt

Nagwa L. Badr
Ain Shams University, Egypt

Mohamed F. Tolba
Ain Shams University, Egypt

ABSTRACT

Cloud computing is an emerging computing paradigm that is rapidly gaining attention as an alternative to other traditional hosted application models. The cloud environment provides on-demand, elastic and scalable services, moreover, it can provide these services at lower costs. However, this new paradigm poses new security issues and threats because cloud service providers are not in the same trust domain of cloud customers. Furthermore, data owners cannot control the underlying cloud environment. Therefore, new security practices are required to guarantee the availability, integrity, privacy and confidentiality of the outsourced data. This paper highlights the main security challenges of the cloud storage service and introduces some solutions to address those challenges. The proposed solutions present a way to protect the data integrity, privacy and confidentiality by integrating data auditing and access control methods.

INTRODUCTION

Cloud computing can be defined as a type of computing in which dynamically scalable resources (i.e. storage, network, and computing) are provided on demand as a service over the Internet. The service delivery model of cloud computing is the set of services provided by cloud computing that is often referred to as an SPI model, i.e., Software as a Service (SaaS), Platform as a Service (PaaS) and Infrastructure as a Service (IaaS). In a SaaS model, the cloud service providers (CSPs) install and operate application

DOI: 10.4018/978-1-5225-8176-5.ch058

Copyright © 2019, IGI Global. Copying or distributing in print or electronic forms without written permission of IGI Global is prohibited.

software in the cloud and the cloud users can then access the software from cloud clients. The users do not purchase software, but rather rent it for use on a subscription or pay-per-use model, e.g. Google Docs (Attebury, George, Judd, & Marcum, 2008). The SaaS clients do not manage the cloud infrastructure and platform on which the application is running. In a PaaS model, the CSPs deliver a computing platform which includes the operating system, programming language execution environment, web server and database. Application developers can subsequently develop and run their software solutions on a cloud platform. With PaaS, developers can often build web applications without installing any tools on their computer, and can hereafter deploy those applications without any specialized system administration skills (Tim, Subra, & Shahed, 2009). Examples of PaaS providers are Windows Azure (Chambers, 2013) and Google App Engine (Pandey & Anjali, 2013). The IaaS model provides the infrastructure (i.e., computing power, network and storage resources) to run the applications. Furthermore, it offers a pay-per-use pricing model and the ability to scale the service depending on demand. Examples of IaaS providers are Amazon EC2 (Gonzalez, Border, & Oh, 2013) and Terremark (Srinivasan, 2014).

Cloud services can be deployed in four ways depending upon the clients' requirements. The cloud deployment models are public cloud, private cloud, community cloud and hybrid cloud. In the public cloud (or external cloud), a cloud infrastructure is hosted, operated, and managed by a third party vendor from one or more data centers (Tim, Subra, & Shahed, 2009).The network, computing and storage infrastructure is shared with other organizations. Multiple enterprises can work simultaneously on the infrastructure provided. Users can dynamically provide resources through the internet from an off-site service provider (Bhadauria & Sanyal, 2012). In the private cloud, cloud infrastructure is dedicated to a specific organization and is managed either by the organization itself or third party service provider. This emulates the concept of virtualization and cloud computing on private networks. Infrastructure, in the community cloud, is shared by several organizations for a shared reason and may be managed by themselves or a third party service provider. Infrastructure is located at the premises of a third party. Hybrid cloud consists of two or more different cloud deployment models bound together by standardized technology, which enables data portability between them. With a hybrid cloud, organizations might run non-core applications in a public cloud, while maintaining core applications and sensitive data in-house in a private cloud (Tim, Subra, & Shahed, 2009).

A cloud storage system (CSS) can be considered a network of distributed data centers which typically uses cloud computing technologies like virtualization, and offers some kind of interface for storing data (Borgmann, *et al.*, 2012). Data may be redundantly stored at different locations in order to increase its availability. Examples of such basic cloud storage services are Amazon S3 (Berriman, *et al.*, 2013) and Rackspace (Garg, Versteeg, & Buyya, 2013). One fundamental advantage of using a CSS is the cost effectiveness, where data owners avoid the initial investment of expensive large equipment purchasing, infrastructure setup, configuration, deployment and frequent maintenance costs (Abo-alian, Badr, & Tolba, 2015). Instead, data owners pay for only the resources they actually use and for only the time they require them. Elasticity is also a key advantage of using a CSS, as storage resources could be allocated dynamically as needed, without human interaction. Scalability is another gain of adopting a CSS because Cloud storage architecture can scale horizontally or vertically, according to demand, i.e., new nodes can be added or dropped as needed. Moreover, a CSS offers more reliability and availability, as data owners can access their data from anywhere and at any time (Abo-alian, Badr, & Tolba, 2016). Furthermore, Cloud service providers use several replicated sites for business continuity and disaster recovery reasons.

Despite the appealing advantages of cloud storage services, they also bring new and challenging security threats towards users outsourced data. Since cloud service providers (CSPs) are separate administrative entities, the correctness and the confidentiality of the data in the cloud is at risk due to the following reasons: First, since cloud infrastructure is shared between organizations, it is still facing the broad range of both internal and external threats to data integrity, for example, outages of cloud services such as the breakdown of Amazon EC2 in 2010 (Miller, 2010). Second, users no longer physically possess the storage of their data, i.e., data is stored and processed remotely. So, they may worry that their data could be misused or accessed by unauthorized users. For example, a dishonest CSP may sell the confidential information about an enterprise to the enterprise's closest business competitors for profit. Third, there are various motivations for the CSP to behave disloyally towards the cloud users regarding their outsourced data status. For example, the CSP might reclaim storage for monetary reasons by discarding data that has not been or is rarely accessed or even hide data loss incidents to maintain a reputation (Cong, Ren, Lou, & Li, 2010). In a nutshell, although outsourcing data to the cloud is economically attractive for long term large scale storage, the data security in cloud storage systems is a prominent problem. Cloud storage systems do not immediately offer any guarantee of data integrity, confidentiality, and availability. As a result, the CSP should adopt data security practices to ensure that their clients' data is available, correct and safe from unauthorized access and disclosure.

Downloading all the data and checking on retrieval is the traditional method for verifying the data integrity but it causes high transmission costs and heavy I/O overheads. Furthermore, checking data integrity when accessing data is not sufficient to guarantee the integrity and availability for all the stored data in the cloud because there is no assurance for the data that is rarely accessed. Thus, it is essential to have storage auditing services that verify the integrity of outsourced data and to provide proof to data owners that their data is correctly stored in the cloud.

Traditional server-based access control methods such as Access Control List (ACL) (Shalabi, Doll, Reilly, & Shore, 2011) cannot be directly applied to cloud storage systems because data owners do not fully trust the cloud service providers. Additionally, traditional cryptographic solutions cannot be applied directly while sharing data on cloud servers because these solutions require complicated key management and high storage overheads on the server. Moreover, the data owners have to stay online all the time to deliver the keys to new users. Therefore, it is crucial to have an access control method that restricts and manages access to data and ensure that the outsourced data is safe from unauthorized access and disclosure.

In this paper, an extensive survey of cloud storage auditing and access control methods is presented. Moreover, an evaluation of these methods against different performance criteria is conducted. The rest of the paper is organized as follows. Section 2 overviews various cloud storage auditing methods. Section 3 presents some literature methods for cloud access control. A comparative analysis of some existing data security methods in cloud computing is provided in section 4. Section 5 discusses the limitations of different data security methods in cloud computing and provides some concluding remarks that can be used in designing new data security practices. Finally, we conclude in section 6.

DATA STORAGE AUDITING METHODS

This section first defines the system model and security model of data storage auditing schemes within cloud computing. Then, the existing data storage auditing methods that are classified into different categories are presented.

Data storage auditing can be defined as a method that enables data owners to check the integrity of remote data without downloading the data or explicit knowledge of the entire data (Blum, Evans, Gemmell, Kannan, & Naor, 1994). Any system model of auditing scheme consists of three entities as mentioned in (Liu, Zhang, & Lun, 2013):

1. **Data Owner:** An entity which has large data files to be stored in the cloud and can be either individual consumers or organizations.
2. **Cloud Storage Server (CSS):** An entity which is managed by a Cloud Service Provider (CSP) and has significant storage space and computation resources to maintain clients' data.
3. **Third Party Auditor or Verifier (TPA):** An entity which has expertise and capabilities to check the integrity of data stored on CSS.

In the security model of most data auditing schemes, the auditor is assumed to be honest-but-curious. It performs honestly during the entire auditing protocol but it is curious about the received data. So, it is essential to keep the data confidential and invisible to the auditor during the auditing protocol, but the cloud storage server could be dishonest and may launch the following attacks (Yang & Xiaohua, 2014):

1. **Replace Attack:** The server may choose another valid and uncorrupted pair of the data block and data tag (m_k, t_k) to replace the challenged pair of the data block and data tag (m_i, t_i), when it has already discarded m_i or t_i.
2. **Forge Attack:** The server may forge the data tag of the data block and deceive the auditor if the owner's secret tag keys are reused for the different versions of data.
3. **Replay Attack:** The server may generate the proof from the previous proof or other information, without retrieving the actual owners' data.

As illustrated in Figure 1, a data auditing storage scheme should basically consist of five algorithms (Abo-Alian, Badr, & Tolba, 2016):

1. **Key Generation:** It is run by the data owner. It takes as input security parameter 1^λ and outputs a pair of private and public keys (sk, pk).
2. **Tag Generation:** It is run by the data owner to generate the verification metadata, i.e., data block tags. It takes as inputs a public key pk, a secret key sk and the file blocks b. It outputs the verifiable block tags T_b.
3. **Challenge:** It is run by the auditor in order to randomly generate a challenge that indicates the specific blocks. These random blocks are used as a request for a proof of possession.
4. **Response/Proof:** It is run by the CSP, upon receiving the challenge, to generate a proof that is used in the verification. In this process, the CSP proves that it is still correctly storing all file blocks.
5. **Verify:** It is run by the auditor in order to validate a proof of possession. It outputs TRUE if the verification equation passed or FALSE otherwise.

The existing data storage auditing schemes can be basically classified into two main categories:

Figure 1. Structure of an auditing scheme

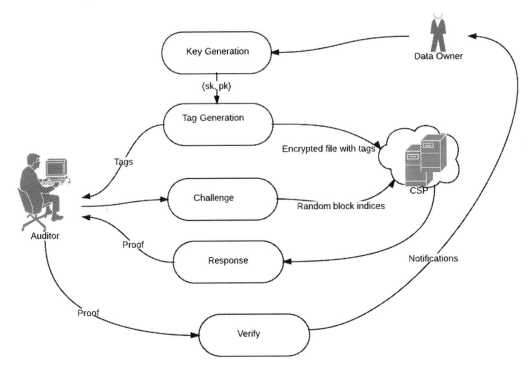

1. **Provable Data Possession (PDP) Methods:** For verifying the integrity of data without sending it to untrusted servers, the auditor verifies probabilistic proofs of possession by sampling random sets of blocks from the cloud service provider (Ateniese, *et al.*, 2007).
2. **Proof of Retrievability (PoR) Methods:** A set of randomly valued check blocks called sentinels are embedded into the encrypted file. For auditing the data storage, the auditor challenges the server by specifying the positions of a subset of sentinels and asking the server to return the associated sentinel values (Juels & Kaliski, 2007).

The existing data storage auditing methods can be further classified into several categories according to:

1. **The Type of the Auditor/Verifier:** Public auditing or private auditing.
2. **The Distribution of Data to be Audited:** Single-copy or multiple-copy data.
3. **The Data Persistence:** Static or dynamic data.

Public Auditing vs. Private Auditing

Considering the role of the auditor in the auditing model, data storage auditing schemes fall into two categories; private auditing and pubic auditing (Zheng & Xu, 2012). In private auditing, only data owners can challenge the CSS to verify the correctness of their outsourced data (Yang & Jia, 2012).Unfortunately, private auditing schemes have two limitations: (a) They impose an online burden on the data owner to verify data integrity and (b) The data owner must have huge computational capabilities for auditing.

Examples of auditing schemes that only support private auditing are (Chen & Curtmola, 2012; Chen & Curtmola, 2013; Mukundan, Madria, & Linderman, 2012; Etemad & Kupcu, 2013). In public auditing or third party auditing (Zhu, Ahn, Hu, Yau, An, & Hu, 2013), data owners are able to delegate the auditing task to an independent third party auditor (TPA), without the devotion of their computational resources. However, pubic auditing schemes should guarantee that the TPA keeps no private information about the verified data. Several variations of PDP schemes that support public auditing such as (Chen & Curtmola, 2013; Mukundan, Madria, & Linderman, 2012; Fujisaki & Okamoto, 1999; Abo-alian, Badr, & Tolba, 2015), were proposed under different cryptographic primitives.

Auditing Single-Copy vs. Multiple-Copy Data

For verifying the integrity of outsourced data in the cloud storage, various auditing schemes have been proposed which can be categorized into:

1. Auditing schemes for single-copy data.
2. Auditing schemes for multiple-copy data.

Auditing Schemes for Single-Copy Data

Shacham and Waters (Shacham & Waters, 2013) proposed two fast PoR schemes based on an homomorphic authenticator that enables the storage server to reduce the complexity of the auditing by aggregating the authentication tags of individual file blocks. The first scheme is built from BLS signatures and allows public auditing. The second scheme is built on pseudorandom functions and allows only private auditing but its response messages are shorter than those of the first scheme, i.e., 80 bits only. Both schemes use Reed-Solomon erasure encoding method (Plank, 1997) to support an extra feature which allows the client to recover the data outsourced in the cloud. However, their encoding and decoding are slow for large files.

Yuan and Yu (Yuan & Yu, 2013) managed to suppress the need for the tradeoff between communication costs and storage costs. They proposed a PoR scheme with public auditing and constant communication cost by combining techniques such as constant size polynomial commitment, BLS signatures, and homomorphic linear authenticators. On the other hand, their data preparation process requires (s+3) exponentiation operations where s is the block size. However, their scheme does not support data dynamics.

Xu and Chang (Xu & Chang, 2011) proposed a new PDP model called POS. POS requires no modular exponentiation in the setup phase and uses a smaller number, i.e., about 102 for a 1G file, of group exponentiation in the verification phase. POS only supports private auditing for static data and its communication cost is linear in relation to the number of encoded elements in the challenge query.

Ateniese *et al.* (Ateniese G., *et al.*, 2011) introduced a PDP model supported with two advantages: Lightweight and robustness. Their challenge/response protocol transmits a small, and constant amount of data, which minimizes network communication. Furthermore, it incorporates mechanisms for mitigating arbitrary amounts of data corruption. On the other hand, it relies on Reed-Solomon encoding scheme in which the time required for encoding and decoding of n-block file is $O(n^2)$.

Lou *et al.* (Cao, Yu, Yang, Lou, & Hou, 2012) proposed a public auditing scheme that is suitable for distributed storage systems with concurrent user's access. In order to efficiently recover the exact form of any corrupted data, they utilized the exact repair method (Rashmi, Shah, Kumar, & Ramchandran,

2009) where the newly generated blocks are the same as those previously stored blocks. So, no verification tags need to be generated on the fly for the repaired data. Consequently, it relieves the data owner from the online burden. However, their scheme increases the storage overheads at each server, uses an additional repair server to store the original packets besides the encoded packets, and does not support data dynamics.

Auditing Schemes for Multiple-Copy Data

Barsoum and Hasan (Barsoum & Hasan, 2011; Barsoum & Hasan, 2012) proposed two dynamic multi-copy PDP schemes: Tree-Based and Map-Based Dynamic Multi-Copy PDP (TB-DMCPDP and MB-DMCPDP, respectively). These schemes prevent the CSP from cheating and maintaining fewer copies, using the diffusion property of the AES encryption scheme. TB-DMCPDP scheme is based on Merkle hash tree (MHT) whereas MB-DMCPDP scheme is based on a map-version table to support outsourcing of dynamic data. The setup cost of the TB-DMCPDP scheme is higher than that of the MB-DMCPDP scheme. On the other hand, the storage overhead is independent of the number of copies for the MB-DMCPDP scheme, while the storage overhead is linear with the number of copies for the TB-DMCPDP scheme. However, the authorized users should know the replica number in order to generate the original file which may require the CSP reveal its internal structure to the users.

Zhu *et al.* (Zhu, Hu, Ahn, & Yu, 2012) proposed a co-operative provable data possession scheme (CPDP) for multi-cloud storage integrity verification along with two fundamental techniques: Hash index hierarchy (HIH) and homomorphic verifiable response (HVR). Using the hash index hierarchy, multiple responses of the clients' challenges that are computed from multiple CSPs, can be combined into a single response as the final result. Homomorphic verifiable response supports distributed cloud storage in a multi-cloud storage environment and implements an efficient collision-resistant hash function.

Wang and Zhang (Wang & Zhang, 2014) proved that the CPDP (Zhu, Hu, Ahn, & Yu, 2012) is insecure because it does not satisfy the knowledge soundness, i.e., any malicious CSP or malicious organizer is able to pass the verification even if they have deleted all the stored data. Additionally, the CPDP does not support data dynamics.

Etemad and Kupcu (Etemad & Kupcu, 2013) proposed a distributed and replicated DPDP (DR-DPDP) that provides transparent distribution and replication of the data over multiple servers where the CSP may hide its internal structure from the client. This scheme uses persistent rank-based authenticated skip lists to handle dynamic data operations more efficiently, such as insertion, deletion, and modification. On the other hand, DR-DPDP has three noteworthy disadvantages: First, it only supports private auditing. Second, it does not support the recovery of corrupted data. Third, the organizer looks like a central entity that may get overloaded and may cause a bottleneck.

Mukundan *et al.* (Mukundan, Madria, & Linderman, 2012) proposed a Dynamic Multi-Replica Provable Data Possession scheme (DMR-PDP) that uses the Paillier probabilistic encryption for replica differentiation so that it prevents the CSP from cheating and maintaining fewer copies than what is paid for. DMR-PDP also supports efficient dynamic operations such as block modification, insertion, and deletion on data replicas over cloud servers. However, it supports only private auditing and does not provide any security proofs.

Chen and Curtmola (Chen & Curtmola, 2013) proposed a remote data checking scheme for replication-based distributed storage systems, called RDC-SR. RDC-SR enables server-side repair and places a minimal load on the data owner who only has to act as a repair coordinator. In RDC-SR, each replica constitutes a masked/encrypted version of the original file in order to support replica differentiation. In order to overcome the replicate-on-the-fly (ROTF) attack, they make replica creation a more time-consuming process. However, RDC-SR has three remarkable limitations: First, the authorized users must know the random numbers used in the masking step in order to generate the original file. Second, it only supports private auditing. Third, it works only on static data.

Static vs. Dynamic Data Auditing

Considering the data persistence, existing auditing schemes can be categorized into: Auditing schemes that support only static archived data such as; (Chen & Curtmola, 2013; Shacham & Waters, 2013; Yuan & Yu, 2013) and auditing schemes that support data dynamics such as; insertion, deletion and modification (Abo-alian, Badr, & Tolba, 2016). For enabling dynamic operations, existing data storage schemes utilize different authenticated data structures including: (1) Merkle hash tree (Merkle, 1980), (2) balanced update tree (Zhang & Blanton, 2013), (3) skip-list (Pugh, 1990; Goodrich, Tamassia, & Schwerin, 2001; Erway, Küpçü, Papamanthou, & Tamassia, 2009) and (4) map-version table (index table) (Chen & Curtmola, 2013; Fujisaki & Okamoto, 1999) that are illustrated in detail, as follows:

Merkle Hash Tree

Merkle Hash Tree (MHT) (Merkle, 1980) is a binary tree structure used to efficiently verify the integrity of the data. As illustrated in Figure 2, the MHT is a tree of hashes where the leaves of the tree are the hashes of the data blocks. Wang *et al.* (Wang, Wang, Ren, Lou, & Li, 2011) proposed a public auditing protocol that supports fully dynamic data operations by manipulating the classic MHT construction for

Figure 2. Merkle hash tree
Merkle, 1980.

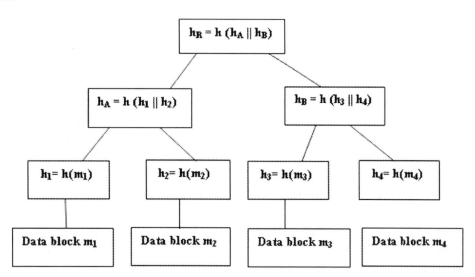

block tag authentication in order to achieve efficient data dynamics. They could also achieve batch auditing where different users can delegate multiple auditing tasks to be performed simultaneously by the TPA. Unfortunately, their protocol does not maintain the data privacy and the TPA could derive user's data from the information collected during the auditing process. Additionally, their protocol does not support data recovery in case of data corruption.

Lu *et al.* (Liu, Gu, & Lu, 2011) addressed the security problem of the previous auditing protocol (Wang, Wang, Ren, Lou, & Li, 2011) in the signature generation phase that allows the CSP to deceive by using blocks from different files during verification. They presented a secure public auditing protocol based on the homomorphic hash function and the BLS short signature scheme which is publicly verifiable and supports data dynamics, it also preserves privacy. However, their protocol suffers from massive computational and communication costs.

Wang *et al.* (Wang, Chow, Wang, Ren, & Lou, 2013) proposed a privacy-preserving public auditing scheme using random masking and homomorphic linear authenticators (HLAs) (Ateniese, Kamara, & Katz, 2009). Their auditing scheme also supports data dynamics using MHT and it enables the auditor to perform audits for multiple users simultaneously and efficiently. Unfortunately, their scheme is vulnerable to the TPA offline guessing attack.

Balanced Update Tree

Zhang and Blanton (Zhang & Blanton, 2013) proposed a new data structure called" balanced update tree," to support dynamic operations while verifying data integrity. In the update tree, each node corresponds to a range of data blocks on which an update (i.e., insertion, deletion, or modification) has been performed. The challenge with constructing such a tree was to ensure that: (1) a range of data blocks can be efficiently located within the tree and (2) the tree is maintained to be balanced after applying necessary updates caused by clients queries, i.e., the size of this tree is independent of the overall file size as it depends on the number of updates. However, it introduces more storage overhead on the client. Besides, the auditing scheme requires the retrieval, i.e., downloading, of data blocks which leads to high communication costs. Figure 3 illustrates an example of balanced update tree operations.

Skip List

A skip list (Pugh, 1990) is a hierarchical structure of linked lists that is used to store an ordered set of items. An authenticated skip list (Goodrich, Tamassia, & Schwerin, 2001) is constructed using a collision-resistant hash function and keeps a hash value in each node. Due to the collision resistance of the hash function, the hash value of the root can be used later for validating the integrity. Figure 4 (Erway, Küpçü, Papamanthou, & Tamassia, 2009) illustrates an example of a rank-based authenticated skip list, where the number inside the node represents its rank, i.e., the number of nodes at the bottom level that can be reached from that node.

Lu *et al.* (Liu, Gu, & Lu, 2011) used the skip list structure to support data dynamics in their PDP model that reduces the computational and communication complexity from log(n) to constant. However, the use of a skip-list creates some additional storage overheads, i.e., about 3.7% of the original file at the CSP-side and 0.05% at the client-side. Additionally, it only supports private auditing.

Figure 3. Example of balanced update tree operations
Zhang & Blanton, 2013.

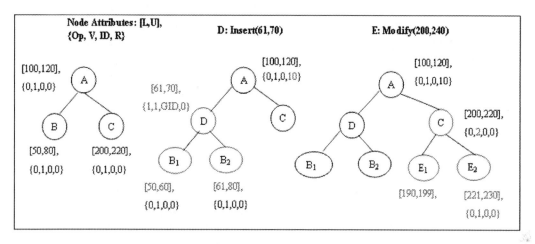

Figure 4. Rank-based authenticated skip list
Erway, Küpçü, Papamanthou, & Tamassia, 2009.

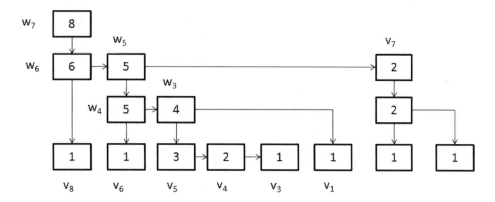

Index Table

A map-version table or an index table is a small data structure created by the owner and stored on the verifier side to validate the integrity and consistency of all file copies stored by the CSP (Barsoum & Hasan, 2011). The map-version table consists of three columns: Serial number (SN), block number (BN), and version number (VN). The SN represents an index to the file blocks that indicates the physical position of a block in a data file. The BN is a counter used to make logical numbering/indexing to the file blocks. The VN indicates the current version of file blocks.

Yang *et al.* (Li, Chen, Tan, & Yang, 2012; Li, Chen, Tan, & Yang, 2013) proposed a full data dynamic PDP scheme that uses a map-version table to support data block updates. Then, they discussed how to extend their scheme to support other features, including public auditing, privacy preservation, fairness, and multiple-replica checking.

Recently, Yang and Xiaohua (Yang & Xiaohua, 2014) presented Third-party Storage Auditing Scheme (TSAS) which is a privacy preserving auditing protocol. It also supports data dynamic operations using Index Table (ITable). Moreover, they add a new column to the index table, T_i, that is the timestamp used for generating the data tag to prevent the replay attack. They applied batch auditing for integrity verification for multiple data owners in order to reduce the computational cost on the auditor. However, this scheme moved the computational loads of the auditing from the TPA to the CSP, i.e., pairing operation, which introduced high computational cost on the CSP side.

ACCESS CONTROL METHODS

Despite the cost effectiveness and reliability of cloud storage services, data owners may consider them as an uncertain storage pool outside the enterprises. Data owners may worry that their data could be misused or accessed by unauthorized users as a reason of sharing the cloud infrastructure. An important aspect for the cloud service provider is to have in place an access control method to ensure the confidentiality and privacy of their data, i.e., their data are safe from unauthorized access and disclosure (Abo-alian, Badr, & Tolba, 2016).

Generally, access control can be defined as restricting access to resources/data to privileged/authorized entities (Menezes, Van Oorschot, & Vanstone, 1996). Various access control models have emerged, including Discretionary Access Control (DAC) (Li N., 2011), Mandatory Access Control (MAC) (McCune, Jaeger, Berger, Caceres, & Sailer, 2006), and Role-Based Access Control (RBAC) (Ferraiolo, Kuhn, & Chandramouli, 2003). In these models, subjects (e.g. users) and objects (e.g. data files) are identified by unique names and access control is based on the identity of the subject or its roles. DAC, MAC, and RBAC are effective for closed and relatively unchangeable distributed systems that deal only with a set of known users who access a set of known services where the data owner and the service provider are in the same trust domain (Cha, Seo, & Kim, 2012).

In cloud computing, the relationship between services and users is more ad hoc and dynamic, service providers and users are not in the same security domain. Users are usually identified by their characteristics or attributes rather than predefined identities (Cha, Seo, & Kim, 2012). Therefore, the cryptographic solution, such as data encryption before outsourcing, can be the trivial solution to keep sensitive data confidential against unauthorized users and untrusted CSPs. Unfortunately, cryptographic solutions only are inefficient to encrypt a file to multiple recipients, and fail to support fine-grained access control, i.e., granting differential access rights to a set of users and allowing flexibility in specifying the access rights of individual users. Moreover, traditional ACL-based access control methods require attaching a list of authorized users to every data object. When ACLs are enforced with cryptographic methods, the complexity of each data object in terms of its ciphertext size and/or the corresponding data encryption operation is linear to the number of users in the system, and thus makes the system less scalable (Yu, 2010).

The following sub-sections overview the existing access control methods and highlight their main advantages and drawbacks.

Traditional Encryption

One method for enforcing access control and assuring data confidentiality is to store sensitive data in encrypted form. Only users authorized to access the data have the required decryption key. There are two main classes of encryption schemes: 1) Symmetric key encryption and 2) Public key encryption (Fujisaki & Okamoto, 1999).There are several schemes (Kallahalla, Riedel, Swaminathan, Wang, & Fu, 2003; Vimercati, Foresti, Jajodia, Paraboschi, & Samarati, 2007; Goh, Shacham, Modadugu, & Boneh, 2003) proposed in the area of access control of outsourced data addressing the similar issue of data access control with conventional symmetric-key cryptography or public-key cryptography. Although these schemes are suitable for conventional file systems, most of them are less suitable for fine-grained data access control in large-scale data centers which may have a large number users and data files. Obviously, neither of them should be applied directly while sharing data on cloud servers, since they are inefficient in encrypting a file to multiple recipients in terms of key size, ciphertext length and computational cost for encryption. Moreover, they fail to support fine-grained attribute-based access control and key delegation.

Broadcast Encryption

In the broadcast encryption (BE), a sender encrypts a message for some subset S of users who are listening on a broadcast channel, so that only the recipients in S can use their private keys to decrypt the message. The problem of practical broadcast encryption was first formally studied by Fiat and Naor in 1994 (Fiat & Naor, 1994). The BE system is secure against a collusion of k users, which means that it may be insecure if more than k users collude.

Since then, several solutions have been described in the literature such as schemes presented in Boneh *et al.* (Halevy & Shamir, 2002) and Halevy and Shamir (Boneh, Gentry, & Waters, 2005) which are the best known BE schemes. However, the efficiency of both schemes depends on the size of the authorized user set. Additionally, they also require the broadcaster/sender to refer to its database of user authorizations.

Paillier *et al.* (Delerable, Paillier, & Pointcheval, 2007) proposed a dynamic public-key broadcast encryption that simultaneously benefit from the following properties: Receivers are stateless; encryption is collusion-secure for arbitrarily large collusions of users and security is tight in the standard model; new users can join dynamically (i.e. without modification of user decryption keys and ciphertext size).

Recently, Seberry *et al.* (Kim, Susilo, Au, & Seberry, 2013) proposed a semi-static secure broadcast encryption scheme with constant-sized private keys and ciphertexts that improves the scheme introduced by Gentry and Waters (Gentry & Waters, 2009). They reduce the private key and ciphertext size by half. In addition, the sizes of the public key and the private key do not depend on the total number of users. Unfortunately, it is only secure against adaptive chosen plaintext attacks (CPA).

Apparently, a BE system achieves a one-to-many encryption with general performance. However, it may not be applied directly while sharing data on cloud servers, since it fails to support attribute-based access control and key delegation.

Identity-Based Encryption

Identity-based encryption (IBE) was proposed by Shamir in 1984 (Boneh, Gentry, & Waters, 2005). But, IBE remained an open problem for many years until a fully functional identity-based encryption (IBE) scheme proposed by Boneh and Franklin (Halevy & Shamir, 2002). It can be defined as a type of public-key cryptography (PKC), in which any arbitrary string corresponding to unique user information is a valid public key such as; an email address or a physical IP address. The corresponding private key is computed by a trusted third party (TTP) called the private key generator (PKG) as illustrated in Figure 5 (Wikipedia, 2014).

Figure 5. Example of an identity- based encryption
Wikipedia, 2014.

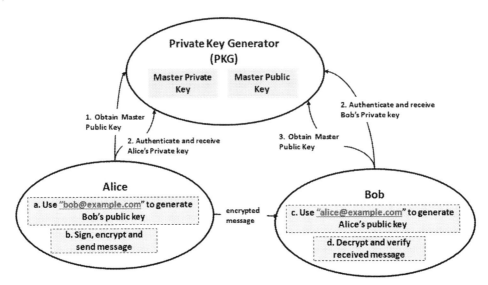

Compared with the traditional PKC, the IBE system eliminates online look-ups for the recipients authenticated public key. However, an IBE system introduces several problems: First, there is only one PKG to distribute private keys to each user which introduces the key escrow problem, i.e., the PKG knows the private keys of all users and may decrypt any message. Second, the PKG is a centralized entity; it may get overloaded and can cause a bottleneck. Third, if the PKG server is compromised, all messages used by that server are also compromised. Recently, Lou *et al.* (Li J., Chen, Jia, & Lou, 2013) proposed a revocable IBE scheme that handles the critical issue of overhead computation at the Private Key Generator (PKG) during user revocation. They employ a hybrid private key for each user, in which an AND gate is involved to connect and bond the identity component and the time component. At first, the user is able to obtain the identity component and a default time component, i.e., PKG can issue his/her private key for a current time period. Then, unrevoked users need to periodically request a key update for the time component to a newly introduced entity named Key Update Cloud Service Provider (KU-CSP) which introduces further communication costs.

Hierarchical Identity-Based Encryption

Horwitz and Lynn (Horwitz & Lynn, 2002) introduced the concept of a Hierarchical identity-based encryption (HIBE) system in order to reduce the workload on the root PKG. They proposed a two-level HIBE scheme, in which a root PKG needs only to generate private keys for domain-level PKGs that, in turn, generates private keys for all the users in their domains at the next level. That scheme has a chosen ciphertext security in the random oracle model. In addition, it achieves total collusion resistance at the upper levels and partial collusion resistance at the lower levels.

Gentry and Halevi (Gentry & Halevi, 2009) proposed an HIBE scheme with total collusion resistance at an arbitrary number of levels, which has chosen ciphertext security in the random oracle model under the BDH assumption and key randomization. It is noteworthy that their scheme has a valuable feature which is one-to-many encryption, i.e., an encrypted file can be decrypted by a recipient and all his ancestors, using their own secret keys, respectively. However, the length of ciphertext and private keys, as well as the time of encryption and decryption, grows linearly with the depth of a recipient in the hierarchy.

Figure 6 (Gagné, 2011) illustrates an example of HIBE in which the root PKG generates the system parameters for the HIBE system and the secret keys for the lower-level PKGs, which, in turn, generate the secret keys for the entities in their domains at the bottom level. In other words, a user public key is an ID-tuple, which consists of the user's identity (ID) and the IDs of the user's ancestors. Each PKG uses its secret keys (including a master key and a private key) and a user public key to generate secret keys for each user in its domain.

Liu *et al.* (Liu, Wang, & Wu, 2010) utilized the 'one-to-many' encryption feature of (Gentry & Halevi, 2009) and proposed an efficient sharing of the secure cloud storage services scheme. In their scheme, a sender can specify several users as the recipients for an encrypted file by taking the number and public keys of the recipients as inputs of an HIBE system. Using their scheme, the sender needs to encrypt a file only once and store only one copy of the corresponding ciphertext regardless of the number of intended recipients. The limitation of their scheme is that the length of ciphertexts grows linearly with the number of recipients so that it can only be used in the case of a confidential file involving a small set of recipients.

Recently, Zhang *et al.* (Mao, Zhang, Chen, & Zhan, 2013) presented a new HIBE system where the ciphertext sizes as well as the decryption costs are independent of the hierarchy depth, i.e., constant length of ciphertext and a constant number of bilinear map operations in decryption. Moreover, their scheme is fully secure in the standard model. The HIBE system obviously achieves key delegation and some HIBE schemes achieve one-to-many encryption with adequate performance. However, it may not be applied directly while sharing data on cloud servers because it fails to efficiently support fine-grained access control.

Figure 6. Hierarchical identity-based encryption
Gagné, 2011.

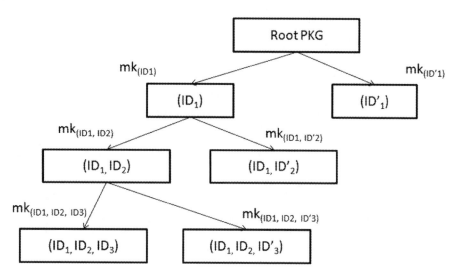

Attribute-Based Encryption

An Attribute-Based Encryption (ABE) scheme is a generalization of the IBE scheme. In an IBE system, a user is identified by only one attribute, i.e., the ID. While, in an ABE scheme, a user is identified by a set of attributes, e.g. specialty, department, location, etc. Sahai and Waters (Sahai & Waters, 2005) first introduced the concept of the ABE schemes, in which a sender encrypted a message, specifying an attribute set and a number d so that only a recipient who has at least d attributes of the given attributes can decrypt the message. Although their scheme, which is referred to as a threshold encryption, is collusion resistant and has selective-ID security, it has three drawbacks: First, it is difficult to define the threshold, i.e., the minimum number of attributes that a recipient must have to decrypt the ciphertext. Second, revoking a user requires redefining the attribute set. Third, it lacks expressibility which limits its applicability to larger systems.

As an extension of the ABE scheme, two variants are proposed in the literature: 1) the Key Policy based ABE (KP-ABE) scheme and 2) the Ciphertext-Policy based ABE (CP-ABE) scheme.

Key-Policy Attribute-Based Encryption

A key policy attribute-based encryption (KP-ABE) scheme was first proposed by Goyal *et al.* (Goyal, Pandey, Sahai, & Waters, 2006) which supports any monotonic access formula consisting of AND, OR, or threshold gates. Their scheme is considered a fine-grained and expressive access control. KP-ABE is a scheme in which the access structure or policy is specified in the users' private keys, while ciphertexts are associated with sets of descriptive attributes.

As stated in (Waters, 2011), any monotonic access structure can be represented as an access tree over data attributes. For example, Figure 7 presents an access structure and attribute sets that can be generated in a healthcare application (Yu, Wang, Ren, & Lou, 2010). The data owner encrypts the data file using a selected set of attributes (e.g., diabetes, A, Asian, etc.) before uploading it to the cloud. Only users, whose access structure specified in their private keys matching the file attributes can decrypt the file,

Figure 7. Key-policy attribute-based encryption in a healthcare system
Yu, Wang, Ren, & Lou, 2010.

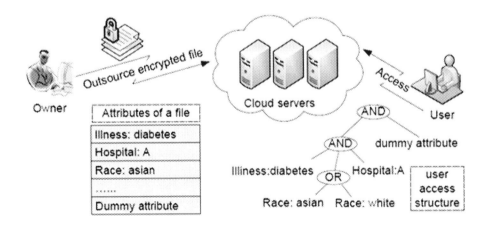

in other words, a user with access structure as follows: diabetes Λ (Asian V white) can decrypt the data file encrypted under the attributes diabetes and Asian.

In recent times, authors of (Yu, Wang, Ren, & Lou, 2010; Si, Wang, & Zhang, 2013) proposed a user private key revocable KP-ABE scheme with non-monotonic access structure, which can be combined with the XACML policy (di Vimercati, Samarati, & Jajodia, 2005) to address the issue of moving the complex access control process to the cloud and constructing a security provable public verifiable cloud access control scheme.

All of the prior work described above assume the use of a single trusted authority (TA) that manages, e.g., add, issue, revoke, etc., all attributes in the system domain. This assumption not only may create a load bottleneck but also suffers from the key escrow problem as the TA can decrypt all the files, causing a privacy disclosure. Thus, Chase (Chase, 2007) provided a construction for a multi-authority ABE scheme which supports many different authorities operating simultaneously, and each administering a different set of domain attributes, i.e., handing out secret keys for a different set of attributes (Li, Yu, Ren, & Lou, 2010). However, his scheme is still not ideal because there are three main problems: first, there is a central authority that can decrypt all ciphertexts because it masters the system secret keys and thus a key escrow problem is aroused; second, it is very easy for colluding authorities to build a complete profile of all of the attributes corresponding to each global identifier (GID); third, the set of authorities is predetermined.

Chase and Chow (Chase & Chow, 2009) proposed a more practical multi-authority KP-ABE system, which removes the trusted central authority to preserve the user's privacy. Their scheme allows the users to communicate with AAs via pseudonyms instead of having to provide their GIDs. Moreover, they prevent the AAs from pooling their data and linking multiple attribute sets belonging to the same user.

Yu *et al.* (Yu, Wang, Ren, & Lou, 2010) exploited the uniquely combined techniques of ABE, proxy re-encryption (PRE) (Goh, Shacham, Modadugu, & Boneh, 2003), and lazy re-encryption (LRE) (Blaze, Bleumer, & Strauss, 1998) to allow the data owner to delegate most of the computation tasks involved in user revocation to untrusted CSPs without disclosing the underlying data contents. PRE eliminates the need for direct interaction between the data owner and the users for decryption key distribution, whereas LRE allows the CSP to aggregate the computation tasks of multiple user revocation operations. For example, once a user is revoked, the CSP just record that. If only there is a file data access request from a user, the CSP then re-encrypts the requested files and updates the requesting user's secret key.

Recently, Zeng *et al.* (Li, Xiong, Zhang, & Zeng, 2013) propose an expressive decentralizing KP-ABE scheme with a constant ciphertext size, i.e., the ciphertext size is independent of the number of attributes used in the scheme. In their construction, there is no trusted central authority to conduct the system setup and the access policy can be expressed as any non-monotonic access structure. In addition, their scheme is semantically secure in so-called Selective-Set model based on the n-DBDHE assumption.

Hohenberger and Waters (Hohenberger & Waters, 2013) proposed a KP-ABE scheme in which ciphertexts can be decrypted with a constant number of pairings without any restriction on the number of attributes. However, the size of the user's private key is increased by a factor of the number of distinct attributes in the access policy. Furthermore, there is a trusted single authority that generates private keys for users which violates the user privacy and causes a key escrow problem.

Unfortunately, in all KP-ABE schemes, the data owners have no control over who has access to the data they encrypt, except by their choice of the set of descriptive attributes for the data. Rather, they must trust that the key issuer issues the appropriate keys to grant or deny access to the appropriate users.

Additionally, the size of the user's private key and the computation costs in encryption and decryption operations depend linearly on the number of attributes involved in the access policy.

Ciphertext-Policy Attribute-Based Encryption

In the ciphertext-policy ABE (CP-ABE) introduced by Waters *et al.* (Bethencourt, Sahai, & Waters, 2007), the roles of the ciphertexts and keys are reversed in contrast with the KP-ABE scheme. The data owner determines the policy under which the data can be decrypted, while the secret key is associated with a set of attributes. Most of the proposed CP-ABE schemes incur large ciphertext sizes and computation costs in the encryption and decryption operations which depend at least linearly on the number of attributes involved in the access policy. Therefore, Chen *et al.* (Chen, Zhang, & Feng, 2011) proposed two CP-ABE schemes, both have constant size ciphertext and constant computation costs for an access policy containing AND Gate with a wildcard. The first scheme is provably CPA-secure in standard model under the decision n-BDHE assumption while the second scheme is provably CCA-secure in a standard model under the decision n-BDHE assumption and the existence of collision-resistant hash functions.

Yan Zhu at al. (Zhu Y., Hu, Ahn, Huang, & Wang, 2012; Zhu Y., Hu, Ahn, Yu, & Zhao, 2012) proposed a comparison-based encryption scheme that support a complete comparison relation, e.g., $=$, $\neq$, $\leq$, $\geq$, in the policy specification to implement various range constraints on integer attributes, such as temporal and level attributes. They combined proxy re-encryption (with CP-ABE to support key delegation and reduce computational overheads on lightweight devices by outsourcing the majority of decryption operations to the CSP. Their scheme provides O (1) size of private key and ciphertext for each range attribute. Additionally, it is also provably secure under the RSA and CDH assumption. However, their scheme depends on a central single authority to conduct the system setup and manage all at- tributes. And, they do not provide a mechanism for efficient user revocation.

Zhang and Chen (Zhang & Chen, 2012) proposed the idea of" Access control as a service" for public cloud storage, where the data owner controls the authorization, and the PDP (Policy Decision Point) and PEP (Policy Enforcement Point) can be securely delegated to the CSP by utilizing CP-ABE and proxy re-encryption. However, it incurs high communication and setup costs.

The main limitations of most traditional CP-ABE schemes are: First, compromising the user's privacy since the access structure is embedded in the ciphertext that may reveal the scope of the data file and the authorized users who have access. The obvious solution to this problem as proposed by Nishide *et al.* (Nishide, Yoneyama, & Ohta, 2008), is to hide ciphertext policy, i.e., hidden access structure. Subsequently, there are various efforts to improve the traditional CP-ABE scheme and to support privacy-preserving access policy such as in (Doshi & Jinwala, 2012; Qian, Li, & Zhang, 2013; Jung, Li, Wan, & Wan, 2013). The other limitation of the traditional CP-ABE schemes is depending on a single central authority for monitoring and issuing user's secret keys. Recently, many CP-ABE schemes consider multi-authority environments (Jung, Li, Wan, & Wan, 2013; Li, Yu, Zheng, Ren, & Lou, 2013; Yang, Jia, Ren, & Zhang, 2013).

To achieve fine-grained and scalable data access control for personal health records (PHRs), Lou *et al.* (Li, Yu, Zheng, Ren, & Lou, 2013) utilized CP-ABE techniques to encrypt each patient's PHR file while focusing on the multiple data owner scenario. Moreover, they adopted proxy re-encryption and lazy revocation to efficiently support attribute and user revocation. However, the computational costs of the key generation, encryption, and decryption processes are all linear with the number of attributes.

Hierarchical Attribute-Based Encryption

The Hierarchical Attribute-Based Encryption (HABE) model, as described in (Wang, Liu, & Wu, 2010; Wang, Liu, Wu, & Guo, 2011), integrates properties in both an HIBE model (Gagné, 2011) and an ABE model (Sahai & Waters, 2005). As illustrated in Figure 8, it consists of a root master (RM) and multiple domains, where the RM functions as the TTP, and the domains are enterprise users. More precisely, a domain consists of many domain masters (DMs) corresponding to the internal trusted parties (ITPs) and numerous users corresponding to end users. The RM, whose role closely follows the root PKG in an HIBE system, is responsible for generation and distribution of system parameters and domain keys. The DM, whose role integrates both the properties of the domain PKG in an HIBE system and the AA in an ABE system, is responsible for delegating keys to the DMs at the next level and distributing secret keys to users.

Wang *et al.* (Wang, Liu, & Wu, 2011) proposed fuzzy and precise identity-based encryption (FPIBE) scheme that supports the full key delegation and requires only a constant number of bilinear map operations during decryption. The FPIBE scheme is able to efficiently achieve a flexible access control by combining the HIBE system and the CP-ABE system. Using the FPIBE scheme, a user can encrypt data by specifying a recipient ID set, or an access control policy over attributes, so that only the user whose ID belongs to the ID set or attributes satisfying the access control policy can decrypt the corresponding data. However, the ciphertext length is proportional to the number of authorized users and encryption time. As well as, the size of a user's secret key is proportional to the depth of the user in the hierarchy.

For supporting compound and multi-valued attributes in a scalable, flexible, and fine-grained access control, Wan *et al.* (Wan, Liu, & Deng, 2012) proposed hierarchical attribute-set-based encryption (HASBE) by extending the ciphertext policy attribute-set-based encryption (CP-ASBE) with a hierarchical structure of users. HASBE employs multiple value assignments for access expiration time to deal with user revocation more efficiently. However, the granting access operation is proportional to the number of attributes in the key structure.

Figure 8. Hierarchical attribute-based encryption model
Wang, Liu, Wu, & Guo, 2011.

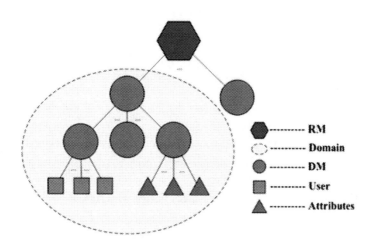

Zhou *et al.* (Chen, Chu, Tzeng, & Zhou, 2013) proposed a new hierarchical key assignment scheme, called CloudHKA, that addresses a cryptographic key assignment problem for enforcing a hierarchical access control policy over cloud data. CloudHKA possesses many advantages: 1) Each user only needs to store one secret key, 2) Each user can be flexibly authorized the access rights of Write or Read, or both, 3) It supports a dynamic user set and access hierarchy, and 4) It is provably secure against collusive attacks. However, the re-key cost in the case of user revocation is linear with the number of users in the same security class. CloudHKA does not consider the expressive user attributes, so it can be considered coarse-grained access control scheme.

Qin Liu *et al.* (Wang, Liu, & Wu, 2014) recently extended the hierarchical CP-ABE scheme (Wang, Liu, & Wu, 2010; Wang, Liu, Wu, & Guo, 2011) by incorporating the concept of time to perform automatic proxy re-encryption. More specifically, they proposed a time-based proxy re-encryption (TimePRE) scheme to allow a user's access right to expire automatically after a predetermined period of time. In this case, the data owner can be offline in the process of user revocations. Unfortunately, TimePRE scheme has two drawbacks: first, it assumes that there is a global time among all entities. Second, the user secret key size is O(mn), where m is the number of nodes in the time tree corresponding to the user's effective time period and n is the number of user attributes.

Role-Based Access Control

In a Role-Based Access Control (RBAC) system, access permissions are assigned to roles and roles are assigned to users/subjects (Wikipedia, 2014). Roles can be created, modified or disabled according to the system requirements. Role-permission assignments are relatively stable, while user-role assignments change quite frequently (e.g., personnel moving across departments, reassignment of duties, etc.). So, managing the user-role permissions is significantly easier than managing user rights individually (Ferrara, Madhusudan, & Parlato, 2013).

Zhou *et al.* (Zhou, Varadharajan, & Hitchens, 2011) proposed a role-based encryption (RBE) scheme for secure cloud storage. This scheme specifies a set of roles assigned to the users, each role having a set of permissions. Roles can be defined in a hierarchy, which means a role can have sub-roles (successor roles). The owner of the data can encrypt the private data to a specific role. Only the users in the specified role or predecessor roles are able to decrypt that data. The decryption key size still remains constant regardless of the number of roles that the user has been assigned to. However, the decryption cost is proportional to the number of authorized users in the same role.

COMPARATIVE ANALYSIS OF SECURITY METHODS ON CLOUD DATA STORAGE

This section evaluates the performance of auditing and access control methods, that were presented in the previous sections, against different performance criteria.

Performance Analysis of Data Storage Auditing Methods

This sub-section assesses the different characteristics of some existing data storage auditing schemes such as auditor type, supporting dynamic data, replication/multiple-copy and data recovery, as illustrated in Table 1. In addition, it evaluates their performance in terms of computational complexity at the CSP and the auditor, storage overheads at the CSP and the auditor, communication complexity between the auditor and the CSP, as illustrated in Table 3.

As shown in Table 1, most auditing schemes focus on a single copy of the file and provide no proof that the CSP stores multiple copies of the data owners file. Although data owners many need their critical data to be replicated on multiple servers across multiple data centers to guarantee the availability of their data, only few schemes (Etemad & Kupcu, 2013; Barsoum & Hasan, 2012; Zhu, Hu, Ahn, & Yu, 2012) that support auditing for multiple replicas of data owner's file.

Table 2 gives more notations for cryptographic operations used in the different auditing methods. Let r, n, k denote the number of replicas, the number of blocks per replica and the number of sectors per block (in the case of block fragmentation), respectively. s denotes the block size. c denotes the number of challenged blocks. Let λ be the security parameter which is usually the key size. Let p denote the order of the groups and $\varphi(N)$ denotes the Euler Function on the RSA modulus N.

Table 1. Characteristics of data storage auditing schemes

Scheme	Auditor Type	Dynamic Data	Replication	Data Recovery
(Liu, Zhang, & Lun, 2013)	Public	Yes	No	No
(Yang & Xiaohua, 2014)	Public	Yes	No	No
(Ateniese, *et al.*, 2007)	Public	No	No	No
(Wang, Chow, Wang, Ren, & Lou, 2013)	Public	Yes	No	No
(Shacham & Waters, 2013) (BLS)	Public	No	No	Yes
(Shacham & Waters, 2013) (RSA)	Public	No	No	Yes
(Shacham & Waters, 2013) (MAC)	Private	No	No	Yes
(Yuan & Yu, 2013)	Public	No	No	Yes
(Xu & Chang, 2011)	Public	No	No	Yes
(Barsoum & Hasan, 2012)	Public	Yes	Yes	No
(Zhu, Hu, Ahn, & Yu, 2012)	Public	No	Yes	No
(Etemad & Kupcu, 2013)	Private	Yes	Yes	No

Table 2. Notations of cryptographic operations

Notation	Cryptographic Operation
MUL	Multiplication in group G
EXP	Exponentiation in group G
ADD	Addition in group G
H	Hashing into group G
MOD	Modular operation in Z_N
Pairing	Bilinear pairing; e (u, v)
SEncr	Stream Encryption

Table 3. Performance analysis of different auditing schemes

Scheme	Computational complexity		Storage Overhead		Communication Complexity
	CSP	Auditor	CSP	Auditor	
(Liu, Zhang, & Lun, 2013)	1 SEncr + O(c) [MUL+ EXP + ADD]	O(c) [MUL+ H+ EXP] + 2 Pairing	(1+1/k) n	O (1)	O (1)
(Yang & Xiaohua, 2014)	O(c) [ADD + MUL + EXP] + O(k) [EXP + Pairing]	O(c) [H+ EXP+ MUL] + 2 Pairing	s. n/k	O (1)	O(c)
(Ateniese, *et al.*, 2007)	O(c) [H+ MUL + EXP]	O(c) [H + MUL+ EXP]	n · |N|	O(λ)	O (3|N|)
(Wang, Chow, Wang, Ren, & Lou, 2013)	O(c) [MUL+ EXP + ADD] +H + 1 Pairing	O(c) [MUL+ H+ EXP] + 2 Pairing	(1+1/k) n)	O(1+1/k)	O(kc)
(Shacham & Waters, 2013) (BLS)	O(c) [ADD + MUL +EXP]	O(k) [MUL + EXP] + O(c) [H + EXP] + 2 Pairing	n.|p|	O(λ)	O(c+|p|)
(Shacham & Waters, 2013) (RSA)	O(c) [ADD + MUL +EXP]	O(k) [MUL + EXP] + O(c) [H + EXP]	n.|N|	O(λ)	O (c+|N|+ s)
(Shacham & Waters, 2013) (MAC)	O(c)	O(c)H	n.|p|	N/A	O (c+|p|+ s)
(Yuan & Yu, 2013)	O(c+s) [MUL+ EXP)	O(c) [MUL+ EXP] + 4 Pairing	(1+1/s) n	O (1)	O (1)
(Xu & Chang, 2011)	O(s) EXP	3EXP + O(c) [ADD + MUL + PRF]	(1+1/s) n	O (1)	O(λ)
(Barsoum & Hasan, 2012)	O(c) [EXP + MUL + ADD]	O(c) [H+ MUL+ EXP] + O(k) [MUL+ EXP] + O(r)ADD+ 2 Pairing	2n	O(2n)	O(kr)
(Zhu, Hu, Ahn, & Yu, 2012)	O(c) Pairing + O(ck) EXP	3 Pairing + O(k) EXP	n.|p|	O(λ)	O (c + k)
(Etemad & Kupcu, 2013)	O (1+ log nr) [EXP+ MUL]	O (1+ log nr) [EXP+ MUL]	log nr	O (1)	O (log nr)

As shown in Table 3, MAC-based schemes (Shacham & Waters, 2013) require storage overheads of metadata, i.e., block tags, as long as each data block size. On the other hand, they have efficient computational complexity at the CSP and the auditor. The homomorphic tags based on BLS signatures (Ateniese, *et al.*, 2007; Shacham & Waters, 2013) are much shorter than the RSA-based homomorphic tags (Shacham & Waters, 2013). While the verification cost, i.e., the computational cost at the auditor in the BLS-based auditing schemes is higher than that of RSA-based auditing schemes due to the bilinear pairing operations which consume more time than other cryptographic operations.

To reduce the storage overheads, the data owner can store the tags together with the data blocks only on the CSP. Upon challenging the CSP, the CSP generates the data proof and the tag to the auditor instead of only the data proof. But this solution will increase the communication cost between the CSP and the auditor. In fact, there is a tradeoff between the storage overheads at the auditor and the communication costs between the CSP and the auditor.

The scheme of Yuan and Yu (Yuan & Yu, 2013) omits the tradeoff between communication costs and storage costs. The message exchanged between the CSP and the auditor during the auditing procedure consists of a constant number of group elements. However, it requires 4 Bilinear pairing operations for proof verification that result in high computational cost at the auditor. The communication cost can be reduced by using short homomorphic tags such as BLS tags (Mukundan, Madria, & Linderman, 2012; Etemad & Kupcu, 2013) that enable the CSP to reduce the communication complexity of the auditing by aggregating the authentication tags of individual file blocks into a single tag. Batch auditing (Yang & Xiaohua, 2014; Wang, Chow, Wang, Ren, & Lou, 2013) can further reduce the communication cost by allowing the CSP to send the linear combination of all the challenged data blocks whose size is equal to one data block instead of sending them sequentially.

Auditing schemes that support dynamic data (Yang & Xiaohua, 2014; Etemad & Kupcu, 2013; Barsoum & Hasan, 2012; Wang, Chow, Wang, Ren, & Lou, 2013; Liu, Zhang, & Lun, 2013) add more storage overheads at the auditor. MHT-based schemes (Wang, Chow, Wang, Ren, & Lou, 2013) keep the metadata at the auditor side (i.e. the root of the MHT) smaller than schemes that utilize the index table (Yang & Xiaohua, 2014; Barsoum & Hasan, 2012), as the total number of index table entries is equal to the number of file blocks. On the contrary, the computational and communication costs of the MHT-based schemes are higher than those of the table-based schemes. During the dynamic operations of the MHT-based schemes, the data owner sends a modification request to the CSP and receives the authentication paths. The CSP updates the MHT according to the required dynamic operations, regenerates a new directory root and sends it to the auditor. On the other hand, for the table-based schemes, the data owner only sends a request to the CSP and updates the index table without the usage of any cryptographic operations. However, auditing schemes based on the index table (Yang & Xiaohua, 2014; Barsoum & Hasan, 2012) suffer a performance penalty during insertion or deletion operations, i.e. O(n) in the worst case, because the indexes of all the blocks after the insertion/deletion point are changed, and all the tags of these blocks should be recalculated. While the complexity of insertion or deletion operations when using skip lists (Etemad & Kupcu, 2013) is O (log n).

Performance Analysis of Access Control Methods

This sub-section presents an evaluation of different access control methods in terms of the ciphertext size, user's secret key size, decryption cost, user revocation cost and the existence of multiple authorities.

As illustrated in Table 4, user revocation is a very challenging issue in access control methods that requires re-encryption of data files accessible to the revoked user, and may need updates of secret keys for all the non-revoked users. So the user revocation requires a heavy computation overhead on the data owner and may also require him/her to be always online. Access control methods that utilize the proxy encryption can efficiently perform the user revocation operation such as (Zhang & Chen, 2012; Li, Yu, Zheng, Ren, & Lou, 2013; Yang, Jia, Ren, & Zhang, 2013; Chen, Chu, Tzeng, & Zhou, 2013). To further improvement on the complexity of user revocation, hierarchical access control methods such as (Wan, Liu, & Deng, 2012; Zhou, Varadharajan, & Hitchens, 2011) use the concept of key delegation.

Ciphertext and secret key sizes are other challenging issues in current access control methods that may cause high storage overhead and communication cost. Ciphertext and secret key sizes usually grow linearly with the number of attributes in the system domain. Methods of (Zhang & Chen, 2012; Doshi & Jinwala, 2012; Wan, Liu, & Deng, 2012; Chen, Chu, Tzeng, & Zhou, 2013; Zhou, Varadharajan, & Hitchens, 2011) have constant ciphertext sizes while only the methods of (Doshi & Jinwala, 2012; Zhou, Varadharajan, & Hitchens, 2011) achieve constant secret key size.

Table 4. Performance analysis of different access control methods

Access Control Method	Approach	Ciphertext Size	User Key Size	Decryption Cost	User Revocation Cost	Multiple Authority
(Hohenberger & Waters, 2013)	KP-ABE	Linear with no. of attributes	Linear with no. of attributes	Constant no. of pairings	N/A	No
(Doshi & Jinwala, 2012)	CP-ABE	Constant	Constant	Constant no. of pairings,	N/A	No
(Qian, Li, & Zhang, 2013)	CP-ABE with fully hidden access structure	Linear with no. of attributes	Linear with total no. of attributes	Linear with no. of attribute authorities	N/A	Yes
(Li, Yu, Zheng, Ren, & Lou, 2013)	CP-ABE with proxy encryption and lazy re-encryption	Linear with no. of attributes and no. of AA	Linear with no. of attributes in the secret key.	Linear with total no. of attributes	Linear with no. of attributes in the secret key.	Yes
(Yang, Jia, Ren, & Zhang, 2013)	CP-ABE with proxy encryption	Linear with no. of attributes in the policy	Linear with the total no. of attributes	Constant	Linear with no. of non-revoked users who hold the revoked attribute	Yes
(Wang, Liu, & Wu, 2011)	HIBE + CP-ABE	Linear with no. of users and the max. the depth of the hierarchy.	Linear with no. of attributes of a user	Constant	N/A	Yes
(Wan, Liu, & Deng, 2012)	CP-ABE + HIBE	Constant	Linear with no. of attributes of a user	Linear with no. of attributes in the key	Constant	Yes
(Chen, Chu, Tzeng, & Zhou, 2013)	HIBE with proxy encryption	Constant	Read and Write keys independent of number of ciphertexts	Linear with the depth of the user in hierarchy	Linear with no. of authorities and no. of ciphertext accessed by revoked user.	Yes
(Zhou, Varadharajan, & Hitchens, 2011)	Hierarchical RBAC	Constant	Constant	Linear with no. of users in the same role.	Linear with no. of roles	Yes
(Zhang & Chen, 2012)	CP–ABE + proxy encryption	Constant	Linear with no. of attributes	Constant no. of pairings	Constant	No

In most of the access control methods, decryption cost scales with the complexity of the access policy or the number of attributes which is infeasible as in the case of lightweight devices such as mobiles. Some access control methods such as (Hohenberger & Waters, 2013; Zhang & Chen, 2012; Chen & Curtmola, 2013; Yang, Jia, Ren, & Zhang, 2013; Doshi & Jinwala, 2012; Wang, Liu, & Wu, 2011) have constant decryption costs. Some access control methods, e.g. (Hohenberger & Waters, 2013; Zhang & Chen, 2012; Doshi & Jinwala, 2012), assume the use of a single trusted authority (TA) that manages (e.g., add, issue, revoke, etc.,) all attributes in the system domain. This assumption not only may create a load bottleneck but also suffers from the key escrow problem as the TA can decrypt all the files, causing a privacy disclosure. Instead, recent access control methods, such as (Wang, Liu, & Wu, 2011; Wan, Liu, & Deng, 2012; Chen, Chu, Tzeng, & Zhou, 2013), consider the existence of different entities, called attribute authorities (AAs), responsible for managing different attributes of a person, e.g.

the Department of Motor Vehicle Tests whether you can drive, or a university can certify that you are a student, etc. Each AA manages a disjoint subset of attributes, while none of them alone is able to control the security of the whole system.

DISCUSSIONS AND CONCLUDING REMARKS

From the extensive survey in the previous sections, we conclude that data security in the cloud is one of the major issues that is considered as a barrier to the adoption of cloud storage services. The most critical security concern is about data integrity, availability, privacy, and confidentiality. For validating data integrity and availability in cloud computing, many auditing schemes have been proposed under different security levels and cryptographic assumptions.

Most auditing schemes are provably secure in the random oracle model. The main limitations of existing auditing schemes can be summarized as follows: (1) Dealing only with archival static data files and do not consider dynamic operations such as insert, delete and update, (2) Relying on spot checking that can detect if a long fraction of the data stored at the CSP has been corrupted but it cannot detect corruption of small parts of the data, (3) Relying on Reed-Solomon encoding scheme to support data recovery feature in case the data is lost or corrupted. It leads to inefficient encoding and decoding for large files, (4) Supporting only private auditing that impose computational and online burdens on the data owners for periodically auditing their data, (5) verifying only single copy data files and not considering replicated data files, and (6) Incurring high computational costs and storage overheads.

Therefore, to overcome the prior limitations, an ideal auditing scheme should have the following features:

1. **Public Auditing:** To enable the data owners to delegate the auditing process to a TPA in order to verify the correctness of the outsourced data on demand.
2. **Privacy-Preserving Assurance:** To prevent the leakage of the verified data during the auditing process.
3. **Data Dynamics:** To efficiently allow the clients to perform block-level operations on the data files such as insertion, deletion, and modification while maintaining the same level of data correctness assuring and guaranteeing data freshness.
4. **Robustness:** To efficiently recover an arbitrary amount of data corruptions.
5. **Availability and Reliability:** To support auditing for distinguishable multi-replica data files to make sure that the CSP is storing all the data replicas agreed upon.
6. **Blockless Verification:** To allow TPA to verify the correctness of the cloud data on demand without possessing or retrieving a copy of challenged data blocks.
7. **Stateless Verification:** Where the TPA is not needed to maintain a state between audits.
8. **Efficiency:** To achieve the following aspects:
   a. Minimum computation complexity at the CSP and the TPA.
   b. Minimum communication complexity between the CSP and the TPA.
   c. Minimum storage overheads at the CSP and the TPA.

For ensuring data confidentiality in the cloud computing, various access control methods were proposed in order to restrict access to data and guarantee that the outsourced data is safe from unauthorized access. However, these methods suffer many penalties such as (1) Heavy computation overheads and a cumbersome online burden towards the data owner because of the operation of user revocation, (2) Large ciphertext and secret key sizes as well as high computation costs in the encryption and decryption operations which depend at least linearly on the number of attributes involved in the access policy, (3) Compromising the users privacy by revealing some information about the data file and the authorized users in the access policy, and (4) Relying on single authority for managing different attributes in the access policy which may cause a bottleneck and a key escrow problem.

Consequently, we propose that the ideal access control methods should satisfy the following requirements:

1. **Fine-Grained:** Granting different access rights to a set of users and allowing flexibility and expressibility in specifying the access rights of individual users.
2. **Privacy-Preserving:** Access policy does not reveal any information to the CSP about the scope of the data file and the kind or the attributes of users authorized to access.
3. **Scalability:** The number of authorized users cannot affect the performance of the system.
4. **Efficiency:** The method should be efficient in terms of ciphertext size, user's secret key size, and the costs of encryption, decryption, and user revocation.
5. **Forward and Backward Security:** The revoked user should not be able to decrypt new ciphertexts encrypted with the new public key. And, the newly joined users should be able to decrypt the previously published ciphertexts encrypted with the previous public key if they satisfy the access policy.
6. **Collusion Resistant:** Different users cannot collude each other and combine their attributes to decrypt the encrypted data.
7. **Multiple Authority:** To overcome the problems of load bottleneck and key escrow problems, there should be multiple authorities that manage the user attributes and issue the secret keys, rather than a central trusted authority.

CONCLUSION

Cloud storage services have become extremely promising due to its cost effectiveness and reliability. However, this service also brings many new challenges for data security and privacy. Therefore, cloud service providers have to adopt security practices to ensure that the clients' data is safe. In this paper, the different security challenges within a cloud storage service are introduced and a survey of the different methods to assure data integrity, availability and confidentiality is presented. Comparative evaluations of these methods are also conducted according to various pre-defined performance criteria. Finally, we suggest the following research directions for data security within cloud computing environments: (1) Integrate attribute-based encryption with role-based access control models such that the user-role and role-permission assignments can be separately constructed using access policies applied on the attributes of users, roles, the objects and the environment. (2) Develop a context-aware role-based control model and incorporate it to the Policy Enforcement Point of a cloud, and enable/activate the role only when the user is located within the logical positions time intervals and under certain platforms in order to prevent the malicious insiders from disclosing the authorized user's identity. (3) Integrate efficient access control and auditing methods with new hardware architectural and virtualization features that can help protect the confidentiality and integrity of the data and resources. (4) Incorporate the relationship between auditing and access control for guaranteeing secure cloud storage services. (5) Extend current auditing methods with data recovery features.

REFERENCES

Abo-alian, A., Badr, N., & Tolba, M. (2015b). Keystroke dynamics-based user authentication service for cloud computing. *Concurrency and Computation.*

Abo-alian, A., Badr, N., & Tolba, M. (2016d). Hierarchical Attribute-Role Based Access Control for Cloud Computing. *The 1st International Conference on Advanced Intelligent System and Informatics (AISI2015),* 381-389.

Abo-alian, A., Badr, N. L., & Tolba, M. F. (2015a). Auditing-as-a-Service for Cloud Storage. *Intelligent Systems, 2014,* 559–568.

Abo-alian, A., Badr, N. L., & Tolba, M. F. (2016a). Authentication as a Service for Cloud Computing. *Proceedings of the International Conference on Internet of things and Cloud Computing* (pp. 36-42). ACM. 10.1145/2896387.2896395

Abo-alian, A., Badr, N. L., & Tolba, M. F. (2016b). Integrity as a service for replicated data on the cloud. *Concurrency and Computation.*

Abo-Alian, A., Badr, N. L., & Tolba, M. F. (2016c). Integrity Verification for Dynamic Multi-Replica Data in Cloud Storage. *Asian Journal of Information Technology, 15*(6), 1056–1072.

Ateniese, G., Burns, R., Curtmola, R., Herring, J., Khan, O., Kissner, L., ... Song, D. (2011). Remote Data Checking Using Provable Data Possession. *ACM Transactions on Information and System Security, 14*(1), 121–155. doi:10.1145/1952982.1952994

Ateniese, G., Burns, R., Curtmola, R., Herring, J., Kissner, L., Peterson, Z., & Song, D. (2007). Provable data possession at untrusted stores. *The 2007 ACM Conference on Computer and Communications Security* (pp. 598-609). ACM.

Ateniese, G., Kamara, S., & Katz, J. (2009). *Proofs of Storage from Homomorphic Identification Protocols. In Advances in Cryptology–ASIACRYPT* (pp. 319–333). Springer Berlin Heidelberg.

Attebury, R., George, J., Judd, C., & Marcum, B. (2008). Google Docs: A Review. *Against the Grain, 20*(2), 14–17.

Barsoum, A. F., & Hasan, M. A. (2011). *On Verifying Dynamic Multiple Data Copies over Cloud Servers.* IACR Cryptology ePrint Archive.

Barsoum, A. F., & Hasan, M. A. (2012). Integrity verification of multiple data copies over untrusted cloud servers. *The 12th IEEE/ACM International Symposium on Cluster, Cloud and Grid Computing* (pp. 829-834). IEEE Computer Society.

Berriman, G. B., Deelman, E., Good, J., Juve, G., Kinney, J., Merrihew, A., & Rynge, M. (2013). *Creating A Galactic Plane Atlas With Amazon Web Services.* arXiv preprint arXiv:1312.6723

Bethencourt, J., Sahai, A., & Waters, B. (2007). Ciphertext-Policy Attribute-Based Encryption. *IEEE Symposium on Security and Privacy* (pp. 321-334). IEEE.

Bhadauria, R., & Sanyal, S. (2012). Survey on Security Issues in Cloud Computing and Associated Mitigation Techniques. *International Journal of Computers and Applications, 47*(18), 47–66. doi:10.5120/7292-0578

Blaze, M., Bleumer, G., & Strauss, M. (1998). *Divertible protocols and atomic proxy cryptography. In Advances in Cryptology—EUROCRYPT'98* (pp. 127–144). Springer Berlin Heidelberg. doi:10.1007/BFb0054122

Blum, M., Evans, W., Gemmell, P., Kannan, S., & Naor, M. (1994). Checking the correctness of memories. *Algorithmica, 12*(2), 225–244. doi:10.1007/BF01185212

Boneh, D., Gentry, C., & Waters, B. (2005). Collusion resistant broadcast encryption with short ciphertexts and private keys. *Advances in Cryptology–CRYPTO, 2005,* 258–275.

Borgmann, M., Hahn, T., Herfert, M., Kunz, T., Richter, M., Viebeg, U., & Vowe, S. (2012). *On the Security of Cloud Storage Services.* Fraunhofer-Verlag.

Cao, N., Yu, S., Yang, Z., Lou, W., & Hou, Y. T. (2012). *LT Codes-based Secure and Reliable Cloud Storage Service. In Processing of 2012 IEEE INFOCOM* (pp. 693–701). IEEE.

Cha, B., Seo, J., & Kim, J. (2012). Design of attribute-based access control in cloud computing environment. *The International Conference on IT Convergence and Security,* 41-50.

Chambers, J. (2013). *Windows Azure Web Sites.* John Wiley & Sons.

Chase, M. (2007). *Multi-authority attribute based encryption. In Theory of Cryptography* (pp. 515–534). Springer Berlin Heidelberg.

Chase, M., & Chow, S. (2009). Improving privacy and security in multi-authority attribute-based encryption. *The 16th ACM conference on Computer and communications security* (pp. 121-130). ACM.

Chen, B., & Curtmola, R. (2012). Robust Dynamic Provable Data Possession. *The 32nd International IEEE Conference on Distributed Computing Systems Workshops* (pp. 515-525). IEEE.

Chen, B., & Curtmola, R. (2013). Towards self-repairing replication-based storage systems using untrusted clouds. *The 3rd ACM conference on Data and application security and privacy* (pp. 377-388). ACM.

Chen, C., Zhang, Z., & Feng, D. (2011). *Efficient ciphertext policy attribute-based encryption with constant-size ciphertext and constant computation-cost. In Provable Security* (pp. 84–101). Springer Berlin Heidelberg.

Chen, Y., Chu, C., Tzeng, W., & Zhou, J. (2013). *Cloudhka: A cryptographic approach for hierarchical access control in cloud computing. In Applied Cryptography and Network Security* (pp. 37–52). Springer Berlin Heidelberg.

Cong, W., Ren, K., Lou, W., & Li, J. (2010). Toward publicly auditable secure cloud data storage services. *IEEE Network*, 24(4), 19–24. doi:10.1109/MNET.2010.5510914

Delerable, C., Paillier, P., & Pointcheval, D. (2007). Fully collusion secure dynamic broadcast encryption with constant-size ciphertexts or decryption keys. *Pairing-Based Cryptography–Pairing, 2007*, 39–59. doi:10.1007/978-3-540-73489-5_4

di Vimercati, S. D., Samarati, P., & Jajodia, S. (2005). *Policies, models, and languages for access control. In Databases in Networked Information Systems* (pp. 225–237). Springer Berlin Heidelberg. doi:10.1007/978-3-540-31970-2_18

Doshi, N., & Jinwala, D. (2012). *Hidden access structure ciphertext policy attribute based encryption with constant length ciphertext. In Advanced Computing, Networking and Security* (pp. 515–523). Springer Berlin Heidelberg.

Doshi, N., & Jinwala, D. (2012). *Hidden access structure ciphertext policy attribute based encryption with constant length ciphertext. In Advanced Computing, Networking and Security* (pp. 515–523). Springer Berlin Heidelberg.

Erway, C., Küpçü, A., Papamanthou, C., & Tamassia, R. (2009). Dynamic provable data possession. *The 16th ACM conference on Computer and communications security* (pp. 213-222). ACM.

Etemad, M., & Kupcu, A. (2013). Transparent Distributed and Replicated Dynamic Provable Data Possession. *The 11th international conference on Applied Cryptography and Network Security* (pp. 1-18). Springer Berlin Heidelberg.

Ferraiolo, D., Kuhn, D. R., & Chandramouli, R. (2003). *Role-based access control*. Artech House.

Ferrara, A., Madhusudan, P., & Parlato, G. (2013). *Policy analysis for self-administrated role-based access control. In Tools and Algorithms for the Construction and Analysis of Systems* (pp. 432–447). Springer Berlin Heidelberg.

Fiat, A., & Naor, M. (1994). *Broadcast encryption. In Advances in Cryptology—CRYPTO'93* (pp. 480–491). Springer Berlin Heidelberg. doi:10.1007/3-540-48329-2_40

Fujisaki, E., & Okamoto, T. (1999). *Secure integration of asymmetric and symmetric encryption schemes. In Advances in Cryptology* (pp. 537–554). Springer Berlin Heidelberg.

Gagné, M. (2011). *Identity-Based Encryption. In Encyclopedia of Cryptography and Security* (pp. 594–596). Springer Science Business Media.

Garg, S. K., Versteeg, S., & Buyya, R. (2013). A framework for ranking of cloud computing services. *Future Generation Computer Systems*, 29(4), 1012–1023. doi:10.1016/j.future.2012.06.006

Gentry, C., & Halevi, S. (2009). *Hierarchical identity based encryption with polynomially many levels. In Theory of Cryptography* (pp. 437–456). Springer Berlin Heidelberg.

Gentry, C., & Waters, B. (2009). Adaptive security in broadcast encryption systems (with short ciphertexts). *Advances in Cryptology-EUROCRYPT, 2009*, 171–188.

Goh, E., Shacham, H., Modadugu, N., & Boneh, D. (2003). Sirius: Securing remote untrusted storage. *Network and Distributed System Security (NDSS) Symposium*, 131-145.

Gonzalez, C., Border, C., & Oh, T. (2013). Teaching in amazon EC2. *The 13th annual ACM SIGITE conference on Information technology education* (pp. 149-150). ACM.

Goodrich, M. T., Tamassia, R., & Schwerin, A. (2001). Implementation of an authenticated dictionary with skip lists and commutative hashing. *DARPA Information Survivability Conference* (pp. 68-82). IEEE. 10.1109/DISCEX.2001.932160

Goyal, V., Pandey, O., Sahai, A., & Waters, B. (2006). Attribute-based encryption for fine-grained access control of encrypted data. *The 13th ACM conference on Computer and communications security* (pp. 89-98). ACM.

Halevy, D., & Shamir, A. (2002). *The LSD broadcast encryption scheme. In Advances in Cryptology—CRYPTO 2002* (pp. 47–60). Springer Berlin Heidelberg. doi:10.1007/3-540-45708-9_4

Hohenberger, S., & Waters, B. (2013). Attribute-based encryption with fast decryption. *Public-Key Cryptography–PKC, 2013*, 162–179.

Horwitz, J., & Lynn, B. (2002). *Toward hierarchical identity-based encryption. In Advances in Cryptology—EUROCRYPT 2002* (pp. 466–481). Springer Berlin Heidelberg. doi:10.1007/3-540-46035-7_31

Juels, A., & Kaliski, B. (2007). Pors: Proofs of retrievability for large files. *The 2007 ACM Conference on Computer and Communications Security* (pp. 584-597). ACM.

Jung, T., Li, X., Wan, Z., & Wan, M. (2013). *Privacy preserving cloud data access with multi-authorities. In The 2013 IEEE INFOCOM* (pp. 2625–2633). IEEE.

Kallahalla, M., Riedel, E., Swaminathan, R., Wang, Q., & Fu, K. (2003). Plutus: Scalable Secure File Sharing on Untrusted Storage. *2nd usinex conference on file and storage technologies*, 29-42.

Kim, J., Susilo, W., Au, M. H., & Seberry, J. (2013). Efficient Semi-static Secure Broadcast Encryption Scheme. *Pairing-Based Cryptography–Pairing, 2013*, 62–76.

Li, C., Chen, Y., Tan, P., & Yang, G. (2012). An Efficient Provable Data Possession Scheme with Data Dynamics. *The International Conference on Computer Science & Service System* (pp. 706-710). IEEE.

Li, C., Chen, Y., Tan, P., & Yang, G. (2013). *Towards comprehensive provable data possession in cloud computing. Wuhan University Journal of Natural Sciences*.

Li, J., Chen, X., Jia, C., & Lou, W. (2013). Identity-based Encryption with Outsourced Revocation in Cloud Computing. *IEEE Transactions on Computers*, 1–12.

Li, M., Yu, S., Ren, K., & Lou, W. (2010). *Securing personal health records in cloud computing: Patient-centric and fine-grained data access control in multi-owner settings. In Security and Privacy in Communication Networks* (pp. 89–106). Springer Berlin Heidelberg.

Li, M., Yu, S., Zheng, Y., Ren, K., & Lou, W. (2013). Scalable and secure sharing of personal health records in cloud computing using attribute-based encryption. *IEEE Transactions on Parallel and Distributed Systems*, 24(1), 131–143. doi:10.1109/TPDS.2012.97

Li, N. (2011). Discretionary Access Control. In Encyclopedia of Cryptography and Security (pp. 864-866). Springer US.

Li, Q., Xiong, H., Zhang, F., & Zeng, S. (2013). An expressive decentralizing kp-abe scheme with constant-size ciphertext. *International Journal of Network Security, 15*(3), 161–170.

Liu, F., Gu, D., & Lu, H. (2011). An improved dynamic provable data possession model. *The IEEE International Conference on Cloud Computing and Intelligence Systems* (pp. 290-295). IEEE.

Liu, H., Zhang, P., & Lun, J. (2013). Public Data Integrity Verification for Secure Cloud Storage. *Journal of Networks, 8*(2), 373–380. doi:10.4304/jnw.8.2.373-380

Liu, Q., Wang, G., & Wu, J. (2010). Efficient sharing of secure cloud storage services. *The 10th International Conference on Computer and Information Technology (CIT)* (pp. 922-929). IEEE.

Mao, Y., Zhang, X., Chen, M., & Zhan, Y. (2013). Constant Size Hierarchical Identity-Based Encryption Tightly Secure in the Full Model without Random Oracles. *The 2013 Fourth International Conference on Emerging Intelligent Data and Web Technologies (EIDWT)* (pp. 652-657). IEEE.

McCune, J. M., Jaeger, T., Berger, S., Caceres, R., & Sailer, R. (2006). Shamon: A system for distributed mandatory access control. *22nd Annual Computer Security Applications Conference* (pp. 23-32). IEEE. 10.1109/ACSAC.2006.47

Menezes, A. J., Van Oorschot, P. C., & Vanstone, S. A. (1996). *Handbook of applied cryptography.* CRC Press. doi:10.1201/9781439821916

Merkle, R. C. (1980). Protocols for public key cryptosystms. *IEEE Symposium on Security and Privacy* (pp. 122-122). IEEE Computer Society.

Miller, R. (2010). *Amazon Addresses EC2 Power Outages Data Center Knowledge.* Retrieved from http://www.datacenterknowledge.com/archives/2010/05/10/amazon-addresses-ec2-power-outages/

Mukundan, R., Madria, S., & Linderman, M. (2012). Replicated Data Integrity Verification in Cloud. *A Quarterly Bulletin of the Computer Society of the IEEE Technical Committee on Data Engineering, 35*(4), 55–64.

Nishide, T., Yoneyama, K., & Ohta, K. (2008). *Attribute-Based Encryption with Partially Hidden Encryptor-Specified Access Structures. In Applied cryptography and network security* (pp. 111–129). Springer Berlin Heidelberg.

Pandey, U. S., & Anjali, J. (2013). Google app engine and performance of the Web Application. *International Journal (Toronto, Ont.), 2*(2).

Plank, J. S. (1997). A Tutorial on Reed-Solomon Coding for Fault-Tolerance in RAID-like Systems. *Software, Practice & Experience, 27*(9), 995–1012. doi:10.1002/(SICI)1097-024X(199709)27:9<995::AID-SPE111>3.0.CO;2-6

Pugh, W. (1990). Skip lists: A probabilistic alternative to balanced trees. *Communications of the ACM, 33*(6), 668–676. doi:10.1145/78973.78977

Qian, H., Li, J., & Zhang, Y. (2013). Privacy-Preserving Decentralized Ciphertext-Policy Attribute-Based Encryption with Fully Hidden Access Structure. Information and Communications Security (pp. 363-372). Springer International Publishing.

Rashmi, K. V., Shah, N. B., Kumar, P. V., & Ramchandran, K. (2009). Explicit construction of optimal exact regenerating codes for distributed storage. *47th Annual Allerton Conference onCommunication, Control, and Computing* (pp. 1243-1249). IEEE. 10.1109/ALLERTON.2009.5394538

Sahai, A., & Waters, B. (2005). Fuzzy identity-based encryption. *Advances in Cryptology–EUROCRYPT*, *2005*, 457–473.

Shacham, H., & Waters, B. (2013). Compact Proofs of Retrievability. *Journal of Cryptology*, *26*(3), 442–483. doi:10.100700145-012-9129-2

Shalabi, S. M., Doll, C. L., Reilly, J. D., & Shore, M. (2011). *Patent No. U.S. Patent Application 13/311,278.* Washington, DC: US Patent Office.

Si, X., Wang, P., & Zhang, L. (2013). KP-ABE Based Verifiable Cloud Access Control Scheme. *The 12th IEEE International Conference on Trust, Security and Privacy in Computing and Communications (TrustCom)* (pp. 34-41). IEEE.

Srinivasan, S. (2014). *Cloud Computing Providers. In Cloud Computing Basics* (pp. 61–80). Springer New York. doi:10.1007/978-1-4614-7699-3_4

Tim, M., Subra, K., & Shahed, L. (2009). *Cloud security and privacy*. O'Reilly & Associates.

Vimercati, S. D., Foresti, S., Jajodia, S., Paraboschi, S., & Samarati, P. (2007). Over-encryption: Management of Access Control Evolution on Outsourced Data. *The 33rd international conference on Very large databases* (pp. 123-134). VLDB Endowment.

Wan, Z., Liu, J., & Deng, R. H. (2012). HASBE: A hierarchical attribute-based solution for flexible and scalable access control in cloud computing. *IEEE Transactions on Information Forensics and Security*, *7*(2), 743–754. doi:10.1109/TIFS.2011.2172209

Wang, C., Chow, S. S., Wang, Q., Ren, K., & Lou, W. (2013). Privacy-Preserving Public Auditing for Secure Cloud Storage. *IEEE Transactions on Computers*, *62*(2), 362–375. doi:10.1109/TC.2011.245

Wang, G., Liu, Q., & Wu, J. (2010). Hierarchical attribute-based encryption for fine-grained access control in cloud storage services. *The 17th ACM conference on Computer and communications security* (pp. 735-737). ACM.

Wang, G., Liu, Q., & Wu, J. (2011). Achieving fine-grained access control for secure data sharing on cloud servers. *Concurrency and Computation*, *23*(12), 1443–1464. doi:10.1002/cpe.1698

Wang, G., Liu, Q., & Wu, J. (2014). Time-based proxy re-encryption scheme for secure data sharing in a cloud environment. *Information Sciences*, *258*, 355–370. doi:10.1016/j.ins.2012.09.034

Wang, G., Liu, Q., Wu, J., & Guo, M. (2011). Hierarchical attribute-based encryption and scalable user revocation for sharing data in cloud servers. *Computers & Security, 30*(5), 320-331.

Wang, H., & Zhang, Y. (2014). On the Knowledge Soundness of a Cooperative Provable Data Possession Scheme in Multicloud Storage. *IEEE Transactions on Parallel and Distributed Systems, 25*(1), 264–267. doi:10.1109/TPDS.2013.16

Wang, Q., Wang, C., Ren, K., Lou, W., & Li, J. (2011). Enabling Public Auditability and Data Dynamics for Storage Security in Cloud Computing. *IEEE Transactions on Parallel and Distributed Systems, 22*(5), 847–859. doi:10.1109/TPDS.2010.183

Waters, B. (2011). Ciphertext-Policy Attribute-Based Encryption: An Expressive, Efficient, and Provably Secure Realization. *Public Key Cryptography–PKC, 2011,* 53–70.

Wikipedia. (2014a, April). *ID-based encryption.* Retrieved from http://en.wikipedia.org/wiki/ID-based_encryption

Wikipedia. (2014b). *Role-based access control.* Retrieved from http://en.wikipedia.org/wiki/Role-based_access_control

Xu, J., & Chang, E. C. (2011). *Towards efficient provable data possession.* IACR Cryptology ePrint Archive.

Yang, K., & Jia, X. (2012). Data storage auditing service in cloud computing: Challenges, methods and opportunities. *World Wide Web (Bussum), 15*(4), 409–428. doi:10.100711280-011-0138-0

Yang, K., Jia, X., Ren, K., Zhang, B., & Xie, R. (2013). Dac-macs: Effective data access control for multi-authority cloud storage systems. *IEEE Transactions on Information Forensics and Security, 8*(11), 1790–1801. doi:10.1109/TIFS.2013.2279531

Yang, K., & Xiaohua, J. (2014). *TSAS: Third-Party Storage Auditing Service. In Security for Cloud Storage Systems* (pp. 7–37). Springer New York. doi:10.1007/978-1-4614-7873-7_2

Yu, S. (2010). *Data sharing on untrusted storage with attribute-based encryption* (PhD dissertation). Worcester Polytechnic Institute.

Yu, S., Wang, C., Ren, K., & Lou, W. (2010). *Achieving secure, scalable, and grained data access control in cloud computing. In The 2010 IEEE INFOCOM* (pp. 1–9). IEEE.

Yuan, J., & Yu, S. (2013). Proofs of retrievability with public verifiability and constant communication cost in cloud. *Proceedings of the 2013 international workshop on Security in cloud computing* (pp. 19-26). ACM. 10.1145/2484402.2484408

Zhang, Y., & Blanton, M. (2013). Efficient dynamic provable possession of remote data via balanced update trees. *The 8th ACM SIGSAC symposium on Information, computer and communications security* (pp. 183-194). ACM.

Zhang, Y., & Chen, J. (2012). Access control as a service for public cloud storage. *32nd International Conference on Distributed Computing Systems Workshops (ICDCSW)* (pp. 526-536). IEEE. 10.1109/ICDCSW.2012.65

Zheng, Q., & Xu, S. (2012). Secure and Effcient Proof of Storage with Deduplication. *The second ACM conference on data and application security and privacy* (pp. 1-12). ACM.

Zhou, L., Varadharajan, V., & Hitchens, M. (2011). Enforcing role-based access control for secure data storage in the cloud. *The Computer Journal, 54*(10), 1675–1675. doi:10.1093/comjnl/bxr080

Zhu, Y., Ahn, G., Hu, H., Yau, S., An, H., & Hu, C. (2013). Dynamic Audit Services for Outsourced Storages in Clouds. *IEEE Transactions on Services Computing, 6*(2), 227–238. doi:10.1109/TSC.2011.51

Zhu, Y., Hu, H., Ahn, G., Huang, D., & Wang, S. (2012). *Towards temporal access control in cloud computing. In The 2012 IEEE INFOCOM* (pp. 2576–2580). IEEE.

Zhu, Y., Hu, H., Ahn, G., Yu, M., & Zhao, H. (2012). Comparison-based encryption for fine-grained access control in clouds. *The second ACM conference on Data and Application Security and Privacy* (pp. 105-116). ACM.

Zhu, Y., Hu, H., Ahn, G. J., & Yu, M. (2012). Cooperative Provable Data Possession for Integrity Verification in Multicloud Storage. *IEEE Transactions on Parallel and Distributed Systems, 23*(12), 2231–2244. doi:10.1109/TPDS.2012.66

This research was previously published in the Handbook of Research on Machine Learning Innovations and Trends edited by Aboul Ella Hassanien and Tarek Gaber, pages 61-93, copyright year 2017 by Information Science Reference (an imprint of IGI Global).

Chapter 59
Digital Forensics in Distributed Environment

Asha Joseph
VIT University, India

K. John Singh
VIT University, India

ABSTRACT

This chapter is about an ongoing implementation of a digital forensic framework that could be used with standalone systems as well as in distributed environments, including cloud systems. It is oriented towards combining concepts of cyber forensics and security frameworks in operating systems. The framework consists of kernel mechanisms for data and event monitoring. The system monitoring is done in kernel mode by various kernel modules and forensic model mapping is done in user mode using the data collected by those kernel modules. Further, the authors propose a crime model mapping mechanism that makes use of rule sets that are derived from common cyber/digital crime patterns. The decision-making algorithm can be easily extended from a node in a computing cluster, to a cloud. The authors discuss the challenges to digital forensics in distributed environment and cloud extensions and provide some case studies where the proposed framework is applied.

INTRODUCTION

This chapter is about an ongoing implementation of the framework in the field of digital forensic which could be used with the standalone system as well as for forensics in the distributed environment. It is oriented towards combining the concepts of cyber forensics, security frameworks in Operating Systems, digital forensic support integrated with Operating Systems, challenges of digital forensics and proposed solution for such challenges in a typical distributed computing environment.

Digital forensics is around for a while and is rapidly becoming a specialized and accepted investigative technique with its own tools and legal precedents that validate the discipline. The aim of digital forensics is not to prevent the crime as and when it happens, but to identify the victim and criminal either proactively or after the attack or incident occurs in the system or in the network; analyze it in depth

DOI: 10.4018/978-1-5225-8176-5.ch059

Copyright © 2019, IGI Global. Copying or distributing in print or electronic forms without written permission of IGI Global is prohibited.

and record it for further reference. Computer forensics can be defined as "the application of computer investigation and analysis techniques in the interests of determining potential legal evidence"; while digital forensics can be defined as "the application of scientifically established methods in preserving, collecting, validating, identifying, analysing, interpreting and presenting digital evidence to the court of law after obtaining the evidence from reconstruction of events if possible". Digital forensics can be categorized into different groups such as Cyber Forensics, Disk Forensics, Memory Forensics, Cloud Forensics, Network forensics etc. And the attackers are usually referred as cyber criminals not as digital criminals and the crime is referred as cybercrime.

BACKGROUND

Digital Forensics

The application of scientifically established methods in collecting, preserving, validating, identifying, analyzing, interpreting and presenting digital evidence to the court of law after obtaining the evidence from the reconstruction of events if possible.

Memory Forensics

It is the forensic analysis of a computer's memory dump. Advanced computer attacks will use stealth techniques to avoid leaving traceable evidence data on the computer's non-volatile memory (hard drive, SSD etc). In those situations, the computing system's memory (RAM) dump is taken using OS tools or third-party tools for further forensic analysis. Using OS tools and symbolic debugging information of the OS components, it is possible to substantially recreate the state of the computing system to a reasonable analysis at the process and resource level.

Disk Forensics

It is the analysis of storage devices which comes in numerous categories in terms of physical interfaces and storage technologies. The forensic analysis of disks mainly consists of the application and operating system logs, picture analysis, signature/keyword analysis of known digital entities of criminal nature, timeline analysis, mailbox, databases, cookies, registry – virtually any persistent data that is commonly used by various application software and operating system.

Network Forensics

It is all about the monitoring and analysis of computer network traffic for evidence collection, information gathering or even intrusion detection. Compared to the other areas of digital forensics, network forensics deal with more volatile data and thus it is considered as a proactive approach to forensic investigation (Sammons, 2015)

Network security should be a huge concern to all of us since the networks are under near-constant attack from lone hackers, organized criminals, and foreign countries. Cybercrime, Cyberwar, and cyberterrorism are major problems threatening not only our countries and companies but our personal computers as well. Networks represent a far greater challenge, from a forensic standpoint. They vary wildly in size and complexity. There are several tools to help us protect our critical network infrastructure, including firewalls and intrusion detection systems. Smart organizations plan for security breaches enabling them to respond efficiently and effectively minimizing the damage and increasing the odds that they can identify the perpetrator(s) (Shrivastava et al., 2016; Shrivastava, 2016).

Cloud Forensics

Cloud computing can be viewed as digital computing using the shared collection of networked resources. So, it is evident that cloud forensics is closely related to network forensics. In a cloud, resources are shared and often duplicated (to avoid data losses) and a cloud service provider typically has hundreds to thousands of tenants from various jurisdictions whose computing needs are satisfied by the shared networked resources that the service provider owns. Information security in terms of privacy and access control to these shared resources are of paramount importance in such a multi-tenant environment. Further to complicate the matters, huge sets of resources can be provisioned and de-provisioned dynamically in a cloud. Thus, it is apparent that legacy methods of digital forensics tend to be lesser effective in a cloud environment. Instead of trying to analyze the huge amount of data for evidence – which itself may require a cloud service in terms of required computing power, a proactive approach will be more practical. In a proactive approach (as we saw in network forensics), we monitor and analyze the cloud system in real time using a distributed monitoring framework. We will see more of this proposed framework as we progress through the chapter.

Digital forensic tools are application programs and utilities that automate various or specific digital forensic functions. These tools are credited for amongst other things reducing the time required to analyze large volumes of data, case management, and standardized reporting and making it possible to carry out tasks that would otherwise have been impossible to complete manually. It is acknowledged that automation results in the reduction in costs and significantly shortens the time needed for training forensic professionals (Saxena et al., 2012).

David Bennett (2011) states that legal evidence might be sought to constitute a wide range of computer crimes or misuses such as child pornography, use of abusive languages, audio or video, including theft of trade secrets, theft of or destruction of intellectual property and fraud. Usually, digital evidence is the event logs generated by application software as well as operating system software. In modern Operating Systems, any application process will be running in a much-closed environment and Operating System will make sure that an application has minimal knowledge of any other application process that is running in the system. So, naturally, evidence data as event logs generated by such application processes lack the overall system perspective. The data discovered is important in forensic analysis and in solving various computer crimes through the proper log or record preservation, which leads to profiling.

The Statistics

These are some of the statistics of the study conducted on cyber-crimes in India. In the last 2+ years, about 200 zero-day exploits unleashed.11.6 million mobile devices are infected at any given time. In 2014, more than 348 million identities stolen. Overall, about 594 million people were affected by cybercrime. The statistics followed by the predictions by cyber security analysts are as follows:

It was predicted that 2017 would be the year of online extortion. More than 30% of crimes by criminal networks will involve the theft or use of stolen data moved across international boundaries. Cyber/digital crime will cost the global economy over the US $650 billion, climbing over to over US$1 trillion by 2020. It would be more than 1.5 billion people will be affected by data breaches by 2020.A graphical representation of rising crime rate in India and specifically in the southern part of India are given in Figure 1.

The following are some of the statistics by the study conducted by National Cyber/digital Safety and Security Standards Summit, India:

The cybercrime rate has reached its peak in the year 2015. Cyber security analysts predict that 2016 will be the year of online extortion. By 2019, more than 30% of crimes committed by transactional criminal networks will involve the theft or use of stolen data moved across international boundaries (Joseph & Singh, 2016). By 2020, more than 1.5 billion people will be affected by data breaches. The following Figure 2 represents the recent statistics.

More Recent Findings

Small and midsized organizations (SMBs), defined as those with 100 to 1,000 employees, are hardly immune to cyber/digital crime.

According to the recent Keeper Security's "The State of SMB Cybersecurity" report, a staggering 50 percent of small and midsized organizations reported suffering at least one cyber-attack in the last 12

Figure 1. Rise of crime rate in Southern India

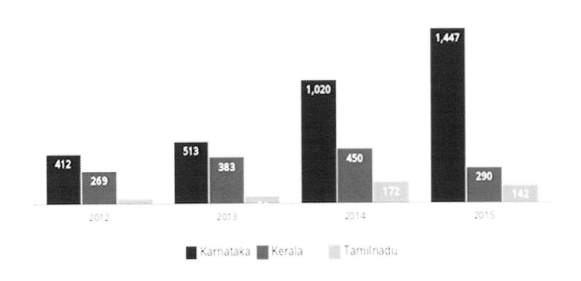

Total Cyber Crime Cases Reported

Figure 2. Number of cybercrime cases reported

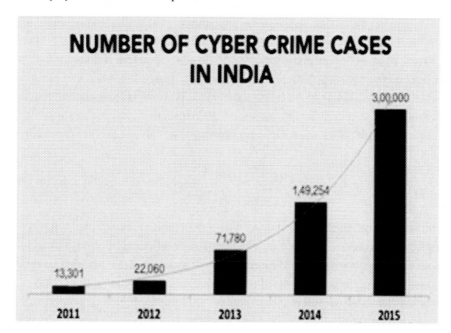

months. The average cost of a data breach involving theft of assets totaled $879,582 for these SMBs. They spent another $955,429 to restore normal business in the wake of successful attacks. For these SMBs, 60 percent of employees use the exact same password for everything they access. Meanwhile, 63 percent of confirmed data breaches leverage a weak, default or stolen password. (Techpayments, 2016)

Research Challenges in the Field of Digital Forensics

Constant developments in Information Technology and communication have posed many challenges in the field of digital forensics. Based on the advancements existing digital forensic models (Shrivastava, 2017), these are some of the major challenges in this field:

1. The lack of real data sources for study and analysis purposes (Baggili & Breitinger, 2015)
2. The lack of efficient and readily available tools for data acquisition and analysis
3. The limitation of the operating environment during the acquisition of data
4. The accessibility to the data – especially if the data is on distributed systems
5. The volume of data and the time is taken to undertake an investigation
6. The ultimate lack and differences of laws across the countries
7. Multitude of OS platforms and file systems
8. Cloud system that has multi-tenancy and involves multiple jurisdictions

Legal support and forensic standardization are also challenges encountered in network forensics. As stated by Chen et al. (2015) real-time and comprehensive audits in distributed environments like cloud are very difficult and post audits can be rather challenging. The capacity of comprehensive investigations and the collection of web exception information are also limited.

Evidence disappearance is also a major challenge in the distributed digital environment, especially in cloud networks. Environmental or regional factors such as, the collection of evidence should be in accordance with local laws and regulations that may increase the difficulty in time and costs of forensic investigations. Privacy issues of legitimate users are again a problem that is encountered in digital forensics. In a multi-tenant environment, how to qualify forensics range to protect the privacy of legitimate users is still a challenge that needs to be faced. Evidence fixation/collection/preservation can be very complex in the cloud and distributed environments, because investigation involves non-standard data sets, such as processes, workflow information etc. Long-term preservation of evidence is a huge challenge.

PROPOSED WORK

Crime follows humanity from the Garden of Eden and human being is confronted with interesting mental conflicts such as whether to declare the world he is dared to commit a crime and get away with it or protect himself. This conflict, deepest in our minds manifests itself in actions: the criminal commits mistake and leaves traces, always; evidence is the digital footprint left out during the commission of cyber/digital/ digital crimes such as terrorism, fraud identity theft or child pornography. Considering these aspects to get more from the interpretation of digital evidence, suggests for a new method - "crime and criminal profiling". Nykodym (2008) Point out that "the idea that an individual committing the crime in cyber space can fit a certain outline (a profile) may seem far-fetched, but evidence suggests that certain distinguishing characteristics do regularly exist in cyber/digital criminals". Therefore, the possibility of using the tools and techniques discussed by Tennakoon (2016) might be worth testing in a practical scenario.

The steps/stages in criminal profiling are shown in Figure 3 (Adapted from Tennakoon,2016)

The criminal profiling has six stages:

1. Understanding what aspect of the victim attracted the criminals ("criminology")
2. Identification of a motive
3. Identification of characteristics of the criminal (expert, script-kiddie)
4. Collecting Evidence
5. Analysis of evidence
6. Repeat the above to refine the deductions.

From the research point of view, this analysis should give insights into what all data is to be collected from the system in the first place.

The rest of this chapter is dedicated to the proposed framework, explaining the fundamental concepts and technologies behind its operation. It is to be noted that the system is designed to be scalable and can be easily tailored from a single host solution to a distributed digital forensic system that can be an integrated part of a cluster, grid or even a cloud.

Typical Scenario

To illustrate the fundamental concepts on which the proposed architecture is conceived, the following scenario is considered:

Figure 3. Stages in criminal profiling

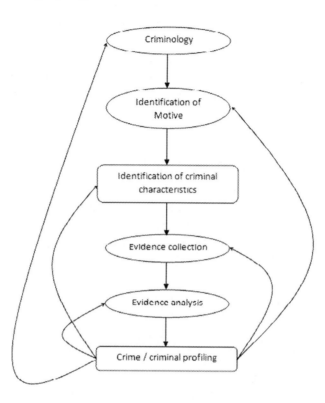

An attacker gets all the credentials of a victim's internet banking account - including his mobile phone or an illegally duplicate SIM. With the security measures currently in practice, such an attacker can have open access to the victim's bank account - because even the 2-factor authentication using mobile One Time Password (OTP) will be circumvented by the attacker. However, the proposed architecture can detect, log and even alert the authorities in runtime when this happens. This is how it is proposed to achieve:

The proposed system is installed on the server where the banking application server runs. The banking server application does not have any dependency or relation with the proposed software framework. For simplicity, we are assuming that the server is not part of a distributed system. To maintain anonymity, such an attacker will usually try to login to the bank account from many public proxies available on the Internet. We can get an exhaustive database of such proxy servers from many government authorities' private sources. Have such a database ready for the forensic model-matching component (fraud detection) in the architecture (Shrivastava & Gupta, 2014). The kernel network subsystem hook detects that a TCP connection is initiated to a socket belonging to the banking server process and notifies the model-matching component that a connection attempt is made to the banking server process. The model-matching component notes that the connection is made from one of the proxies in its database. The username and password information is encrypted end to end from the attacker's host to the server process and hence our framework cannot access such details, but we do have a kernel process subsystem hook, which can monitor file access and network access of each process in the server. The security model-matching component tells this process subsystem hook to watch out for imminent local or network database access from the banking server process.

In the cases, such as, the scope of the digital crime is not limited or only if the OS kernel has access to all events; a trigger is made by the model-matching component as soon as these happen in a configurable time window (some hundreds of milliseconds). The logs generated by the banking server process and all other relevant logs for that time is tagged and archived for further analysis. This way, the evidence of a possible crime is collected in real time, without the burden of a huge data set and low rate of false positives. More than that, none of the existing server applications are to be modified (Shrivastava et al., 2012).

The Role of Operating System

The operating system is the most powerful software, the brain of the computer system, so how can it assist in cyber/digital forensics? From a conventional criminal forensics perspective, it is very well equivalent to the most intelligent and knowledgeable person assisting an autopsy. Being the master software running on a digital computing platform, it is evident that Operating System software has the ultimate knowledge and control over an event that is happening in the system. In other words, any software running as a part of Operating Systems has the capability to monitor all events from a system-wide perspective. At the same time, popular general-purpose Operating Systems has minimal security mechanisms enforced by default because it will affect the overall system experience by the end user (e.g. the infamous User Authentication Module – UAM – in Windows) and event logging from a cyber/digital-forensic perspective is not even a secondary priority of popular Operating Systems.

Many server applications are not configured or maintained properly for security and security oriented auditing. The scope of a digital crime may not be limited to the event logs generated by a single server/user application. It may be spread across much different software (and even hardware) and at present, there is no centralized entity to co-relate and then analyze them to make a coherent security decision. Only the operating system kernel has access to all the events in the system and hence a kernel-oriented approach is required for the effective generation and logging of security events in a host/server system.

The authentication and authorization enforced by popular operating systems do not enforce the security policies on many user actions that can potentially be a security threat. This is usually justified in terms of user-friendliness and system performance. The amount of data to be analyzed for finding a valid evidence of the crime is huge. This is primarily because all usual logging schemes are very primitive in nature and do not differentiate between normal logs and logs that can be potential candidates for cyber/digital forensic evidence. Many digital services are cloud-based and are inherently distributed across host machine boundaries. From a cyber forensic point of view, coordinated monitoring of potential security threats and related events in such a distributed system is virtually non-existing.

It is evident from the above-listed reasons that, digital evidence collection can only be performed satisfactorily by a security-enhanced operating system kernel, which has the following capabilities: It should have a subsystem to enforce security policies based upon one or more digital forensic models. It also should have a subsystem for monitoring the logs from such policy enforcement and logically coordinate them using one or more digital forensic models.

In this work, a new security architecture for is proposed, which tries to incorporate the above capabilities into a typical operating system kernel. For this purpose, Linux Operating System is selected and existing methods for enhancing securities and enforcing security policies in Linux kernel are studied. Various digital forensic models are analyzed and suitable mechanisms to incorporate them as policies into the said subsystem are identified. A mechanism to collect events generated from enforcing these policies is also identified and possibilities to make the system distributed are discussed.

The Targets of Proposed Framework

The target of the proposed work is to find out and classify if there is any cyber security / digital forensic models in place for general purpose Operating Systems at present. If there are, in what all ways it can be further improved and made more effective? If not, propose a practical approach and model for it. It is noted that for profiling crimes and criminals, access to evidence digital data is most important. Since real life evidence data for analysis of cybercrimes are difficult to come by, - a problem that is practically very difficult to take care of - mechanisms that can enable sophisticated logging and tracing in existing systems is identified as a very important area where much research is yet to happen.

Primarily, it is difficult to get access to the run-time state of the systems, and as a result, there can be important information that is not part of the analysis, such as network connections, encryption keys, decrypted data, process lists, and modified code running in memory. It is also noted that in recent times more and more data are stored and managed in distributed hosts (mostly hosted in clouds using virtualized hosts). Hence, the monitoring and logging of events that are related to cyber security in a distributed environment are getting more and more importance. The work mentioned by Chou (2009) opens a new methodology for securing the logs using virtualization tools and comparing it with kernel module approach. It is noted that evidence data acquisition from a computer system can be accomplished in two distinct methods:

One is using logs generated by the applications like web server, FTP server etc. and the another method is using kernel mode analysis and logging system that functions as a part of operating system and thus having exclusive access to all events and data in the system.

The second approach is significantly different from the first because, in operating system kernel, the data and events can be analyzed from the perspective of the whole system – whereas in the first case the information in the logs is severely limited by the scope of the concerned application. However, the second approach involves the additional complexity of kernel mode implementation (that is significantly more advanced and less documented than application level implementations).

The problem further extends to how the event logs generated by the Operating System can be used for forensic analysis. In other words, how the above-described security mechanisms and models can be further extended so that the evidence is made more useful in criminal profiling, another related domain in cyber forensics. Obviously, this work needs access to design and development details of a typical general-purpose Operating System. Considering the Open Source development model that gives us complete access to all such information, Linux is selected as the platform for all practical purposes for this work. The research area of evidence data acquisition system in kernel mode is briefly mentioned in Chou (2009).

Proposed Framework

In this work, security architecture is proposed, which tries to incorporate Information Flow Control and provenance approaches (Pohly et al. 2012) into a typical operating system kernel – and the target of this work is evidence collection and application of digital forensic modeling on the collected evidence. For this purpose, Linux Operating System is selected and existing methods for enhancing securities and enforcing security policies in Linux kernel are studied (Wright, Cowan & Smalley, 2002; Wright, Cowan & Morris, 2002). Various digital forensic models are analyzed and suitable mechanisms to incorporate them as policies into the said subsystem are identified. A mechanism to collect events generated from enforcing these policies is also identified and possibilities to make the system distributed are discussed.

The framework consists of kernel mechanisms for data and event monitoring that encompasses virtually all subsystems of the OS kernel. In addition, a user mode entity is defined that can monitor, classify and store these data and events. This user mode entity can make decisions based on predefined forensic models. We have designed such a system where whole system monitoring is done in the kernel by various kernel modules and forensic model mapping of the provenance data collected by those kernel modules is done by the user mode application modules, shown in Figure 4.

The Linux Security Modules (LSM) allows the Linux kernel to support a variety of computer security models while avoiding favoritism toward any single security implementation. The framework is licensed under the terms of the GNU General Public License and is the standard part of the Linux kernel since Linux version 2.6. AppArmor, SELinux, Smack, TOMOYO Linux, and Yama are the currently accepted modules in the official kernel.LSM was designed to provide the specific needs of everything needed to successfully implement a mandatory access control module while imposing the fewest possible changes to the Linux kernel (Bates, Tian & Butler, 2016). LSM avoids the approach of system call interception. Instead, LSM inserts "hooks" (upcalls to the module) at every point in the kernel where a user-level system call is about to result in access to an important internal kernel object.

LSM Module for Forensics

This is one of the two core components of the proposed architecture. This module acts as a kernel mode counterpart of the Forensic Model Matching (FFM) component that is a user mode component. It es-

Figure 4. The framework

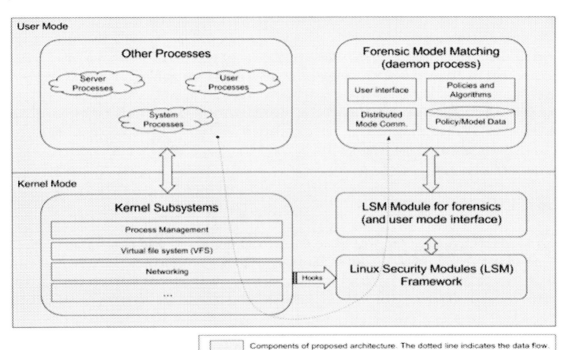

sentially uses the LSM framework to monitor all relevant creation and access of kernel objects (files, network interfaces, network data packets, IPCs) by other processes in the system. The processes and other objects to be monitored are set by the user mode counterpart (FFM) which does it based upon policies currently set.

Forensic Model Matching (Daemon Process) (FMMD)

This is the most important component in the designated architecture. This module runs as a privileged (as root) daemon process. It provides the configuration interface using which policies pertaining to a particular forensic model, which can be further defined and set. It also implements necessary algorithms for implementing that model. As described in the previous section, it uses the kernel mode counterpart to facilitate the required fine-grained access to all objects maintained by the kernel in the system.

The access control rules enforced on the user by the OS is assumed to be in place. The model does not include those rules in the crime model mapping. This is because digital crimes are made regardless of the access controls in place. Criminals either find loopholes in the access restrictions in place (administrative errors) or exploits the vulnerabilities in a process or system (bugs in software) to gain access to the targeted resource. From a cyber forensics point of view, the model to identifies a crime as and when it is committed rather than trying to prevent it (even though this model can be extended for

Figure 5. Crime model mapping module

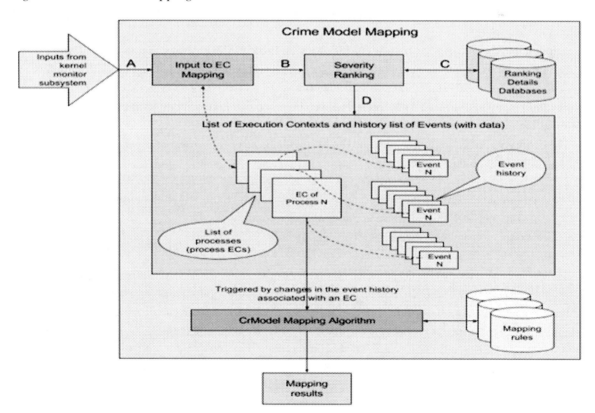

that purpose). Another reason to exclude the access control enforced by the system from this model is to avoid too many unknowns and variables in the model that system administrators have the multitude of ways to set access controls for processes and users.

The Crime Model Mapping Algorithm

The crime model-mapping algorithm makes use of rule-sets, which are derived from common cyber/digital crime patterns. Each of these patterns has parameters that are readily available in the EC and event history associated with it. This includes (but not limited to) the list of known server processes in the system, the database of safe IP addresses which can act as valid source and destinations of network connections, the list of blacklisted IP addresses which are generally proxy IP addresses and attack sites, the network ports to which connections are made from outside, the network ports to which connections are made from the host, the checksum of known malicious binaries and so on.

Cloud and Other Distributed Computing Environments

Distributed computing, especially cloud computing presents some hard challenges for digital forensics. One of the major challenges is that the evidentiary material could be distributed over many servers that can be located in countries (or even continents). This implies a multi-jurisdiction and multi-tenancy environment, which can hinder or delay the investigation severely. Another problem is that the servers can be provisioned and unallocated in a matter of minutes. Because of this dynamic nature of the cloud resources, data (and logs) for multiple customers can be spread across a volatile set of hosts and data centers in the cloud.

Another major problem for traditional forensics applied on the cloud is that users will most likely choose not to store local copies of their data on the local storage of their PCs and other digital devices, given the security, synchronization and share features offered by the cloud. Interaction with data stored in the cloud is normally carried out through a web browser. So, hardly any useful evidence data can be obtained from the storage of a client device.

The discussion so far logically points to the following three options for carrying out effective forensic investigations in a cloud system:

1. Collect evidence data from client devices known to have connected to the cloud
2. Eavesdrop network traffic between client and the cloud
3. Get evidence from the cloud server by legal means

These observations are pointing at the requirement of having a proactive forensic framework - such as the proposed framework discussed here - built into the popular end-user Operating Systems so that a forensic system is in place before and during the attacks. Such a framework can provide effective evidence data with scarcely any performance impact on the devices. We will now see that that the proposed framework can fulfill these requirements and it can be implemented in two distinctly different ways as follows:

1. The framework implemented in each Virtual Machine in the cloud
2. The framework implemented in the client devices of the cloud

The first implementation is more intrusive as it requires the cloud infrastructure changes whereas the second implementation is less intrusive as it involves only the client side of the cloud. We will see each of these approaches in detail as follows:

The Proposed Framework Implemented in Cloud

The system we discussed so far has the boundaries set solely by the host on which it is implemented. The decision-making algorithm can be easily extended to be a node in a computing cluster, grid or even a cloud. Here in this chapter, we are considering cloud environment for such an analysis. We will analyze a proposed technology and framework to monitor and manage resources in a cloud environment which can be readily extended to include the previously explained forensic features.

In cloud computing, the underlying large-scale computing infrastructure is often heterogeneous, not only because it's not economical and reliable to procure all the servers, network devices, and power supply devices in one size and one time, but because different application requires different computer hardware, e.g. workflow extensive computing might need standard and cheap hardware; scientific computing might need specific hardware other than CPU like GPU or ASIC.

There are kinds of resources in the large-scale computing infrastructure need to be managed, CPU load, network bandwidth, disk quota, and even type of operating systems. To provide the better quality of service, resources are provisioned to the users or applications, via load balancing mechanism, high availability mechanism and security and authority mechanism. To maximize cloud utilization, the capacity of application requirements shall be calculated so that minimal cloud computing infrastructure devices shall be procured and maintained. Given access to the cloud-computing infrastructure, applications shall allocate proper resources to perform the computation with time cost and infrastructure cost minimized.

To implement flexible and fine-grained resource monitoring and management in a cloud deployment scenario, such an Advanced Resource Management and Monitoring System (ARMS) must have the following characteristics:

Firstly, it should provide a well-defined method for the cloud operator and his clients to properly communicate with each other and arrive at a set of Service Level Agreements in terms of resource usage.

Secondly, the heterogeneous nature of physical resources (in physical hosts) shall be manageable by a resource management paradigm, which can be used to define the conceptual entity, which can be used uniformly by the resource allocation algorithm. This paradigm must be made simple enough so that the cloud operator and clients can use the underlying concept in their resource negotiations.

Thirdly, the system shall be distributed across the cloud so that it must run in each of the host systems where virtual machines are run by one or more hypervisors. This component integrates itself with host OS as well as the hypervisor (and hence the VMs and virtual networks present in the host), providing complete control over the host system and hosted VMs. The distributed system shall be able to communicate together in the cloud whenever a resource management decision is taken which has the global impact on the cloud operation. This also can be used to take system snapshots as described in Alamulla, Iraqi, and Jones, (2013).

Finally, the resource management system must be able to run in a heterogeneous environment of different operating systems and different hypervisors. Thus, the implementation shall be portable across popular server class operating systems and it shall be able to support all popular hypervisors. This earlier work, in the field of cloud, was to realize these requirements by the design and development of such an advanced resource management system (ARMS) for clouds.

The fine-grained control and monitoring capabilities over resource usage such as bandwidth and memory based upon user-defined rules and conditions demand some components that are a part of the host operating system. Without direct interaction of the host OS as well as with the hypervisor, this kind of control is not possible in a virtual hosting environment. This kind of a component as shown in Figure 6 is the key part of the proposed solution.

To provide the complete access control over the cloud system, it is required to have control over the physical network of hosts within the cloud (the real LAN of hosts) as well as over the virtual networks managed by the hypervisors residing in the hosts. In order to achieve this, ARMS is designed as a distributed system, running on all physical hosts in the cloud setup. This distributed nature of ARMS is also illustrated in Figure 6.

Thus, ARMS have access control and resource management over the whole cloud in a physical and virtual level by distributing itself over the host network of the cloud. Also, being present on the edge host device (gateway), ARMS can also act as a highly efficient firewall, which has reached to the whole host network with its distributed architecture, as shown in Figure 7.

Figure 6. ARMS architecture

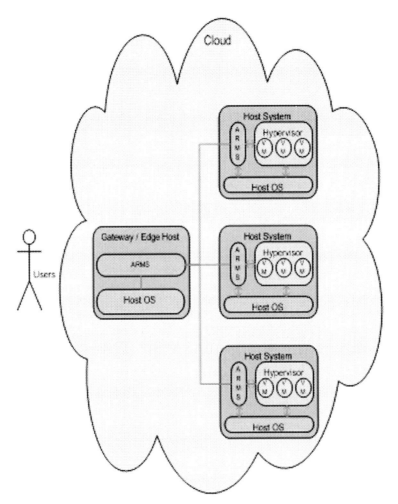

Figure 7. ARMS system architecture

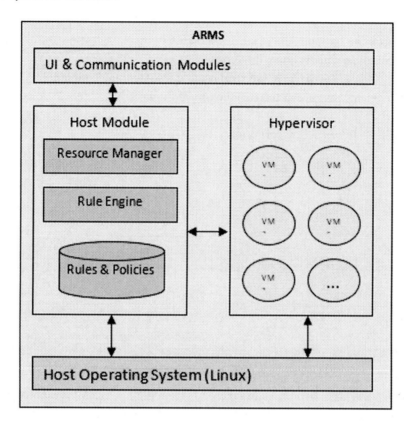

This is particularly effective in a cloud environment as a proactive forensic approach if it can be integrated with the cloud resource provisioning system as shown in ARMS where resource usage allocation and monitoring are implemented using agent software running on each physical host in the cloud. If the proposed system is integrated with the agent module of a system such as ARMS, it has the potential to become a viable solution as a proactive digital forensic framework for any distributed system.

The Proposed Framework Implemented in Cloud Client

Here we will have a case study, where the proposed framework will be able to show that by searching local artifacts, it is possible to find interesting evidentiary material about the user-cloud interaction.

Case Study: Dropbox Client

Dropbox is a very popular cloud-based storage system where the user can install a software application that acts as a client to Dropbox cloud storage service. The user can typically define a directory (folder) on his device (PC or mobile). We will call this folder as his "Dropbox local folder". The client software application will monitor the "Dropbox local folder" for changes and keep the contents of it synchronized with the storage allocated for the user in Dropbox storage servers.

In this case study, the following scenario is considered:

1. The user is installing Dropbox client software on his Linux workstation and "MyDropbox" as his "Dropbox local folder" in his home directory.
2. The user is creating a new a file in the Dropbox local folder and saving it.
3. The user then deletes that file in the Dropbox local folder.

The FFMD has this simple policy definition:

```
[policy]
name=cloud_local_client;
id=1001;
type=file_monitor;
process=dropbox;
monitor=open,read,write,execute,delete;
directory=$home/*;
rank=1;
dependency=nil;
action=log;
```

Note that the policy definition is relatively straightforward. It has a name and id and specifies which process is of interest and what action it can take on files in the folder "MyDropbox" that is present in any of the user's home folder. This rule need not be matched with further and it is indicated by the "nil" dependency attribute of the policy, its rank (importance) is highest and action to be taken is simple logging.

When the user carries out the above described operations, the following is the output log of the framework:

```
Event: Policy match: name=cloud_local_client, id=1001, type=file_monitor
timestamp= 1488643352 (03/04/2017 4:02pm UTC)
process=dropbox, proc id: 12876, user: ashajoseph2015
file_path=/home/ashajoseph2015/MyDropbox/test.txt
file_action=open [flags: read | write] [success]
```

As we can see, the kernel file monitor and process monitor together has hooked the file created by "Dropbox" process and passed it as an event to FFMD module. It analyzed the event using the simple policy and logged the event with all relevant details such as process id, user id, time, file path etc.

```
Event: Policy match: name=cloud_local_client, id=1001, type=file_monitor
timestamp= 1488643693 (03/04/2017 4:08pm UTC)
process=dropbox, id: 12876, user: ashajoseph2015
file_path=/home/ashajoseph2015/MyDropbox/test.txt
file_action=unlink (delete) [success]
```

Again, the kernel file monitor and process monitor together has hooked the file deletion by "Dropbox" process and passed it as an event to FFMD module. It analyzed the event using the simple policy and logged the event with all relevant details.

Case Study: Google Documents Accessed via Web Browser

1. User logs on docs.google.com
2. User creates a word document
3. User deletes a word document

In this case, the FFMD has this simple policy definition:

```
[policy]
name=cloud_local_client;
id=1002;
type=network_monitor;
process=*firefox*,*chrome*;
monitor=connect,disconnect,timeout;
server=docs.google.com/*;
url=*;
protocol=http,https;
rank=1;
dependency=nil;
action=log;
```

The policy describes the browser processes to look for (namely processes that have 'firefox' or 'chrome' in their process names) and asks the framework to monitor the network for HTTP and https communications with the server under docs.google.com. This simple policy has no dependencies; its rank (importance) is highest and the action to be taken is simple logging.

The following is the output log of the framework implementation:

```
Event: Policy Match: name=cloud_local_client, id=1002, type=network_monitor
timestamp= 1488648660 (03/04/2017 5:31pm UTC)
process=firefox, id: 12876, user: ashajoseph2015
url: https://docs.google.com/document/u/0/create?usp=docs_home&ths=true
type: request
rank=1;
dependency=nil;

Event: Policy Match: name=cloud_local_client, id=1002, type=network_monitor
timestamp= 1488648662 (03/04/2017 5:31pm UTC)
process=firefox, id: 12876, user: ashajoseph2015
url: https://docs.google.com/document/u/0/create?usp=docs_home&ths=true
type: response 302
```

```
rank=1;
dependency=nil;

Event: Policy Match: name=cloud_local_client, id=1002, type=network_monitor
timestamp= 1488648665 (03/04/2017 5:31pm UTC)
process=firefox, id: 12876, user: ashajoseph2015
url: https://docs.google.com/document/u/0/d/1CdAfCImh-0oIIWOEM8w1PXZtwsBC56Wd-
pjUNaq5WmSU/edit
type: request
rank=1;
dependency=nil;

Event: Policy Match: name=cloud_local_client, id=1002, type=network_monitor
timestamp= 1488648669 (03/04/2017 5:31pm UTC)
process=firefox, id: 12876, user: ashajoseph2015
url: https://docs.google.com/document/u/0/d/1CdAfCImh-0oIIWOEM8w1PXZtwsBC56Wd-
pjUNaq5WmSU/edit
type: response 200
rank=1;
dependency=nil;
```

These logs clearly show the creation of a new file with an id *1CdAfCImh-0oIIWOEM8w1PXZtwsB-C56WdpjUNaq5WmSU* by the user ashajoseph2015 at 03/04/2017 5:31 pm UTC.

This case study showcases some important limitations of the client-side network monitoring. Because the connection is HTTPS (secure HTTP), after the initial HTTPS handshaking, all communication will be encrypted. So the forensically useful information is only the URL. However, the positive side is that the URL itself will give some important clues such as the document ID as seen in the logs above. With this information and the IP address of this device, it is legally possible to obtain rest of the details such as file name, its owner, and contents from Google.

CONCLUSION

Forensic computing and cyber/digital crime investigation emerged because of increase in digital crime due to the development of the Internet and proliferation of computer technology. In this chapter, we reviewed the literature in computer forensics and identified many categories of active research in computer forensics. A few research categories are framework, trustworthiness, computer forensics in networked /virtualized environments and acquisition and analysis of evidence data. The advances such as components, approaches, and the process of each category have been reviewed and discussed.

After conducting the extensive literature review, it is understood that lack of effective mechanisms in place to collect the data, lack of effective frameworks to classify the data, the volume of evidence data and the time taken to undertake an investigation based upon the data are key limiting factors for future advancements in this domain. Further exploring techniques and technologies for potentially reducing these issues resulted in focusing on approaches such as criminal profiling and better methods of tracing and logging events in the system under observation.

In this chapter, we put forth a proposal, which accomplishes the crime and criminal profiling, using the data collected from a sophisticated operating system level evidence acquisition scheme thus achieving integrity and correctness of the forensic analysis results from distributed and non-distributed systems. If the proposed system is integrated with the agent module of a system such as ARMS, it has the potential to become a viable solution as a proactive digital forensic framework for any distributed system.

REFERENCES

Alamulla, S., Iraqi, Y., & Jones, A. (2013). A Distributed Snapshot Framework for Digital Forensics Evidence Extraction and Event Reconstruction from Cloud Environment. *Proceedings of IEEE International Conference on Cloud Computing Technology and Science*, 699-704. 10.1109/CloudCom.2013.114

Baggili, I., & Breitinger, F. (2015). Data Sources for advancing cyber forensics: What the social world has to offer. *Proceedings of AAAI Spring Symposium*, 6-9.www.aaai.org/docs

Bates, A., Tian, D., & Butler, K. R. B. (2016). Trustworthy Whole-System Provenance for the Linux Kernel. *Proceedings of 24th USENIX Security Symposium*, 319-334.

Bennett, D. W. (2011). *The Challenges Facing Computer Forensics Investigators in Obtaining Information from Mobile Devices for Use in Criminal Investigations*. Retrieved from http://articles.forensicfocus.com

Chen, L., Xu, L., Yuan, X., & Shashidhar, N. (2015, February). Digital forensics in social networks and the cloud: Process, approaches, methods, tools, and challenges. In *Computing, Networking and Communications (ICNC), 2015 International Conference on* (pp. 1132-1136). IEEE.

Chou, B. H., & Tatara, K. (2009). A Secure Virtualized logging scheme for digital Forensic in comparison with Kernel Module approach. *Proceedings of the international conference of ISA*.

Hu, L., Zhang, X., Wang, F., Wang, W., & Zhao, K. (2012). Research on the Architecture Model of Volatile Data Forensics. *Procedia Engineering*, 29, 4254–4258. doi:10.1016/j.proeng.2012.01.653

Joseph, A. (2012). Cloud Computing with Advanced Resource Management. *International Journal of Advanced Technology and Engineering Research*, 4, 21–25.

Joseph, A. (2013a). *Enhanced Resource Management on cloud systems using Distributed Policy and Rule Engines* (Master's Thesis). VTU Bangalore, India.

Joseph, A. (2013b). Enhanced Resource Management using Distributed Policy and Rule Engines. *Proceedings of International Conference on Advanced Computing and Information Technology*.

Joseph, A. (2017). Provenance of Digital Assets-Blockchains and Bitmarks. *IEEE ComSocNwesletter*, 1, 5.

Joseph, A., & Singh, K. J. (2016). The latest Trends and challenges in cyber forensics. *Proceedings of International Conference ICMCECE*, 107.

Morris, J., Smalley, S., & Kroah-Hartman, G. (2002, August). Linux security modules: General security support for the Linux kernel. *USENIX Security Symposium*.

Nykodym, N., Ariss, S., & Kurtz, K. (2008). Computer addiction and cyber-crime. *Journal of Leadership, Accountability and Ethics*, *35*, 55–59.

Pohly, D., McLaughlin, S., McDaniel, P., & Butler, K. (2012). Hi-Fi: Collecting High-Fidelity Whole-System Provenance. *Proceedings of Annual Computer Security Applications Conference*.

Sammons, J. (2015). *The Basics of Digital Forensics - The Primer for Getting Started in Digital Forensics. 2nded*. Syngress Publications.

Saxena, A., Shrivastava, G., & Sharma, K. (2012). Forensic investigation in cloud computing environment. *The International Journal of Forensic Computer Science*, *2*, 64-74.

Shinder, D. (2010). *Profiling and Categorizing Cyber Criminals*. Retrieved October 2016, from www.TechRepublic.com/blog/it-security

Shrivastava, G. (2016, March). Network forensics: Methodical literature review. In *Computing for Sustainable Global Development (INDIACom), 2016 3rd International Conference on* (pp. 2203-2208). IEEE.

Shrivastava, G. (2017). Approaches of network forensic model for investigation. *International Journal of Forensic Engineering*, *3*(3), 195–215. doi:10.1504/IJFE.2017.082977

Shrivastava, G., & Gupta, B. B. (2014, October). An encapsulated approach of forensic model for digital investigation. In *Consumer Electronics (GCCE), 2014 IEEE 3rd Global Conference on* (pp. 280-284). IEEE. 10.1109/GCCE.2014.7031241

Shrivastava, G., Sharma, K., & Dwivedi, A. (2012). Forensic computing models: Technical overview. *CCSEA, SEA, CLOUD, DKMP, CS & IT*, *5*, 207–216.

Shrivastava, G., Sharma, K., & Kumari, R. (2016, March). Network forensics: Today and tomorrow. In *Computing for Sustainable Global Development (INDIACom), 2016 3rd International Conference on* (pp. 2234-2238). IEEE.

TechPayments. (2016). *20 Eye-Opening Cybercrime Statistics*. Retrieved from http://www.fitech.com/news/20-eye-opening-cybercrime-statistics/

Tennakoon, H. (2016). *The need for a comprehensive methodology for profiling cyber-criminals*. Retrieved on November 2016, from http://www.newsecuritylearning.com

Watson. (2013). *ExtremeXOS Operating System*. Technical Specification Report. The University of Cambridge.

Wright, C., Cowan, C., Morris, J., Smalley, S., & Kroah-Hartman, G. (2002, June). Linux security module framework. In *Ottawa Linux Symposium* (*Vol. 8032*, pp. 6-16). Academic Press.

Zhang, S., Meng, X., & Wang, L. (2016). An Adaptive Approach for Linux Memory Anaysis based on Kernel Code Reconstruction. *Eurasip Journal of Information Security, 14*, 13.

This research was previously published in the Handbook of Research on Network Forensics and Analysis Techniques edited by Gulshan Shrivastava, Prabhat Kumar, B. B. Gupta, Suman Bala, and Nilanjan Dey, pages 246-265, copyright year 2018 by Information Science Reference (an imprint of IGI Global).

Chapter 60
Cloud Auditor Loyalty Checking Process Using Dual Signature

Divya Thakur
Samrat Ashok Technological Institute (SATI), India

ABSTRACT

We apply dual signature method. Providing security to the data from auditor during remote data possession checking by applying dual signature. Basically dual signature is a mechanism that is used to provide security during secure electronic transition protocol. The function of dual signature is to provide authenticity and integrity of the data. It links two message wished for two different recipient. In the case of providing security from auditor we use this methodology because it works on the basic of providing two links for two different recipients. In the case of dual signature customer wants to send order information to the trader and payment information to the bank. Here we use two links but not for the purpose of secure transaction but for the purpose of secure information exchange in remote possession checking.

INTRODUCTION

Since cloud provides greater storage capacity in virtual environment so mostly organizations use cloud to store their data without leaving a copy in their local device. However along with many benefits of cloud computing, it also brings new summons to create security (A. Atayero and O. Feyisetan 2011) and reliable data storage and ensuring the integrity of the data stored in the cloud is one of them. This is because data loss could happen in any infrastructure, no matter how high degree of reliability the cloud service provider commit to the user.

Here author are taking about dual signature based method (B. J. Brodkin, N. W. Cloud, S. Risks, C. Computing and G. A. Engine 2008) that is a technique under digital signature it provides two links for transaction purpose.

Digital signatures are a fundamental technique for verifying the authenticity of a digital message. The Significance of digital signatures in cryptography is also amplified by their use as building blocks for more complex cryptographic protocols. Recently, we have seen several pairing based signature schemes that are both practical and have added structure which has been used to build other primitives ranging

DOI: 10.4018/978-1-5225-8176-5.ch060

Copyright © 2019, IGI Global. Copying or distributing in print or electronic forms without written permission of IGI Global is prohibited.

Figure 1. Cloud computing logical diagram

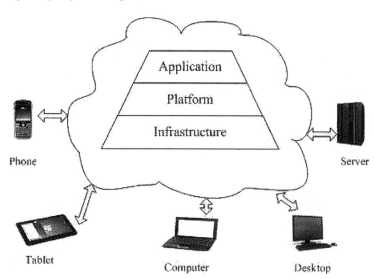

from Aggregate Signatures to Oblivious Transfer. Ideally, for such a fundamental cryptographic primitive we would like to have security proofs from straightforward, static complexity assumptions.

Now by improving this technique we can apply it to provide security from static assumptions for new signature schemes as well as pre-existing schemes. Providing new proofs for these existing schemes serve a meaningful sanity check as well as new insight into their security. This kind of security check is valuable not only for schemes proven in the generic group model, but also for signatures that require extra checks to rule out trivial breaks since these subtleties can easily be missed at first glance. Although users can use the traditional remote data possession checking method to check the integrity of their outsourced data, the two-party based checking method could not fully meet the properties of cloud computing for the following reasons: First, the users have to be online to conduct the checking procedure, which is feasible in many cases for example the user is travelling on the ocean; Second, the users' computation and communication resources are limited and it will take much of the users' resource to conduct the checking procedures themselves (C. C. Basics 2009).

Therefore, third-party auditing becomes the natural choice for auditing the cloud storage, which has been widely adopted. A third-party auditor (TPA), who owns expertise and capabilities, can do a more efficient and unbiased work. For the third-party auditing, it allows a third- party auditor to auditing the integrity of data in the cloud on behalf of the users. Recently, a number of auditing protocols were proposed to meet all kinds of properties: public auditing, privacy-preserving, high efficiency and so on. There some existing auditing protocols in terms of the type of cryptography, the data dynamics, the costs of communication and computation, the need for challenge-updating (G. Ateniese, K. Fu, M 2005).

In Cloud Computing, the remotely stored electronic data might not only be accessed however additionally updated by the clients, e.g., through block modification, deletion, insertion, etc. Unfortunately, the state of the art within the context of remote data storage mainly target static data files and therefore the importance of this dynamic data updates has received limited attention. According to the role of the verifier within the model, all the schemes out there fall into two categories: private confirmable and public confirmable. Achieving higher efficiency, schemes with private verifiability impose computational burden on clients. On the other hand, public verifiability alleviates clients from acting a lot of computation for guaranteeing the integrity of data storage. To be specific, clients are ready to delegate a third party to perform the verification without devotion of their computation resources. To ensure cloud data storage security, it is vital to enable a TPA to evaluate the service quality from an objective and independent perspective. Public audit-ability additionally permits clients to delegate the integrity verification tasks to TPA whereas they themselves may be unreliable or not be able to commit necessary computation resources performing continuous verifications. Another major concern is the way to construct verification protocols that may accommodate dynamic data files. The service is totally managed by the provider. This on demand service is provided at cloud service providers are creating a substantial effort to secure their systems, so as to reduce the threats of insider attacks, and reinforce the confidence of customers. In the cloud scenario if third party auditor itself get hacked then the authorized won't receive any notification of unauthorized access of its data. One of the most important issues with cloud data storage is that of data integrity verification at un-trusted servers (Huth and J. Cebula 2011). Public audit-ability for storage correctness assurance: to permit anyone, not simply the clients who originally stored the file on cloud servers, to posses the capability to verify the correctness of the stored data on demand.

Dynamic data operation support: to permit the clients to perform block-level operations on the data files whereas maintaining identical level of data correctness assurance. The design should be as efficient as possible therefore on make sure the seamless integration of public audit-ability and dynamic data operation support. Block less verification: no challenged file blocks should be retrieved by the verifier (e.g., TPA) throughout verification process for efficiency concern. The major issues related in cloud computing environment as involved concerning to security and a few other issues.

SECURITY ISSUES

The security is a major issue in cloud computing. It is a sub field of computer security, network security or data security. The cloud computing security refers to a broad set of policies, technology & controls conclude to protect data, application & the associated infrastructure of cloud computing. Some security and privacy problems that require to be considered are as follows (J. Bethencourt, A. Sahai and B. Waters 2007):

- **Authentication:** Only authorized user can access data within the cloud.
- **Correctness of Data:** This is the method through which user will get the confirmation that the data stored within the cloud is secure.
- **Availability:** The cloud data should be simply available and accessible with no burden. The user should access the cloud data as if he is accessing local data. No storage Overhead and easy maintenance: User doesn't need to worry concerning the storage demand & maintenance of the data on a cloud.
- **No Data Leakage:** The user data stored on a cloud will accessed by only authorize the user or owner. Therefore all the contents are accessible by only authorize the user.
- **No Data Loss:** Provider might hide data loss on a cloud for the user to take care of their reputation. In cloud computing, cloud data storage contains two entities as cloud user and cloud service provider cloud server. With the popularity of cloud computing, there have been increasing involvements about its security and privacy. Since the cloud computing environment is distributed

and un-trusted, data owners have to encrypt outsourced data to enforce confidentiality, Nowadays, as an emerging and efficient computing model, cloud computing has attracted widespread attention and support in many fields. In the cloud computing environment, much applicability such as resource renting, application hosting, and service outsourcing show the core concept of an on-demand service in the IT field. In recent years, many IT tycoons are developing their business cloud computing system, e.g. Amazon'sEC2, Amazon's S3, Google App Engine and Microsoft's Azure etc. Cloud computing can provide flexible computing potential, reduce costs and capital expenditures and charge according to usage (L. Cheung and C. Newport 2007).

Although the cloud computing paradigm brings many benefits, there are many unavoidable security problems caused by its inherent characteristics such as the dynamic complexity of the cloud computing background, the openness of the cloud platform and the high concentration of resources. One of the important problems is how to ensure the security of user data. Security problems, such as data security and privacy protection in cloud computing, have become serious obstacles which, if not appropriately addressed, will prevent the development and wide application of cloud computing in the future. In cloud computing, users store their data files in cloud servers. Thus, it is compelling to prevent unauthorized access to these resources and realize secure resource sharing. In classic access control methods, we generally assume data owners and the storage server are in the same secure field and the server is fully trusted. However, in the cloud computing background, cloud service providers may be attacked by malicious attackers. These attacks may leak the private information of users for commercial interestsasthe data owners commonly store decrypted data in cloud servers. How to realize access control to the encrypted data and ensure the confidentiality of data files of users in an entrusted background are problems that must be solved by cloud computing technologies and applications. Moreover, since the number of users is large in a cloud computing background, how to realize scalable, flexible and fine-grained access control is strongly desired in the service-oriented cloud computing model (M. Armbrust, A. D. Joseph, R. H. Katz and D. A. Patterson 2009).

SYSTEM MODEL

Now we are taking about system model of cloud data storage system. In the Cloud system, we have three entities (P. Mell, T. Grance and T. Grance 2011): Cloud Clients have large data files to be stored and rely on the cloud for data management and computation. They can be either individual consumers or commercial organizations. Cloud Servers virtualizes the resources according to the requirements of clients and expose them as storage pools. Typically, the cloud clients may lease storage capacity from cloud servers, and store their individual data in these bought or rented spaces for future utilization. Auditor which helps clients upload and check their outsourced data maintains a Map Reduce cloud and acts like a certificate authority. This assumption presumes that the auditor is correlated with a pair of public and private keys. Its public key is made available to the other entities in the system.

The Cloud system supporting auditing and file-level reduplication includes the following three protocols respectively highlighted by red, blue and green in Figure 2.

Figure 2. Cloud architecture

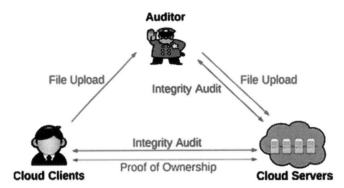

File Uploading Protocol

The purpose of this protocol is allowing clients to upload files via the auditor. Defiantly, the file uploading protocol includes three phases:

- **Phase 1 (Cloud Client! Cloud Server):** Client achieves the duplicate check with the cloud server to check if such a file is stored in cloud storage or not before uploading a file. If there is a duplicate, another protocol called proof of professorship will be run between the client and the cloud storage server. Else the following protocols (including phase 2 and 3) are run between these two entities.
- **Phase 2 (Cloud Client! Auditor):** Client transmit files to the auditor, and receives a stub from auditor.
- **Phase 3 (Auditor! Cloud Server):** Auditor helps generate a set of tags for the uploading file, and send them along with this file to cloud server.

Integrity Auditing Protocol

It is a reciprocal protocol for uniqueness verification and allowed to be initialized by any entity neglecting the cloud server. In this agreement, the cloud server plays the role of proofer, while the auditor or client works as the verifier. This protocol leads two steps:

- **Phase 1 (Cloud Client/Auditor! Cloud Server):** Verifier (i.e., client or auditor) creates a set of task and sends them to the proofer (i.e., cloud server).
- **Phase 2 (Cloud Server! Cloud Client/Auditor):** Based on the stored files and file tags, proofer (i.e., cloud server) tries to prove that it absolutely owns the target file by sending the proof back to verifier (i.e., cloud client or auditor). At the end of this protocol, verifier results true if the integrity verification is passed.

Proof of Ownership Protocol

This protocol initialized at the cloud server for certifying that the client exactly owns a claimed file. This protocol is normally triggered along with file uploading protocol to reduce the effluence of side channel information (Qiasi Luo1 and Yunsi Fei 2011). On the contrast to integrity auditing protocol, in the cloud server works as verifier, while the client plays the role of proofer. This protocol has two phases

- **Phase 1 (Cloud Server! Client):** Cloud server produce a set of challenges and sends them to the client.
- **Phase 2 (Client! Cloud Server):** The client reacts with the proof for file ownership, and cloud server finally checks the validity of proof. This is over all procedure preformed whenever any data is stored over cloud. Above we have detailed the entire procedure step that are involved in cloud system model. All the phases are declared here.

DUAL SIGNATURE

An important invention introduced in SET; the dual Signature (R. V Agalya and K. K. Lekshmi 2014). The Moto of the dual signature is the similar to standard electronic signature: to assuarity the authentication and uniqueness of data. In this case, the customer wants to send the order information (OI) to the dealer and the payment information (PI) to the bank. The dealer does not need to know the customer`s credit card`s number, and the bank does not want to know the information of the customer`s order. The customer is afforded extra security in terms of privacy by keeping these two items individually. However, the two items must be linked in this way that can be used to solve disputes if required. The link is needed so that the customer can prove that this payment is done for this order and not for some other goods and service.

Figure 3 shows the model of dual signature. When the dual signature is designed, it gets the hash of the sum hashes of OI (Order) and PI (Payment Information) as inputs. The dual signature is the encrypted MD of the concatenated MD's of PI and OI. The dual signature is Information sent to both the dealer and the bank. The protocol arranges for the dealer to see the MD of the PI without checking the PI itself, and the bank sees the MD of the OI but not the OI itself. The dual signature can be checked using the MD of the OI or PI. It doesn't require the OI or PI. Its MD does not acknowledge the content of the OI or PI, and thus privacy is maintained. Within the SET protocols there is a condition where the cardholder communicates with both the dealer and payment gateway in a single message. The message consist of an order section, with details of the products to be purchased, plus a payment section. The

Figure 3. Dual signature

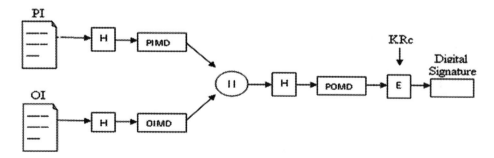

payment detail will be used by the banker and the order information by the dealer, but the messages are both sent collectively this means that the message packaging must:

1. Prohibit the dealer from seeing the payment instruction.
2. Prohibit the banker from seeing the order instruction.
3. Link the two parts of the message, so that they can only be used as a pair.

In this condition, SET uses a technique called dual signature. When the order and payment information are sent by the cardholder, the dealer will be able to read the order information, and the banker is able to read only the payment information. The dealer will not see the cardholder's account information. In a SET transaction, the transfer of money and offer are linked allowing the money to be transferred to the dealer only if the cardholder agrees the offer. The bond is needed so that the customer can claim that this payment is done for this order and not for some other goods and service below Figure 3 shows the model of dual signature. The cardholders create a dual signature by passing the order instruction (OI) and payment instruction (PI) through a hash function. The two message digests generated (OI message digest and PI message digest) are summed. The resulting message is run wound up a hash function and is encrypted with the cardholder private signature key using RSA signature generation algorithm. The dual signature is sent to both the dealer and the bank. The protocol is designed for the dealer to see the MD of the PI without seeing the PI itself, and the bank checks the MD of the OI but not the OI itself. The dual signature can be established by using the MD of the OI or PI. It doesn't require the OI or PI itself. Its MD does not show off the content of the OI or PI, and thus privacy is maintained.

Here we are taking that we are extending dual signature approach for checking the auditor's loyalty. For this purpose we can use two links as follows: In the dual signature the link that is used for payment information can be used as a link for the actual auditor's identity. And That means in this link we can store some identity proof of actual auditor this identity may be any personal question or may b any other task. That will proof that the auditor is behaving like the original one or not. And in the second link will store information about the currently active auditor. This is shown in Figure 4.

Figure 4. Dual signature for checking auditor loyalty

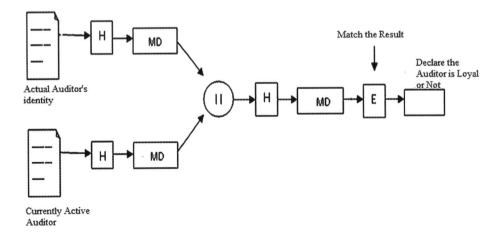

Now when the currently active auditor will try to interrupt your data that is stored over cloud it will immediately inform to the other link and that link may either ask any question or perform any task if the it reply as the program wants and do that specific task according to the system that will proof that the auditor is loyal and if it does not it means auditor is not loyal. It the auditor is loyal then it will allow the auditor to interrupt your data if the auditor is not then it will deny auditor to interrupt your data (S. Agarwal, J. Dunagan, N. Jain, S. Saroiu, A. Wolman and H. Bhogan 2010). There are lots of advantages of adopting this method that are as follows:

Advantage

- **Integrity:** Quality of truthfulness and accuracy is generally known as integrity. Our proposed approach provide integrity of the data because in our approach we calculate the message digest and then store that digested message into a single file and after that we again calculate the digest of digested message it will filter our approach and will maintain the integrity of data.
- **Non-Repudiation:** Since user will digitally sign the complete package including data plus message digest using their own private key it maintains non-repudiation. As we know that the non repudiation means legal setting wherein the authenticity of a signature is challenged for uniqueness.
- **Confidentiality:** Generally confidentiality is always used in terms of privacy and security in our proposed approach digitally signed data plus message digest is again encrypted using private key with the help of cryptography. Hence confidentiality is maintained in our approach.
- **Authentication:** Normally authentication is a state of confirming the actuality of the data's identity. Since in our approach all the data and their message digest are separately appended in a file so their identity can be easily confirmed on the basis of that file.

CONCLUSION AND FUTURE DIRECTION

Security in the cloud is a very essential term as well as a benefit and also a challenge. Security in the cloud is a greatest challenge that is very closely related with service providers and users. 70% of cloud user's admitted security is major concern in cloud storage data. It is apparently vital condition within the cloud cannot be over emphasized due to threats from within and outside of the cloud environments. Confidentiality, personal data integrity and data Security responsibilities within the cloud should be a collaborative effort between both vender and users. These responsibilities differ by the type of cloud services been accessed. The cloud service provides is on responsible service to make sure the security, integrity and non-redundancy of cloud data storage and to confirm maximum protection. Vender have the responsibility to ensure the public data integrity and isolation protections are put in place to extenuate the risks users create to one another in terms of data loss, misuse, or privacy violation within the cloud. Now from the cloud service provider's position, there should be an effective supervising mechanism in place to allow for effective planning and implementation of services. This facilitate as a séance to respond to events quickly and more efficiently. Cloud users on the other hand must sure and be clear about their responsibility for their security key generation. The process of shared key generation used two different part CSS and TPA. The CSA and TPA used the randomized key generation technique for the processing of user authentication. The proposed model validates the genuine and fake user. For the minimization of attack possibility the CSS server automatic generates fake file for unauthorized user. The fake user accept the fake file and not hit the sever next time and save the computational time of server. The proposed model validates in RMI server for remote machine and also validates the key generation process technique. Our experimental result shows better performance instead of pervious algorithm. The analysis enabled us to draw some conclusions. Majority of the already accessible models area unit mature enough, but, they do not give versatile security choices for encoding based on data sensitivity for data storage over cloud.

In Future this scheme can be applied with actual cluster of machines to form a cloud in local area network using tool like Hadoop. Then the results can be captured in real time. To achieve the assurances of cloud data integrity and availability and enforce the quality of dependable cloud storage service for users, an effective and flexible distributed scheme with explicit dynamic data support, including block update, delete and append is being implemented. Our aims to extend the protocol to support data level dynamics at minimal costs.

REFERENCES

Atayero, A., & Feyisetan, O. (2011). Security Issues in Cloud Computing: The Potentials of Homomorphic Encryption. *Journal of Emerging Trends in Computing and Information Sciences*, 2(10), 546–552.

Brodkin. (2008). *Seven cloud-computing security risks*. Gartner.

Cloud Computing basics for non-experts. (2015, May). *Cloudweeks*, 1–8.

Armbrust, J. Katz, & Patterson. (2009). Above the Clouds: A Berkeley View of Cloud Computing. University of California at Berkeley.

Ateniese, Fu, Green, & HohenBerger. (2005). Improved proxy re-encryption schemes with applications to secure distributed storage. *Proc. NDSS*, 1-15.

Huth & Cebula. (2011). *The Basics of Cloud Computing*. Carnegie Mellon University.

Bethencourt, J., Sahai, A., & Waters, B. (2007). Cipher text-policy attribute-based encryption. *Proceedings of IEEE Symposium on Security and Privacy*, 321-334.

Cheung, L., & Newport, C. (2007). Provably secure cipher- text policy ABE. *Proceedings of the ACM conference on Computer and communications security*, 456-465.

Mell, Granceand, & Grance. (2011). *The NISTD definition of Cloud Computing*. Recommendations of the National Institute of Standards and Technology.

Luo & Fei. (2011). Algorithmic Collision Analysis for Evaluating Cryptographic System and Side-Channel Attacks. *International Symposium on H/w- Oriented Security and Trust*, 1-10.

Agalya & Lekshmi. (2014, August). A Verifiable Cloud Storage using Attribute Based Encryption and Outsourced Decryption with Recoverability. *International Journal of Engineering and Innovative Technology*, 10-21.

Agarwal, S., Dunagan, J., Jain, N., Saroiu, S., Wolman, A., & Bhogan, H. (2010). Volley: Automated data placement for geo-distributed Cloud services. *Proceedings of the 7th USENIX conference on Networked systems design and implementation*, 155-170.

This research was previously published in Detecting and Mitigating Robotic Cyber Security Risks edited by Raghavendra Kumar, Prasant Kumar Pattnaik, and Priyanka Pandey, pages 126-134, copyright year 2017 by Information Science Reference (an imprint of IGI Global).

Chapter 61
Security in Cloud of Things (CoT)

Bashar Alohali
Liverpool John Moores University, UK

ABSTRACT

With IoT era, development raises several significant research questions in terms of system architecture, design and improvement. For example; the requirement of virtual resource utilization and storage capacity necessitates making IoT applications smarter; therefore, integrate the IoT concept with cloud computing will play an important role. This is crucial because of very large amounts of data that IoT is expected to generate. The Cloud of Things (CoT) is used to connect heterogeneous physical things to the virtual domain of the cloud. Despite its numerous advantages, there are many research challenges with utilization of CoT that needs additional consideration. These include high complexity, efficiency, improving reliability, and security. This chapter introduces CoT, its features, the applications that use CoT. CoT, like all other networked functions, is vulnerable to security attacks. The security risks for CoT are listed and described. The security requirements for CoT are identified and solutions are proposed to address the various attacks on CoT and its components.

INTRODUCTION

Through the years, the era of information technology and pervasiveness of digital technologies have showed an exponential growth. The rising number of technological improvements offers a wealth of new services. Recently, Internet of Things (IoT) has attracted attention since it involves several applications, including smart grid, control systems, remote healthcare, smart mobility, traffic flow management and so on. In addition, it is expected to grow in terms of its deployment as well as its applicability in various application areas. The term IoT was coined by Kevin Ashton in 1999, which meant any entity that has a chip placed inside it or addressable on a network with an IP-address and can connect to wireless or wired network infrastructure (Gratton, 2013). These are everyday objects with ubiquitous connectivity and communicating and operating constantly. The use of IoT leads to a smart world with ubiquitous computing and provides services that enables remote access and intelligent functionality (Chaouchi, 2013). IoT enables real-time analysis of data flows that could improve efficiency, reliability and economy

DOI: 10.4018/978-1-5225-8176-5.ch061

Copyright © 2019, IGI Global. Copying or distributing in print or electronic forms without written permission of IGI Global is prohibited.

of systems. For example, connecting all appliances in the smart house can save electricity by efficient monitoring. Thus, IoT provides convenience in day-to-day living and makes an intelligent use of resources in a home (Parwekar, 2011).

CoT represents an important extension of IoT. CoT refers to the virtualization of IoT infrastructure to provide monitoring and control. IoT deployments typically generate large amounts of data that require computing as well as storage. A cloud infrastructure that can provide these resources can effectively offload the computing and storage requirements within the IoT network to the cloud. An added benefit is the ability to virtualize the underlying IoT infrastructure to provide monitoring and control from a single point. An application using IoT could therefore become a smart application. A CoT connects heterogeneous appliances to the virtual cloud domain. Both tangible and intangible objects (home appliances, sensor-based and network-enabled) and surrounding people can be integrated on a network or into a set of networks (Sun, Zhang, & Li, 2012).

CoT suggests a model consisting of a set of services (or commodities) that are delivered just like the traditional commodities. In other words, CoT can provide a virtual infrastructure which can integrate analytic tools, monitoring devices and visualization platforms (Parwekar, 2011). Moreover, CoT is a recent technological breakthrough that can enable end-to-end service provisioning for users and businesses to directly access applications on demand from anywhere, anytime (Sun et al., 2012). The emerging CoT services will enable a new generation and intelligent use of a collection of applications that will be fed with real time and analysis.

CoT, as a connected universe of things, can become a tangible reality in the future. Connected devices and things, ranging from sensors to public transport, will send huge of data that should be effectively managed and processed. However, cyber-attacks on critical infrastructure, recently, have highlighted security as a major requirement for CoT. A compromise of the CoT can have drastic effects, sometimes nation-wide and on people's lives. So, a CoT infrastructure should be secure. This chapter will present an overview of some of the concepts related to CoT. After introducing CoT, it continues to present the architecture and the applications of CoT. In addition, the security requirements for the CoT are discussed and the security challenges are highlighted. Specifically, the threats to the CoT are discussed. The chapter concludes with a discussion on the existing security solutions and a mention of the open research issues.

BACKGROUND

Overview of CoT

IoT on which CoT is based, is a new IT paradigm that describes an imagined reality of trillions of things connected to each other. It is transmitting valuable data that is stored, processed and analyzed by computers to control and addresses all sorts of human activities, ranging from healthcare, road traffic, emergency management, retail, crime prevention, lighting, energy and power and/or transportation. IoT is closely linked with the concepts of "smart city", "ubiquitous computing" (Vasseur & Dunkels, 2010), and other paradigms that describe new technological reality in which sensors and microcontrollers are embedded in various things and integrated into human living. This results in increased comfort and security. IoT unites several individual technologies, including machine-to-machine (M2M), supervisory control and data acquisition (SCADA), a system designed for industrial remote monitoring & control of equipment, wireless sensor networks (WSN) and radio-frequency identification (RFID). All these systems and technologies have diverse and complex functionalities that include monitoring, sensing, tracking, locating, alerting, scheduling, controlling, protecting, logging, auditing, planning, maintenance, upgrading, data mining, trending, reporting, decision support, back office applications, and others (Gubbi, Buyya, Marusic, & Palaniswami, 2013).

One of the main differences of IoT paradigm from machine-to-machine technologies (M2M) technologies is remote sensing (McGrath & Scanaill, 2013). Its significance on prospective creation of complex and all-embracing network architecture with its unique protocols, storage capacities, software applications and users is similar to the Internet.

The main idea behind cloud computing is that cloud providers offer a shared access to multiple users to physical computing infrastructure and software. Cloud computing formed into three different service scopes, namely, Infrastructure as a Service (IaaS), Platform as a Service (PaaS) and Software as a Service (SaaS) (Kifayat, Merabti, & Shi, 2010). These models may be deployed as a private, public, and community or hybrid clouds. From the technological viewpoint, key characteristics of cloud technologies, such as on-demand service, broad network access, resource pooling, rapid elasticity and measured service are enabled by virtualization process. Through virtualization single system images may be created from cluster machine infrastructure, which provides a unified user interface and efficient utilization of resources. Virtualization in cloud services is enabled by middleware. Given its huge storage, computing and sharing capabilities IT clouds are regarded as enablers for implementation of IoT networks. Cloud of Things is a real-world mixture between IoT paradigm and cloud technology. Both of them have three layers - IoT includes devices, connection and management (DCM) layers, whereas cloud computing has SaaS, PaaS and IaaS (SPI) layers (see Figure 1). IoT can be organized as Intranet of Things, Extranet of Things or Internet of Things, as clouds can be deployed as private, public or hybrid clouds.

However, these successful examples of technology application, implementation of the CoT require further transformation of cloud technologies. In fact, current storage infrastructure and file, systems cannot be used in IoT context that will require processing, analysis and response to sensitive data that handles dynamic real-world infrastructures and processes. In this view, considerations of security and protection become fundamental in the CoT framework.

CoT has a potential of integrating a large number of connected devices; including GPSs, mobile phones, broadband, TV and outgrow the number of human subscribers in a cloud. Therefore, implementation of

Figure 1. Components of cloud computing

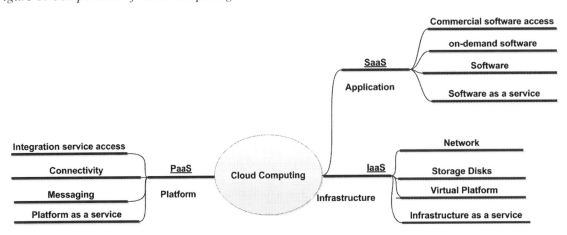

cloud based on IoT paradigm requires the development of complex infrastructure and software architecture to fit with IoT characteristic and requirements. Currently, M2M connectivity, data storage, processing and interchange with other machines are limited, because the majority of IoT devices exist in Intranet and Extranet. M2M is normally regulated by systems that focus on connectivity and monitoring, rather than data sharing and data interchange with other machines. Few IoT networks are currently accessible on the Internet and most of the projects have been experimental (Parwekar, 2011).

Architectural Elements of CoT

The elements of the CoT architecture are presented in this section. They are mentioned using a high level taxonomy to help in identifying and defining the components required by CoT. It requires three components that can enable continuous ubiquitous computing:

1. Hardware consisting of embedded communication hardware, sensors and actuators,
2. Middleware which is responsible for 'on demand' storage and computing tools for data analytics
3. Visualization and analysis tools that are user-friendly and available on different platforms and for different applications (Distefano, Merlino, & Puliafito, 2012).

This section briefly discusses a few enabling technological developments in these categories that make up the 3 components indicated above.

Figure 2. System architecture for the CoT

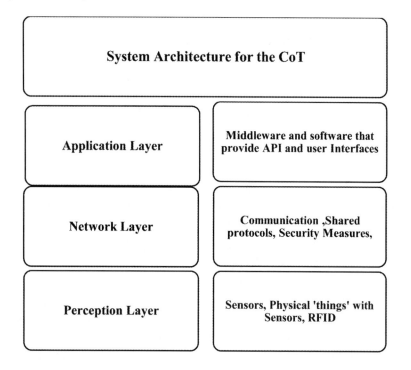

Hardware

The first CoT architectural element is the Radio Frequency IDentification (RFID). RFID act as an e-barcode providing a capability to automatically identify anything that they are attached to. RFID "tags" are of two types – inactive tags and active tags. Inactive tags are not powered with a battery but they utilize the power from the RFID reader's interrogation signal. Such tags are typically used in the Retail and Supply-Chain Management sector. An example that can be given to explain this procedure better are the applications used in transportation, such as the registration stickers or the replacement of tickets. RFID active tags are powered from their own battery and are able to initiate communication. Such tags are used in port containers to monitor the movement of cargo (Hwang, Dongarra, & Fox, 2013). Sensors are similar to active RFIDs but they have better onboard storage and computing capability.

Another necessary architectural element of CoT is Wireless Sensor Networks (WSNs). They are cost-effective, efficient and low power, miniature electronic devices used in remote sensing applications. WSN components include WSN hardware, a WSN communication stack, a WSN middleware and a secure data aggregation (Emary & Ramakrishnan, 2013). WSNs consist of a large number of intelligent sensors and can collect, process and analyze the distribution of valuable data and information that are gathered in a variety of environments. Specifically, the data from the sensors are shared between sensor nodes and thereafter sent to a centralized (or distributed) system for analysis. However, the technical challenges that must be addressed in order to exploit WSNs' huge potential are multidisciplinary and substantial in nature.

WSN core hardware is a node consisting of power supply, multiple sensor interfaces and Analogue/Digital convertors, a transceiver and processing units. The sensors interconnect into a WSN in an ad-hoc mode and applications ride over the network. On a sensor, the MAC layer predominantly used is the IEEE 802.15.4. The network layer, in recent past, is moving towards an IP based implementation such as 6LoWPAN and ZigBee over IP. WSN nodes communicate with each other to propagate information to an aggregation/storage point in the network (also termed as "gateway"). They can use either a single-hop path or a multi-hop path to reach such a point in the network. Routing protocols are necessary to route data to the destination. The aggregation point could provide the connecting link to the Internet. The WSN, therefore, becomes a sub-network connected to the Internet.

Middleware

WSN middleware is a mechanism that is necessary to combine the sensor network infrastructure and the Service Oriented Architecture (SOA) to provide an independent access to other heterogeneous sensor resources. To achieve this, a platform-independent middleware is needed. One leading example is the Open Sensor Web Architecture (OSWA) which is developed upon a uniform set of standard data representations and operations (Emary & Ramakrishnan, 2013).

The fourth component of WSN is the secure data aggregation methodology that is required to ensure that the data collected by the several sensors are reliable. This component is necessary for WSNs as they are open to several malicious attacks that can cause node failures. In such an event, the impact of the node failures must be minimal and the rest of the WSN must continue to function. Hence, the WSN must have the capability to heal itself and ensure secure and authentic data over the network.

Addressability is a requirement since each device/sensor requires to be uniquely addressed (Zhou, 2013). Thus, addressing is another architectural element of CoT. This mechanism allows the network to uniquely identify millions of devices and control remote devices through the Web. The features that must be taken into account in order to develop and implement a unique address are the scalability, the persistence, the reliability and the uniqueness. In other words, the target here is every single connected element to the network must be identified by its identity, functionality, and location.

Data Storage, Analytics, and Visualization

The data storage and analytics is one of the most important architectural elements of CoT as the development of an unprecedented amount of data is compulsory in this emerging field. In other words, as mentioned above the data gathered within the CoT must be stored and used intelligently for smart actuation and monitoring purposes. This can be achieved through the development of various Artificial Intelligence (AI) algorithms (such as novel fusion algorithms), which will be centralized based on the need. These algorithms, in combination with temporal machine learning methodologies based on evolutionary algorithms, should make sense of the data gathered as well as must be able to achieve automated decision making.

The last CoT architectural element relates with visualization which is crucial for a CoT application as it allows a better interaction between the end-user and the environment/s. The visualization must be attractive and easy for the end-user to fully benefit from the CoT revolution. Luckily, this is achieved through the years since most information is provided in meaningful ways to consumers. Raw data is processed and converted into knowledge. This knowledge helps in fast decision-making, especially in applications where the decision-making is automated and is in real-time. The meaningful information extraction from raw data is non-trivial. Raw data, along with event detection information is generated according to the needs of the users (Chao, 2012).

CoT Applications

CoT involves several applications that can be classified based on the network availability type, heterogeneity, repeatability coverage, scale, user involvement and impact. Thus, CoT applications can be categorized into 4 application domains:

1. Personal and home,
2. Enterprise,
3. Utilities and
4. Mobile

Personal and Home

This concerns the information gathered by the sensor from the ambience of a home or from that of a personal space such as a body area network (BAN). Only those who own the network use the data that is collected. For example, nowadays it is possible for a smartphone with iOS, Android or Windows Phone operating system to communicate with the several interfaces (Bluetooth, Bluetooth LE, Wi-Fi) for interconnecting sensors that measure physiological parameters. In addition to this, applications can allow the control of home equipment such as fridges, air conditioners, lighting, and other appliances providing an ease of energy and functional management of a home. This involves customers in the

CoT revolution (Zhou, 2013). Such applications could use Twitter-like approach where the individual 'things' in the house could periodically tweet the readings that could be easily followed from anywhere by developing a TweetOT (Gubbi et al., 2013). However, such services require a common framework for using the cloud for information access. The security requirements for these services would require a new approach to provide privacy, authentication secrecy and integrity.

Enterprise

Enterprise-based applications mainly relate with businesses and deals with the NoT (Network of Things) within a business environment. The data and the information gathered by these networks are selectively released and their owners only use them. For instance, the data generated and gathered by an application to keep track of the number of residents within a building (for environmental reasons), is utilized by the environment control agency. A light sensor can automate this counting/monitoring activity and feed the data into a larger system that controls the environment. The same input can also be extrapolated to track resident movement from a security functional requirement. Similarly, the sensors can be enhanced to perform additional sensing functions and the application can be enhanced to provide this functionality. The CoT approach provides this application/implementation with the flexibility of making changes to parts of the system (adding areas of coverage) or changing the devices, enhancing the functionality of the application and so on.

Utilities

CoT applications, such as the one mentioned above, introduce users to a smarter environment that can provide security, convenience and automation. The term "Smart Cities" has gained relevance in this context and there are various test beds that are being implemented as proof-of-concept. The bases of the Smart City implementations are CoT based applications in various domains. Such applications, both large and small scale, have been implemented and tested on test bed infrastructure for the last few years. The test beds consist of several subsystems and involve multiple focus (user) groups with an objective to share the collected data. Some of the applications address larger community issues such as pollution, health and well being and transportation (Gubbi et al., 2013). These applications are also used for the safety and physical security. An example is a surveillance application that can help identify intrusions/ illegal access and identify wary activities, both with and without visual sensors such as cameras.

The need for service optimization is another driver for CoT based applications. Applications are used by several utility organizations mainly to manage their resources, to optimize their services, e.g. Cost of Electricity delivery vs profit margin. Such a CoT application predominantly works at the front-end on the sensing infrastructure and requires interworking with other applications at the back-end to cooperatively deliver the service optimization targeted for. Usually, such networks are used by large businesses (on a national scale) that have the resources for large network infrastructure. A typical example is networks labeled as critical infrastructure, such as power generation and distribution grids, water distribution grids, transportation networks, railroad network, Logistics and so on. With resource optimization, CoT applications are deemed to enhance environment friendliness – efficient use of power/water and delivery, pollution monitoring and control, etc., are typical applications that enhance environment friendliness. (Bandyopadhyay & Sen, 2011).

Mobility

The final CoT application deals with the mobility (such as transportation and traffic) (Gubbi et al., 2013). In fact, urban traffic is what causes the traffic noise pollution as well as the degradation of the air quality. In addition, the traffic congestion, the supply-chain efficiencies and the productivity are directly related and can result in high-costs due to delays and delivery schedule failures. Therefore, CoT application for mobility uses multi-dynamic traffic information that provides the capability for better planning and improved scheduling. Large-scale WSNs are used to feed the sensed information to such applications that are used for the online control of travel times, queue lengths and noise emissions. The CoT application replaces the existing automated physical systems, comprising networks of inductive loop vehicle detectors, to monitor and sense the traffic data.

CoT applications can be enhanced by the implementation of scenario-based models that attempt to plan and design mitigation and alleviation plans. The availability of Bluetooth devices affects the penetration of such applications in a number of smart products such as the smartphones and the navigation systems (GPS) (Zhou, 2013). Bluetooth devices release signals with a nomadic media access ID number that can be read by Bluetooth sensors within a particular coverage area enabling the movement identification of devices. If this is also complemented by other data sources i.e. bus GPS, then problems such as vehicle travel time on motorways would be addressed, as these applications would be able to provide accurate and reliable real time transport information.

Another important application in mobile CoT domain is logistics management dealing with the efficient transportation planning and scheduling. It involves monitoring the items being transported. The monitored items are sensed and the data is fed into the large-scale, back-end network that includes other sensing networks such as a transportation-monitoring network. The monitored items physically transit through various physical locations and the sensing network feeds the item's location information to the back-end network that does the tracking.

In summary, we observe that CoT based applications have implementations across several application domains. They often form elements of the front-end network and communicate with a large-scale back-end network to provide a service. They have helped to make services both efficient as well as innovative and in almost all cases provide a means of replacing existing infrastructure with greener solutions. A distinctive feature of these applications is overall cost reductions and increased revenue margins. Consequently, it is expected that the proliferation of such applications will only increase.

CoT for a Smart Grid

Smart grid is considered as an intelligent network of meta-systems and subsystems to provide energy cost-effectively and reliably. Figure 3 illustrates the communication network of a smart grid. It has a hierarchical structure, comprising three areas, Home Area Network (HAN), Neighbor Area Network (NAN) or Field Area Network (FAN) and Wide Area Network (WAN). Smart Grids derive benefit from the fact that homes can be automated using ubiquitous computing and such automation can help in energy monitoring. It is the embedded Internet of things that provide several services linked to physical devices or resource monitors and enable the management of energy consumption of devices and appliances (Xi, Jianming, Xiangzhen, Limin, & Yan, 2011). The occupant expects to be able to monitor and control various systems in a home using a Home Management System, a typical CoT application. The operation is based on real-time data and two-way communication with renewable power generation (Alohali,

Figure 3. CoT for a smart grid

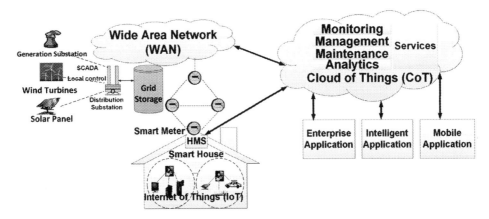

Merabti, & Kifayat). One of the main purposes of smart home is to adapt to the movements of green, energy saving, environment-friendly concepts that have emerged in recent years.

There are many applications involved with smart home, including demand response, dynamic pricing, system monitoring, cold-load pick-up, and the mitigation of greenhouse gas emissions (Karnouskos, 2013). CoT for HAN is expected to play an important role in smart grids. The obvious benefits of deploying a CoT based on smart grid are improved storage, computing offload from the sensors and devices and faster access via the Internet (Karnouskos, 2013).

The following are the summarized benefits of utilizing CoT on a smart grid:

- Better-quality storage ability, memory, and maintenance of the resources.
- Reduced energy consumption of devices.
- Real time control and fast, extensive analytics.
- Capability to support several platforms and OS.

Security Challenges of CoT

The infrastructure for a CoT is built using the combination of IoT levels (intranet, extranet or internet) and cloud computing. CoT security, therefore, has a similar set of security threats, vulnerabilities and objectives. Primarily, the data exchange between elements of the CoT need to be checked for their integrity and kept private. In addition, the data itself requires to be checked for validity and freshness. Apart from this, there is the factor of security provided by the Cloud service provider, within the cloud infrastructure, which includes data storage, data access and data isolation. The impact of failure of hardware or a potential service breakdown due to security reasons (malicious intrusions) is intense on a community, especially if it is in relation to a CoT deployed as a Critical Infrastructure (Electricity, Water, Gas, Telecom, Healthcare, etc.).

Connected things are resource-limited devices with reduced storage capacity and energy, which makes them vulnerable to a number of potential attacks and risks. This means that sensitive data may be blocked and manipulated. Avoiding requires that Security be addressed as part of the basic design of a service deployed as a CoT application. In order to improve things' against attacks new security protocols, encryption methods and algorithms are being developed taking into consideration memory and computing limitations of connected devices. Several such schemes already exist in the context of security in WSNs and could possibly be adapted to the CoT scenario requirements. Security architecture of CoT should also address the issue of fault tolerance, since device failures may be quite common in CoT system. Filtering bogus and manipulated data and securing data identity are critical tasks for robust CoT security system (Aazam, Khan, Alsaffar, & Eui-Nam, 2014).

Connected devices generate large volumes of data that should be transmitted, processed and managed. In a focused CoT, data management is primarily realized by cloud computing systems. Therefore, the security of this data depends on security measures undertaken by cloud service providers. Data security in cloud systems depends on protection of virtualization process and safe allocation and reallocation of resources. Recall that the Cloud is made up of shared as well as distributed computing and storage resources. The hypervisor and virtual machine should be organized/configured sufficiently to prevent data exposure when resources are reallocated from one virtual machine (VM) to another. Data security may be also compromised by the malicious traffic going from one VM to another. In order to avoid this risk, traffic monitoring and firewalls between VMs may be used as effective counter-measures. Another technique is segregation and isolation of different VMs classes from each other (Cucurull & Guasch, 2014). Anomaly detection is used to monitor behavior and detect deviations. Those deviating the agreed code of conduct are either debarred from further use or quarantined. This helps to prevent potential security incidents.

In addition to the security concerns mentioned so far, there are a few distinct to CoT. These security challenges originate from the features of embedded computer devices, RFID, networks and M2M communication. The key challenges and obstacles to practical security of CoT and available technology solutions are outlined below:

1. **Dynamic Activity Cycle:** Security challenges of CoT are linked with a difference of roles and functions that may be realized by connected devices. They may be a waste in some situations and active in others (Gál et al., 2014). They may transmit data immediately to cloud servers or to other devices. Things may just receive data from other devices serving as an intermediary storage capacity in the network. The variability of roles played by connected devices, which are frequently different from CRUD tasks made by computers, makes it necessary to develop new security approaches and techniques address these challenges (Oh & Kim, 2014).

2. **Heterogeneous Interactions:** The domain of connected devices is extremely heterogeneous, because different manufacturers with different standards, protocols and technical requirements make many of them. So, it is unlikely that all home devices fit homogeneity and interoperability criteria achieved in the computer industry; the standards are evolving. This is especially true for device network's points of connection with external networks, such as Internet. This connection frequently requires gateways or proxies, which makes end-to-end communication problematic. Different protocols and technical features of connected devices make it necessary to implement qualitatively new cryptographic algorithms that lightweight and offer an end-to-end secure communication channel (Sharma et al., 2014).

3. **Anti-Virus Provision:** In classic computer networks, PCs are normally protected from malware and attacks by advanced and memory-consuming anti-virus suites (Shon, Cho, Han, & Choi, 2014). Provision of connected devices with such anti-virus protection is a challenge due to memory and computing power constraints of CoT.

4. **Small Packets Vulnerability:** Connected devices are normally built based on IEEE 802.15.4 standard created for low-rate wireless personal area network (LR-WPANs). The standard supports 127-byte packets at the physical layer (Saha & Sridhar, 2012). This architecture may cause fragmentation of large packets of security protocols, which results in opening of new attack, especially for DoS attacks. The implications of these attacks may be particularly adverse in case of key exchange messaging by connected devices (Chaouchi, 2013).

Attacks on CoTs

Attackers with different motives and skills can take advantage of the security weaknesses of the cloud of things, and can cause various levels of damage to the network. Attackers at the top level include online hackers, terrorists, employee's opponents, or users, and so on. Thus with developments in the security of networks and computers, we are currently facing more and more complex and advanced attacks and threats. In this section, we will describe and discuss attacks and threats as they relate to CoTs. However, the majority of these attacks are related to those that apply to traditional networks. We will briefly illustrate attacks, which are dangerous and can potentially tend towards significant harm to the network.

1. **Denial of Service (DoS):** DoS is defined as stopping the system or network from providing normal service. It involves an attack that reduces or removes a network's capacity to execute its expected function through hardware failures/crashes, software bugs, resource (memory/computing) exhaustion, malicious broadcasting of high-energy signals or complex interaction between these points. CoT is especially vulnerable to DoS attacks due to the small memory, processing and power limitations of devices. These attacks may only be noticed after the service is blocked or becomes unavailable due to memory or battery exhaustion (Medaglia & Serbanati, 2010).
2. **Jamming:** Things in CoT are also especially vulnerable to electromagnetic interference based on the same frequency-band signals as in the attacked devices. This attack is known as jamming and is typically prevented by anti-jamming (Chen & Gong, 2012).
3. **Brute-Force Attack:** A brute-force attack usually involves an exhaustive key search, where an adversary goes against any block cipher in a search for the key. In general, cryptanalysis on the key leads to an exhaustive key search attack in which every possible combination of bits in the key is tried in turn (Smith & Marchesini, 2007). This can lead to compromise of the communication of an entire network. Therefore, the stronger the key is, the greater the key length and the longer it will take for the attacker to discover the valid key and decrypt the message. However, long keys impact both storage and computing on the embedded devices and therefore the design of the security mechanisms require to strike a fine balance between the security objectives and the limited resources available on the devices.
4. **Replay Attack:** This is where an attacker can capture the network traffic and resend the packets at a later time to obtain unauthorized entry to the resources. In a common method of replay attack, a malicious user can eavesdrop on communications and resend old packets again multiple times in order to spoof information or gain access/trust to/of another device. It can also waste node or system resources (Miri, 2013) thereby inducing a mild DoS as well.
5. **Malware:** CoT devices may also be attacked by malware that includes viruses, Trojan horses, worms and other programs that are designed to damage the appliance. Penetration of these threats into the network is usually addressed by antivirus software and firewalls, at the perimeter.

Security Methods for Cloud of Things

The existing methods of securing the cloud of things include using the private cloud with enterprise parameter, content encryption, session containers, cloud access brokers and runtime security visualization.

SECURITY REQUIREMENTS

CoT and the networks it hosts need a multi-layered approach to security starting at powering up. The security requirements must be addressed through the device's entire lifecycle. In this section, a general and brief review about security requirement in CoTs is presented.

1. Confidentiality

Confidentiality is one of the primary aims of security. One of the best ways to achieve confidentiality, data integrity and non-repudiation of communication is by encrypting data and establishing a shared secret key among nodes. In cryptography, the most crucial and challenging step is key management. Key management is a critical challenge, and to obtain proper security, the key's length should be sufficiently long to meet the security objectives and at the same time not drain the embedded system's resources. Furthermore, the key's lifetime should fit with the security requirement. A keying relationship can be used to facilitate cryptographic mechanisms in CoT communication.

Table 1.

Private Clouds	Content Encryption	Session Containers	Cloud Access Brokers	Runtime Security Visualization
Involve establishing a virtual infrastructure inside currently existing corporate firewall	Designed to ensure that cloud resident content is not retrievable through plain text by ATP malware	Secures the public clouds by making the user to initiate a relatively secure connection that maintains end-to-end closure as opposed to HTML5	Involves the use of a broker, which monitors the authentication path from users and provide enhanced security	Involve the dynamic establishment of runtime security visualization. Reasoning being, the storage and other computing infrastructure are embedded on in virtual runtime systems and that makes security systems be embedded too.
Accessible to only authenticated users	Works only if the underlying algorithm cannot be broken and are based strong ciphers	Supports multiple personas	Allows flexible integration of emerging security capacities	Provide a virtual WAF to protect an HTTP application
Provides easy access to members yet restrictive	Ensures significant data secrecy and have malware resistance platform	Session containers provides client system data wipe that ensures the user data is not retrieved by another user	Provide passive security observation that may be desirable to the users. It also offers active security measure in that it accesses the proxies in active mode.	Benefits include providing security for dynamic objects and handle different assets at a go

Cryptographic techniques make use of two types of keys, either symmetric or asymmetric. Symmetric cryptography relies on a shared secret key between two nodes to enable secure communication. Asymmetric cryptography applies a pair of keys per node, a private key and a public key. The public key is used for encryption and can be published. The private key is used for decryption and is known only to the node and no one else. From a computational point of view, asymmetric cryptography requires many orders of magnitude more resources than symmetric cryptography (Stavroulakis & Stamp, 2010). In general, key management involves the following four sorts of keys: one-time session symmetric keys, public keys, private keys and passphrase-based symmetric keys. The session keys are used once and are generated for each new message. The public keys are used in asymmetric encryption. On the other hand, private keys are also used in asymmetric encryption. Passphrase-based keys are used to protect private keys. A single node can have multiple public or private key pairs (Alfred J. Menezes, Oorschot, & Vanstone, 1996).

2. Secure Booting

Secure booting deals with the integrity and the authenticity of the software packages on the devices that can be verified by using cryptographically generated digital signatures (Chandramouli, Iorga, & Chokhani, 2014). The digital signature must be attached to the software to ensuring that only the particular software is authorized to run on that device. Although the foundation of trust has been already established, CoT devices still need protection from several run-time threats and/or malicious purposes.

3. Access Control

Access control involves the application of various forms of access control and resource. These controls are usually built into the device's operating system, therefore limiting the device component's privileges in accessing only the resources needed in order to do only their assigned tasks. However, in the case where a component is compromised, this security requirement (access control) can assure that the intruder has minimal access to other system components as possible. The least privilege's principle commands that only the minimal access expected to perform a function should be endorsed to minimize the effectiveness and efficiency of any security breach (A Younis, Kifayat, & Merabti, 2014).

CoT devices also need a firewall mainly to control traffic, which will terminate at the cloud device. Therefore, firewalling is another one crucial security requirement for CoT (Zhou, 2013). The firewall and deep packet check capability have unique protocols that can direct how such devices can communicate to each other. At the same time, these tools have the strength to identify malicious payloads hiding in non-IT protocols (daCosta, 2013).

4. Authentication

When a device is plugged into the network, it must be able to authenticate itself prior to receiving or transmitting data and information (Swaminatha & Elden, 2003). This is necessary embedded devices do not have end-users sitting behind computers, waiting to type the identifications required to access the network (Bhattasali, Chaki, & Chaki, 2013). Thus, in order for the devices to access a network, they must automatically and correctly identify their credentials, securely, prior to authorization by using several machine authentication techniques.

5. Privacy

One of the most security concerns in CoT relates to privacy. Privacy attacks may target individual privacy (identification of a user's location, private information and preferences) and group privacy. To improve privacy protection, which is especially crucial as more things carrying sensitive user data enter the CoT, privacy-enhancing technologies may be utilized (Rosado, Mellado, & Piattini, 2013).

6. Updates and Patches

The final security requirement concerns the updates and patches. When the device is in operation it should start to receive software updates and patches to work properly. The devices must be ready to authenticate the patches which are received from their operators (Amies & Alex Amies, 2012). However, this authentication must not damage the functional safety of the device. This is critical when multiple devices in the field are performing crucial operations and are dependent on security patches to defend against vulnerability that escapes into the wild. Therefore, both the software updates and the security patches must be provided in a way so that they can save the limited bandwidth and the periodic connectivity of an embedded device and reduce the possibility of compromising functional safety.

A SECURE SCHEME FOR CLOUD OF THINGS (CoT)

Figure 4 details the network model elements and how they communicate. The IoTs consists of devices that are grouped into two. One group is prepared for devices that require basic operation (basically one-way communication) and is called Group 1. The other is reserved for devices that can be monitored and controlled, thus requiring two-way communication, and is termed Group 2. Each group has a group leader with which the appliances in each group interconnect. The group leaders connect with the cloud of things (CoT).

CoT has access for monitored data from the appliances in the IoTs and can send control commands to the devices. Smart phones access the CoT via the Internet. The utility provider also uses a cloud infrastructure for its services. Any data regarding the IoTs is sourced from the CoT. The group leaders communicate with the cloud using a public data network such as the Internet via wired broadband links. The IoTs appliances in each group, as well as and each group leader, will communicate using technologies like ZigBee or WiFi. The objective of our solution is to provide effective resources for secure communication.

Given the functionality and interaction mentioned, the functional security requirements are as follows:

1. The IoTs appliances must be physically secured to the greatest extent possible. Physical compromise of a device cannot be permitted and can cause the loss of functionality of portion of the network.
2. The data sent or received should be protected sufficiently to prevent sniffing packets on the wireless channels from decrypting the data.

The assumptions made for designing the solution are:

Figure 4. The network model

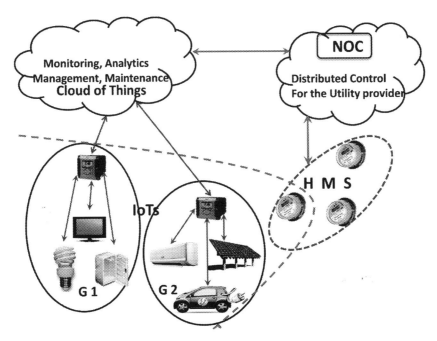

1. The IoT devices in the two groups, as well as both group leaders, use unicast communication.
2. The group leaders are trusted devices.
3. The CoT interface is registered with the group leaders.
4. The appliances in each group are connected as a tree with the appliances as leaf nodes.
5. An attacker could eavesdrop on all traffic or replay messages since the IoTs uses wireless technologies.
6. Time stamps are applied for data freshness testing.
7. The devices are tamper-resistant; any attempt to manipulate the device to access stored information will result in that information being destroyed and the device becomes inactive.

Symmetric key cryptography is installed for secure interaction between the appliances in each group and each group leader as well as for interaction between the group leaders and the cloud. The objectives of the scheme are to provide a means for secure data exchange among the communicating components of each of the groups with CoT. The scheme benefits from the following points – all data is encrypted, the encryption key changes with time, the encryption key distribution is secure and the limitation of resources on the IoTs are considered.

The security scheme works as follows: The communication between the CoT and the appliances in the groups are shown in the Figures 5, 6. In Group 1, the communication is between the CoT and the appliance and is typically in the form of ON/OFF commands. The CoT first forms the data, D, to be sent to the appliance in Group 1. Recall that the data to the appliance in Group 1 is sent via group leader 1 (GL1). The CoT generates a triplet of the ID of the Group 1 appliance, the command text for the appliance and a time stamp. The command and the time stamp are privately sent to the appliance in Group 1 via GL1. Therefore, the command and time stamp are encrypted using the symmetric key shared between the CoT and the appliance in Group 1(Figure 5), Group Key 3 (GK3). This message is now packaged

Box 1.

Pre-deployment Phase

1. *Assign a unique ID to every appliances in Group 1 and Group 2 and the two group leaders*

2. **In Group 2**:

   a. *Assign a unique group key to group leader of Group 2. This group key is shared with all appliances in the group*

   b. *Use the group key and the ID of the device to generate a unique key for each appliances in Group 2*

3. **In Group 1**:

   a. *Assign a unique key to the group leader for Group 1*

   b. *Assign the same key to every appliances in Group1*

   c. *Assign the shared key provided by the CoT*

4. **Group Leaders 1, 2**:

   a. *Assign the group key shared with the group*

   b. *Assign a different group key shared by the CoT*

5. **CoT**

   a. *Register the unique IDs of the Group 1, Group 2 appliances and the group leaders in the CoT*

   b. *Share a unique group key with the group leaders*

   c. *Share a unique key with all appliances in Group 1*

Figure 5. CoT to Group 1 device interaction via the Group Controller 1

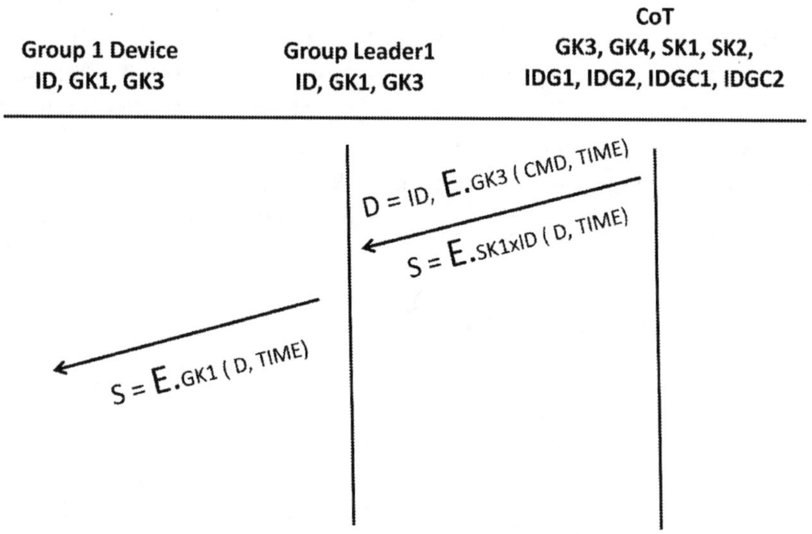

Group 1 Device	Group Leader1	CoT
ID, GK1, GK3	ID, GK1, GK3	GK3, GK4, SK1, SK2, IDG1, IDG2, IDGC1, IDGC2

$D = ID, E._{GK3} (CMD, TIME)$

$S = E._{SK1xID} (D, TIME)$

$S = E._{GK1} (D, TIME)$

Figure 6. CoT to Group 2 device and Group 2 device to CoT Interaction via the Group Controller ?

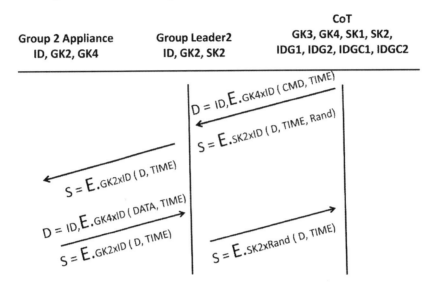

and destined to GL1, which is the next immediate recipient. A triplet of D, a time stamp and the ID of GL1 is formed. D and the time stamp need to be encrypted for privacy. The CoT generates an encryption key using the shared key with GL1, SK1 and the ID of GL1. D and the time stamp are encrypted using the generated key and sent to GL1.

GL1 determines that the message has arrived from the CoT. It now generates the decryption key using the shared key with the CoT, SK1 and its ID and decrypts the message. If the message is successfully decrypted, it verifies the time to confirm that the value is greater than the earlier value it received from the CoT. It then reads D to identify the ID of the Group 1 appliance to which the message is designated. GL1 then sends the message to the appliance by encrypting D and its time stamp using the shared key with the Group 1 appliance, GK1. On receiving this message, the Group 1 appliance decrypts the message using GK1 to retrieve D, verifies the time stamp, decrypts D using the shared key with CoT, GK3, retrieves the time stamp, validates it and then takes the command sent by the CoT.

In Group 2 (Figure 6), the communication is from the CoT to the Group 2 appliance via the GL2. The data packaging is similar to that for Group 1 devices, except for the addition of a random number generated by the CoT. GL2 registers the random value, which is used with SK2 to generate a key for sending data to the CoT. When the Group 2 appliance asks to send data to the CoT, the same two-step process is followed. Applying the random value confirms that the key is refreshed each time the CoT receives some data.

Open Research Issues for Securing CoT

The security challenges and research open issues concerning CoT are the reliability in privacy and security, the efficiency in participatory sensing, the data analytics (or data mining), the quality of service and the Geographic Information Services (GIS)-based visualization. The final goal of CoT is the ability to deploy smart objects, get them to interact with similar smart object networks as well as Internet infrastructure, seamlessly. An extension of this is to be able to deploy sensor-based networks and be able to run multiple applications over them. These applications should be able to use the infrastructure, both interchangeably as well as concurrently. Standardization plays an important role in the realizing such an objective, given the heterogeneous nature of the devices and their operations.

1. Reliable Secure Reprogrammable Networks and Privacy

Reliable security and privacy are major concerns for the networks, especially if they are deployed on a large scale. A network or service, when vulnerable will be attacked causing the network to have inoperative parts as well as harbor the possibility of invalid data being injected into the network, leading to undesirable consequences. The three main architectural elements of CoT, which are the cloud, the RFID and WSN, are highly vulnerable to such attacks. Therefore, a primary line of defense in protecting these networks against the data exploitation is the cryptography (Bhattasali et al., 2013).

Cryptography is an effective and efficient solution as it can use cryptographic methodologies that can ensure the data confidentiality, integrity and authenticity. Embedded systems often need to update/ upgrade the software that they run as part of the CoT application. Such updates are centrally "pushed" onto the devices. These must be applied to all nodes in the network. CoT adopts a secure reprogramming protocol, which allows the nodes to authenticate every single code update resulting in the prevention of potentially malicious installations. Addressing these issues of secure reprogramming and insider attacks is a potential area of research.

The security issues in the cloud, is somewhat similar to the re-programming problem. The data, within the cloud, moves across virtual hosts and these hosts themselves can move between several locations (servers/data centres). The means to ensure data privacy across the cloud is an active research area and continues to address this issue. Particularly, this issue holds a higher risk in the database-based applications that involve personal information.

2. Efficient Participatory Sensing

CoT indicates the development and use of efficient participatory sensing platforms mainly to reduce the sensing costs. In addition to this, the participatory sensing can give the nearest indication concerning environmental parameters experienced by the end-users. In other words, these platforms derive from the environmental data gathered by the end-users that form a social currency (Wang et al., 2009). This is also, at times, associated with the term "crowd sensing".

The consequence of this phenomenon is that the more timely data that are generated to be directly compared with the available data through a fixed infrastructure sensor network. In either case, the importance here is for the end-users to be able to give an experience feedback in regards to a given environmental parameter. Unfortunately however, the end-users meet difficulties to do this and these limitations might place a new implication on the reference data role offered by a fixed infrastructure CoT as a backbone (Wang et al., 2009).

If one were to attempt to rely on the crowd-sensed data alone, it limits the ability to produce significant information and data for policy decisions. Addressing these problems in terms of security, reliability of data as well as data analytics within a mobile cloud (formed in an ad-hoc manner with smartphones, for example) are current areas of research.

3. Data Analytics (or Data Mining)

CoT uses a complex sensing environment. Extracting useful data, transforming that data into knowledge is a challenge. Data availability is asynchronous and has a varied time and spatial resolution. This makes the data extraction a reasonably tough challenge. In addition, data validity has to be continuously established. Research studies that have been conducted in the recent past have adopted methodologies using light learning methods that allowed data anomalies and pre-defined events to be extracted through the use of supervised and unsupervised learning. Then, there is the issue of simultaneously learning events, activities and their representations at multiple levels of complexity (Qian, Ruicong, Qi, Yan, & Weijun, 2010; Shen, Liu, & Wang, 2010).

4. Proper Security Risk Mitigation

Mitigating possible security threats is critical to creating a relatively secure and effectivity among CIOs and CISOs, which facilitate migration of applications and data to the cloud-computing platform. Most of the existing data, applications and systems possess variable security thresholds. In a way of example, web, social and mobile systems can be migrated to the virtual server without similar level of security concerns compared to the highly regulated information or sensitive applications. The decision as to whether a product, application or service is for the cloud server depends on the kind of data or application at hand, the service level agreement and the associated security environment. Therefore, the decision to migrate to the clouds primarily depends on the data sensitivity and the degree of security the cloud provider is offering, especially in public clouds. Business organizations must therefore establish whether the overall value achieved offset the risk when making the decision to go clouds in their data storage and management.

5. Adequate Understanding of the Cloud Service Provider

Many companies are facing the challenge in adequately understanding the cloud service provider before to getting the environment. Some providers may not be aware of the data security requirements that the customer requires. Therefore, the cloud service providers need comprehensive auditing to confirm how secure they are. However, few institutions having the auditing capacity currently exist in the market; hence, most organizations blindly enter into agreements to move to the clouds without considering the security implications their actions may impose on their data. The technology arena and the government should research and develop clear regulations for the cloud service providers. Additionally, proper policies relating to data breach in the cloud of things need clear statement to secure the cloud users.

Quality of Service

Taking into consideration that CoT is comprised of several heterogeneous networks that provide multiple services, there are multiple traffic types within the network. It is essential that this single network is able to support all the types of traffic (and therefore all applications on the network) without quality of service compromise. There are two application classes: i) the bandwidth and delay sensitive inelastic traffic such as the traffic monitoring and ii) the delay tolerant elastic traffic such as the monitoring of weather parameters at low sampling rates. All the traffic has to be securely delivered and their temporal characteristics have to be maintained end-to-end. However, due to the segments that often constitute 'gaps' in resource guarantee, it is not easy to provide quality of service guarantees in wireless networks (El-Sayed, Mellouk, George, & Zeadally, 2008).

As a result of these, the quality of service in cloud computing is an open research issue requiring more and more attention and research as the data and tools continuously become available on clouds (A Vouk, 2008).

GIS-Based Visualization

In many cases, CoT directly relates with new display technologies as well. Therefore, as long as these display technologies emerge, creative visualization will be enabled. Touch-based interfaces have given the opportunity to end-users to navigate the data better than even before, as well as the ability to directly operate with the display objects. However, the data arising from the ubiquitous computing (such as CoT) is not always ready for handling and consumption using visualization platforms, therefore they have to undergo further processing. This phenomenon makes the entire situation very complex for heterogeneous spatial and temporal data (Zhou, 2013).

Thus, there is a need for new visualization schemes which must be able to represent the heterogeneous sensors in a 3D landscape that varies temporally (Ren, Tian, Zhang, & Zhang, 2010). Finally, another challenge that emerges concerning the visualization of data gathered within CoT is that these data are usually geographically-related and are sparsely distributed in the cloud (Ning, 2013) and, therefore to cope with this, a framework based on Internet GIS is required (Ren et al., 2010).

CONCLUSION

The concept of the Internet of Things (IoT) is an interconnection of distinguishable objects and defines a thing within the Internet or similar IP structure. The things refer to physical objects, such as home appliances, medical devices, intelligent devices and so on. Those things are enhanced with computing and communication technology and have the ability to interconnect and communicate through embedded RFID chips, barcodes, sensors, or other networks. The Cloud of Thing (CoT) is a conceptual model used by Internet of Things (IoT) that provides smart things functions as process of analyzing, developing, controlling and maintaining of multiple applications (Seong Hoon & Daeyoung, 2013). It is combination between IoT paradigm and modern cloud technology. However, current storage infrastructure and file, systems cannot be used in IoT that will require processing, analysis and response to sensitive data that handles huge real-world infrastructures and processes. Therefore, considerations of security and protection become critical related with the specific technical characteristics of CoT things, networks and cloud technologies compatible with IoT architecture.

This chapter demonstrated the creation of CoT system faces many challenges and risks linked with specific technical and network characteristics of things. In particular, security threats and available solutions connected with resource-constrained nature of CoT devices were discussed and new security requirements that tackle the issue of CoT network were addressed. The future research should address the issue of CoT architecture deployment and implementation focusing on specific features of IoT integration with cloud computing services.

RECOMMENDATIONS

In order to achieve the goal of world cloud ecosystem, the stakeholders in the ICT sector needs to enact policies that embed the cloud computing in the global market and the business environment. The policies should further ensure timely address of issues affecting the cloud of things and encourage the business sector to embrace the new computing platform. To achieve the above, the global ICT stakeholders should consider implementing the following recommendations:

First, the ICT should intensify the progress in cloud research. The current clouds are based on the broader domain of computing utility, which overlap into other associated domains that are a result of several years of research and development. Consequently, there is significant risk that the research and development in the ICT sector may be repeated as opposed to being improved in the cloud computing. Therefore, the progress in the cloud computing field research should specifically focus on the cloud computing and the challenges currently affecting it. In other words, holistic approach is necessary to facilitate collaboration and use of results between associated domains such as grids, high performing computing and web services.

Two, the industry and research should concentrate on concerns facilitates long-term relevance. Therefore, any short term measures in research poses the risk of obsolesce in the near future instead of spearheading diversification and essential realization in the cloud of things capability. To avoid the ambiguity of the long-term relevance, the commercial interest needs to be clear in indicating the benefit and significant impact of such a long-term investment in the cloud-computing field.

Three, the ICT stakeholders need to facilitate smooth transition to the cloud of things arena. Many developers do not get enough support to test the possible cloud computing applications and services. That implies that we already have the cloud computing yet the necessary tools of trading are lacking. Similarly, the trading organizations also find it quite difficult to migrate their data to the clouds because of the security challenge. Evidently, the ICT sector has a lot more work to do in making the transition work.

Lastly, Cloud of things stakeholders need to encourage the establishment and adoption of standards. This will ensure that the developers of cloud applications, the cloud service providers and other parties offering cloud related services adhere to specific standards. That give confidence to the general public and other participants that the cloud computing is safe for use. Both the large scale SMEs and the Large-scale players will have equal platform to compete in cloud service provision.

REFERENCES

Aazam, M., Khan, I., Alsaffar, A. A., & Eui-Nam, H. (2014, January 14-18). Cloud of Things: Integrating Internet of Things and cloud computing and the issues involved. *Paper presented at the 2014 11th International Bhurban Conference on Applied Sciences and Technology (IBCAST)*.

Alohali, B., Merabti, M., & Kifayat, K. A New Key Management Scheme for Home Area Network (HAN) In *Smart Grid*.

Amies, A., Sluiman, H., Guo Tong, Q., & Ning Liu, G. (2012). *Developing and Hosting Applications on the Cloud*. IBM Press/Pearson.

Bandyopadhyay, D., & Sen, J. (2011). Internet of Things: Applications and Challenges in Technology and Standardization. *Wireless Personal Communications*, 58(1), 49–69. doi:10.100711277-011-0288-5

Bhattasali, T., Chaki, R., & Chaki, N. (2013, December 13-15). Secure and trusted cloud of things. *Paper presented at the 2013 Annual IEEE India Conference (INDICON)*.

Chandramouli, R., Iorga, M., & Chokhani, S. (2014). *Cryptographic Key Management Issues and Challenges in Cloud Services*. Springer. doi:10.1007/978-1-4614-9278-8_1

Chao, L. (2012). *Cloud Computing for Teaching and Learning: Strategies for Design and Implementation*. Information Science Reference. doi:10.4018/978-1-4666-0957-0

Chaouchi, H. (2013). *The Internet of Things: Connecting Objects*. Wiley. doi:10.1002/9781118600146

Chen, L., & Gong, G. (2012). *Communication System Security*. Taylor & Francis.

Cucurull, J., & Guasch, S. (2014). *Virtual TPM for a secure cloud: fallacy or reality? daCosta, F. (2013). Rethinking the Internet of Things: A Scalable Approach to Connecting Everything*. Apress.

Distefano, S., Merlino, G., & Puliafito, A. (2012, July 4-6). Enabling the Cloud of Things. *Paper presented at the 2012 Sixth International Conference on Innovative Mobile and Internet Services in Ubiquitous Computing (IMIS)*.

El-Sayed, H., Mellouk, A., George, L., & Zeadally, S. (2008). Quality of service models for heterogeneous networks: overview and challenges. *Annals of telecommunications, 63*(11-12), 639-668. doi:10.100712243-008-0064-z

Emary, I. M. M. E., & Ramakrishnan, S. (2013). *Wireless Sensor Networks: From Theory to Applications*. Taylor & Francis. doi:10.1201/b15425

Gál, Z., Almási, B., Dabóczi, T., Vida, R., Oniga, S., Baran, S., & Farkas, I. (2014). *Internet of Things: application areas and research results of the FIRST project*.

Gratton, D. A. (2013). *The Handbook of Personal Area Networking Technologies and Protocols*. Cambridge University Press. doi:10.1017/CBO9780511979132

Gubbi, J., Buyya, R., Marusic, S., & Palaniswami, M. (2013). Internet of Things (IoT): A vision, architectural elements, and future directions. *Future Generation Computer Systems, 29*(7), 1645–1660. doi:10.1016/j.future.2013.01.010

Hwang, K., Dongarra, J., & Fox, G. C. (2013). *Distributed and Cloud Computing: From Parallel Processing to the Internet of Things*. Elsevier Science.

Karnouskos, S. (2013, February 25-28). Smart houses in the smart grid and the search for value-added services in the cloud of things era. *Paper presented at the 2013 IEEE International Conference on Industrial Technology (ICIT)*.

Kifayat, K., Merabti, M., & Shi, Q. (2010). Future security challenges in cloud computing. *International Journal of Multimedia Intelligence and Security*, *1*(4), 428–442. doi:10.1504/IJMIS.2010.039241

McGrath, M. J., & Scanaill, C. N. (2013). *Sensor Technologies: Healthcare, Wellness and Environmental Applications*. Apress. doi:10.1007/978-1-4302-6014-1

Medaglia, C., & Serbanati, A. (2010). An Overview of Privacy and Security Issues in the Internet of Things. In D. Giusto, A. Iera, G. Morabito, & L. Atzori (Eds.), *The Internet of Things* (pp. 389–395). Springer New York. doi:10.1007/978-1-4419-1674-7_38

Menezes, A., van Oorschot, P., & Vanstone, S. (1996). Handbook of Applied Cryptography.

Miri, A. (2013). *Advanced Security and Privacy for RFID Technologies*. Information Science Reference. doi:10.4018/978-1-4666-3685-9

Ning, H. (2013). *Unit and Ubiquitous Internet of Things*. Taylor & Francis. doi:10.1201/b14742

Oh, S. W., & Kim, H. S. (2014). Decentralized access permission control using resource-oriented architecture for the Web of Things. *Paper presented at the 2014 16th International Conference on Advanced Communication Technology (ICACT)*. 10.1109/ICACT.2014.6779062

Parwekar, P. (2011, September 15-17). From Internet of Things towards cloud of things. *Paper presented at the 2011 2nd International Conference on Computer and Communication Technology (ICCCT)*.

Ren, L., Tian, F., Zhang, X., & Zhang, L. (2010). DaisyViz: A model-based user interface toolkit for interactive information visualization systems. *Journal of Visual Languages and Computing*, *21*(4), 209–229. doi:10.1016/j.jvlc.2010.05.003

Rosado, D. G., Mellado, D., & Piattini, M. (2013). *Security Engineering for Cloud Computing: Approaches and Tools*. Information Science Reference. doi:10.4018/978-1-4666-2125-1

Saha, D., & Sridhar, V. (2012). *Next Generation Data Communication Technologies: Emerging Trends*. Information Science Reference. doi:10.4018/978-1-61350-477-2

Seong Hoon, K., & Daeyoung, K. (2013, June 28-July 3). Multi-tenancy Support with Organization Management in the Cloud of Things. *Paper presented at the 2013 IEEE International Conference on Services Computing (SCC)*.

Sharma, S., Shuman, M. A. R., Goel, A., Aggarwal, A., Gupta, B., Glickfield, S., & Guedalia, I. D. (2014). Context aware actions among heterogeneous internet of things (iot) devices: Google Patents.

Shon, T., Cho, J., Han, K., & Choi, H. (2014). Toward Advanced Mobile Cloud Computing for the Internet of Things: Current Issues and Future Direction. *Mobile Networks and Applications*, *19*(3), 404–413. doi:10.100711036-014-0509-8

Smith, S., & Marchesini, J. (2007). *The Craft of System Security*. Pearson Education.

Stavroulakis, P., & Stamp, M. (2010). *Handbook of Information and Communication Security*. Springer. doi:10.1007/978-3-642-04117-4

Sun, E., Zhang, X., & Li, Z. (2012). The internet of things (IOT) and cloud computing (CC) based tailings dam monitoring and pre-alarm system in mines. *Safety Science, 50*(4), 811–815. doi:10.1016/j.ssci.2011.08.028

Swaminatha, T. M., & Elden, C. R. (2003). *Wireless Security and Privacy: Best Practices and Design Techniques*. Addison-Wesley.

Vasseur, J. P., & Dunkels, A. (2010). *Interconnecting Smart Objects with IP: The Next Internet*. Elsevier Science.

Vouk, A. (2008). Cloud computing–issues, research and implementations. *CIT. Journal of Computing and Information Technology, 16*(4), 235–246. doi:10.2498/cit.1001391

Wang, Y., Lin, J., Annavaram, M., Jacobson, Q. A., Hong, J., Krishnamachari, B., & Sadeh, N. (2009). A framework of energy efficient mobile sensing for automatic user state recognition. *Paper presented at the Proceedings of the 7th international conference on Mobile systems, applications, and services*, Kraków, Poland. 10.1145/1555816.1555835

Xi, C., Jianming, L., Xiangzhen, L., Limin, S., & Yan, Z. (2011, October 14-16). Integration of IoT with smart grid. *Paper presented at the IET International Conference on Communication Technology and Application (ICCTA 2011)*.

A Younis, Y., Kifayat, K., & Merabti, M. (2014). An access control model for cloud computing. *Journal of Information Security and Applications*.

Zhou, H. (2013). *The Internet of Things in the Cloud: A Middleware Perspective*. Taylor & Francis.

KEY TERMS AND DEFINITIONS

Asymmetric Cryptography: Also known as public-key cryptography, asymmetric cryptography is a model of cryptography whereby a pair of keys is used in the encryption and decryption of a message for safe transfer. One key is used to encrypt a message, and all intended recipients can get the decryption key from a public database.

Data Mining: This involves analyzing Big Data in the search for patterns or relationships between variables.

Field Area Network (FAN): This is a combination of Neighborhood Area Networks and local devices, attached to a Field Area Router that offers a backhaul WAN interface.

Home Area Network (HAN): This is a network that is set up within a home. It entails a connection between digital devices, multiple computers, to telephones, televisions, home security systems, and other smart appliances wired into the network.

Internet of Things: This is a scenario where people, animals and other objects have unique identifiers, and are able to transfer data over a network without the need for human-to-computer or human-to-human interaction.

Neighbor Area Network (NAN): This is an offshoot of Wi-Fi hotspots and other wireless local area networks (WLANs) that enable users to share one access point to connect to the internet.

Secure Booting: This is a standard that was developed to make sure that a computer system boots only with a software that is trusted by the device manufacturer.

Virtualization: This is the creation of a virtual version of a computer hardware platforms, network resources, and even operating systems.

Wide Area Network (WAN): This is a telecommunications network covering a wide area, of a half mile or a mile radius.

This research was previously published in Managing Big Data in Cloud Computing Environments edited by Zongmin Ma, pages 46-70, copyright year 2016 by Information Science Reference (an imprint of IGI Global).

Chapter 62
Data Security in Wired and Wireless Systems

Abhinav Prakash
University of Cincinnati, USA

Dharma Prakash Agarwal
University of Cincinnati, USA

ABSTRACT

The issues related to network data security were identified shortly after the inception of the first wired network. Initial protocols relied heavily on obscurity as the main tool for security provisions. Hacking into a wired network requires physically tapping into the wire link on which the data is being transferred. Both these factors seemed to work hand in hand and made secured communication somewhat possible using simple protocols. Then came the wireless network which radically changed the field and associated environment. How do you secure something that freely travels through the air as a medium? Furthermore, wireless technology empowered devices to be mobile, making it harder for security protocols to identify and locate a malicious device in the network while making it easier for hackers to access different parts of the network while moving around. Quite often, the discussion centered on the question: Is it even possible to provide complete security in a wireless network? It can be debated that wireless networks and perfect data security are mutually exclusive. Availability of latest wideband wireless technologies have diminished predominantly large gap between the network capacities of a wireless network versus a wired one. Regardless, the physical medium limitation still exists for a wired network. Hence, security is a way more complicated and harder goal to achieve for a wireless network (Imai, Rahman, & Kobara, 2006). So, it can be safely assumed that a security protocol that is robust for a wireless network will provide at least equal if not better level of security in a similar wired network. Henceforth, we will talk about security essentially in a wireless network and readers should assume it to be equally applicable to a wired network.

DOI: 10.4018/978-1-5225-8176-5.ch062

Copyright © 2019, IGI Global. Copying or distributing in print or electronic forms without written permission of IGI Global is prohibited.

INTRODUCTION

Although a wireless network offers multifold advantages, albeit it is also vulnerable to several security and privacy threats as itis a dynamic open medium (Kaufman, Perlman, & Speciner, 1995). Different types of clients such as laptops, cell phones, smart devices, etc. can join or leave the network anytime they wish. This opens up issues like fake registrations and packet sniffing. This chapter deals with the issues of security and privacy of a network in great detail by discussing countermeasures for different kinds of attacks. Weseparately discuss privacy and its importance also known as network anonymity that is usually achieved by employing redundancy at the cost of some associated overheads. We start off with the introduction of the basic idea in data security, then discuss available standards for different types of networks and powerful tools like Encryption. From there, we build up to known types of attacks and a brief study of major data breaches of recent times. We also discuss various experimental measures and proposed solutions. We end the chapter with our projections on data security and the summarize what to expect in future.

GOALS OF SECURITY

Data Authentication

This implies verifying and guaranteeing the identity of the sender and receiver of the data before any data transmission is initiated.

Data Confidentiality

This feature is the core of secured communication and this mechanism assures that the data being transferred is only divulged to the authenticated sender and receiver. Attributes like date, time, content type, etc. are included in the data.

Data Integrity

This property assures that the data remains intact in its original form during the transmission from the sender to receiver. This means that no one is able to modify the data along the way during transmission which should also be verifiable at both the ends of communication. Checksum is one example of such a service.

Non-Repudiation

This is generally a combination of Authentication and Integrity of the data. This service facilitates proof of origin and integrity of data. In other words, no user can falsify the true ownership of data. Digital Signature is an example of such a service.

Data Availability and Reliability

In addition to all these earlier features, security mechanism should also guarantee certain threshold level of quality of service (QoS) while vide all such features could possibly add overheads. By having measures for intruder detection and combating various networks attacks provide uninterrupted service at required QoS level.

DATA ENCRYPTION

Encryption is the cryptography process in which messages or information are encoded in such a way that only authenticated people can interpret it (Gordon, Loeb, Lucyshyn, & Richardson, 2006). An encrypted message can be intercepted along the propagation path of transmission. But, by the inherent characteristics of the process, it renders useless to an interceptor, and no meaningful information can be divulged. The process of encoding is referred as encryption and decoding as decryption. The original data in its true form is referred to as plaintext. The data received after performing an encryption algorithm on the plaintext is called ciphertext. A small key portion of the algorithm in the form is a seed value for the decryption algorithm, and works as a missing secret piece of the puzzle. This secret is called a Key which is essential to decrypt a ciphertext to plaintext and is shared only with authorized people. Anyone in the possession of this key can decrypt all the ciphertext being transmitted. The harder it is to crack the key or the encryption algorithm, better is the encryption algorithm. Technically, two factors are most important for reverse engineering for an encryption algorithm to crack it, time and computation power required. Any good encryption algorithm designer tries to keep both these values as high as possible. Encryption schemes can be divided into two main categories, symmetric and asymmetric.

Symmetric-Key Encryption

In a symmetric encryption scheme the same key is used to encrypt a message as well as to decrypt it. This being the major weakness of this scheme (Figure 1). If the secret symmetric key is captured by an inter-

Figure 1. Symmetric encryption

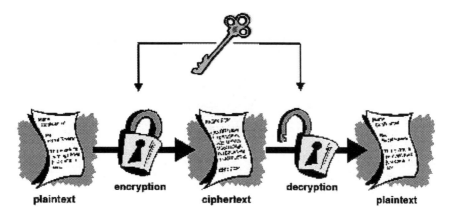

ceptor, the whole system fails and information transmitted is no more secure. In a symmetric key scheme, the sender and receiver have to first agree on using a specific unique key for encryption/decryption. This phase is called key establishment phase which should be done over a secured medium of communication. In a network of N nodes, the number of possible sender-receiver pairs can be N(N-1)/2, requiring a unique key for each pair. This number grows rapidly with an increase in the number of nodes in the network. Hence, requiring a very large number of keys for secure communication in the network makes it poor for scalability point of view. All these factors make symmetric encryption schemes vulnerable to linear cryptanalysis, known-plaintext attacks, chosen plaintext attacks, differential cryptanalysis, etc.

Asymmetric-Key Encryption

Also known as Public-Key Encryption, asymmetric encryption employs two keys. One known as the public key which is published publically and the second secret key known as the private key which is only known to the person it is created by. Asymmetric encryption was the landmark invention in the field of cryptography. Most of the well known robust encryption schemes even today are based on asymmetric keys. As shown in Figure 2, public and private keys are used for encryption and decryption respectively. This is made possible by using sophisticated complex mathematical structures which are discussed in detail further. But, as a result of higher complexity, asymmetric keys require significantly more computing power as compared to symmetric encryption.

Asymmetric encryption does have a major advantage over symmetric encryption, possessing better scalability as number of required keys grows only linearly with the size of the network. A majority of modern schemes generally employ a hybrid approach where a symmetric key is established for communication during the key establishment phase using asymmetric channel.Once asymmetric encryption facilitates the communicating nodes with a secure channel for key sharing then further communication can take place over a secure channel using only the symmetric key which has lower overheads.

Figure 2. Asymmetric encryption

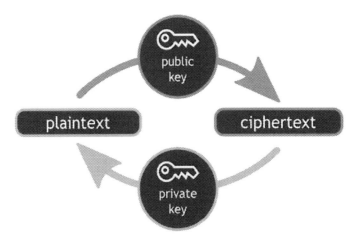

STREAM CIPHER AND BLOCK CIPHER

Stream Cipher

When using a stream cipher, encryption or decryption is done one bit or character at a time and hence the name.The plaintext stream is hashed together using the key stream using the encryption algorithm to output a ciphertext stream. This function can be as simple as a XOR operation. A key stream can be formed in several ways either use a predetermined array of keys or generate one key at a time using an algorithm at a required required frequency. When designing such a key generation algorithm, dependencies of key values on plaintext, ciphertext or earlier used keys can be added to make the scheme robust (Robshaw & Billet, 2008). Figure 3 shows the concept behind a stream cipher.It can be observed that both the source and the destination should have the same key stream and the index needs to be synchronized for the process of encryption or decryption. Stream cipher is also known as state cipher as encryption of each character is dependent on the current state of the cipher.It is intuitive that in case the receiver doesn't have the correct state of the key stream even though it possesses the correct key stream, it might not be able to decipher the message.

Block Cipher

Whereas, in a Block Cipher, the plaintext of size n characters is broken into equal m sized blocks. Each individual block of plaintext is encrypted with a key of size k bits. Figure 4 shows the basic idea behind block ciphers (Shor, 1994). It can be observed that a block cipher in its simplest formworks like a stream cipherif the block size m=1. However, an application block cipher has several other differences from a stream cipher, making it much more versatile. Block cipher is the foundation of most of the cryptographic algorithms of recent times (Table 1) (Jakimoski & Kocarev, 2001).

Figure 3. An example of Stream cipher

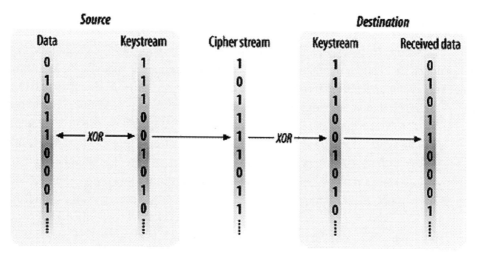

Figure 4. A Block cipher

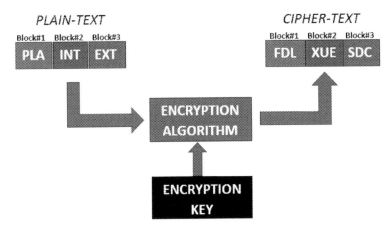

Table 1. Stream cipher vs block cipher

Stream Cipher	pros	**Fast Processing**: Encryption/Decryption takes linear time and constant amount of memory space. **Low error propogation**: One bit error does not effect the following bits in the sequence.
	cons	**Low diffusion property**: Any change in one bit does not effect the change of any other bit in the sequence. **Prone to Man-in-the-middle attack:** No integrity protection or authentication provided. Message can be modified along the way by a malicious node.
Block Cipher	pros	**Avalanche effect:** High level of diffusion is provided as effect of even one bit is spread over several bits. **Message Integrity:** Makes availability of integrity protection. Malicious node detection possible. **Versatile:** Can be used as a building block for a universal hash function or a pseudo-random number generator.
	cons	**Slow:** High computation and memory requirements. Can only work with certain block size. **Lower error resilience:** Error in a single bit can render the whole block useless. **Padding:** Last un-even sized block requires padding in order to extend the last plaintext block to the cipher's block size.

CONFUSION AND DIFFUSION

Confusion and Diffusion are the two quantifiers for the efficiency of a good Cryptographic system. These were first introduced by Claude Shannon in 1945. To create confusion, each character of the ciphertext should depend on several different parts of the key in different ways. It means that there exists an involved and complex relationship between plaintext, key, and ciphertext. An eavesdropper should not be able to guess a deterministic relationship that can predict the effect of changing one chatracter in plaintext has on the encrypted ciphertext (Shannon, 1949). The major goal of confusion is to make it impossible to generate the key even if the eavesdropper has a large number of plaintext and ciphertext pairs that has been created by using the same key. Diffusion means a very slight change in the input which can be expressed as change in one bit of plaintext should have a very large impact on the ciphertext. Further, since encryption is an invertible process, this should also be true in the reverse direction. A slight change in ciphertext should also effect in a huge change in the plaintext produced when decrypted. As quoted by Claude Shannon, "diffusion refers to dissipating the statistical structure of plaintext over the bulk of ciphertext". In practice both confusion and diffusion properties are achieved by using bit substitution and permutation of the order of bitsrespectively. A Substitution-permutation network is a very good example of such a structure that provides robust encryption by iteratively performing substitution and permutation in a specific order (Goldreich, 2003). Shannon also describes this in terms of *information entropy*, the lower the amount of information that is divulged related to the plaintext by a data packet sniffed by an eavesdroppe, higher is the entropy of the packet. Higher entropy is desired from a good security scheme which is achieved by maximizing confusion and diffusion. For a good cryptosystem, it means it would require a very large number of packets by an adversary to reverse engineer it.

MALLEABILITY

A cryptographic algorithm posseses malleability if an encrypted known ciphertext when replaced by another ciphertext (chosen specifically to attack) by an adversary followed by decryption using the algorithm gives meaningful result. This meaningful result could be a function of original plaintext, hence it is related or close to the original plaintext (Dolev, Dwork, & Naor, 2003). In this case, even though the original plaintext is not revealed, some parts of information is leaked which can be exploited by a malicious node to intelligently modify the original message in the data stream.

That is, for a given message M and the corresponding ciphertext$C$ = Encrypt(M), it is possible to generate C' = $F'(C)$ so that$Decrypt(C')$ = P' = $F'(P)$ with arbitrary, but known, functions F and F'.

Generally speaking, malleability is considered as a flaw in a cryptographic system and can be used to define weakness of a particular block/stream encryption scheme. However in some cases, this is a desired property from a cryptosystem which is known as *Homomorphic encryption* where the objective is to build to be malleable (Jajodia & Tilborg, 2011). This property allows computations to be performed on data without decrypting it, which empowers the use of homomorphic systems in the field of cloud computing to guaranty confidentiality of the processed data. For example, encrypted search terms can be examined in an encrypted database without having to decrypt the whole database and in-turn causing a vulnerability. Homomorphic algorithms have also been deployed to perform computations securely for private information retrieval, collision-resistant hash functions, and secured electronic voting systems.

SUBSTITUTION-PERMUTATION NETWORK

To further our understanding of block ciphers, we must recognize a Substitution-permutation network (SPN) which is a sequence of chained mathematical operations used in block cipher algorithms. Such a network accepts a block of the plaintext and the encryption key as input, and applies several iterations known as "rounds" of substitution boxes (S-boxes) and permutation boxes (P-boxes) to generate the ciphertext block. Now several combinations of S and P boxes can be generated for each round. Figure 5 shows how they are used in a SPN.The S-boxes and P-boxes convertsblocks of input bits into output bits. This operation can be as simple as a XOR operation followed by bitwise rotation (Paar & Pelzl, 2010). A different round key is used in each round to encrypt the input bits. Decryption is done by performing the inverses of the S-boxes and P-boxes and applying the round keys in reversed order.

Figure 5. A Substitution-permutation network (SPN)

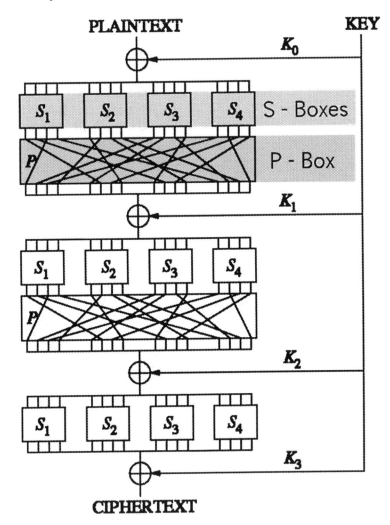

Substitution Box

An S-box works like a lookup table, when given an input of m bits, it returns n bits as an output. Generally speaking, it is not necessary for m to be equal to n. This substitution should have the property of one to one mapping in order for the S-box to be invertible which is essential for decryption. This substitution step is essential to provide obscurity to the key and the resultant cipher hence introduces the property of confusion. A good S-box is supposed to possess a quality known as avalanche effect. This means that a very small change in the input for the S-box greatly changes the output given (Delfs & Knebl, 2002). Under the strict avalanche criterion when a single input bit is changed to the S-box, the probability of each output bit changing should be 50%. In simple terms, it is desired from a good S-box to change even 1-bit of the input should affect atleast half of the output bits.

Permutation Box

A P-box is basically a shuffling of all the input bits coming from different sources as in our case it will be from different S-boxes and then sending them to the next set of S-boxes as shown in the SPN network Figure 5. A desired property of a good P-box is that it divides the bits coming from one particular S-box to as many different S-boxes possible in the next round. To enhance security, the output of the P-box is hashed together with the round key using some operation which can be as simple as XOR.

A P-box could be imagined as a transposition cipher, whereas, an S-box could be perceived as a substitution cipher. Individually when used by itself, they do not provide much security to the cipher. But, when used in combination together as shown in an SPN, they provide pretty high level of security.

ENCRYPTION STANDARDS

Data Encryption Standard (DES)

Even though DES is deemed obsolete now, it did inspire several successful cryptographic schemes. DES is a symmetric key algorithm with 56-bit key size (Biham & Shamir, 1990). In DES a unique symmetric key is used to encode and decode a message. So, both the source and the receiver must securely establish a shared private key among each other. Now, DES has been superseded by the more secure Advanced Encryption Standard (AES) algorithm as DES is considered to be insecure for many applications. The advent of Data Encryption Standard opened up the field of cryptography and the development of better encryption algorithms. It was invented at IBM during early 70's but was kept open to public unlike its predecessors that were kept private by military and government intelligenceorganizations. This ensured anyone interested in security could study how the algorithm worked and try to crack it.

DES is a typical block cipher which takes a fixed-length string of plaintext bits and converts it through a sequence of complex operations into a ciphertext, which is a string of the same length as the plaintext (Figure 6). DES uses 64-bit block size hence the original plaintext is broken into 64-bit blocks.A shared private 64-bit key is also hashed during this transformation to ensure security. Even though the key has a length of 64-bits, only 56-bits are used for the actual key. Rest of the eight bits are used for checking parity.The DES modified and used by NSA had a structure of S-boxes the complete details are still kept a secret. This secrecy led lot of people to believe that NSA had built in a backdoor for itself in DES (Daemen & Rijmen, 2002).

Advanced Encryption Standard (AES)

In the year 2001 DES was replaced by much more secure standard called AES. It uses a SPN network for encryption unlike DES which uses a Feistal network. AES is also a symmetric key algorithm hence same key is used for encoding and decoding. AES is a variant of Rijndael algorithm which has a fixed block size of 128 bits, and a key size of 128, 192, or 256 bits. Further, AES is found to be very fast in hardware as well as software (Biryukov, Cannière, & Quisquater, 2004). The decryption algorithm fol-

Figure 6. Overall structure of DES

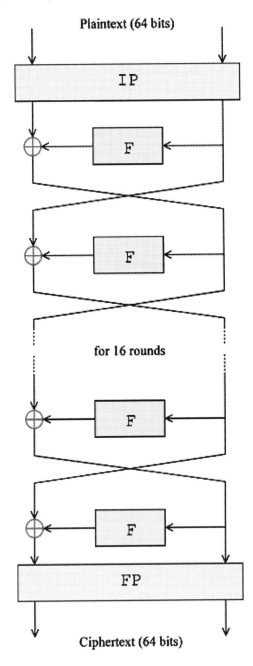

lows a similar path as the encryption algorithm, only replacing the steps by their inverses. The round keys of have to be used in the reverse order during decryption. Brute force attack or slightly improved versions of a brute force attack are the only known successful attacks for AES, although even today, none of these known attacks are computationally feasible in realtime (Paterson & Watson, 2008).

RC4

RC4 (ARC-Four) was the most widely used stream cipher. RC4 was designed by Ron Rivest of RSA Security in 1987. It was used with secure socket layer (SSL), which was used to secure private information and money transfers over the Internet. Furthermore, it is used in WEP (Wired Equivalent Privacy) which is liable for securing wireless data (Fluhrer, Mantin, & Shamir, 2001). RC4 showed that it is secured enough for certain systems, but it was found out that it does not offer that level of security to wireless communications, making it fall short for many security applications. Remarkable for its simplicity and speed in software, multiple vulnerabilities have been discovered in RC4, rendering it insecure. Transport Layer Security (TLS) is a protocol that ensures privacy between communicating applications and their users on the Internet. TLS is the successor to the Secure Sockets Layer (SSL). Several organizations and companies like Microsoft and IETF have recommended not to use RC4 with TLS due to security concerns (Trappe & Washington, 2006).

WIRELESS STANDARDS

Wired Equivalent Privacy (WEP)

WEP is a standard network protocol that augments security to 802.11 wireless networks while working at the data link layer (Edney & Arbaugh, 2004). The idea behind WEP was to provide the similar level of security on a wireless link comparable to a wired network. Nevertheless, the fundamental technology behind WEP has been confirmed to be pretty insecure as compared to newer protocols like WPA (McClure, Kurtz, & Scambray, 2009). WEP exploits a data encryption systemnamed RC4 with a mixture of user- and system-generated key values. The original applications of WEP used encryption keys of length 40 bits and 24 additional bits of initialization vector (IV) to form the RC4 key (64 bits in total). In an effort to escalate security, these encryption techniques were modified to accomodate longer keys of length 104-bit (128 bits of total data), 152-bit and 256-bit (Bittau, Handley, & Lackey, 2006).

In Shared Key authentication, the WEP key is used for authentication in a four-step challenge-response handshake (Figure 7) (Lashkari, Danesh, & Samadi, 2009). In the first step, client directs an authentication request to the Access Point (AP), in response to which AP responses with a clear-text challenge.

Figure 7. WEp encryption

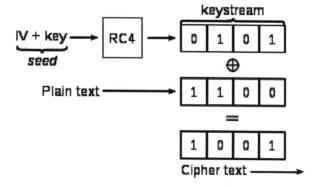

Then, the client encodes the challenge-text using the established WEP key and sends it back in another authentication request. Finally, the AP decrypts the message received. If this is found to be same as the challenge text, the AP sends back a positive response.After the authentication and association phase, the pre-established WEP key is also used for encoding the data frames using RC4.

Wi-Fi Protected Access (WPA)

The Wi-Fi Alliance introduced WPA as an intermediate fix to take the place of WEP which had serious security concerns (Arbaugh, 2003). Temporal Key Integrity Protocol (TKIP) was implemented for WPA under 802.11i standard. WEP used a 40-bit or 104-bit encryption key that was manually entered at the wireless APs and clients and was not changed. TKIP uses a new key for each data packet, it dynamically generates a new 128-bit key using the RC4 cipher for each packet and thus thwarts the types of attacks that rendered WEP insecure.

WPA uses a message integrity check algorithm named Michael to verify the integrity of the packets. Michael provides a sufficiently strong data integrity guarantee for the packets and it is much stronger than a Cyclic Redundancy Check (CRC) which was used in WEP and later found to be weak.

802.11i (WPA2)

WPA2 was introduced to replace WPA. It is even more robust than WPS as it supports CCMP (CTR mode with CBC-MAC Protocol) instead of TKIP which is an AES based encryption mode with stronger security. This was a compulsory requirement of WPA2 under the accepted guidelines of 802.11i by the Wi-Fi alliance (Stallings, 1999).

SECURITY ATTACKS

As stated earlier, the main difference among wired and wireless network is the medium used for data transmissions. The open air broadcast characteristic of a wireless network makes it easy for everybody to attack the network if not properly secured, due to the nonexistence of physical hurdles, where the range of wireless signalcan be from 100meters to 1000meters (Hamed & Al-Shaer, 2006). Lack of need for a physical medium and easy setup helped an exponential growth of wireless networks which proved to be another hurdle in augmenting the network security. A lot of times establsishing network security can be time consuming or cost expensive which can be a deterrent for people. Lack of proper knowledge or education can also prevent people from having good network security. All these factors can lead to vulnerabilities and attacks which can be categorized in several different categories (Preneel, Rijmen, & Bosselaers, 1998).

Active Attacks: Masquerading, Replay, Message Modification, DoS, Etc.

An active attack in a network where a hacker attempts to make changes to data on the target or data enroute to the target (SANS, 2002). Types of active attacks include masquerade attack where an intruder pretends to be a particular user of a system to gain access or to gain greater privileges than currently authorized (Gurkas, Zaim, & Aydin, 2006).

Passive Attacks: Eavesdropping, Traffic Analysis

It is a type of attack wherein adversaries "listen in" on packets that are in transit. Even though it seems the simplest kind of attack, passive eavesdropping can prove very dangerous over aperiod of time (Manley, Mcentee, Molet, & Park, 2005). When paired with advanced and aggressive probabilistic algorithms, the data collected over time can help crack almost any encryption algorithm out there. For this very reason, keys are desired to be dynamic in any good security scheme which should be renewed frequently, well before its integrity becomes questionable.

Side-Channel Attacks

In the year 1996, one of the best examples of a side-channel attack was discovered by a cryptographer named Paul Kocher, in which he measured electric power consumption of microprocessors. In a side-channel attack, an attacker instead of using a brute force approach or targeting theoretical vulnerabilities of the cryptosystem, algorithmic information is gathered related to the physical implementation parameters. For example, parameters like amount of electric power being consumed by the processor (Katz & Lindell, 2008), runtime of the algorithm, electromagnetic emanation from a smartcard, etc. In Paul Kocher's attack, he exploited the power consumption amounts of the microprocessor and plotting it on a curve, he could deterministically identify which conditional branch was followed by the algorithm. Further, it has been found that if the identified conditional branch depends on a secret key, then a lot of information about the key is divulged (Schiller, 2000). In another case, similar side-channel attacks were able to completely hack smart cards, forcing the manufactures to withdraw their product and causing huge losses. Several popular security algorithms have been found to be prone to these attacks by losing the secret key to hackers and hence rendered useless. In his work of '96 Paul talks about timing attacks on implementations of Diffie-Hellman, RSA, DSS, and other systems.

Man in the Middle Attack

A man-in-the-middle attack is one in which a malicious usercovertlycaptures and relays data packetsamong two users who trust they are connecting directly (Peterson & Davie, 2000). It's a form of eavesdropping but the entire communication is controlled by the man in the middle, who even has the capability to modify each data packet (Figure 8). Sometimes, referred to as a session hijacking attack, it is successful if the man in the middle can impersonate each user to the satisfaction of the other. This attack poses a serious threat to online security because it gives the attacker the capability to sniff and control sensitive information in real-time while pretending to be a trusted user during all communications (Pfleeger, 1997).

Modern Attacks

Adware

Such advertising-supported software is a routine that automatically shows advertisements for marketing purposes and in turn, generates money for the server. The ads can be in the user interface of the software or on a screen presented to the user during the installation.

Figure 8. Man-in-the-middle attack

Man in the Middle Attacker

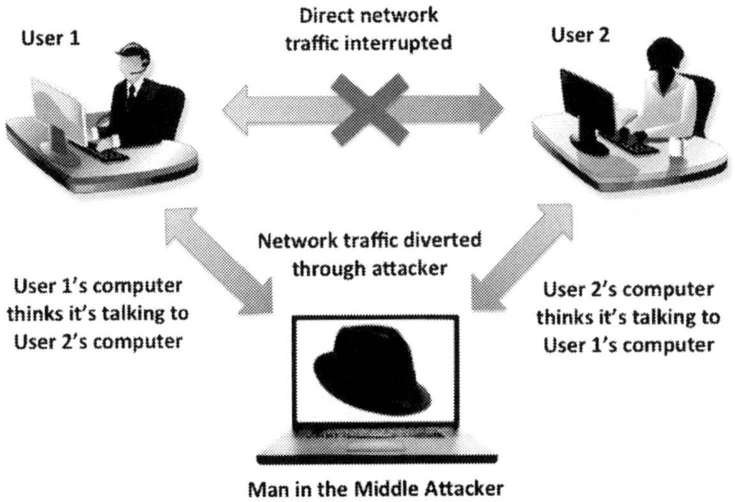

Backdoor

A backdoor in a computer system or a cryptosystem is a technique of bypassing customary authentication, obtaining unauthorized remote access to a computer, or attaining access to plaintext while trying to stayconcealed.

Bluejacking

This is the distribution of unsolicited messages over Bluetooth to Bluetooth-enabled devices such as mobile phones, PDAs or laptop computers, sending a vCard which usuallyholds a message in the name field (bluedating or bluechat) to another Bluetooth-enabled device by means of the OBEX protocol.

Bluesnarfing

This means an unauthorized access of data from a wireless device over a Bluetooth connection, frequently between phones, desktops, laptops, and PDAs (Petros, Luo, Lu, & Zhang, 2001).

Boot Sector Virus

A boot sector virus is a virus that infects the master boot record of a storage device, usually a hard drive, but occasionally a CD. These can be sometimes very hard to remove.

Botnet

Zombie army is a number ofcomputers connected to the Internet thatforward transmissionswithout any knowledge of the original owner, which could be a spam or virus to other computers on the Internet.

Browser Hijackers

This is a form of unwanted software that changes a web browser's settings without user's authorization so as to insertannoying advertising into the user's browser. A browser hijacker may switch the existing home page, error page, or search page with its own.

Chain Letters

Chain letters are letters/emailsthatassureanunbelievable return in exchange for a very small effort. The simplest form of a chain letter contains a list of x people. You are supposed to send something to the top person on the list. Then, you remove the top person on the list, sliding the second person into the top position, add yourself in the bottom position, make y copies of the letter, and mail them to your friends. The assurance is that you will ultimately receive x times y of somethingas an award.

Cookies

Session hijacking, at times also known as "cookie hijacking" is the manipulation of a valid computer session, sometimes also called a session key, thatachieves unauthorized access to data or services in a computer system. Specifically, it is used to refer to the theft of a magic cookie used to authenticate a user to a remote server.

Crimeware

This is intended to commit identity theft using social engineering or technical stealth in order to steal a computer user's financial accounts for the purpose of taking funds from those accounts or making unauthorized online purchases. On the other hand, crimeware may well steal confidential or sensitive corporate data. Crimeware signifies a rising problem in network security as many malicious code threats seek to steal confidential information.

DDoS

This is a type of DoS attack where multiple hijacked internet devices, frequently infected with a Trojan, are exploited to target a single system triggering a Denial of Service (DoS) attack (Wood & Stankovic, 2002).

Dropper

A dropper is an executable file that drops a document to disk, opens it, and silently executes an attacker's payload in the background stealthily. Droppers can carry viruses, backdoors and other malicious scripts so they can be executed on the hijacked device.

Exploit

An exploit is a piece of software, a chunk of data, or a sequence of commands that exploit vulnerability or a bug in order to cause unintended or unanticipated behavior to be present in a computer software and/or hardware. Such behavior often includes attacks like attaining control of a computer system, sanctioning privilege escalation, or a DoS attack.

Fake AV or Scareware

This is a Trojanthat intentionally misrepresents the security status of a computer. These programs try to persuade the user to purchase security software in order to remove non-existent malware or security risks from the computer.

Keylogger

A keylogger is a type of surveillance spyware software that has the ability to record every keystroke made on the keyboard to a log file. A keylogger recorder can record instant messages, e-mail, and any information typed at any time using the keyboard. The log file created by the keylogger can then be sent to a specified receiver.

Mousetrapping

Mousetrapping is a procedure used by some malicious websites to keep visitors from leaving their website, either by launching an endless series of pop-up ads or by re-launching their website in a window that cannot be easily closed. Many websites that do this also employ browser hijackers to change the user's default homepage.

Obfuscated Spam

Obfuscated spam is email that has been disguised in an attempt to bypassor avoid detection by the anti-spam software. By obfuscating the key terms used by the anti-spam software to filter spam messages and can be achieved by inserting unnecessary spaces between the letters of key spam words.

Pharming

This is a cyber attack planned to forward a website's traffic to another, fake site. Pharming can be conducted either by altering the hosts file on a victim's computer or by exploitation of a vulnerability in DNS server software.It is a form of online fraud very similar to phishing as pharmers rely upon the same bogus websites and theft of confidential data.

Phishing

This is an attempt to acquire sensitive infoin an electronic communicationsuch as usernames, passwords, and credit card details (and sometimes, indirectly, money), often for malicious reasons, by masquerading as a trustworthy entity.

Spyware

This is software that aims to gather information in a sneakyway about a person or organization and that may send such information to another entity without the user's consent, or that takes control over a computer without the user's knowledge. Spyware is of four types: system monitors, trojans, adware, and tracking cookies.

SQL Injection

This is a code injection technique, used to attack data-driven applications, in which malicious SQL statements are inserted into an entry field for execution (e.g., to dump the database contents for an attacker).

Trojan

This is any malicious computer program to convince a victim to install by misrepresenting itself as useful, routine, or interesting.

Virus

This is a malware program thatafter execution reproducescopies of itself into other computer programs, data files, or the boot sector of the hard drive and when this duplication succeeds, the affected areas are then said to be "infected."

Wabbits

A Wabbit, Rabbit, or Computer Bacterium is a type of self-replicating computer program. Unlike viruses, wabbits do not infect host programs or documents. Unlike worms, wabbits do not use network capabilities of computers to spread. Instead, a wabbit constantlyduplicates itself on a local computer. Wabbits can be programmed to have malicious side effects.

Worms

A computer worm is a standalone computer malware that replicates itself in order to spread to other computers. Often, it uses a computer network to spread itself, relying on security failures of the target computer to access it. Unlike a computer virus, it does not need to attach itself to an existing program.

Linear Cryptanalysis

This is a general form of cryptanalysis based on finding affine approximations to the action of a cipher.

Chosen Plaintext Attacks

A chosen-plaintext attack (CPA) is an attack model for cryptanalysis which presumes that the attacker can obtain the ciphertexts for arbitrary plaintexts. The goal of the attack is to gain information which reduces the security of the encryption scheme.

Known-Plaintext Attacks

The known-plaintext attack (KPA) is an attack model for cryptanalysis where the attacker has access to both the plaintext and its encrypted version (ciphertext). These can be used to reveal further secret information such as secret keys and code books.

Differential Cryptanalysis

Differential cryptanalysis is a form of an attack targeted mainly towards block ciphers (Huang, Shah, & Sharma, 2010). Stream ciphers and hash functions are found to be equally prone too. In the broadest sense, it is the study of how differences in information input can affect difference in resulting output. In the case of a block cipher, it refers to a set of techniques for tracing differences through the network of transformations, learning where the cryptosystemdisplays non-random behavior, and misusing such attributes to recover the secret key.

SECURITY IN WMAN (802.16)

The WMAN (Wireless Metropolitan Area Network) or WiMAX was introduced as the "last mile" network bringing connectivity to far off remote areas. The 802.16 standard has beenaccepted and released in Dec 2001. Thereafter, serious security flaws in the 802.11 WEP security protocol were widely known and acknowledged.Although the designers of 802.16 security module were aware of security loop holesprevalent in 802.11 WEP design, they still had several shortcomings in the security design.Since the telecommunications standard,Data Over Cable Service InterfaceSpecifications (DOCSIS) was introduced to solve the "last mile" problem for cable communication, itwas incorporated in the 802.16 standard.However, wired networks greatly differ from wireless ones, 802.16 fails to protect the 802.16 communication and has serious vulnerabilities.

Physical Layer Attacks

The 802.16 standard relies completely on MAC layer security and has no security provisions for the physical layer. Due to this vulnerability, 802.16 network is highly prone to attacks like radio jamming and an attacks named"water torture" in which the attacker sends a seriesof data packets to drain the victim's battery charge.

No Base Station Authentication

A major defect in the authentication process used by WiMAX's privacy and key management (PKM) protocol is the absence of base station (BS) or service provider authentication. All authentications are one way and the key is also generated by the BS and the user has to trust the BS not to be malicious. This makes WiMAX networks vulnerable to man-in-the-middle attacks, exposing users to numerous confidentiality and availability attacks. The 802.16e amendment augmentedprovision for the Extensible Authentication Protocol (EAP) to WiMAX networks. However, EAP protocol provision is currently optional for service providers.

PKM Authorization Drawbacks

Insufficient key length and flawed use of cipher modes providing weak security. WiMAX uses DES-CBC cipher with 56-bit key length whichnecessitatesan unpredictable initialization vector to initialize CBC mode. TEK uses 3DESencryption, but uses it in ECB mode which has vulnerabilities.

Lack of Integrity Protection

The SA (Security Associations) initialization vector is a constant and its TEK is public information. Additionally, the PHYsynchronization field is extremely repetitive and predictable and the MPDU initialization vector is also predictable.IEEE 802.16 fails to provide data authenticity.

Small KeyID for AK and TEK

AK-ID is only 4-bit long, where TEK-ID is only2-bit long. This createsthe chance of reusing keys without detection.

Due to these major flaws in 802.16 protocol, it is known to be highly prone to the following attacks:

- Rouge Base Station
- DoS Attacks
- Data Link-Layer attacks
- Application Layer attacks
- Physical Layer attacks
- Privacy Sub-Layer attacks
- Identity Theft
- Water Torture
- Black hat attacks

Due to the obvious vulnerabilities in PKM, a newer and better version PKMv2 was introduced. PKMv2includes a solution to mutual authentication between BS and SS. It also provides a key hierarchy structure for AK derivation. Availability of two authorization modes RSA and EAP. AK is derived from PAK in RSA mode and PMK in EAP mode.

CLOUD SECURITY

Cloud computing provides users and organizations with numerous capabilities to store and process their large amount of data in third-party data centers (Hassan, Riad, & Hassan, 2012). Organizations use the Cloud in a range of diverse service models (SaaS, PaaS, and IaaS) and deployment models (Private, Public, Hybrid, and Community). There are many security issues/concerns linked with cloud computing but these issues fall into two general categories: security issues faced by cloud providers (organizations providing software-, platform-, or infrastructure-as-a-service via the cloud) and security issues faced by their customers (companies or organizations who host applications or store data on the cloud). The accountability goes both ways, however, the service providershave a greater responsibility to ensure that their infrastructure is secure and that clients' data and applications are secureat all times while the end user must take measures to strengthen their applications by using strong passwords and authentication methods.

Cloud data is stored in huge servers that are purpose built and stored in large secure physical locations know as data centers. When an organization stores data over the cloud, they lose the physical control over the location (Yu, Wang, Ren, & Lou, 2010). Hence, it is of utmost importance to secure the physical locations of data centers. It has been learned from recent data center attacks that most of them were conducted with the help of an inside attacker. Subsequently, it is very important to conduct extensive background checks before hiring employees at the data center.

Clouds serve multiple clients sometimes in the same domain handling sensitive consumer data. It is similar to a bank safety deposit box. Just like the banks cloud service providers need to protect the stored data not only from outside attackers but also preventing one customer's data to be accessed by other customers unless authorized for such an access by the original owner of the data. On top of big data manipulation algorithms, cloud providers need to deploy robust protocols for logical storage segregation (Takabi, Joshi, & Ahn, 2010). This means access rights and rules should be strictly enforced.

The broad use of virtualization in employing cloud server infrastructure introduces novel security apprehensions for customers or users of a public cloud service. Virtualization modifies the connection between the Operating System and underlying hardware be it computing, storage or even networking. This presents an additional layer of virtualization that itself must be properly configured, managed and secured. Major concern with virtualization is that it is a logical implementation and not physical hence bugs or loopholes can be disastrous if exploited. An attacker can exploit such a loophole to gain administrator access to the cloud which gives full access and control over the cloud bypassing the virtualization layer. For example, a breach in the administrator workstation with the management software of the virtualization software can cause the whole datacenter to go down or be reconfigured by an attacker.

Cloud security protocol is effective only if the robust security implementations are enforced. Agood cloud security architecture should identify the issues that can arise with security management. The security management addresses these issues with security controls (Mather, Kumaraswamy, & Latif, 2009). These controls are put in place to protect any weaknesses in the system and reduce the effect of an attack. Further, if such an attack is detectedit should be dealt with immediately. Although there are many types of controls for a cloud security architecture, they can be categorized in one of the following categories:

Deterrent Controls

These controls are envisioned to diminish attacks on a cloud system (Winkler, 2011). Much like a warning sign on a fence or a private property, deterrent controls typically reduce the threat level by informing potential attackers that there will be adverse consequences for the wrongdoer. This type of control can be considered a subset of preventive controls.

Preventive Controls

This fortifies the cloud system against attacks and effort are made to minimize if not completely eliminating vulnerabilities and weaknesses present in the system. Strict policies for authentication of cloud users, for example, makes it less probable that unauthorized users can access the cloud, and more probable that cloud users are positively identified.

Detective Controls

Detective controls are intended to detect and combat appropriately to any suspicious activity that occur. In the event of an attack, a detective control will warn the preventative or corrective controls to address the issue immediately. System and network security monitoring, including intrusion detection and prevention measures, are normally employed to detect attacks on cloud systems and the supporting communications infrastructure.

Corrective Controls

Corrective controls minimize the negative impact of an incident, typically by controlling the damage. They come into action while or immediately after an incident. Restoring cloud system backups in order to reconstruct a compromised system is an example of a corrective control.

PRIVACY

Privacy is a very important issue to be dealt with in anycomputer network, specifically the location privacy. In several cases, it is very critical to hide the location of a client in the network as there could be a physical threator a threat of losing sensitive information to an adversary (Smailagic & Kogan, 2002). For example, in most cases, a node would notlike it to be disclosed that it is the one in the network initiating a sensitive bank transaction. Since most ofthe connections in a wireless network are over wireless channels which can easily be sniffed and vulnerable to packetsniffing attacks. In this way, the adversary works in a passive way by just sniffing the data being transferredover a wireless connection. This information can be collected and be used to crack the transaction keys byperforming statistical analysis. The biggest threat comes in the form of a global attacker whichhas access to all the ongoing wireless connections and keeps collecting data packets on them to analyzethem to get information like keys, etc., in order for a future active attack. An active global attacker can be even more dangerous as an active global active attacker not only sniffs packets beingtransmitted globally but it also devises dynamic methods or algorithms in order to identify the targeted nodeinitiating the sensitive communication by using data like transmission event duration, time taken by thepacket to traverse from source to destination, packet size etc. Hence, it is very important to come up withprivacy schemes to keep the client nodes anonymous in a network.

The Onion Routing (TOR)

For a computer network, Onion Routing was invented by Michael G. Reed, Paul F. Syverson, and David M. Goldschlag to provide anonymity (figure 9). In this scheme, The path is pre-computed at the source and the data packet is encrypted in multiple layers with the public key of the forwarding node along the path to destination in a sequential order and each node removes their layer of encryption after receiving the packet and forward the remaining packet called the onion to the next hop and finally the decrypted data with all the layers of encryption removed is received by the destination (Syverson, Goldschlag, & Reed, 1997). Using this approach, each node is only aware of the previous or next hop node which ensures anonymity of the source and the destination.

The list of nodes are maintained by a directory node. Directory node shares this list with users of the network. The path and its members are always computed by the source. Hence, no node in the network knows its location in the chain except the exit node which is the final node in the chain. When the chain of communication route is established, the source can send data over the Internet anonymously. When the destination of the data sends data back, the intermediary nodes continue the same link back to the source, with data again encrypted in layers, but in reverse such that the final node this time removes the first layer of encryption and the first node removes the last layer of encryption before sending the data, for example a web page, to the source.

THOUGHTS ON SECURITY

Best Practices

Careful planning and precautionscan protect against majority of the security threats (Zorzi, Gluhak, Lange, & Bassi, 2010). Following are some of the most important precautionary steps an individual can take to protect themselves:

Figure 9. An Onion packet

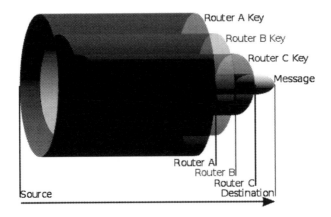

- **Security Software:** This is one of the most important preventive actions that can save from an attack. Modern security softwares come in different flavors like firewalls, antivirus protection, email-protection, malware-protection, web-protection, etc. Generally it's a good idea to get a comprehensive suite from a reputable merchant like Norton, Mcafee, etc. These softwares are always running in the background and monitor any suspicious activity. Whenever any illegal activity is observed the suspected file is blocked and quaranteened and the user is asked for permission to permanently disinfect by deletion.

- **Principle of Least Privilege (PoLP):** Administrator access should be strictly used on need only basis. Account privileges of all users should be closely monitored, people who are not authorized, should not be given admin rights. User account with limited access/rights should be used for basic daily use.

- **Keeping Softwares and Operating System Current:** Regular update checks should be performed to keep the OS and softwares state current. Specifically it is very important to keep antivirus definition files updated to latest version. These files make sure the antivirus software is fully equipped to detect and thwart any new and recent attacks discovered. Softwares can be updated by applying the latest service packs and patches. It is also very important to verify the source of these updates by verifying their digital certificates before installation.

- **Creating System Backup/Restore Points:** Even after taking all the previous steps a system still might get infected which sometimes can lead to losing all the data on the system. It is a very good idea to keep multiple backups of datawhich can save a lot of frustration.In case of an operating system crash, hardware failure, or virus attack the system can be recovered to last known stable state easily by using the backup file.

Additional Suggested Precautions

- Avoid opening email attachments from unknown people.
- Deploy encryption whenever it is available.
- Do not click random links.
- Do not download unfamiliar software off the Internet.
- Do not forward virus hoaxes or chain mail.
- Log out or lock computer when not in use.
- Never share passwords or passphrases.
- Remove/Uninstallprograms or services not needed.
- Restrict/Disable remote access.
- Secure home network with a strong password.

RECENT PROPOSALS

Internet of Things (IoT) is the biggest new development in the field of wireless networks this year (Guinard, Trifa, & Wilde, 2010). As the name implies it's the network of physical objects embedded with electronic hardware and software along with network capabilities. In IoT each entity or "thing" is uniquely distinguishable through its embedded computing harware but is able to function within the existing Internet infrastructure. The Internet of Things empowers objects to be controlled remotely and collect data from sensors utilizing existing network infrastructure, creating prospects deeper integration between the physical world and the digital cyber world, and subsequently promising enhanced efficiency, reliability, accuracy and financial gains.

IoT guarantees the automation of pretty much every field of life by interconnecting virtually everything. IoT gives the capability of converting every day to day mundane object into smart devices and communicating with each other. This helps deployment of advanced applications like Smart Grid and taking it to the next level to create a smart city. At the advent of Internet and other groundbreaking networking inventions the biggest question was Security and Privacy. Similarly, IoT raises very similar questions, but this time the problem is literally huge. IoT proposes to include 20 billion devices by the year 2020. This brings us to the issue of capturing, manipulating and securing a humongous of data. This data set is so big that there is a whole new field of study for handling extremely large data sets known as "Big Data".Currently the internet community doesn't really know for sure how to handle security in such a complex domain. So for now, IoT has been rolled out with very basic security protocols at hand. Several scholars have expressed serious concerns related to security and privacy issues in IoT and makes them wary of this new age ubiquitous computing revolution as this would literally effect the life of everyone present everywhere. People are also concerned about issues related to environmental impact and effect of IoT on younger people and children. Not only does IoT promises to bring remote access and control via internet to every step of our daily life, it also brings issues like cyber attacks and cyber bullying right into our bedrooms. This means security is the biggest issue related to IoT. Advanced algorithms need to be developed to guarantee security and privacy with low overheads since most of the IoT things have low resources.

SUMMARY

In this chapter we discussed various aspects of network security. It is a very broad field that requires extensive in depth study even for a basic understanding of concepts related to it. With time networking technologies keep evolving providing faster connectivity to even the farthest places on earth and beyond. This keeps presenting new challenges for the network security designers. Newer hybrid networks like the Mesh (Akyildiz, X. Wang, & W. Wang, 2005), Smart Grid, IoT, WiMax (Ghosh, Wolter, Andrews, & Chen, 2005), etc. create unlimited possibilities while creating new security challenges. There would always be a need for newer, better, smarter and faster security architectures.

REFERENCES

Akyildiz, I. F., Wang, X., & Wang, W. (2005). Wireless mesh networks: A survey. *Computer Networks*, *47*(4), 445–487. doi:10.1016/j.comnet.2004.12.001

Arbaugh, W. (2003). Wireless security is different. *Computer*, *36*(8), 99–101. doi:10.1109/MC.2003.1220591

Biham, E., & Shamir, A. (1990). Differential Cryptanalysis of DES-like Cryptosystems. *Advances in Cryptology-CRYPT0' 90. Lecture Notes in Computer Science*, 2–21.

Biryukov, A., Cannière, C. D., & Quisquater, M. (2004). On Multiple Linear Approximations. *Advances in Cryptology – CRYPTO 2004. Lecture Notes in Computer Science, 3152,* 1–22. doi:10.1007/978-3-540-28628-8_1

Bittau, A., Handley, M., & Lackey, J. (2006). The final nail in WEP's coffin. *2006 IEEE Symposium on Security and Privacy (S&P'06).* 10.1109/SP.2006.40

Daemen, J., & Rijmen, V. (2002). *The design of Rijndael: AES-the Advanced Encryption Standard.* Berlin: Springer. doi:10.1007/978-3-662-04722-4

Delfs, H., & Knebl, H. (2002). *Introduction to cryptography: Principles and applications.* Berlin: Springer. doi:10.1007/978-3-642-87126-9

Dolev, D., Dwork, C., & Naor, M. (2003). Nonmalleable Cryptography. *SIAM Rev. SIAM Review, 45*(4), 727–784. doi:10.1137/S0036144503429856

Edney, J., & Arbaugh, W. A. (2004). *Real 802.11 security: Wi-Fi protected access and 802.11i.* Boston, MA: Addison-Wesley.

Fluhrer, S., Mantin, I., & Shamir, A. (2001). Weaknesses in the Key Scheduling Algorithm of RC4. *Selected Areas in Cryptography Lecture Notes in Computer Science,* 1-24.

Ghosh, A., Wolter, D., Andrews, J., & Chen, R. (2005). Broadband wireless access with WiMax/802.16: Current performance benchmarks and future potential. *IEEE Commun. Mag. IEEE Communications Magazine, 43*(2), 129–136. doi:10.1109/MCOM.2005.1391513

Goldreich, O. (2003). *Foundations of cryptography.* Cambridge, UK: Cambridge University Press.

Gordon, L. A., Loeb, M. P., Lucyshyn, W., & Richardson, R. (2006). 2006 CSI/FBI computer crime and security survey. *Computer Security Journal, 22*(3).

Guinard, D., Trifa, V., & Wilde, E. (2010). *A resource oriented architecture for the Web of Things.* IOT.

Gurkas, G., Zaim, A., & Aydin, M. (2006). Security Mechanisms And Their Performance Impacts On Wireless Local Area Networks. *2006 International Symposium on Computer Networks.* 10.1109/ISCN.2006.1662520

Hamed, H., & Al-Shaer, E. (2006). Taxonomy of conflicts in network security policies. *IEEE Commun. Mag. IEEE Communications Magazine, 44*(3), 134–141. doi:10.1109/MCOM.2006.1607877

Hassan, Q. F., Riad, A. M., & Hassan, A. E. (2012). Understanding Cloud Computing. *Software Reuse in the Emerging Cloud Computing Era,* 204-227.

Huang, X., Shah, P. G., & Sharma, D. (2010). Protecting from Attacking the Man-in-Middle in Wireless Sensor Networks with Elliptic Curve Cryptography Key Exchange. *2010 Fourth International Conference on Network and System Security.* 10.1109/NSS.2010.15

Imai, H., Rahman, M. G., & Kobara, K. (2006). *Wireless communications security.* Boston: Artech House.

Jajodia, S., & Tilborg, H. C. (2011). *Encyclopedia of cryptography and security.* New York, NY: Springer.

Jakimoski, G., & Kocarev, L. (2001). Chaos and cryptography: Block encryption ciphers based on chaotic maps. *IEEE Trans. Circuits Syst. I. IEEE Transactions on Circuits and Systems. I, Fundamental Theory and Applications*, 48(2), 163–169. doi:10.1109/81.904880

Katz, J., & Lindell, Y. (2008). *Introduction to modern cryptography*. Boca Raton, FL: Chapman & Hall/CRC.

Kaufman, C., Perlman, R., & Speciner, M. (1995). *Network security: Private communication in a public world*. Englewood Cliffs, NJ: PTR Prentice Hall.

Lashkari, A. H., Danesh, M. M., & Samadi, B. (2009). A survey on wireless security protocols (WEP, WPA and WPA2/802.11i). *2009 2nd IEEE International Conference on Computer Science and Information Technology*.

Manley, M., Mcentee, C., Molet, A., & Park, J. (2005). Wireless security policy development for sensitive organizations. *Proceedings from the Sixth Annual IEEE Systems, Man and Cybernetics (SMC) Information Assurance Workshop*. 10.1109/IAW.2005.1495946

Mather, T., Kumaraswamy, S., & Latif, S. (2009). *Cloud security and privacy*. Sebastopol, CA: O'Reilly.

McClure, S., Kurtz, G., & Scambray, J. (2009). *Hacking exposed 6: Network security secrets & solutions*. New York, NY: McGraw-Hill.

Paar, C., & Pelzl, J. (2010). *Understanding cryptography: A textbook for students and practitioners*. Heidelberg: Springer. doi:10.1007/978-3-642-04101-3

Paterson, K. G., & Watson, G. J. (2008). Immunising CBC Mode Against Padding Oracle Attacks: A Formal Security Treatment. *Lecture Notes in Computer Science Security and Cryptography for Networks*, 340-357.

Peterson, L. L., & Davie, B. S. (2000). *Computer networks: A systems approach*. San Francisco, CA: Morgan Kaufmann.

Petros, Z., Luo, H., Lu, S., & Zhang, L. (2001). Providing robust and ubiquitous security support for mobile ad-hoc networks. *Proceedings Ninth International Conference on Network Protocols ICNP 2001 ICNP-01*.

Pfleeger, C. P. (1997). *Security in computing*. Upper Saddle River, NJ: Prentice Hall PTR.

Preneel, B., Rijmen, V., & Bosselaers, A. (1998). Recent Developments in the Design of Conventional Cryptographic Algorithms. State of the Art in Applied Cryptography Lecture Notes in Computer Science, 105-130.

Robshaw, M., & Billet, O. (2008). *New stream cipher designs: The eSTREAM finalists*. Berlin: Springer. doi:10.1007/978-3-540-68351-3

Schiller, J. H. (2000). *Mobile communications*. Harlow: Addison-Wesley.

Shannon, C. E. (1949). Communication Theory of Secrecy Systems. *The Bell System Technical Journal*, 28(4), 656–715. doi:10.1002/j.1538-7305.1949.tb00928.x

Shor, P. (1994). Algorithms for quantum computation: Discrete logarithms and factoring. *Proceedings 35th Annual Symposium on Foundations of Computer Science.* 10.1109/SFCS.1994.365700

Smailagic, A., & Kogan, D. (2002). Location sensing and privacy in a context-aware computing environment. *IEEE Wireless Commun. IEEE Wireless Communications, 9*(5), 10–17. doi:10.1109/MWC.2002.1043849

Stallings, W. (1999). *Cryptography and network security: Principles and practice.* Upper Saddle River, NJ: Prentice Hall.

Syverson, P., Goldschlag, D., & Reed, M. (1997). Anonymous connections and onion routing. *Proceedings. 1997 IEEE Symposium on Security and Privacy (Cat. No.97CB36097).* 10.1109/SECPRI.1997.601314

Takabi, H., Joshi, J. B., & Ahn, G. (2010). Security and Privacy Challenges in Cloud Computing Environments. *IEEE Security & Privacy Magazine IEEE Secur. Privacy Mag., 8*(6), 24–31. doi:10.1109/MSP.2010.186

The SANS Institute. (2002). *Auditing networks, perimeters and systems* [Lecture notes]. Retrieved from https://www.sans.org/course/auditing-networks-perimeters-systems

Trappe, W., & Washington, L. C. (2006). *Introduction to cryptography: With coding theory.* Upper Saddle River, NJ: Pearson Prentice Hall.

Winkler, J. R. (2011). *Securing the cloud: Cloud computer security techniques and tactics.* Waltham, MA: Syngress.

Wood, A., & Stankovic, J. (2002). Denial of service in sensor networks. *Computer, 35*(10), 54–62. doi:10.1109/MC.2002.1039518

Yu, S., Wang, C., Ren, K., & Lou, W. (2010). Achieving Secure, Scalable, and Fine-grained Data Access Control in Cloud Computing. *2010 Proceedings IEEE INFOCOM.*

Zorzi, M., Gluhak, A., Lange, S., & Bassi, A. (2010). From today's INTRAnet of things to a future INTERnet of things: A wireless- and mobility-related view. *IEEE Wireless Communications, 17*(6), 44–51. doi:10.1109/MWC.2010.5675777

This research was previously published in the Handbook of Research on Modern Cryptographic Solutions for Computer and Cyber Security edited by Brij Gupta, Dharma P. Agrawal, and Shingo Yamaguchi, pages 1-27, copyright year 2016 by Information Science Reference (an imprint of IGI Global).

APPENDIX: ACRONYMS

AAA: Authentication, Authorization and Accounting
AES: Advanced encryption Standard
AP: Access Point
AS: Authentication Server
BSS: Basic Service Set
BWA: Broadband Wireless Access
CBC: Chain Block Chaining Mode
CRC: Cyclical Redundancy Checking
DES: Data Encryption Standard
DoS: Denial of Service
EAP: Extensible authentication Protocol
EAPOL: Extensible Authentication Protocol over LAN
ECB: Electronic Codebook Mode
ESS: Extended Service Set
GMK: Group Master Key
IBSS: Independent BSS
IR: Infrared Frequency
IV: Initialization Vector
KSG: Key Stream Generator
LLC: logical Link Control
MAC: Medium Access Control
NIST: National Institute of Standards and Technology
OFB: Output Feedback Mode
PKC: Public Key Cryptography
RADIUS: Remote Authentication Dial-In User Service
RF: Radio Frequency
SSID: Service Set ID
SSL: Secure Socket Layer
WEP: Wired Equivalent Privacy
WIFI: Wireless Fidelity
WIMAX: Worldwide Interoperability for Microwave Access
WLAN: Wireless Local Area Network
WMAN: Wireless Metropolitan Area Network
WPA: WiFi Protected Access

Chapter 63
Cloud Computing Applications in the Public Sector

Amir Manzoor
Bahria University, Pakistan

ABSTRACT

Cloud computing brings key advantages to the governments facing conflicting IT challenges. However, the cloud paradigm is still fragmented and concerns over data privacy and regulatory issues presents significant barriers to its adoption. Cloud computing is expected to provide new ways to run IT in public sector. At the same time, it presents significant challenges for governments, and to make the most of cloud, public sector organizations need to make some important decisions. Governments planning to migrate to the cloud are actively moving to harness digital services but with different focus, reasons, and strategy. However, the degree of cloud adoption by the public sector around the globe varies significantly. Most governments are piloting cloud computing but there are huge differences between each country. This chapter explores the state of the art of cloud computing applications in the public sector; various implications and specific recommendation are also provided.

INTRODUCTION

The shift from client-server computing to the cloud computing is bringing a paradigm change in Information Technology (IT). Cloud computing provides cheaper, faster, easier, more flexible, and more effective IT. Where this paradigm will take us, is difficult to anticipate. However, the rising tide of emerging IT technologies is carrying both private and public sectors, both locally and globally, into territories, which are new and uncharted. This is the era of open data, and the consumerization of IT. We see a transformation of dynamics between public sector and users of public services. With increasing user expectations, several IT-related issues have become more significant than ever before. These issues include service delivery, efficiency, transparency, and quality of service etc. With the evolution of technology, while the technological capabilities are rising, the technology deployment risks are reducing. Governments are finding technology deployments easier and less expensive and continuing to leverage technology to provide modern services to their citizens. However, a world that is increasingly connected than ever

DOI: 10.4018/978-1-5225-8176-5.ch063

Copyright © 2019, IGI Global. Copying or distributing in print or electronic forms without written permission of IGI Global is prohibited.

before pose serious challenges for the governments. Increasing amounts of data poses serious issues related to access, storage, and use of this data including sovereignty, security, and privacy (Lori, 2009). The biggest challenge for governments is to find ways to leverage technology while meeting the above-mentioned challenges and adhering to standards of compliance and security.

Cloud computing has emerged as a solution for a broad array of computing needs and requirements such as custom software environments (Armbrust et al., 2010; Erl et al., 2013). As such, cloud computing has drawn significant attention from both industry and research scientists. Cloud services, both public and private, has demonstrated potential of providing scalable and cost-effective services that can handle various enterprise and web workloads and can be pooled so that a large number of users can access them economically (Pokharel & Park, 2009; Bojanova et al., 2013).

Governance Challenges for Governments

In a bid to serve their citizens better, governments continue to look for use of modern technologies. This use of technology, however, brings two conflicting demands. First, enough investment is required maintain and improve standards. Second, they need to come up with customized technology solutions that best meet their needs, under tighter budgets. The situation gets further complicated given that governments also have legacy IT software and infrastructures. The compartmentalized IT infrastructures are inflexible and expensive. Therefore, governments need to think of new, innovative ways of providing services in order meet the demands of citizens. Cloud computing is an agile approach that is also cost-effective, scalable, flexible, and secure. The critical question now is not whether governments are using cloud computing, but how. While private sector has placed the use of cloud computing at the center of their IT strategy, public sector has just started to adopt cloud computing (Cellary & Strykowski, 2009).

However, a few important decisions must be taken by governments before they decide to leverage the use of cloud computing paradigm. First question is about the governance of cloud computing, the leadership of cloud adoption effort, and the assurance that the desired impact of cloud computing actually occurs. The second question relates to the business question of cloud adoption that will show the clear benefits of cloud adoption and win the support from all stakeholders for cloud adoption.

With respect to the governance of cloud computing, we first need to look at today's governments where three bodies are usually responsible for running the IT functions: 1) a president's office is usually responsible for any changes to government services; 2) various departments or ministries are responsible to source and develop their own IT systems to meet their own specific needs; 3) a core IT function is the responsibility to make IT efficient, consistent and standardized. However, these three components seldom work together and try to protect their autonomy and budgets while avoiding sharing of data because of data security concerns. This non-collaborative approach runs against increasing efficiency and enhanced service delivery. Cloud computing can cuts through the inefficient segregation of IT infrastructure using reusable components and shared architectures and applications. Cloud computing promotes collaboration among people and delivers convenient and flexible services to end users across any government. With their segregated IT infrastructures, public sector organizations have duplicate resources that push up costs. Use of cloud computing allows governments at every level (e.g. local, regional, national) to benefit from the scalable resources and pay-per-use costing of cloud (Wyld, 2009). With systems consolidation, cost savings and greater speed and agility, cloud makes a compelling business case (West, 2010). This brings us to the second area that governments have to address before moving to cloud environments i.e. making a strong business case for cloud computing and its adoption.

Cloud Computing Benefits for Public Sector

When it comes to the business case, there are four main reasons why more and more public sector organizations are now thinking about and adopting the cloud computing paradigm:

- **Cost Reduction**: Use of cloud computing results in reduced costs, lower capital, and operational costs. Pay-as-you-go pricing let public sector organizations pay for what they use.
- **Scalability**: Cloud computing is scalable and capacity can be adjusted when needed e.g. during peaks and troughs in demand.
- **Speed**: Cloud computing is fast. Piloting, testing, and delivery of new projects is much quicker because cloud fosters rapid test-and-learn cultures.
- **High Performance**: The cloud offers more capacity than traditional technology infrastructure. Public sector organizations can benefit from "infinite" capacity if the need arises.

Realization of economies of scale and cutting costs are the most important reasons most public sector organizations have been investing in cloud. However, sole focus on cost cutting has caused most public sector organizations neglect the true potential of cloud to transform the services. The benefits than can be derived from this transformation are dramatic. For instance, the Norwegian government's Altinn4 cloud platform has been used by nearly 90% of companies for submitting documents to public bodies. Another disadvantage of this focus on cost cutting is that public sector organizations are concentrating on private clouds. However, private cloud is just the first step towards cloud falls far short of transforming services. The move towards private clouds should be taken as way to help people get used to the cloud experience and create a platform for moving towards transformation in the future.

With more and more compelling arguments emerging in favor of cloud computing, it is now the time for public sector organizations to proactively plan for utilization of cloud provision. European Commission published its Cloud Strategy in September 2012, which has shown how cloud computing could boost productivity, growth, and jobs. The strategy showed how cloud could create 2.5 million new jobs across Europe, as well as an extra 160 billion Euros per annum/annually to European Union's GDP by 2020 (Hustinx, 2012).

With such opportunities available, the proactive approach of cloud adoption by public sector organizations makes sense. Public sector organizations around the globe are planning to move to cloud but with different speeds and in different directions. Cloud computing would help these organizations meet mission requirements, solve the problem of tight budgets with cost-effective capabilities, and deliver secure, shared services for mobile workers and citizens (Jaeger et al., 2008). For public sector organizations, cloud computing is the 21st century tool for fostering innovation in public services. Public sector organizations are moving to the cloud to optimize internal processes, to accelerate deployment of mission-specific capabilities, and to redefine how public sector delivers services for citizens. Recent research by IDC showed that Spain and the UK were leading cloud adoption in Europe. The UK government has arguably the most mature approach to cloud computing among all Western European governments (IDC, 2013a).

The main objective of this chapter is to explore the applications of cloud computing and related technologies for public sector to discover some visible trends of successful cloud computing applications. The chapter further provides some implications and suggestions to replicate this success in public sectors in other spheres of life, in other parts of the world.

CLOUD COMPUTING: ACHIEVING TRANSFORMATION OF PUBLIC SECTOR

Jansen & Grance (2011) provide a formal definition of cloud computing as follows: "Cloud computing is a model for enabling ubiquitous, convenient, on-demand network access to a shared pool of configurable computing resources (e.g., networks, servers, storage, applications, and services) that can be rapidly provisioned and released with minimal management effort or service provider interaction."

According to NIST (2011), there are five essential characteristics of cloud computing:

- **On-Demand Self-Service**: A consumer can use cloud services, such as an email account, as needed without any human interaction with the cloud provider.
- **Ubiquitous Network Access**: The cloud provider's capabilities are available over the network and can be accessed through standard mechanisms such as the Internet using a ubiquitous client (e.g. a web browser) from a range of client devices (e.g. smartphones, tablets, laptops).
- **Resource Pooling**: A cloud provider can serve its consumers via a multi-tenant model to serve multiple customers. The assignment and reassignment of physical and virtual resources is based on consumer demand.
- **Rapid Elasticity**: A cloud provider can scale resources both up and down as needed. This scaling, sometimes automatically, is based on demand. To the consumer, cloud resources appears to be "infinite". The consumer can purchase as much or as little computing power as they need.
- **Measured Service**: A cloud provider can control and monitor aspects of the cloud service. Customers only pay for resources they use.

Cloud computing can help public sector organizations work faster, more efficient than ever before, more connected to the end user, be more agile and save money. According to Accenture (2013a), the move to cloud has many key implications for how public sector organizations run their IT. Cloud computing can help transform governments in many ways:

- **Citizen Services**: Using cloud data services, public sector organizations can drive innovation that citizens can reuse such as data mash-ups.
- **Infrastructure**: Cloud computing allow public sector organizations to get IT resources from a service provider. Public sector organization pay the price only for the actual resources used. This price paid is a fraction of the cost of traditional IT services. Therefore, upfront capital expenditures are eliminated and IT administrative burden dramatically reduced. IT budgets and facilities can be consolidated due to hardware efficiencies.
- **Flexibility**: Public sector organizations can scale up and down the cloud resources as per their requirements. Onsite data can also be offloaded to the cloud to improve operational efficiencies. Since the cloud is Internet-based, cloud resources can be accessed from anywhere, supporting remote work and continuity of operations.
- **Collaboration**: Cloud can store both data and applications. That allows multiple users at various geographical locations to work together on the same project.
- **Disaster Recovery/Continuity of Operations:** Since cloud provides centralized data and application storage, the data management, backups, recovery can be much quicker in case of any business disruption.

- **Applications and Content**: Cloud provides centralized software and services. Using cloud, public sector organizations can get latest releases of software without waiting for software procurement. This way, public sector organizations can focus on their mission.
- **Policies and Regulations**: Using cloud computing, government can implement proper processes to meet various compliance requirements.
- **Creative IT**: With centrally managed cloud services, governments do not need to worry about keeping the services running all the time. The government employees get more time to foster creative problem solving.

Delivery Models of Cloud Computing

There are three generally agreed service models for service delivery in Cloud Computing. These are Infrastructure-as-a-Service (IaaS), Platform-as-a-Service (PaaS), and Software-as-a-Service (SaaS) (Gong et al., 2010; Rastogi, 2010). However, in the literature, many other service delivery models have also been suggested. Following is the brief description of the three generally accepted approaches, plus one more, along with some real world examples for each (Department of Internal Affairs, 2014).

Software as a Service (SaaS)

In this delivery model, the consumer uses standardized applications (e.g. customer relationship management) only. The operating system, hardware, or network infrastructure on which applications are running is managed and maintained solely by the cloud provider. The customer accesses the applications using a web browser or thin client application and pricing is based on a pay-per-use basis. Consumers can only make predefined configuration changes to the application and manage user permissions to their own data. Examples of SaaS offerings include the government Office Productivity as a Service (OPaaS), Microsoft Office 365, Google Apps, Salesforce.com and Oracle Applications Cloud.

Platform as a Service (PaaS)

In this service delivery approach, the consumer uses a hosting environment for their applications. The consumer controls the applications that run in the environment (and possibly has some control over the hosting environment), but does not control the operating system, hardware or network infrastructure on which they are running. The platform is typically an application framework. The service provider provides standardized operating systems and application services (e.g. web server or database platform) delivered on IaaS services to enable customers to deploy and run their own applications developed using programming languages supported by the service provider. The service provider is responsible for managing and maintaining the underlying infrastructure hardware, virtualization hypervisor, operating systems and standard application services. Usually, customers can only make predefined configuration changes to the standard operating systems and application services but remain responsible for managing and maintaining their applications. Examples of PaaS offerings include the government Desktop as a Service (DaaS), Google App Engine, Microsoft Windows Azure, Force.com, and Oracle Database Cloud.

Infrastructure as a Service (IaaS)

In this delivery model, the consumer uses fundamental computing resources (i.e. processing, memory, storage, networking components, or middleware) to allow the customer to deploy and run their own operating systems and applications. The consumer can control the operating system, storage, deployed applications and possibly networking components such as firewalls and load balancers, but not the cloud infrastructure beneath them. Typically, virtualization technologies are used to enable multiple customers to share the computing resources. The service provider is only responsible for managing and maintaining the underlying infrastructure hardware and virtualization hypervisor. Examples of IaaS offerings include the government IaaS platforms, Amazon Web Services (AWS), Elastic Cloud Compute (EC2), Google Compute Engine and Rackspace Compute.

Business Process as a Service (BPaaS)

Business Process as a Service (BPaaS) refers to any business process (both horizontal and vertical) that is delivered through the cloud service model, which includes multi-tenant, self-service provisioning, elastic scaling, usage metering and internet-enabled (IBM, 2012). The cloud services can include three foundational cloud services (as mentioned before) i.e. Software as a Service (SaaS), Platform as a Service (PaaS), and Infrastructure as a Service (IaaS). The BPaaS service is configurable and sits on top of these three cloud services. A BPaaS service has a wee-defined API and easily connects to related services. BPaaS services support multiple deployment environments to accommodate future changes in business processes. BPaaS is scalable and can support a very large number of processes. Examples are processes for employee benefit management, business travel and procurement, as well as IT-centric processes.

Deployment Models of Cloud Computing

These refer to the way the services are deployed in various cloud environments. Following are the generally accepted deployment models of cloud computing (Peng et al., 2009; Department of Internal Affairs, 2014).

Public Cloud

In simple terms, public cloud services are characterized as being available to clients from a third party service provider via the Internet. Service provider hosts, operates, and manages the cloud services. Public cloud services are typically delivered over the Internet from one or more of the service provider's data centers. The term "public" does not always mean free, even though it can be free or inexpensive to use. A public cloud does not mean that a user's data is publically visible; public cloud vendors typically provide an access control mechanism for their users. They are offered to the public and rely on multi-tenancy (i.e. multiple customers sharing the service providers resources) to drive economies of scale and deliver the maximum potential cost efficiencies. Public clouds provide an elastic, cost effective means to deploy solutions. However, they usually offer a low degree of control and oversight of the security provided by the service.

Private Cloud

A private cloud offers many of the benefits of a public cloud-computing environment, such as being elastic and service based. The difference between a private and a public cloud is that in a private cloud-based service, data and processes are managed within the organization without the restrictions of network bandwidth, security exposures, and legal requirements that using public cloud services might entail. In other words, the provision of services exclusively for the use of a single organization (i.e. there is no multi-tenancy). In addition, private cloud services offer the provider and the user greater control of the cloud infrastructure, improving security and resiliency because user access and the networks used are restricted and designated.

A number of private cloud patterns have emerged and the following provides an overview of the most common patterns:

- **Dedicated Cloud**: In this cloud, the service is owned, operated and managed by the organization and is hosted within its premises or co-located within a data center facility.
- **Managed Cloud**: Here, the service is owned by the organization but is operated and managed on its behalf by a service provider. The service may be hosted within the organization's premises or co-located within the service provider's facility.
- **Virtual Cloud**: In this cloud, the service is owned, operated, managed, and hosted by a service provider but the organization is logically isolated from other customers.

When compared to the other deployment models, private clouds (usually with the exception of virtual private clouds) provide a greater degree of control and oversight of the security provided by the service. However, they also provide the lowest cost efficiencies because the organization must invest capital to purchase the hardware and software required to meet its anticipated peak usage. Further, costs to maintain hardware over time as it is superseded or falls out of warranty may also be borne directly by the Customer.

Community Cloud

A community cloud is essentially a private cloud that is controlled and used by a group of organizations that have shared interests, such as specific security requirements or a common mission and similar business objectives and/or requirements such as different government agencies within a specific sector. They attempt to achieve a similar level of security control and oversight as those provided by private clouds whilst trying to offer some of the cost efficiencies offered by public clouds. The members of the community share access to the data and applications in the cloud.

Hybrid Cloud

A hybrid cloud is a combination of a public and private cloud that interoperates. A hybrid cloud is created when an organization uses a combination of two or more of the other cloud deployment models to implement its cloud strategy. In this, model users typically outsource nonbusiness- critical information and processing to the public cloud, while keeping business-critical services and data in their control. For example, an organization might choose to publish its websites from the public cloud at the same time as it continues to deliver its business critical applications from an in-house private cloud.

Public "Sovereign" Cloud

This is a new type of cloud gaining popularity. This cloud environment has been developed to address cloud data privacy concerns and access of cloud data by third country authorities. In a sovereign cloud, the data and processing is kept within a specific jurisdiction to comply with regulations (Accenture, 2013a).

Most governments are already investing in virtualization and private cloud infrastructures and keen to realize some of the low-risk benefits of cloud (Accenture, 2013a; Kshetri, 2010; Lee & Kim, 2013). The next logical step after private cloud would be the shared community clouds. These community clouds would be shared with government bodies to encourage cloud use and bring cost benefits. Governments at various levels can benefits form community clouds. For example, central governments can use community clouds to handle non-core tasks. A municipal government can use community clouds for eliminating duplication. In future, cross-border community clouds may emerge to help tackle cross-border issues such as border control, anti-terrorism or international policing and defense. In this regard, Cloud for Europe is a promising initiative of 11 European countries to set up procurement requirements for the public sector.

Cloud environments can expand to provide further cost savings and services that are more agile. Governments are moving for cloud adoption at different speeds. However, the next step taken by any government would depend on government's approach. For example, some governments may move very quickly from IaaS to widespread adoption of external cloud services. Other governments may move from internal clouds to external clouds. Irrespective of the choice of the by a government for cloud adoption, the end result would be a hybrid environment that would consist of private and cross-government community clouds, legacy systems, some public cloud. With this end-result in mind, governments should focus first on developing private clouds with options open for transition towards a hybrid environment.

Cloud Computing Governance Models for Public Sector

Government organizations are transitioning to cloud computing to address their requirements through a variety of governance models (Cisco, 2013). Some of these ae briefly discussed below.

Agency-Led Cloud

One agency or ministry takes a lead role in providing cloud services to other government organizations. In many countries, the Ministry of Interior or the Ministry of Finance takes this role. For example, in France, DILA (Directorate of Legal and Administrative Information) is responsible for ensuring public access to laws, citizen rights and duties, and the information needed to conduct business with the government. DILA is transitioning from paper-based processes to a cloud infrastructure-as-as-service (IaaS) solution.

Government ICT Provider

In many countries, the ministry-led model has evolved to one in which an independent provider provides cloud computing services. An example is the Bundesrechenzentrum GmbH (BRZ), Federal Computing Centre of Austria, which redesigned the cloud-computing architecture with the objective of increasing availability, speed, and ease of operations.

Government Broker

To help them stay focused on their core mission, many government agencies use public cloud services where it makes sense (for example, to provide workspace as a service). The model ranges from a classic central procurement model (such as apps.gov in the United States) to an integrated self-service portal for services. In UK, the government's strategy is focused achieving direct cost savings through fundamental change to the way that the public sector specifies, procures, and operates. The UK government embodied this change into two key programs namely the Public Services Network (PSN) and G-Cloud (Government Cloud).

CLOUD COMPUTING APPLICATIONS IN LEADING E-GOVERNMENTS

Today, we are seeing implementations of cloud computing across the public sector all around the world. Indeed, in many instances, governments will be the leading sector in the development of cloud computing across the wider economies. This section offers a survey of cloud computing applications in leading e-governments to determine the emerging trends and models that the follower government can adopt.

United States

The General Services Administration (GSA) provides cloud-based federal government's primary e–government portals - USA.gov - and its Spanish–language companion site, GobiernoUSA.gov (GSA). The two sites draw in excess of 140 million visits annually. Adoption of cloud computing allowed GSA to increase capacity as needed and make changes to the site in a day as compared to six months (Nagesh, 2009). GSA was able to half the agency's administration costs for the sites and cut its infrastructure costs by 90 percent, while delivering improved and scalable web services (Beizer, 2009; Town, 2009; Jackson, 2009).

GSA envisioned to be able to provide Infrastructure as a Service (IaaS) on demand for all federal agencies through prequalified vendors who have been certified for their security, privacy, and operational capabilities (Hoover, 2009a; Hoover, 2009b; Stegan, 2009). To make provisioning cloud-based services as easy as possible, GSA established Apps.gov, a cloud computing storefront that mirrored best practices from the private sector, such as those of Amazon and eBay (Weigelt, 2009; Urquhart, 2009). Apps.gov was criticized, however, for its limited offerings and for not going far enough to make acquiring cloud-based offerings as easy as it was in the commercial world (Weigelt, 2009).

The NEBULA cloud (nebula.nasa.gov) launched by NASA, was designed to allow for greater transparency and public involvement with space efforts. This cloud was aimed at serving as a seamless, self-service platform that will not just consolidate the agency's web offerings into a single portal, but provide NASA personnel with high capacity computing, storage, and network connectivity and a virtualized, scalable approach to achieve cost and energy efficiencies (National Aeronautics and Space Administration, 2014). NEBULA consolidated NASA's many websites, promoting the public to be more actively engaged with NASA's space missions, and allowing for user-generated blogs, wikis, and other content (Atkinson, 2009). NEBULA platform served as a turnkey Software-as-a-Service (SaaS) experience that could also serve in Platform-as-a-Service (PaaS) or Infrastructure-as-a-Service capacities (IaaS) (National Aeronautics and Space Administration 2014). NEBULA uniquely made use of open-source components as major building blocks of its cloud offerings. NEBULA platform offered NASA, super-computer class storage with capacity of hundreds and thousands of terabytes, with nearly unlimited individual file sizes (National Aeronautics and Space Administration 2014; Naone, 2009). All data from NASA missions could be loaded into the NEBULA cloud (Foley, 2009). NEBULA also creates a number of possibilities for NASA to provide cloud services both within the space agency (possibly allowing the agency to consolidate the 70 internal data centers), and quite possibly, to allow NASA to provide cloud computing services to other federal agencies (Sternstein, 2009).

BioSense 2.0 was the first Department of Health and Human Services system to move completely to a distributed cloud-computing environment. With cloud computing, participating health departments easily managed on-demand access to a shared pool of configurable computing resources such as networks, servers, software, tools, storage, and services, with limited need for additional IT support (Memon et al., 2014). With these common resources, BioSense 2.0 users gained significant efficiency, cost reduction, and information-sharing capabilities. With distributed cloud computing, each BioSense 2.0 participant controlled its portion of the cloud and its data. BioSense 2.0 also provided local and state users free secure data storage space, an easy-to-use data display dashboard, and, most importantly, a shared environment where users could collaborate and advance public health surveillance practice. The BioSense 2.0 cloud-computing environment was governed jointly by local, state, and federal public health representatives.

The U.S. Department of Interior's National Business Center (NBC) is a service provider for numerous federal agencies. NBC introduced several cloud-based human resource management applications, including web-based training, staffing, financial, procurement, and recruitment programs. For NBC, shifting to cloud-based programs produced both marked gains in productivity and significant savings in power consumption. NBC established a cloud portal (www.cloud.nbc.gov/) to consolidate its cloud offerings (Lohr, 2009; U.S. Department of the interior, 2009).

The U.S. Census Bureau employed SaaS by Salesforce.com to manage the activities of about 100,000 partner organizations (Hart, 2009). The White House had taken steps to integrate cloud-computing tools into its operations. It made use of Google Moderator, a simple tool that helped groups determine which questions should be asked, to solicit questions from the public and then allow for public voting to determine what questions would be asked of President. The cloud-based application allowed for hundreds of thousands of votes to be cast on the almost ten thousand questions that were submitted for possible use in the live event with the president (Arrington, 2009; Sternstein, 2009).

Data.gov was a flagship Administration initiative intended to allow the public to easily find, access, understand, and use data that are generated by the Federal government. It was the world's largest open government, data-sharing website. Data.gov operates at two levels. The website was the public presence, delivering on the government's commitment to transparency. On the policy level, Data.gov was about increasing access to data that agencies already make available and making available additional data sources that have not been freely presented to the public in the past. For data that were already available, the emphasis was improved search and discovery as well as provisioning of data in more usable formats. For data that had not been widely available due to current business processes and policies, the focus was on providing data in a more timely and granular manner while still protecting privacy, confidentiality, and security. At an operational level, Data.gov's focus had been on creating the website and associated architecture designed to catalog Federal datasets, improve search capabilities, and publish information designed to allow the end user to determine the fitness for use of a given dataset for a particular application. The goal was to create an environment that fosters accountability and innovation (Federal Chief Information Officers Council, 2009).

Apps.gov is the official online Cloud Computing Storefront for the Federal Government. The site featured a comprehensive listing of all GSA approved Cloud services (business, infrastructure, productivity, and social media applications) available to federal agencies. The site provided information about cloud computing and how to procure/use cloud services. It helped create sustainable, more cost-effective IT Services for the Federal Government (Jensen, 2013). It was built on open source (Office of Citizen Services and Innovative Technologies, 2010). Apps.gov provided a centralized storefront where agencies can easily browse and compare cloud offerings from previous Multiple Award Schedule (MAS) contract holders. Tools such as these would reduce the burden on agencies to conduct their own RFP processes and would concentrate investments in the highest-performing cloud providers (Kundra, 2011). Apps.gov encouraged and enabled the adoption of cloud computing solutions across the Federal Government. It eliminated unnecessary research, analysis and redundant approvals, requisitions and service level agreements across the government by providing agencies a fast, easy way to buy the tools they need.

Magellan was a research and development effort, funded through the U.S. Department of Energy (DOE) Office of Advanced Scientific Computing Research (ASCR), to establish a nationwide scientific mid-range distributed computing and a test bed for data analysis. The goal of Magellan was to investigate how the cloud computing business model can be used to serve the needs of mid-range computing and future data-intensive computing workloads for the DOE Office of Science that are not served through DOE data center facilities today (Ramakrishnan, 2013). Magellan had two sites (NERSC and ALCF) with multiple 10's of teraflops and multiple petabytes of storage, as well as appropriate cloud software tuned for moderate concurrency. Today, the system was being used to push the limits of technical cloud computing (Openstack.org, 2013).

New York City's "Roadmap for the Digital City" highlighted requests from residents to "Create a public cloud using the city's existing IT infrastructure". The Roadmap also explained that developers are calling for a cloud-based application-programming interface for public data and services (City of New York, 2011).

United Kingdom

In the UK, cloud technologies helped to cut central government costs, and helped small and medium-sized enterprises, (SMEs) sell more services to the public sector. A new core IT group called Government Digital Services was driving departments to rapidly transform their information technology. The group was attached to the UK Cabinet Office, and encouraging departments to cut costs and rationalize data centers, while also introducing competition between internal and external providers to bring down costs (GOV.UK, 2013).

The UK government also developed G-cloud, which was a government-wide cloud-computing network (Glick, 2009). The aim of Digital Britain strategy of UK government was to give the country the tools to succeed and lead the way in the economy of the future (Government of the United Kingdom, 2009). An important aspect of the Digital Britain strategy was to improve governmental IT and allow more services to migrate online. To support this action, the UK's IT procurement efforts focused on enabling the government to become a leading force in the use of cloud computing. The Digital Britain team had an official forum, where interested parties could learn more about the plan and comment on it, located at http://digitalbritainforum.org.uk/. The UK government developed a CloudStore where government agencies could buy cloud services from over 700 companies. Over 80% of these were SMEs. The government also expanded its G-Cloud supplier framework in 2013 and introduced a "cloud first" policy.

This meant that anyone in the public sector looking to buy IT must look to the cloud first. For central government, there was no other option, while for the wider public sector it was strongly recommended. The UK government's auditor, the National Audit Office, had pointed out that the UK government's IT reforms and spending controls had saved the taxpayer £316 million in 2011 to 2012 alone. The UK government was looking at how it governed IT to see if it could be more agile and more efficient. Teesside University, UK, Centre for Digital Excellence and Entrepreneurship was encouraging new technology, R&D and open innovation.

Denmark

The debate about the use of cloud computing in Denmark started in early 2009. According to KPMG (2012), Denmark was one of the leading countries regarding the adoption of cloud computing in the public sector. In 2011, a Danish municipality planned to use Google Apps Services such as calendar or e-mail in their school systems. In addition, a Danish procurement organization of a Danish municipality moved procurement services into the cloud in 2011. Although Denmark still struggles with security and privacy issues, the Danish Data Protection Agency judged the cloud service of Microsoft - Office 365 - to be compliant with the EU and Danish legislations. In addition, cloud.dk offers public cloud services fully compliant with the Danish data legislation. According to Statistics Denmark, 37% of public companies in Denmark used cloud-computing solutions to a higher or lower degree (Danmarks Statistik, 2010). A recent Danish study showed a rapid adoption of cloud computing to more than 35% in both the public and private sector (Møberg, et al., 2010). In Denmark, the National IT and Telecom Agency shifted two of its systems, Digitalisér.dk and NemHandel, from a traditional in-house environment to cloud hosting resulting in significant cost and energy savings through the effort (Petrov, 2009; Government of Denmark, IT and Telecom Agency, 2009). National IT and Telecom Agency was working with Local Government Denmark (LGDK), a voluntary association consisting of all 98 Danish municipalities, to explore using cloud computing as part of their national and local IT strategies (ePractice Editorial Team, 2009).

Japan

The state of cloud computing in Japan makes for an interesting read as there exists various oddities within the country with regard to the technology. Japan stood at first place in the Business Software Alliance (BSA) Global Cloud Computing Scorecard. This Scorecard looked at a country's accumulated points based on several different aspects of cloud computing and then graded countries accordingly. The factors considered in the scoring consisted of legislative readiness, management of intellectual property rights, anti-cybercrime laws, interoperability, and international harmonization of cloud computing rules. It was a remarkable achievement considering the fact that Japan had a track record for being a slow adopter of new, non-Japanese technology (The Cloud is a product of Western IT landscape). Several Japanese policymakers had shown a willingness to encourage the proper development and deployment of cloud computing, while ensuring that the rights of end users. Due to the ability of cloud computing to represent various sectors, such as networking, hardware, applications, and platforms, no single policy can effectively cover all of the issues it could bring with regard to business models and technologies. Thus, Japan's policies related to data privacy and the cloud tend to be flexible and adaptable. However, there was a need for public-private alliances as well as industry-backed voluntary actions that would help design policies for specific concerns, along with practices that are driven by laws and contracts (Kar, 2012).

Kasumigaseki Cloud, a major cloud computing initiative consolidating all governmental IT under a single cloud infrastructure, was named for the section of Tokyo where many Japanese government ministerial offices are located (Hicks, 2009a). The initiative sought to develop a private cloud environment that would eventually host all of the Japanese government's computing. The Kasumigaseki Cloud was expected to provide greater information and resource sharing, promote more standardization and consolidation in the government's IT resources, reduced costs, operational benefits, and more environmentally friendly IT operations (Rosenberg, 2009). The Kasumigaseki Cloud was part of the Digital Japan Creation Project. This represented a governmental effort aimed at using IT investments (valued at just under 100 trillion yen) to help spur economic recovery by creating several hundred thousand new IT jobs in the next few years and doubling the size of Japan's IT market by 2020 (Government of Japan, Ministry of Internal Affairs and Communications, 2009; Hoover, 2009c).

Even though Japan recently embraced cloud technology, local telecom companies were aggressively building cloud-computing infrastructures in order to cater to the rapidly increasing demands of the domestic market, as well as in the hopes of expanding globally with their offerings. On the SME side, many Japanese SMEs were considering cloud adoption. For SMEs, the availability of cloud services would only lead to improvements in both a more streamlined workforce, and the reduction of unnecessary costs. SMEs could also expand further as the cloud provides scaled resources for them.

China

Cloud computing is growing rapidly in China with heavy support from the government. The country's overall cloud-computing value chain will be worth at least $122 billion by 2015, according to the China Software Industry Association. The nation accounted for less than 3% of global cloud computing market share but was growing with an annual rate of 40% (Jones, 2012). Easy data storage and low maintenance costs were the factors driving the adoption of cloud computing in China. There existed a lot of room for expansion. China had the world's largest population of Internet users, and by the end of 2013, it was expected that there would be 500 million smartphones, which utilize software and applications based in the cloud, online in China (Larson, 2013). Expanding cloud computing in China was declared a top priority in the government's 12th Five-Year Plan, released in 2011. In 2013, there were at least 40 public cloud projects under way in China. Beijing alone received more than $8 billion to support constructing servers and other infrastructure. Moreover, it is just the beginning.

The National Cloud Computing Industry initiated 'China Cloud'. This development plan was approved by the State Council in 2012. This plan covered a wide range of cloud strategies, including a development strategy, key tasks, technology roadmap, supporting systems for China's cloud computing industry during the 12th Five-Year Period (2011 to 2015). The Ministry of Industry and Information Technology, along with other national departments also announced instructions on developing innovative cloud computing services through pilot and demonstration projects in the second half of 2010. Five cities including Beijing, Shanghai, Shenzhen, Hangzhou and Wuxi were listed as pioneering regions for developing cloud computing services.

In another push for the industry, China approved the National Financial Support Program for Cloud Computing Demonstration Projects. This program provided allocation of a maximum of 1.5bn CNY to

12 key projects from the first five cloud computing cities. In 2012, China planned to develop about ten cloud computing demonstration enterprises in the next three years as part of this program. This plan was expected to make China's cloud computing market worth 200bn CNY.

Cloud computing efforts in China has also been spearheaded by local leaders. The city of Dongying started an IBM-developed cloud computing initiative called the Yellow River Delta Cloud Computing Center. This initiative aimed at improving not only its e-government offerings but economic development (Hicks, 2009b). In the southeastern city of Wuxi, the municipal government set up an IBM developed "cloud services factory" to improve the computing resources available to local companies and to attract more firms to its economic development project. This cloud provided on-demand computing resources to the firms. Firms could readily access the computer resources they require for projects. Participating firms had a ready-made, on-demand computing infrastructure, freeing financial resources for other needs and making the start-ups more likely to thrive and create new economic wealth and jobs in the city (IBM, 2009).

First major use of cloud computing technology in China was expected by the government. Cloud computing based e-government systems were seen as an important enabler for the public sector, helping with workplace efficiency and providing better services to citizens. Chinese government set strategic direction for e-government development. With this strategic direction, many key projects started by China's public sector. In March 2011, the Health Cloud System of Shibei Hospital in the Zhabei District, Shanghai, was put into use. This was the first health cloud for China. In May 2011, the Qingao Municipal Government announced its plans to build a private cloud-computing platform for E-government affairs, the first of its kind for China's public sector. Moreover, in July 2011, the High-tech District of Xi'an City declared its Dual Cloud Deployment Strategy and the Xi'an Software Park built the first cloud-computing center in Northwest China for providing Infrastructure-as-a-Service (IaaS) for enterprises and companies within the park. IT investment by China's public sector was expected to grow from 46.4 billion CNY in 2011 to 50.29bn CNY in 2012 (Jones, 2012).

European Union

In the autumn of 2012, the European Commission launched the Cloud Computing Strategy for the European Union as a first step to stimulate the adoption and increase of the use of cloud technologies within the European single market. The European Commission encouraged legislators to develop a generous global approach to cloud computing to ensure that both cloud computing European users and providers would enjoy the full benefits of this market growth. EuroCloud Europe was a federation of independent European non-profit organizations, present in 30 European countries, which adhered to the general mission and objectives of EuroCloud: to promote and raise awareness of the benefits of the cloud computing market in Europe. Through the annual events they organize, EuroCloud facilitated knowledge sharing, creation of a contact network and the establishment of strategic alliances with the European industry. Through its office in Brussels, EuroCloud Europe participated in the working groups on the standardization of cloud industry in the European Commission (trust, certification, interoperability). In less than two years, EuroCloud had been present in 27 European countries with legally established organizations in 18 countries, including Romania. The directors of the boards of the organizations from these countries are members of the EuroCloud Europe and have one vote each in the decisions to be taken at European level (Railway Informatics, 2013).

France

In France, government was slow in adopting cloud due to government's desire to avoid the social effects of cutting spending and jobs too quickly. Government of France was committed to keeping all data and services hosted within its borders but took a slower approach to cloud adoption, basing the move mainly on internal transformation. The strategy of government has two strands. First, the Directorate of Legal and Administrative Information (DILA), one of the branches of the prime minister's central administration, to be tasked to build a private cloud. This private cloud would be used by DILA and other government ministries. Second, the government would sponsor creation of two private sector "sovereign clouds" managed and run by major communications operators. This sponsorship was meant to ensure that public, multi-tenant cloud services were available to French private and public sector organizations within France. The two sponsored clouds were CloudWatt, managed by Orange, and Numergy, run by SFR (Accenture, 2013b). In Paris, the municipality joined forces with a third party to build a cloud-based intranet. Secondary schools were using the cloud to share course materials and other information (IDC, 2013b).

France favored the development and installation of a nation-wide cloud for governments, a so-called G-Cloud (Governmental Cloud). France started its development of the G-Cloud named "Andromeda" in 2011. This G-Cloud, a IaaS platform for governments, was set up and implemented by the two companies Orange and Thales. The main aim of developing a G-Cloud in France was in relation to data protection and legislative issues. A cloud especially developed for France could guarantee full compliance with national law in terms of data protection and security. Such compliance might not be achieved by e.g. adopting US-based services. Government of France was building up some kind of G-Cloud for the French Directorate of Legal and Administrative Information (DILA). This cloud would offer French citizens fast and performing access to French public services.

Belgium

In Belgium, the government moved to cloud environment gradually, creating key digital building blocks like digital identity, signature and archive functions. It would then use these blocks to support new cloud infrastructure, applications and services. Meanwhile, government organizations were introducing cloud projects and pilots at all levels, including federal, regional and city administrations. The central government issued requests for information (RFIs) for external providers to help them move applications to the cloud and provide back up and disaster recovery. Government was also looking for a service provider to define and manage service levels for cloud solutions, similar to a "cloud broker". For example, the city of Ghent worked to introduce SAP's cloud-based Success factors for human capital management. At a regional level, the Flanders region took steps to outsource systems infrastructure, and aimed to become an "infrastructure-light" cloud broker.

The Belgian Federal Public Service of Health, Food Chain Safety and Environment used a cloud-based storage and collaboration environment to ensure that its own staff as well as external users could jointly manage the European Presidency (Microsoft, 2011). Using Huddle, which lets you connect and work securely with other people online, the FPS Social Security's EU 2010 Presidency Team was organizing conferences, meetings and preparing relevant documents for negotiations. Colleagues from national and local public institutions, non-governmental organizations (NGO), research centers and universities could work together on files, share discussions, manage approvals and schedule events.

In view of giving governmental institutions a legally compliant and reliable framework through which they could buy ad-hoc commodity services on a pay-per-use basis, the Belgian government developed a G-Cloud framework, similar to what the UK already did. The G-Cloud was a hybrid combination of public and private cloud, i.e. the existing consolidated data centers of the federal government and commercial cloud services, which could be ordered through a self-service portal. The federal ICT ministry selected a market player that it considered solid for this purpose. In addition, the Belgian Privacy Commission announced that it was preparing an opinion on the privacy aspects of offering and using cloud services, in particular about the risks connected to the development of a cloud strategy by public authorities. It would also issue a recommendation about the use of cloud computing by companies (World IT Lawyers, 2013).

Germany

Germany stood 4th in the BSA ranking of 2013 (BSA, 2013). Germany's government has held back from adopting cloud services, mainly because citizens were worried about data privacy and security. Germany had comprehensive cybercrime legislation and up-to-date intellectual property protection in place. The combination of these laws provided reasonable protection for cloud computing services in Germany. While the government talked about consolidating contracts with its five biggest IT providers into a structure like the UK's G-Cloud, no decisive actions were taken. There was some continuing uncertainty about whether Web-hosting businesses and access providers are liable under the Civil Code for copyright breaches that occur on their systems. Germany also has modern electronic commerce and electronic signature laws in place. Like most European countries, Germany has comprehensive privacy legislation, but it includes onerous registration requirements that may act as a cost barrier for the use of cloud computing. In addition, Germany has 17 data protection authorities, which leads to uncertainty in the application of the law. Germany has a strong commitment to international standards and interoperability and making good progress on extending broadband access to the population.

Some examples of migration to cloud at the federal level exist, as some data centers have been virtualized, and some cloud pilots are underway. However, states and cities are taking to cloud much more readily. One good example is goBerlin, a cloud-based marketplace that gave Berlin's residents secure access to public and commercial services. The project built on the existing cloud infrastructure of public IT services provider ITDZ Berlin. By providing Software as a Service (SaaS) for small and medium-sized businesses and local authorities, it would help these entities play a key role in developing and using IT services. During a pilot period across the Berlin metropolitan area, residents made the most of the integrated cloud service using an e-identity card. A key goal of the project was to create strong user and developer communities, which will encourage goBerlin to thrive and grow (FOKUS, 2013).

To ensure the secure and reliable use of cloud computing in Germany, a number of problems need to be solved. Current IT concepts have to be adapted to specific requirements, particularly in data security and protection, standardization, interoperability and service quality. Legal problems include liability issues and aspects of contractual law as well as legal assurance of data protection and security. Cloud computing calls for new business models in the German ICT industry.

Spain

There is still very limited adoption of cloud computing in the public sector in Spain. Reasons are information integrity, privacy, and legal concerns. The central government was not the driving force behind cloud computing adoption but moreover local governments were. Local governments had a limited financial capacity in contrast to the central government and here cloud computing could tremendously help in saving costs. However, many governments had adopted cloud computing. The favored deployment model in Spain was the private cloud (approx. 58%), followed by the public cloud (approx. 31%) and the hybrid cloud (app. 17%). The private cloud was favored because of higher control in terms of security and privacy. The community cloud model was generally seldom used in Spain because it targeted a fusion of specific sector applications (e.g. health), which seemed to be undesired (Zwattendorfer & Tauber, 2013).

The government of Catalonia in Spain signed a $67 million contract with HP to transform the government's data centers to a cloud-based infrastructure in order to operate its compute services more efficiently. The agreement runs for 10 years (InformationWeek, 2013). In fact, the Public Administration took the first steps in cloud computing, drawing on the infrastructure available: the SARA network. On 15 January 2013, the High Council for E-Government designated SARA as a priority project to start building the private cloud of the Public Administration in Spain. SARA connected and provided services to the General Administration as well as to Regional and Local Governments. Currently, it offers widespread-shared services in the Spanish Public Administration, such as the @firma platform for e-certificate validation and the data mediation platform (Government of Spain, Ministry of Finance and Public Administration, 2013).

Ireland

Ireland is rapidly becoming a dominant force in Cloud Computing, building on its international reputation as a leader in ICT. Many key players have already been attracted to Ireland while a wide spectrum of technology companies with Irish operations are actively expanding into and researching the Cloud. Ireland anchored cloud computing in their national governmental strategy. This strategy of the Irish government with the name "Technology Actions to Support the Smart Economy" was introduced by the Ministry of Energy and Communications and the Ministry of State in 2009. The Irish government's comprehensive strategic approach to develop the sector in recognition of Ireland's potential to become a world leader in Cloud Computing attracted world leaders, such as EMC, Citrix and Dropbox. Supportive Infrastructure, competitive costs, and Data/IP protection were the main drivers behind cloud computing progress in Ireland. (IDA Ireland.com, 2014).

Ireland saw cloud computing as one of the key drivers for economic growth in Ireland. They estimated high reductions in server and energy costs by expecting high value job generation at the same time. Therefore, Irish government released a separate "Cloud Computing Strategy" paper in 2012. Irish government planned several governmental services based on cloud computing offered to their citizens, aiming on increased productivity by decreasing public expenditures at once. The Irish government also provided some kind of guidance for businesses when adopting cloud computing. This guidance entitled "SWiFT 10: Adopting the Cloud – Decision Support for Cloud Computing" consisted of a set of standards which would help businesses to lower obstacles when moving services into the cloud.

The Irish Centre for Cloud Computing and Commerce (IC4) was focused on developing an internationally recognized industry-led center of excellence for innovation and applied research. An industry panel, including Intel, IBM and Microsoft, guided its activities. Cloud R&D centers have also been developed by US technology companies, including Dell, HP, IBM and EMC.

Pakistan

In the developing world, Pakistan is an important example of a country making headways in cloud implementation. Cloud computing is ideal for countries like Pakistan. Pakistani businesses and organizations have started to look for ways to integrate cloud computing it into their operations. Telecom, electronic, print media, education and banking sectors possess exceptional potential to utilize cutting-edge technologies in their businesses and many are already using cloud infrastructure for database and business applications. Many global firms, such as Oracle and Microsoft, are getting into cloud computing market of Pakistan. However, the market is still not fully mature for cloud computing. There are in excess of 20,000 small organizations in Pakistan and these will need these services to enhance their productivity, as they grow further. There are a large number of Pakistani vendors offering the Cloud Computing Services which are hosting there data storage and processing services within Pakistan.

Microsoft, in collaboration with Fujitsu, launched cloud services for Pakistan in 2013. The key targets of these services were local businesses. In May 2014, Pakistan Telecommunication Company Limited (PTCL) announced that it was ready to transform human resource operational processes with cutting-edge cloud computing technology. The announcement was made at SAP Forum in Karachi. In the first deal of its kind in the country, PTCL employed a series of solutions from SAP Company "Success Factors" to streamline vital HR processes and unlock new avenues of employee productivity. The move was set to add additional momentum to the company's ambitious and expansive business strategy, which recently helped deliver a 31 percent increase in the first quarter as compared to the same period of last year. The telecommunications market in Pakistan is fiercely competitive, and only those with the vision and ability to adapt with latest technology especially with people's capability management will stand out.

In 2012, CyberNet, a leading Internet Service Provider of Pakistan, launched RapidCompute, Pakistan's first cloud computing service. RapidCompute was an Infrastructure-as-a-Service (IaaS) platform that combined enterprise class infrastructure with the deep-dive expertise and strong support. RapidCompute offered a high performance, standards-based, flexible and robust cloud solution. Using RapidCompute, customers could comfortably operate and manage their virtual machines (called RapidMachines), quickly scale up and down as per their business needs and get the true cloud experience.

ENABLERS AND BARRIERS TO CLOUD COMPUTING IMPLEMENTATION

There is no doubt that cloud computing offers the potential to deliver significant benefits to the organizations who adopt this technology – not only seen from a pure economical point of view, but also in terms of agility and innovation. However, success is not to be taken for granted; certain factors are imperative for achieving the desired effects from a cloud computing initiative. First, developing a cloud computing strategy and making sure that it is well anchored. The strategy should disclose the current state in terms of drivers and barriers across the (political) landscape with regard to ICT maturity, infrastructure and (political) needs. Secondly, articulating and communicating the whys and desired effects of your initiative i.e. making it a realistic and relevant "burning platform" for change (Montemayor et al., 2014; West, 2010). Below are some of the other enablers and barriers identified in the present research.

Enablers

The conditions for fast adoption of cloud computing are already in place in many developed countries, e.g. telecom infrastructure, IT infrastructure and visions of use of IT and IT services in the public sector (The Economist Intelligence Unit, 2010).

Another enabler towards cloud computing is the green power (hydroelectric power and geothermal energy) and cooling at an attractive cost that can be provided by e.g. the appropriate climate and environment. For example, in the Nordic countries – especially where low-cost "green" electricity and natural cooling due to the cold climate are at hand – a relatively big part of the interest in cloud computing is concentrated around building data centers to be used for cloud computing services. Since the cost of electric power is one of the largest operating costs for data centers, keeping these costs down will be vital for the success of cloud computing providers. Google has built a data center in Finland, Microsoft has been in dialogue with Greenland about a data center establishment, and Facebook builds their new data center in Luleå, Sweden. Another enabler is the high-speed data lines. However, there are also challenges in data center offerings. Challenges can be in areas of national taxes or legal requirements.

Barriers

According to Nordic Council of Ministers (2012), the most significant barrier to using cloud computing is the issues surrounding security and privacy of personal data. Take an example of the case of the municipality of Salem in Sweden. The Swedish Data Inspection Board, on 28 September 2011, stated that the standard Google agreement used between Salem and Google did not fulfil the legal requirements in the Swedish Personal Data Act (Datainspektionen, 2011). The conclusion was comparable to preliminary conclusions in the Narvik case in Norway (Digi.no, 2011) and in the Odense case in Denmark (Datatilsynet, 2010).

The laws on personal data in many European countries state that personal information can only be transferred to countries in the European Union (EU), as long as a proper security level is maintained. Data can also be transferred to some countries outside EU if the country agrees to meet EU standards under the directive's Safe Harbor principles. There are EU mechanisms to overcome data transfer restrictions but not all countries have recognized these mechanisms or have imposed additional requirements on their use. In some countries, there are specific restrictions on transferring certain types of public sector data out of the country, thus preventing the uptake of public cloud services based outside of the country. The public companies have to make sure that cloud service providers have the security and infrastructure in place for the company to live up to security level and national laws, and the governance can be very difficult because of the distributed nature of cloud computing.

As a means to overcoming this barrier, the National IT and Telecom Agency in Denmark published a guide for legal aspects of cloud computing usage, including an evaluation of cloud services against the Personal Data Act. Many of the aspects in the guide were related to the lack of a clear legislation model regarding jurisdiction over the hosted data, its distribution in other countries etc. (IT & Telestyrelsen, 2011).

The European countries are comparable concerning laws for securing personal data. Legal issues with cloud computing are comparable to legal issues for normal IT hosting. The difference is that global providers (Google, Amazon, Microsoft etc.) are not able to physical locate data, and localization is an essential legal requirement that all European countries must fulfil.

In the cases involving national security, law enforcement authorities of many countries can access personal information hosted by third parties. This issue has raised serious concerns over use of public clouds. Data protection laws hold a cloud customer responsible for the security of data in the cloud. In practice, cloud customers face many difficulties in securing contractual data security requirements for commoditized cloud services. The ultimate data security comes down to security of the encryption keys needed to access the data. In this regard, European Union has developed data protection rules to clarify things and establish a Europe-wide set of rules under which European citizens' data can be stored in the cloud. Governments can further strengthen the security of cloud data by providing encryption for both the data stored in the cloud and data in transit.

In Europe, the government IT operations tend to be segregated with each department developing its separate budgets and plans. Ministries generally avoid sharing data and applications over concerns of data control and security. To make cloud work in situations like this, governments need to adopt a more open approach by taking control of data and ensuring privacy and security are up to the job. Doing so would encourage departments share information among themselves and beyond. This would also help develop a connected government for citizens.

The ownership of applications available in the cloud is another issue. This issue is more important in cases where an application works only on a particular cloud platform. Users refrain from using such applications because they are uncertain as to who owns the applications. A sound management of cloud platforms and applications can enable governments to address any such issues of intellectual property.

According to Accenture (2013a), recent security breaches and debates over personal data showed that US citizens were still not 100% happy about digital society. While some people may be against further digitization of public services, many people are hoping for more digital public services. In Europe, there already exists a large number of digital public services users looking forward for more digital services.

TRENDS OF PUBLIC SECTOR ADOPTION OF CLOUD COMPUTING

Governments planning to migrate to cloud are actively moving to harness digital services but with different focus, reasons, and strategy (Accenture, 2013a; Liang et al., 2011). Based on their strategies, the governments migrating to cloud computing can be divided into three categories: cutters, builders, and enhancers. The governments' cloud adoption strategies were influenced by their goals and the degree of the centralization of their existing operations.

Countries classified as Cutters are those developed high GDP economies that are hit severely by the volatility of global economy. These are the countries going through a period of sluggish growth with high budget deficit and looking to cut down government expenditures. In these countries, the expenditure on information and communications technology (ICT) is on the rise, though at a slow rate. Some examples of cutters include Spain, UK, USA, France, Italy, and Netherlands. Among cutters, we also have quick cutters (i.e. those countries looking to achieve quick cost reduction and higher productivity) and slow cutters (i.e. those countries focusing on the transformation of their internal operations). UK is an example of quick cutter while France is an example of slow cutter. Quick cutters can migrate to a full cloud solution by first using IaaS and replacing any legacy applications with PaaS and SaaS. They can then consolidate their applications and final move towards introducing cloud-based services.

Countries classified as Builders are those developing economies with strong economic growth looking to build their infrastructure for their future needs. These countries have high GDP growth with moderate budget deficit and the expenditure on information and communications technology (ICT) is on the rise at a high rate. Brazil, China, India, Indonesia, Mexico, Saudi Arabia, and South Africa are some examples of Builders. These countries look to gain quick benefits from cloud computing. Builders can migrate to a full cloud solution by first accelerating the development of government technology infrastructure by using PaaS and/or SaaS solutions. They can then build a cloud broker to consolidate their services and finally roll out new cloud services over time.

Countries classified as Enhancers, are those developed economies with a moderate GDP growth rate and a lower budget deficit. These countries have relatively high per-capita GDP relatively unaffected by the financial crisis. They intend to increase gradually the expenditure on ICT. Some examples of Enhancers include Austria, Belgium, Denmark, Malaysia, Singapore, South Korea, and Germany. One way Enhancers can move to cloud computing is that one public organization take a lead and other use cloud services produced by the former.

Cloud-based consumer applications (such as Facebook and iPhone applets) used successfully in commercial sector may find their use in public sector (Marston et al., 2011; Davies et al., 2010). Greater cross-governmental sharing is expected in future which will allows citizens access to government services using a unified storefront. Public sector use of pre-approved cloud-based platforms and preconfigured applications will increase in future. These will be used by public sector organization to develop applications for their operations. Just like the energy market, it is expected that a competitive, real-time market for cloud services will emerge and public sector organizations will use it to get the services desired. The data security in the government cloud will become level-based that would be determined by setting access levels based on rules defined in the cloud (Liu et al., 2014). Governments are expected to increase their data analytics capabilities to detect data errors. Governments may also promote clouds as a low cost way to provide IT services to non-governmental organizations, community organizations or small start-up businesses.

To measure all the ways cloud computing will change operation of public sector is difficult. Public sector decision makers will require a thorough assessment to understand how clouds can help them. More specifically, the decision makers need to investigate what new services should be pursued using cloud computing given the current technological capabilities. This will help ensure strategic ambitions do not outrun the capabilities of the technology. Public sector organizations also need to enhance the maturity of their systems, management, operations tools, and processes so that they could be part of a hybrid environment in the future.

CLOUD COMPUTING FOR PUBLIC SECTOR: IMPLICATIONS AND RECOMMENDATIONS

Implications

To adopt cloud computing, governments need to have a clear long term strategy, clear feasibility study and a will to resolve the many inherent issues. Some of the issues are national structural issues e.g. fragmented procurement, contracting, and budgeting of IT services. Some of the issues are of global nature e.g. concerns over data security and changing data privacy regulations.

A single digital environment, such as the cloud, can provide many benefits to countries and their citizens. As the people's lives more and more digitized, citizens expect that their transactions with public sector should take place online. There are obvious reasons for these expectations. Digital citizens feel empowered with control of their interactions with public sector organizations. For governments, cloud provides better engagement with citizens, increased trust between public sector organizations and the citizens, and reduced costs of interaction with the citizens.

Currently, cloud policies of many governments are undeveloped and unproven. There exist various questions marks with respect to the governments' ability to successfully identify and manage the risks of working in a cloud environment. In this situation, any government moving for cloud adoption should proceed with caution until policies, standards, and technical proficiency are addressed to avoid any un-needed risks. The conventional wisdom at this point suggests that without deliberate planning in scope, deployment, management, privacy, security, and the other considerations, the cloud is a "red herring" that demands a wait-and-see approach.

In order for the government to have the ability to identify opportunities for cloud technologies, and implement them within the governmental IT and policy structures without exposing the departments to unwanted or unforeseen risk, an appropriate governance structure seems necessary (Paquette et al., 2010). Without an appropriate governance structure, the cloud implementation will most probably lead to unpredictable and undesirable consequences to the government.

Cloud computing provides compelling paradigm for managing and delivering services over the Internet and rapidly changing the landscape of IT (Zhang et al., 2010). Nevertheless, the current technologies are not matured enough to realize full potential of cloud computing. Many key challenges, such as automatic resource provisioning, power management and security management, still need to be addressed.

Recommendations

According to an estimate, most government agencies require 18-24 months to redirect funding required for transition to cloud computing. Even if government agencies take advantage of public clouds, some up-front investment will be required. Cloud implementations may take several years, depending on the size of the agency and the complexity of the cloud model it selects (i.e., public, private, or hybrid). It could take as long as 4 years before accumulated savings offset the initial investment costs in cloud computing. An improperly planned or inefficiently executed cloud implementation can prolong this period. To be economically feasible, cloud implementation requires proper planning and efficient execution. To help build momentum and support for migration to cloud computing, government agencies should identify the IT workload that can be transitioned to the cloud in the near term. Around the globe, cloud computing has received the backing of executives of government agencies. For government agencies, cloud-computing offers clear opportunities significantly reduce growing data center and IT hardware expenditures.

For migration of low-sensitivity data to the cloud, public clouds should be preferred by the government agencies. This is based on the assumption of a constant IT workload over the next three years. If government agencies require maintaining control of infrastructure and data, private clouds should be preferred. This is based on the assumption that the transition to the new cloud environment will occur steadily over 3 years, existing facilities will be used, and IT workload would remain constant. A hybrid cloud should be used when a government agency intends to use a private cloud to handle the majority of its IT workload and a public cloud for low-sensitivity data. This is based on the assumption that majority of workload will be transferred to the private cloud and existing facilities will be used.

An active pursuit of "cloud first" policy is the need of the hour for governments. Governments should develop private clouds with ultimate transition to become cloud broker. Since scale efficiencies provided by cloud computing produces significant impacts, government agencies should explore the potential of a private cloud approach for interdepartmental and interagency collaboration and investment. Governments should invest in common infrastructure, services, and pilot projects. Governments should develop a platform to consume government-wide services. Governments should consider individual targets for cloud-based government services. To attract and encourage private investment in cloud implementation projects, governments should proactively provide the IT governance frameworks for cloud implementation at various government levels (such as local, regional, or city level). Governments need to boost data privacy and security at a national and international level while providing clarity regarding the concerns over data security and privacy.

FUTURE RESEARCH AREAS

Despite the recent cloud computing adoption by the public sector around the globe, the research on cloud computing is still in its nascent stages. New challenges keep emerging from existing applications while many existing issues still need to be fully addressed.

Virtualization can provide significant benefits in cloud computing by enabling virtual machine migration to balance load across the data center (Zhang et al., 2010). In addition, virtual machine migration enables robust and highly responsive provisioning in data centers. The major benefits of virtual machine migration are to avoid hotspots. Detecting workload hotspots and initiating a migration lacks the agility to respond to sudden workload changes. This question needs further investigation.

Improving energy efficiency is another major issue in cloud computing. It has been estimated that the cost of powering and cooling accounts for 53% of the total operational expenditure of data centers. In USA alone, data centers consumed more than 1.5% of the total energy generated in 2006. This figure was expected to grow to grow 18% annually. This situation puts infrastructure providers under enormous pressure to reduce energy consumption. How this energy consumption can be reduced while meeting government regulations and environmental standards? That requires future investigation.

Analysis of data traffic is important for today's data centers. To optimize customer experiences, many web applications rely on analysis of traffic data. In order make their management and planning decisions, network operators need to understand traffic flows through the network. Currently, there is not much work on measurement and analysis of data center traffic. This area needs further research.

Data security is another important research topic in cloud computing (Subashini & Kavitha, 2011). Service providers typically do not have access to the physical security system of data centers. Service providers rely on the infrastructure provider to achieve full data security (Paquette et al., 2010; Rittinghouse & Ransome, 2009). Even for a virtual private cloud, the service provider can only specify the security setting remotely, without knowing whether it is fully implemented.

CONCLUSION

Governments across the globe face two conflicting challenges: investment of large amount of funds to provide public services and work with ever-tightening budgets. Harnessing new technology is the only way forward for governments to reconcile these two challenges and provide their citizens with more efficient and effective services. Legacy IT infrastructure of many governments and located across departments, presents an additional hurdle where governments cannot work more efficiently because systems, information, and costs cannot be easily shared.

Citizens expect low-cost, high-quality public services. To provide cost-effective, scalable, and responsive services, in a flexible and secure manner, require governments to adopt an innovative approach. Cloud computing not only brings these benefits together but also provides more benefits. Cloud computing involves lower capital and operating costs and provide flexible capacity, which is needs-based. New services can be brought to market quickly. Cloud computing also provides high performance computing power. For governments to become "digital governments", cloud computing provides tremendous opportunities.

Most governments are piloting cloud computing and there exists significant differences among these piloting efforts. While some governments have begun to virtualize for private cloud infrastructure, most governments are switching to cloud independently. This approach of independent cloud implementation does not take into account the bigger picture or the chance to share information in the future. Thus far, the common objective of cloud implementation seems to be cost cutting and movement towards a digital environment.

In most governments, the responsibility of IT management is generally shared between three bodies: a president's office, ministries or departments, and an IT infrastructure. President's office normally focusses on overall government reforms. Ministries or departments focus on meeting their own needs. IT infrastructure works across the government to provide efficiency and operational standards. For these three bodies, cloud computing can provide a new, more efficient way of working. Presently, the three bodies initiate individual cloud implementations with following a more coordinated approach.

Government initiatives for cloud implementation are further hindered by concerns over compliance with data protection laws. Another issue is data location in the cloud and its access by authorities of another country. The same concerns have made European governments wary of using public cloud services. With proposals to update data protection rules, it is expected that decision makers will have greater clarity and decision-making on the use of cloud services will be easier. Constantly improving cloud security continues to eliminate existing weak spots in IT infrastructure and provide tighter controls.

With respect to the cloud paradigm, a public service organization can be a user, a provider, or both. It is expected that, with the evolution of market, governments will be able to decide what role is best for them. Involvement of all the important stakeholders, including local government, citizens, and service providers, cloud can help to bring "digital government". This digital government, while cutting costs, will deliver flexible and responsive public services. Cities of many countries are working towards cloud implementation, while governments are working to overcome the security challenges.

Cloud implementation will affect the governments in three important ways i.e. speedy service delivery, the agility to react to events and a consistent long-term strategy. While the importance of IT service skills will decline in future, the importance of the vision of service strategy and management of technology suppliers will become very significant in future.

With respect to the cloud implementation, the countries can be classified as Cutters, builders and enhancers. Most governments are already investing in cloud infrastructures with virtualization as the first step. The natural progression would be move to sharing community clouds with other government bodies. Governments can use secure cross-border community clouds to meet some of the challenges. Cloud for Europe initiative is a joint initiative of 11 countries that will develop a set of procurement requirements together. Over the time, it is expected that governments will build their own cloud-based solutions with ultimately moving towards a hybrid solution. This hybrid solution will be a mix of private and cross-government community cloud, as well as legacy systems and public cloud. The Defense Information Systems Agency (DISA), created by the US Department of Defense (DoD), provides a model for the future cloud services broker of DoD. It is expected that European countries will follow suit.

This chapter has, hopefully, added to the existing knowledge of the state-of-the-art of cloud computing in public sector, covering its various applications, essential concepts, deployment/delivery models, prominent characteristics, as well as future research directions. More importantly, a comparison of leading e-governments' strategies and trends of could computing usage and specific recommendations are provided that would be helpful for follower e-governments in establishing their respective roadmaps for cloud computing implementation. As the development of cloud computing technology is still at an early stage, this work will hopefully provide a better understanding of the challenges of cloud computing in public sector, and pave the way for further research in this area.

REFERENCES

Accenture. (2013a). *Achieving Digital Excellence in Public Service: Accenture Research and Insights 2013.* Retrieved from http://www.accenture.com/us-en/Pages/insight-achieving-digital-excellence-public-service-summary.aspx

Accenture. (2013b, September 23). *European Public Services - Cloud Changes the Game.* Retrieved from http://www.accenture.com/us-en/Pages/insight-european-public-services-cloud.aspx

Armbrust, M., Fox, A., Griffith, R., Joseph, A. D., Katz, R., Konwinski, A., & Stoica, I. (2010). A view of cloud computing. *Communications of the ACM, 53*(4), 50–58. doi:10.1145/1721654.1721672

Arrington, M. (2009, March 24). *White House Using Google Moderator For Town Hall Meeting. And AppEngine. And YouTube.* Retrieved from http://techcrunch.com/2009/03/24/white-house-using-google-moderator-for-town-hall-meeting/

Atkinson, N. (2009, June 4). *NASA Creates a New NEBULA: Cloud Computing Project.* Retrieved from http://www.universetoday.com/32013/nasa-creates-a-new-nebula-cloud-computing-project/

Beizer, D. (2009, February 23). *USA.gov will move to cloud computing -- FCW.* Retrieved from http://fcw.com/Articles/2009/02/23/USAgov-moves-to-the-cloud.aspx

Bojanova, I., Zhang, J., & Voas, J. (2013). Cloud computing. *IT Professional, 15*(2), 12–14. doi:10.1109/MITP.2013.26

BSA. (2013). *2013 BSA Global Cloud Computing Scorecard.* Retrieved from http://cloudscorecard.bsa.org/2013

Cellary, W., & Strykowski, S. (2009). E-government based on cloud computing and service-oriented architecture. In *Proceedings of the 3rd international conference on Theory and practice of electronic governance* (pp. 5–10). ACM. 10.1145/1693042.1693045

Cisco. (2013). *21st Century Digital Government: Secure, Connected, Mobile.* Retrieved from http://www.cisco.com/web/strategy/docs/gov/brochure_cisco_cloud_government.pdf

City of New York. (2011). *Road Map for the Digital City*. Retrieved from http://www.nyc.gov/html/media/media/PDF/90dayreport.pdf

Datainspektionen. (2011, September 30). *Risker med otydliga avtal för molntjänster*. Retrieved from Datainspektionen: www.datainspektionen.se/press/nyheter/risker-med-otydliga-avtal-for-molntjanster/

Datatilsynet. (2010, June 26). *Udtalelse i forbindelse med anmeldelse af "Google Apps –online kontorpakker med kalender og dokumenthåndtering"*. Retrieved from Datatilsynet: http://datatilsynet.dk

Davies, G., Greenway, A., Harris, J., & Alter, A. (2010). *Six questions every government executive should ask about cloud computing*. Academic Press.

Department of Internal Affairs. (2014). *Cloud Computing*. Retrieved from http://www.ict.govt.nz/assets/ICT-System-Assurance/Cloud-Computing-Information-Security-and-Privacy-Considerations-FINAL2.pdf

Digi.no. (2011, July 7). *Narvik må svare for Google Apps*. Retrieved from Digi.no IT-bransjens nettavis: http://www.digi.no/873387/narvik-maasvare-for-google-apps

ePractice Editorial Team. (2009, August 17). *DK: Public discussion in implementing cloud computing services in the Danish public sector | ePractice*. Retrieved from http://www.epractice.eu/en/news/292790

Erl, T., Mahmood, Z., & Puttini, R. (2013). *Cloud Computing: Concepts, Technology & Architecture*. Pearson Education.

Federal Chief Information Officers Council. (2009). *Data.gov Concept of Operations Draft*. Retrieved from http://ideascale.com/userimages/sub-1/736312/ConOpsFinal.doc

Fokus, F. (2013). *goBerlin – Marketplace for trustworthy governmental and business services*. Retrieved from http://www.fokus.fraunhofer.de/en/elan/projekte/national/go_berlin/index.html

Foley, J. (2009, May 22). *NASA Launches "Nebula" Compute Cloud*. Retrieved from http://www.informationweek.com/government/enterprise-architecture/nasa-launches-nebula-compute-cloud/217600714

Glick, B. (2009, July 28). *Digital Britain commits government to cloud computing*. Retrieved from http://www.computing.co.uk/ctg/news/1816113/digital-britain-commits-government-cloud-computing

Gong, C., Liu, J., Zhang, Q., Chen, H., & Gong, Z. (2010). The characteristics of cloud computing. In *Proceedings of Parallel Processing Workshops (ICPPW)* (pp. 275–279). IEEE. 10.1109/ICPPW.2010.45

Government of Denmark. (n.d.). *IT and Telecom Agency, Press Release: Launching a dialogue on cloud computing in government, July 17, 2009*. Retrieved from: www.itst.dk/nyheder/nyhedsarkiv/2009/opleg-til-dialog-om-cloud-computing-i-detoffentlige

Government of Japan, Ministry of Internal Affairs and Communications (MIC). (2009, May). *Press release: MIC announces the outline of Digital Japan Creation Project (ICT Hatoyama Plan)*. Retrieved from: http://www.soumu.go.jp/main_sosiki/joho_tsusin/eng/Releases/NewsLetter/Vol20/Vol20_01/Vo

Government of Spain, Ministry of Finance and Public Administration. (2013). *Towards a Cloud Computing Strategy in the Public Administration*. Retrieved from https://administracionelectronica.gob.es/pae_Home/dms/pae_Home/documentos/OBSAE/pae_Notas_Tecnicas/2013-02_nota_tecnica_CLOUD_EN.pdf

Government of the United Kingdom, Department for Business Innovation & Skills and Department for Culture, Media and Sport. (2009). *Digital Britain: The Final Report, June 16, 2009*. Retrieved from: http://www.culture.gov.uk/images/publications/digitalbritain-finalreportjun09.pdf

GOV.UK. (2013, May 5). *Government adopts "Cloud First" policy for public sector IT*. Retrieved from https://www.gov.uk/government/news/government-adopts-cloud-first-policy-for-public-sector-it

Hart, K. (2009, March 31). Tech Firms Seek to Get Agencies on Board With Cloud Computing. *The Washington Post*. Retrieved from http://www.washingtonpost.com/wp-dyn/content/article/2009/03/30/AR2009033002848.html

Hicks, R. (2009b). The future of government in the cloud. *FutureGov, 6*(3), 58-62.

Hicks, R. (2009a). Chinese city builds public cloud to aid innovation. *FutureGov Asia Pacific: Transforming Government + Education + Healthcare, 29*(Sep). Available http://www.futuregov.net/articles/2009/sep/29/oil-rich-chinesecity-buildspublic-cloud-aid-inno/

Hoover, J. N. (2009a, May 14). *Federal Government Considering Cloud Computing*. Retrieved from http://www.informationweek.com/government/enterprise-architecture/federal-government-considering-cloud-com/217500172

Hoover, J. N. (2009b, May 15). *Japan Hopes IT Investment, Private Cloud Will Spur Economic Recovery*. Retrieved from http://www.informationweek.com/services/business-process/japan-hopes-it-investment-private-cloud/217500403

Hoover, J. N. (2009c, June 12). *General Services Administration's CIO Looks To The Cloud*. Retrieved from http://www.informationweek.com/government/cloud-saas/general-services-administrations-cio-loo/217800986

Hustinx, P. (2012). *Opinion of the European Data Protection Supervisor on the Commission's Communication on "Unleashing the potential of Cloud Computing in Europe"*. Brussels: European Data Protection Supervisor.

IBM. (2009). *White Paper - Seeding the Clouds: Key Infrastructure Elements for Cloud Computing, Feb 2009*. Available: ftp://ftp.software.ibm.com/common/ssi/sa/wh/n/oiw03022usen/OIW03022USEN.PDF

IBM. (2012, March 28). *Delivering Business Process as a Service (BPaaS) on the IBM SmartCloud, Part 1: Using ICON to extend Business Process Manager cloud images [CT316]*. Retrieved from http://www.ibm.com/developerworks/websphere/library/techarticles/1203_lau/1203_lau.html

IDC. (2013a, January). *Business Strategy: Western Europe Government Sector IT Cloud Computing Trends, 2012–2013*. Retrieved from http://www.idc.com/getdoc.jsp?containerId=GIPP12U

IDC. (2013b, May). *Perspective: Government Hits the Road–CEE Governments on Their Way to Cloud*. Retrieved from http://www.idc.com/getdoc.jsp?containerId=CEMA19764

InformationWeek. (2013, June 26). *HP Wins $67 Million Spain Government Cloud Contract*. Retrieved from http://www.informationweek.com/cloud/software-as-a-service/hp-wins-$67-million-spain-government-cloud-contract/d/d-id/1110543?

Ireland, I. D. A. com. (2014). *Cloud Computing in Ireland - IDA Ireland* Retrieved from http://www. idaireland.com/en/business-in-ireland/industry-sectors/cloud-computing/

IT & Telestyrelsen. (2011). *Cloud Computing og de juridiske rammer – En vejledningom lovgivningskrav og kontraktmæssige forhold i forbindelse med cloud computing*. IT & Telestyrelsen.

Jackson, J. (2009, May 18). *But is it really cloud computing? -- GCN*. Retrieved from http://gcn.com/ blogs/gcn-tech-blog/2009/05/gsa-cloudy.aspx

Jaeger, P. T., Lin, J., & Grimes, J. M. (2008). Cloud computing and information policy: Computing in a policy cloud? *Journal of Information Technology & Politics*, *5*(3), 269–283. doi:10.1080/19331680802425479

Jansen, W., & Grance, T. (2011). Guidelines on security and privacy in public cloud computing. *NIST Special Publication*, *800*, 144.

Jensen, A. (2013). *Federal Cloud Computing: Elements*. Issues and Implementation Challenges.

Jones, P. (2012, May 21). *China's growing cloud industry | Datacenter Dynamics*. Retrieved from http:// www.datacenterdynamics.com/focus/archive/2012/05/china%E2%80%99s-growing-cloud-industry

Kar, S. (2012, July 31). *BSA Study: Strong Cloud Adoption in Emerging Markets | CloudTimes*. Retrieved from http://cloudtimes.org/2012/07/31/bsa-study-strong-cloud-adoption-emerging-markets/

KPMG. (2012). *Exploring the Cloud: A Global Study of Governments' Adoption of Cloud*. Available: http://images.forbes.com/forbesinsights/StudyPDFs/exploring-cloud.pdf

Kshetri, N. (2010). Cloud computing in developing economies. *Computer*, *43*(10), 47–55. doi:10.1109/ MC.2010.212

Kundra, V. (2011). *Federal cloud computing strategy*. Academic Press.

Larson, C. (2013, September 10). Will Cloud Computing in China Be a Boon or Peril for Business? *BusinessWeek: Technology*. Retrieved from http://www.businessweek.com/articles/2013-09-10/will-cloud-computing-in-china-be-a-boon-or-peril-for-business

Lee, H.-O., & Kim, M. (2013). Implementing cloud computing in the current IT environments of Korean government agencies. *Interaction*, *4*, 5.

Liang, D.-H., Liang, D.-S., & Wen, I.-J. (2011). Applications of Both Cloud Computing and E-government in Taiwan. *International Journal of Digital Content Technology and Its Applications*, *5*(5).

Liu, B. F., Zhong, H. H., & Wang, M. (2014). How to Design the Cloud Computing Used in E-Government's Information Security. *Applied Mechanics and Materials*, *536*, 616–619.

Lohr, S. (2009, June 15). IBM to Help Clients Fight Cost and Complexity. *The New York Times*. Retrieved from http://www.nytimes.com/2009/06/15/technology/business-computing/15blue.html

Lori, M. (2009). *Data security in the world of cloud computing*. Co-Published by the IEEE Computer And Reliability Societies.

Marston, S., Li, Z., Bandyopadhyay, S., Zhang, J., & Ghalsasi, A. (2011). Cloud computing—The business perspective. *Decision Support Systems*, *51*(1), 176–189. doi:10.1016/j.dss.2010.12.006

Memon, A. A., Naeem, M. R., Tahir, M., Aamir, M., & Wagan, A. A. (2014). A New Cloud Computing Solution for Government Hospitals to Better Access Patients' Medical Information. *American Journal of Systems and Software*, 2(3), 56–59.

Microsoft. (2011, March 31). *Belgium used cloud computing to collaborate with partners during EU Presidency*. Retrieved from http://www.microsoft.com/eu/impact-on-society/multimedia/belgium-used-cloud-computing-to-collaborate-with-partners-during-eu-pr.aspx

Møberg, E., Danielsen, A. H., Damgaard, T. T., Christensen, S., Weeke, S., & Bundgaard, N. (Eds.). (2010). *Strategi, trends og erfaringer i danske virksomheder*. Rambøll Management Consulting A/S.

Montemayor, A. D. S., López, J. F., & Álvarez, J. C. (2014). Critical factors affecting the utilization of cloud computing. In *CBU International Conference Proceedings* (Vol. 2, pp. 324–329). CBU. 10.12955/cbup.v2.481

Nagesh, G. (2009, September 29). *USA.gov's successful shift to cloud computing could become the model*. Retrieved from http://www.nextgov.com/cloud-computing/2009/09/usagovs-successful-shift-to-cloud-computing-could-become-the-model/44915/

Naone, E. (2009, June 23). *The Standards Question*. Retrieved from http://www.technologyreview.com/article/413985/the-standards-question/

National Aeronautics and Space Administration. (2014). *NASA - Flagship Initiatives*. Retrieved from http://www.nasa.gov/open/plan/nebula.html

NIST. (2011, October 25). *Final Version of NIST Cloud Computing Definition Published*. Retrieved November 8, 2014, from http://csrc.nist.gov/publications/PubsSPs.html#800-145

Nordic Council of Ministers. (2012). *Nordic Public Sector Cloud Computing – a discussion paper*. Nordic Council of Ministers. Retrieved from http://norden.diva-portal.org/smash/record.jsf?pid=diva2:701433

Office Of Citizen Services and Innovative Technologies. (2010). *Federal Cloud Computing Initiative*. Available: http://www.nist.gov/itl/cloud/upload/NIST_Cloud_Computing_Briefing_2010_sbGSA.pdf

Openstack.org. (2013). *Building High Performance Clouds*. Retrieved October 18, 2014, from http://www.openstack.org/user-stories/argonne-national-laboratory-us-department-of-energy/

Paquette, S., Jaeger, P. T., & Wilson, S. C. (2010). Identifying the security risks associated with governmental use of cloud computing. *Government Information Quarterly*, 27(3), 245–253. doi:10.1016/j.giq.2010.01.002

Peng, J., Zhang, X., Lei, Z., Zhang, B., Zhang, W., & Li, Q. (2009). Comparison of several cloud computing platforms. In *Proceedings of Information Science and Engineering (ISISE)* (pp. 23–27). IEEE. 10.1109/ISISE.2009.94

Petrov, O. (n.d.). *Backgrounder: Financial crisis and cloud computing - Delivering more for less. Demystifying cloud computing as enabler of government transformation, World Bank, Government Transformation Initiative, June 16, 2009*. Available: http://siteresources.worldbank.org/INTEDEVELOPMENT/Resources/BackgrounderFinancialCrisisCloudComputing.doc

Pokharel, M., & Park, J. S. (2009). Cloud computing: future solution for e-governance. In *Proceedings of the 3rd international conference on Theory and practice of electronic governance* (pp. 409–410). ACM. 10.1145/1693042.1693134

Railway Informatics, S. A. (2013). *Impact of Cloud Computing on Electronic Government*. Author.

Ramakrishnan, L. (2013). Magellan: experiences from a Science Cloud. *eScholarship*. Retrieved from http://escholarship.org/uc/item/6rz9893s

Rastogi, A. (2010). A model based approach to implement cloud computing in e-Governance. *International Journal of Computers and Applications*, *9*(7), 15–18. doi:10.5120/1399-1888

Rittinghouse, J. W., & Ransome, J. F. (2009). *Cloud computing: implementation, management, and security*. CRC Press.

Statistik, D. (2010, January 24). *Nyt fra Danmarks Statistik Nr. 32*. Retrieved from Danmarks Statistik: http://www.dst.dk/pukora/epub/Nyt/2011/NR032.pdf

Stegan, D. (2009, July 16). *Vivek: One stop cloud shop - Tech Bisnow (DC) - Bisnow*. Retrieved from https://www.bisnow.com/archives/newsletter/tech/vivek-one-stop-cloud-shop

Sternstein, A. (2009, July 24). *White House mulls making NASA a center for federal cloud computing*. Retrieved from http://www.nextgov.com/cloud-computing/2009/07/white-house-mulls-making-nasa-a-center-for-federal-cloud-computing/44369/

Subashini, S., & Kavitha, V. (2011). A survey on security issues in service delivery models of cloud computing. *Journal of Network and Computer Applications*, *34*(1), 1–11. doi:10.1016/j.jnca.2010.07.006

The Economist Intelligence Unit. (2010). *Digital Economy Rankings 2010. Beyond e-readiness*. The Economist Intelligence Unit Limited.

Towns, S. (2009, May 1). *Federal Web Portal Moves to Cloud Computing Platform*. Retrieved from http://www.govtech.com/enterprise-technology/Federal-Web-Portal-Moves.html

Urquhart, J. (2009, September 18). *Five ways that Apps.gov is a trendsetter*. Retrieved from http://www.cnet.com/news/five-ways-that-apps-gov-is-a-trendsetter/

U.S. Department of the Interior. (2009, August). *Department of the Interior National Business Center (NBC) - Cloudbook Government Profile*. Retrieved from http://www.cloudbook.net/directories/gov-clouds/us-doi-national-business-center--nbc

Weigelt, M. (2009, July 31). *Kundra aids search for procurement leader -- FCW*. Retrieved from http://fcw.com/articles/2009/08/03/week-kundra-aids-ofpp-search.aspx

West, D. M. (2010). *Saving money through cloud computing*. Governance Studies at Brookings.

World, I. T. Lawyers. (2013, November 12). *Belgium develops a government cloud similar to the UK, by Geert Somers (time.lex) | WorldITLawyers - A network of specialists in ecommerce law, privacy and data protection, etc*. Retrieved from http://www.worlditlawyers.com/belgium-develops-government-cloud-similar-uk-geert-somers-time-lex-2/

Wyld, D. C. (2009). *Moving to the cloud: An introduction to cloud computing in government.* IBM Center for the Business of Government.

Zhang, Q., Cheng, L., & Boutaba, R. (2010). Cloud computing: State-of-the-art and research challenges. *Journal of Internet Services and Applications, 1*(1), 7–18.

Zwattendorfer, B., & Tauber, A. (2013). The public cloud for e-government. *International Journal of Distributed Systems and Technologies, 4*(4), 1–14. doi:10.4018/ijdst.2013100101

KEY TERMS AND DEFINITIONS

Business Process as a Service: Business Process as a Service (BPaaS) is a form of business process outsourcing (BPO) that employs a cloud computing service model.

Cloud: A cloud service has three distinct characteristics that differentiate it from traditional hosting. It is sold on demand, typically by the minute or the hour; it is elastic i.e. a user can have as much or as little of a service as they want at any given time; and the service is fully managed by the provider.

Cloud Migration: The process of transitioning all or part of a company's data, applications and services from on-site premises behind the firewall to the cloud, where the information can be provided over the Internet on an on-demand basis.

Cloud Provider: A service provider who offers customers storage or software solutions available via a public network, usually the Internet.

Cloud Testing: Cloud testing is a subset of software testing in which simulated, real-world Web traffic is used to test cloud-based Web applications. Cloud testing also verifies and validates specific cloud functions, including redundancy and performance scalability.

Community Cloud: A community cloud is a cloud service model that provides a cloud computing solution to a limited number of individuals or organizations that is governed, managed and secured commonly by all the participating organizations or a third party managed service provider.

Hybrid Cloud: A hybrid cloud is an integrated cloud service utilizing both private and public clouds to perform distinct functions within the same organization. All cloud computing services should offer certain efficiencies to differing degrees but public cloud services are likely to be more cost efficient and scalable than private clouds. Therefore, an organization can maximize their efficiencies by employing public cloud services for all non-sensitive operations, only relying on a private cloud where they require it and ensuring that all of their platforms are seamlessly integrated.

Infrastructure as a Service: Infrastructure as a service (IaaS) is a standardized, highly automated offering, where compute resources, complemented by storage and networking capabilities are owned and hosted by a service provider and offered to customers' on-demand. Customers are able to self-provision this infrastructure, using a Web-based graphical user interface that serves as an IT operations management console for the overall environment. API access to the infrastructure may also be offered as an option.

Multi-Tenant: Multi-tenancy is an architecture in which a single instance of a software application serves multiple customers. Each customer is called a tenant. Tenants may be given the ability to customize some parts of the application, such as color of the user interface (UI) or business rules, but they cannot customize the application's code.

Platform as a Service: Platform as a Service (PaaS) is a concept that describes a computing platform that is rented or delivered as an integrated solution, solution stack or service through an Internet connection. The solution stack may be a set of components or software subsystems used to develop a fully functional product or service, such as a Web application that uses an OS, Web server, database and programming language. More generically, the solution stack may deliver an OS, middleware, database or application.

Private Cloud: A private cloud is a particular model of cloud computing that involves a distinct and secure cloud based environment in which only the specified client can operate. As with other cloud models, private clouds will provide computing power as a service within a virtualized environment using an underlying pool of physical computing resource. However, under the private cloud model, the cloud (the pool of resource) is only accessible by a single organization providing that organization with greater control and privacy.

Public Cloud: A public cloud is one based on the standard cloud-computing model, in which a service provider makes resources, such as applications and storage, available to the public over the Internet. Public cloud services may be free or offered on a pay-per-usage model.

Software as a Service: Software as a Service (SaaS) is a software distribution model in which applications are hosted by a vendor or service provider and made available to customers over a network, typically the Internet.

This research was previously published in Cloud Computing Technologies for Connected Government edited by Zaigham Mahmood, pages 215-246, copyright year 2016 by Information Science Reference (an imprint of IGI Global).

Chapter 64
Data Integrity in Mobile Cloud Computing

Abhishek Majumder
Tripura University, India

Samir Nath
Tripura University, India

Avijit Das
Tripura University, India

ABSTRACT

With the help of cloud computing Mobile Cloud Computing (MCC) overcomes the limitations of a mobile device such as security, performance and environment. But, security of the data stored in the cloud is a very challenging issue. Since the cloud cannot be fully trusted, data stored in the cloud is not fully secured. Integrity of the stored data is very important for the data owner. Therefore, it is a big problem to maintain the integrity of the data stored in the cloud environment. This chapter discusses existing schemes for data integrity in the mobile cloud environment. In this chapter a scheme has been proposed for enhancing data integrity in Mobile Cloud Environment. To make integrity checking fast the size of the data file is used. It has also been shown that how fast the integrity loss can be detected if the file size is considered. Finally, the proposed scheme is compared with some of the existing scheme.

INTRODUCTION

The data storage and processing has been shifted to the centralized and powerful systems located inside the cloud from the mobile devices because of the platform provided by the Mobile cloud computing (MCC). MCC (Dinh, 2013, Chetan et al., 2010; Gupta et al., 2012; Mane et al., 2013) offers an infrastructure where data processing and storage is performed outside the mobile device. By this way, the services of MCC can be provided not only to the smart phone users but also to much wide range of mobile users. An example of MCC is shown in Figure 1.

DOI: 10.4018/978-1-5225-8176-5.ch064

Copyright © 2019, IGI Global. Copying or distributing in print or electronic forms without written permission of IGI Global is prohibited.

Figure 1. Mobile cloud computing architecture

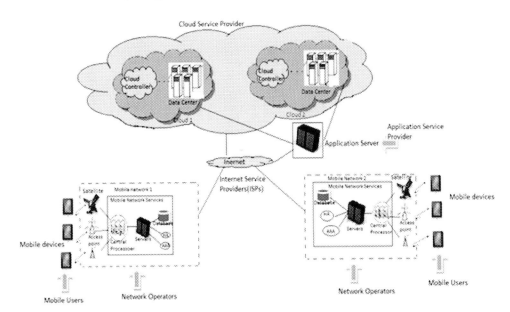

In MCC Mobile Client gets relived from the burden of computation and storage because most of their data files are put into the cloud. But it gives rise to some new problems and challenges. The owners of the data are often worried about the integrity of the data stored in the cloud because, when the data is stored, owners do not have full control over the data. The cloud cannot be fully trusted; therefore, the data stored in the cloud is not fully secured. CSP can be dishonest and can disclose or manipulate the stored information. This kind of activities will not be acceptable to data owner. Mishaps such as tempering and information disclosure can take place with the data while residing in the cloud. So, data confidentiality and security is very important for the owner. If data is altered by any unauthorized person, the integrity of the data gets severely damaged. Therefore, for the clients it is very vital to guarantee that their data is correctly maintained and stored in the cloud. So, maintaining the integrity of the user data is a challenging issue in mobile cloud environment.

The main objective of this chapter is to design a mechanism to ensure the data integrity as well as the confidentiality of the user's data stored in cloud in MCC environment. In this scheme the objective is to make the data secret not just from the cloud service provider (CSP) but also from trusted third party (TPA). Secondly, to build a simple and efficient mechanism through which the resource constrained mobile device can also be benefited by offloading most of the tasks like encryption, decryption and integrity verification tasks to the TPA.

MOBILE CLOUD COMPUTING

In today's world, handheld devices such as, smart phone, tablet PCs have emerged as an integral part of human life as they are very convenient and effective tools for communication at any place and at any time. The users have the expectation that all the information should be accessible at their fingertips anytime anywhere. But, compared to conventional processing devices such as PCs and laptops mobile devices have lack of resources (e.g. bandwidth, storage and battery life).

For overcoming the limitations of handheld devices, a new technology named mobile cloud computing has emerged which combines both cloud computing and mobile computing. The concept of mobile has been introduced not much after the launch of cloud computing in mid-2007. Since mobile cloud computing reduces the cost for development and running of mobile applications, it has attracted the attention of large number of industrialist (Soyata et al., 2013).

Advantages of Mobile Cloud Computing

- **Extending Battery Lifetime:** Intensive computations and complicated processing are moved from resource-constrained mobile devices to resourceful servers of the cloud. It will relieve mobile devices from long execution time of the processes. This in turn, reduces the power consumption and increases battery life of mobile device.
- **Improving Data Storage Capacity and Processing Power:** Limited storage capacity is a deficiency of the mobile devices. MCC has been developed to enable the mobile devices for storing and retrieving large amount of data to and from the cloud using the wireless media. Few of the existing services are: ShoZu, Flickr, Image Exchange, Amazon Simple Storage Service (Amazon S3).
- **Improving Reliability:** The reliability of the stored data and application in the cloud is more because the content is stored and backed up on multiple systems. This will reduce the chances of data or application loss if mobile device crashes or is lost.

Application

- **Mobile Commerce (M-Commerce):** It provides a business model for commerce utilizing mobile devices.
- **Mobile Learning:** Conventional applications of m-learning have disadvantages in terms of (a) High device and network cost. (b) Limited resources for education. (c) Low network transmission rate. For solving these limitations cloud-based m-learning applications have been developed. For example, the applications offer users much enhanced services with respect to longer battery life, higher processing speed and much enriched services in terms of data using a cloud having high processing ability and huge storage capacity.

Table 1.

Application Classes	Type	Examples
Mobile Shopping	B2B (Business to Business) B2C (Business to Customer)	Using a mobile device order or locate specific products.
Mobile Advertising	B2C	Based on user's current location sending of custom made advertisement.
Mobile Financial application	B2B, B2C	Mobile-user fees, brokerage firms, banks.

- **Mobile Healthcare:** For reducing limitation of conventional medical treatment, MCC can be applied. Resources (e.g. patient healthcare records) can be accessed very fast and easily using mobile healthcare (m-healthcare). Healthcare centers and hospitals can access many on-demand services instead of maintaining a standalone application in its local server.
- **Mobile Gaming:** For service providers, a lucrative market to obtain large revenue is Mobile game (m-game). The game engine is completely offloaded by M-game form the mobile device to the cloud servers. The screen interface on the device is used by the user to interact. The energy of the mobile device is saved through offloading of multimedia. So, the game playing time of mobile device increases.

Issues

Though mobile devices have very limited computation capacity but the cloud has very large storage capacity and computation ability. Therefore, implementation of cloud computing for mobile is very challenging (Alizadeh et al., 2013; Qi et al., 2012). Some of the issues with mobile cloud computing are:

- **Limited Resources:** Since the mobile devices have limited resources, using cloud computing in mobile device is very challenging. Some of the limited resources are: low quality display, limited battery and limited computing power.
- **Network Related Issues:** The processing of data is carried out in the cloud through the network. Therefore, the issues related to network such as heterogeneity, availability and bandwidth create challenge in MCC.
- **Security:** Large number of security issues is faced by the mobile device since data is stored in the cloud. For addressing this issue many mechanisms have been developed. But, still there are lot of challenges related to the security of the stored data. Moreover privacy of the user is also a challenging issue. The use of Global Positioning System (GPS) in the handheld device reveals the position of the user.

SECURITY IN MOBILE CLOUD COMPUTING

The primary concerns of mobile cloud computing security (Khan et.al., 2013; Chaturvedi et al., 2011; Garg et al., 2013; Huang et al., 2011; Ruebsamen et al., 2012, Zissis et al., 2012):

- **Security of Data/Files:** One of the important concerns of mobile cloud computing is to secure the data stored by the mobile users in the cloud. The data/file stored in the cloud is very vulnerable to the threats. An unauthorized person may access and change the stored data. Therefore, maintenance of the security of the stored data/file is very essential since the data may be confidential as well as important for the user.
- **Security of Mobile Applications:** The services are provided by application model to the mobile users by using cloud resources. Therefore, it is very important to secure the mobile application and application model. The capacity of the mobile device is increased by the use of mobile application model.

Data Integrity

Protecting data from unauthorized fabrication, modification and deletion is known as data integrity (Khaba et al., 2013; Khatri et al., 2012). Mobile users' data storage capacity is increased by uploading the files in the cloud. But the mobile device loses physical control over the stored data. So, a mechanism should be there for ensuring the correctness of user's uploaded data. Through integrity verification, the correctness of the uploaded files can be verified.

Different Security Threats

User's data residing in the cloud may face different security threats. Some of the attacks are discussed through Table 2.

RELATED WORK

To solve the problem of data integrity in mobile cloud computing many schemes has been proposed. In this section, some of the existing schemes have been discussed.

Energy Efficient Framework for Integrity Verification

Using the concept of trusted computing and incremental cryptography, Itani et al. (December, 2010) proposed an energy efficient framework for handheld devices to ensure the integrity of the mobile users' data/files stored on the cloud server. There are three main entities in the system design: mobile client, cloud service provider, and trusted third party. The storage services offered by the cloud service provider are used by the mobile user. Efficient management, allocation and operation of the resources are the responsibility of the cloud service provider. Installation of tamperproof coprocessors on the remote cloud is the responsibility of the trusted third party. Multiple registered mobile clients are associated with each coprocessor. The Secret Key (SK) is distributed with associated mobile clients by the coprocessor. On behalf of the mobile client, the coprocessor generates a message authentication code. Figure 2 shows the interaction among different entities:

Table 2. The different security threats in MCC

Name of the Attack	Description
Identity Spoofing	In this attack a person impersonate as someone who is the owner of the data.
Viruses and worms	These are very known attacks. These are the codes whish degrade the performance of any application.
Repudiation	When a person refused after sending a message that he did not send it.
Tampering	When any unauthorized person does some changes in other user's data.
Information disclosure	The secure information of owner is disclosed to any unauthorized user.

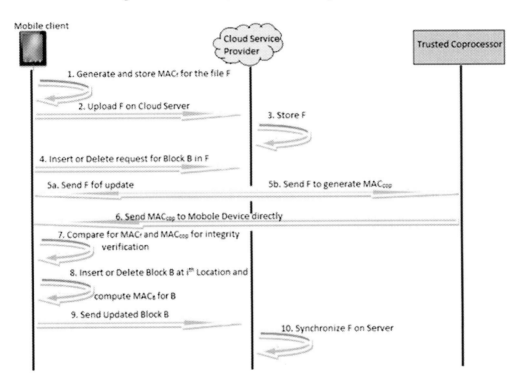

Figure 2. Interaction among the mobile client, CSP and trusted processor

The processes of uploading, insertion of block, deletion of block and verification for integrity of files in the MCC are discussed by the authors. To upload a file in the cloud server, the mobile client creates an incremental Message Authentication Code (MAC_f) using SK.

$$MAC_f = \sum_{i=1}^{k} HMAC\left(F_i, SK\right) \tag{1}$$

where, MAC_f is the sum of increment message authentication codes, Fi represents the ith part of the file and k is the total logical partition of file. MAC_f is stored on local storage by the mobile client. The files are uploaded on the cloud server.

Insertion, deletion and updation operations on the uploaded file(s) are performed by the mobile client at any time. For insertion or deletion of the block at j^{th} position of a file, the mobile client sends request to a cloud server for the file. The file is transferred to the trusted coprocessor and the mobile client by the cloud server. MAC_{cop} is reconstructed by the trusted coprocessor and sent to the mobile client. MAC_{cop} as well as the file is received by the mobile client from trusted coprocessor and cloud server respectively. The mobile client compares the stored MAC_f with MAC_{cop} for integrity verification. If he values of recalculated and received MACs are same, the integrity of the file is confirmed. When the integrity of the file is verified, the block at j^{th} location of the file is inserted or deleted by the mobile client. Then the value of MAC_f is recalculated using SK, old MAC_f and inserted or deleted blocks. For

Figure 3. Entities in mobile cloud computing

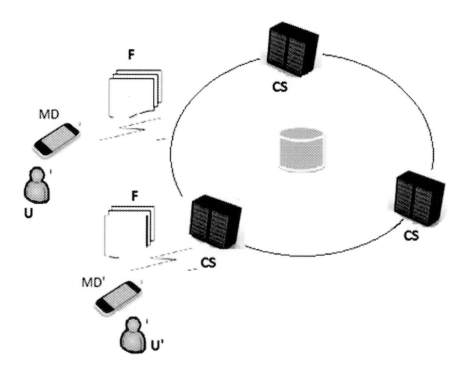

reducing communication overhead, only the location information and the updated block are sent to the cloud server to synchronize storage. The integrity of the files stored in the cloud storage can be verified by the mobile client. The process for integrity verification is initiated by the mobile client through sending of a request to the cloud server. After receiving the request the files are transferred from the cloud servers to the trusted coprocessor. The incremental authentication code for each message is computed by coprocessor and sent to the mobile client. To verify the integrity, the stored MAC_f and received MAC_{cop} needs to be compared by the mobile client.

Encryption Based Scheme (EnS)

The encryption based scheme is proposed by Ren et al. (2011). In this scheme, integrity checking as well as file encryption is carried out by Mobile Device (MD) itself. Three major entities or operators of MCC scenarios are:

1. **Mobile Device (MD):** MDs are the devices capable of wireless communication, storage and computing. Some examples of MDs are: wireless sensor node, tablet PC, smart phone etc.
2. **Cloud Server (CS):** CS generally offers computing and storage services to the clients. This scheme considers storage service only. This service can further be divided into two categories: back-end CS and portal CS. MD directly accesses the back-end CS. On the other hand, portal CS accesses the back-end CS.

3. **User (U):** MD is manipulated by the user. There may be multiple users who desire to access the same data or file in CS. Data or file is the operated object both are denoted as F. A file is downloaded (uploaded) from (into) CS.

Uploading Process

The process for uploading is given as follows:

1. MD prompts to ask U to input a password before the file F is uploaded. The password is denoted by PWD.
2. MD creates integrity key IK = H(FN ‖ PWD‖FS) and encryption key EK= H(PWD‖FN ‖ FS), where H(.) is hash function, FS is the file size and H(.) and FN is the file name.
3. F is encrypted by MD with EK as F′ = ENC(F, EK), where symmetric key encryption function is denoted by ENC(.,.).
4. File integrity authentication code is generated by MD. It is denoted as MAC = {H(F, IK)}.
5. MD sends {F′ ‖ H(FN) ‖MAC} to portal CS.
6. MD stores T = ⟨FN⟩ locally and deletes EK and IK.

Downloading Process

The downloading process is as follows:

1. Let MD desires to fetch F with the name FN. Then H(FN) is sent to CS by MD. CS searches in ⟨F′,H(FN),MAC⟩. Then it sends back {F′ ‖MAC} that matches H(FN) to MD.
2. U is asked to input corresponding PWD for the FN. This process is prompted by MD.
3. MD creates integrity key IK = H(FN ‖ PWD ‖FS) and encryption key EK= H(PWD ‖FN ‖ FS), where FS is the size of F′, which has |F′ |=|F |= FS .
4. MD decrypts out F = DEC(F′,EK), and checks whether MAC = H(F, IK) is held, where, DEC(.,.) is the symmetric key decryption function.
5. If the values of calculated and received MACs are same, the integrity of the file is confirmed.

Provable Data Possession Scheme

The scheme is proposed by Yang et al. (2011). In this scheme, there are three main entities in the system model:

1. **Mobile End-User:** The mobile end-user contains a Trusted Platform Model (TPM) chip. It stores data files into the cloud and expects to get trusted storage validation.
2. **Trusted Third Party Auditor (TPA):** TPA is credible to the clients. In this scheme, it performs authentication tasks as well as encryption.
3. **Cloud Storage Service Provider (CSP):** CSP provides storage services to the clients. The storage capacity of the CSP is very large. Proof of data possession can also be provided by the CSP when needed.

Figure 4. System structure model

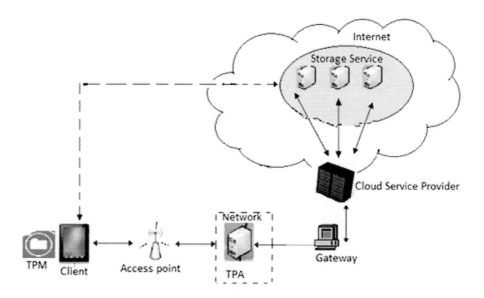

In case of mobile clients, the device's ability of computation and storage is very limited. But, mobile device can user TPM chip for producing and storing secret key. The TPA is located between the gateway of the IP network services and the mobile access point. The TPA is required to have limited storage space and high computing ability. The memory is used to only store a small part of information of the client and current session message. To provide services, the connection between TPA and the client should be secure. Using internet, the CSP provides redundant and high-capacity storage services. Generally, the CSP is malicious as well as unsafe entity. Which means, for some financial interests, the user's original data can be read, deleted or tempered. The proof of data possession can also be forged. There, encrypted files should be sent to the CSP. The scheme assumes that all the parties communicate through authenticated, reliable and secure channels.

Following functions are performed in this scheme:

- **KenGen(1k) → (pk,sk):** An initial secure parameter 1k is taken by this algorithm. It returns the private key sk and the public key pk. In this scheme, the keys are generated by the end-user and maintained in TPM chip.
- **Encapek(F) → F':** This algorithm is used by the TPA for encrypting the raw file F using the seal key ek and encoding it with erasure codes. the sealed file F' is returned.
- **SigGen_Clientsk (F') → Sigsk (H(R)):** End user runs this algorithm. The hash value of the root of the Merkle hash tree (MHT) is taken as input. The end user's signature is outputted as metadata.
- **SigGen_TPA(F') → Φ:** TPA runs this algorithm. Each of the data blocks {mi} of the sealed file F' is taken as input. The signature collection Φ= { σi } on {mi} is outputted.
- **GenProof (chal,F', Sigsk(H(R)), Φ) → (P):** Storage server runs this algorithm. It takes the signature set Φ, the metadata signature, the stored file F' and the verification challenge message"chal" generated by TPA as input and returns the possession proof P.

- **Verify(P, chal)→ {TRUE|FALSE}:** Using the proof P returned from the server, the random challenge chal and some metadata of the end-user, the TPA verifies the integrity of the data file. If the output is TRUE, the integrity of the file is correct otherwise, integrity of the data is incorrect.
- **Decapdk(F')→F:** A request is sent by the end user to extract a file F. The corresponding sealed file F' is retrieved by the TPA. The the file F' is decoded and decrypted with the decryption key (dk) to get F. After that F is sent to end-user.

Setup

In this phase it is assumed that the remote identification with the TPA is completed by the TPM which resides in the end-user. A trusted communication channel is also set up.

- At first Diffie-Hellman key exchange is completed. After that, the TPA and the client share a symmetric key $g^{\alpha\beta}$.
- The original file F is encrypted using the key. The file is then sent to the TPA.
- On receiving the original file F from the client, the pair of asymmetric keys (ek, dk) are created by invoking KenGen(*), where (dk) is for decrypting the file and (ek) for encrypting the file.
- Using $Encap_{ek}$(F), the file is encrypted by TPA. Then it is divided into small blocks and encoded with erasure codes.
- H(R) is then calculated by TPA.
- After encrypting H(R) and dk with the shared key $g^{\alpha\beta}$, the TPA sends them to the client.
- The client signs H(R) using $Singen\_Client_{sk}$(F'). Then it sends the signature of H(R) back to the TPA.
- The signature collection of each blocks of F' is calculated by the TPA using SinGen_TPA(F'). Then {Sigsk (H(R)), F', Φ} is sent to the cloud storage servers.

Integrity Verification

Following steps are executed for integrity verification:

- A verification challenge is sent from the TPA or the client to the cloud storage service provider (CSP).
- Based on the challenge, the proof of verification is computed by CSP. Then the CSP sends the proof of verification to the TPA.
- The TPA sends the result to the client after verification of the proof.

TPA generates the challenge message "chal". c random numbers are chosen in the set [1, N] by the TPA for constituting a sequence subset I . For each i∈I, the TPA chooses a random element vi∈Zp. The number i and the corresponding vi compose the challenge message sent to CSP. The CSP uses GenProof(chal, F, Sigsk (H(R)), Φ) for creating the proof after receiving the "chal". It contains the corresponding hash value H(mi) of the data blocks {mi} for every i∈I. In addition to that it also contains information Ωi to rebuild the root H(R) of the MHT.

File Retrieval

Before retrieving the file, through Diffie-Hellman key exchange protocol the TPA and the client negotiates to form a symmetric session key (Ks).

- After encrypting the decryption key (dk) using Ks, the client sends it to the TPA. Then the CSP is requested by TPA to extract the file F'.
- F' is sent to the TPA by the CSP.
- For getting the raw file F the TPA runs $Decap_{dk}(F')$. Then it sends F to the end-user using the secure communication channel.

Efficient and Secure Data Storage Operations for MCC

Based on Attribute Based Data Storage (ABDS) system and Privacy Preserving Cipher text Policy Attribute Based Encryption (PP-CP-ABE) Zhou et al. (October, 2012) developed a scheme for secure and efficient data storage operations. Encryption and decryption operations can be securely outsourced by lightweight mobile devices to the CSP using PP-CP-ABE.

Following entities are there in this scheme:

- **Data Owner (DO):** A sensor or wireless mobile device can be a DO. Storage service of the cloud is used by the DO.
- **Trust Authority (TA):** The responsibility of cryptographic key distribution lies on TA. It is very trusted.
- **Encryption Service Provider (ESP):** Without the knowledge of actual encryption key, ESP performs encryption of data owner's file.
- **Decryption Service Provider (DSP):** Decryption service is offered to the data owner by DSP. But it does not have any information about actual content.
- **Storage Service Provider (SSP):** Storage services are provided by the client by SSP. The ESP encrypts the file before uploading it on the cloud. Figure 5 shows the system model of the scheme.

Setup and Key Generation Phase

- **A Bilinear Map E:** $G0 \times G0 \rightarrow G1$ of prime order p having generator g is chosen by trusted authority to set up PP-CP-ABE. The public parameters are:

$PK = \{G0, g, h = g\beta, f = g1/\beta, e(g, g)\alpha\}$.

where, α, β are randomly selected α, $\beta \in Zp$. Master Key $MK = (\beta, g\alpha)$ is only known to TA.

Private Key $(SK) = \{ D = g(\alpha+r)/\beta$; for all $j \in S$: $Dj = gr \times H(j)ri$; $Dj = grj\}$.

where, $r \in ZP$ and $rj \in ZP$ are randomly selected for each attribute $j \in S$. SK is sent to Data Owner by TA using a secure channel.

Figure 5. System architecture

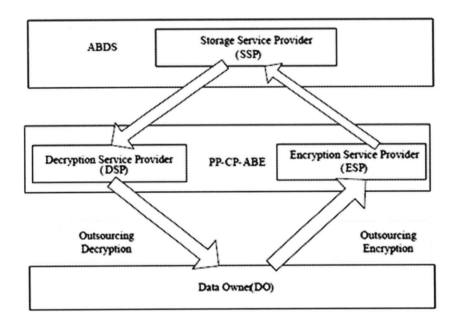

Encryption Phase

For outsourcing encryption, a policy tree $T = TESP \wedge TDO$ is defined by DO, Where, TESP and TDO are two sub trees and $\wedge$ is logical AND operator. The data access policy controlled by DO is denoted by TDO. On the other hand, data access policy controlled by ESP is denoted by TESP.

- **ESP Produces Cipher Text:** $CTESP = \{ y \in YESP: Cy = gqy(0), C'y = H(att(y))qy(0)\}$.

where, YESP is set of leaf nodes in TESP.

- DO computes $CTDO = \{y \in Y2: Cy = gqy(0), Cy = H(att(y))qy(0)\}$, $\hat{C} = M\ e(g, g)\alpha s$ and $C = hs$, where the message is denoted by M. DO sends $\{CTDO, C, \hat{C}\}$ to ESP.

when ESP receives message from DO, it generates Cipher Text $CT = \{T = TESP \wedge TDO; \hat{C} = M\ e(g, g) \alpha s; C = hs; y \in YESP\ U\ YDO: Cy = gqy(0), C'y = H(att(y))qy(0)\}$ and sends CT to SSP.

Decryption Phase

Following steps are carried out when decryption phase is executed:

At first, a private key is built by DO as $SKblind = \{ Dt = gt(\alpha+r)/\beta, \forall\ j \in S: Dj = gr\ .\ H(j)rj, Dj = grj\}$. where, $t \in ZP$ and $Dt = gt(\alpha+r)/\beta$.

DO checks if the access policy tree is satisfied by its attributes. If no, DO sends request to SSP for the encrypted file else it sends SKblind to DSP.

- Now, SSP sends CT= { T; C = hs ; ∀ y ∈ Y1 U Y2: Cy = gqy(0), Cy= H(att(y))qy(0)} where, CT' is subset of CT.
- When DSP receives SKblind and CT, decryption of the encrypted file is carried out and sent to DO. After that, DO can obtain the original message M.

A Framework for Secure Data Service in MCC

A secure data service has been proposed by Jia et al. (April, 2011) to outsource security and data to cloud in trusted mode. Through the secure data service the mobile users can share as well as move data into the cloud without disclosing any information. The proposed network model has three main entities: (a) cloud service provider, (b) data owner, and (c) data sharer. The network model is shown in Figure 6.

The files are shared by the data owner. Access is also granted by the DO. For data storage and retrieval both data owner and data sharer utilize the cloud storage service.

For achieving secure data service, identity base encryption and proxy re-encryption schemes are used. In proxy re-encryption scheme, the cipher text encrypted using A's public key is converted into another

Figure 6. Proposed framework's network model

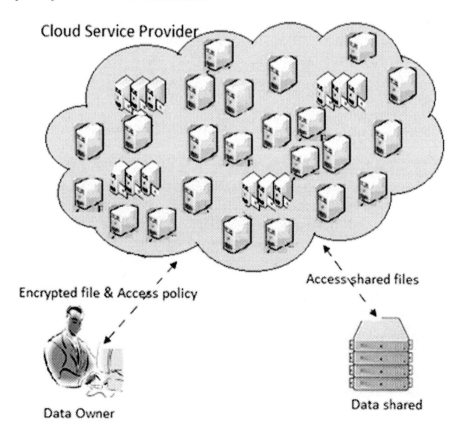

cipher text using B's public key by a semi trusted proxy. The bilinear mapping is used in identity based encryption scheme. A bilinear map can be defined as:

$$e: G_1 \times G_1 \to G_T \tag{2}$$

The bilinear map with the properties of non-degeneracy, computability and bilinearity is represeinted in Eq. (2). The G_1 and G_T are the multiplicative cyclic groups with prime order q and g is the generator of the G_1. The scheme uses two independent hash functions: H_1 and H_2.

$$H1: \{0, 1\}^* \to G1, H2: GT \to G1 \tag{3}$$

There are six phases in this scheme:

1. **Setup Phase:** During this phase, system parameters (G_1, G_T, g, g^s) as well as system Master Key (MK) is generated, where $s \in Z_q$ is randomly selected. The information about MK is by the authority only. The system parameters are public and disseminated among mobile users.
2. **Key Generation Phase:** For obtaining SK mobile users need to register in the system. SK is computed based on H_1 and mobile users' identity using MK. Eq. 4 shows the computation of SK_{ID}.

$$SK_{ID} = H_1(ID)^{MK}, \text{ where } ID \in \{0, 1\}^* \tag{4}$$

3. **Encryption Phase:** The file is divided into n chunks by the Mobile user. m_i represents each chunk. m_i is encrypted under owner identity (ID_{owner}) as a public key. The encryption under identity is known as identity based encryption.

$$EF = (g^r, m_i \cdot e(g^s, H_1(ID_{owner})^r)) \text{ where } 1 \leq i \leq n \tag{5}$$

Here, $r \in Z_q$ is selected randomly. The Encrypted File (EF) is then uploaded on the cloud server.

4. **Re-Encryption Key Generation Phase:** Re-encryption keys are generated by the mobile user after EF is uploaded. These keys are generated to enable authorized users to access the file.
5. **Re-Encryption Phase:** To encrypt the EF utilizing proxy re-encryption scheme, the re-encryption keys are sent to the cloud. Then the proxy re-encryption scheme converts the cipher text encrypted using the owner's public key into a cipher text encrypted using the sharer's public key.
6. **Decryption Phase:** The cloud server is requested by the sharer for obtaining the re-encrypted file. The validity is verified by the cloud after checking the re-encryption key for the sharer. The corresponding re-encrypted file is sent to the sharer by the cloud server, if a key is found. Because of the cipher text transformation, the file can be decrypted by the sharer without involving the data owner.

The scheme provides data privacy as well as access control. It has minimized the cost incurred for communication and updation of access policy.

Framework for Secure Storage Services in MCC

For ensuring the integrity and security of the mobile users' file stored in cloud server Hsueh et al. (June, 2011) proposed a scheme for smart phones. For authenticating the owner of the uploaded file the scheme has introduces an authentication mechanism. There are three modules in the framework: mobile device, cloud service provider, certification authority and telecommunication module. The interaction between different modules is shown in Figure 7.

Cloud service is utilized by mobile device. To authenticate the mobile user certification authority is responsible. The password and related information is generated and kept by the telecommunication module for using cloud service. It has been assumed that the Session Key (SK), Public Key (PK) and Secret Key (SK) are distributed securely among certification authority, telecommunication module and mobile devices. Using certification authority, a mobile user needs to register in the telecommunication module for using the cloud services. After successful registration, a Password (PWD) is issued for mobile device by the telecommunication module. The PWD is used by the mobile device for using cloud resources. The registration request can be represented as:

$$MD \rightarrow CA: E_{PK\,T}\,E\,(MU, Num, TK)$$

$$U_N, S_{SK\,MU}\,(H\,(MU, Num)), H(MU, Num) \tag{6}$$

where, H represents a standard hash function, U_N is randomly generated number for the proof of identity, Num is the mobile user's number, MU represents the mobile user's name, TK represents the combination of the Num and PWD, $S_{SK\,MU}$ produces a signature for the mobile user using a cryptographic function on the passed value and SK of the mobile device and $E_{PK\,TM}$ represents encryption with the PK of telecommunication module. When the certification authority receives the message from the mobile

Figure 7. Framework for secure storage

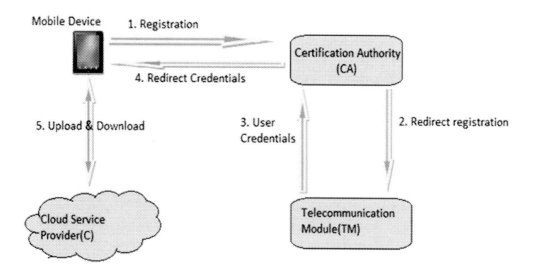

device, using the received signature it validates the message authenticity. Following message is sent by the certification authority to the telecommunication module if the message is received from a valid user.

$$CA \rightarrow TM: E_{PK\,TM} \,(MU, Num, TK)$$

$$U_N, S_{SK\,CA} \,(H\,(MU, Num)) \tag{7}$$

Using S_{SKCA} the certification authority is authenticated by the telecommunication module. When the certification authority is authenticated successfully, the mobile user gets registered in the telecommunication module. The information of the mobile user is stored in the local database of telecommunication module. In the future, this stored information can be used for verification. The telecommunication module has the responsibility of generating PWD for the mobile user to access the resources. The mobile user's information is encrypted by telecommunication module using the mobile device's PK. This is done to securely deliver PWD to the mobile device. Again, TK is used to encrypt PWD again so that only authorized mobile user can decrypt the password. The encrypted information is forwarded to the mobile device by the telecommunication module through the certification authority.

$$TM \rightarrow CA: E_{PK\,MU} \,(MU, Num, U_N, ETK\,(PWD))$$

$$CA \rightarrow MD: E_{PK\,MU} \,(MU, Num, U_N, ETK\,(PWD)) \tag{8}$$

The file is encrypted using SEK by the mobile device. Then it is uploaded in the cloud along with S_{SKMU}, MU and PWD.

$$MD \rightarrow C: PWD, MU, ESEK\,(Data)$$

$$S_{SK\,MU} \,(H\,(MU \parallel SV \parallel ESEK\,(Data))) \tag{9}$$

where secret value created by the mobile device is denoted by SV. It is assumed that telecommunication module, cloud and mobile device know SV. The mobile device sends H(MU ‖ SV), MU and PWD to the cloud for downloading a file. Using SV and MU the hash value is regenerated by the cloud. The signature received is compared with the newly computed hash value to authenticate the mobile device's request. The cloud sends the signature as well as the encrypted file to the mobile device after authentication is successful.

$$C \rightarrow MD: E_{SEK} \,(Data), H\,(E_{SEK} \,(Data) \parallel SV) \tag{10}$$

The signature is verified by the mobile device. Then the file is decrypted using SEK. A secure file sharing mechanism is also introduced in this scheme. The mechanism is used to share the file between two users, A and B. The user B needs to inform A about PWD_B, Num_B and MU_B for accessing the file if it wants to share some file with A. On the basis of a signature stored with the encrypted file, the owner of the file can be authenticated by A when it is received from B. Through sharing mechanism, A can know B's secret information. The secret information of B can be used by A for impersonating B in future.

PROPOSED SCHEME

Limited processing power, storage and battery life are the primary limitations of mobile devices. For benefiting resource constrained mobile devices MCC has been introduced. Offloading more tasks to the cloud for saving the processing power and battery life is the main objective of MCC.

Offloading is carried out in this scheme to minimize the burden of the. In this scheme, all the encryption, decryption and integrity verification has been moved to a remote third party called third party auditor, which will perform all this on behalf of the mobile and will minimize the burden of the mobile device.

All the schemes already discussed above which uses the third-party auditor for the purpose of encryption and decryption as well as integrity checking of user's data, assumes that TPA is fully trusted one and the cloud service provider is untrusted. But as the TPA is also a third party and beyond the reach of owner of the data, so there is a chance that TPA can be curious about the user's data and can be dishonest also (Gupta et al., 2013). So, though TPA is trusted one, but we cannot consider it fully trusted.

So, if the TPA becomes dishonest, then what should be the way that can protect the user's data? For addressing this problem, a technique has been proposed in this section.

In this scheme the main objective is to make the whole data secret not only to the CSP, but also to the TPA. By user-side encryption this can be achieved. The mobile device (MD) will encrypt the file with password (PW) which will be provided by the user (U), and will send this encrypted data to the TPA through a secure channel. While receiving the data, MD will decrypt the data/file with the same PW. The only thing is that, the mobile device has to do the work encryption/decryption at the client side. As only the mobile device is the only one which is fully trusted, so it will be beneficial for us i.e. client side encryption/decryption. Nowadays, mobile phones are coming with high configurations according to their CPU, RAM and large battery life. So, it is possible for the mobile device to do this task easily.

After receiving the encrypted data, TPA will a perform encryption, decryption and integrity verification tasks over the data before uploading it to the cloud.

Secondly for integrity verification of user's data, in this scheme the size of the file has been considered. The idea behind considering the file size is that; If the data being changed or damaged or any unauthorized person does something with the intention to destroy the data (tempering), then the size of the data changes. Any deletion, modification, updation of the data affects the file size. So, this simple change can be a factor to check the integrity of data which have been proposed in this scheme.

Entities

In the proposed scheme three entities are used:

1. **Mobile Device (MD):** User utilizes the services offered by cloud through this. It performs encryption and decryption over user data through PW. It is a trusted one.
2. **Third Party Auditor (TPA)**: Performs encryption, decryption and integrity verification over user data. Though it trusted one, but in this scheme, it is considered as semi trusted.
3. **Cloud Service Provider (CSP):** Provides storage services to clients. It is responsible for operating, managing and allocating cloud resources. It is untrusted one.

Process

Data owner uses the mobile device to access the cloud. He/she then uses the mobile devices to store / retrieved files from the cloud. It has been assumed that the user has already completed the authentication tasks with the CSP. Whole process divided into two parts:

1. Uploading process
2. Downloading process

Uploading Process

The different steps during the uploading process has been described below:
   Steps:

1. Mobile device first encrypts file with the password provided by the user. MD sends the encrypted file to the TPA.
2. TPA calculates the size of the received file.
3. TPA than calculates the hashes of the received file. This hash values will be used for integrity checking. Any changes in the data will change the hash value of the same file.
4. TPA then encrypts the file and sends the encrypted file to the CSP.

Downloading Process

The different steps during the downloading process have been described below:
   Steps:

1. User first requests for the intended file through TPA to the CSP.
2. CSP sends the file to the TPA.
3. TPA decrypts the file.
4. For integrity verification TPA performs the following tasks:
   a. TPA first calculates the size of the received file. If the file size is matched with the previously stored one
      i. TPA calculates the hash of the received file and matches it with the stored one.
      ii. If it matches then data integrity is maintained.
      iii. Else then data integrity is not maintained
   b. Else
      i. Integrity of the file has been lost.
5. After verification TPA sends the data to MD if its integrity is not lost.
6. MD decrypts the file with the same password as provided by the user.

Figure 8. Remote data integrity through third party auditor

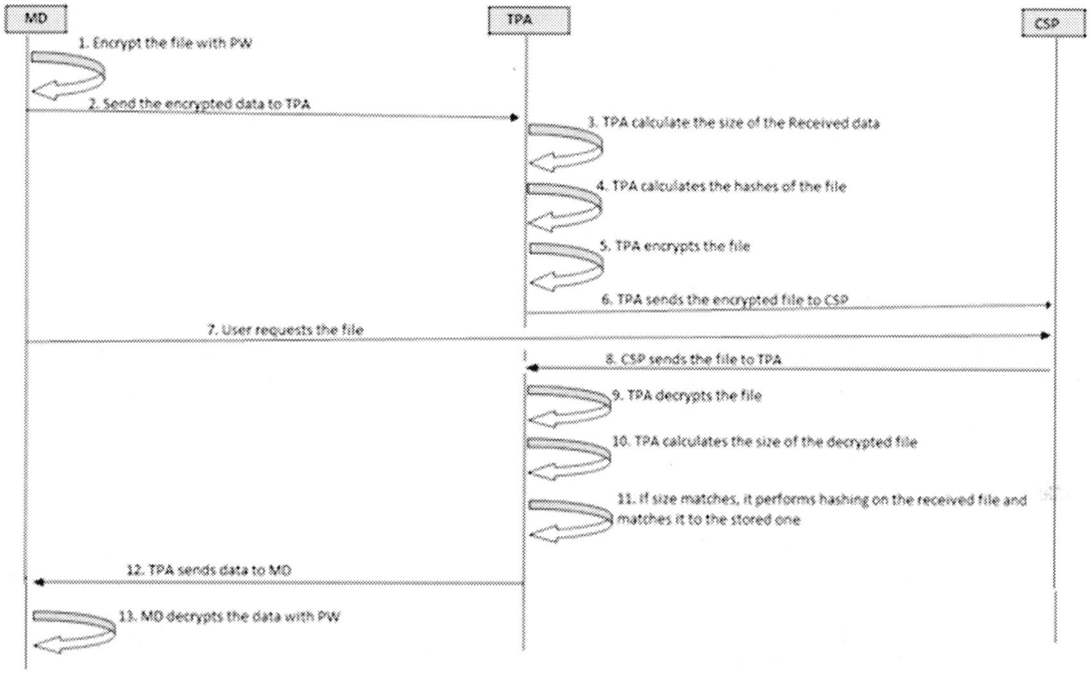

IMPLEMENTATION

For performance evaluation, the proposed scheme has been implemented through Java socket programming. The experiment has been carried out in the Computer Science & Engineering laboratory of Tripura University. Three PCs connected through LAN are considered in this experiment. One PC is marked as client and other two as TPA and cloud storage respectively. For simplicity, only the string type data has been taken as user data to implement the scheme. The string name has also been considered to be unique. The data is stored on the cloud with respect to the string name. In case of retrieval of data, the same name is used. A swing interface at the client side has been designed through which the client store and retrieves his data stored on the cloud.

For the client side, there is two processes:

1. **Data Store:** The user stores data with respect to a name.
2. **Data Retrieve:** The user requests his data to the cloud by the name.

The configuration of PCs is given as: Processor: Core i5 (2.6 GHz), Hard disk: 260 GB, RAM: 2GB (DDR 3), OS: Windows 7.

Figure 9. Simple scenario of the implementation

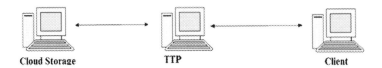

Following tables are used by different entities:

- **TTP Table:** TTP maintains a table for every user's data. TTP maintains a database of the fields which is necessary for the purpose of integrity checking of the data. The entities of the table are:
  - Name Size MD Key
  - Where,
  - Name is the unique name given to the data.
  - Size is the length of the data (String data).
  - MD is the message digest of the data and used an MD5 algorithm to generate the message digest of the user's data.
  - Key is the unique key used by the TTP to encrypt/decrypt the data. The TTP uses the key to encrypt the data before sending the data to the cloud and the same key to decrypt while retrieval.
- **Cloud Service Provider Table:** CSP also maintains a table to store the user data. The entities of the table are:
  - Name Data
  - Where,
  - Name is the unique name given to the data.
  - Data is the actual data of the user which is in encrypted from.

RESULT AND COMPARISON

In the propose scheme there are two cases for the purpose of data checking, one is through the size of the data and another is the message digest of the data. Here for the string type of data the length of the message has been considered as size and for message digest the MD5 algorithm has been used which generates unique message digest for every unique data.

The data stored on the cloud is in encrypted from. Though the data is in encrypted from the data is not safe. The attacker can access the data and can do the following with the intension to modify, delete the data. If the attacker does the following, then there may be two cases:

1. The attacker can temper the data by deleting. The whole data or a part of the data.
2. The attacker can modify the data.

The solutions of two cases have been discussed.

Case 1

Suppose the data is "University" with the name UNIV. Table 3 shows the TPA table.

Table 4 shows the Cloud.

Here the attacker can modify the data by deleting the whole data or some of the characters of the data as seen Table 5.

If the attacker does so, the size of the data changes. Then the size will not match with the previously stored one and this will result an error that means the integrity of the data has been lost. There is no need to run the MD5 algorithm to check the integrity of the message. The TPA then sends a message confirming that the integrity of the message has been lost.

Case 2

The attacker is somehow able to modify the data by maintaining the data size (see Table 6).

The characters of the above table have been replaced/modified like that: & -> A, 8 -> 9, Y -> Z

Table 3.

Name	Size	MD	Key
UNIV	21	ef03714edac9a27853b66cfcc21657b7	Key

Table 4.

Name	Data
UNIV	&Y⌐˩¶♫E┼↑E8♀‼˥◀Y/˩

Table 5.

Name	Data
UNIV	&Y⌐˩¶8♀‼˥◀Y/˩

Table 6.

Name	Data
UNIV	&Y⌐˩¶♫E┼↑E8♀‼˥◀Y/˩

Table 7.

Name	Data
UINV	AY|⌐ ¶♫E╀↑E9♀‼¬ ◀Z/⌐

Though the size of the data remains same but the message digest of the data will not match with the previously stored one and it will result as an error and a message will be sent to the client confirming that the integrity of the message has been lost.

Time Comparison

In this scheme for the purpose of integrity verification at first the data/file size is considered. Then the message digest is considered. The size of any file is computed by the operating system automatically when it is created and any change in the file also changes the file size. So, in the proposed scheme file size is calculated and stored in the database for the purpose of integrity verification.

Let the original file F and size of the file is S1. S1 is stored on the TPA's database. Let the file size is modified to F' and the size becomes S2.

Here, for integrity verification TPA simply calculates the S2 and matches it to S1. If S1≠S2 then integrity of the file is lost.

On the other hand, calculating message digest of any file is a complex process and it takes more time compared to calculating the file size. Any message digest algorithm goes through several rounds of interaction and so forth consumes more time. So, if we consider that time to generate the message digest of any file F is t1 and to calculate the length of the file is t2, then always t1>t2.

For example, time to calculate the MD5 of the data "My name is Avijit Das" is 71820664 ns (approx). But time to calculate the size (length) of the data "My name is Avijit Das" is 9938 ns (approx). That means, t1>t2.

Secondly, like the existing schemes, the proposed scheme also checks the integrity of the message considering message digest to counter the case when the file size remains same after modification.

Comparison

1. In energy efficient frame work for integrity verification, discussed in the related work section, it can be observed that the mobile device generates the MAC code of the data/file during uploading of the data to the cloud as well as during the downloading process. MAC code is stored in the local database of the mobile device. The burden on the mobile device is increased. Therefore, the mobile device needs to perform lots of task on the client's side (MAC code generation).

For retrieving the file a request is sent to the CSP. In response, the CSP sends one copy of file/data to the mobile client and the other to the trusted coprocessor (TC). The file's MAC code is then generated by TC. The MAC code is sent from the TC to the client. The client compares the previously stored MAC with the newly received MAC. In this way, also the burden of the mobile phone increases because it has to do all the integrity verification tasks.

But in this scheme instead of sending data twice to the mobile client and TC, the data is sent to the TPA first and then to the client after verification. The TPA does all the encryption, decryption and integrity verification tasks on behalf of the mobile device. This way it relieves the mobile device from the burden of all computations.

2. In Encryption based scheme, it has seen that all the encryption, decryption as well as the integrity verification tasks are performed by the mobile device. The cloud simply stores the data and there is no third party in between. This way the burden of the mobile device increases.

But in proposed scheme offloads all of the tasks to the third party which is in between the client and CSP. The third party does all the encryption, decryption as well as integrity verification tasks while uploading and downloading the data from the cloud and thus relieves the mobile device from the burden of computations.

3. The proposed scheme performs encryption as well as decryption with the help of a password (user given) at the mobile side considering that the TPA can also be dishonest some time and can lick the data also. Nowadays, the mobile phones are coming with much high configuration (smart phones, tablets, etc.). So, the task can be easily done at the client side for better security of the data.

CONCLUSION AND FUTURE WORK

MCC allows the user to get benefitted by the services offered by the cloud. Through MCC user of the mobile device can access his/her data stored on the cloud at anytime, anywhere if there is an internet connection. Users of the cloud are not aware of the physical location of their data on the cloud. As a result data security is the major concern of the cloud consumers. Customer do not want to lose their private information or do not want any change on their data without their permission as a result of malicious insiders in the cloud. So data integrity is the most important issue related to security risks of cloud as well as MCC. Data stored on the cloud may suffer from any damage occurring during transition from cloud to mobile, while residing on the cloud etc. So it is very essential to ensure the integrity i.e. correctness of the data. In this chapter a scheme has been proposed to solve the problem of data security specially data integrity. The proposed scheme has been implemented and its performance has been analyzed. The proposed scheme has been compared with some of the existing schemes. The future work remains as improvement of the scheme in more realistic way and to analyze the performance of the proposed scheme in a large network.

REFERENCES

Alizadeh, M., Hassan, W. H., Behboodian, N., & Karamizadeh, S. (2013). A brief review of mobile cloud computing opportunities. *Research Notes in Information Science*, *12*, 155–160.

Chaturvedi, M., Malik, S., Aggarwal, P., & Bahl, S. (2011). Privacy & Security of Mobile Cloud Computing. *Ansal University Sector, 55*.

Chetan, S., Kumar, G., Dinesh, K., Mathew, K., & Abhimanyu, M. A. (2010). Cloud computing for mobile world. Retrieved from chetan.ueuo.com

Dinh, H. T., Lee, C., Niyato, D., & Wang, P. (2013). A survey of mobile cloud computing: architecture, applications, and approaches. *Wireless communications and mobile computing, 13*(18), 1587-1611.

Garg, P., & Sharma, V. (2013). Secure data storage in mobile cloud computing. *International Journal of Scientific & Engineering Research, 4*(4), 1154–1159.

Gupta, P., & Gupta, S. (2012). Mobile cloud computing: The future of cloud. *International Journal of Advanced Research in Electrical. Electronics and Instrumentation Engineering, 1*(3), 134–145.

Gupta, V., & Rajput, I. (2013). Enhanced data security in cloud computing with third party auditor. *International Journal of Advanced Research in Computer Science & Software Engineering, 3*(2), 341–345.

Hsueh, S. C., Lin, J. Y., & Lin, M. Y. (2011, June). Secure cloud storage for convenient data archive of smart phones. In *Proceedings of IEEE 15th International Symposium on Consumer Electronics (ISCE)*. (pp. 156-161). 10.1109/ISCE.2011.5973804

Huang, D., Zhou, Z., Xu, L., Xing, T., & Zhong, Y. (2011, April). Secure data processing framework for mobile cloud computing. In *Proceedings of IEEE Conference on Computer Communications Workshops (INFOCOM WKSHPS)*. (pp. 614-618). 10.1109/INFCOMW.2011.5928886

Itani, W., Kayssi, A., & Chehab, A. (2010, December). Energy-efficient incremental integrity for securing storage in mobile cloud computing. In *Proceedings of International Conference on Energy Aware Computing (ICEAC)* (pp. 1-2). 10.1109/ICEAC.2010.5702296

Jia, W., Zhu, H., Cao, Z., Wei, L., & Lin, X. (2011, April). SDSM: a secure data service mechanism in mobile cloud computing. In *Proceedings of IEEE Conference on Computer Communications Workshops (INFOCOM WKSHPS)* (pp. 1060-1065).

Khaba, M. V., & Santhanalakshmi, M. (2013). Remote Data Integrity Checking in Cloud Computing. *International Journal on Recent and Innovation Trends in Computing and Communication, 1*(6), 553–557.

Khan, A. N., Kiah, M. M., Khan, S. U., & Madani, S. A. (2013). Towards secure mobile cloud computing: A survey. *Future Generation Computer Systems, 29*(5), 1278–1299. doi:10.1016/j.future.2012.08.003

Khatri, T. S., & Jethava, G. B. (2012, November). Survey on data Integrity Approaches used in the Cloud Computing. *International Journal of Engineering Research and Technology, 1*(9), 1–6.

Mane, Y. D., & Devadkar, K. K. (2013). Protection concern in mobile cloud computing–a survey. *IOSR Journal of Computer Engineering, 3*, 39-44.

Qi, H., & Gani, A. (2012, May). Research on mobile cloud computing: Review, trend and perspectives. In *Proceedings of Second International Conference on Digital Information and Communication Technology and it's Applications (DICTAP)* (pp. 195-202).

Ren, W., Yu, L., Gao, R., & Xiong, F. (2011). Lightweight and compromise resilient storage outsourcing with distributed secure accessibility in mobile cloud computing. *Tsinghua Science and Technology, 16*(5), 520–528. doi:10.1016/S1007-0214(11)70070-0

Ruebsamen, T., & Reich, C. (2012). Enhancing mobile device security by security level integration in a cloud proxy. In *Proceedings of Third International Conference on Cloud Computing, GRIDs and Virtualization* (pp. 159-168).

Soyata, T., Ba, H., Heinzelman, W., Kwon, M., & Shi, J. (2013). Accelerating mobile cloud computing: A survey. In *Communication Infrastructures for Cloud Computing* (pp. 175-197). Hershey, PA: IGI Global.

Yang, J., Wang, H., Wang, J., Tan, C., & Yu, D. (2011). Provable data possession of resource-constrained mobile devices in cloud computing. *JNW, 6*(7), 1033–1040. doi:10.4304/jnw.6.7.1033-1040

Zhou, Z., & Huang, D. (2012, October). Efficient and secure data storage operations for mobile cloud computing. In *Proceedings of 8th international conference and 2012 workshop on systems virtualiztion management (svm), Network and service management (cnsm)* (pp. 37-45).

Zissis, D., & Lekkas, D. (2012). Addressing cloud computing security issues. *Future Generation Computer Systems, 28*(3), 583–592. doi:10.1016/j.future.2010.12.006

ADDITIONAL READING

Ali, M. (2009, December). Green cloud on the horizon. In *Proceedings of the IEEE International Conference on Cloud Computing* (pp. 451-459).

Buyya, R., Yeo, C. S., Venugopal, S., Broberg, J., & Brandic, I. (2009). Cloud computing and emerging IT platforms: Vision, hype, and reality for delivering computing as the 5th utility. *Future Generation Computer Systems, 25*(6), 599–616. doi:10.1016/j.future.2008.12.001

Cai-dong, G., & ... . (2010, November). The investigation of cloud-computing-based image mining mechanism in mobile communication WEB on Android. In *Proceedings of the 9th International Conference on Grid and Cooperative Computing (GCC)* (pp. 408-411). 10.1109/GCC.2010.85

Chen, Y. J., & Wang, L. C. (2011, September). A security framework of group location-based mobile applications in cloud computing. In *Proceedings of 40th International Conference on Parallel Processing Workshops* (pp. 184-190). 10.1109/ICPPW.2011.6

Chow, R., Jakobsson, M., Masuoka, R., Molina, J., Niu, Y., Shi, E., & Song, Z. (2010, October). Authentication in the clouds: a framework and its application to mobile users. In *Proceedings of the 2010 ACM workshop on Cloud computing security workshop* (pp. 1-6). 10.1145/1866835.1866837

Cuervo, E., Balasubramanian, A., Cho, D. K., Wolman, A., Saroiu, S., Chandra, R., & Bahl, P. (2010, June). MAUI: making smartphones last longer with code offload. In *Proceedings of the 8th International Conference on Mobile Systems, Applications, and Services* (pp. 49-62). 10.1145/1814433.1814441

Davis, J. W. (1993, May). Power benchmark strategy for systems employing power management. In *Proceedings of the International Symposium on Electronics and the Environment* (pp. 117-119). 10.1109/ISEE.1993.302825

Di Fabbrizio, G., Okken, T., & Wilpon, J. G. (2009, November). A speech mashup framework for multimodal mobile services. In *Proceedings of the 2009 International Conference on Multimodal Interfaces* (pp. 71-78). 10.1145/1647314.1647329

Dong, Y., Zhu, H., Peng, J., Wang, F., Mesnier, M. P., Wang, D., & Chan, S. C. (2011). RFS: A network file system for mobile devices and the cloud. *Operating Systems Review*, *45*(1), 101–111. doi:10.1145/1945023.1945036

Doukas, C., Pliakas, T., & Maglogiannis, I. (2010, August). Mobile healthcare information management utilizing Cloud Computing and Android OS. In *Proceedings of Annual International Conference of the IEEE on Engineering in Medicine and Biology Society (EMBC)* (pp. 1037-1040).

Gao, H. Q., & Zhai, Y. J. (2010, October). System design of cloud computing based on mobile learning. In *Proceedings of 3rd International Symposium on Knowledge Acquisition and Modeling* (pp. 239-242).

Garcia, A., & Kalva, H. (2011, January). Cloud transcoding for mobile video content delivery. In *Proceedings of International Conference on Consumer Electronics (ICCE)* (pp. 379-380). 10.1109/ICCE.2011.5722637

Hoang, D. B., & Chen, L. (2010, December). Mobile cloud for assistive healthcare (MoCAsH). In *Proceedings of IEEE Asia-Pacific Services Computing Conference (APSCC)* (pp. 325-332).

Huang, D., Zhang, X., Kang, M., & Luo, J. (2010, June). MobiCloud: building secure cloud framework for mobile computing and communication. In *Proceedings of Fifth IEEE International Symposium on Service Oriented System Engineering (SOSE)* (pp. 27-34). 10.1109/SOSE.2010.20

Huerta-Canepa, G., & Lee, D. (2010, June). A virtual cloud computing provider for mobile devices. In *Proceedings of the 1st ACM Workshop on Mobile Cloud Computing & Services: Social Networks and Beyond*. 10.1145/1810931.1810937

Jin, X., & Kwok, Y. K. (2010, December). Cloud assisted P2P media streaming for bandwidth constrained mobile subscribers. In *Proceedings of 16th International Conference on Parallel and Distributed Systems (ICPADS)* (pp. 800-805).

Keahey, K., Tsugawa, M., Matsunaga, A., & Fortes, J. (2009). Sky Computing. *IEEE Internet Computing*, *13*(5), 43–51. doi:10.1109/MIC.2009.94

Koukoumidis, E., Lymberopoulos, D., Strauss, K., Liu, J., & Burger, D. (2011, March). Pocket cloudlets. In *Proceedings of the 16th International Conference on Architectural Support for Programming Languages and Operating Systems (ASPLOS)* (pp. 171-184).

Lagerspetz, E., & Tarkoma, S. (2010, March). Cloud-assisted mobile desktop search. In *Proceedings of 8th IEEE International Conference on Pervasive Computing and Communications Workshops (PERCOM Workshops)* (pp. 826-828).

Li, L., Li, X., Youxia, S., & Wen, L. (2010, October). Research on mobile multimedia broadcasting service integration based on cloud computing. In *Proceedings of International Conference on Multimedia Technology* (pp. 1-4). 10.1109/ICMULT.2010.5630979

Li, Y. C., Liao, I. J., Cheng, H. P., & Lee, W. T. (2010, December). A cloud computing framework of free view point real-time monitor system working on mobile devices. In *Proceedings of International Symposium on Intelligent Signal Processing and Communication Systems (ISPACS)* (pp. 1-4).

Liu, L., Moulic, R., & Shea, D. (2010, November). Cloud service portal for mobile device management. In *Proceedings of 7th International Conference on e-Business Engineering (ICEBE)* (pp. 474-478). 10.1109/ICEBE.2010.102

Nkosi, M. T., & Mekuria, F. (2010, November). Cloud computing for enhanced mobile health applications. In *Proceedings of IEEE Second International Conference on Cloud Computing Technology and Science (CloudCom)* (pp. 629-633). 10.1109/CloudCom.2010.31

Oberheide, J., Cooke, E., & Jahanian, F. (2007, August). Rethinking Antivirus: Executable Analysis in the Network Cloud. In *Proceedings of the 2nd USENIX workshop on Hot topics in security (HOTSEC)*.

Oberheide, J., Cooke, E., & Jahanian, F. (2008, July). CloudAV: N-Version Antivirus in the Network Cloud. In *Proceedings of the USENIX Security Symposium* (pp. 91-106).

Papakos, P., Capra, L., & Rosenblum, D. S. (2010, November). Volare: context-aware adaptive cloud service discovery for mobile systems. In *Proceedings of the 9th International Workshop on Adaptive and Reflective Middleware* (pp. 32-38). 10.1145/1891701.1891706

Rahman, M., & Mir, F. A. M. (2005, November). Fourth Generation (4G) mobile networks-features, technologies & issues. In *Proceedings of 6th IEE International Conference on 3G and Beyond* (pp. 1-5).

Samimi, F. A., McKinley, P. K., & Sadjadi, S. M. (2006). Mobile service clouds: A self-managing infrastructure for autonomic mobile computing services. In *Proceedings of the 2nd International Workshop on Self-Managed Networks, Systems, and Services* (pp. 130-141).

Satyanarayanan, M. (1996, May). Fundamental challenges in mobile computing. In *Proceedings of the fifteenth annual ACM symposium on Principles of distributed computing* (pp. 1-7). 10.1145/248052.248053

Stoer, M., & Wagner, F. (1997). A simple min-cut algorithm. *Journal of the ACM, 44*(4), 585–591. doi:10.1145/263867.263872

Subashini, S., & Kavitha, V. (2011). A survey on security issues in service delivery models of cloud computing. *Journal of Network and Computer Applications, 34*(1), 1–11. doi:10.1016/j.jnca.2010.07.006

Tang, W. T., Hu, C. M., & Hsu, C. Y. (2010, October). A mobile phone based homecare management system on the cloud. In *Proceedings of 3rd International Conference on Biomedical Engineering and Informatics (BMEI)* (pp. 2442-2445). 10.1109/BMEI.2010.5639917

Wang, S., & Dey, S. (2010, December). Rendering adaptation to address communication and computation constraints in cloud mobile gaming. In *Proceedings of Global Telecommunications Conference (GLOBECOM)* (pp. 1-6). 10.1109/GLOCOM.2010.5684144

Wang, S., & Wang, X. S. (2010, May). In-device spatial cloaking for mobile user privacy assisted by the cloud. In *Proceedings of Eleventh International Conference on Mobile Data Management (MDM)* (pp. 381-386). 10.1109/MDM.2010.82

Yang, X., Pan, T., & Shen, J. (2010, July). On 3G mobile e-commerce platform based on cloud computing. In *Proceedings of 3ʳᵈ IEEE International Conference on Ubi-media Computing (U-Media), 2010* (pp. 198-201).

Ye, Z., Chen, X., & Li, Z. (2010, October). Video based mobile location search with large set of SIFT points in cloud. In *Proceedings of the 2010 ACM Multimedia Workshop on Mobile Cloud Media Computing.* (pp. 25-30). 10.1145/1877953.1877962

Zhao, W., Sun, Y., & Dai, L. (2010, August). Improving computer basis teaching through mobile communication and cloud computing technology. In *Proceedings of 3ʳᵈ International Conference on Advanced Computer Theory and Engineering* (pp. V1-452-V1-454).

Zhenyu, W., Chunhong, Z., Yang, J., & Hao, W. (2010, August). Towards cloud and terminal collaborative mobile social network service. In *Proceedings of IEEE Second International Conference on Social Computing (SocialCom)* (pp. 623-629). 10.1109/SocialCom.2010.97

KEY TERMS AND DEFINITIONS

Certification Authority: Certification authority provides digital certificate. This digital certificate certifies the ownership of the public to a particular subject. This certificate allows others to rely on the signature of the subject done by using his private key. A certification authority is trusted by subject or the owner of the public key and the party which rely on the certificate.

Cloud Computing: It is the facility through which computing services such as software, networking, database and Storage are delivered to the users through the internet. Companies which are providing the services to the clients are known as cloud service provider. The users are charged by the cloud service providers based on the usage.

Cloud Service Provider: It is an organization that offers cloud computing based solutions and services to the customers. The services it can provide may be rented and maintained by the service provider. The services may be computation hardware, platform for hosting website or application software. Since cloud is scalable and cost effective the services of the cloud isare becoming increasingly desirable.

Data Security: The technique through which unauthorized access to websites, databases and computer gets prevented is known as data security. It also protects the data from corruption. It is very necessary for any organization of any size. It is a critical issue in case of cloud computing.

Mobile Device: It is a hand held device designed to be extremely portable. Using the services of the cloud, the users can perform large set of tasks through these hand held device.

Third Party Auditor: The primary role of Third Party Auditor (TPA) is to check periodically whether the CSP is complying to or deceiving from the service layer agreement. TPA can also perform the integrity check of the data stored in the cloud on demand of the user. It is an entity which acts on behalf of the client.

This research was previously published in Cloud Computing Technologies for Green Enterprises edited by Kashif Munir, pages 166-199, copyright year 2018 by Business Science Reference (an imprint of IGI Global).

Chapter 65
Cloud Security Using 2-Factor Image Authentication Technique

Ratish Agarwal
UIT-RGPV, India

Anjana Pandey
UIT-RGPV, India

Mahesh Pawar
UIT-RGPV, India

ABSTRACT

Cloud computing is being anticipated as the infrastructural basis of tomorrow's IT industry and continues to be a topic of interest of many new emerging IT firms. Cloud can deliver resources and services to computers and devices through internet. Since Cloud Computing involves outsourcing of sensitive data and critical information the security aspects of cloud need to be dealt carefully. Strong authentication, focusing mainly on user-authentication, acts as a pre-requisite for access control in the cloud environment. In this paper we discuss an efficient authentication mechanism to deal with the security threats that are faced by cloud. The method proposed in this paper prevents the confidential data and information of end users stored in a private cloud from unauthorized access by using a two-factor authentication involving shared image concept in addition with encrypted key authentication.MD5 hashing technique is used which takes binary pixel value of image as input and convert it into a 128-bit hash value. The overall process of authentication has been shown through experimental result and implementation which shows a series of snapshots taken from the chapter.

INTRODUCTION

Cloud computing is a type of computing that uses the internet to allow the sharing of resources and data to other computers and devices as per the demands of clients. This technology provides users and enterprises with various capabilities to store and process their data in third-party data centers. It has become a highly demanded utility as it provides high computing power, cheap cost of services, high

DOI: 10.4018/978-1-5225-8176-5.ch065

Copyright © 2019, IGI Global. Copying or distributing in print or electronic forms without written permission of IGI Global is prohibited.

performance, scalability, accessibility as well as availability. The technology which is responsible for cloud computing is termed as virtualization, which divides a single physical computing device into multiple "virtual" devices, which are independent of each other and can be used and managed easily for performing computations on different tasks. A cloud can be deployed into three main types Public Cloud, Private Cloud and Hybrid Cloud, according to the types of its user.

There are a number of security concerns associated with cloud computing. These issues fall into two broad categories: security issues faced by cloud providers and security issues faced by their customers. The security issues faced by end users can be reduced by using authentication mechanisms at their end. Authentication is a process in which the credentials provided are compared to those on file in a database of authorized users' information on a local operating system or within an authentication server. If the credentials match, the process is completed and the user is granted authorization for access. Two-factor authentication mechanisms are more robust as compared to traditional password authentication.

- **Cloud Computing:** We will also concentrate on fundamental concepts of Cloud Computing and its related technologies. Computing phenomenon itself, to be considered totally virtualized, must let the computers to be built from physically distributed components like storage, processing, data, and software resources. Technologies like cluster, grid and recently cloud computing, have altogether allowed accessing to huge amounts of computing resources by integrating computing and physical resources in a fully virtualized way and have offered in single system view to the end user. The end users use the computing and physical resources in Utility manner which describes a business framework for delivering the services and computing power on-demand basis. And according to the need of the user, Cloud Service Providers (CSPs) have aimed to deliver the services and cloud users have to pay the service providers based on their usage that means "pay-per-use" or "pay-as-you-go". As we discussed in the previous chapter that in electric grid, the users just use the electricity which is coming from the power stations and users have to pay how much they have used the electricity. Likewise in Cloud Computing environment, users need not to know the underlying architecture for getting the services; they just have to pay according to their usage. Cloud is basically an infrastructure which is maintained by some Cloud Service Providers and end-users are getting the services on-demand from the service provider and they have to pay the required money for their usage. Service Provider giants like Amazon, Microsoft, Google, IBM offer on-demand resource and computing services to the user commercially.
- **Evolution of Cloud Computing:** Cloud computing evolved when we started thinking about what we actually need. Cloud computing is not a new technology. In fact, it is the most used technology whenever we work on our computers. The difference that has occurred now is the way we see and utilize cloud computing. The beginning of what we call the concept of cloud computing can be traced back to the mainframe days of the 1960s when the idea of "Utility Computing" was coined by MIT computer scientist and Turing award winner John McCarthy. He remarked that "Computation may someday be organized as public utility". In 1961, while speaking at the MIT Centennial he suggested.

Utility computing concept is very simple. Utility computing can be defined as a service provisioning model where a service provider makes computing resources and infrastructure management available to the customer as needed. This approach is like pay-per-use or metered service that means customer can pay as their usage for internet service, file sharing, web site access and other applications. In 1966,

Douglas F Parkhill published the book "The Challenge of the Computer Utility". He explored elastic provisioning and resource sharing concept in his book.

In early days of IT industry, in 1957, IBM brought into light 704 as the first mainframe computer that had the function of floating-point arithmetic. Sequentially, in 1964 the IBM System/360 came up in the market. This product family has drawn attention to the industry that the peripheral components were transferable and that the software unit was executable on all computers of this product family (Based on Bashe 1986). The miniaturization of these computers and further developments led to the independent machines, suppose the 'minicomputers' such as DEC's Minicomputer PDP-8 in 1964 or Xerox's Alto in 1974 (According to Freiberger et al. 2000).

The advancement of the PC (Personal Computer) began in the age of 1970ies, constructed with the first microprocessor 4004 in 1967 and the later microprocessor 8008 introduced by Intel in 1971. The first Home computer, the Micral invented by Andre Thi Troung in 1973 (Freiberger et al 2000) on the basis of microprocessor 8008. Construction manuals for the Mark 8 or TV Typewriter were initially aimed Hobbyists. In this era of personal computers, marketing concept has been introduced as Altair 8800 had been sold as the construction set by MITS in 1975. This computer was one of the initial home computers. On the basis of this concept, a BASIC interpreter (According to Freiberger et al. 2000) has been developed by Microsoft. Sequentially, Apple, Commodore, Atari and others has come up in the home computer's market. IBM entered in the market phase and invented the name PC (Personal Computer). Microsoft entered as an operating system developer and for IBM-PC has developed the operating system which eventually came into use as the standard platform, which became compatible with many other PC-manufacturers. Sequentially many phases of the developments and advancements was going on, significant performance developments were hitting the market. With the invention of graphical user interface (GUI), development leads to the further advanced approach.

When considering more development for connecting multiple PCs, then another milestone came up in the industry and that is Internet. The Advanced Research Chapters Agency (ARPA) has introduced the concept of Internet as a research chapter. While considering internet, every connecting point regarded as a node. In support of the US ministry of defense, a communication system has been developed in such a way that if one of the nodes would be broken, the communication system remained stay connected. Eventually, out of this chapter, the ARPAnet was developed and around 200 institutions were connected though this network. In 1983, TCP/IP concept has been introduced and the net's protocol was switched to TCP/IP which helps to connect the entire subnet to the ARPA net. Now the Internet has been called as network of networks. With the invention of World Wide Web (WWW) by British engineer and computer scientist Sir Tim Berners-Lee in 1989, internet finally got a breakout success. Sir Tim Berners-Lee has given the concept of a system to manage the information for CERN (European Organization for Nuclear Research) where hyperlinks were used. Eventually, in respect to the end users there was need for web browsers. So World Wide Web achieved high popularity when web browser Mosaic came in the market (Freiberger et al. 2000; Berners-Lee 1989).

Now, the entire IT industry has put the effort towards designing the quality web browser. Increasing bandwidths and technologies also helps to develop this kind of browser. Java, PHP or Ajax all made it possible to be able to create more and more detailed and user-interactive sites. This kind of developments leads the industry towards making many multimedia websites, user-friendly applications.

Meanwhile, in the age of 1990ies the concept of grid computing came up in the academia. Ian Foster and Carl Kesselman published "The Grid: Blueprint for a New computing Infrastructure", a book, in which the new analogy was similar to electrical grid concept. We can explain the concept with our daily life example. When we plug an electric appliance into an electrical outlet, we don't care how electric power is generated or how it is getting to the outlet. We just use it. This is the basic concept of virtualization. We need not to know the underlying architecture or the procedure and how the resources are coming to the end-users. They just utilize it. Here electricity is virtualized; virtualization hides a huge distribution grid and power generation stations. Technologies like cluster, grid and now cloud computing, all the technologies have targeted at allowing access to huge amount of computing resources in a fully virtualized pattern. It makes a single system view by collecting resources in a aggregate pattern. All these technologies are delivering the services to the users or customers as a "pay-per-use" or "pay-as-you-go" pattern (payment based on usage).

In 1999 Sales force initiated to start delivering applications to the customers using a simple website. The real-time applications were delivered to the enterprises and distributed over the internet; thus the computing as utility-basis has been started and that has came to reality. In 2002 Amazon Started its milestone creating Amazon Web Services (AWS), and delivering services like storage, computations etc. Amazon is going to allow customers to blend their own website with its huge online data. These types of services and computing facility grew gradually on demand. Eventually in 2006, Amazon introduced its Elastic cloud (Amazon EC2), a web service for commercial use, which allows individuals as well as small industries to rent infrastructure (resources, storage, memory) on which they can deploy and run their own applications. After the launching of Amazon storage (Amazon S3), they have used the "pay-per-use" model for pricing of usage of their service. And form the point of that, cloud computing pricing model has came up in the market. Gradually Google Apps Engine, Force.com, Eucalyptus, Windows Azure, Aneka and other clouds are became the big players in the cloud industry.

- **Related Technologies:** Technologies Related to Cloud computing are mostly Cluster Computing and Grid Computing which are the parts of distributed computing. Cloud computing requires bare metal virtualization which is a component of system hardware & resource virtualization. And Web Services acts as the interface to the user and various Internet technologies helps to build up Web Services.

In the next section, we will discuss about Cluster computing, Mobile computing, and Grid computing.

- **Cluster Computing:** Let's start with the basic concept of cluster computing According to N. Sadashiv and S. M Dilip Kumar. A computer cluster can be defined as a set of loosely coupled computers working together in such a way that all the machines can be viewed as a Single System image (SSI). Computer clusters emerged as an output of convergence of a huge number of computing movement including the accessibility to high speed networks, microprocessors at a low price, and software for delivering high performance distributing computing.

- **The Architecture of Computer Cluster:** Now we concentrate on the architecture of the computer cluster so that we can understand easily how different machines can be viewed as Single System Image. In, R. Buyya has elaborately explained the key components of a computer cluster which includes multiple standalone computers, an operating system, and communication software, a high performance interconnecting medium, middleware and different application. A computer node can be a single or single or multiprocessor system (PCs, SMPs, workstations) with memory, I/O facilities, and operating system. The Cluster middleware stays in between the multiple PC/

Workstations and applications. It works as a Single System Image maker and availability infrastructure. Programming environments offer efficient, portable, and easy-to-use tools for application development. Computer cluster can also be used for the execution of parallel and sequential application.

- **Components of Computer Cluster:** A typical computer cluster has some prominent components, which are used to do a specific task.
- **Grid Computing:** Cloud computing is the gradually development of cluster computing and grid computing. It also includes parallel and distributed computing. In short, we can say that cloud computing is the basic realization of all these concepts. Already we have discussed about computer cluster, its underlying architecture and its application. Now we are moving into Grid concept.

Grid computing was first coined in 1990s by Cart Kesselman and Ian Foster and succinctly defined as: Grid computing is coordinated resource sharing and problem solving in dynamic, multi-institutional virtual organizations". When we explain grid computing it is essential to distinguish it from clusters. These clusters are spread across locally and compelled to utilize a common hardware and operating system, whereas the grids include the heterogeneous computers that are linked to each other and spread across globally. Even the hardware and operating system can be distinct from each other.

Grid computing is a complex phenomenon which has evolved via earlier developments in parallel, distributed and HPC (High Performance computing) (Weishaupl et al., 2005 and Harms et al. 2006). The real Grid problem was identified to be the support provided by the development for generic sharing of IT resources.

According to Foster, "The real and specific problem that underlies the Grid concept is coordinated resource sharing and problem solving in dynamic, multi-institutional virtual organizations. The sharing that we are concerned with is not primarily file exchange but rather direct access to computers, software, data, and other resources, as is required by a range of collaborative problem-solving and resource brokering strategies emerging in industry, science, and engineering." (Foster et al., 2001, p2).

Computing grids are conceptually and logically like electrical grids. In an electrical grid, wall outlets allow us to connect to an infrastructure of resources which generate and distribute the electricity. When we connect to the electrical grid, we don't even need to know where the power plant is situated or how the electricity gets to us. Likewise, in the IT industry, in order to co-ordinate different IT resources grid computing uses the middleware, thus enabling them to function and work as one virtual device. The main aim of grid computing, just like the electrical grid, is to grant users the permission to use the resources as per their requirement, and to provide access to the assets of IT, and combined processing power from any remote location. According to S. Zhang, X. Chen et al, Grid imparts a series of resources for distributed computing with the help of WAN or LAN to the application of the end user, which makes it look like he is using a super virtual computer. This idea would be secured and safe and organize as well as co-ordinate the sharing of resources among people, business circles, resources and organizations, and will provide an organization which is both virtual and dynamic. Grid computing is thus a type of distributed computing. It requires unlimited power production by hardware, software, locations and organizations. Its aim is to allow anyone that is a part of grid to co-ordinate, co-operate and exchange information amongst them. Although grid computing has all these properties but cloud computing is still considered better. Cloud computing is itself derived from grid computing and so allows the users to access on-demand resources and the resources are provisioned according to their application.

- **Grid Related Technologies:** Grid Computing connects the machines that are located in different geographical remote areas and forms a single network to emerge (from user point of view) as a virtual supercomputer by linking both the resource and computational power of all systems on a single grid. A grid computing network consists of geographically and physically linked network including machines, peripheral devices, switches, data and connecting cable instruments. All the resources can be accessed by each user using only single login account. Different resources may own the physical resources. Distributed computing and Peer to Peer computing are said to be the cousins of Grid computing.

- **Distributed Computing:** The main purpose of introducing this computing is to divide the workload of a program among different processes. The main aim of distributing computing is to divide and deal out the problems into different computers connected through a common network. A distributing system comprising of multiple autonomous computers, communicate with each other via a computer network. The computer works together in order to attain a common goal. Here we will describe some typical characteristics of distributed system:

- **Fault Tolerance:** Each computer within the distributed system has to tolerate failures i.e. the system should have the potential for fault tolerance.

- **Heterogeneous Atmosphere:** The structure of the distributed system (network latency, network topology, network connections, and total number of participating computers) is not predefined. The distributed system may comprise of distinct kinds of computers and heterogeneous network links. While executing a program, the system structure may change in order to achieve the goal.

- **Separate Participation:** Each and individual computer has its distinct participation and has limited view of complete system. Each computer may only know the some module or some part of the whole program or input. We can see that distributed systems are groups of computers interlinked with each other through a communication network and each computer containing processor and memory, have the same goal for their work. Depending on the workload and the execution type of the program, network topology and the total number of participating computers have been dynamically arranged.

- **Peer-to-Peer Computing:** Peer-to-Peer computing is a technique in which every computer can share the physical resources and services by directly exchanging between the systems and each computer can act as servers and clients for the other computers connected to the network. Which computer can act as a client or server depends upon the role which is most trustworthy and productive for the network. In peer-to-peer computing, content is typically exchanged in the direct way over the fundamental Internet Protocol (IP) network. The main advantage of peer-to-peer (P2P) computing is that there is chance of central point of failure and decentralized coordination maintains how to keep the global state consistent. There are 6 nodes such as Node A, B, C, D, E, and F. Each of the nodes represents itself a machine and they can share the physical resources and services directly exchanging among the nodes and communicate with each other. Each node can act as a server and client for the other nodes connected to the network.

In P2P systems, computing resources like storage space, computing power, and bandwidth are provided by clients. The main advantage of P2P computing is that lack of centralized system administrator eliminates the problem of single point of failure which is the basic pitfalls of centralized system. Hence there is a provision of data and system back up among the nodes. But main loopholes of P2P system is that security issue. A node may download a virus file which may infect the other systems; in that concern, P2P system is vulnerable to unsigned and unsecure codes which lead to unsecure environment due to lack of centralized administrator.

- **Connectivity: Communicating Securely and Easily:** This layer defines the fundamentals of protocols of authorization, communication and authentication that the grid-specific network transactions require. The data exchange among the fabric layer resources requires communication protocols. Routing, transport and naming are the basic requirements for communication. Authentication protocols are required for communication services for providing secure mechanisms for validating the authentication of users and resources. Connectivity layer provides authentication services which consist of the following features:
- **Single Sign On:** All the users must be allowed to validate themselves ("log on") just once and only after that they will be allowed to access the multiple grid resources described in the fabric layer.
- **Delegation:** Any user should be able to run the program on his behalf, so that the accessing of the resources of the grid will be authenticated.
- **Integration with Various Local Security Solutions:** Each resource provider or the site should be integrated with various local security solutions. Grid security solutions must be able to combine with multiple local security solutions and map itself to the local environment.
- **User-Based Trust Relationships:** If the right to access the resources from distinct sites or resource providers is given to the user, then he should be able to use the sites together without requiring the interaction of the administrators of the providers.
- **Resource: Sharing Single Resources:** The resource layer stays over the connectivity layer communication and authentication protocols to identify protocols for the initiation, monitoring, secure negotiation, accounting, control and payment of sharing operations on individual resources. Resource layer implements these protocols upon fabric layer to access and control local resources. The resource layer protocols consist of two main classes:
- **Information Protocol:** These types of protocols are used to get information about the structure and states of resources like usage policy, current load and its configuration.
- **Management Protocols:** The negotiation of access to the physical resources that are shared, resource requirement specification and the monitoring of operations that are to be performed is carried out by these protocols. While executing or controlling the operations, the on-going status of that operation may also be held up.
- **Collective: Coordinating Multiple Resources:** The next layer is focused towards the protocols and services that are associated with global resource and interact with collections of resources. That's why we have referred the next layer of the grid architecture stack as the collective layer.
- **Directory Services:** Directory services allow its users to make queries for resources by type, availability or load-sharing demand. Resource-level protocols are used to construct directories.
- **Co-Allocation, Scheduling, and Brokering Service:** These kind of services allow participants to request the allotment of tasks one or more physical resources for a particular purpose and the scheduling of tasks over the suitable resources.
- **Monitoring and Diagnostics Services:** These particular services monitor the resource allotment, overload management, and also keep attention to the attacks.

- **Data Replication Services:** Data replication services support the storage management to maxi mize the data access performance and minimize the response time and cost.
- **Workload Management Systems:** This management service manages the usage, description, status of the task and multi-component workflows.

PROPOSED METHODOLOGY

Here in this chapter we use a cryptographic technique to generate ciphers - MD5 which stands for Message Digest algorithm 5. It is a widely used cryptographic hash function that takes up the data (text or binary) as an input and generates a fixed size "hash value" as the output. In this work, we have used this algorithm to convert binary value associated with each pixel of image into a hexadecimal value which is mapped by both- client and server. The main concept and sequential methodology regarding our work is enlisted below as a DFD in Figure 1. The DFD given in Figure 1 is further explained step-by-step in Algorithm 1.

Figure 1.

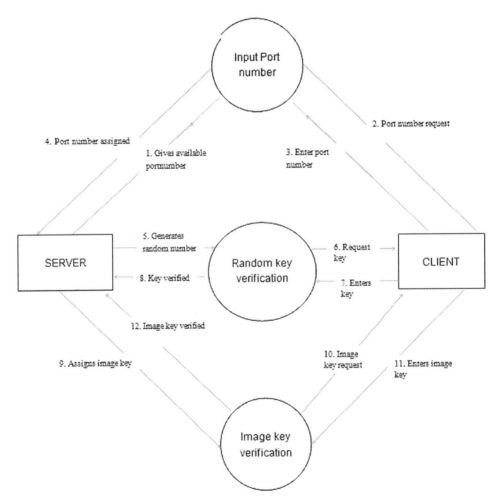

Algorithm 1.

```
Step 1. Run Cloud_main.java()
Step 2. Enter the values for Cloud parameters.
Step 3.end if any parameter=0
Step 4. Enter the port number x on the server side.
Step 5. Enter the port number y on client side.
Step 6. end if port numbers do not match.
Step 7. /* random key generation on the server side */
showMessageDialog("Random No. generated "+value);
Step 8. Enter the Random number on the client Side.
Step 9. Select Generate key.
Step 10. /* Master Key generated*/
Step 11. Match key on the Server side
Step 12. if matched
showMessageDialog("Key Verified")
Step 13. Select Image key on the server side.
Step 14. Select image key on the Client Side
Step 15. if image key matched
showMessageDialog("User Authenticates");
Step 16. if image key not matched
showMessageDialog(null,"Invalid user")
System.exit(0)
Step 17. Communication established successful
```

EXPERIMENTAL RESULT

In this chapter a cloud environment has been simulated using CloudSim simulation tool which is a framework for modeling and simulation of cloud computing infrastructures and services. It is completely written in JAVA, which includes various packages and classes used for simulation of cloud. The four main entities here are – Data Centres, Brokers, Cloudlets and Vms. Data centre helps in creation of hosts with an appropriate amount of characteristics like Ram, PE's, CPU's, bandwidth, mips (milli instructions per second) etc. Broker helps in the sequential execution of tasks and acts the mediator for interaction between cloudlets and server by providing access to virtual machines. Cloudlet is an entity of cloud computing environment that is located at the edge of the Internet. VM is a self-contained operating environment that behaves as a separate computer. In this work, we have used Xen hypervisor. A window as shown in Figure 2 appears in which number of data centres, brokers, cloudlets and vm's are entered to create a cloud. The simulation starts. Afterwards the Server window appears as shown in Figure 3.A port number is entered in the text field to which the server will be listening to when started. ClientGUI1. java file is run. This will generate the Client Window as shown in Figure 4.Same port number is entered in the client window. If the port numbers match client request is accepted as shown in Figure 5.

Figure 2.

Figure 3.

Figure 4.

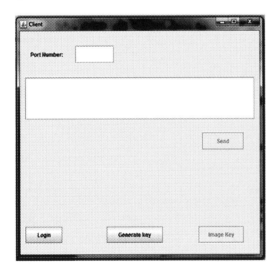

Figure 5.

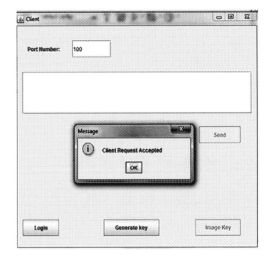

CONCLUSION

Cloud computing is now coming up as a new technology which is being used by companies of all sizes. Irrespective of the size of the company, they demand a secure cloud. Thus security in cloud is the most important factor. Still, there is a need for better mechanisms to provide organized authentication. Here in this chapter we proposed an efficient authentication mechanism to deal with the threats of security that are faced by the cloud. The proposed technique implemented can prevent the data stored from various types of attacks such as identity disclosure attack, outsider attack or password impersonation. In order to find new schemes and methods in the cloud environment to provide a proper authentication for the users, research is still in progress. The method that we proposed here takes less storage cost and has less time complexity. Moreover, it provides public verifiability to each user in the cloud. It also lays a proper base to continue with the development and research in the cloud security field.

REFERENCES

Agarwal. (2012). Multi-level Authentication Technique for Accessing Cloud Services. *International Conference on Computing, Communication and Applications*, 1-4.

Chow, Masuoka, Molina, Niu, Shi, & Song. (2010). Authentication in the Clouds: A Framework and its Application to Mobile Users. CCSW'10, Chicago, IL.

Kim & Hong. (2011). *One-Source Multi-Use System having Function of Consolidated User Authentication.* YES-ICUC.

Pawle & Pawar. (2013). Face Recognition System (FRS) on Cloud Computing for User Authentication. *International Journal of Soft Computing and Engineering, 3*(4).

Quorica. (2009). *Business Analysis Evolution of Strong Authentication.* Retrieved from: http://quocirca.com/sites/default/files/reports/092009/452/CRYPTOCard.pdf

Schneier, B. (2009). Be careful when you come to put your trust in the clouds. *Guardian.* Retrieved from: http://www.guardian.co.uk/technology/2009/jun/04/bruce-schneier-cloud-computing

Shen, Z., Li, L., Yan, F., & Wu, X. (2010). Cloud Computing System Based on Trusted Computing Platform. *International Conference on Intelligent Computation Technology and Automation, 1,* 942-945. 10.1109/ICICTA.2010.724

Ziyad, & Rehman. (2014). Critical Review of Authentication Mechanism in Cloud Computing. *International Journal of Computer Science Issues 11*(3).

This research was previously published in Detecting and Mitigating Robotic Cyber Security Risks edited by Raghavendra Kumar, Prasant Kumar Pattnaik, and Priyanka Pandey, pages 135-147, copyright year 2017 by Information Science Reference (an imprint of IGI Global).

Chapter 66
Challenges of Cloud Computing Adoption From the TOE Framework Perspective

Omar Al-Hujran
Princess Sumaya University for Technology, Jordan

Enas M. Al-Lozi
Al-Zaytoonah University of Jordan, Jordan

Mutaz M. Al-Debei
The University of Jordan, Jordan

Mahmoud Maqableh
The University of Jordan, Jordan

ABSTRACT

Cloud computing can be classified as a third-generation computing platform which refers to on-demand delivery of computing infrastructure and services via a network, usually the Internet. Cloud computing promises to provide several advantages to its adopters such as: cost advantage, availability, scalability, flexibility, reduced time to market and dynamic access to computational resources. Notwithstanding the numerous advantages of cloud computing, its implementation and adoption in developing countries is still limited and surrounded by variety of issues. Hence, the main objective of this article is to identify the main challenges facing the utilization of these services in developing countries, particularly Jordan. To achieve the above-mentioned objective, six in-depth interviews with ICT officials and experts in the domain of cloud computing were used as the main data collection method. The challenges of cloud computing adoption emerged in this study are classified into technological, organizational and environmental factors.

DOI: 10.4018/978-1-5225-8176-5.ch066

Copyright © 2019, IGI Global. Copying or distributing in print or electronic forms without written permission of IGI Global is prohibited.

1. INTRODUCTION

The highly dynamic business environment and the increasingly competition pressures urge organizations to adopt various state-of-the-art information systems/information technologies (IS/IT) in order to improve their business operations and performance (Sultan, 2010; Pan and Jang, 2008), to advance there IS/IT innovativeness and to sustain themselves in the competitive marketplace (Wu et al., 2013). One of the recent and advanced innovative technologies is cloud computing, which is increasingly being considered as a technology that has the potential of changing how business can be conducted and how information systems are presently operated and used within organizations. According to the National Institute of Standards and Technology (NIST), cloud computing is defined as "…a model for enabling convenient, on-demand network access to a shared pool of configurable computing resources (e.g., networks, servers, storage, applications, and services) that can be rapidly provisioned and released with minimal management effort or service provider interaction…" (Mell and Grance, 2011). Cloud computing service models are classified based on the computing requirements of the end-users into three different layers including: software as a service (SaaS), infrastructure as a service (IaaS), and platform as a service (PaaS) (Alshamaila et al., 2013). However, the deployment models of cloud computing are usually classified as: public cloud, private cloud, hybrid cloud, and community cloud.

The emergence of the cloud computing as a disruptive technology has the potential of changing how business operations can be conducted and how computing services are developed, deployed, operated, maintained, and paid for (Gangwar et al., 2015). Recently, we are witnessing a big movement toward adopting innovative technologies, such as cloud computing, so as to gain competitive advantages that would help organizations in vanquishing the high levels of competition in many industries. Indeed, each organization has its own unique drivers to adopt cloud computing, but they generally fall into some general categories: cost savings, availability, scalability, flexibility, time-to-market, and others (EMC, 2011). Moreover, cloud computing has the potential to bring substantial benefits to organizations especially for small and medium-sized enterprises (SMEs) which usually cannot afford high investment in ICT infrastructure.

Without a doubt, the rapid emergence, prevalence and potential impact of cloud computing has sparkled a significant amount of interest amongst Information Systems/Information Technology (IS/IT) industry and research. However, and despite the rapid emergence of cloud computing, empirical research on cloud computing adoption is still quite limited (Alharbi, et al., 2016; Gupta et al., 2013; Morgan and Conboy, 2013). In addition, there has been less focus on adoption at the organizational level compared to the excessive one at the individual level (Marston et al., 2011). Further, despite the numerous advantages of cloud computing, its implementation and adoption in developing economies is still limited and surrounded by a variety of risks and challenges. These include: security, reliability, performance and integration issues (Gangwar et al., 2015). Moreover, the cultural differences between developed and developing countries are acknowledged. Many organizations in developing countries have deeply entrenched cultural diversities and norms compared to those in developed countries. These societal culture-based differences influence the diffusion of innovation and transfer of technology across nations (Sabi et al., 2017). Therefore, the main objective of this research is to explore the technological, organizational, and environmental factors that hinder the adoption of cloud computing technology by organizations in a culturally different part of the world, particularly Jordan.

The rest of this paper is organized as follows. Section 2 provides a theoretical background. Section 3 describes the research design and methodology applied in this study. In Section 4, we present the results of the study and offers justified interpretations and discussions in regard to the results. Section 5 provides theoretical and practical implications. Finally, the paper concludes in Section 6.

2. THEORETICAL BACKGROUND

2.1. Technology-Organization-Environment (TOE) Framework

The technology-organization-environment (TOE) is an organisation-level theory and multi-perspective framework that was developed by Tornatzky and Fleischer (Tornatzky and Fleischer, 1990). Based on this framework, the adoption process of a technology innovation is influenced by technological, organizational and environmental dimensions of an organization's context (Alharbi, et al., 2016; Alshamaila et al., 2013). The inclusion of technological, organizational and environmental factors has made TOE advantageous over other adoption models in studying technology adoption, use and value creation from technology (Gangwar et al., 2015). In addition, TOE framework is free from industry and firm-size restrictions (Wen and Chen, 2010). Moreover, TOE framework has been widely tested in IT/IS adoption studies and has reported consistent empirical support (Oliveira et al., 2014). The framework is also comprehensive and thus allows examining the adoption phenomenon and its impact on value chain activities from a holistic picture (Gangwar et al., 2015). As summarized in Zhu et al. (2006), the current literature validated the usefulness of the TOE framework for understanding the diffusion of a complex IS/IT innovation. Therefore, this framework.is adopted as a theoretical background in this study.

2.2. Cloud Computing Adoption: Technology Context

The technology context describes the characteristics of both internal and external technologies related to an organization. Internal technologies represent technologies that are currently in use by the organization while external technologies represent technologies that are available in the marketplace but not currently in use by the organization. Several technological factors that affect an organization's decision to adopt cloud technology have been identified in the literature. Frequently used constructs include: *security* (Aleem and Sprott, 2013; Gupta et al., 2013; Lian et al., 2014), *relative advantage* (Oliveira et al., 2014; Alshamaila et al., 2013; Borgman et al., 2013; Morgan and Conboy, 2013; Low et al., 2011), uncertainty (Alshamaila et al., 201), compatibility (Oliveira et al., 2014; Lian et al., 2014; Borgman et al., 2013; Morgan and Conboy, 2013; Low et al., 2011), complexity (Oliveira et al., 2014; Lian et al., 2014; Alshamaila et al., 2013; Borgman et al., 2013; Morgan and Conboy, 2013; Low et al., 2011), and trialability (Alshamaila et al., 2013; Morgan and Conboy, 2013).

2.3. Cloud Computing Adoption: Organization Context

The organization context refers to the characteristics and resources of an organization that impact the adoption and implementation decisions of an innovation (Oliveira et al., 2014), where in this case the innovation is represented by cloud computing technology. Common organization characteristics affecting the adoption decision of cloud computing including firm size, top management support, organization structure, organization culture, and the availability of human and slack resources (Oliveira et al., 2014; Alshamaila et al., 2013; Low et al., 2011). For example, top management support plays an essential role in cloud computing adoption because its implementation may involve integration, allocation of resources and reengineering of business processes (Low et al., 2011). Therefore, support from top management is critical in cloud computing adoption as they have the ability to make the change and influence the organization's members to implement this change (Oliveira et al., 2014). The size of the organization is another critical determinant of cloud computing adoption. Organization's size is usually determined by its capital, the number of its employees, the amount of investment involved, the annual revenue and the target market. It is often argued that large firms tend to adopt more innovations, largely because they have more resources, skills, experience and their ability to take risk (Alshamaila et al., 2013; Low et al., 2011).

2.4. Cloud Computing Adoption: Environment Context

The environment context refers to the settings in which an organization conducts its business; it can be related to surrounding conditions of the organization such as industry nature, competitors, regulations, geographical locations, and interactions with the government (Lian et al., 2014; Oliveira et al., 2014). Competitive pressures, for example, may encourage organizations to adopt new and innovative IS/IT systems to provide better services, gain competitive advantages (Lian et al., 2014), or at least to ensure survival. Regularity support is another important environmental factor that might influence cloud computing adoption by organizations. Indeed, government regulations can positively or negatively impact cloud computing adoption (Borgman et al., 2013). On the one hand, the government can support cloud computing adoption by providing tax advantages such as introducing regulation that force firms to comply with certain technology standards (Borgman et al., 2013). On the other hand, the non-compliance and violation of regulations may result in extra transactions cost on organizations and may involve strict liability (Delmas, 2002).

2.5. Challenges of Cloud Computing

Cloud computing represents a major shift in IS/IT and promises to bring substantial benefits to how organizations conduct their business. Cloud computing promises to dramatically reduce upfront and operating costs of ICT services (Marston et al., 2011; Venters and Whitley, 2012). Cloud computing also promises to deliver scalability (Aleem and Sprott, 2013), availability (EMC, 2011), agility (Armbrust et al., 2010), flexibility and other benefits to business enterprises so as to allow enterprises to focus on core business processes, while leaving the IT activities to the cloud provider (Salleh et al., 2012). However, despite the numerous benefits of cloud computing, there are several challenges that need to be resolved before it can be recognized as a viable ICT choice for organizations and especially in developing countries. Previous research indicated that loss of physical control of the data that is put on the cloud, security issues, privacy concerns, reliability of the internet connection, lack of standards and regulations represents the major concerns that are highly anticipated by potential cloud computing adopters (Mather et al., 2009; Aleem and Sprott, 2013). Based on the conducted review of literature, the main challenges of cloud computing are summarized in Table 1.

Table 1. Cloud Computing Challenges

Challenge	Brief Description	References
Lack of Regulations	Regulations regarding cloud computing are till now not clear enough for cloud customers to know their legal status and the jurisdiction.	Aleem and Sprott (2013); EMC (2011); Marston et al. (2011)
Lack of Standards	There is a lack of open standards between cloud computing providers. Switching from one cloud provider to another gets to be truly confounded.	EMC (2011); Shimba (2010); Marston et al. (2011); Nuseibeh (2011).
Lock-in	Customer will be locked into a specific service that is rendered by the provider.	Armbrust et al (2010); Salleh et al. (2012); Prince (2011)
Loss of Control	Organizations adopting cloud computing may face risk of losing a level of control over their companies, instead of controlling the IT environment directly they manage it through relationships with CSPs (cloud service providers) and SLA (service level agreement). Freedom of customers becomes limited because as they will be more reliant on the service provider.	Armbrust et al. (2010); Marston et al. (2011); Salleh et al. (2012); Prince (2011)
Privacy Concerns	Privacy is not a barrier but it must be taken into consideration. For example, customers need to know if their data is going to be disclosed by the cloud operator and subsequently used by third parties.	Office of the Privacy Commissioner of Canada (2007); Marston et al. (2011); Svantesson and Clarke (2010); Prince (2011)
Reliability	Cloud computing services are usually delivered via the Internet. Issues related to Internet connections such as bottlenecks (e.g. response time, latency and packet-loss) remain a big concern of cloud customers toward procuring cloud services.	Armbrust et al. (2010); Aleem and Sprott (2013); EMC (2011); Kim et al. (2009); Marston et al. (2011); Prince (2011); Qian et al. (2009)
Security Concerns	While companies prefer to keep their data within private corporate network under their control and security mechanisms, usage of cloud computing force companies to communicate their data over public internet, this in turn increase data vulnerability. In addition to the fact that CSP have to deal with huge amount of data, work load management issue becomes difficult among geographically dispersed machines which makes it ambiguous for the customer to know where the data is located and how is protected.	Armbrust et al (2010); Aleem and Sprott (2013); EMC (2011); Marston et al. (2011); Mujinga and Chipangura, (2011); Office of the Privacy Commissioner of Canada, (2007); Kim et al. (2009); Prince (2011); Qian et al. (2009); Zhang et al., (2010)

2.6. Cloud Computing Adoption

Unsurprisingly, there is a noticeable gap in terms of investments in advanced technologies as well as the adoption of such innovative technologies between developed and developing countries. The low levels of investments and adoption in developing countries can be attributed to the continuous socio-economic and political challenges in addition to the unique characteristics of developing countries' cultures (Sabi et al., 2017; Fong, 2009). Thus, we believe that introducing a technology to a new context successfully requires proper considerations of important cultural, socio-economic, and political differences (Al-Hujran et al., 2015).

Cloud computing innovation is widely seen as a solution to the digital divide between developed and developing countries and also to the innovation adoption problems faced by developing countries (Purkayastha and Braa, 2013; Sabi et al., 2017). This is because cloud computing innovation offers organizations in developing countries the accessibility and usage opportunities of advanced technologies which are available to organizations operating in the developed countries. By doing so, organizations operating in developing countries become more globally competitive than ever before (Kshetri, 2011). Indeed, the adoption and usage of cloud computing technology would help in bridging the digital divide, and in providing a cost-effective platform for organizations operating in developing countries to access global markets (Sabi et al., 2017).

On the basis of Technology-Organization-Environment (TOE) framework and the Diffusion of Innovation (DOI) theory, Oliveira et al. (2014) investigated the adoption of cloud computing by manufacturing and services organizations in Portugal and concluded that complexity, relative advantage, technological readiness, firm size and top management support have a direct effect on the adoption of cloud computing. In another study and by utilizing TOE framework and Human-Organization-Technology fit theory, Lian et al. (2014) indicated that the five most critical factors affecting the decision to adopt cloud computing technology were cost, security, perceived technical competence, top manager support, and complexity. Similarly, Low et al. (2011) used the TOE framework and DOI to examine the adoption of cloud computing in the Taiwanese high-tech industry. Findings of their study discovered that top management support, relative advantage, firm size, competitive pressure, and trading partner pressure characteristics have a noteworthy impact on the adoption of cloud computing technologies. By adopting the TOE framework as a theoretical base, Alshamaila et al. (2013) conducted semi-structured interviews among 15 key decision makers from different small and medium enterprises (SMEs) and service providers in the north east of United Kingdom. Their qualitative assessment indicated that compatibility, relative advantage, firm size, uncertainty, geo-restriction, trial-ability, top management support, innovativeness, prior experience, industry, supplier efforts, market scope, and external computing support were main determinants of SME adoption of cloud-based solutions. Gupta et al. (2013) presented five factors affecting the usage of cloud computing by SMEs in Singapore. These factors were: ease of use, convenience, security, privacy and cost reduction. Trigueros-Preciado et al. (2013) identified the main barriers to cloud adoption in Spain. They found that the knowledge about cloud computing is limited among the surveyed organizations, and that ignorance of the technology amongst these organisations was the major obstacle to adopt cloud computing technologies. Mohammed (2011) discussed the most key drivers and constraints for secure cloud computing from a societal and technological perspective. In his paper, he highlighted the most important societal issues such as: trust, privacy, and user behavior and how security affects these factors. In addition, the paper discussed the key technological issue such as: scalability, reliability, encryption, data rights, and transparency.

In the e-government context, Lian (2015) developed an integrated model which is based on the Unified Theory of Acceptance and Use of Technology 2 (UTAUT2) to identify the main factors that influence cloud-based e-invoicing service in Taiwan. The paper has examined seven factors: performance expectation, effort expectation, social influence, facilitating conditions, trust in e-government, security concerns and perceived risk. Relevant hypotheses were developed in this study. To empirically test these hypotheses, the paper utilized a questionnaire-based survey to collect. Findings from 251 valid responses of this study revealed that effort expectation, social influence, trust in e-government, and perceived risk have a significant effect on the adoption of the e-invoicing service. In addition, the results indicated that perceived risk and trust in e-government mediates the relationship between security concerns and behavioral intention to adopt the e-invoicing service. However, surprisingly findings of this study found that performance expectation and facilitating conditions were not significant factors. In another context, Sabi et al. (2017) investigated the factors that impact diffusion, adoption, and usage of cloud computing at educational institutions in sub-Saharan Africa. Results of this study found that socio-cultural factors, usefulness, results demonstrability and data security significantly impact ICT experts and decision makers' propensity to recommend adoption of cloud computing in the universities.

3. RESEARCH DESIGN AND METHODOLOGY

This research aims at investigating the determinants prohibiting Jordanian organizations from moving to the cloud. Cloud computing paradigm is still quite new to the most of Jordanian organizations. In addition, there is lack of research in this area and this is more evident in developing countries. Due to the insufficient empirical work in the cloud computing field and a notably need to get rich data, this study was considered exploratory in nature, so that a qualitative approach mainly using semi-structured interviews was adopted as the main data collection tool for this research. The use of qualitative methods, such as interviews, has been suggested for exploratory research when little is known about the phenomenon of interest and when there is a need to identify unanticipated or new issues in regard to the area of study (Sekaran and Bougie, 2010). In this research, therefore, six full-length interviews were conducted with key ICT officials and experts within the Jordanian landscape of cloud computing were conducted. Open-ended questions were chosen to put the interviewee at ease giving them the ability to respond in their own words using their own structure. Data also came from secondary sources that included published work in peer reviewed academic journals, high impact journals and reviews, media releases and websites, in addition to documents obtained from the sample's officials.

An interview protocol was prepared to guide the interviewing process. Data collection took place between November 2015 and February 2016. As mentioned earlier, six direct face-to-face full-length semi-structured interviews were conducted with ICT officials and cloud computing experts of a set of firms operating in different industries in the Jordanian market in an attempt to meet the main objectives of this research. Every target out of the whole six firms has a different field of business than the other; this is demonstrated in Table 2, and all the targets are located in Amman, the capital city of Jordan as a matter of determining the geographical coordinates of the target. The interviews have been performed at each firm's location. The interviews lasted between 40 and 60 minutes. All interviews were audio recorded but only after all participants approved the recording. Data was then transcribed, proof-read, and then analyzed using content analysis techniques as described by (Miles and Huberman, 1994; Al-Debei and Avison, 2010).

Having all interviews in hands, the transcribed data of the six interviews went through preparation and editing processes to make it ready for the analysis. The resulted textual data was then aggregated with the hand notes of the researchers and the joined content was qualitatively analyzed. The analysis procedure has been performed using NVIVO 10.0 software. It has been widely advised to use different computer-aided examination for qualitative data interpretation and analysis as supported by Charmaz

Table 2. List of Interviewees

ID	Interviewee's Position	Industry	Interview Date	Duration
1	ICT Consultant	Telecommunications	Nov 25, 2015	40 min
2	Executive Director	Consultancy	Nov 30, 2015	50 min
3	Director of ICT	ICT	Dec 3, 2015	60 min
4	Business Development Manager	ICT	Dec 30, 2015	60 min
5	IT Manager	Banking	Jan 20, 2016	45 min
6	CIO	Aviation	Feb 2, 2016	60 min

(2000). This route of data analysis has been selected due to the proven efficacy, accuracy and minimum amounts of systemic errors of the resulting outcomes when compared to conventional old-fashioned analysis approaches.

NVIVO is a computer assisted qualitative data analysis package, settled by QSR International (Bazeley and Richards, 2000). This software offers a set of functions that support the coding and recovery of text. Another remarkable privilege is that it assists researches to write down memos during the analysis process (Gibbs, 2002). In an attempt to conquer reliable and informative data out of the interviews, each single interview has skillfully created a transcript that was saved in a distinct word processor document. This has enabled sustaining fertility of the interviews data. Afterwards, all documents were imported in NVIVO for reading, analysis and coding. The main objective of the analysis was to transform data into insights and findings so as to make a sense out of it. During the analysis, as list of ideas emerge, ideas were grouped based on significant headings to form the concepts. Next, related concepts were aggregated in categories to form the themes that constitute the results of this research. The emerging themes were then examined based on their intensity, depth, and specificity with the research questions, with additional emphasis given to comments that were frequently repeated or refuted by the interviewees (Marshall and Rossman, 1999; Al-Debei and Avison, 2010). The results are then presented in a narrative form granting detailed insights into the main factors hindering cloud computing adoption by organizations in Jordan.

4. RESULTS AND DISCUSSION

4.1. Technological Factors

The main factors hindering the adoption of cloud computing in Jordan was found to be related to security, privacy, trust, and compatibility & integration requirements. Security risks can be described as risks associated with remote data hosting, virtualized and shared resources, and data transfer over the Internet (Subashini and Kavitha, 2011). Our analysis revealed that there are huge concerns about data confidentiality and security risks when it comes to cloud computing adoption by organizations in Jordan. Consistent with previous studies (e.g. Lian et al., 2014; Aleem and Sprott, 2013; Gupta et al., 2013; Kshetri, 2013), our analysis revealed that security risks present key challenges for widespread adoption of cloud in Jordan. For example, interviewee 1 explained that, "Security and privacy are considered as the most important barriers to adopt cloud computing. The level of security and privacy must be listed in the Service Level Agreement (SLA), usually the authentication mechanism implies high level of security, providers must enhance security over the rendered applications in different ways such as username and passwords, biometrics and card plus password, as otherwise data will be easy to be unofficially disclosed or hacked". Interviewee 6 also explained that "One of the reasons of dealing with global service provider is that we must follow specific security standards, and the global provider commit and achieve that", interviewee 4 comported with interviewee 6 by saying "I think that global provider such as Amazon will invest much more on security aspects than our organization regarding our data". While interviewee 5 opposed with the two previous interviewees and connected security with trust when he said, "Our provider is local because this gives us higher trust and security…" Indeed, security concerns have been highlighted as a main technological issue in cloud adoption literature (Lian et al., 2014; Aleem & Sprott, 2013; Gupta et al., 2013; Kshetri, 2013; Marston et al., 2013; Morgan & Conboy, 2013; Mohammed, 2011; Sultan, 2011; Zhang et al., 2010). Security remains a major obstacle for many enterprises to migrate to the cloud. A recent survey conducted by the International Data Corporation reviled that security was the main cloud computing adoption concern and about 75% of respondents reported that they had significant concerns about security (Sultan, 2011). Cloud computing security risk incident has happened when Google, a major cloud computing provider had its systems attacked and hacked (Markoff and Barboza, 2010). Therefore, securing both data and communication is really important for both cloud service providers and consumers.

Privacy is also still an area of concern to organizations in Jordan when it comes to cloud computing. In public cloud model, service providers manage the physical location(s) of the data that are being stored. Therefore, consumers have real concerns about privacy, data security, data ownership and audit, especially if these providers are located in another country (Kshetri, 2013; Marston et al., 2013). Data privacy and protection barriers are keeping down wide scale of cloud adoption by organizations in general. Our analysis also revealed that there are many issues related to the concept of trust in service providers. This can be referred to as Institution-based trust which can be described as the degree to which the organization believes that effective third-party guarantees are in place to assure the fulfillment of the client's expectations (Gefen et al., 2006). One of trust related issues that was highlighted in our study is the nature of cloud service provider based on its location; whether it is local or global provider. Findings regarding this issue were conflicting. For example, when interviewee 2 was asked if they trust local provider more than global provider, he replied: "I had an experience with global service provider and also with a local service provider and the global one was more reliable from my own perspective" then he noted: "the principles of cloud are not tied to a specific geographic area". However when interviewees 1 and 5 were asked the same question, answers were different from the previous one and they agreed that local provider can be more trusted; interviewee 1 said: "Despite the fact that global provider can provide you with better prices and service, you will feel more safe to deal with local provider also some problems could be solved easily due to personal relationships". Interviewee 5 said: "Our provider is local because this gives us higher levels of trust and security". Then he pointed out to a problem they have faced and that it was solved easily because their provider is local. Another issue is that the decision of adopting cloud might be related to the concept of trust; Interviewee 6 stated: "Adoption of cloud computing is based on two main factors: risk and trust. Perceived value can be also added as a third factors…" Our analysis also revealed that the concept of trust can be related to other concepts such as, reliability, availability and security. For example, regarding the relation with availability and reliability, interviewee 6 said: "We are dealing with a trusted and reliable provider such as Microsoft to guarantee service availability and avoid time down cases". Interviewee 2 agreed with him when he said: "One of the risks is to lose service then you do not know where to go after this so we need trusted providers". Regarding relation with security interviewee 2 also said: "Risks of security and trust will rise because of the distributed nature of cloud". Trust can be considered as a determinant or a challenge to adopt cloud when it comes to Supply Chain Management (SCM) and Customer Relationship Management (CRM) systems, interviewee 1 stated: "It is very difficult for cloud to support SCM, because within SCM you do not have your information only but your suppliers' information as well so you need their approval to put this information on the cloud". The same idea is for CRM, organizations need to get the approval of their customers to put their data over cloud thus they can maintain trust-based relationship.

Compatibility and Integration requirements was also identified as one of the factors hindering the adoption of cloud computing in Jordan. Compatibility is the extent to which an innovation or new technology is recognized as harmonious with current values, past experience and the requirements of potential adopters (Rogers, 1995, p. 240). Compatibility can be considered as an essential factor in the decision of adopting an innovation (Rogers, 1995; Ching and Ellis, 2004). When enterprises think about adopting cloud, compatibility with existing applications would be a noticeable concern (Dargha, 2012; Heinle and Strebel, 2010). This concern stems from the little control that cloud customers have over the rendered computing platforms by the provider, this in turn force providers to assure flexibility, nevertheless, providers can change the rendered platforms whenever they want without having the customer approval (Leavitt, 2009). From the developer side, there is a growing attention toward compatibility, which is centered on achieving a high level of integration for the new technology (Kamal, 2006). Organizations need to integrate applications and data for variety of reasons such as adopting diverse separate service providers. Thus integration might become an important issue. This is what our analysis has revealed as interviewee 1 stated that "If cloud service provider renders certain services, then companies will be forced to go for different service provider. It is the same for websites and so on; this point has a positive aspect in which customer can distribute risk between all providers which in turn will decrease the risk. On the other hand, when taking all services from one provider, the risk will be higher because the customer will be highly dependent on the provider. On the other hand, dealing with one provider only makes it easier to integrate, coordinate and manage. If data will move from one system to another, many questions could be raised such as: how will the integration be done? Who will be in charge for the integration process? Is it possible that it will be an integrator cloud service provider which it's role to integrate between two different services? If we take two different services from two different providers and they are not compatible in term of technology, who will be responsible for that? Is there a need for integrator? All of these questions will be explicated in the future". Interviewee 6 noted about integration "When we deal with a big company like Microsoft, they commit to the SLA, integration is not big issue and small problems might occur but not major problems such as service down". The finding of this study is in line with previous studies such as (Alshamaila et al., 2013; Safari et al., 2015). However, this result in inconsistent with some of previous studies as well. For example, Low et al. (2011) found that compatibility has no significant effect on the adoption of cloud computing in Taiwan. One possible justification for this inconsistency is that the industries are different as the previous study focused on high-tech industry while the current study focused on ICT industry.

4.2. Organizational Factors

The main factors identified in this study as barriers for cloud computing adoption in Jordan from an organizational standpoint are: organizational culture in addition to top management support and the characteristics of CEOs. This study finds that organizational culture is one of the main significant organizational factors in adoption and implementation of cloud computing. This is consistent with previous studies which indicated that culture is one of the critical success factors for implementing IS/IT systems (Al-Hujran et al., 2015; Morgan and Conboy, 2013; Rosenberg, 2001). The deployment of a cloud computing service leads to drastic changes in the way IS/IT services are invented, developed, deployed, scaled, maintained and delivered. As a result, resistance to change from business users and more specifically the IT officials always emerges as one of the most noticeable barriers facing the successful utilization of cloud computing services (Marston et al., 2013; Morgan and Conboy, 2013). In this research, one of the points that have emerged from our analysis is IT officials' resistance to change their traditional IT environment because of their fear of losing control on ICT environment or losing their jobs. Interviewee 1 confirmed this point by stating: "IT officials are the people who usually recommend the implementation of new IT/IS systems. However, I believe that they would not recommend something that conflict with their interest. Also, people usually do not like to lose their knowledge power and to start learning new systems". On the same level of importance, IT officials assume that cloud computing would replace them and therefore would increase the possibility of losing their jobs. Interviewee 1 contemplated, "IT officials might think that they will lose their jobs and therefore they will not recommend cloud systems for their companies".

Other organizational factors that impact cloud computing adoption are top management support and the characteristics of CEOs. The results of this study is in line with previous studies such as (Oliveira et al., 2014; Alshamaila et al., 2013; Low et al., 2011). For example, Low et al. (2011) found that top management support has a significant effect on the adoption of cloud computing. Implementing cloud computing may involve business process reengineering and resources integration, therefore, top management support is necessary to boost commitment and to create a positive environment toward this innovation (Low et al., 2011). In this research, most of the interviewees indicate that a decision to adopt IS/IT system including cloud computing service is usually made by top management. This means that the adoption of cloud computing is heavily dependent on the top management knowledge and attitude toward this technology, whether as inhibitors or facilitators. Interviewee 1 stressed the importance of top management support and senior managers' characteristics by stating: "I worked in the IT industry for long time and I know that most of decision makers in different public and private organization here in Jordan do not see the value of implementing new technologies on their businesses. I believe that, the mentality of mangers in eastern part of the world is different than that of managers in the western part. Many of senior managers in this part of the world perceive that investment in technology is wasting of resources as they do not see the potential value of technology for businesses". He continued, "I strongly believe that this factor will be a strong barrier in front of cloud computing adoption, especially for large enterprises".

4.3. Environmental Factors

The main environmental factors negatively affecting the adoption of cloud computing technology in Jordan are regulatory frameworks and SLAs as contractual agreements between the cloud services provider and the company getting the service. Our result that suggest regulatory framework as one of the main impediments of cloud computing in Jordan is consistent with previous studies such as (Marston et al., 2013; Morgan and Conboy, 2013). However, this result in inconsistent with some of previous studies as well. For example, Oliveira et al. (2014) found that regulatory framework has no significant effect on the adoption of cloud computing in Portugal. A plausible justification for this inconsistency in the importance of regulatory framework in cloud computing adoption could be related to the fact that Jordan represents late adopters' context for cloud computing technology as opposed to early adopters' context of European counterparts.

As an environmental factor, regulations can be considered as a main issue when adopting cloud computing (Morgan and Conboy, 2013). For instance, central bank of Jordan does not allow Jordanian banks to store their critical data (core banking) on the cloud. In addition, Delmas (2002) remarked that organizational non-compliance with surrounded regulations may transform extra transaction expenses and potential legitimate conclusions coming about because of these activities. Here in Jordan we do not have specific regulations or regulatory framework that deal with cloud computing aspects, which may limit many customers from adopting the cloud. According to our interviewees, interviewee 3 stated "Cloud in Jordan is still in its infancy stage, we still have many barriers related to laws and regulations, and customers may wonder who can take backup for my data? Who will be accountable in the case of my data loss? How can I guarantee that my data will not be disclosed to a third-party or being sold to my competitors? There must be regulations and laws to organize all of that". When he was asked if there is a tendency from Jordanian government toward stating a regulatory framework for the cloud, he replied "There is a tendency, but we in general are slow in taking actions, we still need the regulators to be more aware of the cloud computing technology. I think it will take a long time to develop regulatory framework regarding cloud computing in Jordan". He added "Regulations play a critical role in public cloud because in this case, there are two separate parties that need regulations and laws to govern their relationship, while in the private cloud, instructions will be enough because it is internally". Interviewee 6 noted "Regulations limit us from hosting our core banking on the cloud". When he was asked if the bank will be more relaxed in case of regulations existence, he replied "maybe yes, because the bank will be more safe if its data is stored and managed internally, the reason of that that I have storage for my data in addition to a maintenance contract with our hardware supplier and insurance in the case of any danger, there will be a company that will compensate us, but when giving our data to local provider what will be the insurance and guarantee?". Interviewee 4 stated "Regulations can be considered as a benefit and a threat at the same time". He added "I know about six banks in Jordan using virtualization because at the end of the day it is economically much more cost effective. They are just not ready to give piece of their core banking out to the public cloud, because of security perspective, things like that and regulations as well, like for example I was working with a bank in Jordan that have branches in Palestine so I told them why do you have two separate data centers: one for the branches in Jordan and another for the branches in Palestine. The answer was very much about regulations as the regulations in Palestine monetary authority does not allow them to store and manage their data outside the country. Interviewee 2 agreed interviewee 4 by saying "Regulations considered as double edge; sometimes regulations become bottleneck. However, being just completely free and acting without any regulations is a problem".

Our research also revealed that SLAs are vital aspects that need to be carefully considered before moving to the cloud. Based on our qualitative research, we found out that SLAs are considered to be a hindering factor affecting the adoption of cloud computing in Jordan. SLAs are contractual arrangements between the cloud services provider and the customer that specifies many terms such as availability, serviceability, quality of service (QoS), penalties in case of violation terms, and are considered as a support for the pay-per-consumption. However, SLAs constitute a big impediment in front of cloud customers toward procuring cloud services (Mujinga and Chipangura, 2011). Sometimes it is difficult to enforce and monitor SLAs (Keller and Ludwig, 2003). In addition, each cloud provider has its own terminologies and concepts that maybe misleading and misunderstood by the customer. In addition, cloud providers may manipulate the terms to favor their desired selling points. For example, Aleem and Sprott (2013) reported that 65.7 percent of respondents agree that SLAs are viewed as being unsatisfactory forms of protection that weigh heavily in favor of the cloud provider. This in turn makes it challenging for customers to identify the right provider that will perfectly suite their needs and help them in achieving their desired business goals. SLA varies from one provider to another according to the rendered services provided by those providers. As such, it is challenging to make all providers agree on a standardized framework for modelling SLAs (i.e. writing the same terms and concepts). In this context, interviewee 3 highlighted the significances and the need for a clear and formal methodology to handle cloud computing SLAs, he stated: "SLA is very important when it comes to cloud computing. This contract will be the main reference for both; consumers and service providers. Therefore, to avoid disputes, cloud customers need to manage this document properly. Before signing, IT department has to check technical and quality of service issues, legal department has to check legal issues carefully, and senior management has to review business aspects". Interviewee 4 also commented about the importance of SLA by stating: "SLAs are very important, I am using something outside my organization, so I need to have a contract which states what can I expect, and for example, I am working with cloud service provider and services are down for a day, then I am out of business for a day. Accordingly, we must have a really good agreement on what you can expect from each other with of course penalties…" Accordingly, we believe that cloud computing SLA vetting process is very critical as potential clients need to be thoroughly aware of the terms and conditions and perhaps legal council should be involved at this stage (Aleem and Sprott, 2013).

5. IMPLICATIONS

5.1. Theoretical Implications

Organizations in developing countries lag behind their Western counterparts due to lack of cutting edge technology required for running their businesses (Sabi et al., 2017). However, while the current literature (refer to Section 2.6) provides a better understanding of cloud computing technologies usage in Western countries and countries in the Asian-Pacific region, empirical research that rigorously explore the proposed factors that might influence the adoption of cloud computing in other parts of the world such as the Arabian Peninsula is needed. This gap is significant given cultural and social characteristics of Arab nations differ significantly from those of the Western nations (Baker et al, 2010). Our literature review also revealed that there is a limited number of studies have evaluated the adoption of cloud computing on the organizational level. Although cloud computing has different service and deployment model, the literature has not focused on identifying the adoption of different models. In addition, prior research on cloud computing adoption has largely focused on the operational and technological aspects of cloud computing and their impact on cloud computing adoption (Schneider and Sunyaev, 2016). While the current literature provides a fundamental understanding of cloud computing, empirical studies that comprehensively explain the diffusion and adoption of cloud computing in organizations from socio-technical perspectives are still required (Alharbi, et al., 2016; Marston et al., 2011; Low et al., 2011; Lin and Chen, 2012; Hsu et al., 2014; Oliveira et al., 2014). Moreover, and based on our extensive literature review, we found out that most of previous studies explored cloud computing adoption from the viewpoint of the individual user (e.g. Arpaci, 2017; Sharma et al., 2016), but very little attention has been given to investigate cloud computing adoption from an organizational perspective.

5.2. Practical Implications

Our study results suggest that security, privacy, trust, in addition to compatibility and integration requirements are the main technological impediments for cloud computing adoption in Jordan. As security is a major concern for organization in Jordan, service providers should come up with new approaches that tackles these concerns. This might include partnerships to be established with local governmental agencies such as the ministry of information and communication technologies. In this case, cloud computing services will be offered by the service provider but through the local governmental agency which will be responsible for governance. This solution might help in significantly reducing consumers' security risks and concerns and in building trust in such services. Moreover, workshops and seminars can be held on a continuous basis by service providers to announce new developments and innovations related to security on the cloud. This would be also beneficial in raising the awareness of customers in this particular domain. As for data privacy, we believe that service providers need to highlight their approaches and strategies to handle data privacy in a very clear way to customers. Moreover, they might come up with innovative approaches to handle this. One idea is to allow customers to host data within their data center but to host or use their applications on the cloud. Another idea is that to have key management system or the encryption system hosted at the customer side and before data is transferred to the cloud it gets encrypted using the locally hosted key management system and then in its way back to the customer side where it gets decrypted.

The third identified challenge to cloud computing adoption in Jordan is trust. It was revealed in our study that some organizations in Jordan would have higher trust in service providers if the service providers host their data and applications on local cloud computing data centers. This implies that major service providers such as Amazon, Oracle, and Microsoft need to seriously think about expanding their cloud computing data centers' territories to include Middle East in general and the Arab world in particular for higher adoption rate of cloud computing technology. The fourth technological impediments that was identified in our study is related to compatibility and information requirements. This implies that organizations in Jordan need to adjust their organizations along with their processes to become compatible with cloud computing systems. Organizations need to effectively address their management style, culture of the organization, structure and integration of the processes to successfully utilize cloud computing solutions. This is essential as cloud computing should be compatible with the organization's policy, technology development environment, and business needs (Lin and Chen, 2012). Managers need also to work on changing existing business processes to be fully aligned with cloud computing solutions. It is also very critical that organizations work on establishing transparent information flow for better utilization of cloud computing.

Our study results also suggest that organizational culture, top management support, and characteristics of CEOs are the main organizational impediments for cloud computing adoption in Jordan. Indeed, the choice to deploy a cloud computing solution would lead to significant changes in the way technological services and products are designed, developed, deployed, scaled, maintained and delivered. Therefore, such a decision is usually confronted with significant resistance to change coming from technological resources within the organization as they might fear from losing their jobs. This implies that management need to manage the transition to cloud very carefully by allowing their IT personnel to adjust their skills and capabilities to suit the cloud computing landscape. Regular meetings with IT personnel in which management illustrates their cloud computing strategy and keeps IT personnel in their future plans would help in moving to the cloud more smoothly. Further, our study revealed that top management support and the characteristics of CEOs is critical to cloud computing adoption. Indeed, the adoption of cloud computing is heavily dependent on the top management knowledge and attitude toward this technology. This implies that cloud service providers need to focus on highlighting cloud computing technology along with its benefits and value to top managements within organizations in Jordan. One idea is to frequently design roundtable events with C-level personnel within organizations in Jordan to make sure that they have enough knowledge about this innovative platform and positive attitudes towards cloud computing technology. This would help in making top management within Jordanian organizations perceive cloud computing as an asset of high strategic importance and value which is helpful to them in enabling their organizations to sustain their competitive advantages. This is significant as otherwise top management within Jordanian organization might delay their investments in cloud computing until they learn more about it.

Finally, our study results revealed that regulatory framework and SLA are two key environmental impediments of cloud computing adoption in Jordan. Regulatory framework is very critical to cloud computing adoption and especially in developing countries. This implies that Jordan should develop its legislations in the domain of cloud computing so to support and at the same time protect the use of cloud computing. The existence of such legislations and regulatory framework would facilitate the adoption of cloud computing solutions by Jordanian organizations. Another important environmental factor that significantly and negatively affects the adoption of cloud computing in Jordan is related to SLAs. This implies that cloud service providers need to write their SLA in a more clear form and to reduce Jargon and complex terminologies. SLAs need also to be fair and to include articles for the benefits of both; the provider and the customer to achieve a win-win situation. We also recommend that cloud service providers to include warranties for customers to encourage them to confidently move into the cloud landscape.

6. CONCLUSION AND LIMITATIONS

This study aimed at identifying the factors hindering cloud computing adoption by organizations in Jordan. Findings of this study revealed that cloud computing utilizations by Jordanian companies still at its early stages. Indeed, it was clear that there is a low-level of cloud computing adoption by Jordanian companies. According to interviewees, both service providers and consumers still immature enough to adopt cloud computing. Some of organizations in Jordan implement virtualization as the first level of cloud computing. Other organizations adopt mail and hosting services. On the other hand, service providers in Jordan are also still immature in the area of cloud computing and offer only limited cloud computing services. Major players in the Jordanian IT industry such as IT providers and telecommunication companies are offering the basic levels of cloud computing such as data center visualization, servers, virtual firewall and websites hosting. Only few of them offer advance cloud services such as SaaS. This issue has been explicitly expressed as Interviewee 1 stated: "In the area of cloud computing we have many IT companies who provide visualization and hosting services while very few offer software and application as a service which we really need". Interviewee 3 confirmed this point by saying: "Many companies and IT professionals in Jordan talk about cloud computing, but few of them know exactly what they want and need from cloud computing. Although our institution is considered as a high-tech institution in Jordan and therefore should be one of the early adopters of technological innovations, only mail hosting service is implemented".

Interestingly and despite the lack of adoption of cloud computing technology in Jordan, it was found out that cloud computing is perceived useful by Jordanian companies. Consistent with previous literature (e.g. Alshamaila et al., 2013; Gupta et al., 2013; Sultan, 2011), our findings have shown that cloud computing is economically feasible solution for SME's because they have limited resources and financial capabilities to invest in IT. According to interviewees, most of the start-ups use global cloud computing providers where they host their applications, website or cloud service. Cost savings is the first perceived advantage of cloud computing, and thus cloud computing may seem very attractive to SME's, as interviewee 1 stated "SME's do not have the financial capability to buy software applications and the needed infrastructure, thus cloud computing gives them a competitive advantage in which it lowers the cost of applications and the needed infrastructure, need for less manpower (people) to manage, maintain applications. Moreover, with cloud computing, SMEs do not have to buy licenses for the software itself, all of this will be the responsibility of the provider". He added that "SMEs usually have a small number of employees so if they will not use the cloud, the utilization of applications will be decreased, in this case cost of the application will outweigh the benefit of the application, but when using the cloud, it will be more feasible and the benefit will outweigh the cost". Interviewee 3 claimed "let us assume I want to initiate a company and I want to decide which will be more efficient solution to be considered, adopting the cloud or having the service within my company, I will find out that cloud computing option is less costly and as a start-up will go for it". All interviewees also agreed that in the near future SMEs will be the early adopters of cloud computing as it is a cost-effective option for them. as interviewee 4 stated "if you examine SMEs, you can easily find out that the majority do not have the budget for the IT infrastructure needed so as to run the business smoothly". He added "I think when people start using cloud computing services then they can start perceiving the associated benefits. interviewee 1 confirmed that by saying "I think that SMEs will be the pioneers in adopting cloud computing in Jordan; not the large enterprises because they are modest in terms of economics (financial capabilities), that means that they sometimes take risk because they have no other choices, they will go to cloud over building needed infrastructure for their applications".

To summarize, results revealed that cloud computing makes eminent sense for SMEs; however, there are significant technical, organizational and environmental issues which need to be tackled before cloud computing services are effectively used by organizations in Jordan. Based on applying TOE framework, findings of this study were classified into several technological, organizational and environmental factors that adversely impact cloud computing adoption. The identified technological factors were security, privacy concerns, trust, and compatibility. On the other hand, the main identified organizational factors were culture, top management support, and characteristics of CEOs. Finally, the main identified factors that are hindering cloud computing adoption by organizations in Jordan from environmental standpoint were the need for regulatory framework and SLAs contractual agreements.

As with all studies, this study is not free of limitations. The major limitation is derived from the sample size and the geographical location of the sample which is limited to only six full-length interviews that were conducted with ICT officials and cloud computing experts of a set of firms operating located in Jordan. Although these findings are believed to be applicable to other organizations in Arab countries that share demographic characteristics with Jordan, our limited-number of interviews may not be representative of the entire country or the Arab region. Further study in other countries would most likely strengthen and validate the findings of this study. Second, this study investigated the determents of cloud computing adoption in general and did not specify a cloud computing service model. However, determinant factors may diverge according to the cloud service model. In other words, the determinant factors of decisions to adopt SaaS model may considerably differ from the determinant factors of decisions to adopt IaaS or PaaS service models (Schneider and Sunyaev, 2016). Therefore, this paper calls for further research on the adoption of a specific cloud service model as well as a comparative research on the adoption of different cloud computing service models.

REFERENCES

Al-Debei, M. M., & Avison, D. (2010). Developing a unified framework of the business model concept. *European Journal of Information Systems*, *19*(3), 359–376. doi:10.1057/ejis.2010.21

Al-Hujran, O., Chatfield, A., Migdadi, M., & Al-Debei, M. (2015). Strategic Imperative of Influencing Citizen Attitude in Increasing E-government Adoption and Use: An Empirical Study. *Computers in Human Behavior*, *53*, 189–203. doi:10.1016/j.chb.2015.06.025

Aleem, A., & Sprott, C. R. (2013). Let me in the cloud: Analysis of the benefit and risk assessment of cloud platform. *Journal of Financial Crime*, *20*(1), 6–24. doi:10.1108/13590791311287337

Alharbi, F., Atkins, A., & Stanier, C. (2016). Understanding the determinants of Cloud Computing adoption in Saudi healthcare organisations. *Complex & Intelligent Systems*, *2*(3), 155–171. doi:10.100740747-016-0021-9

Alshamaila, Y., Papagiannidis, S., & Li, F. (2013). Cloud computing adoption by SMEs in the north east of England: A multi-perspective framework. *Journal of Enterprise Information Management*, *26*(3), 250–275. doi:10.1108/17410391311325225

Armbrust, M., Fox, A., Griffith, R., Joseph, A. D., Katz, R., Konwinski, A., & Zaharia, M. (2010). A view of cloud computing. *Communications of the ACM*, *53*(4), 50–58. doi:10.1145/1721654.1721672

Arpaci, I. (2017). Antecedents and consequences of cloud computing adoption in education to achieve knowledge management. *Computers in Human Behavior*, *70*, 382–390. doi:10.1016/j.chb.2017.01.024

Baker, E., Al-Gahtani, S., & Hubona, G. (2010). Cultural impacts on acceptance and adoption of information technology in a developing country. *Journal of Global Information Management*, *18*(3), 35–58. doi:10.4018/jgim.2010070102

Bazeley, P., & Richards, L. (2000). *The Nvivo Qualitative Project Book*. London: Sage Publications. doi:10.4135/9780857020079

Borgman, H. P., Bahli, B., Heier, H., & Schewski, F. (2013, January). Cloudrise: Exploring cloud computing adoption and governance with the TOE framework. In *46th Hawaii International Conference on System Sciences* (pp. 4425–4435). Washington, DC: IEEE. 10.1109/HICSS.2013.132

Charmaz, K. (2000). Grounded theory: objectivist and constructivist methods. In N. K. Denzin & Y. S. Lincoln (Eds.), *Handbook of Qualitative Research* (2nd ed., pp. 509–535). Thousand Oaks, CA: Sage.

Ching, H. L., & Ellis, P. (2004). Marketing in cyberspace: What factors drive e-commerce adoption? *Journal of Marketing Management*, *20*(3-4), 409–429. doi:10.1362/026725704323080470

Dargha, R. (2012). Cloud computing: from hype to reality: fast tracking cloud adoption. In *Proceedings of the International Conference on Advances in Computing, Communications and Informatics* (pp. 440-445). ACM. 10.1145/2345396.2345469

Delmas, M. A. (2002). The diffusion of environmental management standards in Europe and in the United States: An institutional perspective. *Policy Sciences*, *35*(1), 91–119. doi:10.1023/A:1016108804453

EMC. (2011). *Cloud Infrastructure and Services Student Guide*. EMC Education Services.

Fong, M. W. (2009). Technology leapfrogging for developing countries. In *Encyclopedia of Information Science and Technology* (2nd ed., pp. 3707–3713). IGI Global. doi:10.4018/978-1-60566-026-4.ch591

Gangwar, H., Date, H., & Ramaswamy, R. (2015). Understanding determinants of cloud computing adoption using an integrated TAM-TOE model. *Journal of Enterprise Information Management*, *28*(1), 107–130. doi:10.1108/JEIM-08-2013-0065

Gibbs, G. (2002). *Qualitative Data Analysis: Explorations with Nvivo*. London: Open University Press.

Gupta, P., Seetharaman, A., & Raj, J. R. (2013). The usage and adoption of cloud computing by small and medium businesses. *International Journal of Information Management*, *33*(5), 861–874. doi:10.1016/j.ijinfomgt.2013.07.001

Heinle, C., & Strebel, J. (2010). IaaS adoption determinants in enterprises. In Economics of Grids, Clouds, Systems, and Services (pp. 93-104). Springer Berlin Heidelberg. doi:10.1007/978-3-642-15681-6_7

Hsu, P. F., Ray, S., & Li-Hsieh, Y. Y. (2014). Examining cloud computing adoption intention, pricing mechanism, and deployment model. *International Journal of Information Management*, *34*(4), 474–488. doi:10.1016/j.ijinfomgt.2014.04.006

Kamal, M. M. (2006). IT innovation adoption in the government sector: Identifying the critical success factors. *Journal of Enterprise Information Management*, *19*(2), 192–222. doi:10.1108/17410390610645085

Keller, A., & Ludwig, H. (2003). The WSLA framework: Specifying and monitoring service level agreements for web services. *Journal of Network and Systems Management*, *11*(1), 57–81. doi:10.1023/A:1022445108617

Kim, W., Kim, S. D., Lee, E., & Lee, S. (2009). Adoption issues for cloud computing. In *Proceedings of the 7th International Conference on Advances in Mobile Computing and Multimedia* (pp. 2–5). New York, NY: ACM.

Kshetri, N. (2013). Privacy and security issues in cloud computing: The role of institutions and institutional evolution. *Telecommunications Policy*, *37*(4), 372–386. doi:10.1016/j.telpol.2012.04.011

Leavitt, N. (2009). Is cloud computing really ready for prime time? *Computer*, (1): 15–20.

Lee, J. (2004). Discriminant analysis of technology adoption behavior: A case of Internet technologies in small businesses. *Journal of Computer Information Systems*, *44*(4), 57.

Lian, J. W. (2015). Critical factors for cloud based e-invoice service adoption in Taiwan: An empirical study. *International Journal of Information Management*, *35*(1), 98–109. doi:10.1016/j.ijinfomgt.2014.10.005

Lian, J. W., Yen, D. C., & Wang, Y. T. (2014). An exploratory study to understand the critical factors affecting the decision to adopt cloud computing in Taiwan hospital. *International Journal of Information Management*, *34*(1), 28–36. doi:10.1016/j.ijinfomgt.2013.09.004

Lin, A., & Chen, N. C. (2012). Cloud computing as an innovation: Perception, attitude, and adoption. *International Journal of Information Management*, *32*(6), 533–540. doi:10.1016/j.ijinfomgt.2012.04.001

Low, C., Chen, Y., & Wu, M. (2011). Understanding the determinants of cloud computing adoption. *Industrial Management & Data Systems, 111*(7), 1006–1023. doi:10.1108/02635571111161262

Markoff, J., & Barboza, D. (2010). Researchers Trace Data Theft to Intruders in China. *The New York Times.*

Marshall, C., & Rossman, G. (1999). *Designing Qualitative Research.* London: Sage.

Marston, S., Li, Z., Bandyopadhyay, S., Zhang, J., & Ghalsasi, A. (2011). Cloud computing—The business perspective. *Decision Support Systems, 51*(1), 176–189. doi:10.1016/j.dss.2010.12.006

Mather, T., Kumaraswamy, S., & Latif, S. (2009). *Cloud security and privacy: An enterprise perspective on risks and compliance.* Sebastopol, CA: O'Reilly Media.

Mell, P., & Grance, T. (2011). The NIST Definition of Cloud Computing. *Communications of the ACM, 53*(6), 50.

Miles, M., & Huberman, A. (1994). *Qualitative Data Analysis: An Expanded Sourcebook.* California: Sage Publications.

Mohammed, D. (2011). Security in cloud computing: an analysis of key drivers and constraints. *Information Security Journal: A Global Perspective, 20*(3), 123-127.

Morgan, L., & Conboy, K. (2013). Key factors impacting cloud computing adoption. *Computer, 46*(10), 97–99. doi:10.1109/MC.2013.362

Mujinga, M., & Chipangura, B. (2011). Cloud computing concerns in developing economies.

Nuseibeh, H. (2011). Adoption of cloud computing in organizations. In *AMCIS Proceedings.*

Office of the Privacy Commissioner of Canada. (2007). *Fact sheet: Privacy impact assessments.* Retrieved from http://www.privcom.gc.ca/

Oliveira, T., Thomas, M., & Espadanal, M. (2014). Assessing the determinants of cloud computing adoption: An analysis of the manufacturing and services sectors. *Information & Management, 51*(5), 497–510. doi:10.1016/j.im.2014.03.006

Pan, M.-J., & Jang, W. (2008). Determinants of the adoption of enterprise resource planning within the technology-organization-environment framework: Taiwan's communications. *Journal of Computer Information Systems, 48*(3), 94–102.

Prince, J. D. (2011). Introduction to cloud computing. *Journal of Electronic Resources in Medical Libraries, 8*(4), 449–458. doi:10.1080/15424065.2011.626360

Purkayastha, S., & Braa, J. (2013). Big data analytics for developing countries–using the cloud for operational BI in health. *The Electronic Journal on Information Systems in Developing Countries, 59.*

Rogers, E. M. (1995). *Diffusion of innovations* (4th ed.). New York, NY: Free Press.

Rosenberg, M. J. (2001). *E-learning: Strategies for delivering knowledge in the digital age* (Vol. 3). New York: McGraw-Hill.

Sabi, H. M., Uzoka, F. M. E., Langmia, K., Njeh, F. N., & Tsuma, C. K. (2017). A cross-country model of contextual factors impacting cloud computing adoption at universities in sub-Saharan Africa. *Information Systems Frontiers*.

Safari, F., Safari, N., & Hasanzadeh, A. (2015). The adoption of software-as-a-service (SaaS): Ranking the determinants. *Journal of Enterprise Information Management*, *28*(3), 400–422. doi:10.1108/JEIM-02-2014-0017

Salleh, S. M., Teoh, S. Y., & Chan, C. (2012). Cloud enterprise systems: A review of literature and its adoption. In PACIS (p. 76). Association for Information Systems. AIS Electronic Library (AISeL).

Schneider, S., & Sunyaev, A. (2016). Determinant factors of cloud-sourcing decisions: Reflecting on the IT outsourcing literature in the era of cloud computing. *Journal of Information Technology*, *31*(1), 1–31. doi:10.1057/jit.2014.25

Sekaran, U., & Bougie, R. (2010). *Research Methods for Business: A Skill Building Approach*. UK: John Wiley and Sons.

Sharma, S. K., Al-Badi, A. H., Govindaluri, S. M., & Al-Kharusi, M. H. (2016). Predicting motivators of cloud computing adoption: A developing country perspective. *Computers in Human Behavior*, *62*, 61–69. doi:10.1016/j.chb.2016.03.073

Shimba, F. (2010). *Cloud computing: Strategies for cloud computing adoption*. Unpublished master's thesis, Dublin Institute of Technology, Dublin.

Sultan, N. (2010). Cloud computing for education: A new dawn? *International Journal of Information Management*, *30*(2), 109–116. doi:10.1016/j.ijinfomgt.2009.09.004

Sultan, N. A. (2011). Reaching for the "cloud": How SMEs can manage. *International Journal of Information Management*, *31*(3), 272–278. doi:10.1016/j.ijinfomgt.2010.08.001

Svantesson, D., & Clarke, R. (2010). Privacy and consumer risks in cloud computing. *Computer Law & Security Review*, *26*(4), 391–397. doi:10.1016/j.clsr.2010.05.005

Tornatzky, L. G., & Fleischer, M. (1990). *The processes of technological innovation*. Lexington, MA: Lexington Books.

Trigueros-Preciado, S., Pérez-González, D., & Solana-González, P. (2013). Cloud computing in industrial SMEs: Identification of the barriers to its adoption and effects of its application. *Electronic Markets*, *23*(2), 105–114. doi:10.100712525-012-0120-4

Venters, W., & Whitley, E. A. (2012). A critical review of cloud computing: Researching desires and realities. *Journal of Information Technology*, *27*(3), 179–197. doi:10.1057/jit.2012.17

Wen, K. W., & Chen, Y. (2010). E-business value creation in Small and Medium Enterprises: A US study using the TOE framework. *International Journal of Electronic Business*, *8*(1), 80–100. doi:10.1504/IJEB.2010.030717

Wu, W. W., Lan, L. W., & Lee, Y. T. (2013). Factors hindering acceptance of using cloud services in university: A case study. *The Electronic Library*, *31*(1), 84–98. doi:10.1108/02640471311299155

Zhang, Q., Cheng, L., & Boutaba, R. (2010). Cloud computing: State-of-the-art and research challenges. *Journal of Internet Services and Applications*, *1*(1), 7–18. doi:10.100713174-010-0007-6

Zhu, K., Dong, S., Xu, S. X., & Kraemer, K. L. (2006). Innovation diffusion in global contexts: Determinants of post-adoption digital transformation of European companies. *European Journal of Information Systems*, *15*(6), 601–616. doi:10.1057/palgrave.ejis.3000650

This research was previously published in the International Journal of E-Business Research (IJEBR), 14(3); edited by Payam Hanafizadeh and Jeffrey Hsu, pages 77-94, copyright year 2018 by IGI Publishing (an imprint of IGI Global).

Chapter 67
The Benefits of Cloud Computing:
Evidence From Greece

Georgios Chatzithanasis
Harokopio University, Greece

Christos Michalakelis
Harokopio University, Greece

ABSTRACT

Cloud computing is gaining ground in the global ICT market and day by day a significant number of Small and Medium Enterprises (SMEs) are adopting cloud services with sole purpose to improve their business environment and become more efficient, competitive and productive. Migrating a business IT infrastructure to the cloud offers reduction on server and storage costs, software maintenance expenditures, network and energy expenses as well as costs associated with disaster recovery. Since the cloud computing model works on a "pay-as-you-go" basis, it provides the option to pay for what is used. Thus, its adoption can offer slow start-up or expansion costs, creating an environment for rapid innovation and development. Into that context, this article presents the Greek side of cloud evolution through two representative case studies, the migration of an IT system of a Greek industry, from an in-house data center to Google Cloud and a study of the "in-house" IT infrastructure of the National Confederation of Hellenic Commerce. Findings from the Greek industry, indicate that the cloud proposal could cost 50%, or 24% less per month (depending on the solution). As far as the National Confederation of Hellenic Commerce is concerned, the article proposes only a new measure of security using Cloud services for reasons that will be discussed at the case study. Both case studies take into account the present costs of the IT system (energy consumption, third party contracts and maintenance) and propose alternatives through cloud migration. Results indicate that cloud computing offers benefits and significant cost savings for both studied cases, showing promising ways for the successful adoption of the cloud.

DOI: 10.4018/978-1-5225-8176-5.ch067

Copyright © 2019, IGI Global. Copying or distributing in print or electronic forms without written permission of IGI Global is prohibited.

1. INTRODUCTION

According to (Mell & Grance, 2011) cloud computing is a model for enabling ubiquitous, convenient, on-demand network access to a shared pool of configurable computing resources (e.g., networks, servers, storage, applications, and services) that can be rapidly provisioned and released with minimal management effort or service provider interaction.

This cloud model is composed of five essential characteristics, three service models, and four deployment models. At this time of its expansion, everybody should be familiar with the benefits and risks cloud computing bears. Before this paper analyses the two Greek adoption case studies, a short introduction to the cloud is included, for the sake of completeness. Briefly, according to (Hassan, 2011) these attributes characterize cloud computing:

- **On-demand Computing Model:** Organizations are able to escape from complex and expensive in-house infrastructure and choose the amount of resources they require for their operation;
- **Autonomous:** Clients are separated from the technical details of the cloud services they use;
- **Predefined Quality of Service:** Cloud providers state QoS terms in their service level agreements to inform clients about expected level of service;
- **Internet-based:** All cloud services are hosted beyond organizations and delivered over the Internet;
- **Easy-to-use:** Cloud providers offer easy-to-use interfaces that enable clients to make use of their services;
- **Scalable:** Clients are not limited with fixed amounts of resources. They can scale up and down at free will;
- **Inexpensive:** Cloud computing offers small-and-medium-sized enterprises (SMEs) a significantly lower-cost option than building an in-house infrastructure;
- **Subscription-based Model:** Clients subscribe to services they are interested in, and they are charged accordingly.

The architecture of cloud computing is pyramid shaped, starting with IaaS as a foundation and on top, SaaS (Varia, 2010). The main logic behind the pyramid shape, is that on the road to the top, the user is not required to know in detail how things work in the cloud:

- **Infrastructure-as-a-Service (IaaS):** IaaS provides hardware such as CPUs, memory, storage, networks, and load-balancers. The next architectures are based on IaaS in order to work;
- **Platform-as-a-Service (PaaS):** Supplies users with development and administration platforms that provide on-demand access to available hardware resources. Many PaaS platforms are available to enable access to IaaS resources;
- **Data-as-a-Service (DaaS):** Frees organizations from buying high-cost database engines and mass storage. This service offers database capabilities for storing client information;
- **Software-as-a-Service (SaaS):** The ultimate form of cloud resources that delivers software applications to clients in terms of accessible services. With SaaS, clients subscribe to applications offered by providers rather than building or buying them.

If the first pillar of this paper is the cloud computing, the second is the enterprises. The cloud services offer great amount of options, so every organization can enjoy the aspects of cloud it needs.

According to (Eurostat, 2016), 19% of EU enterprises proceeded with the adoption of cloud computing in 2014, mostly for hosting their e-mail systems and storing files in electronic form. 46% of those firms used advanced cloud services relating to financial and accounting software applications, customer relationship management or to the use of computing power to run business applications. In 2014, almost twice as many firms used public cloud servers (12%) as private cloud servers (7%), i.e. infrastructure for their exclusive use. Four out of ten enterprises (39%) using the cloud reported the risk of a security breach as the main limiting factor in the use of cloud computing services. A similar proportion (42%) of those not using the cloud reported insufficient knowledge of cloud computing as the main factor that prevented them from using it.

As shown in Figure 1, between two years (2014-2016) the EU-28 countries have increased their use of cloud computing by 2%. Greece should make an honest effort to untie itself from the 9% and harvest the potential of cloud computing.

2. THE CLOUD(Y) GREECE

Around the world other case studies have tried to estimate the cloud adoption diffusion in the private as well as the public sector. Additionally, new frameworks are proposed for a better understanding on the ways cloud computing can be encapsulated in every organization. In Australia for example, 24% of regional government councils around the country have implemented some adoption of cloud computing on their services. 14% have already made a full adoption of some public services (Ali, Soar, & Yong, 2016). In England efforts were made for the development of a cloud computing adoption model for SMEs (Alshamaila, Papagiannidis, & Li, 2013).

Figure 1. Use of cloud computing services, by economic activity and size, EU-28, 2014 and 2016

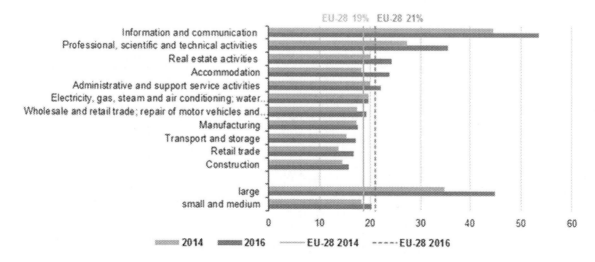

According to Eurostat, Table 1, in 2014 Greece has the 27th place among the European countries that buy Cloud services used over the internet. Unfortunately, 8% of Greek enterprises have adopted cloud computing on 2014. 2015 gave a spark of hope, with a small increase of 1% from 2014, but it is still stuck even in 2016. Greece is struggling to recover from the economic wounds that the Great Recession

Table 1. Eurostat findings (2016)

Country	2014	2015	2016
Finland	51	53	57
Iceland	43	-	-
Italy	40	-	22
Sweden	39	-	48
Denmark	38	37	42
Norway	29	38	40
Ireland	28	35	36
Netherlands	28	-	35
United Kingdom	24	-	35
Croatia	22	22	23
Belgium	21	25	28
Slovakia	19	20	18
Malta	17	25	28
Czech Republic	15	-	18
Estonia	15	-	23
Slovenia	15	17	22
Spain	14	15	18
Lithuania	13	16	17
Luxembourg	13	-	19
Portugal	13	-	18
France	12	-	17
Austria	12	-	17
F.Y.R.O.M	12	-	7
Germany	11	-	16
Cyprus	10	13	15
Bulgaria	8	5	7
Greece	8	9	9
Hungary	8	11	12
Latvia	6	8	8
Poland	6	7	8
Romania	5	8	7
Serbia	4	-	-

caused. It is only logical that many Greek enterprises are not paying any attention to new technological advances and they try to avoid extra costs in order to survive.

According to the Foundation for Economic and Industrial Research (Danchev, Tsakanikas, & Ventouris, 2011) cloud computing can bring substantial gains to the Greek economy. Cloud computing can generate savings amounting to € 4.8 billion over the next 10 years with the reduction of costs for equipment and maintenance. Through increased scalability and reduced barriers for new markets, cloud computing can boost Greek economy by € 5 billion. As a result of Cloud Computing adoption, more than 38,000 job openings by the end of 2020 will be created. In order to achieve these benefits, Greek businesses (and the public sector as a facilitator) should adopt cloud computing at least as fast as the country's major competitors in the global markets. If Greece achieves a 5-year transition to the cloud, while its competitors follow a 10-year transition path, the cloud dividend can reach € 21 billion with substantial employment gains over the medium term. In contrast, if technophobia and self-pity continues, the competitive position of Greece will continue to slide down and the cloud dividend will only extend to about € 5 billion with little employment gains during the difficult 6-7 years that lie ahead.

"Diffusion of cloud computing can potentially change the way business information systems are developed, scaled up, maintained and paid for. This not only applies to large organizations, but also increasingly to small and medium-sized businesses" - (Alshamaila, Papagiannidis, & Stamati, 2013). Although, a large number of Greek enterprises do not adopt cloud services. According to Eurostat, the lack of technical knowledge regarding the cloud computing, creates an obstacle large enough to obstruct any kind of cloud migration. Unfortunately, this situation is not limited only to one sector but to the majority of Greek businesses and organizations. The technology is not the only "black box" that enterprises are skeptical and hesitant about. The legal and contractual aspects as well as the final way to the implementation of a cloud migration are enemies of any change towards the cloud. Furthermore, the security of cloud computing poses a great threat on adopting cloud services and migrating business-critical applications and data, especially when a business is not very familiar with the concept and function of cloud.

Greece needs to put a great amount of effort in order to leverage the benefits of the cloud computing in both the public and the private sectors, despite the fact that cloud adoption may face substantial difficulties.

3. CASE STUDIES

After gathering useful data from (Katsantonis, Filiopoulou, Michalakelis, & Nikolaidou, 2015) with a startup case study, this paper advanced into actual organizations. As mentioned earlier, two organizations were studied and evaluated for the context of this work. The first is a bookbinding, newspaper-wrapping company, sharing the same industrial premises with a para-pharmaceutical wholesale dealer. The second organization is the National Confederation of Hellenic Commerce (ESEE). The National Confederation of Hellenic Commerce is a confederate organization representing Greek commerce on both domestic and international levels. In order to evaluate the research, this study is using guidelines from the C.A.T "Cloud Adoption Toolkit" (Khajeh-Hosseini, Greenwood, Smith, & Sommerville, 2012). Briefly, the steps are the following:

- **Technology Suitability Analysis:** Supports decision makers in determining whether cloud computing is the right technology to support their proposed system (Services, Leader, Capex, & Spend, 2016);
- **Risk and Benefit Analysis:** The potential cost savings of using cloud computing have to be examined in the wider context of other benefits and risks. (Lock, Storer, & Sommerville, 2009);
- **Cost Modeling:** Cost modeling gathers all the useful information about the company's CAPEX, OPEX and compares it with the corresponding cost of a potential it infrastructure. (Services et al., 2016);
- **Energy Consumption Analysis:** The purpose of Energy Consumption Analysis is to support decision makers in determining the optimum energy consumption of their own private cloud infrastructure. Additional information on energy consumption was found in (De Alfonso, Caballer, Alvarruiz, & Moltó, 2013). For the study of the companies, only the consumption of the present IT infrastructure was measured;
- **Stakeholder Impact Analysis:** The purpose of Stakeholder Impact Analysis is to support decision makers in determining the socio-political viability, or benefits and risks, of a proposed IT system. (Khajeh-Hosseini, Greenwood, & Sommerville, 2010);
- **Responsibility Modeling:** The purpose of responsibility modeling is to support decision makers in determining the operational viability of a proposed IT system.

3.1. General Pack S.A / SPM Pharma

General Pack S.A. operates since 1984, achieving great success in the industry of magazine and newspaper wrapping, as well as at the services of direct mail and press products finishing. SPM Pharma operates in the wholesale and retail of consumable items for pharmacies, medical clinics and medical stores.

The companies' current requirements for their IT services are:

- ERP (Enterprise Recourse Planning) software;
- Mass storage for user files;
- Two websites, one for each company, which are outsourced and hosted by a third-party company.

These requirements are quite representative for a large part of businesses in Greece. It is obvious that the companies have great mobility prospects to the Cloud. The reason of such a claim is the attempt -to be made- in order to integrate all services for cost saving and optimization of services. Besides the cost advantages, the companies can update the ERP system with new lower-cost options and additional functionality. The next picture shows the companies' server room. The companies have three servers that were purchased a decade ago (the fiscal year 2006-2007):

- Server 1:
  - SEN E.R.P (used by General Pack);
  - File Server;
- Server 2:
  - File Server Backup (this server is out of order);
- Server 3:
  - SEN E.R.P (used by SPM).

Using the Cloud Adoption Toolkit, the cost of the IT equipment of the companies is shown in Table 2.

3.1.1. Costs

Energy costs (€/kWh) were calculated based on the energy bill of the factory. The calculation where based on the companies' invoice from the Public Power Corporation (P.P.C Useful Customer Information, 2014). The total costs are shown in Table 2.

3.1.2. Findings / Proposal

The companies rely on legacy IT system that needs to be entirely replaced. An in-house IT system is not cost efficient, because the needs of the organization are fairly basic. Research findings indicate that for a successful cloud migration the companies should add an IoS (Internet over Satellite) connection. The reason is that area has really poor internet connection (1.5 mb/s). This problem is caused by the old and badly maintained copper lines of OTE (Organization of Telecommunications of Greece). In the industrial zone of Koropi (where the companies are located) there are no plans for optic fiber expansion, so the satellite internet is an inevitable step for cloud migration. The cost of IoS from Cosmote (Greek telecommunication Company) is € 80 per month without any additional costs of installation.

The companies' proposal insisted on moving the 10 emails that are used at the moment to Google in order to gain additional cloud storage (Google Drive 30GB) for file sharing between employees. In addition, Google offers the capability to mask the "…@gmail.com" with the companies' website name like "…@generalpack.gr". The cost is € 1.77 per user and per month.

The sites will be hosted on a server chosen between competitors (Table 3). Google is the best choice for the case study, because of the low cost, high availability prices and competitive server specs. The suitability analysis of the Cloud adoption toolkit helped on deciding about the Cloud Provider. Also, the decision involved the SLA's (Hoehl, 2015) of the candidate providers. Table 3 sums up the specs of the most prevalent cloud providers for this case study. The prices are based on the website Cloudorado (cloudorado.com, 2015).

Table 2. IT infrastructure cost

Item / Serv	Watt	75% *	kWh / Day	Cost (€)	Cost (€) / Month
Maint.	-	-	-	-	175.00
Site GP	-	-	-	110.00	9.17
Site SPM	-	-	-	108.00	9.00
SEN (Lic.)	-	-	-	2,000	166.67
Pc1	650	487.5	11.7	-	27.75
Pc2	500	375	9	-	21.35
Pc3	500	375	9	-	21.35
A/C	633	474.75	11.39	-	27.02
UPS	910	60**	1.44	-	3.42
Total Cost:					**460.73**

* Making the assumption that the PC's were using 75% of the total power.
** The specific UPS on idle uses around 60W.

Table 3. Cloud cost

Providers	RAM (GB)	CPU (Unit)	Storage (GB)	Cost (€) / Month
Google	**5.5**	**6**	**200**	**114.00**
GoGrid	4	4	200	118.00
Cloud Sigma	4	4	200	152.30
Elastic Hosts	4	4	200	199.00

The last pillar of the companies' cloud migration proposal included a new ERP/CRM software that has new capabilities than the legacy that is being used. The suggested option is Odoo (formerly known as OpenERP). Odoo offers three different software editions Free Odoo, Odoo Enterprise, Odoo Cloud. The first is the free version of the Software that adds no extra cost providing the basic functionality needed. The Enterprise version is a complete version that can be hosted by any server and Odoo Cloud is similar to the Enterprise version but it is hosted in Odoo's cloud servers.

The final costs are displayed in Figure 2. It is easily observable, that two out of three solutions are below the maintenance costs of the IT infrastructure of the companies. The study has concluded that the companies are able to support their business activities even with Odoo Community, without spending extra capital on another version of ERP. Present IT cost is € 460.71, Hosting Odoo (Community) € 227.90, Odoo Cloud € 755.40, Hosting Odoo (Enterprise) € 350.90.

3.2. National Confederation of Hellenic Commerce

ESEE is the higher, nationwide and internationally, representative organization of Greek trade. It is based on the cooperation of large local trade associations active in the Greek society from the 19th and

Figure 2. Price comparison (Odoo Pricing, 2015)

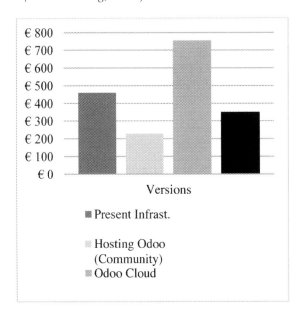

early 20th century. The effort for nationwide representation went through several stages, initially taking informal forms. Thus, in 1961 the Coordinating Council of Trade Associations was established.

ESEE has its offices in the city of Athens. The IT department has developed a well-designed and successfully maintained IT infrastructure, with the specifications shown in Table 4.

Before April 2016 ESEE used instead of the equipment in Table 4, three Hewlett Packard ML350 Gen5. The organization's current requirements for their IT services are: Mail Server, Storage, Antivirus and ERP.

A NAS (Network Attached Storage) is also available, used to back up all the business-critical documents. Unfortunately, the size quickly becomes insufficient. The current IT infrastructure operating without any flaws and the required functionality for all the business processes has been achieved. As mentioned before, one of the major factors that causes some problems on the company's operation and IT expansion is the internet connection bandwidth. The company is forced to use five different internet connections (5 different modem-routers), each one only achieves 24 Mbp/s. The result is that the end users can only achieve a bandwidth of about 4 Mbp/s on their desktop. Using the Cloud Adoption Toolkit, the cost of the IT equipment of the company is estimated and shown in the Table 5.

3.2.1. Costs

Energy costs (€/kWh) were calculated based on the energy bill of the organizations.

Table 4. ESEE IT infrastructure

Model	CPU	RAM	Storage	Software
HP - DL350 Gen10	Intel Xeon	32 GB	600 GB	Windows Server 2012 (Hyper Visor)
HP - DL350 Gen10	Intel Xeon	32 GB	600 GB	Windows Server 2012 (Hyper Visor)
EMC - VNXe 1600	Intel Xeon	16 GB	10 TB	Operating Environment 3.1.3

Table 5. ESEE IT costs

Info	Watt (60%)	Cost (€)	Cost (€) / Month
Internet Connections	-	1,500.00	125.00
Major Events *	-	1,500.00	125.00
www.esee.gr	-	400.00	33.33
www.kaele.gr	-	400.00	33.33
www.inemy.gr	-	-	-
ERP License	-	1,500.00	125.00
HP - DL350 Gen10	300	-	21.93
HP - DL350 Gen10	300	-	21.93
EMC - VNXe1600	240	-	17.54
A/C (24.000 BTU)	4,219.80	-	308.47
A/C (24.000 BTU)	4,219.80	-	308.47
Total / Month	-	-	**1,120.00**

Major events consist of disk failures, offline server and any other malfunction that may occur.

3.2.2. Findings / Proposal

ESEE has a "rock-solid" infrastructure and at the moment because the new equipment is not yet amortized, from a financial point of view the cloud migration is not wise choice. A partial migration could be a feasible solution though (hybrid cloud). The monthly cost of a complete migration of the servers into the Cloud is displayed in Table 6. As before, for the calculations the pricing data from Cloudorado. com were used.

According to the calculations in Table 6, the best solution is the Google Cloud Platform. As far as the EMC server is concerned, the cost is at a level of € 243.13. In the case of a complete cloud migration the yearly cost will be:

$$2*Cost\_HP\_Cloud\_Equivalent + 1*Cost\_EMC\_Cloud\_Equivalent = 4,898.88 + 2,917.56 = € 7,816.44$$
/ year (€ 651.37 / month)

From Table 5, a large part of the monthly expenses is fully eradicated with the use of cloud computing. The power consumption of the servers is no longer a concern. The cloud bandwidth of these servers is capable of hosting the three websites, reducing the monthly bill of ESEE. The comparative Table 7 was created to compare the two configurations.

As shown in the Table 4, the major malfunctions are no longer a concern. The second air condition is now superfluous so it will not be needed. The server room will still keep the telephone line switches and additional equipment this is why the usage of the A/C is required.

Table 6. Cloud providers costs

Provider	Cost (€) / Month
Google	**204.12**
Amazon Web Services	319.49
Windows Azure	474.80

Table 7. ESEE cloud IT costs

Info	Watt	Watt (60%)	Cost (€)	Cost (€) / Month
Internet Connections	-	-	1,500.00	125.00
ERP License	-	-	1,500.00	125.00
Cloud Servers			7,816.44	651.37
A/C (24.000 BTU)	7,033	4,219.80	-	308.47
Total / Month	-	-	-	**1,209.84**

Comparing the two Tables (7 – 5), switching to a cloud infrastructure will cost € 1,078.08 (difference between total/month multiplied by 12) more annually. Although the cost difference for an enterprise might be insignificant additional training for the cloud and the migration procedure itself could induce additional costs that are not measured in this paper.

According to (Andrikopoulos, Strauch, & Leymann, 2013) decision support is of great importance as well as the C.A.T mentioned before any step towards cloud migration. Especially for a migration that has not clear financial benefits such as this. An additional consideration is also the effort required for the adaptation from the IT department, the staff and the management in order for. Following the C.A.T a risk and benefit analysis was conducted with a questionnaire from PlanForCloud.gr. The results indicate that the full-scale adoption for cloud had more risks than potential benefits.

After interviewing the IT management of ESEE, the solution that was proposed was not a complete cloud migration, but a hybrid cloud implementation for backup purposes. The cloud infrastructure that will be setup as a backup server for business-critical data. The data will be safely stored in an encrypted form using a Google Storage server.

At the moment, the IT administrators need about 1.5 TB for the data, so a solution based on these figures was created (see Table 8).

Each class consists of the commands shown in Table 9. The commands are calculated per million. The first month, when the first backup requires a major bandwidth in order to be completed. During the next 9 and 2 months, only the storage size changes. The calculations were made based on an annual contract.

The total cost of this backup server is € 141.10 per month. Also, the IT stuff already know how to schedule backups on Windows Server 2012 so no training or additional cost is required.

Table 8. Backup server costs

Duration (Month)	Storage (TB)	Bandwidth (TB)	Class A	Class B	Cost (€)
1	3	1.5	0.1	1	228.85
9	3	0.5	0.05	0.7	1,123.29
2	4	0.7	0.08	0.9	340.18
Total:	-	-	-	-	**1,692.32**

Table 9. Commands classification (Google Storage Pricing, 2016)

Operation	Class
GET Service GET Bucket (when listing objects in a bucket) PUT POST	Class A
GET Bucket (when retrieving bucket configuration) GET Object HEAD	Class B
DELETE	Free

4. CONCLUSION

Greece due to its crisis, can have some very important benefits with the proper leverage of cloud computing. After the thorough examination of two completely different enterprises and their needs, it is only reasonable to say that cloud computing is something that every company needs. Some companies can harvest and enjoy all of the benefits cloud computing provides and others -due to their well-maintained IT infrastructure- only need some extra functionality that can be achieved with the use of cloud.

The findings point out clearly that the cloud proposal could cost 50%, or 24% less per month for the General Pack. As far as ESEE is concerned, the complete cloud migration is not necessary. Also, the costs have not significant differences. Although a hybrid cloud solution for a backup server could be ideal. With a monthly cost that does not exceed € 150, ESEE can maintain a backup of business-critical data out of the boundaries of the organization for greater security and availability. The significance of the cloud adoption should be a major concern for all companies, especially Greek. Reduced income and a small budget for investment IT make Greece a very prosperous ground for cloud to expand and help SMEs to reduce internal costs and be more competitive to the European and the Global market as well.

Future research can focus on the additional cost that a migration to the cloud can hide. Analysis for the impact that affects stakeholders and the responsibility modeling is needed in order to better understand cloud migration. Costs like training and disruption of the company's operation.

An additional research like this, can help decision-makers to conduct an in-depth cloud migration assessment for the enterprise that they represent. The star of cloud computing shines bright and hopefully every company will embrace some of its aspects.

REFERENCES

Ali, O., Soar, J., & Yong, J. (2016). An investigation of the challenges and issues influencing the adoption of cloud computing in Australian regional municipal governments. *Journal of Information Security and Applications*, *27*, 19–34.

Alshamaila, Y., Papagiannidis, S., & Li, F. (2013). Cloud computing adoption by SMEs in the north east of England A multi-perspective framework. doi:10.1108/17410391311325225

Alshamaila, Y., Papagiannidis, S., & Stamati, T. (2013). Cloud computing adoption in Greece. In Proceedings of the UK Academy for Information Systems Conference (pp. 5–22).

Andrikopoulos, V., Strauch, S., & Leymann, F. (2013). Decision support for application migration to the cloud : challenges and vision this publication and contributions have been presented at decision support for application migration to the cloud.

Benefits and Risks of Using the Cloud. (2016). Retrieved from http://www.planforcloud.com/

Cloud Server (2015). Retrieved from www.cloudorado.com

Danchev, S., Tsakanikas, A., & Ventouris, N. (2011). Cloud Computing: A Driver for Greek Economy Competitiveness. *Foundation for Economic & Industrial Research*, (November).

De Alfonso, C., Caballer, M., Alvarruiz, F., & Moltó, G. (2013). An economic and energy-aware analysis of the viability of outsourcing cluster computing to a cloud. *Future Generation Computer Systems*, *29*(3), 704–712. doi:10.1016/j.future.2012.08.014

Hassan, Q. F. (2011). Demystifying Cloud Security. *Crosstalk*, 16–21. Retrieved from http://www.crosstalkonline.org/storage/issue-archives/2011/201101/201101-Hassan.pdf

Hoehl, M. (2015). Interested in learning SANS Institute InfoSec Reading Room Proposal for standard Cloud Computing Security SLAs - Key Metrics for Safeguarding Confidential Data in the Cloud.

Katsantonis, K., Filiopoulou, E., Michalakelis, C., & Nikolaidou, M. (2015). Cloud computing and economic growth. In *Proceedings of the 19th Panhellenic Conference on Informatics PCI '15* (pp. 209–214). 10.1145/2801948.2802000

Khajeh-Hosseini, A., Greenwood, D., Smith, J., & Sommerville, I. (2012). The Cloud Adoption Toolkit: Supporting cloud adoption decisions in the enterprise. *Software, Practice & Experience*, *43*(4), 447–465. doi:10.1002pe.1072

Khajeh-Hosseini, A., Greenwood, D., & Sommerville, I. (2010). Cloud migration: A case study of migrating an enterprise IT system to IaaS. In *Proceedings of the 2010 IEEE 3rd International Conference on Cloud Computing CLOUD '10* (pp. 450–457). 10.1109/CLOUD.2010.37

Lock, R., Storer, T., & Sommerville, I. (2009). Responsibility modelling for risk analysis. Retrieved from http://eprints.gla.ac.uk/71594/

Mell, P., & Grance, T. (2011). The NIST definition of cloud computing. *NIST*. doi:10.1136/emj.2010.096966

Odoo Pricing. (2016). Retrieved from https://www.odoo.com/pricing

Services, C., Leader, E., Capex, D., & Spend, U. T. (2016). Understanding CapEx vs. OpEx in a Cloud Computing World.

Use of cloud computing services (2016). Retrieved from Eurostat http://ec.europa.eu/eurostat/statistics-explained/index.php/Cloud_computing_-_statistics_on_the_use_by_enterprises

Useful customer Information. (2014). Retrieved from https://www.dei.gr/documents2/customer.pdf

Varia, J. (2010). Migrating your Existing Applications to the AWS Cloud.

XML API operation classes. (2016). Retrieved from https://cloud.google.com/storage/pricing

This research was previously published in the International Journal of Technology Diffusion (IJTD), 9(2); edited by Ali Hussein Saleh Zolait, pages 61-73, copyright year 2018 by IGI Publishing (an imprint of IGI Global).

Chapter 68
Mobile Cloud Gaming and Today's World

Hallah Shahid Butt
National University of Sciences and Technology (NUST), Pakistan

Sadaf Jalil
National University of Sciences and Technology (NUST), Pakistan

Sajid Umair
National University of Sciences and Technology (NUST), Pakistan

Safdar Abbas Khan
National University of Sciences and Technology (NUST), Pakistan

ABSTRACT

Mobile cloud computing is the emerging field. Along-with different services being provided by the cloud like Platform as a Service, Infrastructure as a Service, Software as a Service; Game as a Service is new terminology for the cloud services. In this paper, we generally discussed the concept of mobile cloud gaming, the companies that provide the services as GaaS, the generic architecture, and the research work that has been done in this field. Furthermore, we highlighted the research areas in this field.

INTRODUCTION

In past few decades, people like to work on desktop computers. But with the evolution in technology, people are most interested to use mobile devices since it is handy and portable. Moreover, mobile is satisfying the needs of user by providing them facility to play games and providing them online video streaming etc. Mobile devices are now the major source of entertainment for the users Cai and Leung (2013).

According to the survey (Netimperative, 2015), in China, 8% of the total mobile subscribers were increased within one year till January 2015 and 15% of growth was observed in number of active mobile social users. Moreover, the web traffic requested by mobiles till August 2015 was 136% increased. Figure 1 presents the stats of mobile gaming in China by August, 2015.

DOI: 10.4018/978-1-5225-8176-5.ch068

Copyright © 2019, IGI Global. Copying or distributing in print or electronic forms without written permission of IGI Global is prohibited.

Figure 1. Increasing trends of mobile users in China
Netimperative, 2015.

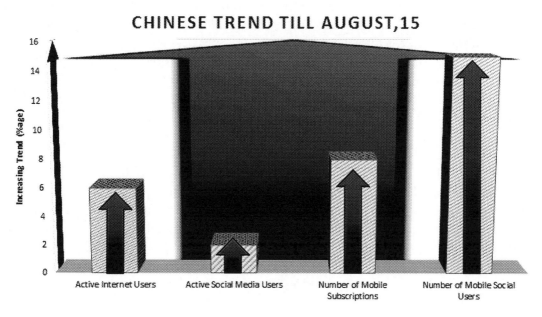

This signifies that the use of internet resources via mobile in increased. This leads to the need to fulfill or meet the needs of users accordingly. According to Cai and Leung (2013), along with the social activities, mobile devices are also used to play different games. These games can be browser based (Mobile Browser Game- MBG) or it can be video based (Mobile Video Gaming). Mobile cloud computing (MCC) - an emerging field- is there to help out such users. Since clouds provide different services based on their infrastructure like Infrastructure as a Service (IaaS), Platform as a Service (PaaS); similarly, Game as a Service (GaaS) is new service being provided by the clouds environment. One interesting advantage of cloud gaming is that it updates games instantly with the web without downloading a new version of the game. By having the ability to push patches to a game, it can be personalized much easier. One of the examples is "The Walking Dead" game, which releases new episodes after two weeks. As each episode is released the data is analyzed and their teams make real-time decisions on how to improve the user experience. The next episode that comes out will be better than the last. (Decker, 2016) The chapter describes the MCG definition, cloud gaming companies, frameworks or models used for it and research areas in this domain.

In this chapter first we will discuss the introduction of mobile cloud gaming which is followed by the identification of cloud gaming companies. General architecture of mobile cloud environment is discussed. Related literature work is also described in this chapter.

MOBILE CLOUD GAMING

Definition

Cloud services are on-demand services. Similarly, gaming on clouds is games on demand service. It is new and emerging trend. Mobile Cloud Gaming is known as collective gaming exhausting mobile devices that connects with the cloud as an outsider system for dealing with game interactions and scenarios. It enables innovative features such as heterogenic-platform processing, power saving, and computational or processing capacity enhancement (Cai and Leung, 2013). MCG have many advantages like scalability to overwhelmed end user hardware constraints, cost-effectiveness for software development along with its distribution, flexible business model to earn profit, providing effective antipiracy solution and providing the facility to click and play games (Cai et al., 2014).

Advantages of MCG

Advantages of mobile cloud gaming are shown in Table 1.

According to the blog (Miica 2016), energy efficiency is an important but relatively unexplored aspect of cloud gaming. However, (Miica 2016) have done research in NomadicLab Ericsson. Remote desktop client is the only software is to be installed that handles the controls and multimedia streaming from a remote server, where the actual video and audio for the desktop are generated. This "thin-client" approach can also be utilized in other contexts, like remote gaming. Nvidia Shield, In-home teaming from Valve Stream, and PlayStation Now are examples of existing products that support remote streaming of game content either from local home PCs or from the cloud (Miica, 2016).

Drawbacks of MCG

Disadvantages of MCG are also shown in Table 2.

Table 1. Advantages of MCG

Advantages	Description
Thin Client	There is no need to install games on mobile devices. Users can access gaming facility using mobile.
Potential Battery Conservation	Since the cloud deals with the rendering and computing of games, power consumption for processing is greatly reduced.
Unlimited Resources	The cloud server hosting the gaming engines, which means that the game has unlimited storage and other computing resources.
Less Chance of Loss	Game data resides in the cloud. This means that, when and where gamers connected to the game, the game content and status, it is still the same. Thus, the player may have seamless game across multiple networks.

Tayade, 2014.

Table 2. Drawbacks of MCG

Drawbacks	Description
Bandwidth Consumption	Clients connect to the cloud via network (internet). Rendering frames of video consume more bandwidth.
Network Dependency	Users are totally dependent on network availability. They are unable to play games if there is no internet connection. Their games may burden the network and cause congestion.
Resource Limitation	Browser games have limitations. Sometimes resources are required for video rendering which might not be visible on mobile browsers.

Tayade, 2014.

Cloud Gaming Companies

The following companies are the providers of cloud gaming.

- **OnLive:** It was one of the commercialized companies to provide cloud games (Cai and Leung 2013). On April 30, 2015, all services provided by OnLive was come to an end since Sony acquired important parts of OnLive (OnLive, 2016).
- **OTOY:** Cai and Leung (2013) and OTOY (2015) mentioned that OTOY is US based company that delivers media and entertainment organizations around the world. They provide GPU-based software solutions that aid in the creation and delivery of digital content. From capture to render to stream, they provide an integrated pipeline for making and distributing 3D content.
- **Gaikai:** According to Cai and Leung (2013) and Gaikai (2013), they provide solutions to stream video games at high quality with low latency. They built the world's fastest interactive entertainment network and won a Guinness World Record for it.
- **G-Cluster:** G-cluster offered operators of the gaming platform in the cloud deployed whiter label that allows users to play through television and various mobile devices. G -cluster instantly becomes corresponding television top box with portable multi-platform cloud gaming on television, PC and tablet. They develop AAA games (Cai and Leung, 2013). Now company is dissolved (G-Cluster, 2016).
- **Playcast Media System:** Cai and Leung (2013) and GTC (2010) mentioned that They developed the first system for providing online on-demand gaming services on live cable network.
- **StreamMyGame:** In Cai and Leung (2013) and StreamMyGame (2012) is declared as only solution that allows applications and games to play remotely. It is free to join online community, by making two sets of current games and video recording. It is the fundamental revolutionary computer game industry, because users can play high-end games low-end equipment.

GENERAL ARCHITECTURE OF MOBILE CLOUD ENVIRONMENT

While discussing mobile cloud architecture, we can say that it is four tier architecture generally. More tiers can be added in this architecture for instance, to ensure security. First tier can be named as client tier in which clients connected with mobile devices can access the network. The improved features in interfaces can help the players to play with ease. This interface is important especially for MBG where web browser is acting as interface. Cai and Leung (2013) Network tier consists of access points and the mobile network service providers. Different networks have their own bandwidths. With different Internet speeds provided by different technologies like 3G and latest 4G, multi-gaming sessions' players are increasing day-by-day (Bose and Saddar, 2015). Clients connect with the Internet tier via access points or mobile network service providers, which in turn connects with the cloud tier. Pictorially, it is represented in the Figure 2.

RELATED WORK

In this section, we tried to cover the proposed solutions to the problems in MCG domain. Innovative framework of cloud-based e-learning games can be a source to enhance students learning in any time

Figure 2. General architecture of mobile cloud computing
Source: (Cai and Leung, 2013).

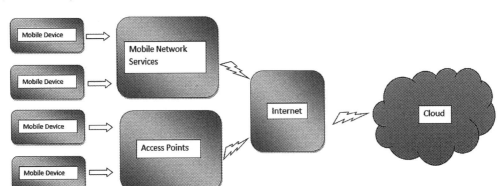

space. Mobile quiz game is developed on the idea of game rooms with real- time synchronization and the client-server model, by members of University of Hong Kong, whose design is illustrated as: Suggested system, i.e. iGame@Cloud, is designed including the components; Interactive E-Learning Game Server running on the Cloud platform, Administration Console Portal, E-Learning Game Portal and Mobile Devices. After registration, each user logs in our cloud-based ELearning Game Server via the wireless network through the user interaction screen already loaded and displayed onto their mobile devices. During the time of scheduling, the E-Learning Game Server will push some questions for the answer. Each user will be given with 3 options. In each round, those users who had given the wrong answers for three times would be required to quit the current game session. The server will only show the right answer for each round only when all the answers are received from the registered mobile phone. Thus, our cloud based e-learning game platform is a round-based game that requires synchronization of data on the server side (Tam et al., 2013).

Zamith et al. (2011) describe that mobile games are applications that run on mobile devices as smart-phones and tablets. The characteristics of current mobile devices make it reality to design extensive game experiences. By using an approach based on distributed processing or computing, games would have lighter requirements regarding hardware. With the idea of cloud computing, games could depend on other terminals to help in processing their assigned tasks. This presents game-loop architecture for 1-player or more than 1-player games, using automatic load balancing and distributing game logic computation among several computers. This focuses at having low-powered devices taking part into complex and difficult games as well as allowing many players to play together through their mobile devices and let the game quality be improved. The current implementation uses HTML 5 for the mobile client (user interface, prompt input and connect to the server cluster) and C plus plus (C++) with Message Protocol Interface (MPI) for processing tasks. The web server is Apache. The component responsible for cluster computing has two parts: the master process, who is assigned to answer client requests, and the slave process, who runs the distributed game loop. For each and every game loop step, the master process gets the current game state from a client, and updates it in each slave process, dividing the problem with all slave processes. Then, the master process amalgamates the solution of each slave process, creating a new game state. In the end, the master process sends to client this new game state. Proposed architecture is illustrated in the Figure 3.

Figure 3. Proposed architecture
Zamith et al., 2011.

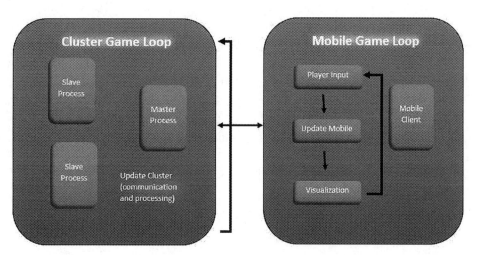

This strategy includes four main components: load balancing; applies the scripting approach and thus analyzes the hardware performance dynamically and adjusts the number of tasks to be processed by the resources, mobile architecture; the input task classes handle user input that comes from several sources. The presentation task and subclasses are responsible for presenting information to the user. The update task classes are assigned to update the game loop state, the network update task; it is responsible for communicating with distributed architecture and updating the game state according to the data received from it, the distributed architecture; the core of the proposed architecture relates to the task manager and the hardware check class, that schedules tasks and changes which processor handles them whenever it is needed.

Kim (2013) says, Client-server architectures are less flexible and scalable, because the bandwidth requirements have grown with the increase in number of gaming user increases. The proposed architecture ensures that a game cloud can provide scalability that enables to host hundreds of mobile games users to have the advantages of cloud computing and local resources for the high quality of games. Following is the architecture proposed, i.e. Efficient Scaling Scheme in the Cloud. Unlike general approach where mobile devices connect to the access network, there presents a mobile network service layer between the wireless access network and mobile cloud computing. Game servers act as proxies for managing the set of their gaming users. Gaming users have no information about interest sets, and are exposed only to enough game state as provided by their server. Using updates published in the low frequency topic, each server periodically determines the interest set of each of its gaming users. The cloud provides an idea of infinite processing power with a highly reliable service, thus removing the need for costly provisioning required resources for mobile games. Although the game state is distributed amongst multiple hosts or nodes, all information resides in the same data center. The size of the set of the gaming users affects game quality and performance. As the interest set size reduces, workload on the cloud is reduced; similarly, large interest sets will result in give an idea of game quality due to frequent updates, but may cause update latencies due to a more workload.

User satisfaction is also important in gaming. Users play games in order to get relax and enjoy. Huang et al. 2014 did experiment in order to quantify the user satisfaction in mobile cloud systems using real game GamingAnywhere which is an open source game. They setup their experiment by connecting desktop client and mobile client with GamingAnywhere server. Desktop client is connected with LAN and mobile client with wi-fi access point. They set up their own GamingAnywhere server on a Windows 7 desktop, Intel Core i7-870 (8 MB cache and 2.93 GHz) and 8 GB of main memory. The desktop client has Windows 7 installed with Intel Core 2 Quad processor Q9400 (6 MB cache and 2.66 GHz) and 4 GB of memory while the mobile client Samsung Galaxy Nexus has 1.2 GHz Dual CPU, 1 GB RAM, 4.65 -inch AMOLED screen, 720P) and Android 4.2.1 features. Desktop Client and Mobile clients connected to the server via the Gigaset Ethernet LAN and Wireless LAN 802.11, respectively. They believed that the two LANs are used in accordance with fair comparison experiments. Figure 4 show the setup of experiment.

They performed their experiment on selected games. Those were:

1. Limbo.
2. Super Smash Bros.
3. Mario Kart 64
4. Super Mario 64
5. To study Customer Satisfaction, they considered four parameters:
   a. Video resolution
   b. Encoding bitrate
   c. Network latency
   d. Frame rate.

They conducted their studies on mobile and desktop clients. Graphics, control and smoothness were rated in their studies. Moreover, impact of selected parameters on above mentioned rated parameters. The results showed that

- The players are more satisfied with sound and graphics quality in mobile devices and quality control on the desktop.
- The network latency, bit rate and frame rate affect graphic quality and smoothness.
- Control quality depends upon the devices being used.

Figure 4. Experiment setup
Kim, 2013.

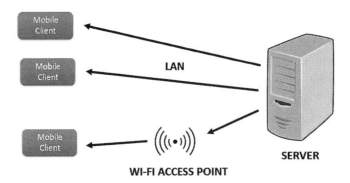

Hossain et al. 2015 proposed an architecture for cloud gaming with emotions- awareness. They tackled the issue of tradeoff between player emotion or feeling with resource consumption, which is affected by game screen. The proposed architecture for emotion-aware cloud gaming framework uses emotion technology and remote display technology to give players good experience. For cloud-based video games, game-screens are rendered on servers and streamed to client's devices whereas emotions of users are sent back to the cloud servers to show-off better display screens. The architecture is shown in Figure 5. The player responses, interactions and commands are recorded and sent to emotion -detection engine (server).

Emotion detection function identify the emotions and send a message to remote display server to change the screens. Components of proposed architecture can be summarized as follows:

- **Cloud Manager:** That manages the overall system by web services. Responsibilities of cloud manager includes maintaining player's profile, game and client's device information, user identification and registration and managing the game sessions.
- **Resource Allocation Manager:** Responsible for assigning virtual machines (VM) required for running the game sessions. The VM is responsible for emotion detection, game state updates, streaming and rendering, audio-video playback and screen-effect control. Their system worked in two phases, first is the learning phase, in which the system learns the emotions and classify them. In the second phase, i.e. the operating stage, a linear programming (LP) model is applied to change the screens based on detected emotions.

They claimed that bearable amount of workload has been transferred to the cloud server, which may not harm or disturb the processing of server.

Figure 5. Player's emotion detecting architecture
Hossain et al., 2015.

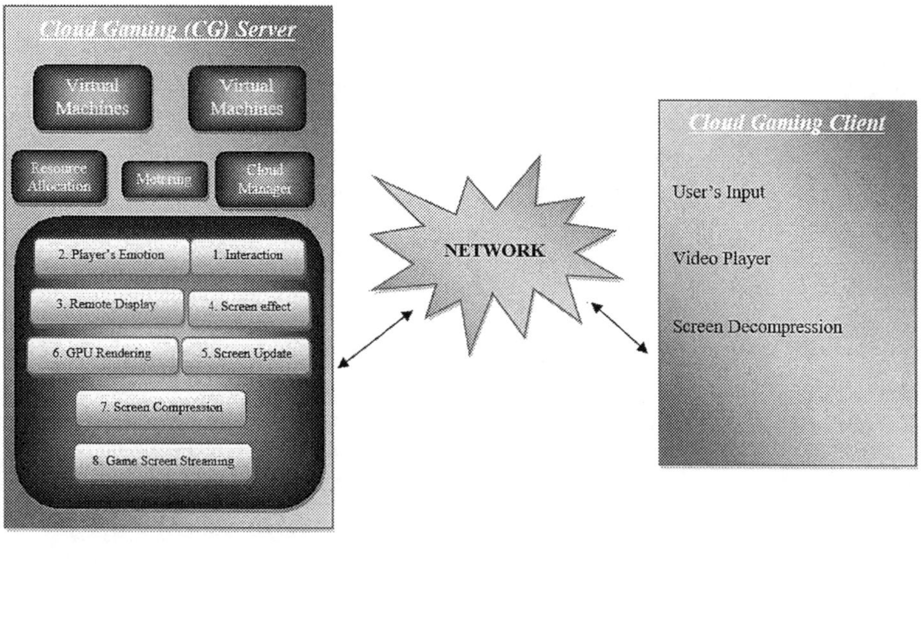

Chen 2015 proposed a game theoretic technology for achieving effective and efficient processing offloading for MCC. They adopted the decentralized computation offloading decision making problem among mobile device users as a decentralized computation offloading game. The main contributions of this research are summarized as follows:

- Decentralized processing or computing offloading game formulation.
- Analysis of game structure.
- Decentralized mechanism for achieving Nash equilibrium.

The results showed that the proposed mechanism can achieve the valuable computation offloading work and is scalable as system size increase

FUTURE RESEARCH DIRECTIONS

MCG is new and emerging field. We can have different research directions specifically considering the security and privacy in clouds. Many researchers have proposed different architectures to solve the issue but the work is still insufficient to cope up with the problem. Moreover, supply of user friendly gaming environment over network is also a problem. Change in architectures that can handle network issues should be implemented.

CONCLUSION

We studied the new emerging paradigm of MCG. In this chapter, we defined the term MCG, its types i.e. MCVG and MBG, the companies that provide cloud based games solutions to users. We described the general cloud environment that how the clients are connected with the cloud and get the services of the clouds. We also described the architecture of StreamMyGame. We tried to describe the proposed frameworks for MCG. Despite of research being done in this field, there are still some research areas where we have to focus. As discussed in related work, the emotion-aware screens are displayed which requires constant message passing between client and server. Client's game information along- with their emotions' information have to send time-to-time which may cause the load on server if there are hundreds of players playing games. Moreover, the security of the cloud is a strong research area. Maintaining security and privacy in clouds is a difficult task.

ACKNOWLEDGMENT

The authors would like to thank Dr. Safdar Abbas Khan, Assistant Professor, School of Electrical Engineering and Computer Sciences (SEECS), National University of Sciences and Technology (NUST) Islamabad Pakistan for their complete support, help and guidance.

REFERENCES

Cai, W., Chen, M., & Leung, V. C. M. (2014). Toward Gaming as a Service. *IEEE Internet Computing, 18*(3), 12–18. Retrieved August 08 2016 from http://ieeexplore.ieee.org/xpls/abs_all.jsp?arnumber=6818918 doi:10.1109/MIC.2014.22

Cai, W., & Leung, V. C. M. (2013). Next Generation Mobile Cloud Gaming. *Proceedings of the IEEE Seventh International Symposium on Service-Oriented System Engineering*, 550-559. Retrieved August 04, 2016 from http://www-users.cselabs.umn.edu/classes/Spring-2015/csci8980/papers/Applications/gaming.pdf

Chen, X. (2015). Decentralized Computation Offloading Game For Mobile Cloud Computing. *IEEE Transactions on Parallel and Distributed Systems, 26*(4), 974–983. Retrieved July 28 2016 from http://ieeexplore.ieee.org/xpl/articleDetails.jsp?tp=&arnumber=6787113 doi:10.1109/TPDS.2014.2316834

G- Cluster. (2016). Retrieved July 30, 2016 from http://www.gcluster.com/eng

Gaikai (2013). Retrieved on July 30, 2016 from http://www.gaikai.com

GTC. (2010). Retrieved July 30, 2016 from http://www.nvidia.com/content/GTC-2010/pdfs/4004B GTC2010.pdf

Hossain, M. S., Muhammad, G., Song, B., Hassan, M. M., Alelaiwi, A., & Alamri, A. (2015). Audio-Visual Emotion-Aware Cloud Gaming Framework. *Proceedings of the IEEE Transactions on Circuits and Systems for Video Technology* (pp. 2105-2118). Retrieved July 20, 2016 from http://ieeexplore.ieee.org/xpls/abs_all.jsp?arnumber=7122897

Huang, C., Hsu, C., Chen, D., & Cheni, K. (2014). Quantifying User Satisfaction in Mobile Cloud Games. *Proceeding of Workshop on Mobile Video* Delivery. Retrieved August 01, 2016 from http://ieeexplore.ieee.org/xpls/abs_all.jsp?arnumber=7122897

Huang, C., Hsu, C., Chen, D., & Cheni, K. (2014). Quantifying User Satisfaction in Mobile Cloud Games. *Proceedings of Workshop on Mobile Video Delivery*. Retrieved August 01, 2016 from http://ieeexplore.ieee.org/xpls/abs_all.jsp?arnumber=7122897

Kim, H. (2013). Mobile Games with an Efficient Scaling Scheme in the Cloud. *Proceedings of the 2013 International Conference on Information Science and Applications (ICISA)*. Retrieved August 09, 2016 from http://ieeexplore.ieee.org/xpls/abs_all.jsp?arnumber=6579356

Kim, H. (2013). Mobile Games with an Efficient Scaling Scheme in the Cloud. *2013 International Conference on Information Science and Applications (ICISA)*, 1-3. Retrieved on August 09, 2016 from http://ieeexplore.ieee.org/xpls/abs_all.jsp?arnumber=6579356

Netimperative (2015). China digital trends in 2015: Huge shift to mobile as growth slows. Retrieved August 01, 2016 from http://www.netimperative.com/2015/09/china-digital-trends-in-2015-huge-shift-to-mobile-as-growth-slows/

OnLive. (2016). Retrieved July 30, 2016 from http://onlive.com/

OTOY. (2015). Retrieved on July 30, 2016 from http://www.home.otoy.com

StreamMyGame. (2012). Retrieved August 01, 2016 from http://streammygame.com/smg/index.php

Tam, V., Yi, A., Lam, E. Y., Chan, C., & Yuen, A. H. K. (2013). Using Cloud Computing and Mobile Devices to Facilitate Students Learning Through E-Learning Games. *Proceedings of the IEEE 13th International Conference on Advanced Learning Technologies* (pp. 471 – 472). Retrieved August 03, 2016 from http://ieeexplore.ieee.org/xpls/abs_all.jsp?arnumber=6601990

Tayade, D. (2014). Mobile Cloud Computing: Issues, Security, Advantages, Trends. *International Journal of Computer Science and Information Technologies, 5*(5), 6635-6639. Retrieved August 11, 2016 from http://citeseerx.ist.psu.edu/viewdoc/download?doi=10.1.1.660.8874&rep=rep1&type=pdf

Zamith, M., Joselli, M., Esteban, W. G. C., Montenegro, A., & Regina, C. P. Leal-Toledo; Luis Valente; Bruno Feijó (2011). A Distributed Architecture for Mobile Digital Games Based on Cloud Computing. *Proceedings of the 2011 Brazilian Symposium on Games and Digital Entertainment (SBGAMES)* (pp. 79-88). Retrieved August 02, 2016 from http://ieeexplore.ieee.org/xpls/abs_all.jsp?arnumber=6363221

Zamith, M., Joselli, M., Clua, E. W. G., Montenegro, A., Leal-Toledo, R. C. P., Valente, L., & Feijo, B. (2011). A Distributed Architecture for Mobile Digital Games Based on Cloud Computing. *Proceedings of the 2011 Brazilian Symposium on Games and Digital Entertainment (SBGAMES)* (pp. 79-88). Retrieved August 02, 2016 from http://ieeexplore.ieee.org/xpls/abs_all.jsp?arnumber=6363221

ADDITIONAL READING

Bose, R. & Sarddar, D. (2015). A new approach in mobile gaming on cloud-based architecture using Citrix and VMware technologies. *Brazilian Journal of Science and Technology.* Retrieved November 23, 2016 from http://link.springer.com/article/10.1186/s40552-015-0012-1

Chen, D. Z. H. (2012, March 23). Data security and privacy protection issues in cloud computing. *Paper presented at the International Conference on Computer Science and Electronics Engineering,* Hangzhou, China. Retrieved July 7, 2016 from http://ieeexplore.ieee.org/xpls/abs_all.jsp?arnumber=6187862

Chuah, S. P., & Cheung, N. M. (2014). Layered Coding for Mobile Cloud Gaming. *Proceedings of International Workshop on Massively Multiuser Virtual Environments MoViD'14.* Retrieved August 10, 2016 from http://dl.acm.org/citation.cfm?id=2577395

Cocking, L. (2012). *The future of mobile cloud infrastructure.* Retrieved July 9, 2016 from http://www.guardtime.com/2012/08/13/the-future-of mobile cloud- infrastructure/

Decker, B. (2016). Cloud gaming – what is it and what's the impact of it? *Digitalriver.com.* Retrieved November 21, 2016 from https://www.digitalriver.com/cloud-gaming-what-is-it-and-whats-the-impact-of-it/

Fernando, N., Loke, S. W., & Rahayu, W. (2013). Mobile cloud computing: A survey. *Future Generation Computer Systems, 29*(1), 84–106. Retrieved July 11, 2016 from http://www.sciencedirect.com/science/article/pii/S0167739X12001318

Galli, H., & Padmanabham, P. (2013). Data security in cloud using hybrid encryption and decryption. *International journal of advanced research in computer science and software engineering.* Retrieved July 10, 2016 from http://www.ijarcce.com/upload/2013/august/23-o-Moni%20Tamil%20-data%20 security%20and%20privacy%20in%20cloud.pdf

Grobauer, B., Walloschek, T., & Stocker, E. (2011). Understanding cloud computing vulnerabilities. *IEEE Security and Privacy*, *8*(2), 50–57. Retrieved July 8 2016 from http://ieeexplore.ieee.org/xpls/ abs_all.jsp?arnumber=5487489 doi:10.1109/MSP.2010.115

Huang, C., Hsu, C., Chen, D., & Cheni, K. (2014). Quantifying User Satisfaction in Mobile Cloud Games. *Proceedings of Workshop on Mobile Video Delivery MoViD'14.* Retrieved August 01, 2016 from http:// ieeexplore.ieee.org/xpls/abs_all.jsp?arnumber=7122897

Jamil, D. H. Z. (2011). Cloud computing security. *International Journal of Engineering Science and Technology*, *3*(4). Retrieved July 8, 2016 from http://link.springer.com/article/10.1007/s00170-012-4163-7

Kevin, H., Khan, L., Kantarcioglu, M., & Thuraisingham, B. (2012). Security issues for cloud computing. In *Optimizing Information Security and Advancing Privacy Assurance: New Technologies.* Retrieved July 8, 2016 from https://books.google.com.pk/books?hl=en&lr=&id=r1-wsl9LbX4C&oi=fnd&pg=PR1& dq=Kevin,+H.,+Khan,+L.,+Kantarcioglu,+M.,+Thuraisingham,+B.+(2012).+Security+issues+for+c loud+computing+Optimizing+Information+Security+and+Advancing+Privacy+Assurance:+New+T echnologies.(&ots=Wcf4wgEAKc&sig=CQlX8ctEGhWCtT5NS_Fk8QrZhho#v=onepage&q&f=false

Kim, H. (2013). Mobile Games with an Efficient Scaling Scheme in the Cloud. *Proceedings of the 2013 International Conference on Information Science and Applications (ICISA).* Retrieved August 09, 2016 from http://ieeexplore.ieee.org/xpls/abs_all.jsp?arnumber=6579356

Kshetri, N. (2013). Privacy and security issues in cloud computing: The role of institutions and institutional evolution. *Telecommunications Policy*, *37*(4-5), 372–386. http://www.sciencedirect.com/science/ article/pii/S0308596112000717 Retrieved July 9, 2016

Leavitt, N. (2009). Is cloud computing really ready for prime time? *Computer*, *42*(1), 15–20. Retrieved July 9 2016 from http://www.hh.se/download/18.70cf2e49129168da0158000123279/1341267677241/ 8+Is+Cloud+Computing+Ready.pdf doi:10.1109/MC.2009.20

Lee, K., Chu, D., Cuervo, E., Kopf, J., Degtyarev, Y., Grizan, S., . . . Flinn, J. (2015). Outatime: Using Speculation to Enable Low-Latency Continuous Interaction for Mobile Cloud Gaming. Retrieved August 10, 2016 from http://research.microsoft.com/en-us/um/people/alecw/mobisys-2015-outatime.pdf

Marinelli, E. (2009, September). Cloud Computing on Mobile Devices using Map Reduce/ Master Thesis Draft, Computer Science Dept., Carnegie Mellon University (CMU) 2009. Retrieved July 8, 2016 from http://oai.dtic.mil/oai/oai?verb=getRecord&metadataPrefix=html&identifier=ADA512601

Miica (2016). Retrieved November 22, 2016 from https://www.ericsson.com/research-blog/cloud/low-energy-mobile-cloud-gaming/

Popovic, K., & Hocenski, Z. (2010). Cloud Computing Security issues and challenges. *Proceedings of the 33rd International convention MIPRO.* USA: IEEE Computer Society Washington DC. Retrieved July 9, 2016 from http://jisajournal.springeropen.com/articles/10.1186/1869-0238-4-5

Ramgovind, S., Eloff, M. M., & Smith, E. (2010). The management of security in cloud computing. *Paper presented at the 2010 Information Security for South Africa, Sandton, and Johannesburg*. Retrieved July 10, 2016 from http://ieeexplore.ieee.org/xpls/abs_all.jsp?arnumber=5588290

Rohit, B., & Sanyal, S. (2012). Survey on security issues in cloud computing and associated mitigation techniques. *International Journal of Computers and Applications*, *47*. Retrieved July 10, 2016 from http://www.ijcaonline.org/archives/volume47/number18/7292-0578

Ruay-Shiung Chang, J. G., & Gao, V. Jingsha He; Roussos, G.; Wei-Tek Tsai. (2013, March 25-28). Mobile cloud computing research - issues, challenges and needs. *Proceedings of the 2013 IEEE 7th International Symposium on Service Oriented System Engineering (SOSE)* (p. 442). Retrieved July 8, 2016 from http://ieeexplore.ieee.org/xpls/abs_all.jsp?arnumber=6525561

Umair, S., Muneer, U., Zahoor, M. N., & Malik, A. W. (2015). Mobile computing: issues and challenges. *Paper presented at the 12th International Conference on High-capacity Optical Networks and Enabling/Emerging Technologies (HONET)*, Islamabad, Pakistan. Retrieved July 6, 2016 from http://ieeexplore.ieee.org/xpls/abs_all.jsp?arnumber=7395438

Umair, S., Muneer, U., Zahoor, M. N., & Malik, A. W. (2016). Mobile Cloud Computing Future Trends and Opportunities. Managing and Processing Big Data in Cloud Computing, 105. Retrieved August 19, 2016 from books.google.com.pk/books?hl=en&lr=&id=9NFYCwAAQBAJ&oi=fnd&pg=PA105&dq=Mobile+Cloud+Computing+Future+Trends+and+Opportunities&ots=fz6JQWOmR5&sig=qPDbyG7woLbqn6-IogYgpNeKlZo#v=onepage&q=Mobile%20Cloud%20Computing%20Future%20Trends%20and%20Opportunities&f=false

Vanhatupa, J. M. (2010). Browser Games for Online Communities. *International Journal of Wireless & Mobile Networks*, *2*(3), 39-47. Retrieved August 18, 2016 from http://airccse.org/journal/jwmn/0203ijwmn03.pdf

Vanhatupa, J. M. (2013). On the Development of Browser Games – Current Technologies and the Future. *International Journal of Computer Information Systems and Industrial Management Applications*. Retrieved on August 18, 2016 from http://www.mirlabs.org/ijcisim/regular_papers_2013/Paper81.pdf

Zamith, M., Joselli, M., Clua, E. W. G., Montenegro, A., Leal-Toledo, R. C. P., Valente, L., & Feijo, B. (2011). A Distributed Architecture for Mobile Digital Games Based on Cloud Computing. *Proceedings of the 2011 Brazilian Symposium on Games and Digital Entertainment (SBGAMES)* (pp. 79 – 88). Retrieved August 02, 2016 from http://ieeexplore.ieee.org/xpls/abs_all.jsp?arnumber=6363221

KEY TERMS AND DEFINITIONS

Cloud Computing: The process of providing shared resources and other services to user on demand, that can be accessed from anywhere provided the internet connection.

Cloud Service: Resources that are delivered over the internet are known as cloud service.

Gaming-as-a-Service (GaaS): Cloud services provided for gaming. Other name for Cloud Gaming.

Infrastructure as a Service (IaaS): Virtualized computing resources available over the internet is the responsibility of infrastructure as a service.

MCG: MCG stands for Mobile Cloud Gaming. It is about that user plays game on his mobile device with all processing done on servers. High quality images are sent to user via wireless network (Chuah and Cheung, 2014).

Mobile Browser Gaming (MBG): Mobile Browser Gaming Playing games on mobile without installing games on mobile device is known as MBG. They provide distinct features like multi-user playing, played on web browser, playing with single account and long duration games (Vanhatupa, 2010).

Mobile Cloud Computing (MCC): Mobile Cloud Computing is the combination of cloud computing, mobile computing and wireless networks to bring rich computational resources to mobile users, network operators, as well as cloud computing providers.

Mobile Video Gaming (MVG): Playing video games on mobile without installing games on mobile device is known as MVG.

Platform as a Service (PaaS): Platform as a service allows the customers to develop, run and manage their applications.

Software as a Service (SaaS): Software as a service is centrally hosted in which software is accredited on subscription basis.

This research was previously published in Exploring the Convergence of Big Data and the Internet of Things edited by A.V. Krishna Prasad, pages 282-295, copyright year 2018 by Engineering Science Reference (an imprint of IGI Global).

Chapter 69

Awareness of Sustainability, Green IT, and Cloud Computing in Indian Organisations

Tomayess Issa
Curtin University, Australia

Girish Tolani
Curtin University, Australia

Vanessa Chang
Curtin University, Australia

Theodora Issa
Curtin University, Australia

ABSTRACT

This chapter examines the level of awareness that organizations in India have of the concepts, strengths and benefits of sustainability, green IT and cloud computing. Very few research papers have examined the sustainability, green IT awareness and cloud computing issues in India, and it has become necessary to ascertain just where Indian organizations stand when it comes to these concerns. Before determining whether these organisations are progressing towards sustainability, green IT and cloud computing, it is first necessary to determine whether, and to what extent, they are aware of these concepts. This research is to obtain answers, which hopefully will be a first step in a shift towards sustainability and green IT, via an online survey. Seventy-five respondents from public and private Indian organizations participated in this survey and confirmed that cloud computing is efficient, flexible and easy to maintain, although security and privacy are major concerns for Indian organizations.

INTRODUCTION

Sustainability, green IT and cloud computing are currently hot topics in research studies as well as in organizations and businesses. Due to the increase of greenhouse gases and global warming, many organizations and businesses are shifting towards becoming green and sustainable. One of the first changes that they implement is in their IT infrastructure because the ICT sector is a major contributor to the

DOI: 10.4018/978-1-5225-8176-5.ch069

Copyright © 2019, IGI Global. Copying or distributing in print or electronic forms without written permission of IGI Global is prohibited.

increase in greenhouse gases which leads to an increase in global warming. The topics of green IT and cloud computing are attracting much discussion and research. These changes in IT infrastructure and the IT sector are taking place all over the world, not just in a few countries. In some countries, governments are promoting green IT and cloud computing by providing policies and guidelines, and encouraging businesses to adopt environment-conscious practices by giving them special benefits. Much research has been conducted on the issues of sustainability, green IT and cloud computing with a common understanding that there is a need to initiate a shift towards sustainability and green IT because of increasing environmental problems and social pressure. Cloud computing is also emerging as a hot topic of research and discussion because it is considered to be the next wave of sustainability and green IT.

Sustainability means using resources wisely to save for the future generation without compromising the needs of the present generation. With technology moving towards sustainability, IT practices and products need to be made greener and safer. Green IT is considered to be the first wave of sustainability. Green IT means implementing green practices in terms of all IT processes and product life cycles. Green IT also includes the use of energy efficient IT products, use of power management software and reusing and recycling IT devices. Cloud computing, on the other hand, is considered as the second wave of sustainability and an extension of green IT which simply is the sharing of resources and applications by a number of people at a single cloud provided by a single vendor.

This conserves power that would otherwise be consumed by huge data centres, and requires less hardware at the user end which results in less wastage of resources. This chapter aims to examine the levels of awareness, regarding sustainability, green IT and cloud computing, of Indian organizations. India is the second largest country in terms of population so it contributes a lot to global warming so it becomes necessary to find out the initiatives and steps taken by the Indian government and organizations in making IT green.

Cloud computing is a relatively new concept in the business world and not many companies in India are thoroughly familiar with it. In actual fact, many Indian-based IT companies are outsourcing cloud computing services to companies in other countries, but have made little effort to introduce this concept in the Indian business world because of cost factors. The conclusion was that the awareness was there but the level of awareness was low or negligible. Some companies have adopted cloud computing in their operations but these are few and far between. The Indian government has done little to promote sustainability, green IT and cloud computing.

IT companies have shown the same lack of effort to promote these concepts in India. The time to take action is now – before it is too late and India is left behind by the more forward-thinking nations. India is also considered to be a technologically advanced country as there are numerous Indian-based IT companies who are actually providing IT services worldwide. In order to collect data for the research work, a survey questionnaire was prepared to determine whether or not Indian organizations are aware of the concepts of sustainability, green IT and cloud computing; and if they are, their level or degree of awareness. Non-probability sampling techniques were used to select the samples; in this case, the snowball technique was used. For the purposes of analysis, the Factor Analysis indicated that Indian organizations are aware of these concepts in their IT operations. They are also a little aware of the benefits of implementing these trends, and the potential harm to their organization by not adopting green IT and IT sustainability as security and privacy are major concerns from the Indian organizations' perspective.

Finally, this chapter aims to examine the level of awareness of Indian organizations' – public and private – about sustainability and cloud computing. This chapter is organized as follows: 1) Introduction;

2) Sustainability and IT; 3) Green IT 4) Cloud Computing; 5) Sustainability and Green IT awareness and Initiatives in India; 6) Chapter Significance; 7) Research Method Design and Research question; 8) Data Collection; 9) Participants; 10) Results; 11) Discussion; 12) Limitations; 13) Conclusion.

SUSTAINABILITY AND IT

Sustainability has emerged as an alarming issue much discussed by scholars and practitioners. This is because the last two decades have brought much economic growth accompanied by increasing concern about both wealth disparity and natural resource depletion (Dao, 2011). The concept of *triple bottom line* has been developed for defining sustainability that includes three components: the natural environment, society and economic performance (Dao, 2011). Sustainability as an issue has increased to the point where there is now a need to guide all businesses towards sustainable development. Consumers now are demanding much more energy-efficient and eco-friendly products, and businesses should recognize the needs of the new consumer that is emerging in the market. During the last two decades, there has been a rapid growth in the ICT sector which has resulted in an increase in the rate of greenhouse gas emissions (Prasad, Saha, P.Misra, B.Hooli, & M.Murakami, 2010).

In 2007, the ICT sector alone was responsible for 0.8 billion tonnes of carbon emission which was 2 per cent of overall emissions and estimation is that it is going to increase to 1.4 billion by 2020 (Prasad et al., 2010). The ICT sector, more than any other sector, needs to seriously consider a shift towards a green and sustainable future. Energy resources need to be used sensibly; irresponsible use will affect the environment and rapidly deplete these resources (Ketting, 1995). Many organizations are not moving towards sustainability as they think that it will increase the cost of production and will erode their competitiveness, but sustainability drives organization towards organizational and technological innovations that yield both top line and bottom line returns (Nidumolu, 2009).

Sustainability should not be confined to IT; it should be applied to the entire business process of an organization. Today, consumers are becoming more environmentally conscious than ever before, so there is a need to incorporate managerial concern with consumer concern about the natural and physical environment; this will contribute to superior business performance and enhance the corporate reputation (Sharma, 2010). Sustainability consists of seven key elements: *governance* which means top management should consist of people who support sustainability; *leadership* which means that the leader responsible for the sustainability agenda must pay attention to how the concept is to be framed and introduced; *business plan* should be made consisting of three diagnostics - situational, goal and implementation; *measure and report* which means activities need to be measured against identified progress and must be reported; *organizational learning* should be encouraged as this helps in speedy transition; *culture* is also necessary for sustainability; and lastly *information systems* - by developing models, information systems can help to achieve sustainability in an eco-efficient, eco-equity and eco-effective way (Smith & Sharicz, 2011). Basically, sustainable IT is also considered as green IT but now is the time to move on to the second wave of sustainable IT which would be more externally focussed and service oriented, allowing IT to exploit both enterprise and customer opportunities while addressing broader societal problems (Harmon & Demirkan, 2011).

GREEN IT

Green IT presents new concepts of manufacturing and recycling computers and devices with minimal impacts on the environment. Currently, data centre and servers are using green IT technology to reduce energy and cost, provide an effective performance, promote recyclability, and reduce the use of hazardous materials. Currently, several companies locally and globally are using green IT technology in their organizations to improve energy efficiency to protect our planet and saving the current resources for the seventh generation (Newton, 2000; Newton, 2003)

Green computing is intended to reduce hazardous material and maximize energy efficiency and it should be recyclable. Green IT refers to saving energy at various levels including hardware, software and services (Agarwal & Nath, 2011). Data centres should be set up in deserts where there is an abundance of available land and geo-tectonic stability, and non-conventional sources of energy - solar and wind - should be used, although the regulation of temperature and humidity must be considered (Vijaykumar, 2011). Virtualization is also important for green IT. There are three types of virtualization: storage virtualization which condenses several storage spaces to a single storage location; network virtualization divides bandwidth into independent channels and combines computing resources into one; and server virtualization hides the physical server resources (Yamini & Selvi, 2010). Data and programs are being swept away from the desktops and PCs, and software are used as services. The internet is the platform for cloud computing services (Hayes, 2008) and has the advantage of decreasing the amount of storage that individual computers require to store a software. Server and storage virtualization are the third generation of virtualization that brings together server and storage to form a whole entity combined into a dynamic, centrally managed resource pool, where any application or operating system can maintain continuous optimization and high availability status (Xianmin, 2011). Green cloud is also introduced as a new architecture for data centres. It will reduce power consumption and give guaranteed performance to the users by leveraging live virtual machine migration technology. This green cloud architecture uses virtual machines to meet the workload requirements (Liu et al., 2009)

CLOUD COMPUTING

Cloud computing refers to applications that are provided as services on the internet, and the hardware and system software in the data centres that provide those services (Armbrust, 2010). The data centre that provides these services including the hardware and the software is called a "cloud" (Armbrust, 2010). These services, when provided to the general public, are called "public cloud" and the services are called "utility computing" because the user can access services according to his/her requirements without having to know where these services are being hosted and how they are delivered (Buyya, 2009). When a company uses a data centre for its own purposes and this centre is not available to the public, this is called "private cloud" (Armbrust, 2010). It simply means that now the computing world is developing software not just for their own requirements, but for millions of others to consume as a service; this is what is done in cloud computing (Buyya, 2009; Singh & Malhotra, 2012; Zissis & Lekkas, 2012).

Buyya (2009) even compared cluster, grid and cloud computing: Cluster computing is a type of parallel and distributed system, which consists of a collection of inter-connected, stand-alone computers working together as a single, integrated computing resource. Grid computing is a type of parallel and distributed system that enables the sharing, selection, and aggregation of geographically distributed `autonomous' resources dynamically at runtime depending on their availability, capability, performance, cost, and users' quality-of-service requirements. Cloud computing is a type of parallel and distributed system consisting of a collection of inter-connected and virtualized computers that are dynamically provisioned and presented as one or more unified computing resource(s) based on service-level agreements (SLA) established through negotiation between the service provider and consumers.

The hardware and infrastructure required for cloud computing are (Singh & Malhotra, 2012; Velte, Velte, & Elsenpeter, 2010; Weiss, 2007; Zhang & Chen, 2010): firstly, clients- the end user devices which are required to interact with the cloud. There are different types of client: 1) Mobile clients include devices like laptops, PDAs and smart phones. These devices generally are subject to security and speed issues as there are certain places where connections are slow (e.g. hotels, restaurants or WIFI- enabled public places) 2) Thin clients are those clients which lack hard drives and any kind of CD/DVD ROM and display just what is on the server. Thin clients are generally used when the applications or the information can be taken from the cloud and there is no additional requirement of storing on individual systems. These are less expensive and are used in small scale or medium scale businesses.

Security is good as no data is stored on the clients. 3) Thick clients are those which are normally used as desktops with all the required hardware. They are connected to the clouds for some particular applications. When cloud computing is introduced in the organization, if company has a low budget, they can use the desktops that are already present in the organisation instead of getting new thin clients. These are handy when one needs to store files on one's own systems instead of fetching it from clouds every time. Security is an issue as data is stored on the client machine itself.

Secondly, security is another aspect to consider when introducing cloud computing. There is always a concern about the security of data as the data is stored by a third party and not by the client itself. There are certain security benefits of storing data on cloud: for example, there is comparatively less data leakage as the storage is centralised and not spread among various clients; clients never need to worry about the security as this is the responsibility of the cloud provider; there are always new developments that address security issues related to the cloud; and lastly, if there is a security breach, the cloud provider can respond to the incident with less downtime than if this were done by the organisation itself (Marston, Li, Bandyopadhyay, Zhang, & Ghalsasi, 2011; Redmap, n.d)

Cloud computing can bring several benefits to an organisation including technical, user, architectural and organizational advantages as follows: (Aymerich, 2008): firstly, the technical advantages are that it does not require additional hardware to handle peak load situations because of which hardware infrastructure can be highly under-utilised; these resources can be virtualised and presented to customers as virtual servers which they can manage by themselves, but if this is done physically, it might require multiple computers or data centres. Finally, Nandgaonkar and Raut (2014) confirm that cloud computing services depend fully on availability, speed, quality and performance of the internet, which is provided by the service provider.

Secondly, the user is no longer stuck with traditional computing and there is no need to buy special devices such as PDAs or specially-configured phones in order to use a particular application. In future, any device that is internet-enabled will be able to use cloud-based applications. Moreover, when using those applications, the end user will not have to worry at all about capacity or compatibility or other issues apart from device maintenance. There are no concerns about upgrading a software version on the hard disk as the cloud provides the latest version.

Thirdly, cloud computing can be set up in places at lower costs of space and electricity. Furthermore, by using cloud computing, an organisation can achieve efficiency in their hardware and software infrastructure as the related costs will be reduced and resource utilization will be increased, thereby increasing profitability. Furthermore, the resources can be pooled, thereby increasing utilization by delivering them only when they are required.

Fourthly, cloud computing is advantageous for low-capital, small and medium-scale businesses as they will not need to spend a great deal on buying in-house resources and technical equipment. Finally, even large-scale businesses and organizations are adopting cloud computing as it saves costs, can be remotely accessed, is easily available, and allows real-time collaboration.

Finally, cloud computing considers the new smart technology which needs to be adopted by organizations and users to reduce the impact of IT technology on environment from design, energy and e-waste (Brender & Markov, 2013; Johnson, 2013; Singh & Malhotra, 2012)

SUSTAINABILITY AND GREEN IT AWARENESS AND INITIATIVES IN INDIA

India is an emerging economy and IT products and services are used at a greater rate here because of the high population and therefore power consumption rate is equally high. The world is relying heavily on non-renewable sources of energy for its power supply. Eighty-five per cent of the world's power comes from fossil fuels, 9 per cent from hydro, 4 per cent from nuclear and 2 per cent from new renewable sources (Naidu, 1996). In India, there is a pressing need to adopt green IT because of the rapid growth of technology, expected shortages of power supply, huge maintenance of data centres and e-wastage of IT hardware and products (SaniaKhan, AbdulRazak, & KrishnaKumar, 2011). The adoption of green IT in India needs a mind-set wave in education, awareness programs and information, technology and commitment, as environmental issues related to carbon footprints, e-wastage and disposals of IT hardware, data centre maintenance are rarely discussed. However, some companies such as MNC IT and other international customers are trying to do business the green IT way, although it is still difficult to adopt green IT practices in India at every level due to the need for huge investment and a drastic change to the entire IT infrastructure (SaniaKhan et al., 2011). Implementing these approaches in India will increase green IT awareness, and this can lead to a reduction of e-waste and carbon footprints.

CHAPTER SIGNIFICANCE

In terms of its practical significance, this chapter will help organizations to acquire knowledge about sustainability, green IT and cloud computing from the base level. They will become aware of the progress made to date, in terms of adopting these concepts in organizational practice, in the world and in India. It will help them to gain a competitive edge because it will allow them to monitor the progress and they can adopt and implement appropriate practices before any other competitor in the market. The chapter draws its data from a wide range of industries in both the private and public sectors, thereby avoiding bias and providing a complete scenario of every organization. This chapter will enable both large organisations and small businesses to become more aware of these concepts. Also, the research data includes several companies which have already shifted to cloud computing, and this is useful for those who are still unsure of it, or are planning future implementation of cloud computing in their businesses. Vendors who provide cloud computing services will also benefit from this research as it also emphasizes the importance of the services provided by these organizations.

At present, no company in India produces green IT products so this chapter will make companies aware of the potential market for such products that exists in India as it is one of the largest IT hubs in the world. The results of the surveys conducted will help organizations to identify the sectors that are already aware of these concepts and also the advantages and disadvantages of putting these into practice if they adopt them in their businesses. This will help new firms to gain a competitive edge by introducing these concepts in their businesses before entering into the market as they would be already familiar with the current scenario as a result of this research.

As for the theoretical significance, this chapter will help those students studying the issues of sustainability, green IT and cloud computing as it can be used as an article for analysis and evaluation. This will help them understand these concepts more broadly and thoroughly. The discussion presented in this chapter on the concepts of sustainability, green IT and cloud computing has been undertaken after analyzing many research works in the literatures, so students will be able to read one research work comprising various other research works. Researchers in the field of green IT, cloud computing and sustainability will benefit from this research as it takes into consideration these concepts in general and in relation to India in particular. This chapter will be of help to researchers who intend to carry out research on the concepts of sustainability, green IT and/or cloud computing based in India. The results of the research work will help them to analyze the current scenario in India and Indian organizations in regards to sustainability, green IT and cloud computing. The results of the surveys provide secondary data for research work and will familiarize students and researchers with the attitudes of Indian organizations towards sustainability, green IT and cloud computing.

RESEARCH METHOD DESIGN AND RESEARCH QUESTION

A mixed-method approach to data collection is used in this chapter. Quantitative data is gathered by means of an online survey. The online survey allows qualitative data to be collected as respondents are invited to provide personal opinions or comments in a separate text box in the survey itself (Issa, 2013; Sexton, Miller, & Dietsch, 2011). Based on the current literature review, the online survey was developed with the intention of examining Indian organizations' awareness of sustainability and cloud computing. The survey consists of two sections: the formal demographic information followed by a second section containing fourteen statements seeking participants' opinions regarding the risks and opportunities of cloud computing as well as sustainability via a five-point Likert scale with a range of 'Strongly Disagree, Disagree, Neutral, Agree, and Strongly Agree'.

This chapter aims to examine major and minor research questions. The Primary research aims to answer this question: To what extent are Indian organizations aware of sustainability, green IT and cloud computing technology? Furthermore, this chapter will address the following minor research questions: "What is the degree of sustainability and green IT awareness among India organizations? This question aims to identify the degree or level of awareness. Once we know whether or not Indian organizations are aware of sustainability, green IT and cloud computing, it will become easier to ascertain their level or degree of awareness, and whether organizations are just aware of these concepts (i.e. basic awareness) or whether they are planning to implement them (i.e. intermediate level of awareness) or whether they have already implemented them (advanced level of awareness). These levels of awareness will assist with the analysis of the results presented in this chapter.

Furthermore, the second minor research question is "What are the strengths and weaknesses of cloud computing in terms of its potential impact on the performance of Indian companies?" This question concentrates mainly on the level of cloud computing awareness. Responses to this question will indicate if Indian organizations actually have implemented cloud computing in their operations and to identify the advantages outweigh its shortcomings. Cloud computing is considered to be the second wave of sustainability and an extension of green IT, so if businesses and organizations have adopted cloud computing, this implies that they are aware of the concepts of sustainability, green IT and cloud computing and that they are shifting towards sustainability and green IT.

DATA COLLECTION

The data collection techniques include the techniques and procedures for data or sample collection which include the basis on which it was collected, how it was collected and from whom it was collected. Data is the main element of every research. It can be primary which means collected directly from sources such as surveys and samples, or it can be secondary collected from existing research work, magazines, articles, newspapers and theses. For collection of data, a sampling technique is used which includes probability sampling and non-probability sampling.

For the purposes of this study, a non-probability sampling technique was used because firstly, there was no way to select a sample population because our aim was to ascertain the awareness levels among Indian organisations from two sectors of industry, private and public, and from all across the country. Secondly, probability techniques would not have been feasible if a company chosen by the researcher as part of the sample, had not replied, thereby returning a negative result. Thirdly, the researcher did not want to predetermine a particular sample size, since it was desirable to collect as many surveys as possible. Non-probability technique provides flexibility in selecting sample size and the number of responses. It is the best technique to use when sample population is not to be selected on the basis of any factor and one has to take into consideration the entire population in that field. Non-probability techniques include: Quota sampling; Purposive sampling; Snowball sampling; Self-selection sampling; and Convenience sampling.

In this study, snowball sampling was used as a means of data collection. With this method, initial contact is made with a few potential respondents who are in turn invited to pass copies of the survey or the survey link to other individuals or companies who in turn forward these on and so on, creating a snowball effect, so to speak. To avoid sampling bias, the respondent sample included males and females, a range of professions, and a variety of industries from both the private and public sectors. Moreover, the researcher did not focus on only one particular region of the country, but made contact with people residing in different regions. This technique suited the purpose of this study which was to find out the degree of awareness of green IT, cloud computing and sustainable IT among Indian organizations.

PARTICIPANTS

This study was conducted in India to examine the *Awareness of Sustainability, Green IT and Cloud Computing in Indian Organisations*. The survey was distributed to organizations in India and the survey response rate was 83.3%. Table 1 provides a summary of the respondents' details including gender, industry sector type and qualifications.

Table 2 shows the number of survey respondents in public and private organizations in India. It was noted that the majority of respondents work in small, medium and large organizations. Furthermore, the majority of respondents worked in communication services and finance and insurance, 18% to 24% respectively (see Table 3).

Finally, Table 4 indicates confirmation that 61% of personnel in Indian organizations are still unaware of cloud computing applications although 16% are currently using various applications such as Amazon and National Green Database.

Table 1. Summary of the respondents' details

Number and Percentage of Questionnaires	
Questionnaires Distributed	90
Questionnaires Returned (valid)	75
Response Rate	83.3%
Gender	
Male Respondents	61
Female Respondents	27
Sector Type	
Public Sector Organization	14
Private Sector Organization	75
Qualifications	
Bachelor's Degree	38
Master's Degree	46
Doctorate (PhD)	2
Other, Please specify	2

Table 2. Number of employees in public and private organizations in India

0-50	17
51 to 200	16
201 to 500	15
501 to 2000	16
2001 to 8000	13
8001 - 100000	9
Total	86

Table 3. Organization types in India

Organizations	Number	Percentage
Accommodation, Cafes and Restaurants	4	4%
Agriculture, Forestry and Fishing	3	3%
Communication Services	16	18%
Construction	9	10%
Education	7	8%
Electricity, Gas and Water Supply	4	4%
Finance and Insurance	22	24%
Government Administration and Defence	6	7%
Health and Community Services	7	8%
Manufacturing	4	4%
Mining	2	2%
Personal and Other Services	5	6%
Property and Business Services	6	7%
Retail Trade	10	11%
Transport and Storage	3	3%
Wholesale Trade	3	3%

Table 4. Cloud computing usage in private and public organizations in India

Answer	Response
Don't Know	20
No	54
Yes If you answered 'yes' to this question, please provide details in the space below of applications you access via cloud computing.	14

RESULTS

A total of 77 participants from India responded to the online survey. With two responses not accepted because of missing data, this resulted in 75 valid cases of responses for India for the following Factor Analysis. Based on the Mean and STD Deviation results, it was confirmed that the majority of the personnel in Indian organizations agreed that cloud computing services are efficient, flexible and sustainable (see Table 5).

To examine the online survey results further, the researchers adopted principal axis factoring for factor extraction, and oblique rotation was applied using the direct oblimin method to correlate the variables (Costello & Osborne, 2005; Hair, Black, Babin, & Anderson, 2009). To measure the sampling adequacy, researchers carried out specific testing from Cronbach's Alpha, Kaiser-Meyer-Olkin and Bartlett's test. Firstly, the Cronbach's Alpha for all 14 variables was .816, indicating an acceptable internal consistency of the items in the scale (Gliem & Gliem, 2003). Secondly, the Kaiser-Meyer-Olkin measure of sampling adequacy was .739 above the recommended value of .6, indicating that a sufficient sample size has been

Table 5. Descriptive statistics – Mean and STD deviation

	Mean	Std. Deviation
Q8_1 Cloud computing is more flexible than traditional computing	3.68	1.010
Q8_2 Cloud computing is more efficient than traditional computing	3.74	.882
Q8_3 Cloud computing helps organisations become 'greener'	3.59	1.109
Q8_4 Cloud computing helps provide scalable services	3.68	.788
Q8_5 Cloud computing helps provide reliable services	3.44	.963
Q8_6 Cloud computing helps provide ease of maintenance	3.62	.973
Q8_7 Cloud computing makes staffing easier	3.39	.959
Q8_8 Cloud computing decreases operating expenses	3.65	.969
Q8_9 Cloud computing increases operating expenses	3.11	1.097
Q8_10 Cloud computing reduces capital costs	3.32	.947
Q8_11 Cloud computing introduces security problems	3.35	1.060
Q8_12 Cloud computing is more risky than traditional computing	3.27	1.031
Q8_13 Cloud computing reduces organisations' carbon footprint	3.18	1.006
Q8_14 Cloud computing contributes to organisations' sustainability	3.61	.857

obtained from the analysis (Hill, 2012). Thirdly, the Bartlett's test of sphericity is highly significant, X^2 = 396.588, df = 91, p < .000, indicating that the items of the scale are sufficiently correlated to factors to be found (Burns & Burns, 2008). Finally, the communalities were all over .05 (see Table 6) except for statements 11 and 14, as Indian organizations still have some concerns about security and sustainability.

Table 6. Cloud computing – Communalities

	Initial	Extraction
Q8_1 Cloud computing is more flexible than traditional computing	.651	.719
Q8_2 Cloud computing is more efficient than traditional computing	.606	.636
Q8_3 Cloud computing helps organisations become 'greener'	.585	.538
Q8_4 Cloud computing helps provide scalable services	.687	.657
Q8_5 Cloud computing helps provide reliable services	.440	.444
Q8_6 Cloud computing helps provide ease of maintenance	.662	.594
Q8_7 Cloud computing makes staffing easier	.624	.469
Q8_8 Cloud computing decreases operating expenses	.559	.898
Q8_9 Cloud computing increases operating expenses	.555	.646
Q8_10 Cloud computing reduces capital costs	.529	.421
Q8_11 Cloud computing introduces security problems	.375	.325
Q8_12 Cloud computing is more risky than traditional computing	.529	.704
Q8_13 Cloud computing reduces organisations' carbon footprint	.501	.467
Q8_14 Cloud computing contributes to organisations' sustainabiliy	.358	.321
Extraction Method: Principal Axis Factoring		

Furthermore, the researchers used principle components analysis to estimate the factor loading matrix for the factor analysis model as well the standard correlation matrix. The Eigen values are assessed to determine the number of factors accounting for the correlations amongst the variables. As demonstrated in Table 7, this model of eight factors explains a total of 56.398% of the variation. The Eigen values and the amount of variances explained by each of these factors are presented in Table 7 (after rotation).

Furthermore, to measure the regression coefficients (i.e. slopes), the researchers carried out the factor loadings. The *factor loadings* are based on most of the items that have a high loading value and the one with the cleanest factor structure is considered as important. Hair et al (2010) suggested the lowest sample size is 50 cases. If the sample size ranges from 71 to 84, the sufficient factor loading is .60. Items Q8_8 and Q8_11 are shared with other factors (Costello & Osborne, 2005). The Q8_8 under Factor 1 and Q8_11 each has a factor loading below .6 (Hair et al, 2010). The statements 4, 8 and 11 were excluded and are highlighted in light blue.

The Pattern Matrix revealed three factors. However, factoring requires at least more than one variable or item grouped in the same factor, referred to share commonness or correlations (Hair et al, 2010). With this, only Factor 1 can be fit for labelling, as Factor 2 and Factor 3 each has only one variable which is Q8_12 and Q8_9 respectively. A score was calculated for this factor by averaging across each individual item. The mean and standard deviation of the factor average is presented below in Table 9.

Overall, it became evident that those who already know about 'cloud computing' even to a limited extent, think of such technology as efficient, flexible, scalable, reliable, easy to maintain. However, the survey outcomes confirmed that although cloud computing usage in India has brought various benefits, there is nevertheless some concern regarding the issue of risk and security of cloud computing as well as sustainability.

Table 7. Cloud computing - Total variance explained

Factor	Initial Eigenvalues			Extraction Sums of Squared Loadings			Rotation Sums of Squared Loadings (a)
1	Total	% of Variance	Cumulative %	Total	% of Variance	Cumulative %	Total
2	3.247	36.082	36.082	2.791	31.006	31.006	2.770
3	1.821	20.228	56.310	1.571	17.461	48.467	1.454
4	1.027	11.414	67.724	.714	7.931	56.398	.999
5	.853	9.474	77.198				
6	.511	5.681	88.842				
7	.435	4.835	93.677				
8	.346	3.846	97.523				
9	.223	2.477	100.000				
Extraction Method: Principal Axis Factoring							
a. When factors are correlated, sums of squared loadings cannot be added to obtain a total variance							

Table 8. Cloud computing – Pattern matrix

x (a)	Factor		
	1	**2**	**3**
Q8_2 Cloud computing is more efficient than traditional computing	.815		
Q8_1 Cloud computing is more flexible than traditional computing	.758		-.131
Q8_6 Cloud computing helps provide ease of maintenance	.718		.116
Q8_5 Cloud computing helps provide reliable services	.693		
Q8_4 Cloud computing helps provide scalable services	.555	-.244	.318
Q8_8 Cloud computing decreases operating expenses	.425		-.131
Q8_12 Cloud computing is more risky than traditional computing	.116	1.005	
Q8_11 Cloud computing introduces security problems		.459	.208
Q8_11 Cloud computing increases operating expenses		.257	.832
Extraction Method: Principal Axis Factoring Rotation Method: Oblimin with Kaiser Normalization			
a. Rotating converged in 10 iterations			

DISCUSSION

The chapter aims to assess the awareness of green IT, cloud computing and sustainability among Indian organizations. This research was intended to discover the extent to which Indian organizations are aware of green IT, cloud computing and sustainability in IT. The survey results indicated that organizations are aware of these concepts in their IT operations, but they have little awareness of the benefits of implementing these trends, and the potential harm that can be caused to their organization by not adopting green IT and IT sustainability. Cloud computing is a relatively new concept in the business world and not many companies in India are thoroughly familiar with it. In actual fact, many Indian-based IT companies (i.e. Wipro, Infosys, and Tata) are outsourcing cloud computing services to companies in other countries, but have made little effort to introduce this concept in the Indian business world because of cost factors.

According to the survey results, there is some degree of awareness of sustainability, green IT and cloud computing in Indian organisations, although this is very low. This is partly due to the fact that that both the government in India and Indian-based companies have made little or negligible efforts to promote green IT, sustainability or cloud computing in India. There appears to be no logical reason for this apparent indifference which seems to be the main reason for the low level of awareness and adoption of these concepts.

Finally, the results presented in this chapter indicate that the advantages of cloud computing outweighs its disadvantages: it helps organisation to become greener, increase operating profits, and provide more

Table 9. Cloud computing – Descriptive statistics (N=75)

	Mean	**Std. Deviation**
Factor 1: Operational benefits	3.621	0.957

reliable services. Several studies ((Avram, 2014; Oliveira, Thomas, & Espadanal, 2014; Son, Lee, Lee, & Chang, 2014) indicate that cloud computing is more efficient and more flexible than traditional computing; it reduces the carbon footprint and promotes sustainability; it is easy to maintain and staffing requirements are simplified. However, respondents also believed that it is more risky than traditional computing and increases the security threats to the organisation as the data is handled by some other entity that provides these services.

To conclude, it appears that Indian organizations are aware of these concepts of sustainability, green IT and cloud computing, but the level of awareness is very low or negligible. Hence, the government and IT companies need to put more effort into promoting cloud computing (i.e. training, workshops, conferences, newsletters via social networking and other facilities, education and others) as a better alternative to traditional computing in many ways. However, despite its many benefits and advantages, it may pose security risks to companies, of which they should be aware.

LIMITATIONS

The study presented in this chapter was limited to 75 participants from both public and private organizations in India. The rationale behind this study is to assess the Indian organizations' awareness of sustainability, green IT and cloud computing. The online survey responses strongly indicated that Indian organizations are aware of these concepts, although the level of awareness is low. Therefore, further research with larger and more diverse groups of organizations is required in the future to strengthen the research findings.

CONCLUSION

Sustainability, green IT and cloud computing are the current hot topics in the fields of IT research and IT business. This research was conducted with organizations located only in India and no other parts of the world. The results of the surveys were noteworthy, indicating that most of the personnel from organizations who participated in the surveys actually were aware of the terms 'sustainability', 'green IT' and 'cloud computing'. Most of them were even using cloud computing in their organizations. However, it emerged that although they knew about these concepts, none of them actually adopted the principles sustainability and green IT in their operations. The purpose of this research paper was to identify whether organizations in India are aware of the concepts of sustainability, green IT and cloud computing, and if so, what is their level of awareness, do they just know about it, or are they considering adopting it, or they are on their way to adopting it, or they are using it? The second important purpose was to identify whether or not those businesses that have adopted cloud computing actually know its strengths and weaknesses, and whether or not they find cloud computing beneficial for their organization.

The answers to the research questions led to the conclusion that, although businesses are familiar with the concepts of sustainability green IT and cloud computing, their levels of awareness of these concepts are very low or negligible. Although companies have responded to these questions, awareness alone is not enough to make a change. More effort should be made to increase companies' awareness of these concepts and move towards incorporating the notion of sustainability within their organisational and business practices. In order to increase both public and corporate awareness, the government and Indian-based IT companies need to collaborate more effectively to ensure that sustainability and green IT are being implemented in organizations and businesses in India. There is an urgent need to make a transition towards sustainability and green IT because of the alarming rate of increase in carbon foot-prints and global warming. Cloud computing is a second wave towards sustainability and an extension of green IT. According to the survey results presented in this chapter, companies do know the strengths and weaknesses of green IT although few companies have attempted to adopt green IT practices in their businesses.

The security issues related to cloud computing are of concern to large organizations. There is a service level agreement between the vendor and buyer, but the data of the company stored with the vendor is always at risk because the employees working in the vendor's organization can pose a threat to the data. The conclusion of this research paper was that although companies are aware of the concept of sustainability, green IT and cloud computing, they are not actually planning or even considering implementing these concepts in their businesses or organizations. Government and IT companies need to put more effort into sustainability and encourage companies by giving them subsidies or rewards for implementing these concepts. In this way, companies can shift towards a more sustainable future because India needs to keep pace with other countries and global trends which are moving towards sustainability and green IT.

REFERENCES

Agarwal, S., & Nath, A. (2011). *Green Computing - A New Horizon of Energy Efficiency and Electronic Waste Minimization: A Global Perspective.* Paper presented at the Communication Systems and Network Technologies (CSNT), 2011 International Conference on. http://dx.doi.org: doi:10.1109/csnt.2011.148

Armbrust, M., Stoica, I., Zaharia, M., Fox, A., Griffith, R., Joseph, A. D., ... Rabkin, A. (2010). A view of cloud computing. *Communications of the ACM, 53*(4), 50. doi:10.1145/1721654.1721672

Avram, M. G. (2014). Advantages and Challenges of Adopting Cloud Computing from an Enterprise Perspective. *Procedia Technology, 12*(0), 529-534.

Aymerich, F. M. (2008). An approach to a cloud computing network 2008 First International Conference on the Applications of Digital Information and Web Technologies (ICADIWT). 113.

Brender, N., & Markov, I. (2013). Risk perception and risk management in cloud computing: Results from a case study of Swiss companies. *International Journal of Information Management, 33*(5), 726–733. doi:10.1016/j.ijinfomgt.2013.05.004

Burns, R., & Burns, R. (2008). Business Research Methods and Statistics Using SPSS. *Sage (Atlanta, Ga.).*

Buyya, R., Yeo, C. S., Venugopal, S., Broberg, J., & Brandic, I. (2009). Cloud computing and emerging IT platforms: Vision, hype, and reality for delivering computing as the 5th utility. *Future Generation Computer Systems, 25*(6), 599–616. doi:10.1016/j.future.2008.12.001

Costello, A., & Osborne, J. (2005). Best Practices in Exploratory Factor Analysis: Four Recommendations for Getting the Most From Your Analysis. *Practical Assessment, Research & Evaluation, 10*(7), 1–9.

Dao, V., Langella, I., & Carbo, J. (2011). From green to sustainability: Information Technology and an integrated sustainability framework. *The Journal of Strategic Information Systems*, *20*(1), 63–79. doi:10.1016/j.jsis.2011.01.002

Gliem, J., & Gliem, R. (2003). Calculating, Interpreting, and Reporting Cronbach's Alpha Reliability Coefficient for Likert-Type Scales2003 Midwest Research to Practice Conference in Adult, Continuing and Community Education (pp. 82 - 88).

Hair, J., Black, W., Babin, B., & Anderson, R. (2009). *Multivariate data analysis*. Upper Saddle River, NJ: Prentice Hall.

Harmon, R., & Demirkan, H. (2011). The Next Wave of Sustainable IT. *IT Professional*, *13*(1), 19–25. doi:10.1109/MITP.2010.140

Hayes, B. (2008). Cloud computing. *Communications of the ACM*, *51*(7), 9–11. doi:10.1145/1364782.1364786

Hill, B. D. (2012). *The Sequential Kaiser-Meyer-Olkin Procedure As An Alternative For Determining The Number Of Factors In Common-Factor Analysis: A Monte Carlo Simulation* USA: Proquest, Umi Dissertation Publishing

Issa, T. (2013). *Online Survey: Best Practice In Information Systems Research and Exploring Social Artifacts: Approaches and Methodologies* (pp. 1–19). IGI Global;

Johnson, P. E. (2013). A Review of "Cloud Computing for Libraries". *Journal of Access Services*, *10*(1), 71–73. doi:10.1080/15367967.2013.738572

Ketting, N. G. (1995). Towards a sustainable energy future. *Energy Policy*, *23*(7), 637–638. doi:10.1016/0301-4215(95)98219-I

Khan, Razak, & Kumar. (2011). Prioritization of Green IT Parameters for Indian IT Industry Using Analytical Hierarchy Process. *World Journal of Social Sciences*, *1*(4), 179–194.

Liu, L., Wang, H., Liu, X., Jin, X., He, W. B., Wang, Q. B., & Chen, Y. (2009). GreenCloud: a new architecture for green data center. In *Proceedings of the 6th international conference industry session on Autonomic computing and communications industry session* (pp. 29-38). ACM. http://dx.doi.org: doi:10.1145/1555312.1555319

Marston, S., Li, Z., Bandyopadhyay, S., Zhang, J., & Ghalsasi, A. (2011). Cloud computing — The business perspective. *Decision Support Systems*, *51*(1), 176–189. doi:10.1016/j.dss.2010.12.006

Naidu. (1996). Indian scenario of renewable energy for sustainable development. *Energy Policy, 24*(6), 575-581.

Nandgaonkar, S., & Raut, A. B. (2014). A Comprehensive Study on Cloud Computing. *International Journal of Computer Science and Mobile Computing*, *3*(4), 733–738.

Newton, L. H. (2000). Millennial Reservations. *Business Ethics Quarterly*, *10*(1), 291–303. doi:10.2307/3857714

Newton, L. H. (2003). *Ethics and Sustainability, Sustainable Development and the Moral Life*. New Jersey, NY: Prentice-Hall, Inc.

Nidumolu, R. (2009). Why sustainability is now the key driver of innovation.(Sustainability Innovation). *Harvard Business Review, 87*(9), 56.

Oliveira, T., Thomas, M., & Espadanal, M. (2014). Assessing the determinants of cloud computing adoption: An analysis of the manufacturing and services sectors. *Information & Management, 51*(5), 497–510. doi:10.1016/j.im.2014.03.006

Prasad, A. R., Saha, S., P.Misra, B.Hooli, & M.Murakami. (2010). back to green. *Journal of Green Engineering*, 89-110.

Redmap. (n.d). *CloudUp! An analysis of security in the cloud*. Retrieved from http://www.redmap.com/downloads/whitepapers/lo/smartCloud%20-%20Whitepaper%20-%20CloudUp!%20An%20Analysis%20of%20Security%20in%20the%20Cloud.pdf

Sexton, N., Miller, H., & Dietsch, A. (2011). Appropriate uses and considerations for online surveying in human dimensions research. *Human Dimensions of Wildlife, 16*(3), 154–163. doi:10.1080/10871209.2011.572142

Sharma, A., Iyer, G. R., Mehrotra, A., & Krishnan, R. (2010). Sustainability and business-to-business marketing: A framework and implications. *Industrial Marketing Management, 39*(2), 330–341. doi:10.1016/j.indmarman.2008.11.005

Singh, A., & Malhotra, M. (2012). Agent Based Framework for Scalability in Cloud Computing *International Journal of Computer Science & Engineering Technology*, 41 - 45.

Smith, P., & Sharicz, C. (2011). The shift needed for Sustainability. *The Learning Organization, 18*(1), 73–86. doi:10.1108/09696471111096019

Son, I., Lee, D., Lee, J.-N., & Chang, Y. B. (2014). Market perception on cloud computing initiatives in organizations: An extended resource-based view. *Information & Management, 51*(6), 653–669. doi:10.1016/j.im.2014.05.006

Velte, A. T., Velte, T. J., & Elsenpeter, R. (2010). *Cloud Computing - A Practical Approach*. McGraw Hill.

Vijaykumar, N. (2011). Datacenters in the Desert. *Technology and Society Magazine, IEEE, 30*(2), 31-38.

Weiss, A. (2007). *Computing in the Clouds*. Retrieved from http://di.ufpe.br/~redis/intranet/bibliography/middleware/weiss-computing08.pdf

Xianmin, W. (2011). *Application of Server Virtualization Technology in Enterprise Information*. Paper presented at the Internet Computing & Information Services (ICICIS), 2011 International Conference on. http://dx.doi.org: doi:10.1109/icicis.2011.13

Yamini, B., & Selvi, D. V. (2010). *Cloud virtualization: A potential way to reduce global warming*. Paper presented at the Recent Advances in Space Technology Services and Climate Change (RSTSCC), 2010. http://dx.doi.org: doi:10.1109/rstscc.2010.5712798

Zhang, W., & Chen, Q. (2010). From E-government to C-government via Cloud Computing *International Conference on E-Business and E-Government* (pp. 679 - 682). 10.1109/ICEE.2010.177

Zissis, D., & Lekkas, D. (2012). Addressing Cloud Computing Security Issues. *Future Generation Computer Systems, 28*(3), 583–592. doi:10.1016/j.future.2010.12.006

ADDITIONAL READING

Ageron, B., Gunasekaran, A., & Spalanzani, A. (2012). Sustainable Supply Management: An Empirical Study. *International Journal of Production Economics, 140*(1), 168–182. doi:10.1016/j.ijpe.2011.04.007

Amann, B., Caby, J., Jaussaud, J., & Pineiro, J. (2009). Shareholder activism for corporate social responsibility: law and practice in the United States, Japan, France and Spain. In D. McBarnet, A. Voiculescu, & T. Campbell (Eds.), *The New Corporate Accountability - Corporate Social Responsibility and the Law* (pp. 336–364). Cambridge.

Armbrust, M., Fox, A., Griffith, R., Joseph, A. D., Katz, R., Konwinski, A., . . . Zaharia, M. (2009). Above the Clouds: A View of Cloud Computing. 1 Dec 2009,http://radlab.cs.berkeley.edu/w/uploads/2/24/9_-_Above_the_Clouds-_A_View_of_Cloud_Computing_.pdf

Basciani, M. (2011). *Is the Cloud Green?* Zurich, Switzerland.

Bateman, A., & Wood, M. (2009). Cloud Computing. *Bioinformatics (Oxford, England), 25*(12), 1475. doi:10.1093/bioinformatics/btp274 PMID:19435745

Berl, A., Gelenbe, E., Di Girolamo, M., Giuliani, G., De Meer, H., Quan Dang, M., & Pentikousis, K. (2009). Energy Efficient Cloud Computing. *The Computer Journal*, 1–7.

Berl, A., Gelenbe, E., Di Girolamo, M., Giuliani, G., Meer, H., Dang, M., & Pentikousis, K. (2010). Energy-Efficient Cloud Computing. *The Computer Journal, 53*(7), 1046–1051. doi:10.1093/comjnl/bxp080

Chang, V., Issa, T., & Issa, T. (2011). Cloud computing and sustainability: an Australian public sector perspective*XXII - International Society for Professional Innovation Management (ISPIM) Conference, held in Hamburg - Germany*

Elliot, S. (2007). *Environmentally Sustainable ICT: A Critical Topic for IS Research?* Paper presented at the Pacific Asia Conference on Information Systems

Goldsmith, S., & Samson, D. (2006). *Sustainable Development and Business Success*. Melbourne: Thomson.

Grossman, R. L. (2009). The Case for Cloud Computing. Computer.org/ITPro, 23 -27.

Hayward, B. (2012). Sustainable ICT. *Telecommunications Journal of Australia, 62*(5), 1–10. doi:10.7790/tja.v62i5.373

Issa, T., Chang, V., & Issa, T. (2010). The Impact of Cloud Computing and Organizational Sustainability *Cloud Computing and Virtualization 2010, held in Singapore*

Issa, T., Chang, V., & Issa, T. (2010). Sustainable Business Strategies and PESTEL Framework. *GSTF International Journal on Computing*, *1*(1), 73–80.

Issa, T., Issa, T., & Chang, V. (2011). Would teaching sustainable development business strategies shift students' mindsets? An Australian experience. *The International Journal of Environmental, Cultural. Economic & Social Sustainability*, *7*(5), 257–272.

Loorback, D., Bakel, J., Whiteman, G., & Rotmans, J. (2010). Business Strategies for Transitions Towards Sustainable Systems. *Business Strategy and the Environment*, *19*, 133–146.

Mayo, R., & Perng, C. (2009). Cloud Computing Payback: An explanation of where the ROI comes from. 1-20.

Schulz, W. (2009). What is SaaS, Cloud Computing, PaaS and IaaS? 15 Feb 2010,http://www.s-consult.com/2009/08/04/what-is-saas-cloud-computing-paas-and-iaas/

ScottJ.StahelW.LovinsH.GraysonD. (2010). *The Sustainable Business*

Sengers, P., Boehner, K., & Knouf, N. (2009). *Sustainable HCI Meets Third Wave HCI: 4 Themes*. Paper presented at the CHI 2009

Skilton, M. (2010a). 8 ways to measure cloud ROI. May 21st,http://www.itworld.com/it-managementstrategy/109126/8-ways-measure-cloud-roi?page=0%2C2

Skilton, M. (2010b). Building Return on Investment from Cloud Computing.

Wakkary, R. (2009). *A Sustainable Identity: Creativity of Everyday Design*. Paper presented at the CHI2009 10.1145/1518701.1518761

Wirtenberg, J. (2009). *Beyond Green: Going Green and Sustainable Environments Transitioning to Green* Retrieved from http://www.greenbaumlaw.com/Wirtenberg.ppt

Wittow, M., & Buller, D. (2010). Cloud Computing: Emerging Legal Issues for Access to Data, Anywhere, Anytime. *Journal of Internet Law*, *14*(1), 1–10.

KEY TERMS AND DEFINITIONS

Cloud Computing: Is a smart technology used to save energy and reduce carbon emission.
Green IT: Using technology and computer resources in an efficient way.
Opportunities: Advantages and prospects occurred during practice of working with a technology.
Risks: Uncertain aspects occurred during usage or implementation a technology (new or Old).
Sustainability: Sustain and manage resources for the next generations.

This research was previously published in Green Services Engineering, Optimization, and Modeling in the Technological Age edited by Xiaodong Liu and Yang Li, pages 269-287, copyright year 2015 by Information Science Reference (an imprint of IGI Global).

Chapter 70
A Cloud–Based Architecture for Interactive E–Training

Halima E. Samra
La Trobe University, Australia

Alice S. Li
La Trobe University, Australia

Ben Soh
La Trobe University, Australia

Mohammed A. AlZain
Taif University, Saudi Arabia

ABSTRACT

Cloud-based technologies play a significant role in the technology-enhanced learning domain. The adoption of cloud technologies in the educational environment has a positive impact on the learning process by offering new tools and services to improve and support the learning life cycle, including interactivity. In specific fields, such as clinical skills training, that involve computer-intensive training scenarios, there is an increased demand to deliver training services to a larger number of learners, therefore the need for cloud services. However, to date there has been a lack of a formalized framework relating to the use of cloud computing for on-demand interactive e-training resources. This paper is to formalize a theoretical framework for an interactive e-training system particularly for clinical skills training, taking into consideration e-training system requirements and with a focus on applying cloud technologies to ensure the dynamic scalability of services and computing power while maintaining QoS and security

INTRODUCTION

Traditionally, clinical skills training involves the use of face-to-face lectures to teach knowledge, skills and behavior. There is growing interest internationally in clinical skills education, especially shortened graduate programmers, also known as "accelerated programmers," which have been introduced to enhance interest in this field in order to increase the number of skilled people and address the recruitment crisis, particularly in nursing (Bloomfield et al. 2013).

DOI: 10.4018/978-1-5225-8176-5.ch070

Copyright © 2019, IGI Global. Copying or distributing in print or electronic forms without written permission of IGI Global is prohibited.

E-learning is widely regarded as a valuable mechanism for the acquisition of clinical skills where flexible access to e-learning resources and the opportunity to engage in independent learning enables students to practice skills at a time of their own choosing and at their own pace (Bloomfield & Jones, 2013). One of the benefits of utilizing the powerful features of e-learning tools is that it provides valuable feedback to the learners throughout the training process, it allows them to select the learning content; and it enables them to engage in self-assessment and to evaluate the results of their learning. However, resources need to be developed to provide an online and realistic training environment. Therefore, it is important to be able to access virtual resources, such as online simulations and virtual lab repositories, to provide on-demand up-to-date training.

Recently, e-learning systems have faced new challenges and limitations for several reasons, including the growing number of users with frequently changing requirements and educational demands. Moreover, accelerated programs which condense coursework into a shortened learning life cycle limit the training opportunities for learners, especially in practical subjects. Also, the growing volume of educational and training materials presents difficulties in terms of adequate storage and ensuring a secure method of data transmission. Consequently, there is an urgent need for new learning models that offer a pragmatic, immersive experience for trainees which utilize different types of resources and which are accessible to many users concurrently, at any place and at any time. There is also a need for a technologically advanced, adaptive virtual environment to support on-demand network access to use the available virtual distributed resources.

A promising solution to the limitations facing e-learning in relation to scalability to enable it to cope with the increasing number of users and resources is cloud computing, which can provide educational institutions with a distance computing infrastructure and data as a service on-demand over the Internet (Fasihuddin et al., 2012). It also offers educational platforms and services, and virtualization by combining all resources and centralized data storage (Ghazizadeh, 2012).

Particularly, for clinical skills learning where services such as virtual labs, simulations, and multimedia provision are computer-intensive and should be offered in a highly scalable way, the cloud-based environment can enable both students and their instructors to access computing resources on-demand for lectures and labs, according to their learning needs (Gonzalez-Martínez et al., 2015).

However, many challenges associated with cloud deployment may arise, such as data privacy, security, availability, consistency, and transmission. Many research studies have proposed solutions to tackle these problems. One solution for educational institutions is for them to build their own private cloud in which to place their sensitive data under their own management. Other research suggests using a cloud backup for important data and information to ensure the requirements of the Service Level Agreement, which specifies the terms of the contract, are met in relation to the provision of the cloud services (Fasihuddin et al., 2012).

Despite the effective solutions which have been applied to cloud models to fit e-learning environments, there is still a growing need for a customized e-training cloud platform that meets the specific needs of training environments. For this reason, the aim of this paper is to introduce a theoretical framework for a cloud-based e-training system, taking into consideration e-training requirements and utilizing the capabilities of cloud computing to address the challenges, such as QoS in terms of resource provisioning and security in terms of data protection in transmission and storage.

This paper is organized as follows. Section 2 presents an overview of cloud computing concepts. Section 3 discusses some related work in cloud-based e-learning. Section 4 describes the proposed framework architecture.

Cloud Computing Overview

The cloud computing paradigm is a promising solution for the next generation of e-learning methods, such as clinical skills education. It provides efficient on-demand network access to centralized resource sharing, such as networks, storage, servers, applications, and services (Höfer and Karagiannis, 2011). The cloud environment is a scalable infrastructure that supports and interconnects several cloud computing service. This new environment is based on the concept of "dynamic provisioning" which means presenting a group of interconnected and virtualized computers as one or more unified computing resource(s) (Rajkumar et al., 2013). Generally, the definition of cloud computing depends on an understanding of its characteristics and the services that can be deployed as a cloud service. The definition of cloud computing as proposed by the National Institute of Standards and Technology (NTIS) encompasses three main components: key cloud characteristics, deployment models, and service models (Sosinsky, 2010).

The NIST definition of cloud computing outlines the following five key characteristics that every cloud should offer (Rountree & Castrillo, 2013):

- **On-Demand Self-Service**: The client can request and receive access to a service in an automated process without the need for human interaction with the cloud service providers (CSPs).
- **Broad Network Access**: The client only needs a basic network connection in order to access the services and applications in the cloud.
- **Resource Pooling**: CSPs pool their computing resources to serve multiple clients and dynamically assign and reassign both physical and virtual resources to meet their clients' changing requirements. By exploiting virtualization, CSPs can increase their system density.
- **Rapid Elasticity**: The cloud resources can be elastically provisioned upon user demand and needs. This can be achieved by using system scalability to make resources available (Sosinsky, 2010).
- **Measured Service**: Cloud service usage should be measured using metrics, such as the storage size used by the client, the network usage, etc. and should support the "pay as you go" feature.

A deployment model refers to the location and management of the cloud's infrastructure (Sosinsky, 2010). There are four different types of clouds that a user can subscribe to, depending on his requirements:

- **Public Cloud**: The public cloud infrastructure is available for public use and CSPs are responsible for the management and administration of the systems that are used to deliver the service (Rountree & Castrillo, 2013). The client needs to connect to the Internet to access the cloud.
- **Private Cloud**: The private cloud infrastructure is customized for an organization's specific use and can be managed by the organization or a third party (Sosinsky, 2010). The client can access this cloud through a local area network, or a wide area network, but in remote cases, clients can be offered a virtual private network (Rountree & Castrillo, 2013).

- **Community Cloud**: A community cloud is where a cloud has been organized to serve a specific group of organizations which share similar requirements (Sosinsky, 2010). The group can obtain more privacy than is available on a public cloud but the group members share the management and administration responsibilities (Rountree & Castrillo, 2013).
- **Hybrid Cloud**: A hybrid cloud model is a combination of two or more cloud models (Rountree & Castrillo, 2013). Every cloud retains its own characteristics, but they are bound together as one unit. It is a complex environment, but to address this problem, a hybrid cloud may offer standardized and proprietary access to the data or the application (Sosinsky, 2010).

A service model presents a set of definitions that describe the service characteristics and criteria (Sosinsky, 2010). Cloud computing delivers infrastructure, platforms, and software as services. Therefore, these services are generally classified into three classes known as cloud service models:

1. **Infrastructure-as-a-Service (IaaS) model:** The IaaS model provides clients with virtualization platforms, including processing and storage resources (virtual machine, virtual storage, and networking). However, running and maintaining the operating system and the software in these resources is the client's responsibility (Rountree & Castrillo, 2013).
2. **Platform-as-a-Service (PaaS) model:** The PaaS model provides an operating system, a development platform and software and hardware tools which are delivered by CSPs to the client. A client is responsible for installing and managing their deployed application (Sosinsky, 2010).
3. **Software-as-a-Service (SaaS) model:** Complete software applications are delivered by the CSPs over the Internet and are accessed via a web browser so the customer does not need to purchase a software license or worry about maintenance (Sosinsky, 2010).

In the past, technological limitations made it difficult for CSPs to deliver a viable service and cope with growing customer demands. A lack of components, inadequate and expensive servers, and the limited capabilities of applications were obstacles that hindered the development of cloud computing (Rountree & Castrillo, 2013). Now cloud computing has embodied technological advances, such as distributed systems, virtualizations, Web 2.0, and service-oriented solutions to cloud difficulties (Rajkumar et al. 2013).

- **Distributed Systems**: Clouds are large distributed computing components which provide services on demand to clients as a single coherent system. Sharing and utilizing cloud computing resources (infrastructure, runtime environments, and services) has resulted in clouds being characterized in terms of scalability, concurrency, and ubiquity (Rajkumar et al., 2013).
- **Virtualizations**: Clouds have a virtually unlimited capacity by dividing physical resources (hardware, storage, runtime environments, programming language, and networking) into several virtual machines (VMs), using software called hypervisors that create separate virtual machine instances. As a result, it provides clouds with application isolation, quality of service, and protection (Rajkumar et al., 2013).
- **Web 2.0**: At present, the primary web interface that clouds use to deliver their services encompasses new technologies and services which bring interactivity and flexibility to Web pages, making cloud computing an attractive solution for constructing computing systems (Rajkumar et al., 2013).

- **Service Orientation**: Service orientation is the core reference model for cloud computing systems with loosely coupled features where the service is reusable and serves different scenarios (Rajkumar et al., 2013).

RELATED WORK

Cloud-based technologies play a significant role in the technology-enhanced learning domain. Many research studies have contributed to the deployment of cloud technologies in the field of education, in general. As a first step, most research which has been conducted discussed the beneficial aspects of cloud deployment in the field of education (Ghazizadeh, 2012), whereas others tried to utilize cloud computing by introducing services such as TLaaS (Teaching and Learning as a Service) (Radhakrishnan et al., 2012). A pedagogical cloud framework was presented by Chaabouni and Laroussi in (Uden et al. 2014) using the modeling of the pedagogical indicators in a collaborative and cooperative way on a cloud with the SaaS model. The aim was to analyse learner usage and manage indicators on the execution of educational scenarios. Several of the proposed cloud architectures focused on the management of the cloud infrastructure. The BlueSky cloud framework for e-learning was proposed by Dong et al. In (Jaatun et al., 2009). They combine traditional middleware functions, such as load balancing and data caching in their architecture to deliver a reliable, scalable, and cost-effective service to e-learning systems. CloudIA is a project conducted by Doelitzscher et al. (Jaatun et al., 2009) to design and build a private cloud for on-demand computing resources, and running e-learning applications and collaboration software. Snow Leopard, developed by Cayirci et al. (Jaatun et al., 2009), is a private cloud for educational purposes in the military domain. It resolves security challenges in its design, including some mechanisms such as privacy, anonymity and traffic analysis. The Virtual Computing Laboratory (VCL) is a training environment that is attracting increased research interest in the cloud domain. A proposed Virtual Laboratories Cloud System (VLCS) for linking e-learning environments with VCLs offers one possible way to improve the learning process by using cloud computing to offer Virtual Laboratories as a Service (VLaaS) (Rădulescu, 2014). The CLEM project, Cloud E-learning for Mechatronics, was developed by Chao et al. (Chaoa et al., 2015) for remote laboratories in the cloud. They developed an ecosystem for learners and educators to share a platform that allows a large number of distributed mechatronic devices to be pooled and used for e-learning.

Other related work includes:

- Cloud for engineering education of learning networks for effective student engagement (Medhav et al., 2017)
- A cloud-based learning tool for graduate software engineering practice courses with remote tutor support (Ding et al., 2017)

MOTIVATION

Although there is a considerable shift toward research in the use of cloud computing in an educational context from different perspectives as discussed above, there is a lack of a well-defined cloud framework that suits training activities and handles the requirements and services for an e-training environment, in particular for clinical skills training. Therefore, our aim is to contribute to the technology-enhanced learning research area with a theoretical framework for a private cloud for e-training systems which supports computing-intensive learning scenarios by using technological features of clouds, such as virtualization, on-demand resource provisioning, scalability, security, reliability, and quality of service

A FORMALIZED THEORETICAL FRAMEWORK FOR CLOUD-BASED E-TRAINING

E-Training System Description

Online education, particularly involving clinical skills, encompasses practical lectures, using resources such as virtual labs and online simulations. The online education also incorporates an e-learning Management System (LMS) for enrolments and virtual classes where lectures are posted as PowerPoint slides, video clips, and e-library.

E-Training Users' Requirements

There are three categories of users involved in the actual e-training systems:

- Students can enroll in a course, login to their account, attend virtual classes, use the material available in LMS, reserve a virtual lab or simulation for a practical session.
- Lecturers can login to their account, create a course, utilize material available in LMS for the course, reserve a virtual class, reserve virtual lab or participate in a simulation
- Institution Management is responsible for the management of the learning process and for configuring the whole cloud platform.

Cloud-Based E-Training System Requirements

In line with e-training system specifications, we propose a private cloud for an e-training system which supports both the individual trainee and/or collaborative work practices through courses prepared by instructors. The characteristics of such an environment vary from the long-term predication for scheduling regular courses to the periodic nature of an educational event, such as enrolment and examination periods. Training activities are computer-intensive and require a high-scale mechanism and full resource provisions to respond to sudden demand variation (Gonzalez-Martínez et al., 2015). Therefore, by utilizing cloud computing features, such as virtualization and on-demand resource provisioning, our design will support scalability and elasticity where resources can be dynamically added or removed according to the user requirements while maintaining QoS (Rajkumar et al., 2013).

Virtualization

Virtualization is one of the most important underlying technologies that supports cloud models. It abstracts the hardware from the operating system (OS) using a hypervisor or Virtual Machine Monitor (VMM) (Younge et al., 2010). Virtualization is the key management feature of the infrastructure layer.

Infrastructure Management

The lower level of the cloud construction involves resource deployment and the management of the physical resources (computer servers, storage block, desktop, and networks). Virtualization forms the upper level in the infrastructure layer by virtually relocating physical resources to multiple virtual machine instances.

- **Server Virtualization:** One physical server (CPU, memory, desks) can run multiple computing environments where every VM can run multiple operating systems and applications in an isolated environment. This helps with the management of a computing-intensive environment by creating a scalable system of different distributed computing devices and increases system performance. In addition, ensuring each VM is isolated will address the security concerns (Jaatun et al., 2009).
- **Storage Virtualization:** Storage virtualization provides cloud systems with storage pools where all the computing resources from various storage facilities can be viewed as a single resource which can be shared among virtual instances. Storage virtualization is a key component in data management because it helps with resource allocation to users (Jaatun et al., 2009).
- **Desktop Virtualization:** Desktop virtualization creates a desktop image as a virtual machine and provides a comprehensive desktop environment for users. It also reduces the risk of data loss and minimizes security concerns as none of the data stored in the data center will be affected by hardware failure (Portnoy, 2012).
- **Network Virtualization:** Virtual machines can be configured with one or more network interface cards (NICs). The hypervisor supports the creation of a virtual network where the vNICs can be interconnected via virtual switches that provide segmentation and isolation for network traffic, ensuring security and data integrity (Portnoy, 2012).

On-Demand Resource Provisioning

Resource provisioning enables the dynamic provision of on-demand resources which can be achieved by easy scheduling and reservation of computing resources (Rajkumar et al., 2013). In an e-training system, the middleware of the cloud should be designed to support the ability to schedule and reserve virtual labs and simulations.

Middleware Management

The efficient management of a computing platform is essential to provide a good training environment for managing distributed applications. In terms of on-demand resource allocation, the computing platform includes three modules: the user management module, the resource allocation module and the access management module (Tian et al., 2010). In addition to the main controller, there is also a management node which is in charge of resource scheduling, security, monitoring and virtual network management.

User Management

The user module consists of several sub-modules, such as the access management module, the login and authentication module and basic information management that update the user database. The database server manages and maintains the user information, such as authentication, resource availability information, platform state information, and connection information (Tian et al., 2010).

Resource Allocation Management

The core of a platform management system is resource allocation which makes scheduling and reserving a resource easy through the collaboration of the three subsystems:

- Resource usage (reservation) which manages the current users' requirements and reserves resources for prospective ones.
- Resources status (analysis) which manages the maintenance of the status of all resources.
- Resources renewal (runtime environment) which manages the reuse of the resource for the same user.

Access Management

This manages the user's access to resources, including distance access and connection management.

Management Node

The management node is the core of the computing platform that works as an intermediate component between users and their requested services. The management node first verifies the user's account before receiving the user's requests, and then allocates the available real and virtual services to the user for a specified time (Tian et al., 2010). The management node controls the cloud platform, offering efficient mechanisms for scheduling, monitoring, and security management, as shown in Figure 1.

Scheduling

Specific APIs are developed to deal with the scheduling and reservation tasks using the task assignment and execution mechanism.

The MapReduce programming model is used for scheduling and executing tasks where the application task is automatically divided into many multiple tasks, each of which may be executed on any node in the cluster (Jaatun et al., 2009).

Monitoring

An e-training system depends on high reliability and service provisioning to ensure the effectiveness of the training sessions. A heartbeat monitoring mechanism is used where the active system and the stand-by system monitor each other's heartbeat and any system that shows no heartbeat for a period of time is considered to be in shut-down mode. Then the current operation can be transferred to another host without interrupting the operation (Matsumoto & Yutaka, 2011).

Figure 1. Proposed Cloud-based E-training framework and management node

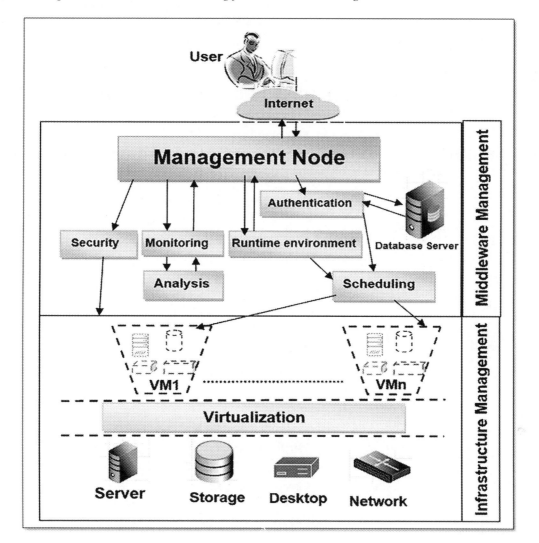

Security Management

For an e-training cloud which is a private cloud, security management issues are lessened due to the proprietary of the infrastructure and the fact that the cloud is managed by the institution. However, data privacy and security still need to be managed by maintaining the e-training environment requirements, such as ensuring that confidential data, such as information on training sessions, examinations and student records are kept private by limiting access to specific users. Also, data traffic must also be secure. Therefore, to provide a secure, controlled execution environment, a reliable flow control mechanism which can be achieved by labelling each data, service, and user with a security classification and authentication level, will ensure that only users with the appropriate security clearance can access the data (Jaatun et al., 2009). Security management for the cloud infrastructure can be done using hypervisors at the hardware level to reinforce the isolation between VMs to prevent data access and provide a secure, multi-tenant environment. The encryption and authentication of communication is essential to avoid data being compromised during transmission. Therefore, access to services can be through secure remote connections, such as the open Secure Shell protocol (OpenSSH) (Tian et al., 2010).

ARCHITECTURE OF THE CLOUD-BASED E-TRAINING SYSTEM

To address the e-training requirements, the proposed theoretical framework includes an infrastructure layer, virtualization layer, platform layer, application layer, and user interface layer in addition to the framework implementation mechanisms and methods for efficiently managing all layers and services, as shown in Figure 2.

Figure 2. Proposed Cloud-based E-training architecture

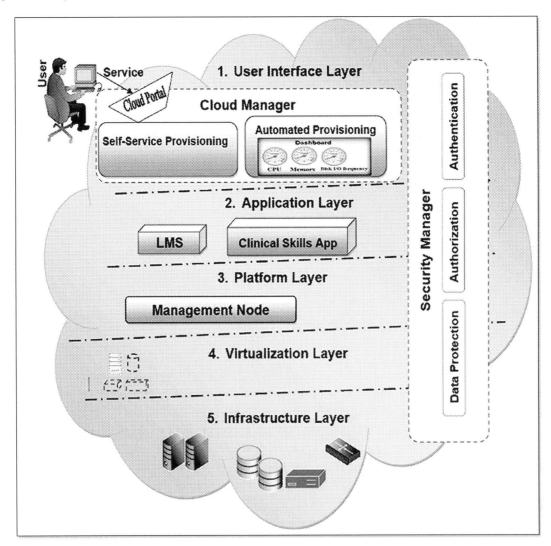

1. **Infrastructure Layer:** The infrastructure layer comprises physical machines in the lower level which provide scalable and elastic computing foundation components that support training sessions with powerful CPUs which constitute the lower layer for the processing layers of the application. The data storage where teaching and training resource materials, being elastic, can dynamically scale up and down to meet the application storage needs. Also, a scalable file storage component constitutes the foundation for the higher-level storage component. Finally, an API for cross-integration enables collaboration between inter-component and inter-application (Zaigham, 2013).
2. **Virtualization Layer:** Virtualization will support our architecture design at the hardware level, operating system level, and network level. Using virtualization, the physical machines in the hardware level can replicated and pooled and dynamically provisioned, based on the current workloads of various applications to achieve on-demand services. Also, it is possible to open more than one operating system platform in a single physical machine for efficient resource sharing and to serve more users (Tian et al., 2010).
3. **Platform Layer:** The platform layer provides an elastic and scalable application development platform through an API. This layer provides an integration platform where various resources that belongs to different platforms in the infrastructure layer (Fasihuddin et al., 2012). In addition to the provision of services such as scheduling and reservation, data services and multi-tenancy support which helps to build scalable cloud applications, and an e-learning LMS framework.
4. **Application Layer:** The application layer provides different types of applications that support the training process where the instructor can use these applications to build their own course by collecting materials from the pool available in the infrastructure layer. Also, it supports multi-users as the application allows many trainees to access the same shared pool of resources.
5. **User Interface Layer:** The interface layer provides various entry points to the e-training cloud, secure access to the functionality of the system, in addition to web-based UIs.

E-TRAINING CLOUD COMPONENTS

The workflow in the e-training private cloud relay in two core components that manages the overall life cycle of the system.

E-Training Cloud Manager

Automated Provisioning Manager

This is a dashboard function which monitors and reports the usage of the CPU, memory, and the disk I/O frequency (Matsumoto & Yutaka, 2011). It is used to visualize resource management by applying important metrics, such as the current number of trainees using the cloud and their requested services to automatically scale the resources and provide services.

E-Training Cloud Portal

The e-training cloud portal provides a template interface for users to access all management-related interactions through self-service provisioning capabilities (Zaigham, 2013). It also enables the administration and monitoring of services. On the back end, the portal will interface with the APIs to easily interact with the other applications and components of the system (Rountree & Castrillo, 2013).

E-Training Cloud Security Manager

The e-training cloud security manager provides security and privacy in terms of a secure authentication and authorization process. User authentication is verified upon login to the cloud using multifactor authentication. Data confidentiality and integrity can be achieved by applying a reliable flow control mechanism using a labelling technique to protect data from unauthorised access or modification. In addition, the security manager will enforce isolation while virtualizing resources to ensure every virtual machine instance operates in an isolated environment. Finally, data can be protected during transmission by applying the OpenSSH protocol.

CONCLUSION

The features of cloud computing, such as dynamic scalability and effective usage of resources, make cloud deployment a logical option for educational environments. The utilization of the powerful virtualization technology enable clouds to auto scale for their computing resources according to the services requested by the user. In the e-training environment, there is a high demand for computing resources during the learning life cycle, and particularly during peak periods, such as enrolment, assignment submission and examination periods. Despite this, no formalized cloud-based e-training framework has been specifically designed for clinical training environments. In this paper, detailed design issues are discussed, mainly focusing on the specific requirements of e-training particularly relating to clinical skills, describing the effectiveness of virtualization, on-demand resource provisioning features, delivering scalable services, achieving QoS and maintaining data security. Accordingly, our input to this area is to propose a formalized theoretical cloud framework for clinical skills education which exploits the features of cloud computing which enables resources to be dynamically available in order to meet the expected QoS requirements that requires automatic scalability and security in terms of data protection during transmission and storage.

REFERENCES

Bloomfield, J., Cornish, J., Parry, A., Pegram, A., & Moore, J. (2013). Clinical skills education for graduate-entry nursing students: Enhancing learning using a multimodal approach. *Nurse Education Today*, *33*(3), 247–252. doi:10.1016/j.nedt.2011.11.009 PMID:22178595

Bloomfield, J., & Jones, A. (2013). Using e-learning to support clinical skills acquisition: Exploring the experiences and perceptions of graduate first-year pre-registration nursing students — A mixed method study. *Nurse Education Today*, *33*(12), 1605–1611. doi:10.1016/j.nedt.2013.01.024 PMID:23473860

Chao, K., James, A., Nanos, A., Chen, J., Stan, S., Muntean, I., ... Capelle, J. (2015). Cloud E-learning for Mechatronics: CLEM. *Future Generation Computer Systems*, 48, 46–59. doi:10.1016/j.future.2014.10.033

Ding, Q., & Cao, S. (2017). RECT: A cloud-based learning tool for graduate software engineering practice courses with remote tutor support.

Fasihuddin, H., Skinner, G., & Athauda, R. (2012). A holistic review of cloud-based e-learning system. *Proceedings of the IEEE International Conference on Teaching, Assessment, and Learning for Engineering (TALE)*. Hong Kong.

Ghazizadeh, A. (2012). Cloud Computing Benefits and Architecture in E-Learning. *Proceedings of the IEEE International Conference on Wireless, Mobile and Ubiquitous Technology in Education*, Takamatsu.

Gonzalez-Martínez, J., Bote-Lorenzo, M., Gomez-Sanchez, E., & Cano-Parra, R. (2015). Cloud computing and education: A state-of-the-art survey. *Computers & Education*, *80*, 132–151. doi:10.1016/j.compedu.2014.08.017

Höfer, C. and Karagiannis, G. (2011). Cloud computing services: taxonomy and comparison. *Journal of Internet Services and Applications*, *2*(2), 81-94.

Jaatun, M., Zhao, G., & Rong, C. (2009). Cloudcom 2009. Springer-Verlag, Berlin Heidelberg.

Madhav, N. & Joseph, M. K. (2017). Cloud for engineering education: learning networks for effective student engagement. *Proceedings of the 2017 IEEE 7th Annual Computing and Communication Workshop and Conference (CCWC)*.

Matsumoto, H., & Yutaka, E. (2011). In Fujitsu. *Sciences et Techniques (Paris)*.

Portnoy, M. (2012). Virtualization Essentials. Hoboken: Wiley.

Radhakrishnan, N., Poorna Chelvan, N., & Ramkumar, D. (2012). *In International of Cloud Computing* (pp. 208–213). Technologies, Applications & Management.

Rădulescu, S.A. (2014). A Perspective on E-learning and Cloud Computing. Social and Behavioral Sciences, 141, 1084–1088.

Rajkumar, B., Christian, V., & Thamarai, S. (2013). Mastering Cloud Computing. Burlington: Elsevier Science.

Rountree, D., & Castrillo, I. (2013). The Basics of Cloud Computing. Burlington: Elsevier Science.

Sosinsky, B. (2010). Cloud Computing Bible. Hoboken: Wiley.

Tian, W., Sheng, S., & Guoming, L. (2010). A Framework for Implementing and Managing Platform as a Service in a Virtual Cloud Computing Lab. *Proceedings of the Education Technology and Computer Science workshop* (pp. 273-279).

Uden, L., Tao, Y.-H., Yang, H.-C., & Ting, I.-H. (Eds.) (2014). *Learning Technology for Education in Cloud - MOOC and Big Data.* Dordrecht: Springer.

Younge, A.J., Von Laszewski, G., Lopez-Alarcon, S., & Carithers, W. (2010). Efficient resource management for cloud computing environments. *Proceedings of the 2010 international Green Computing conference.*

This research was previously published in the International Journal of Knowledge Society Research (IJKSR), 8(1); edited by Miltiadis D. Lytras and Linda Daniela, pages 67-78, copyright year 2017 by IGI Publishing (an imprint of IGI Global).

Chapter 71

Necessity of Key Aggregation Cryptosystem for Data Sharing in Cloud Computing

R. Deepthi Crestose Rebekah
Ravindra college of Engineering for Women, India

Dhanaraj Cheelu
Ravindra college of Engineering for Women, India

M. Rajasekhara Babu
VIT University, India

ABSTRACT

Cloud computing is one of the most exciting technologies due to its ability to increase flexibility and scalability for computer processes, while reducing cost associated with computing. It is important to share the data securely, efficiently, and flexibly in cloud storage. Existing data protection mechanisms such as symmetric encryption techniques are unsuccessful in preventing data sharing securely. This article suggests Key aggregate cryptosystem which produce constant size ciphertexts in order to delegate decryption rights for any set of ciphertexts. The uniqueness is that one can aggregate any number of secret keys and make them as compact as a single key. This compact aggregate key can be easily sent to others with very limited secure storage.

CLOUD COMPUTING ARCHITECTURE

Cloud computing is a model for delivering information technology services in which resources are retrieved from the internet through web-based tools and applications, rather than a direct connection to a servers (Kanchana & Dhandapani, 2013) (Rajasekhara et al., 2014). However, cloud computing structure allows access to information as long as an electronic device has access to web.

DOI: 10.4018/978-1-5225-8176-5.ch071

Copyright © 2019, IGI Global. Copying or distributing in print or electronic forms without written permission of IGI Global is prohibited.

Characteristics of Cloud Computing

The five essential characteristics of cloud computing are On-demand self-service, broad network access, resource pooling, rapid elasticity and measured service:

1. **On-Demand Self-Service:** A service provided by the cloud vendors that enable the provision of cloud resources on demand whenever they are required (Zhang et al., 2010).
2. **Broad Network Access:** The resources hosted on a cloud network that are available for access from a wide range of devices such as smart phones, tablets, personal computers etc., and these resources are accessible from different locations that offer online access. (Prakash, 2013).
3. **Resource Pooling:** The computing resources are pooled by cloud vendors to serve multiple consumers using a multi-tenant model, with different physical and virtual resources dynamically assigned and reassigned according to consumer demand [3]. The examples of resources include storage, processing, memory, network bandwidth and virtual machines.
4. **Rapid Elasticity:** It allows the users automatically control and optimize resource by using a metering capability at some level of abstraction appropriate to the type of services (Mell & Grance, 2014). Resource usage can be monitored, controlled and reported providing transparency for both the provider and consumer of the service.

Service Models of Cloud Computing

Cloud service models describe cloud services are made available to users. Figure 1 explains three service models – SaaS, PaaS and IaaS which provide resources to the users:

1. **SaaS:** It provides the customers with ready to use application running on the infrastructure service provider. The applications are easily accessible from several client devices as on demand services. Salesforce, DocLanding, Zoho, Workday are instances of SaaS are used for different purposes such as email, billing, human resource management etc. (Figure 1),
2. **PaaS**: It provides platform oriented service controlling the installed applications and available hosting environment configuration. Google AppEngine, LoadStorm are the instances of PaaS for running web applications and testing their performance.
3. **IaaS**: It provides infrastructure services such as memory, CPU and storage. The consumer can deploy and run software. It reduces hardware costs. Amazon S3 and FlexiScale, Dropbox are the best examples of IaaS for storing and maintaining virtual servers.

Deployment Models of Cloud Computing

While service models describe the specific capabilities of cloud solutions, deployment models describe where, how, and by whom the cloud's physical servers are managed (Armbrust et al., 2010). Cloud computing may be deployed as private, public and hybrid, which are shown in Figure 2:

1. **Private Cloud:** A private cloud is a particular model of cloud computing that involves a distinct and secure cloud based environment in which on the specific client/ organization can operate.

Figure 1. Service models of cloud

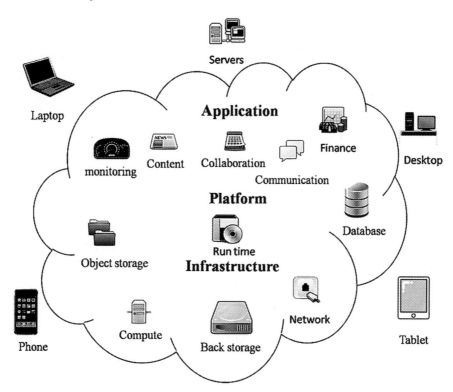

Figure 2. Deployment models of cloud

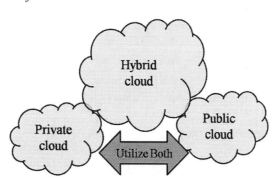

As private cloud is only accessible by a single organization, that organization will have the ability to manage and configure it in line with their needs to achieve a network solution.

Benefits of private cloud are higher security and privacy, cost and energy efficiency and improved reliability.

2. **Public Cloud:** Public cloud is a deployment model under which resources are made generally available to everyone. However, the cloud provider still owns and manages the actual services. Users can self- provision resources from a web interface, in effect renting them from the provider as pay – as – you – use basis (Shelke et al., 2012).

The benefits of public cloud are its on- demand setup and vast scalability.

3. **Hybrid Cloud:** A hybrid cloud is an integrated cloud service utilizing both private and public clouds to perform various functions within the same organization [7]. An organization can maximize their efficiencies by employing public cloud services for non- sensitive operations and private cloud services for sensitive operations and also ensure their platforms seamlessly integrated.

The various services offered by the cloud made the users increasingly opting for cloud storage for saving their data. With the data saved on the cloud, users are no longer required to store their data on local storage devices.

Firstly, in the early days, users used to store data on physical devices. If these devices get lost, users need to purchase new devices and also have to pay for backing up services. Secondly, storing the data on the cloud is more secure than storing it on physical devices. On cloud, data is kept confidential because only authorized people can access the data. On the other hand, if the data stored on physical devices may risk the confidentiality. Thirdly, cloud storage allows the users to share their files or documents from any corner of the world. Through these cloud storage services, users can send their documents to others without necessarily having to meet physically, whereas this cannot happen with traditional storage because users must meet physically with the people they want to share the data with.

Finally, the file backup software provides quick online data backup of any lost data. If the users make any changes on their data, automatic data backup software updates it and therefore it keeps their files secure and updated at all times. However, they can lose their data when they use physical devices.

Considering data privacy, a traditional way to ensure it is to rely on the server to enforce the access control after authentication which means any unexpected privilege escalation will expose all data. In a shared- tenancy cloud computing environment, things become even worse.

Data from different clients can be hosted on separate virtual machines (VM) but reside on a single physical machine. Data in a target VM could be stolen by instantiating another VM co-resident with target one (Mathew et al., 2014). Regarding the availability of files, there are a series of cryptographic schemes which go as far as allowing a third- party auditor to check the availability of files on behalf of the data owner without leakage anything about the data (Wang et al., 2013), or without compromising the data owner's anonymity (Wang et al., 2013).

SECURITY ISSUES OF DATA SHARING IN CLOUD

In this section we explain security issues and challenges in cloud computing.

Cloud computing encompasses many technologies including networks, databases, operating systems, virtualization, resource scheduling, transaction management, load balancing, concurrency control and memory management. Security issues for many these systems and technologies are applicable to cloud computing. For example, the network that interconnects the systems in a cloud has to be secure. Furthermore, virtualization paradigm in cloud computing leads to several security concerns, and mapping the virtual machines to physical machines has to be carried out securely. Data security involves encrypting the data as well as ensuring that appropriate policies are enforced for data sharing (Narkhede et al., 2013). In addition, resource allocation and memory management algorithms have to be secure. Finally, data mining techniques may be applicable for malware detection in the clouds.

There are several types of security threats like are confidentiality, integrity, availability and data sharing to which cloud computing is vulnerable:

- **Confidentiality:** Confidentiality is roughly equivalent to privacy. Measures undertaken to ensure confidentiality are designed to prevent sensitive data from reaching the wrong people, while making sure that the right people can in fact get it, i.e. access must be restricted to those authorized to view the data. Confidentiality of data in cloud may lose due to internal user threats, external attacker threats and data leakage.

Internal user threats are malicious cloud providers, malicious cloud customer users and malicious third party users. External attacker threats are remote software attack of cloud infrastructure, remote software attack of cloud applications, and remote hardware attack against the cloud. Data leakage may happen due to failure of security access rights across multiple domains, failure of electronic and physical transport systems for cloud data and backups.

- **Integrity:** Integrity involves maintaining the consistency, accuracy, and trustworthiness of data. Data must not be changed in transit, and steps must be taken to ensure the data cannot be altered by unauthorized people. Integrity of data may be affected by data segregation, user access and data quality (Cheelu et al., 2013).

Data segregation involves incorrectly defined security perimeters, incorrect configuration of virtual machines and hypervisors. Implementation of poor user access control procedures creates many threat opportunities. The threat of impact of data quality is increased as cloud providers host many customers' data. The introduction of a faulty or misconfigured component required by another cloud user could potentially impact the integrity of data for other cloud users sharing infrastructure.

- **Availability:** Availability is the ability of the user to access data or resources in a specified location and in the correct format. Availability of data may lose due to change management, denial of service threat and physical disruption.

Likewise, cloud users may feel that cloud server is not doing a good job in terms of confidentiality (MohamedInfan, 2014).

CRYPTOGRAPHIC SOLUTIONS FOR DATA SHARING IN CLOUD

To overcome this problem, users can use cryptographic techniques whenever the users don't trust the security of the VM or the honesty of the technical staff. Then users can encrypt their data with their own keys before uploading them to the server.

One of the important functionality of cloud storage is Data sharing. For example, social network users can let their friends view a few of their private pictures; an organization may grant employees access to a portion of sensitive data. The challenging problem is how to share the encrypted data effectively. Obviously, users can download the encrypted data from the cloud storage, decrypt them, and then send them to others for sharing. But it loses the importance of cloud storage.

Imagine that Alice stores all her private photos on Dropbox, and she does not want others to view her photos. Due to various data leakage possibility Alice cannot feel relieved by just relying on the privacy protection mechanisms provided by Dropbox, so she encrypts all the photos using her own keys before uploading. Suppose on one day, Alice's friend, Bob, asks her to share the photos taken over all these years which Bob is appeared in. Alice can then use the share function of Dropbox, but the problem now is how to delegate the decryption rights for these photos to Bob. Certainly, there are two extreme ways for her under the traditional encryption paradigm:

1. Alice can encrypt all the photos with a single encryption key and gives encrypted key to Bob.
2. Alice encrypts photos with different secret keys and sends Bob the corresponding secret keys.

Obviously the first technique is not sufficient since all unchosen data may be also revealed to Bob. For the second method there are practical errors on efficiencies because the number of such keys is as many as number of shared photos.

Encryption techniques come with two techniques, symmetric key encryption and asymmetric key encryption.

1. **Symmetric Key Encryption:** An encryption system in which a single common key is used by the sender and receiver to encrypt and decrypt the message. The symmetric encryption scheme has five ingredients which are present in Figure 3:
    a. **Plaintext:** This is the actual message or data that is fed to the algorithm as input.
    b. **Encryption Algorithm:** The encryption algorithm performs various substitutions and permutations on the plaintext.
    c. **Secret Key:** The secret key is also given as input to the encryption algorithm. The exact substitutions and permutations performed depend on the key used, and the algorithm will produce a different output depending on the specific key being used at the time.

Figure 3. Symmetric encryption

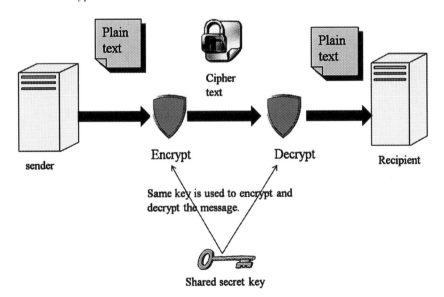

    d.   **Cipher Text:** This the scrambled message produced as output. It depends on the plaintext and the key. The cipher text is an apparently random stream of data, as it stands, is unintelligible.

    e.   **Decryption Algorithm:** This is essentially the encryption algorithm run in reverse. It takes the cipher text and the secret key as input and produces the original plaintext as output.

The problem with the symmetric key encryption is sender and the receiver must have obtained copies of the secret key in a secure fashion and must keep the key secure. If someone can discover the key and knows the algorithm, all communications using this key is readable.

2.   **Asymmetric (Public) Key Encryption:** An encryption system in which a sender uses a public key to encrypt messages and receiver uses a private key to decrypt the messages. The asymmetric encryption scheme has five ingredients which are present in Figure 4:

    a.   **Plaintext:** This is the readable message or data that is fed into the algorithm as input.

    b.   **Encryption Algorithm:** The encryption algorithm performs various transformations on the plaintext.

    c.   **Public and Private Key:** This is a pair of keys that have been selected so that if one is used for encryption, the other is used for decryption. The exact transformation performed by the encryption algorithm depends on the public or private keys that are provided as input.

    d.   **Cipher Text:** This is the scrambled message produced as output after encryption.

    e.   **Decryption Algorithm:** This algorithm accepts the cipher text and the matching key as input and produces the original plaintext.

The use of public key encryption gives more flexibility for our applications. For example, in enterprise settings, every employ can upload encrypted data on the cloud storage server without the knowledge of

Figure 4. Asymmetric encryption

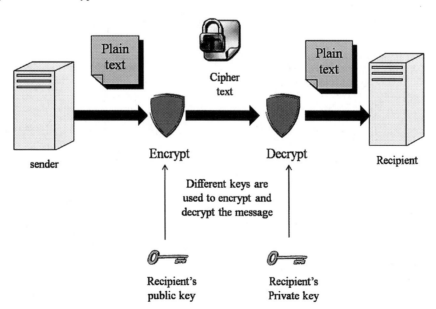

the company's master-secret key (private key). Therefore, the best solution for the above problem is key aggregate cryptosystem (KAC).

In KAC, users encrypt a message not only under a public key, but also under an identifier of cipher text called class. That means the cipher texts are further categorized into different classes. The key owner holds a master secret called master secret key, which can be used to extract secret keys for different classes. More importantly, the extracted key have can be an aggregate key which is as compact as a secret key for a single class, but aggregates the power of many such keys, i.e., the decryption power for any subset of cipher text classes (Chu et al., 2014).

With our solution, Alice can simply send Bob a single aggregate key via a secure e-mail. Bob can download the encrypted photos from Alice's Dropbox space and then use this aggregate key to decrypt these encrypted photos. The scenario is depicted in Figure 5.

That Alice encrypts photos with different public keys but only sends Bob a single (constant size) decryption key. Since the decryption key should be sent via a secure channel and kept secret, small key size is always desirable.

RELATED WORK

This section we compare our basic KAC scheme with other possible solutions on sharing in secure cloud storage.

Figure 5. Alice shares files with identifiers 2, 3, 6, and 8 with Bob by sending him a single aggregate key.

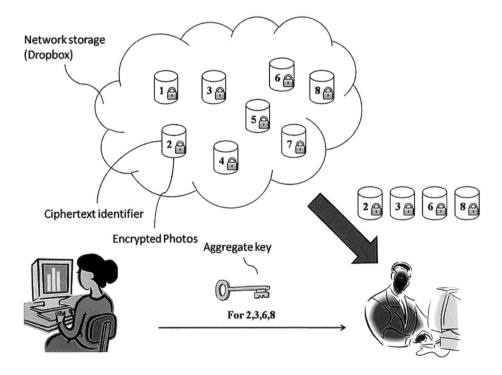

Cryptographic Keys for a Predefined Hierarchy

The main aim of Cryptographic assignment schemes is to minimize the expense in storing and managing secret keys for general cryptographic use (Akl et al., 1983; Chick & Tavares, 1990; Tzeng, 2002; Ram, 2015). By using a tree structure, a key for a given branch can be used to derive the keys of its descendant nodes. Because granting the parent key implicitly grants all the keys of its descendant nodes.

We take the tree structure as an example. Alice can first classify the cipher text classes according to their subjects like Figure 6(a). Each node in the tree represents a secret key, while the leaf nodes represent the keys for individual cipher text classes. Filled circles represent the keys for the classes to be delegated and circles circumvented by dotted lines represent the keys to be granted. Note that every key of the non-leaf node can derive the keys of its descendant nodes.

In Figure 6, if Alice wants to share all the files in the "personal" category, she only needs to grant the key for the node "personal", which automatically grants the delegatee the keys of all the descendant nodes ("photo", "music"). This is the ideal case, where most classes to be shared belong to the same branch and thus a parent key of them is sufficient.

However, it is still difficult for general cases. As shown in Figure 7, if Alice shares her demo music at work ("work"→"casual"→"demo" and "work"→"Confidential"→"demo") with a colleague who also has the rights to see some of her personal data, what she can do is to give more keys, which leads to an increase in the total key size. One can see that this approach is not flexible when the classifications are more complex and she wants to share different sets of files to different people. For this delegate in our example, the number of granted secret keys becomes the same as the number of classes.

Compact Key in Identity-Based Encryption

Identity-based encryption (IBE) is a type of public-key encryption in which the public-key of a user can be set as an identity-string of the user (e.g., an email address). There is a trusted party called private

Figure 6. Compact key is not always possible for a fixed hierarchy.

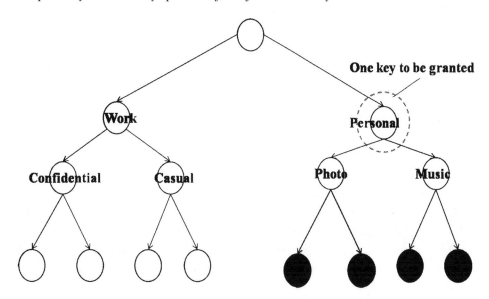

Figure 7. Compact key is not always possible for a fixed hierarchy.

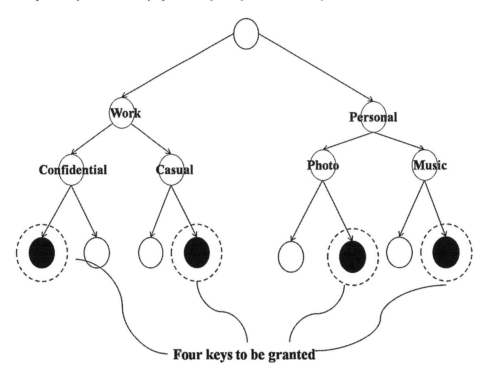

key generator (PKG) in IBE which holds a master-secret key and issues a secret key to each user with respect to the user identity. The encryptor can take the public parameter and a user identity to encrypt a message. The recipient can decrypt this cipher text by his secret key.

Guo et al (2007) and Kate & Potdukhe (2014) tried to build IBE with key aggregation. One of their schemes assumes random oracles but another does not. In their schemes, key aggregation is constrained in the sense that all keys to be aggregated must come from different "identity divisions". While there are an exponential number of identities and thus secret keys, only a polynomial number of them can be aggregated. Most importantly, their key-aggregation comes at the expense of O(n) sizes for both cipher texts and the public parameter, where n is the number of secret keys which can be aggregated into a constant siz(N Bhatt et al., 2013) one. This greatly increases the costs of storing and transmitting cipher texts, which is impractical in many situations such as shared cloud storage.

Key-Policy Attribute-Based Encryption

Attribute-based encryption (ABE) is a paradigm, where messages are encrypted and decryption keys are computed in accordance with a given set attributes and access structure on the set of attributes (Tiplea, 2014). Attribute based encryption allows each cipher text to be associated with an attribute, and the master-secret key holder can extract for a policy of these attributes so that a cipher text can be decrypted by this key if its associated attribute confirms to the policy. The major concern in attribute based encryption is collusion resistance but not the compactness of secret keys. Also the size of the key often increases linearly with the number of attributes it encompasses, or the cipher text-size is not constant.

Proxy Re-Encryption

Instead of sending secret key to the delegate (say Bob) one can delegate the decryption power of some cipher texts by using proxy re-encryption (Canetti & Hohenberger, 2007) (Chu & Tzeng, 2007) (Chu et al., 2009) (Chow et al., 2010).

In proxy re-encryption scheme a delegator (say Alice) and a delegatee (say Bob) generate a proxy key that allows a semi trusted third party (say the Proxy) to convert cipher text encrypted under Alice's public key into cipher text which can be decrypted by Bob.

Proxy re-encryption has various applications including cryptographic file system [25]. However Alice has to trust that according to her instruction the proxy only converts the cipher texts, which is what we want to avoid at the first place. Even, if the proxy conspires with Bob, some forms of Alice's secret key can be recovered which can decrypt Alice's cipher texts without the help of Bob. It means that transformation key of proxy should be safeguarded. Proxy re-encryption makes the secure key storage from delegatee to the proxy. Proxy re-encryption makes the storage requirement from the delegatee to the proxy. Thus it is unacceptable to let proxy reside in the storage server. It is also inconvenient because every decryption requires separate interaction with the proxy.

KEY AGGREGATE ENCRYPTION

We first give the framework and definition for key-aggregate encryption. Then we describe how to use KAC in a scenario of its application in cloud storage.

Framework

A key aggregate encryption scheme consists of five polynomial-time algorithms. Initially the data owner establishes the public system parameter via Setup and generates a public/master-secret key pair via KeyGen. Messages can be encrypted via Encrypt by anyone who also decides which cipher text class is associated with the plaintext message to be encrypted. To generate an aggregate decryption key, the data owner can use the master- secret for a set of cipher text classes via Extract. Now the generated keys can be passed to delegatees securely through secure e-mails or secure devices. Finally, any user with an aggregate key can decrypt any cipher text provided that the ciphertext's class is contained in the aggregate key via Decrypt:

1. **Setup (1^λ, *n*):** This is executed by the data owner to setup an account on an untrusted server. A security level parameter 1^λ and the number of '*n*' cipher text classes (i.e., class index should be an integer bounded by 1^λ and *n*); it outputs the public system parameter '*param*'.
2. **Keygen:** It is executed by the data owner to randomly generate a public/master-secret key pair (*pk, msk*).
3. **Encrypt (*pk, i, m*):** This is executed by anyone who wants to encrypt data. It takes a public key *pk*, an index *i* denoting the ciphertext class and a message *m* as input. It outputs a cipher text *C*.
4. **Extract (*msk, S*):** It is executed by the data owner for delegating the decrypting power for a certain set of cipher text classes to a delegatee. It takes the master secret key *msk* and a set *S* of indices

corresponding to different classes, it output the master-secret key *msk* and a set *S* of indices corresponding to different classes as input; and it outputs the aggregate key for set *S* denoted by K_s.

5. **Decrypt (*Ks, S, i, C*):** This is executed by a delegatee who receives an aggregate key K_s generated by Extract. It takes *Ks*, the set *S*, an index *i* denoting the cipher text class the cipher text *C* belongs to and *C* as input, it outputs the decrypted result *m* if i∈*S*.

    a.   There are two functional requirements:

        i.   Correctness for any integers λ and n, any $S \subseteq \{1,\ldots,n\}$, any index $i \in S$ and any message *m*.
Pr[Decrypt(*Ks,S,i,C*)=m:param←Setup(1^λ,n),(pk,msk)←KeyGen(),C←Encrypt(*pk,i,m*), *Ks*←Extract(*msk,S*)]=1.

        ii.   Compactness For any integers λ, n, any set *S*, any index $i \in S$ and any message *m*; *param* ←Setup(1^λ, *n*),

(*pk, msk*)←KeyGen(),

Ks← Extract(*msk, S*) and C←Encrypt(*pk, i, m*);

|*Ks*| and |*C*| only depend on the security parameter λ but independent of the number of classes *n*.

Sharing Encrypted Data

An authorized application of KAC is data sharing. The key aggregation property is especially useful when we expect the delegation to be efficient and flexible. The schemes enable a content provider to share her data in a confidential and selective way, with a fixed and small cipher text expansion, by distributing to each authorized user a single and small aggregate key.

Here we describe the main idea of data sharing in cloud storage using KAC, illustrated in Figure 2. Suppose Alice wants to share her data m_1, m_2, ...,m_i on the server. She first performs Setup (1^λ, n) to get *param* and execute KeyGen to get the public/master secret key pair (*pk, msk*). The system parameter *param* and public key *pk* can be made public and master secret key *msk* should be kept secret by Alice. Anyone (including Alice herself) can then encrypt each m_i by C_i=Encrypt (*pk, i, m_i*). The encrypted data are uploaded to the server.

With *param* and *pk*, people who cooperate with Alice can update Alice's data on the server. Once Alice is willing to share a set *S* of her data with a friend Bob, she can compute the aggregate key *Ks* for Bob by performing Extract (*msk, S*). Since *Ks* are just a constant size key, it is easy to be sent to Bob via a secure email.

After obtaining the aggregate key, Bob can download the data he is authorized to access. That is, for each $i \in S$, Bob downloads C_i (and some needed values in *param*) from the server. With the aggregate key *Ks*, Bob can decrypt each C_i by Decrpty(*Ks, S, i, C_i*) for each i∈S.

CONCLUSION

Cloud computing is a promising paradigm with growing acceptance, but there is still much work to be done if we want to achieve security in the cloud. The important issue of cloud storage is how to protect user's data privacy. Hence we described a new public key cryptosystem which produce a constant size ciphertext such that efficient delegation of decryption rights for any set of ciphertexts are possible. The uniqueness is that one can aggregate any set of secret keys and make them as compact as single key but encompassing the power of all the keys being aggregated.

The limitation in this work is predefined bound of number of maximum ciphertext classes. In cloud storage the number of ciphertexts usually grows rapidly. So we have reserve enough ciphertext classes for the future extension.

REFERENCES

Akl, S. G., & Taylor, P. D. (1983). Cryptographic solution to a problem of access control in a hierarchy. *ACM Transactions on Computer Systems*, *1*(3), 239–248. doi:10.1145/357369.357372

Akl & Taylor. (1983). Cryptographic Solution to a Problem of Access Control in a Hierarchy. *ACM Transactions on Computer Systems*, *1*(3), 239–248.

Armbrust, M., Fox, A., Griffith, R., Joseph, A. D., Katz, R., Konwinski, A., ... Zaharia, M. (2010). A view of cloud computing. *Communications of the ACM*, *53*(4), 50–58. doi:10.1145/1721654.1721672

Ateniese, G., Fu, K., Green, M., & Hohenberger, S. (2006). Improved proxy re-encryption schemes with applications to secure distributed storage. *ACM Transactions on Information and System Security*, *9*(1), 1–30. doi:10.1145/1127345.1127346

Bhatt, N., Babu, M., & Bhatt, A. (2013). Automation Testing Software that Aid in Efficiency Increase of Regression Process. *Recent Patents on Computer Science*, *6*(2), 107–114. doi:10.2174/2213275911 3069990008

Canetti, R., & Hohenberger, S. (2007, October). Chosen-ciphertext secure proxy re-encryption. In *Proceedings of the 14th ACM conference on Computer and communications security* (pp. 185-194). ACM.

Cheelu, D., Babu, M. R., & Venkatakrishna, P. (2013). A fuzzy-based intelligent vertical handoff decision strategy with maximised user satisfaction for next generation communication networks. *International Journal of Process Management and Benchmarking*, *3*(4), 420–440. doi:10.1504/IJPMB.2013.058268

Chick, G. C., & Tavares, S. E. (1990, January). Flexible access control with master keys. In Advances in Cryptology—CRYPTO'89 Proceedings (pp. 316-322). Springer New York. doi:10.1007/0-387-34805-0_29

Chow, S. S., Weng, J., Yang, Y., & Deng, R. H. (2010). Efficient unidirectional proxy re-encryption. In *Progress in Cryptology–AFRICACRYPT 2010* (pp. 316-332). Springer Berlin Heidelberg.

Chu, C. K., Chow, S. S., Tzeng, W. G., Zhou, J., & Deng, R. H. (2014). Key-aggregate cryptosystem for scalable data sharing in cloud storage. *Parallel and Distributed Systems. IEEE Transactions on*, *25*(2), 468–477.

Chu, C. K., & Tzeng, W. G. (2007). Identity-based proxy re-encryption without random oracles. In *Information Security* (pp. 189–202). Springer Berlin Heidelberg. doi:10.1007/978-3-540-75496-1_13

Chu, C. K., Weng, J., Chow, S. S., Zhou, J., & Deng, R. H. (2009, January). Conditional proxy broadcast re-encryption. In *Information security and privacy* (pp. 327–342). Springer Berlin Heidelberg. doi:10.1007/978-3-642-02620-1_23

Guo, F., Mu, Y., & Chen, Z. (2007). Identity-based encryption: how to decrypt multiple ciphertexts using a single decryption key. In *Pairing-Based Cryptography–Pairing 2007* (pp. 392–406). Springer Berlin Heidelberg. doi:10.1007/978-3-540-73489-5_22

Jain, S. (2014). *An analysis of security and privacy issues, Challenges with possible solution in cloud computing*. National Conference on Computational and Mathematical Sciences (COMPUTATIA-IV), Jaipur, India.

Kanchana, D., & Dhandapani, D. S. (2013). A Novel Method for Storage Security in Cloud Computing. *International Journal of Engineering Science and Innovative Technology*, 2(2), 243–249.

Kate, M. K., & Potdukhe, S. D. (2014). *Data sharing in cloud storage with key-aggregate cryptosystem*. Academic Press.

Mathew, M., Sumathi, D., Ranjima, P., & Sivaprakash, P. (2014). *Secure Cloud Data Sharing Using Key-Aggr egate Cryptosystem*. Academic Press.

Mell, P., & Grance, T. (2014). The nist definition of cloud computing, 2011. National Institute of Standards and Technology Special Publication, 800-145.

Narkhede, A., Dashore, P., & Verma, D (2013). *Graphics Based Cloud Security*. Academic Press.

Infan, Muthurangasamy, & Yogananth. (2014). Resilient Identify Based Encryption for Cloud Storage by Using Aggregated Keys. *International Journal of Advanced Research in Computer Engineering & Technology, 3*(3).

Prakash, K. (2013, February). A Survey On Security And Privacy In Cloud Computing. International Journal of Engineering Research and Technology, 2(2).

Rajasekhara Babu, M., Venkata Krishna, P., & Khalid, M. (2013). A framework for power estimation and reduction in multi-core architectures using basic block approach. *International Journal of Communication Networks and Distributed Systems*, 10(1), 40–51. doi:10.1504/IJCNDS.2013.050506

Ram, N. A., Reddy, N. C. S., & Poshal, G. (n.d.). *An Effective Scalable Data Sharing in Cloud Storage using Key-Aggregate Crypto-system*. Academic Press.

Shelke, M. P. K., Sontakke, M. S., & Gawande, A. (2012). Intrusion detection system for cloud computing. *International Journal of Scientific & Technology Research, 1*(4), 67–71.

Tiplea, F. L., & Dragan, C. C. (n.d.). *Key-policy Attribute-based Encryption for Boolean Circuits from Bilinear Maps*. Academic Press.

Tzeng, W. G. (2002). A time-bound cryptographic key assignment scheme for access control in a hierarchy. *Knowledge and Data Engineering. IEEE Transactions on, 14*(1), 182–188.

Wang, B., Chow, S. S., Li, M., & Li, H. (2013, July). Storing shared data on the cloud via security-mediator. In *Distributed Computing Systems (ICDCS), 2013 IEEE 33rd International Conference on* (pp. 124-133). IEEE. 10.1109/ICDCS.2013.60

Wang, C., Chow, S. S., Wang, Q., Ren, K., & Lou, W. (2013). Privacy-preserving public auditing for secure cloud storage. *Computers. IEEE Transactions on, 62*(2), 362–375.

This research was previously published in Emerging Technologies and Applications for Cloud-Based Gaming edited by P. Venkata Krishna, pages 210-227, copyright year 2017 by Information Science Reference (an imprint of IGI Global).

Section 5
Organizational and Social Implications

Chapter 72
Impact of Technology Innovation:
A Study on Cloud Risk Mitigation

Niranjali Suresh
University at Buffalo, USA

Manish Gupta
University at Buffalo, USA

ABSTRACT

Cloud enables computing as a utility by offering convenient, on-demand network access to a centralized pool of configurable computing resources that can be rapidly deployed with great efficiency and minimal management overhead. In order to realize the benefits of the innovative cloud computing paradigm, companies must overcome heightened risks and security threats associated with it. Security and privacy in cloud is complex owing to newer dimensions in problem scope such as multi-tenant architectures and shared infrastructure, elasticity, measured services, viability etc. In this paper, we survey existing literature on cloud security issues and risks which then guides us to provide a section on auditing based to address the identified risks. We also provide a discourse on risk assessment frameworks to highlight benefits using such structured methods for understanding risks. The main contribution of the paper is investigation of current innovations in cloud computing that are targeted towards assisting in effective management of aforementioned risks and security issues. The compilation of discussed solutions has been developed to cater to specific cloud security, compliance and privacy requirements across industries by cloud service providers, software-as-a-service (SaaS) application vendors and advisory firms.

1. INTRODUCTION

Cloud computing is transforming and redefining the design and procurement of IT infrastructure and software thereby providing attractive services to its users across the globe. The US National Institute of Standards and Technology (NIST) defines cloud computing as "a model for enabling ubiquitous, convenient, on - demand network access to a shared pool of configurable computing resources (e.g. networks,

DOI: 10.4018/978-1-5225-8176-5.ch072

Copyright © 2019, IGI Global. Copying or distributing in print or electronic forms without written permission of IGI Global is prohibited.

servers, storage, applications, and services) that can be rapidly provisioned and released with minimal management effort or service provider interaction" (Mell and Grance, 2011). The technology allows individuals and enterprises to avoid committing large capital outlays when purchasing and managing or operating software and hardware. Cloud reduces strain on developers by allowing them to focus their efforts on coding business logic rather than concerning about over or under provisioning resources for a service based on the market for a service. Large batch oriented tasks can be efficiently executed with minimal resources simply through scalable programming. In cloud, 1000 servers for one hour costs no more than using one server for 1,000 hours. This elasticity of resources, without paying a premium for large scale, is unprecedented in the history of IT. As Heiser and Nicolett (2008) of Gartner mention that cloud computing lacks transparency because it is, for most part, provided by an external entity and is a method for "storing and processing your data externally in multiple unspecified locations, often sourced from other, unnamed providers, and containing data from multiple customers." In the same vein, companies are also advised they consider all the involved risks in moving to cloud and also evaluate all the required controls around the protection of data and processes before migrating to cloud.

One of the main contributions of the chapter is reviewing recent innovations in cloud computing in security space and how they are aligned to manage risks from specific areas of cloud implementation. The discussions on extant literature on cloud, auditing focus areas and risk assessment frameworks help the chapter highlight how recent innovations are poised to manage risks. The primary tenet of the research is innovation in cloud computing. Innovation in IT is one of the widely studied topics (Baregheh et al., 2009) with many acceptable definitions. We use Rogers' (1998) definition as ''introduction of a new product or a 'qualitative change' in a product, a process…''. Not all innovations have the same impact and vary based on type of innovation (Grover et al., 1997; Adomavicius et al., 2007; Christensen et al., 2007; Carlo et al., 2011). Innovation has been linked to higher productivity, growth, and development. (Fagerberg, 2005; Kaplinsky et al., 2009). In recent years, with increasing adoption of IT, the impact of innovations is on rise as well and has been of high interest to researchers (Avgerou, 2008; Xiao et al., 2013).

This chapter is organized in six sections that delve deep into cloud security and innovations. Having introduced cloud computing as a technology platform in the first section, we move on to discuss key risks in cloud, their impact on environmental security and customer's business processes. The third section elaborates on significant aspects of cloud that require additional attention through continuous auditing. Audit challenges and suggested approaches have been delineated in line with industry best practices. This is followed by a description of some of the most prominent cloud computing frameworks and working groups that are widely used accepted across industries and geographies as enablers and benchmarks while setting up cloud systems. The following section briefly examines additional challenges specific to particular cloud computing domains such as banking, medical, and government sectors. The final section discusses recent innovations in cloud computing and its impact on transforming enterprise cloud implementations and managing cloud computing risks. Figure 1 shows how different sections and approach for the study.

2. EXTANT RESEARCH: CLOUD COMPUTING RISKS

Cloud computing is fraught with security risks, according to analyst firm Gartner. Smart customers would consider a third party security assessment before committing their business to a cloud vendor. Gartner

Figure 1. Components and approach of the study

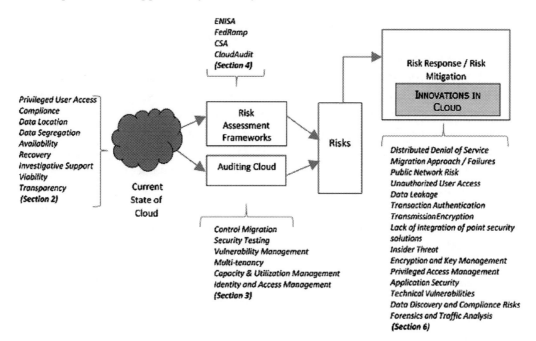

says in a June report titled "Assessing the Security Risks of Cloud Computing" that cloud computing has "unique attributes that require risk assessment in areas such as data integrity, recovery, and privacy, and an evaluation of legal issues in areas such as e-discovery, regulatory compliance, and auditing". Some of the above mentioned areas have been discussed below.

2.1. Privileged User Access

Cloud users, who are also content providers, publish data on cloud and require fine grained access controls. In healthcare, access to patient records stored in cloud would have to be regulated by policies admitted by HIPAA (Yu et al.,2010). In spite of emerging standards, the process of managing identities in cloud environments still presents a level of architectural complexity. Agreement on the implementation of role based and attribute based access controls become difficult to achieve when extended across several agencies and domains. We therefore see the emergence of Identity as a Service (IDaaS) as a potential opportunity to address complexity in IAM in cloud environments. The use of such a service in itself can facilitate the management of identity throughout its lifecycle including the provisioning/de-provisioning and the capture of relevant event information that is required for monitoring and audit purposes as well as the provision of self-service mechanisms for use by end users (Dorey, 2011).

In Cloud, an externally sourced IT service can bypasses the physical, logical and personnel controls that IT normally provides for in-house applications. The cloud service vendors must be requested to state clearly hiring policies and access privileges for data administrators who are allowed to handle the client's' information (Brodkin, 2008). Users, on the other hand, must also consider appointing trustworthy administrators who can be allowed to handle the stored information (Teneyuca, 2011).

2.2. Compliance

Compliance with the regulations is important for businesses. Businesses subject to compliance obligations are audited on a regular basis; and must provide compliance evidence. Any proof of compliance violation or absence of compliance evidence can lead auditors to impose financial fines. These fines may lead to bankruptcy if there are serious violations. Moreover, businesses such as the financial sector publish the results of their compliance audits to increase their client base.

The inability to monitor the cloud directly makes it a very difficult rather impossible choice for businesses to deploy applications as they would not be able meet certain compliance requirements. One specific class of legislations and regulations place restrictions on trans-border data flows and thus places restrictions on the location of data. Many countries in the world ask for the same requirement, the data and applications servers should be located in the country. Compliance also requires meaningful traceability of the various administration actions. These actions should be auditable so that a fine-grained evaluation of the actions can be carried out. The most auditable way of answering this requirement is to produce logs of these actions in a reliable manner. This implies that confidentiality and integrity of these logs should be ensured together with trusted time stamping. Cloud customers should be able to access the logs of every action pertaining to his application on various virtual machines (Massonet, et al., 2011).

Most corporations start using the cloud to launch critical applications without realizing the full impact of putting data in cloud. Cloud providers must therefore ensure environments are secure and intrusion proof in order to maintain users trust. Access guarantee must be provided for client data hosted on cloud. A company hosting sensitive data on cloud might require information on the location of data or may also require the data to be stored only in a particular region. It is advised that a contractual agreement be signed between the provider and user of cloud services to ensure that all consumer data resides on a known server (Kalpana, et al., 2012).

2.3. Data Location

Unique properties of cloud computing such as openness and multi-tenancy have led to the increasing emphasis on data security and privacy protection on cloud environments. In a typical SaaS model customer does not know where the data is stored, hence to avoid the leakage of potentially sensitive information, data privacy laws in many countries including some EU countries forbid certain types of sensitive data to leave the country. In Canada, both the Freedom of Information and Protection of Privacy Act (FOIPPA) in British Columbia and the Personal Information International Disclosure Protection Act in Nova Scotia prohibit the access to, disclosure of, and storage of data outside Canada without consent. This makes locality of data be an extremely important consideration in many enterprise architectures (Kadam, 2011). Organizations that rely on multiple cloud service providers may have little or no control over the movement of their data through different data centers around the world. Similarly, it is not always clear whether the data custodian or the third-party service provider is accountable to protect the data, or which sets of data protection laws apply. To comply with global privacy regulations, organizations need to ensure that their cloud providers implement technical and administrative controls to protect their data. These measures should include adequate technical controls, such as end-to-end encryption or tokenization. Security and privacy SLA's and Data loss prevention tools can also help enforce policies for data movement. For these legal agreements to have practical effect, organizations must also actively manage them. In other words, organizations should require regular reports on the adequacy of their providers' privacy and security measures and database activities, as well as disclosure of any incidents or issues that may put data at risk (Deloitte, 2016).

2.4. Data Segregation

While multi-tenancy maximizes cost benefits to businesses it also allows multiple users to collocate their data using SaaS applications which can lead to intrusion of data of one user by another becomes possible. Hacking a user's application or injecting malicious code in a SaaS system may be called an intrusion. SaaS model should therefore ensure a clear boundary that segregates each user's data at both physical and application layers (Subashini, et al., 2011). The GovCloud service offered by AWS offers an isolated AWS region for hosting highly regulated and sensitive workloads to support compliance requirements such as International Traffic in Arms Regulations (ITAR) and Federal Risk and Authorization Management Program (FedRAMP).

Full data segregation is not possible on cloud, users must come to terms with the fact that their data and VM's share space with other users. Cloud service providers and clients must therefore ensure that encryption is available at all stages, and that these encryption schemes were designed and tested by experienced professionals. Asking for evidence that the encryption implementation was designed and tested by experienced specialists, finding out who performed the protocol analysis and code reviews would be essential. This is important because encryption accidents might lead to lack of availability of critical and sensitive data or might even make the data unusable. Knowing who has access to decryption keys is key while establishing authorised access to data (Brodkin, 2008).

2.5. Availability

A major concern for users with respect to migration to public cloud has been its lack of availability and reliability. There have been several incidences where well-known cloud providers have experienced temporary lack of availability lasting at least several hours and striking loss of personal customer data. For example, Amazon's Elastic Compute Cloud (EC2) service in North America was temporarily unavailable at significant times due to 'lightning storm that caused damage to a single power distribution unit (PDU) in a single availability zone'.

There are three reasons why cloud users must be concerned with the availability of their valued assets in the cloud. First, most cloud providers rent computing and data-center infrastructures from other cloud providers. This means that when one cloud infrastructure is affected (unavailable), most probably, other providers will suffer similar losses, hindering the availability of resources to a wider audience. Second, the possibility that a cloud provider can file for bankruptcy, where the provider goes out of business with consequential financial liability to offset makes the availability of cloud resources a serious issue to consider. Finally, cross-vulnerability in the cloud due to the multi-tenancy implementation of cloud infrastructures and services makes the availability of resources in the cloud an important issue to consider. Users must engage with service providers to understand disaster recovery processes for their cloud based applications. Best practices may include providing backup copies of data on a monthly basis as part of the agreement. Further, users must be aware of their provider's business continuity plans, for instance, whether the provider has hot-standby sites and whether resilience is built as an abstraction to all layers of its services (Onwubiko, 2010).

2.6. Recovery

Disaster recovery and continuity of operations on cloud are among top customer concerns. Cloud providers are expected to replicate user data and application infrastructure across multiple sites to prevent any possibility of total failure. Even if a service provider refuses to divulge the exact location of customer data, it should be able to provide the customer with information on what would happen to their data if cloud data center(s) succumb to a disaster (Brodkin, 2008).

Cloud providers must employ risk models to estimate the number of servers in a data center and determine the distribution of customers across data centers in a manner that minimizes risk. In the event of stress on any single data center due to correlated failures, dynamic migration of a group of customers to another site can be employed. To achieve all of these tasks seamlessly, the cloud provider should be able to treat all of its data centers as a single pool of resources available to its DR customers. To prevent correlated of DR sites (due to factors like electrical grid failure or natural disaster in a geographical location) from stressing any one data center, the cloud provider should attempt to distribute its DR customers across multiple data centers in a way that minimizes potential conflicts—e.g. multiple customers from the same geographic region should be backed up to different cloud data centers (Wood, 2010).

2.7. Investigative Support

In cloud computing, lack of physical access to infrastructure, remote nature of evidence and transparency issues complicate forensics. Gathering forensics data is further restricted by service providers who intentionally avoid providing interfaces for the same. For instance, IaaS providers may not provide images of disks or virtual machines which are of high value during a forensics investigation. Since CSP's are generally dependent on partner CSP's and SaaS providers, investigation must be performed for each link in this dependency chain. It is important for all parties in the chain must be trustworthy, corruption free and willing to support an investigation.

Log records play a significant role in digital forensic analysis of systems. Regulations such as HIPAA, Payment Card Industry Data Security Standard, or Sarbanes-Oxley often require forensically sound preservation of information. Detailed logs may disclose private and sensitive information, hence it must be adequately protected with access controls.

Zonal planning can help determine safe and unsafe zones within a network which could reduce complexities and vulnerabilities of network data transfer in a cloud network. A service provider's own network may be marked as 'safe' while their suppliers or other external networks could be part 'unsafe' (Ko, et al., 2011). CSPs need to adopt and implement efficient mechanisms for the retrieval of data, for backups and to implement a data retention policy. Specific training activities focused in forensic analysis of cloud incidents should be promoted within a cloud service provider organization. CSP should also identify and indicate a "point of contact" to assist a customer with forensic investigation activities. As per the SLA or contract, the CSP should ensure quick and dependable access to the information/data needed at any time during the investigation through specific and documented procedures (ENISA, 2014).

2.8. Viability

The risk of the CSP suddenly going out of business, either through a "soft" cessation (i.e., filing for bankruptcy), or in a more abrupt way (simply ceasing operations and removing assets) concerns the uncertainty about the stability of the CSP. While relying on major CSPs, large enterprises with an insignificant risk of abruptly shutting down, mitigates the problem, the type and cost of service offered by these CSPs might not be suited for the needs of the would-be customer. Small, start-up cloud providers are more subject to market fluctuations, and might at some time decide to stop providing hosting services to their customers, or to move to another business model. In these cases the customer might be left stranded and unable to use the infrastructure anymore without any forewarning (Bartolini, et al., 2015).

Due diligence should be conducted to determine the viability of the vendor/service provider. Consider such factors as vendor reputation, transparency, references, financial (means and resources), and independent third-party assessments of vendor safeguards and processes (Bisong, et al., 2011). To ensure long term viability, issues such as disaster recovery, data portability and exit strategy must be addressed in the service level agreement by both the provider and user. An insurance of the CSP in favor of the customer can reduce the risks by covering the losses suffered by the customer. Software escrow techniques must be revisited for cloud-based services (Bartolini, et al., 2015).

2.9. Transparency

In order to become trusted partners to enterprises, CSP's need to be more transparent about their security practices. Cloud providers have their own firewalls, monitoring and controls to ensure that attacks, APTs, malware and otherwise unauthorized activity, but much of that information is not made available to customers for use in their security and monitoring capabilities. This is a problem that potentially impacts a cloud customers' ability to ensure complete visibility and protection for their own assets by being unable to incorporate all security intelligence and log information from beginning to end of a potential threat vector. While large cloud security providers (CSPs), like Amazon, Rackspace, Verizon's Terremark and Google have well-documented and publicized security practices, several organizations do businesses with smaller service providers in one vertical for purposes like billing or marketing. These vertical-specific CSP's reveal limited security information on their websites and during interactions making it difficult for customers to gain complete insight into their security policies and control implementations (Leinwand, 2016).

One interesting early example of service provider transparency is trust.salesforce.com, a site that salesforce.com, this website provides public information on its performance statistics. The site also guides users on general best practices that can be employed while using salesforce application to avoid attack vectors and comply to legal standards. This website takes the first step towards improved transparency between service provider and customer which is acknowledging that compromise of customer system is indeed possible. The less information that is hidden, the easier it is to trust a provider (Ryoo et al., 2014).

3. AUDITING CLOUD COMPUTING

Decisions to use cloud are generally not part of business road map but are results of economic desire. Lack of adherence to regulatory environment or business not understanding changes in IT introduce significant risk. True cost of cloud implementations, hence need to take into account audit, compliance and risk management. IT audit helps organizations identify and manage compliance and security risk to cloud infrastructure. This in turn reduces cost, improves security and helps make cloud ventures successful. Most cloud providers use core functions, security services and monitoring functions similar to their clients. This enables the use of control frameworks such as COBIT or NIST for auditing systems hosted on cloud. However, it is essential that an auditor recognises the risks to systems as IT moves to cloud and changes that it might bring about to the scope of the audit. Below are some specific areas that an auditor must pay close attention to while auditing cloud.

3.1. Migration of Controls

Migration of an application to cloud involves consideration of certain key factors such as existing IT infrastructure, security architecture and complexity. Security controls would have to adapt and evolve to meet cloud requirements. Existing mechanisms to secure data during rest and transmission, encryption and key management and identity and access management have to be migrated, tested and updated to secure cloud environments. For instance, some corporate systems and data may not be encrypted owing to their reliance on tightly secured internal networks and LAN security. When these systems are moved to cloud they pass over the internet and could be compromised due to lack of secure authentication and data integrity checks (Halpert, Ben 17). Simpler applications such as E Mail can be directly ported to cloud based SaaS applications like Office 365, Google Apps or Lotus live. However, migration of complex applications or legacy systems to cloud might require code changes, elaborate planning and extensive testing (Rashmi, et al., 2012). Migration of a virtual host may also change the legality of actions occurring on that host. In such cases, restrictions and liability of the cloud service provider and user must be clearly stated in contractual agreements.

Ensuring migration of controls must be followed by ensuring application availability and business continuity. Devices that enable network connectivity and data access such as firewalls, traffic-filtering routers and web gateways have to be configured correctly for the application to function as expected. Migration of security policies can be a complex and tedious effort for several organizations despite automation (Reichenberg, 2013).

3.2. Security Testing

Custom applications developed in-house may not be extensively tested for common vulnerabilities of the internet. In a public setting it might be vulnerable to a variety of security incidents like data breaches, malware, bot-nets, worms etc. (Halpert, 2011).

With respect to cloud applications, focus needs to be laid on security testing due to the business implications that come along with security flaws in the application. In a cloud computing environment security testing should be applied on three layers, namely the service, the infrastructure and the platform layer. Testing must be a combined effort by both, the SaaS provider and PaaS or IaaS consumer of cloud services. Application specific code may also introduce risks which have to be resolved by developers or a dedicated security testing team (Zech, et al., 2011). Internal cloud testing to check the quality of infrastructure and cloud capabilities can be done only by the service provider due to their elevated access into cloud systems. Similarly cloud based application system providers must test their services over private, public and hybrid clouds. Engineers must deal with the integration of various SaaS applications through the API's and connectivity protocols provided. Factors such as QoS requirements for applications, testing environment requirements, test models, test adequacy, test techniques and tools for security testing must be addressed and agreed upon by the cloud vendor and client (Gao, J et al., 2011). Auditors must ensure that web applications are carefully tested to ensure adequacy in access, authentication and monitoring (Halpert, 2011).

3.3. Vulnerability Management

Patching is so important that CSIS 20 Critical Security Controls includes as number 4: Continuous Vulnerability Assessment and Remediation (CSIS, 2013). Cloud SaaS applications do not provide much control to a customer where application patching is concerned. A service provider's improper patch management process could have serious ramifications on a user's business. WordPress experienced a serious outage due to a bad patch in the year 2010.

Cloud Security Alliance (CSA) recommends that a service provider and user establish policies, procedures and mechanisms for vulnerability and patch management. A user must employ a risk based approach to prioritize and deploy vendor supplied patches. In PaaS environments, users would have better control over patching, however the biggest challenge lies in environment management. Infrastructure engineers must coordinate with application development, testing teams and cloud service providers while applying patches. In IaaS environments, providers generally install patch management agents which report to a central data center. Apart from these scenarios, cloud service providers are also responsible for fixing vulnerabilities in their API's which are used by customers to access cloud services (Shackleford, 2016)

3.4. Multitenancy

Cloud computing allows greater economy in scale by hosting several virtual machines on a single server, this is known as multi-tenancy. Over provisioning of resources in a multi-tenant environment may cause applications to contend for resources and lead to lack of availability and create a denial of service condition. This could be caused as a result of adverse behaviour of other tenants in a physical server whose application consumes large amount of memory or CPU. Lack of physical controls lead to an excessive dependency on logical controls to prevent tenants from inadvertently interfering with each other's security. Weak logical controls might enable a malicious tenant to compromise the security posture of other tenants. Share services may also be considered a single point of failure when misconfigurations or uncontrolled changes are implemented. Co-mingled tenant data may make data destruction difficult especially if data is stored in shared media (OWASP, 2016).

Auditors must verify that multi-tenant architectures take into account the local segregation of environment, applications, data encryption, key management and storage. Segregation of shared or public cloud can also be achieved through virtual private cloud that allows quarantining virtual infrastructure and linking it back to internal resources via encrypted networks. An auditor should make sure that VPC's are appropriately implemented by the client while configuring cloud setup. They must also advise the client to negotiate isolation of critical and highly sensitive application with the cloud service provider although this may lead to an increase in cost (Ren et al., 2012).

3.5. Capacity and Utilization Management

Cloud service providers charge users according to the resources that they consume. Users are often unable to connect their resource consumption to the amount charged by providers. It is in a multitenant virtualized environment that providers incorrectly apply charges to a user's billing when a software or a bug running on another user's account could be utilizing more than expected resources. A unified mechanism must be in place to fairly measure resource consumption and subsequent charges levied. This mechanism must be able to guarantee the user of the amount of cloud resources that they are likely to consume based on which cloud strategy can be decided (K. Ren et al., 2012).

End-to-End mapping and aggregation of all metered components can be done for specific scenarios like performing a complex business transaction of ordering a product. Many cloud hosting environments do not expose metering information other than the standard billing details accessible to the account owner. Although this allows users to gauge the usage of cloud features within their account, it does not allow users to identify individual application or instance usage. Auditors must ensure that cloud service providers share a granular report of service usage metering and billing. Ensuring accountability for usage and chargeback results in improved services and better alignment between business and IT costs.

3.6. Identity and Access Management

Identity and access management function on cloud must be able to track and provide information on who has access to what information and if this access is monitored or logged by the system. Log of activities, including all authentication and access attempts (success and failed) must be preserved. These metrics must be used by auditors to enforce segregation of duties, identify and prevent access violations and quantify risk exposure (CSA, 2012).

The dynamic nature of cloud requires access management to be flexible enough to support updation of policies dynamically as users enter and leave the system. It is important to keep all roles and data access structures related information confidential and secured. Auditors must monitor and audit compliance with information security policies and best practices to mitigate lack of transparency, if any, among cloud service providers, users and data owners (Habiba, et al., 2013). While some cloud providers may provide a high degree of granularity in access management, auditors must also ensure that these are tested and applied properly to IT systems on cloud. Single, centrally controlled access models such as active directory can become more complicated to implement on cloud (Halpert, 2011)

4. CLOUD CONTROL FRAMEWORKS

Established risk assessment frameworks have been widely used to conduct a through and risk-based auditing of IT and related processes. In recent years, with the emergence of cloud and IOT technologies, these frameworks have also been updated to include auditing criteria and practices for Cloud computing and IOT. Use of a recognized and accepted framework also helps provide assurance that it is objective and independent of biases in evaluation. Below are a few control frameworks that might prove useful for an auditor considering cloud audits.

4.1. ENISA

ENISA is the European Network and Information security agency, papers published by ENSI provide detailed risk assessment models for cloud and specifically advice organizations that do business in the

European Union. Since its inception in 2004, ENISA has been contributing greatly to the development and increasing awareness of network and information security within the European Union. Some solutions delivered by the agency include pan-European Cyber Security Exercises, the development of National Cyber Security Strategies, CSIRTs cooperation and capacity building.

ENISA classifies Cloud Computing (CC) risks into three categories: Organizational, Technical and Legal. Organizational risk pertains to risks to the structure or business of an organization in case of instances such as co-tenant activities or termination of business by cloud service provider. Technical risks arise due to common problems on cloud such as malicious attacks or resource sharing issues which lead to failure of cloud services. Legal risks due to non-adherence of laws or regulations such as privacy law violation due to change in jurisdiction for data in motion (Dahbur, et al.,2011). ENISA (2014b) also studies the cyber threat landscape in cloud and is involved in various issues related to cloud adoption such as privacy, data protection, trust services, emerging technologies etc. The organization also enables optimization of information security by advising on setting up and monitoring service contracts with cloud vendors. In December 2011 ENISA has published a survey and analysis of security parameters in cloud SLAs across the European public sector. Experts across industries work with ENISA to publish papers on cloud computing through a group called ENISA Cloud Security and Resilience Expert Group. The organization also works with public sector, in EU member states, for cloud adoption by understanding current barriers and assisting with solutions and best practices (ENISA, 2014a).

4.2. FedRAMP

FedRAMP is the US government program to apply the Federal Information Security Management Act (FISMA) to cloud computing. The success of FedRAMP has led to its use across East Asia, Northern Europe, and the Americas for cloud security implementations. FedRAMP provides a comprehensive set of cloud security requirements and an independent assessment program backed by the chief information officers (CIOs) of the Department of Defense (DoD), the Department of Homeland Security (DHS), and the GSA. Cloud service providers (CSPs) that implement the required security controls and meet independent assessment requirements can be authorized for use by the federal government. FedRAMP standardized the process of FISMA authorization such that they can be performed once and reused by multiple agencies. This saves both government and private sector CSPs a lot of time and money and enables fast adoption of new systems and services.

FedRAMP also ensures consistency across all government agencies and instills a sense of trust between agencies. An authorized CSP can be leveraged by any agency without having to repeat the process. Continuous monitoring is a critical part of FedRAMP, CSP's must ensure the alignment of business processes like patch management and configuration management across their cloud systems. Authorized CSPs must perform monthly scans and send the scan results to their government authorization point of contact. High vulnerabilities are expected to be mitigated within 30 days and moderate vulnerabilities within 90 days. Failure to mitigate vulnerabilities according to these requirements could lead to a CSP having its authorization suspended or revoked (Taylor, L.,2014). Auditors are allowed to rely on the scope of this certification to forgo independent audits of these systems. The framework stresses the importance of the vendor being a committed partner to meeting standards, monetary security and controls of client's systems (Halpert, Ben, 2011).

4.3. The Cloud Security Alliance (CSA)

The Cloud Security Alliance (CSA) is a nonprofit organization led by industry practitioners, corporations, and other important stakeholders. CSA defines best practices for a secure cloud environment. It aims at enabling customers make an informed decision while transitioning their IT infrastructure to the cloud. In 2010, CSA published the the CSA Governance, Risk Management, and Compliance (GRC) Stack to help customers assess cloud service providers practices against industry standards and their compliance with regulations. In 2013, the CSA and the British Standards Institution launched the Security, Trust & Assurance Registry (STAR), a free, publicly accessible registry in which to publish CSA-related assessments for the reference of cloud users. CSA STAR introduced a control framework covering fundamental security for customers to evaluate overall risk of CSP's, this was called the Cloud Controls Matrix (CCM). CSA STAR self-assessment is open and free for all CSP's while higher levels of assurance through third-party assessments are based on continuous improvement certifications (Microsoft, 2016).

The CSA Top Threats Working Group released the list of top 12 threats in cloud for 2016 called 'The Treacherous 12', specifically related to shared on-demand nature of cloud computing. Risk of data breaches and weak identity management top this list closely followed by insecure API's, system vulnerabilities and account hijacking (Cloud Security Alliance, 2016).

4.4. Cloud Audit

Launched in January 2010 as a CSA working group, CloudAudit is a volunteer cross-industry effort from the best minds and talent in Cloud, networking, security, audit, assurance and architecture backgrounds. There are over 250 participants/interested parties supporting CloudAudit/A6. The "core team" are those that have committed to participate on a regular basis and establish leadership roles within the group. Anyone and everyone is welcome to contribute and participate. CloudAudit provides a common interface for enterprises to streamline their audit process in cloud environments. It also enables providers automate the Audit, Assertion, Assessment, and Assurance of their infrastructure (IaaS), platform (PaaS), and application (SaaS) environments and also allow authorized consumers of their services to do the same through an open, extensible and secure interface and methodology. The group provides light and easy to implement definitions and language structures using HTTP(s) and allow for their extension by providers. CloudAudit assists service providers by automating typically one-off labor-intensive, repetitive and costly auditing, assurance and compliance functions. Consumers, on the other hand, benefit by receiving a consistent and standardized interface to the information produced by the service provider (Cloud Security Alliance, 2010).

While this effort may not alleviate all of the audit concerns, it would begin to provide customers access to data that would differentiate cloud providers based on the information they provide. This will allow customers to partner with providers with whom they can achieve standard compliance. When audit information becomes a differentiating factor for competing service providers, it is possible that companies will continue to improve their work in this area (Rasheed, 2011).

5. DOMAINS

Cloud computing services vary based on industry needs, legal and regulatory requirements. This section provides brief summary of how cloud computing impacts specific industries highlighting main concerns.

5.1. Healthcare Domain

This domain must facilitate sharing of information that is confidential and sensitive. For this purpose medical institutions have started using cloud for sharing. Breach could result in loss to both patients and the institution. Some legal regulations that the medical industry must comply with include Health Insurance Portability and Accountability Act (HIPAA), the Health Information Technology for Economic and Clinical Health (HITECH) Act, the Food and Drug Administration Amendments Act (FDAAA), and the American Recovery and Reinvestment Act (ARRA) of 2009. This gives rise to the need for specifically tailored audit approaches to audit medical cloud systems. Organisations need to cooperate among themselves to tackle cloud security and audits.

5.2. Banking Domain

Owing to high inflow of confidential data, banks would have to update and secure their information incessantly while also making it accessible to customers. Banks can reduce cost by sharing customer information through cloud systems. This could potentially enable reducing interest rates. However, a big security concern faced by banks on cloud is to prevent client information from being misused or stolen. For this, data stored on cloud must be encrypted and access must be restricted by banks. Breach of data of one bank could potentially put other banks data also at risk.

5.3. Government Domain

With government agencies entering cloud domain, auditing cloud service providers is even more important due to sensitive nature of data. Today the Federal Risk and Authorization Management Program (FedRAMP) assesses cloud providers based on visibility, change control process and incident response. CSPs are expected to submit automated data feeds on system performance and reports. CSP's also have to report controls that they have in place to monitor and prevent data breach due to new risks or vulnerabilities (Ryoo et al., 2013).

6. RECENT INNOVATIONS IN CLOUD COMPUTING

While the use of Internet and web-based utilities that companies are embracing for cost savings, productivity and technology agility (Marston et al., 2011) has given them the competitive advantage there is no doubt that they are increasingly becoming more attractive target for hackers (ENISA, 2009). Both the adopting companies and the ones providing cloud services are making strides in implementing processes and technologies based on innovation. However, the providers have the economies of scale and scope on their side to innovate with their services and their security practices. As Kaufman (2009) also explains, larger "providers like Amazon and Microsoft, for example, have the capabilities to deflect and survive cyber-attacks that not all providers have". At the same time, the distributed nature of the cloud with data stored in multiple data centers limits impact from certain kinds of cyber threats (Biswas, 2011). At the same time, potential adopters of cloud services should ensure before signing up for a service that the security that the provider offers meets their risk appetite. There are advancements in underlying technologies that providers have leveraged to offer more robust security solutions around their products. There have been several studies that have explored how companies respond to new innovations in technology and how their adoption of emerging technology is impacted by various factors including evolution of their own offerings, resistance to change and compatibility issues (Nelson and Winter, 1982; Levinthal and March, 1993; Tushman and Anderson, 1986).

Companies also make changes in their management structures and investment decisions to facilitate their ability to innovate in situations that improve their ability to provide more secure offerings (Hargadon, 2003; Sanidas, 2004). Studies have shown failure in the transition to new core technologies to support their own products and services have hampered their own growth (Gilbert, 2005; Taylor and Helfat, 2009). Also, there have been studies to distinguish between types of technological innovation based on divergent requirements and business mandates (Gibson and Birkinshaw, 2004; Gilbert, 2005; Raisch and Birkinshaw, 2008). Innovation in security aspects of cloud offerings also propose differentiated benefits and coverage against known and emerging risks. This section of the chapter investigates how recent technological innovations in managing risks in cloud services have helped both adopters and providers mitigate risks from cloud. Articles were collected from recent media announcements for last one year. These media announcements highlight that providers are keen on spreading the word about their innovation to provide assurance to the world that security is one of their top priorities. We also show how these innovations are mapped to cloud risks that we have identified in section 2 and how specifically they map to audit focus areas from section 3. Table 1 provides a summary of the articles with information on provider company, their services and what cloud risks are being addressed by that service.

Table 1 also shows the references on the media announcements and specific subsection where the announcement is discussed. Table 2 shows how specific cloud risk addressed are mapped to cloud risks that were identified in the section on extant literature on existing cloud computing risks. Table 3 shows mapping of cloud risks and how specific audit focus area can be used to test the control effectiveness and strength of each risk addressed. This will help the auditors and managers understand how the innovation is ranked in terms of providing security that the innovation aims to. At the same time auditors can also see how these specific risks can be incorporated in their overall audit plan when they collectively evaluate the control category to ensure that redundancies are reduced and defence in depth or layered control approach is maintained. The second column in Tables 2 and 3 represent the specific sub-section in Sections 2 and 3, respectively that deals with the specific risk. The first column in these tables is aggregation of similar types of addressed risks. Table 4 shows the cloud risks and specific media announcements that attempt to address them. In the next subsections, each of the announcements are discussed where the section title is also the title(s) of the media announcements that announced the specific innovation.

Table 1. Summary of recent innovations and addressed cloud risks

Cloud Risk Addressed	Provider / Domain	Service(s) / Process(es)	Reference(s)	Chapter Section
Distributed Denial of Service	Amazon Inc	AWS Shield	(Greene and Stevens, 2016; AWS Shield, 2016)	6.1
Migration Approach	Healthcare	Staged Migration	(McKendrick, 2016)	6.2
Public Network Risk	Console Inc.	Console	(Pesek, G, 2016; Hardesty, 2016; Console, 2016)	6.3
Unauthorized User Access & Data Leakage	Various	CASB	(Skyhigh, 2016)	6.4
Transaction Security	IBM	Blockchain network	(Prisco, 2016; Olavsrud, 2016; Castillo, 2016)	6.5
Insider Threat	Various	UEBA, Behavior Analysis	(Sarukkai, 2015)	6.6
Migration Failures	Amazon	AWS Elastic Block Store	(Frank, 2016)	6.7
Encryption and Key Management	Valutive and Gemalto	Safenet	(Vaultive, 2016)	6.8
Privileged Access / Insider Threat	Lieberman	Enterprise Random Password Manager	(Lieberman, 2016a; Lieberman, 2016b)	6.9
Web Application Firewall	Barracuda	Web Application Security	(Barracuda, 2016)	6.10
Public Network Risk	Zscaler	ZScaler Private Access	(Zscaler, 2016)	6.11
Application Security	Amazon	AWS X-Ray	(Amazon, 2016a; (Amazon, 2016c)	6.12
Technical Vulnerabilities	Menlo Security	Isolation Platform	Menlo, 2016)	6.13
Migration Failures	CloudVelox	CloudVelox	(Kepes, 2016)	6.14
Technical Vulnerabilities	Amazon	Amazon Inspector	(Amazon, 2016b)	6.15
Data Discovery and Compliance Risks	Dataguise	DgSecure (Analytics, Governance)	(Amazon, 2016d)	6.16
Insider Threat	Dataguise	DgSecure (RBAC, UEBA)	(Amazon, 2016d)	6.16
Data Encryption	IBM	Z13s servers	(Morgan, 2016; (Bhartiya, 2016; Taft, 2016)	6.17
Forensics and Traffic Analysis	ProtectWise	ProtectWise	(Protectwise, 2016)	6.18
Encryption and Key Management	Google	CSEK	(Vijayan, J, 2016)	6.19

6.1. Amazon Cloud Computing Division Unveils New Cyber Security Service (Greene and Stevens, 2016) / AWS Shield (AWS Shield, 2016)

In wake of the recent Distributed denial of services attack launched against market giants like twitter, PayPal and Netflix, Amazon launches AWS Shield to protect its customers from such attacks that can make websites unreachable for a period of time. AWS shield has been introduced with two tiers – Standard and Advanced. Standard version is free of cost and automatically enabled for all customers of AWS. It protects web applications from commonly known attacks occurring at the network and transport layers.

Table 2. Mapping of cloud risk addressed and current risks focus area

Cloud Risks Addressed	Sub-Sections in 2 (Current Risks)
Distributed Denial of Service	2.3, 2.5, 2.6, 2.7
Migration Approach / Failures	2.2, 2.9
Public Network Risk	2.3, 2.5, 2.9
Unauthorized User Access	2.1, 2.2, 2.4
Transaction Security	2.2, 2.4, 2.7
Data Leakage	2.2, 2.3, 2.4, 2.7
Encryption and Key Management	2.2, 2.3, 2.5, 2.8, 2.9
Privileged Access Management	2.1, 2.2
Web Application Firewall	2.2, 2.7
Application Security	2.2, 2.3, 2.5, 2.6
Technical Vulnerabilities	2.2, 2.3, 2.5, 2.6
Data Discovery and Compliance Risks	2.2, 2.3, 2.4, 2.7, 2.8
Insider Threat	2.1, 2.2, 2.4, 2.6, 2.7
Forensics and Traffic Analysis	2.2, 2.3 2.7, 2.9

Table 3. Mapping of cloud risk addressed and audit focus area

Cloud Risks Addressed	Audit Focus Areas
Distributed Denial of Service	3.5
Migration Approach / Failures	3.1
Public Network Risk	3.4, 3.2
Unauthorized User Access	3.6
Transaction Security	3.6, 3.2
Data Leakage	3.2, 3.6
Encryption and Key Management	3.1, 3.6
Privileged Access Management	3.6
Web Application Firewall	3.3
Application Security	3.3
Technical Vulnerabilities	3.2, 3.3
Data Discovery and Compliance Risks	3.2, 3.4
Insider Threat	3.2, 3.6
Forensics and Traffic Analysis	3.2, 3.5

This is done by analysing incoming traffic to detecting anomalies, malicious code inserts or malware signatures. Inline and automatic mitigation techniques are also available to protect application from impact of attacks. AWS Shield advanced is a paid service and can protect applications from larger and more sophisticated attacks and is integrated with AWS Web Application Firewall (AWS WAF). Enhanced resource specific monitoring, the ability to set proactive firewall rules with AWS WAF and advanced

Table 4. Mapping of cloud risk addressed through innovations

Cloud Risks Addressed	Recent Innovations (Sub-Sections in 6)
Distributed Denial of Service	6.1
Migration Approach / Failures	6.2, 6.7, 6.14
Public Network Risk	6.3, 6.11
Unauthorized User Access	6.4
Transaction Security	6.5
Data Leakage	6.4
Encryption and Key Management	6.8, 6.12, 6.17, 6.19
Privileged Access Management	6.09
Web Application Firewall	6.10
Application Security	6.12
Technical Vulnerabilities	6.13, 6.15
Data Discovery and Compliance Risks	6.16
Insider Threat	6.09, 6.16
Forensics and Traffic Analysis	6.18

automatic mitigation techniques are some key features. AWS Shield advanced provides access to 24*7 DDoS Response team who can be engaged before, during or after attack for specialised services. It also comes with 'DDoS cost protection' which identify spikes on Elastic load balancer that could be caused by a potential DDoS attack and provides service credits for any charges levied because of this spike.

6.2. For Healthcare, Cloud Computing Comes in Measured Doses (McKendrick, 2016)

Health care providers taking to cloud has significantly grown over the past two years despite concerns regarding data protection and HIPPA laws. Most healthcare organizations prefer staged migration to cloud starting with testing cloud platforms with back office applications and then managing analytics and storage on cloud before rolling out patient facing web applications. Companies are opting for a combination of private cloud, for storing sensitive information like patient records, and public cloud for disaster recovery and setting up POC environments.

6.3. Bringing Cloud Security Innovations to the Enterprise (Pesek, G, 2016) / IIX Reinvents Itself as Console (Hardesty, L, 2016) / Console Inc. (Console, 2016)

Console Inc. enables programmable interconnection between two enterprises or an enterprise and a cloud network like Microsoft Azure, Google Cloud platform or AWS via a software platform. With public internet one does not have control over the path taken by data packets, network performance and exposure to threats. A data packet travelling across public internet is, on an average, exposed to four different networks each having several vulnerable points such as routers, switches, gateways etc. Console has a built a global network with 160 points of presence connected by a fibre for direct private connection that can bypass the public internet. Console is the first company to fully automate switching and routing for seamless interconnection, avoiding the risks of sending traffic over the public Internet and providing a more secure, reliable and consistent environment. Console provides other features like social networking among enterprises, SaaS solution providers and business partners. They also provide advanced monitoring that enables an enterprise to repurpose capacity across network ports.

6.4. What Is a Cloud Access Security Broker (CASB) (Skyhigh, 2016)

CASB is an on premise or cloud hosted software that act as policy enforcement points and are placed between cloud service providers and consumers. CASB can combine security policies including Authentication, single sign-on, authorization, credential mapping, device profiling, encryption, tokenization, logging, alerting, malware detection/prevention.

Gartner names cloud access security broker the #1 security technology of 2016 and believes that by 2020, 85% of large enterprises will use CASB for their cloud services.

CASB's can help organizations identify threats and misuse of cloud services by identifying usage of shadow IT cloud services and risks they pose to organizational data. Shadow IT can also pose a threat to the IP of a company when employees put corporate information on cloud during unauthorized deployments. A CASB can monitor data traffic sent between organizational endpoints and cloud applications which will enable IT to uncover rogue deployments and cloud services used by employees.

6.5. IBM Launches Blockchain Cloud Services on High Security Server, LinuxONE (Prisco, 2016) / IBM Building Blockchain Ecosystem (Olavsrud, 2016) / IBM Unveils New Cloud Blockchain Security Service (Castillo, 2016)

IBM has launched a new functionality as part of its cloud services for businesses to test and run blockchain networks. This service will ensure security for private data and is ideal for industries that require strong compliance. Blockchain is a distributed database that can record digital events or transactions. Records cannot be altered and can only be amended. Each block of item in a chain is timestamped and also contains a hash value of the previous block thus creating a link between the two. Each new transaction has to be authenticated by all participants in the distributed network forming the block chain thus providing transparency and creating awareness among stakeholders. IBM looks to improve security of private blockchains running in cloud by securing end points and fighting insider threats. The IBM Blockchain runs on LinuxOne emperor system that can scale up to 8000 VMs and is designed to protect against backdoor attacks. IBM's secure services container technology provides firmware protection and prevents system administrators and root users from accessing the blockchain on cloud. All software built on IBM Blockchain will be encrypted and attested to prevent installation of malware on client systems. It is currently being used to securely track high value goods such as diamonds and artwork. Microsoft has also rolled out BaaS for Microsoft azure.

6.6. How Data Science and Machine Learning Is Enabling Cloud Threat Protection (Sarukkai, 2015)

User and Entity behavioral analytics (UEBA) creates behavior based models for cloud services wherein these models adapt depending on user behavior. Anomalies in user behavior can be easily identified and reported. Machine learning algorithms in UEBA performs data exploration thus enabling prioritization of security incidents. For example, while traditional detection systems might flag every transaction above a certain threshold, UEBA would spot unusual user activities by sifting through large datasets. Given that an average company sees over 2 billion cloud based transactions each day, UEBA can be used against factors such as service action, service action category, number of bytes uploaded/downloaded and rate/time of access of services across a service action or even an entire cloud service provider to identify behavioral anomalies.

Behavior analysis takes security beyond rule writing by looking at activities and behaviors so that even if someone is able to compromise a user's identity, they still have to be able to act like the user, which is when the alarms start to go off. Gartner predicts the UEBA market revenue to rise to approximately US$200 million by the end of 2017.

6.7. Amazon Quietly Launches Tools for Migrating on Premise Apps to Cloud (Frank, 2016)

Migration of legacy and on premise applications to cloud is risky especially if those applications require low downtime. Amazons Server Migration service helps IT replicate on premise VMs to Amazon Cloud by supporting incremental replication. IT administrators install a connector that will analyze their virtualized server environment and collect information about the instances they are using. The AWS Management console provides a view of all operating connectors and virtualized servers in an environment. From there, administrators can create and manage replication jobs to take the contents of a VM and reproduce it as an Amazon Machine Image stored in the AWS Elastic Block Store (EBS) service.

Each incremental replication will sync only what's been changed to minimize network bandwidth use. Allows servers to be tested incrementally. From there, it's possible to spin up a new instance that should be a duplicate of what's running on-premises, either for testing the replicated VM or for getting it running in production. This feature ensures that migration to cloud is simplified. It also allows orchestration of multi-server migrations, incremental testing of migrated servers, supports widely used operating systems and minimizes downtime due to migration.

6.8. Vaultive and Gemalto Team Up to Deliver Increased Cloud Data Security Control for SaaS Applications (Vaultive, 2016)

Vaultive and Gemalto have teamed up to provide an encryption and key management solution by which companies can encrypt data before moving it to cloud and also maintain ownership of encryption keys across SaaS applications. More control over key management allows organization to demonstrate better control of their sensitive data. This approach also allows separation of controls between cloud administrators and security professionals who are responsible for protecting data and keys. Gemalto's SafeNet, which is their multi factor authentication service, can be integrated with this platform for identity and access management.

Some key features of this solution:

1. Rule based policy engine enables rapid integration with SaaS applications and encryption best practices ensures securing data at organizational boundaries;

2.   Cost effective method to secure multiple cloud applications. Ease of deployment across physical, public and virtual cloud environments;

3.   Uses Key Management Interoperability protocol standard and SafeNet can centrally manage and preserve integrity of encryption keys.

6.9. Lieberman Software to Present Cloud Security Session at Gartner Identity and Access Management Summit (Lieberman, 2016a; Lieberman, 2016b)

Some concerns of companies migrating to cloud revolve around the growing number of unmanaged administrator accounts and cryptographic keys. Lieberman Software's cyber security technology automatically discovers privileged accounts in cloud and hybrid environments at scale, and audits access to those accounts. The Enterprise Random Password Manager (ERPM) is a cyber-defense platform that can protect organizations from insider threats, advanced persist threats and cyber-attacks across on-premise and cloud environments. ERPM tracks privileged accounts and provides them with unique and frequently changing credentials. These identities are available only to authorized users on a temporary basis thus preventing unauthorized or anonymous access to critical systems. The software also allows users to configure rules for password complexity, diversity, change frequency and synchronize changes for across dependencies. ERPM can be used to secure identity of super user accounts, service accounts, application credentials, encryption keys and cloud identities on Azure, AWS, Softlayer etc. It also helps organizations meet compliance requirements by providing a comprehensive view of risks across privileged accounts and enforcing credential policies.

6.10. Barracuda Simplifies Web Application Security for AWS Customers (Barracuda, 2016)

Barracuda has released a new metered billing option for its Web Application Firewall that enables customers to deploy an unlimited number of firewalls but pay only for what is consumed. This is in contrast to practices followed by AWS marketplace applications where customer usage is aggregated and charged as part of AWS bill. This offering provides AWS customers greater flexibility and control over operational costs while securing their cloud environments. Meter firewalls allow cost to economically scale with increasing application workloads.

6.11. Zscaler Private Access: Remote Access Without the Security Risks of VPNs (Zscaler, 2016)

VPNs have always been the standard method of providing users remote access to corporate applications on an internal network. However, cost of installation, deployment, maintenance and upgrade is high for VPN. Additional requirements in terms of increased number of datacenters, load balancers, Site-to-Site VPN tunnels and licenses may be required for providing high availability of VPN. The most important risk with VPN is security, since remote access is actually network access. Once in a network malware can propagate and users may be able to gain access to adjacent applications from which they should be restricted.

To address this issue, Zscaler Private Access uses the global Zscaler cloud infrastructure to enable application access independent of network access. Zscaler Private Access decouples applications from the physical network and delivers granular, per-user access to apps and services running in the internal corporate network, in a data center, or in a public cloud like Amazon or Azure. The service is based on Zscaler's global cloud (with over 100 data centers globally), Zscalar App and Zscalar's software connectors, so there is no requirement for additional hardware or upgrades of existing hardware. If there are more than two instances of the same application deployed in two different locations the software will choose the path that provides best performance.

6.12. Amazon Unveils AWS X-Ray and Personal Health Dashboard to Help Monitor Application Health in the Cloud (Amazon, 2016a) / AWS X-Rays (Amazon, 2016c)

With the emergence of distributed systems, ensuring functioning of modules at scale has gained importance. There has been no easy way for developers to "follow-the-thread" as execution traverses EC2 instances, ECS containers, micro-services, AWS database and messaging services. AWS X-Ray is a service that allows developers to debug their distributed applications. X-Ray captures trace data from code running on EC2 instances, AWS Elastic beanstalk AWS Gateway API and more. The data collected at each point is called a segment, and is stored as a chunk of JSON data. A segment represents a unit of work, and includes request and response timing, along with optional sub-segments that represent smaller work units down to lines of code. It allows developers to follow thread execution by adding HTTP headers to requests. The X-Ray UI is built around the concept of filter expressions. The UI is powered by free-form filters that allows to filter results based on response time, duration, service, dates, trace ID, HTTP methods etc.

6.13. Half of the Web Is Vulnerable to Malware (Menlo, 2016)

According to Menlo Software's 'State of the web 2016' report, 46% of internet's top 1 million sites are risky. Menlo considers a site 'risky' if the homepage or associated background sites: is running vulnerable software, is known-bad, or has had a security incident in the last 12 months. Traditional methods like firewalls, anti-virus, network sandboxing or intrusion prevention systems attempt to prevent attacks by distinguishing between "good" and "bad" elements, and then implement policies intended to allow "good" content and block the "bad." However, this strategy has not been effective in eliminating malware and phishing attacks has also generated several false reports.

Menlo Security's cloud based Isolation Platform is aimed at solving the malware problem completely by executing all of the content from the internet in an isolated environment. The application can perform isolation at scale in a distributed cloud environment and render malware free content to the end user without requiring any end point software. The platform is inserted between user and the web and configured via proxy chaining with web gateway or firewall. A user's web request is sent to the platform that browses the web on the users behalf and fetches and executed web content within the platform on the user's behalf. Only 100% safe rendering information is sent to the users device to the native web browser. All of the good or bad content from the web remains in the isolation platform. Platform also helps secure E Mails protecting organization from data theft or fraud.

6.14. CloudVelox Offers Automated Cloud Network Customizations (Kepes, 2016)

CloudVelox software automates migration of on premise applications to public cloud including AWS and Azure with reduced time, complexity and hassle. The software has already automated storage and compute migration and has not added automation for network migration customizations too. Enterprises can "map" their existing networking topologies within a data center and recreate that within a cloud network paradigm. This automation can ease the migration to cloud for large data centers with complex network configurations and enterprise workloads running on specific VLANs and subnets. During migration, Data security and access is managed by SSH, HTTPS, Volume encryption and IPSeC VPN. System security is handled by launching the application in a separate AWS VPC and configuring security groups and virtual access control lists. Application security is ensured by utilizing CloudVelox's ability to authenticate users from LDAP servers running in customer data center, customers can assert control over appropriate resource access in the cloud.

6.15. Amazon Web Services Makes Amazon Inspector Available to All Customers (Amazon, 2016b)

Amazon Inspector identifies potential security issues, vulnerabilities and deviations from security norms to help customers improve security compliance for applications running on AWS cloud servers. This reduces effort required to assess security risks and provides a simplified mechanism for developers to integrate security assessments within the application development cycle. This integration can be done by using API's provided by inspector on specific EC2 instances and associated applications that customers would like to assess. Security tests and duration can be selected and adjusted as required. Once tests are selected, the inspector analyses the application activities and looks for a wide variety of potential vulnerabilities in the system. Information such as application communication flow and channels are gathered and compared against AWS rule packages that comprise of several thousand security vulnerabilities. Once an assessment is completed customers are provided with detailed recommendations for application remediation. This service along with CloudTrail allows auditors to view details and logs of security tests performed thereby simplifying the process of demonstrating compliance for AWS customers.

6.16. Dataguise Shows Security and Compliance Innovations for Cloud-Based Data Infrastructure at AWS Summit in New York (Amazon, 2016d)

Dataguise DgSecure on AWS is a data centric security platform. It scans Amazon S3 (storage) and identifies the location and status of sensitive information that is also accessed via Amazon Elastic MapReduce (Amazon EMR) for data analytics, compliance, and information governance purposes. The solution features transparent, role-based sensitive asset provisioning on the Amazon EMR platform so that users have access to sensitive data hosted on Amazon S3 through DgSecure role-based access policies. The technology also provides detection, monitoring, auditing of sensitive information across cloud based repositories. DgSecure can help businesses understand data breach, privacy and compliance risk, make risk based decisions and provide additional layers of security for data driven initiatives. DgSecure also supports all major distributions including Hortonworks, Cloudera, and MapR as well as major relational databases including Oracle, SQLServer, MySQL, and PostgreSQL. Dataguise also uses machine learning and behavioral analytics to alert administrators when system, device, or human behavior deviates from the norm. It makes sure that any move to the cloud remains compliant with privacy and regulatory requirements by allowing companies to keep track of all the data across the enterprise and ensuring it doesn't fall into the wrong hands.

6.17. IBM's New Cyberframe Is the World's Most Secure Server for Datacenters, Cloud and Mobile (Morgan, 2016) / IBM Encrypts the Cloud With Z13s Mainframes (Bhartiya, 2016) / IBM Takes the Power of Mainframe to Cloud (Taft, 2016)

IBM announced the Z13s (s for security) mainframe servers with speedy encryption, cyber analytics and other security innovations. IBM has spent 5 years and $1 bn on Z13s development efforts. It can process 2.5 bn transactions a day with advanced cryptographic features to encrypt and decrypt data two times faster than previous generation servers with loss in performance. Clients can encrypt data right from the point where order is made on mobile to the financial transactions done in the data center or on cloud. IBM is also offering new analytics service to Z systems that is based on UEBA to identify malicious activity. The Z13 costs half that of public cloud for comparable configuration and equivalent workloads.

The new offerings include IBM Bluemix integration with z Systems. IBM's bluemix environment combined with enhancements to connector technology within bluemix and Z systems now allows enterprises to leverage their own single-tenant version of Bluemix to build applications around their most sensitive data and existing services. IBM also introduced z Systems Hybrid Cloud Connect Test Drive, which enables enterprises to connect their on-premises enterprise systems to a public cloud. IBM z Systems will offer IBM Cloud Manager with OpenStack for the z13 to simplify the management of virtualized environments.

6.18. ProtectWise Achieves Advanced Partner Status in the Amazon Web Services Partner Network (Protectwise, 2016)

ProtectWise offers a cloud detection visibility and response platform that uses software sensors deployed on networks for packet capture of all network traffic. The data is then streamed back to the cloud platform for threat detection and analysis and stored for up to a year, you will know with absolute confidence whether or not events have impacted your environment. The ProtectWise Grid captures high fidelity network traffic, creates a lasting memory for the network and delivers analysis and alerting through a visualizer. The Grid helps users not only understand what is happening in real time, but also to go back in time and show progression in attacks. Users know when and how an attack happens, and are able to pinpoint the attack for rapid remediation. This provides security teams the strategic advantage to hunt and investigate threats through every stage of an attack. The ProtectWise Visualizer is an overview of your network security which allows exploration for collaboration and forensic analysis by cutting through the noise to quickly identify the high-priority threats.

6.19. Google Initiates Customer-Supplied Cloud Data Encryption Keys (Vijayan, J, 2016)

Although many cloud vendors encrypt customer data at rest these days, the fact that they also hold the decryption keys has proved to be an issue for many organizations. Google this week announced general availability of an option that lets customers of its cloud services use their own keys for encrypting sensitive data stored online. Currently, Google's cloud platform encrypts all customer data stored on its servers by default but with this new service Google enables enterprises to bring their own Customer-Supplied Encryption Keys (CSEK) to protect data. The company will only require and hold customer keys temporarily to fulfill requests such as starting a virtual machine or attaching a disk. Google will use CSEK to protect the Google-generated keys used to encrypt and decrypt the data. Any key the customer provides must be 256-bit string encoded in the RFC 4648 standard. Since CSEK's are not stored anywhere by Google, if keys are lost there will be no way for Google to retrieve data encrypted with those keys. Amazon and Box provide similar facilities to its customers for data security.

7. CONCLUSION

It has been evident last few years that cloud computing's offers a lot of promises for small and large enterprises alike. Security risks have been largely seen as main concerns and voiced by companies. Cloud service providers have been on an upward trajectory to improve their offerings' flexibility and scalability and improving security and availability levels. This chapter elaborates on 1) the most important risks inherent to the cloud as are evidenced by extant literature as well as 2) audit focus areas that can provide assurance on control strength of controls that mitigate risks. Companies have taken a hybrid approach with direct and compensating controls for lack of appropriate technology to support their security objectives. This chapter presents how companies (cloud service providers) have responded with innovations in security and how they are in response to risks that have already been highlighted by extant research. This chapter can be useful for managers, auditors and security professionals on how recent innovations are shaping cloud industry and they are providing the much needed respite from the pressure of cloud computing risks. At the same time, it also provides insights into the trend of innovation in security solutions in cloud. As future work on this chapter, we plan on collecting additional data from previous years (older than 2016) and interpret the results to show how the evolution has been for cloud computing. Also, specific risks could be investigated as part of future work to unravel any underlying themes and categories in counter-measures that provide most benefit from the risks that arise due to adoption of cloud computing services.

REFERENCES

Adomavicius, G., Bockstedt, J., Gupta, A., & Kauffman, R. J. (2007). Technology roles and paths of influence in an ecosystem model of technology evolution. *Information Technology Management*, *8*(2), 185–202. doi:10.100710799-007-0012-z

Amazon. (2016a). *Amazon unveils AWS X-Ray and Personal Health Dashboard to help monitor application health in the cloud*. Retrieved online on December 15, 2016 from http://www.geekwire.com/2016/amazon-unveils-aws-x-ray-personal-health-dashboard-help-monitor-application-health-cloud/

Amazon. (2016b). *Amazon Web Services Makes Amazon Inspector Available to All Customers*. Retrieved online on December 15, 2016 from http://www.businesswire.com/news/home/20160419006466/en/Amazon-Web-Services-Amazon-Inspector-Customers

Amazon. (2016c). *AWS XRAY. Amazon Website*. Retrieved online on December 15, 2016 from https://aws.amazon.com/blogs/aws/aws-x-ray-see-inside-of-your-distributed-application/

Amazon. (2016d). *Dataguise Shows Security and Compliance Innovations for Cloud-Based Data Infrastructure at AWS Summit in New York*. Retrieved online on December 15, 2016 from http://www.businesswire.com/news/home/20161205005340/en/Global-Cybersecurity-Confidence-Falls-70-Percent-%E2%80%9CC-%E2%80%9D

Avgerou, C. (2008). Information systems in developing countries: a critical research review. *J. Inform. Technol., 23*(3), 133–146.

AWS Shield. (2016). *AWS Shield: managed DDOS Protection*. Retrieved online on December 15, 2016 from https://aws.amazon.com/shield/

Baregheh, A., Rowley, J., & Sambrook, S. (2009). Towards a multidisciplinary definition of innovation. *Management Decision, 47*(8), 1323–1339.

Barracuda. (2016). *Barracuda Simplifies Web Application Security for AWS Customers*. Retrieved online on December 15, 2016 from http://www.broadwayworld.com/bwwgeeks/article/Barracuda-Simplifies-Web-Application-Security-for-AWS-Customers-20161130

Bartolini, C., El Kateb, D., Le Traon, Y., & Hagen, D. (2015). *Cloud Providers Viability: How to Address it from an IT and Legal Perspective? Economics of Grids*. Clouds, Systems, and Services.

Bhartiya, S. (2016). *IBM encrypts the cloud with Z13s mainframe*. Retrieved online on December 15, 2016 from http://www.cio.com/article/3033967/linux/ibm-encrypts-the-cloud-with-z13s-mainframe.html

Bisong, A., & Rahman, M. (2011). *An overview of the security concerns in enterprise cloud computing*. arXiv preprint arXiv:1101.5613

Biswas, S. (2011, January 20). *Is cloud computing secure? Yes, another perspective* [Web log post]. Retrieved online on January 6, 2017 from http://www.cloudtweaks.com/2011/01/the-question-should-be-is-anything-truly-secure

Brodkin, J. (2008). Gartner: Seven cloud-computing security risks. *InfoWorld, 2008*, 1–3.

Businesswire. (2016). *World First: Outscale Introduces Per-Second Billing to Boost Cloud Adoption*. Retrieved online on December 15, 2016 from http://www.businesswire.com/news/home/20160915005885/en/World-Outscale-Introduces-Per-Second-Billing-Boost-Cloud

Carlo, J. L., Lyytinen, K., & Rose, G. M. (2011). Internet computing as a disruptive information technology innovation: The role of strong order effects. *Information Systems Journal*, *21*(1), 91–122. doi:10.1111/j.1365-2575.2009.00345.x

Castillo, M. (2016). *IBM Unveils New Cloud Blockchain Security Service*. Retrieved from http://www.coindesk.com

Chang, V., Kuo, Y. H., & Ramachandran, M. (2016). Cloud computing adoption framework: A security framework for business clouds. *Future Generation Computer Systems*, *57*, 24–41. doi:10.1016/j.future.2015.09.031

Christensen, C. M., Baumann, H., Ruggles, R., & Sadtler, T. M. (2007). Disruptive Innovation for Social Change. In *Harvard Business Review* (pp. 136–136). Harvard Business School Publication Corp.

Cloud Security Alliance. (2010). *Cloud Audit Working Group*. Retrieved online on December 15, 2016 from https://cloudsecurityalliance.org/group/cloudaudit/

Cloud Security Alliance. (2016). *The Treacherous 12*. Retrieved online on December 15, 2016 from https://downloads.cloudsecurityalliance.org/assets/research/top-threats/Treacherous-12_Cloud-Computing_Top-Threats.pdf

Console. (2016). Console Inc. Retrieved online on December 15, 2016 from https://www.console.to/

Cooper, C. (2016). *Fixing the weakest link in cloud security*. Retrieved online on December 15, 2016 from http://mspmentor.net/cloud-services/fixing-weakest-link-cloud-security

Dahbur, K., Mohammad, B., & Tarakji, A. B. (2011, April). A survey of risks, threats and vulnerabilities in cloud computing. In *Proceedings of the 2011 International conference on intelligent semantic Web-services and applications* (p. 12). ACM. 10.1145/1980822.1980834

Deloitte. (2016). *Data privacy in the cloud Navigating the new privacy regime in a cloud environment*. Retrieved online on December 15, 2016 from http://www.wsj.com/articles/amazon-cloud-computing-division-unveils-new-cyber-security-service-1480620359

Dorey, P. G., & Leite, A. (2011). Commentary: Cloud computing–A security problem or solution?. *Information Security Technical Report, 16*(3), 89-96.

ENISA. (2009). *Cloud Computing: Benefits, Risks and Recommendations for Information Security*. Retrieved online on January 6, 2017 from: http://www.enisa.europa.eu/act/rm/files/deliverables/cloud-computing-risk-assessment

ENISA. (2014a). *Making the cloud more transparent - a boost for secure, trustworthy services*. ENISA.

ENISA. (2014b). *Exploring Cloud Incidents*. Retrieved online on December 15, 2016 from https://www.enisa.europa.eu/publications/exploring-cloud-incidents

Fagerberg, J. (2005). Innovation: a guide to the literature. In J. Fagerberg, D. C. Mowery, & R. R. Nelson (Eds.), *The Oxford Handbook of Innovation* (pp. 1–26). New York: Oxford University Press.

Frank, B. (2016). *Amazon Quietly Launches tools for migrating on premise apps to cloud*. Retrieved online on December 15, 2016 from http://www.pcworld.com/article/3135060/cloud-computing/aws-quietly-launches-tool-for-migrating-on-premesis-apps-to-the-cloud.html

Gao, J., Bai, X., & Tsai, W. T. (2011). Cloud testing-issues, challenges, needs and practice. *Software Engineering: An International Journal, 1*(1), 9–23.

Gilbert, C. (2005). Unbundling the structure of inertia: Resource versus routine rigidity. *Academy of Management Journal, 48*(5), 741–763. doi:10.5465/AMJ.2005.18803920

Greene, J., & Stevens, L. (2016). Amazon Cloud Computing Division Unveils New Cyber Security Service. *Wall Street Journal*. Retrieved online on December 15, 2016 from http://www.wsj.com/articles/amazon-cloud-computing-division-unveils-new-cyber-security-service-1480620359

Greene, T. (2015). *SANS: 20 critical security controls you need to add*. Retrieved online on December 15, 2016 from http://www.networkworld.com/article/2992503/security/sans-20-critical-security-controls-you-need-to-add.html

Grover, V., Fiedler, K., & Teng, J. (1997). Empirical evidence on Swansons tri-core model of information systems innovation. *Information Systems Research, 8*(3), 273–287. doi:10.1287/isre.8.3.273

Habiba, M., Islam, M. R., & Ali, A. S. (2013, July). Access control management for cloud. In *2013 12th IEEE International Conference on Trust, Security and Privacy in Computing and Communications* (pp. 485-492). 10.1109/TrustCom.2013.61

Halpert, B. (2011). *Auditing cloud computing: A security and privacy guide* (Vol. 21). John Wiley & Sons. doi:10.1002/9781118269091

Hardesty, L. (2016). *IIX Reinvents Itself as Console*. Retrieved online on December 15, 2016 from https://www.sdxcentral.com/articles/news/iix-reinvents-itself-console/2016/05/

Hargadon, A. (2003). *How breakthroughs happen: The surprising truth about how companies innovate*. Boston, MA: Harvard Business School Press.

Heiser, J., & Nicolett, M. (2008). *Assessing the security risks of cloud computing*. Stamford, CT: Gartner Research. Retrieved online on January 6, 2017 from http://www.globalcloudbusiness.com/SharedFiles/Download.aspx?pageid=138&mid=220&fileid=12

Kadam, Y. (2011). Security Issues in Cloud Computing A Transparent View. *International Journal of Computer Science Emerging Technology, 2*(5), 316–322.

Kaplinsky, R., Chataway, J., Clark, N., Hanlin, R., Kale, D., Muraguri, L, Papaioannou, T., Robbins, P. and Wamae, W. (2009). Below the radar: what does innovation in emerging economies have to offer other low-income economies? *International Journal Technology Management Sustenance Development, 8*(3), 177–197.

Kaufman, L. M. (2009). Data security in the world of cloud computing. *IEEE Security and Privacy, 7*(4), 61–64. doi:10.1109/MSP.2009.87

Kepes, B. (2016). *CloudVelox offers automated cloud network customizations*. Retrieved online on December 15, 2016 from http://www.networkworld.com/article/3142742/cloud-computing/cloudvelox-offers-automated-cloud-network-customizations.html

Ko, R. K., Jagadpramana, P., Mowbray, M., Pearson, S., Kirchberg, M., Liang, Q., & Lee, B. S. (2011, July). TrustCloud: A framework for accountability and trust in cloud computing. In *2011 IEEE World Congress on Services* (pp. 584-588). 10.1109/SERVICES.2011.91

Kroes, N. (2014). *Making the cloud more transparent - a boost for secure, trustworthy services*. Retrieved online on December 15, 2016 from http://ec.europa.eu.gate.lib.buffalo.edu/commission_2010-2014/kroes/en/content/making-cloud-more-transparent-boost-secure-trustworthy-services

Kwang, T. W. (2016). *Cloud technology for public sector innovation*. Retrieved online on December 15, 2016 from http://www.enterpriseinnovation.net/article/cloud-technology-public-sector-innovation-2130602017

Leinwand, A. (2016). *Transparency in the cloud or the lack of thereof*. Retrieved online on December 15, 2016 from http://cloudtweaks.com/2016/11/transparency-cloud/

Levinthal, D. A., & March, J. G. (1993). The myopia of learning. *Strategic Management Journal, 14*(S2), 95–112. doi:10.1002mj.4250141009

Lieberman. (2016a). *Lieberman Software to Present Cloud Security Session at Gartner Identity and Access*. Retrieved online on December 15, 2016 from http://www.marketwired.com/press-release/lieberman-software-present-cloud-security-session-gartner-identity-access-management-2178865.htm

Lieberman. (2016b). *Enterprise Random Password Manager*. Retrieved online on December 15, 2016 from https://liebsoft.com/products/Enterprise_Random_Password_Manager/

Marston, S., Li, Z., Bandyopadhyay, S., Zhang, J., & Ghalsasi, A. (2011). Cloud computing – the business perspective. *Decision Support Systems, 51*(1), 176–189. doi:10.1016/j.dss.2010.12.006

Massonet, P., Naqvi, S., Ponsard, C., Latanicki, J., Rochwerger, B., & Villari, M. (2011, May). A monitoring and audit logging architecture for data location compliance in federated cloud infrastructures. In *Parallel and Distributed Processing Workshops and Phd Forum (IPDPSW), 2011 IEEE International Symposium on* (pp. 1510-1517). IEEE. 10.1109/IPDPS.2011.304

McKendrick, J. (2016). For healthcare: cloud computing comes in measured doses. *Forbes*. Retrieved online on December 15, 2016 from http://www.forbes.com/sites/joemckendrick/2016/11/27/for-healthcare-cloud-computing-comes-in-measured-doses/#62b6087d6894

Mell, P., & Grance, T. (2011). *The NIST definition of cloud computing: Recommendations of the 33666 Institute of Standards and Technology*. Retrieved online on January 6 from http://csrc.nist.gov/publications/nistpubs/800-145/SP800-145.pdf

Menlo. (2016). *Half of the Web is Vulnerable to Malware*. Retrieved online on December 15, 2016 from http://www.prnewswire.com/news-releases/half-of-the-web-is-vulnerable-to-malware-300376971.html

Microsoft. (2016). *Cloud Security Alliance*. Retrieved online on December 15, 2016 from https://www.microsoft.com/en-us/trustcenter/Compliance/CSA

Morgan, S. (2016). IBM's new cyberframe is the world's most secure server for datacenters, cloud and mobile. *Forbes*. Retrieved online on December 15, 2016 from http://www.forbes.com/sites/stevemorgan/2016/02/16/ibms-new-cyberframe-is-the-worlds-most-secure-server/#e0781e868fa6

Nelson, R. R., & Winter, S. G. (1982). *An evolutionary theory of economic change*. Cambridge, MA: Belknap Press/Harvard University Press.

Olavsrud, T. (2016). *IBM Buiding blockchain ecosystem*. Retrieved online on December 15, 2016. http://www.cio.com/article/3147358/it-industry/ibm-building-blockchain-ecosystem.html

Onwubiko, C. (2010). Security issues to cloud computing. In *Cloud Computing* (pp. 271–288). Springer London. doi:10.1007/978-1-84996-241-4_16

OWASP. (2010). *Cloud-10 Multi Tenancy and Physical Security*. Retrieved online on December 15, 2016 from https://www.owasp.org/index.php/Cloud-10_Multi_Tenancy_and_Physical_Security

Pesek, G. (2016). *Bringing cloud security innovations to the enterprise*. Retrieved online on December 15, 2016 from http://siliconangle.com/blog/2016/12/02/bringing-cloud-security-innovations-enterprise-reinvent/

Prisco, G. (2016). *IBM Launches Blockchain Cloud Services on High Security Server*. Retrieved online on December 15, 2016 from https://bitcoinmagazine.com/articles/ibm-launches-blockchain-cloud-services-on-high-security-server-linuxone-1469043762

ProtectWise. (2016). *ProtectWise Achieves Advanced Partner Status in the Amazon Web Services Partner Network*. Retrieved online on December 15, 2016 from http://www.businesswire.com/news/home/20161201005006/en/ProtectWise-Achieves-Advanced-Partner-Status-Amazon-Web

Raisch, S., & Birkinshaw, J. (2008). Organizational ambidexterity: Antecedents, outcomes, and moderators. *Journal of Management*, *34*(3), 375–409. doi:10.1177/0149206308316058

Rasheed, H. (2011). *Auditing for standards compliance in the cloud: Challenges and directions*. Academic Press.

Rashmi, M. S., & Sahoo, G. (2012). A five-phased approach for the cloud migration. *Int J Emerg Technol Adv Eng*, *2*(4), 286–291.

Ren, K., Wang, C., & Wang, Q. (2012, January-February). Security Challenges for the Public Cloud. *IEEE Internet Computing*, *16*(1), 69–73. doi:10.1109/MIC.2012.14

Rogers, M. (1998). *The Definition and Measurement of Innovation* (Working paper no. 9/ 98). Melbourne Institute of Applied Economic and Social Research. Retrieved online on January 6, 2017 from http://melbourneinstitute.com/downloads/working_paper_series/ wp1998n09.pdf

Ryoo, J., Rizvi, S., Aiken, W., & Kissell, J. (2013). Cloud Security Auditing: Challenges and Emerging Approaches. *IEEE Security & Privacy, 12*(6), 68-74. doi:10.1109/MSP.2013.132

Sanidas, E. (2004). Technology, technical and organizational innovations, economic and societal growth. *Technology in Society*, *26*(1), 67–84. doi:10.1016/j.techsoc.2003.10.006

Sarukkai, S. (2015). *How Data Science And Machine Learning Is Enabling Cloud Threat Protection.* Retrieved online on December 15, 2016 from http://cloudtweaks.com/2015/12/data-science-machine-learning/

Shackleford, D. (n.d.). *How to overcome unique cloud-based patch management challenges* Retrieved online on December 15, 2016 from http://searchcloudsecurity.techtarget.com/tip/How-to-overcome-unique-cloud-based-patch-management-challenges

SkyHigh. (2016). *What is a cloud access security broker.* Academic Press.

Subashini, S., & Kavitha, V. (2011). A survey on security issues in service delivery models of cloud computing. *Journal of Network and Computer Applications, 34*(1), 1–11. doi:10.1016/j.jnca.2010.07.006

Taft, D. (2016a). *IBM takes the power of mainframe to cloud.* Retrieved online on December 15, 2016 from http://www.eweek.com/cloud/ibm-takes-the-power-of-the-mainframe-to-the-cloud.html

Taft, D. (2016b). *IBM Delivers Secure Blockchain Services in the Cloud.* Retrieved online on December 15, 2016 from http://www.eweek.com/cloud/ibm-delivers-secure-blockchain-services-in-the-cloud.html

Taylor, A., & Helfat, C. E. (2009). Organizational Linkages for Surviving Technological Change: Complementary Assets, Middle Management, and Ambidexterity. *Organization Science, 20*(4), 718–739. doi:10.1287/orsc.1090.0429

Taylor, L. (2014). FedRAMP: History and Future Direction. *IEEE Cloud Computing, 1*(3), 10–14. doi:10.1109/MCC.2014.54

Teneyuca, D. (2011). Internet cloud security: The illusion of inclusion. *Information Security Technical Report, 16*(3).

Tushman, M. L., & Anderson, P. C. (1986). Technological discontinuities and organizational environments. *Administrative Science Quarterly, 31*(3), 439–465. doi:10.2307/2392832

Vaultive. (2016). *Vaultive and Gemalto Team Up to Deliver Increased Cloud Data Security Control for SaaS Applications.* Retrieved online on December 15, 2016 from http://www.prnewswire.com/news-releases/vaultive-and-gemalto-team-up-to-deliver-increased-cloud-data-security-control-for-saas-applications-300342211.html

Vijayan, J. (2016). *Google Initiates Customer-Supplied Cloud Data Encryption Keys.* Retrieved online on December 15, 2016 from http://www.eweek.com/cloud/google-initiates-customer-supplied-cloud-data-encryption-keys.html

Wood, T., Cecchet, E., Ramakrishnan, K. K., Shenoy, P. J., van der Merwe, J. E., & Venkataramani, A. (2010). Disaster Recovery as a Cloud Service: Economic Benefits & Deployment Challenges. *HotCloud, 10*, 8–15.

Xiao, X., Califf, C.B., Sarker, S., & Sarker, S. (2013). ICT innovation in emerging economies: a review of the existing literature and a framework for future research. *Journal Information Technology, 28*(4), 264–278.

Yu, S., Wang, C., Ren, K., & Lou, W. (2010). Achieving Secure, Scalable, and Fine-grained Data Access Control in Cloud Computing. *Proceedings IEEE INFOCOM*. 10.1109/INFCOM.2010.5462174

Zech, P. (2011, March). Risk-based security testing in cloud computing environments. In *2011 Fourth IEEE International Conference on Software Testing, Verification and Validation* (pp. 411-414). 10.1109/ICST.2011.23

Zscaler. (2016). *Zscaler Private Access—Remote Access without the Security Risks of VPNs*. Retrieved online on December 15, 2016 from https://www.zscaler.com/press/zscaler-private-access/remote-access-without-security-risks-vpns

This research was previously published in Information Technology Risk Management and Compliance in Modern Organizations edited by Manish Gupta, Raj Sharman, John Walp, and Pavankumar Mulgund, pages 229-267, copyright year 2018 by Business Science Reference (an imprint of IGI Global).

Chapter 73
A Review of Security Challenges in Cloud Storage of Big Data

Sara Usmani
National University of Sciences and Technology (NUST), Pakistan

Faiza Rehman
National University of Sciences and Technology (NUST), Pakistan

Sajid Umair
National University of Sciences and Technology (NUST), Pakistan

Safdar Abbas Khan
National University of Sciences and Technology (NUST), Pakistan

ABSTRACT

The novel advances in the field of Information Technology presented the people pleasure, luxuries and ease. One of the latest expansions in the Information Technology (IT) industry is Cloud Computing, a technology that uses the internet for storage and access of data. It is also known as on-demand computing. The end user can access personal data and applications anywhere any time with a device having internet. Cloud Computing has gained an enormous attention but it results in the issues of data security and privacy as the data is scattered on different machines in different places across the globe which is a serious threat to the technology. It has many advantages like flexibility, efficiency and scalability but many of the companies are hesitant to invest in it due to privacy concerns. In this chapter, the objective is to review the privacy and security issues in cloud storage of Big Data and to enhance the security in cloud environment so that end users can enjoy a trustworthy and reliable data storage and access.

INTRODUCTION

Cloud Computing is considered as the standard for next generation computation. In Cloud Computing, the resources i.e., end user applications, personal data or DBMS (Database Management Systems) are provided by a third party over internet like services. National Institute of Standards and Technology (NIST) defines Cloud Computing as universal, appropriate, on-demand network access to a shared pool

DOI: 10.4018/978-1-5225-8176-5.ch073

Copyright © 2019, IGI Global. Copying or distributing in print or electronic forms without written permission of IGI Global is prohibited.

of configurable computing resources (e.g., networks, servers, storage, applications, and services) that can be rapidly provisioned and released with minimal management effort or service provider interaction (Mell & Grance, 2011). There is a service provider that manages and provides the services over the internet while the clients purchase them according to their needs. The architecture of cloud includes several modules like databases, software competencies, applications, etc. planned to influence the power of cloud resources to solve problems of enterprise. The architecture of cloud includes modules and the relationship between these modules. The cloud architecture has several components like

- Resources on ground cloud resources.
- Software services and components middleware.

The cloud architecture is intended at providing the users with huge bandwidth allowing them continuous access to their data and applications and having the ability to move rapidly and competently between servers or even between clouds. The service model comprises three levels: Software as a Service (SaaS), Platform as a Service (PaaS) and Infrastructure as a Service (IaaS) as described in Figure 1.

In SaaS, applications are accessed via web browsers that are managed by cloud service provider and interfaces available on the end-user side. It removes the need to perform any installation or download on individual devices. In PaaS, applications are built on the platform. The services are provided to the user through a set of programs that can carry out the specific task. It makes the building and deployment of applications quick and economic. IaaS facilitates services through virtual machines. It provides the computer infrastructure with on demand resources. The users do not have to purchase the equipment; they have to purchase the service.

BACKGROUND

Cloud Computing is associated with Grid Computing but they are not the same (Berman, 2003). Grid Computing incorporates different resources together and controls the resources with the incorporated

Figure 1. SPI Cloud Service Delivery Model (Almorsy, 2010)

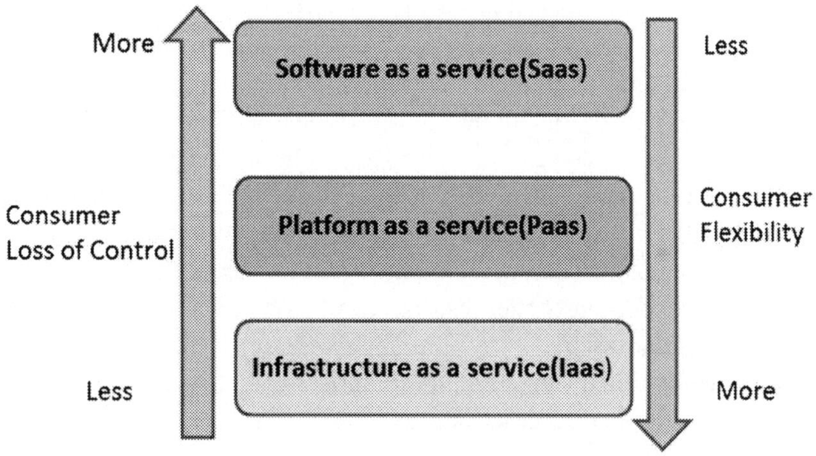

Operating Systems to provide high performance computing services whereas in Cloud Computing, computing and storage resources are controlled by different Operating Systems to provide services such as large data storage and high performance computing to users. The whole representation of Grid Computing has been changed by Cloud Computing. Cloud Computing is very favorable for the Information Technology (IT) applications but some problems still exist while storing data and deploying applications that should be solved for personal users and enterprises. One of the major hurdles in adoption of Cloud Computing is data security which is escorted with issues like compliance, privacy, trust and legal matters (Shah, 2008). Privacy and security is close to the role of institutions and institutional evolution (Kshetri, 2013). A latest survey by International Data Group (IDG) enterprise discuss the three challenges for applying a successful cloud strategy in enterprise vary considerably between IT and line-of-business (LOB).

For IT, security concerns are 66% and out of which 42% were cloud based projects that were cancelled due to security concerns (Berman, 2003). Seven security risks have been acknowledged by Gartner in seven Cloud Computing security risks that are considered vital before making a decision by the enterprise for adopting the Cloud Computing model (Brodkin, 2008). These risks are: 1) Access to authorized users: the risk of exposing the data of the organization over an external processing platform due to restricted physical and logical controls external to the organizations limitations. 2) Conformance to regulations: handling data outside the boundaries of the organization is still subject to accountability measures.3) Storage space: Cloud customer does not know about exact location of their data and thus needs service provider guarantee to comply with privacy limitations. 4) Data separation: Trustworthy and well tested encryption patterns are required as customers data is distributed over shared place. 5) Recovery: A policy should be declared by service providers to handle failures. 6) Investigation: Due to dispersal of data, breach or intrusion attempts are hard to be chased and marked over the cloud. 7) Long-term viability: Assurance of data availability in case of bankruptcy or other issues of service providers. Organization needs guarantee that huge amount of data will not be lost.

Chen (2012) discusses data security and privacy protection issues in Cloud Computing and understanding Cloud Computing vulnerabilities, such as security and privacy concerns were observed regarding Cloud Computing. Risks, the effects of risks and future prospects regarding risks were also discussed. Examples of security concerns included reliability, protection of sensitive data and privacy of data. Cloud computing models exhibit an encouraging future but at the same time there are some flaws and problems. The unresolved issues should be addressed in existing technologies to overcome the flaws. In addition to risks and threats, security should be addressed properly and secure ways should be found to make this emerging technology free of flaws and problems (Almorsy, 2010; Leavitt, 2009; Grobauer, 2011).

Service providers should implement security in all possible ways to satisfy the customers and face and suggest the ways to overcome the flaws that arise during the execution of cloud processes. For that, Popovic (2010) in his paper "Cloud Computing Security Issues and Challenges" discuss the challenges, standards and management methodologies recommended to both cloud engineers and users. Standard way of cloud services security is an important issue that arose due to the increased demand and importance of clouds (Ramgovind, 2010). So, standardized Security Level Agreement (SLA) guarantees assurance which increases the belief among cloud adopting organizations. These standards guarantee support in having mutual trust, reduced risks and better distribution of cloud service among organizations as customers, service providers and investors.

The deployment model of Cloud Computing is comprises of 1) Private Cloud, 2) Public Cloud, 3) Community Cloud, 4) Hybrid Cloud, as described in Figure 2. Public clouds are the ones that are owned by the service providers and the data is provided to the clients on demand. Private clouds are those

Figure 2. Cloud storage model (Ramgovind, 2010)

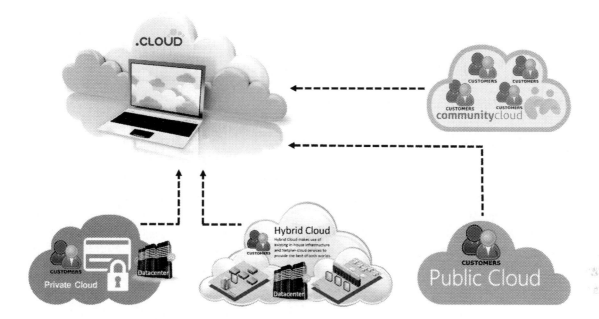

owned by particular organizations and companies. Community Cloud is private too but resources of the cloud are shared among the organizations of same community. Hybrid Cloud is the merge of private and public cloud with applications having less security concerns on public cloud and the one with more on the private ones.

This chapter contains summary of all the reviews of Cloud Computing, the positive and negative aspects of each issue was clearly mentioned (Shaikh, 2011). Popular types of Cloud Computing have been discussed in this chapter. It highlights the threats that are unsafe for Cloud Computing and discusses various solutions of it as well. An example was included in the paper which was about Amazon Virtual Private Cloud (VPC). A Virtual Private Network (VPN) was presented in the chapter that can increase cloud security and also presents firewall solution for cloud security (Jamil, 2011).

A business model has been proposed for data security using encryption and decryption mechanisms. The cloud service providers are responsible for all the tasks but doing so increase the overhead of data computations for cloud server. The major drawback of this technique is that the customer has complete trust of service provider as they have the authority to control the data (Rao, 2013).

Behl (2011) discusses that definition of Distributed Computing has been redefined due to Cloud Computing emergence. Cloud Computing has many benefits but it also has some issues like security threats. The focus of his paper (Behl, 2011) was to discuss security related issues and talk about the methodology used and their drawbacks and contain solutions for numerous security issues and the authors have tried to put forward security strategies that overcomes the existing threats in Cloud Computing. Silva (2013) discusses the security threats that have been published in 661 publications. These include 1) Misuse of Cloud Computing resources, 2) The API's and interfaces of Cloud Computing are insecure, 3) Malicious insiders, 4) the technologies are shared so there are many privacy issues, 5) the issue of data loss, 6) the issue of account or service hacking, and 7) the existence of unknown risks profile.

Among these issues, the last one is most prevalent issue and is present in 377 publications. Standard Deviation (SD) and coefficient of variation techniques are used to reduce the risks of these security threats.

CLOUD COMPUTING CHARACTERISTICS

Following are some Cloud Computing characteristics:

1. **Broad Network Access:** A standard mechanism is used for the delivery of services across the internet and the services can be accessed through various tools.
2. **Resource Pooling:** Pools of computing resources are developed to entertain different variety of client's requests and these resources can be dynamically assigned or unassigned according to customer's requests.
3. **Rapid Elasticity:** The services offered by the cloud providers are limitless and customers have the opportunity to purchase the services in any amount at any time period.
4. **Measured Services:** The use of services by the clients is measurable. All the record of usage of services is maintained by service providers.

CLOUD COMPUTING TECHNOLOGIES

Microsoft Cloud Technologies

Microsoft is the primary cloud service provider. All types of cloud services like SaaS, PaaS and IasS are provided by them. Windows Server is an example of Infrastructure as a Service. Windows Azure is an example of Platform as a Service through which applications can easily be built and hosted in a datacenter while only paying the amount that is used by the user; SQL Server and Visual Studio are other examples of PaaS. Office 365, Customer Relationship Management (CRM) and Exchange servers are examples of Software as a Service. So, a complete deal of services is provided from Microsoft Cloud that can be used at customer's ease.

Oracle Cloud Technologies

Oracle also delivers complete package of cloud services including SaaS, PaaS and IasS. It allows the customer to focus on the business rather than thinking about administrating IT. Database services are offered by Oracle that can be accessed through network connection or customer can have complete development and deployment environment for their services. In the beginning, the cloud service can be used free for 30 days as trial and then the customer can use the offers as per their need and demand. The cloud service offered by Oracle can be used to develop J2EE applications or JavaServer Faces (JSF) or servlet or Enterprise Java Beans (EJB) applications can be developed. Oracle has also introduced a mobile cloud that provides easy interfaces, API's (Application Programming Interface) and option to build mobile apps for the organizations. Notifications and data synchronizations are the important facilities delivered using Oracle mobile cloud.

Google Cloud Technologies

Google also delivers all the services of Cloud Computing like SaaS, IaaS and PaaS. The Google cloud allows the developers to make, test and then deploy applications on the cloud. The ability of Google to serve millions of Gmail customers, return billions of search requests results in milliseconds is due to the usage of cloud services. Using Google apps engine, the customer can run their applications on PaaS using built-in functionality. A lot of common programming languages like java, Python and Hypertext Preprocessor (PHP) can be used for developing applications.

Using compute engine, large scale applications having huge workloads can be run on virtual machines that are hosted by Google by only choosing the machine that fulfills customer's requirement. For database storage, customer can use Cloud-SQL that provides full managed MySQL that can be used for storage and management of data. Google Big Query can be used for analyzing the Big Data. Google Prediction API can be used for forecasting future trends using previous data using Machine Learning algorithms. It can be integrated with different applications and their functionality can be reused.

SECURITY ISSUES IN CLOUD COMPUTING AND STORAGE OF BIG DATA

The issues in Cloud Computing includes Security, Management and Monitoring. At present, there is no standard for developing cloud applications on servers or controlling the access of services in cloud. Many techniques have been formulated but these techniques have some security failures due to Cloud Computing dynamics.

In Cloud Computing, security handling is quite complex as described in Figure 3. The bottom layer indicates the deployment models as discussed above. The service delivery model of Cloud Computing is above the deployment model. The characteristics of these models are shown in top- most layers. These features need security. The challenges of Cloud Computing in security are shown in vertical direction.

Whenever the user sends/receives their data using cloud technology, there are security threats. The hacker can attack the data that is being sent or received by the cloud as shown in following Figure 4.

The data that is being sent or received, if, hacked can be changed and the customer's trust can be broken thus losing the customers. So, data privacy and security are the basic concerns of Cloud Computing. Table 1 shows some risks in Cloud Computing.

Data Integrity

Data integrity is protecting the data from unauthorized access so that the personal data of end users cannot be stolen. For this purpose, authorization can be used to allow the authenticated users to use the cloud and have access to only their data. Wrongly set security perimeters or incorrect virtual machines can be a threat to data integrity in cloud environment. If the access control is poorly managed, then the ex-employees will still have the administrative access to cloud service provider and can cause a great damage to data integrity. The use of faulty application by the cloud client can cause damage to data integrity of others sharing the same infrastructure.

Figure 3. Cloud computing complex security architecture (Chen, 2012)

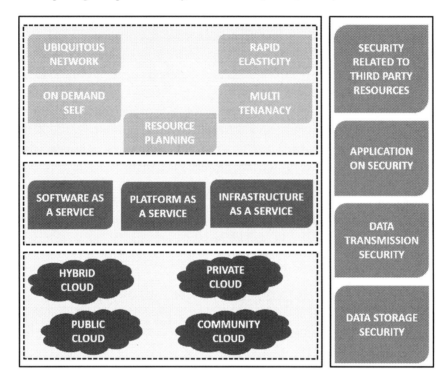

Figure 4. Cloud computing security threats (Shaikh, 2011)

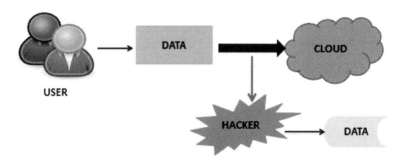

Table. 1 Cloud computing risks (Brodkin, 2008)

Risks	Description
Data confidentiality	Cloud service provider has the access to data stored in the cloud and has control of which entities can access the data. Confidentiality of data can be maintained by encryption of data before entry or through contractual obligation.
Data disposal	Cloud service provider assures high availability of data by keeping multiple copies of data so the risk of data being deleted from backups is increased within the cloud.
Data location and segregation	If the data segregation is not applied, it could result in the loss of information of huge number of customers because of central storage.
Assuring cloud security	Customers are not sure of the systems they are using because they cannot directly interact with the system, so we have to assure the security of the systems to gain trust of customers.

Data Confidentiality

Data Confidentiality is necessary for the end users to maintain and store their confidential information inside cloud service providers or cloud customer or some third party that is helping cloud environment. In SaaS, it could be the administrator or the cloud client. In PaaS, the developers of application or the managers could be the threat to data confidentiality. Third-party consultants could harm the data confidentiality in IaaS. External threats to data confidentiality include software attack of cloud infrastructure and cloud applications. It also includes hardware attack and social engineering. Cloud service providers storing the private data like the details of credit card can be harmed by external attackers especially in private clouds where the user endpoints are easy to target. Data leakage among the organizations using same service provider is a threat to confidentiality of data. It may be possibly because of the failure of hardware or the human error or the poor rights of security in the domain.

Data Availability

It means if network failure occurs or there is disk damage whether the cloud users are able to recover their data and to what degree. Inaccurate change management that could be both software and hardware by cloud service providers can produce negative effects. These could be infrastructure changes or changes in the third-party systems. Denial of Service (DoS) is also a threat to Cloud Computing that will harm the service models. The Denial of Service attack will harm network bandwidth, Domain Name System (DNS), application and data. Disruptions of services can be caused if cloud service providers are unable to secure the large data center. The insecure organization environment and remote working can lead to disruption by insiders or externally. When the cloud users try to recover their own systems in addition to the recovery managed by service providers the threat of improper recovery is produced that will affect the recovery time.

Virtualization and Multi-Tenancy

Both Virtualization and Multi-Tenancy are important factors of Cloud Computing yet they are also a huge security risk. There are different architectures of Virtualization available and these architectures affect the security risks of applications or Cloud Computing services. If the Operating System (OS) of the system is targeted, then it may be possible that the emulated OS is also targeted for the attack. For example, the windows running on Virtual Machine or the windows running on OS are both at risk of attack from outside. So, both normal machines and virtual machines have a risk of attack but securing virtual machines is more difficult than normal machines. This rises from the fact that if one Virtual Machine (VM) gets attacked, then other VM's can also get attacked as there are no security bypass rules since they share the same network. Using antivirus on VM's is a good and easy solution but keeping all the antivirus on all VM's up-to-date is quite a complex task. Another issue might be data leakage that occurs due to shared resources in VM's. It includes both cache based and Random Access Memory (RAM) based attacks. The cause of these attacks is that both cache and RAM does not flush automatically after completing their task. In order to avoid cache based attacks, noise can be injected to flush the data if there is some remaining on the VM. To avoid RAM based attacks, it is necessary to restrict the ability of VM to lock the memory bus. The above mentioned solutions can avoid the attacks but it is better to take steps so that these issues do not occur in the first place.

Data Privacy

Making the data private and secure from unauthorized users as well as making the data free from any malicious attacks is a very tough task. Managing the data privacy is one main issue that the users have no control over the data where it is stored, i.e. the user has no direct access to the server. Data storage in the cloud can be of two types: PasS or SaaS environment and IaaS environment. In IaaS, data is stored on the cloud instead of local hardware such as Amazon Simple Storage Service. In PaaS and SaaS, the data is used in applications, it is not stored for long term. In IaaS, the data security can be achieved by simply doing encryption of data. It can be suitable in some cases but it cannot be suitable in all cases.

Denial of Service

It is one of the biggest security risk in Cloud Comp,uting or in any internet-based application. The Denial of Service attacks includes attackers sending packets in large amounts to make the server performance low and consuming huge bandwidth. Distributed Denial of Service (DDoS) is also very dangerous attack because it uses many computers to attack a server using different attacking techniques. Both the DoS and DDoS attacks can take place through any of IaaS, PaaS and SaaS cloud types and public or private clouds.

The solution to these attacks is the use of firewall. However, the use of firewalls in Cloud Computing have their own challenges and issues. One solution proposed was of centralized firewall but it also has some drawbacks as cloud is offering many different services and each have different rules and managing them having centralized firewall is difficult to manage. To avoid these issues, a solution was proposed of decentralized firewall that is cost effective. This works as grouping multiple servers into clusters and giving the cluster resources to launch the Virtual Machine (VM) that hosts the firewall for specific VM. Now, the customer can use the firewall for their specific application and pay the service providers accordingly.

Deduplication

It means that the server stores only one copy of the file irrespective of how many clients have requested to keep the copy of file. This is done to save the cloud service and usage of network bandwidth. But deduplication can lead to leakage of information. For example, a request has been initiated for the server to save the file but the copy of that file is already stored so server notifies the client that the file is already stored which may be critical for some users as they do not want to share the information or the customer will know that another user already has the same file which is not good in some cases.

User Access Control

Allowing only authorized or subscribed users to use the service is an essential part of any service provider. So a complete authentication mechanism should be available so that no user can use the service that does not belong to him/her. Depending upon different cloud services, different mechanisms are available. In SaaS, as the cloud service provider is responsible for network availability, server and application only control of user is given to the customer. The customer must ensure that only eligible people should be given the access to server. In PaaS, the service provider provides network and server availability, the application's hold is given to the customer and so customers are responsible for providing access to cloud services. In IaaS, all the responsibility is given to the customers so they have to manage security and other aspects of the cloud. The issues include weak passwords which should not be allowed. Resetting the password should be secure so that if user reenters the password, he/she may be able to reuse the service but on the other side it should be secure from potential hackers or attackers. Another technique could be to assign the responsibility of resetting the password to some team and the customers or users can request for resetting the password. It is much secure approach.

SECURITY METHODOLOGY FOR CLOUD STORAGE

There is an essential need to securely handle Big Data in cloud. The major concern in Cloud Computing is that the owner of data does not have control on the security of data and there is greater concern when the user has security critical information stored in Cloud Computing service or has a company's private data. Figure 5 shows the layered view of Cloud Computing security architecture.

Data Center Layer

As data can be placed anywhere in the cloud, these need to be secure so that attacker is unable to access data. Most of the time, cloud provider uses encryption to ensure security at this layer. In encryption, data gets converted into cipher text using key. Encryption have been around about many years, e.g. use of secret code so that only intended party can understand that message. Today's encryption is far more sophisticated. In today's world, it is mostly used in security of data. Firstly, data gets converted into ci-

Figure 5. Layered security architecture of cloud (Rabi, P. et al, 2011)

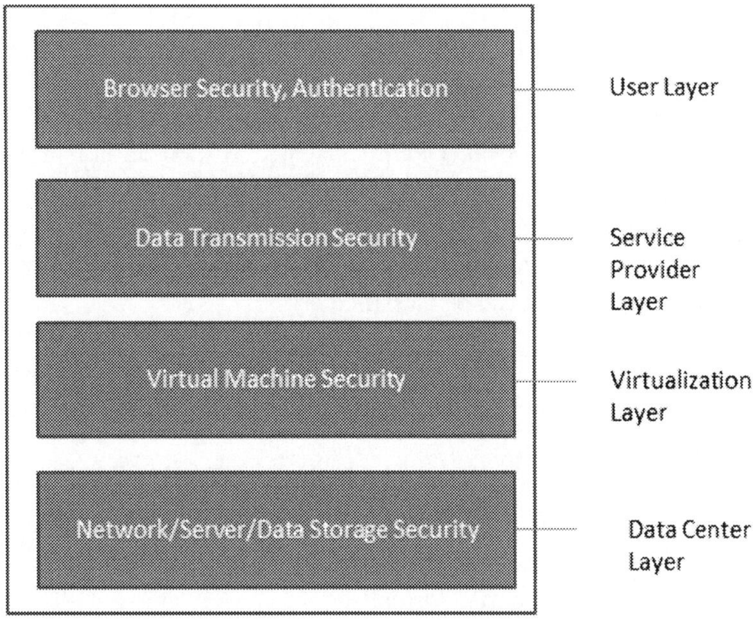

Browser Security, Authentication	User Layer
Data Transmission Security	Service Provider Layer
Virtual Machine Security	Virtualization Layer
Network/Server/Data Storage Security	Data Center Layer

pher text using encryption key and encryption algorithm then only authorized party can decrypt (change cipher text in plain text) it using decryption key. The encryption can be symmetric and asymmetric.

In symmetric key encryption, the encryption and decryption keys are both same. Asymmetric key encryption is also called public key encryption. In this scheme, encryption is available to anyone who wants to encrypt the data but decryption key is only available to authorized party. Cipher text is not easily understood by others except authorized parties. Encryption provides confidentiality, authenticity, integrity, non-repudiation and all these features depend on the efficiency of encryption algorithm provided encryption must correspond to the level of sensitivity of the data that is hosted. If the data is more sensitive so it should be more secure i.e. hard to decipher by attacker. While many providers have implemented encryption to secure data in cloud but they often overlook security of the key. If keys are not protected enough, then they are exposed to security attack.

Key Protection by SCP (Secure Co-Processor)

The author Kevin (2012) proposed Secure Co-Processor (SCP) for the security of keys in Cloud Computing. SCP is temper resistant hardware if there is tampering, SCP clears the internal memory. When installed on the server, it performs the local computations which are hidden from the server. Secure co-processor cannot be used for entire sensitive data due to limited memory and computational power. So, it is not feasible to compute entire data set but we can use temper resistant hardware to store some of the encryption decryption keys so that keys are not vulnerable to attack by attacker through snapshot of system and any attempt to take control of the co-processor results in the co-processor clearing the internal memory. Hence, keys are saved from attacker and secured data can also be handled efficiently by secure co-processor (Rohit, 2012). Figure 6 describes the encryption mechanism used.

Virtualization Layer

Virtualization is fundamental technology that powers Cloud Computing. It allows running multiple OS and applications on a single machine. It provides the flexibility and also reduces the operating cost. Virtualization abstracts the underlying hardware. It utilizes the hardware efficiently by maximizing the job done by single Central Processing Unit (CPU). Currently, virtualization is used in public, private and hybrid cloud.

Many virtualization approaches can be used at various system layers e.g. hardware-like desktop, Operating System and software-like storage, memory, etc. Hardware Virtualization is used to abstract the hardware. Hardware Virtualization can be classified as

- Full Virtualization
- Partial Virtualization
- Para Virtualization

Full Virtualization includes complete abstraction of underlying hardware so it is more efficient approach than other two and mainly used for server virtualization. Full Virtualization can further be classified as bare metal virtualization and hosted virtualization.

In hosted virtualization approach, hypervisor lies on top of host Operating System. However, it increases complexity and security risk.

Figure 6. Encryption mechanism used (Rohit, 2012)

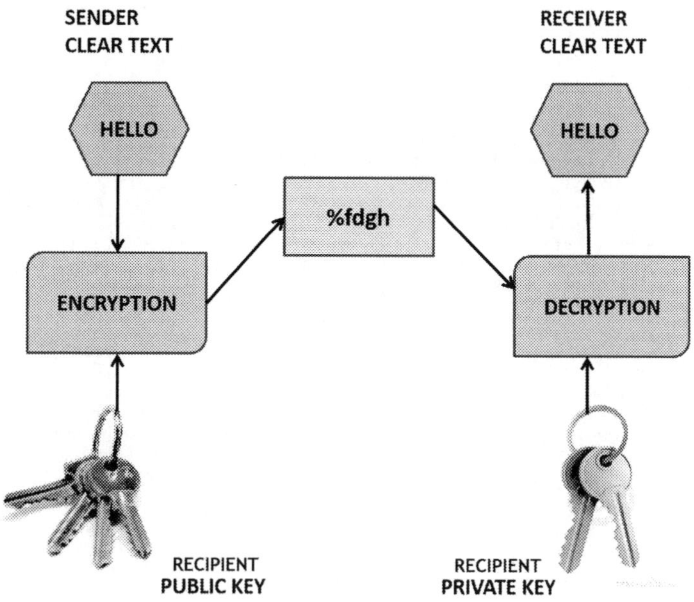

In bare metal virtualization approach, the hypervisor lies directly on top of the hardware so this approach is mainly used for server virtualization in Cloud Computing as it provides more efficiency and robustness.

Hypervisor is known as the controller of VM and acts as a Resource Manager to provide resources to each OS as shown in Figure 7. Many OS share both memory and CPU so an isolating attack can be launched on the hypervisor to gain illegal access to data. Cloud resources are virtualized, different users share the same infrastructure and any unauthorized access can compromise the confidentiality of data. Security at this layer is also important due to various vulnerability of virtualization component i.e. hypervisor, virtual machine and disk images to name a few:

- Hyper jacking.
- VM Escape Attack.
- Attack through worm viruses and botnet.
- Attacker can monitor traffic and by tampering the functionality of Guest VM and exploit security.
- Virtual machine checkpoint attack.
- Virtual machine image sprawl problem.

Hyperjack is an attack where some users can maliciously take control over hypervisor. Hypervisor is used to create the virtual environment in virtual machine host. The purpose of Hyperjack is to target the Operating System. It involves installing a malicious hypervisor that manages the entire host system. Hyperjack attack can be done by

- Injecting a fake hypervisor beneath the original hypervisor.
- Gaining control of original hypervisor.

Figure 7. Virtualization layer architecture (Kevin, 2012)

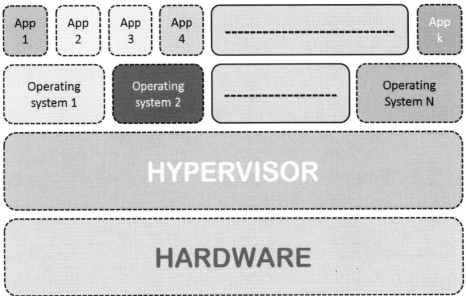

Virtual Machine is designed to run in isolated environment in the host and the Operating System in virtual machine should be unaware that it is virtualized. Also, there should be no way to break out of the virtual environment and interact directly with hypervisor. If the virtual machine "breaks" that virtual environment, then it is called VM Escape.

VM Escape is related to vulnerabilities of the Operating System. When such vulnerabilities are exploited, it allows the attacker to run malicious code and break the boundaries of VM. VM escape attacks can only be accomplished through a local physical environment.

As the number of OS running on hardware increases, security concerns also increases because it is possible that attacker run malicious code on host through guest system so security of hypervisor is of greater concern. Following policies can be used to ensure security at this layer.

- Hypersafe is a system designed to maintain the integrity of hypervisor.
- Security features such as firewall, Host-based Intrusion Prevention System (HIPS), Log Monitoring, Intrusion Prevention Systems (IPS)/ Intrusion Detection and Prevention Systems (IDPS) antimalware protection must be provided at guest OS.
- After migration of VM, it should be ensured that data is removed from old disk.
- Properly configure interaction between host machine and Guest OS.
- Before saving VM, use encryption or hashing of VMs state.
- Apply patches and update to maintain images security. Hypersafe is a system designed to maintain the integrity of hypervisor.
- Security features such as firewall, HIPS, Log Monitoring, IDPS/IPS antimalware protection must be provided at guest OS.
- After migration of VM, it should be ensured that data is removed from old disk.
- Properly configure interaction between host machine and Guest OS.
- Before saving VM, use encryption or hashing of VMs state.

- VM images backup should be maintained and to secure them Cryptography can be used.
- Unnecessary disk images can result in security compromise so unnecessary disk images should be avoided.
- VM Checkpoint attack can be avoided by encrypting them.
- We can use antivirus and Spyware in guest Operating System.
- Apply patches and update to maintain images security.
- Running only necessary resource sharing features.
- Physical cloud environment must be prevented from insider attacks to avoid VM escape attack.

Service Provider Layer

In the cloud, data is transferred through a network which can be shared or dedicated, Local Area Network (LAN) or Wide Area Network (WAN), Virtual Private Network (VPN) and each of them are exposed to different security threats. In discussing network layer security in the cloud, differentiate clouds in private and public. Private cloud is less prone to attack than public cloud as it is mostly implemented using public network such as internet which is exposed to a lot of security issues:

- Sniffer attack
- Reused IP address
- Eavesdropping

So, some security policies should also be implemented such as

- Authentication and confidentiality of data should be ensured especially when using public cloud infrastructure.
- Encryption Algorithm and Tokenization should be used so that only cipher text is transmitted rather than original data.

User Layer

At this layer, security is mostly concerned with authentication of user. Vulnerabilities at this layer may lead to unauthorized access e.g., through cookie poisoning, cookie mainly contain user credentials, cookie poisoning include changing the data of cookie to get unauthorized access. This can be prevented by either the routine cleanup of cookies or adoption of encryption scheme for cookie content. The paper "Comparative analysis of various authentication techniques in Cloud Computing" (Shabnam, 2013) provides comparative analysis of different authentication mechanisms i.e. using Kerberos, using Key distribution center, using public key.

Many protocols used today do not provide any security and many client/ server application rely on the client program to be honest about the identity of user. Kerberos was created to provide strong security. Kerberos provides credential authentication without transmitting the password in either clear or hashed form and hence made offline password cracking impossible.

SECURITY ASSURANCE FROM USER PERSPECTIVE OF CLOUD STORAGE

In Cloud Computing, from the user end we should not ignore the importance of Service Level Agreement (SLA). SLA is a blue print or warranty of mobile and security levels. In SLA, the following points should be considered:

- Details about the system infrastructure and security standards to be maintained by the service provider along with your rights to audit their compliance.
- Affirms your institutions ownership of its data stored on service providers system and specifies your rights to get it back.
- Specifies your rights and cost to continue or discontinue using the service.
- It should specify service guarantee time period which is the duration of time during which service is guaranteed.
- SLA includes service guarantee which specifies the metric or services which service provider tries to meet during service guarantee time period. These metrics include availability, response time, recovery time, etc.
- SLA should include service credit. Service credit is the amount of penalty that provider have to pay or credited to customer if service guarantee is not met.
- Service guarantee exclusion should include the instances that are excluded from service guarantee e.g. downtime related to scheduled maintenance.
- SLA also describes Service violation measurement and reporting. It includes how and who measures and reports the violation of service guarantee.

PRIORITIZE CLOUD SECURITY FOR BIG DATA

There are many benefits if we move towards the cloud. When considering moving towards cloud computing, we should think security in a wider aspect than traditional IT security. New approaches demand new ways and new aspects of thinking. Three things should be considered when considering security in cloud:

1. **Describe Problems Early:** Cloud Computing is like a complex problem, so first of all we should have clear idea of our purpose of why we are shifting towards the cloud. Fixing this will solve a lot of problems later.
2. **Access Control is Essential:** As the data is not stored physically but is somewhere that is not under your reach, a proper access control system should be maintained and implemented. This is the best way to save data.
3. **Vulnerability Testing:** Cloud security requires vulnerable testing. As much testing as possible should be done so that the product will be fulfilling a majority of security aspects.

If these points are considered at the beginning, much of the security risks can be managed and the organizations can adopt Cloud Computing without the barrier of security of private data.

INDUSTRIAL SURVEY OF CLOUD SECURITY TOOLS

Today, many tools are available in market for the security of cloud computing. Use of these tools can be beneficial for us. Here, we will discuss some tools that are available in the market that can be used for the security of clouds of Big Data at different layers.

Cipher Cloud

Cipher Cloud is a software suite for the security of the cloud. It is basically used to encrypt and decrypt data before uploading and downloading. It ensures security at the user layer. It encrypts and tokenizes data at user's business gateway. The keys used for encryption and decryption remain within your business network so if any attacker accesses your data in cloud, he/she will only find cipher text. It also offers malware detection and data loss prevention. Its specific builds are available for commonly used cloud applications such as Office 365, Gmail, SalesForce but it has one build which is available that can be configured to work with any cloud application you want to use.

OKTA

OKTA is another powerful tool that mainly focuses on Identity Management. It provides single sign on. It manages your logins across all of your applications such as Salesforce, Oracle, SAP, Office 365, etc. OKTA offers automatic user management, multifactor authentication, Log Auditing, allows you to set centralized policies. Log auditing allows you to trace user access to cloud app.

Skyhigh Network

Skyhigh Network provides the risk assessment by checking logs of your firewalls, proxies and gateways by discovering which cloud apps are in use and the risks related to these apps. Its analysis tools can discover potential data leaks. Further, it provides 3-click security to allow contextual access to the cloud by providing a reverse proxy approach. It also provides direct access to cloud without actually needing Virtual Private Network or any other device. It can also provide a data encryption facility.

Storage Made Easy (SME)

It is a commercial solution for Cloud Security. It provides many security features such as

- Encryption using AES-256
- File sharing
- Collaboration across other cloud
- Files Versioning
- Authorization of user

Its REST API is also available for developers, and there are also .NET libraries.

FUTURE RESEARCH DIRECTIONS

By using Cloud Computing, many benefits like reduced cost, early deployment and data availability can be achieved. But there are many problems associated with the usage of Cloud Computing that should be overcome to obtain better results. These include Data Confidentiality, Security and privacy issues as discussed above. Much research has been done in this domain but there are still loop holes that are still there making Cloud Computing risky. These issues should be addressed and ways should be figured so that the benefits could be achieved.

CONCLUSION

Usage of cloud computing bears many fruits, e.g., it is cost effective and it has ease of access but there are also practical problems related to it and security is one of them. Lack of security is the main reason users are reluctant to use Cloud Computing for their private and confidential data. In this chapter, a literature review has been conducted on the security issues of Cloud Computing and their possible solutions and based upon this, layered security architecture has been proposed in which we discuss different security issues relevant to each layer and their possible solutions and policies to ensure security. Although in this chapter we have explored the field further, studies are needed to provide other techniques to deal with existing issues. An assessment criteria needs to be proposed through which we can analyze the efficiency of security solution.

ACKNOWLEDGMENT

The authors would like to thank Dr. Safdar Abbas Khan, Assistant Professor, School of Electrical Engineering and Computer Sciences *(SEECS)*, National University of Sciences and Technology *(NUST)* Islamabad Pakistan for their complete support, help and guidance.

REFERENCES

Almorsy, M., Grundy, J., & Müller, I. (2016). An analysis of the cloud computing security problem. In *Proceedings of APSEC 2010 Cloud Workshop, Sydney, Australia.* Retrieved May 21, 2017 from https://www.cs.auckland.ac.nz/~john-g/papers/cloud2010_1.pdf

Behl, A. (2011). Emerging security challenges in cloud computing: An insight to cloud security challenges and their mitigation. In *Proceedings of 2011 World Congress on Information and Communication Technologies (WICT),* 217-222. New Jersey: Institute of Electrical and Electronic Engineers (IEEE). Retrieved July 1, 2016 from http://ieeexplore.ieee.org/document/6141247/

Berman, F., Fox, G., & Hey, A. J. (2003). *Grid computing: making the global infrastructure a reality* (Vol. 2). CA: John Wiley and Sons. Retrieved May 21, 2017 from http://www.dsc.ufcg.edu.br/~sampaio/Livros/Wiley%20Grid%20Computing%20Making%20the%20Global%20Infrastructure%20a%20Reality.pdf

Brodkin, J. (2008). Gartner: Seven cloud-computing security risks. *InfoWorld, 2008*, 1–3. Retrieved May 21, 2017 from http://www.infoworld.com/article/2652198/security/gartner--seven-cloud-computing-security-risks.html

Chen, D., & Zhao, H. (2012). Data Security and Privacy Protection Issues in Cloud Computing. In *Proceedings of 2012 International Conference on Computer Science and Electronics Engineering (ICCSEE)*. Retrieved July 2, 2016 from http://ieeexplore.ieee.org/document/6187862/

Grobauer, B., Walloschek, T., & Stocker, E. (2011). Understanding Cloud Computing Vulnerabilities. *IEEE Security and Privacy, 9*(2), 50–57. Retrieved July 2, 2016 from http://ieeexplore.ieee.org/document/5487489/ doi:10.1109/MSP.2010.115

Hamlen, K., Kantarcioglu, M., Khan, L., & Thuraisingham, B. (2012). Security issues for cloud computing. In H. Nemati (Ed.), *Optimizing Information Security and Advancing Privacy Assurance: New Technologies* (pp. 150-162). Hershey, PA: IGI Global. Retrieved May 21, 2017 from http://www.igi-global.com/chapter/security-issues-cloud-computing/62720?camid=4v1

Jamil, D., & Zaki, H. (2011). Cloud Computing Security. *International Journal of Engineering Science and Technology, 3*(4), 3478–3483. Retrieved July 3, 2016 from http://www.scirp.org/(S(i43dyn45teexjx455qlt3d2q))/reference/ReferencesPapers.aspx?ReferenceID=1091052

Kshetri, N. (2013). Privacy and security issues in cloud computing: The role of institutions and institutional evolution. *Telecommunications Policy, 37*(4-5), 372–386. Retrieved July 3, 2016 from http://www.sciencedirect.com/science/article/pii/S0308596112000717 doi:10.1016/j.telpol.2012.04.011

Leavitt, N. (2009). Is Cloud Computing Really Ready for Prime Time? *Computer, 42*(1), 15-20. New York, NY: ACM. Retrieved May 21, 2017 from http://dl.acm.org/citation.cfm?id=1512163

Mell, P., & Grance, T. (2011). The NIST Definition of Cloud Computing, Recommendations of the National Institute of Standards and Technology. *Computer Security*. Retrieved July 3, 2016 from http://faculty.winthrop.edu/domanm/csci411/Handouts/NIST.pdf

Popović, K., & Hocenski, Ž. (2010). Cloud computing security issues and challenges. In *2010 Proceedings of the 33rd International Convention on Information and Communication Technology, Electronics and Microelectronics (MIPRO)* (pp. 344-349). IEEE. Retrieved May 21, 2017 from http://ieeexplore.ieee.org/document/5533317/

Ramgovind, S., Eloff, M. M., & Smith, E. (2010). The management of security in Cloud computing. In *Information Security for South Africa (ISSA '10)*. New Jersey: Institute of Electrical and Electronic Engineers (IEEE). Retrieved July 4, 2016 from http://ieeexplore.ieee.org/document/5588290/

Rao, G. H., & Padmanabham, P. (2013). Data Security in Cloud using Hybrid Encryption and Decryption. *International Journal of Advanced Research in Computer Science and Software Engineering, 3*(10), 494–497. Retrieved May 21, 2017 from https://www.ijarcsse.com/docs/papers/Volume_3/10_October2013/V3I10-0252.pdf

Rohit, B., & Sanyal, S. (2012). Survey on Security Issues in Cloud Computing and Associated Mitigation Techniques. *International Journal of Computers and Applications, 47*(18), 47–66. Retrieved July 4, 2016 from http://www.ijcaonline.org/archives/volume47/number18/7292-0578 doi:10.5120/7292-0578

Shah, M. A., Swaminathan, R., & Baker, M. (2008). Privacy-Preserving Audit and Extraction of Digital Contents. *IACR Cryptology EPrint Archive*. Retrieved July 5, 2016 from https://pdfs.semanticscholar.or g/8600/5009402ef47f23ee0d2548f73e6aabbe714e.pdf

Shaikh, F. B., & Haider, S. (2011). Security threats in cloud computing. In *Proceedings of 2011 International Conference for Internet Technology and Secured Transactions (ICITST)* (pp. 214-219). IEEE. Retrieved May 21, 2017 from http://ieeexplore.ieee.org/document/6148380/

Sharma, S., & Mittal, U. (2013). Comparative Analysis of Various Authentication Techniques in Cloud Computing. *International Journal of Innovative Research in Science, Engineering and Technology, 2(4)*, 994-998. Retrieved May 21, 2017 from https://www.ijirset.com/upload/april/17_COMPARATIVE.pdf

Silva, C. M. R., da Silva, J. L. C., Rodrigues, R. B., Campos, G. M. M., do Nascimento, L. M., & Garcia, V. C. (2013). Security Threats in Cloud Computing Models: Domains and Proposals. In *Proceedings of 2013 IEEE Sixth International Conference on Cloud Computing (CLOUD)* (pp. 383-389). IEEE. Retrieved May 21, 2017 from https://www.researchgate.net/publication/261450583_Security_Threats_ in_Cloud_Computing_Models_Domains_and_Proposals

Wikipedia. (2016). Virtual Machine. Retrieved July 12, 2016 from https://en.wikipedia.org/wiki/Virtual_machine

ADDITIONAL READING

Cocking, L. (2012). The Future of Mobile Cloud Infrastructure. Retrieved May 21, 2017 from http://www.guardtime. com/2012/08/13/the-future-of mobile cloud- infrastructure/

Cuervo, E., Balasubramanian, A., Cho, D. K., Wolman, A., Saroiu, S., Chandra, R., & Bahl, P. (2010). MAUI: making smartphones last longer with code offload. In *Proceedings of the 8th International Conference on Mobile Systems, Applications and Services* (pp. 49-62). New York City, NY: ACM. Retrieved from http://dl.acm.org/citation.cfm?id=1814441

Fernando, N., Loke, S. W., & Rahayu, W. (2013). Mobile cloud computing: A survey. *Future Generation Computer Systems, 29*(1), 84–106. Retrieved from https://pdfs.semanticscholar.org/b2d2/517acc5fa1f1 3526c77badbdd661f1b2ad0c.pdf doi:10.1016/j.future.2012.05.023

Gao, J., Chang, R. S., Gruhn, V., He, J., Roussos, G., & Tsai, W. T. (2013). Mobile cloud computing research-issues, challenges and needs. In *Proceedings of the 2013 IEEE 7th International Symposium on Service Oriented System Engineering (SOSE)* (pp. 442-453). IEEE. Retrieved from https://asu.pure. elsevier.com/en/publications/mobile-cloud-computing-research-issues-challenges-and-needs

Kosta, S., Aucinas, A., Hui, P., Mortier, R., & Zhang, X. (2011). Unleashing the Power of Mobile Cloud Computing using ThinkAir. arXiv:1105.3232 Retrieved from https://scholar.google.com/citations?view_ op=view_citation&hl=it&user=NOi_xTgAAAAJ&citation_for_view=NOi_xTgAAAAJ:u-x6o8ySG0sC

Kovachev, D., Cao, Y., & Klamma, R. (2011). Mobile Cloud Computing: A Comparison of Application Models. arXiv:1107.4940 Retrieved from https://scholar.google.com/citations?view_op=view_citation &hl=en&user=qhzVptEAAAAJ&citation_for_view=qhzVptEAAAAJ:2osOgNQ5qMEC

Marinelli, E. E. (2009). *Hyrax: Cloud Computing on Mobile Devices using MapReduce* (Doctoral dissertation [Master Thesis Draft]. Carnegie Mellon University. Retrieved from https://www.researchgate.net/publication/238694867_Hyrax_Cloud_Computing_on_Mobile_Devices_using_MapReduce

Qi, H., & Gani, A. (2012). Research on Mobile Cloud Computing: Review, Trend and Perspectives. In *Proceedings of Second International Conference on Digital Information and Communication Technology and it's Applications* (pp. 195-202). IEEE. Retrieved from https://arxiv.org/ftp/arxiv/papers/1206/1206.1118.pdf

Umair, S., Muneer, U., Zahoor, M. N., & Malik, A. W. (2015). Mobile computing: issues and challenges. In *Proceedings of 2015 12th International Conference on High-Capacity Optical Networks and Enabling/Emerging Technologies* (pp. 1-5). IEEE. Retrieved from http://ieeexplore.ieee.org/document/7395438/

Zhong, L., Wang, B., & Wei, H. (2012). Cloud computing applied in the mobile internet. In *Proceedings of 2012 7th International Conference on Computer Science & Education* (pp. 218-221). IEEE. Retrieved from https://www.researchgate.net/publication/261497115_Cloud_computing_applied_in_the_mobile_Internet

KEY TERMS AND DEFINITIONS

Cloud Computing: The process of providing shared resources and other services to user on demand that can be accessed from anywhere provided the internet connection.

Cloud Service: Resources that are delivered over the internet are known as cloud services.

Cloud Storage: The availability of data and keeping the data safe and secure is the responsibility of Cloud Storage.

Host-Based Intrusion Prevention System (HIPS): A Host-based Intrusion Prevention System is a system or a program employed to protect critical computer systems containing crucial data against viruses and other Internet malware.

IaaS: Virtualized computing resources available over the internet is the responsibility of Infrastructure as a Service.

PaaS: Platform as a Service allows the customers to develop, run and manage their applications.

Privacy: Privacy involves keeping the user data and integrity safe from external attack.

SaaS: Software as a Service is centrally hosted in which software is accredited on subscription basis.

Security: Involves policies that protect the data and information linked with Cloud Computing applications

Virtual Machine (VM): An emulation of a particular computer system. Virtual machines operate based on the computer architecture and functions of a real or hypothetical computer, and their implementations may involve specialized hardware, software or a combination of both.

This research was previously published in the Handbook of Research on Big Data Storage and Visualization Techniques edited by Richard S. Segall and Jeffrey S. Cook, pages 175-195, copyright year 2018 by Engineering Science Reference (an imprint of IGI Global).

Chapter 74

Why We Disclose Personal Information Despite Cybersecurity Risks and Vulnerabilities:
Obligatory Passage Point Perspective

Patrick I. Offor
City University of Seattle, USA

ABSTRACT

Is it fair to say that the disclosure of personal information, in an online setting, is voluntary or due to incentivization, cognitive risk-benefit analysis, cognitive predisposition, or based on information sensitivity, whereas our personal information is being collected, knowingly and forcibly most of the time, and unknowingly and inadvertently at other times? While the collection of personal information is necessary to organizations and online users alike, in completing online transactions, the issue is the collection of additional non-pertinent information that serves only organizations' prescriptive and predictive analytics and their business interests, and not the users'. Most study on the phenomenon have centered on voluntary or willful disclosure, and on technical collections. This article examines the phenomenon based on the concept of the obligatory passage point and found that online users disclose their personal information online mostly because the information are designated as required in an online setting, contrary to conventional beliefs.

INTRODUCTION

Personal information or personal data is the heartbeat or the basis for online transaction processing. In other words, the disclosure of personal information is the bedrock upon which electronic activities, over the Internet, flourishes. Personal information includes personal identifiable information, personal financial information, and personal healthcare information. Some personal information can be classified

DOI: 10.4018/978-1-5225-8176-5.ch074

Copyright © 2019, IGI Global. Copying or distributing in print or electronic forms without written permission of IGI Global is prohibited.

as sensitive or confidential. The personal information and online transaction relationship is such that an online user would always be required to provide some sort of personal data in any human-internet interaction for proper identification, authentication, payment, and for ensuring the completeness of the transaction, whether the transaction is for goods or for services. Completeness of a transaction involves all activities from the initiation of a transaction to the receipt of the goods or services.

The numbers of online transactions are on the rise because the number of users of internet capable devices and the number of organizations with online presence have increased dramatically in the U.S., and around the world (Offor, 2016). Therefore, the need for organizations to obtain, store, and use or deploy their online users' personal information in electronic commerce or business (e-commerce or e-business), electronic government (e-government), electronic healthcare (e-healthcare), electronic marketplace (e-marketplace), online banking, and the like has grown exponentially.

Sadly, the same personal information has also become the main target of cybersecurity incidents and attacks, from malicious and non-malicious attackers, because of the central role it plays in advancing online transactions. The largest exposures of data breaches, around the world, have occurred in the last couple of years. Among them are (1) the 3.0 million records exposed at Yahoo in 2016, (2) the 2.0 billion records at DU Caller Group, in China, in 2017, (3) the 1.3 billion records at River City Media, in the U.S., in 2017, (4) the 1.2 billion records at NetEase Incorporated (dba 163.com), in China, in 2017, (5) the 1.1 billion records at Aadhaar database, in India, in 2018, and (6) the 711 million records from a misconfigure spambot database, in the Netherlands, in 2017 (Risk Based Security Report, 2018). Furthermore, the average cost of each lost or stolen record that has sensitive or confidential information was $141 in 2016 and the average total cost of data breach was $3.62 million in the same year, according to the 2017 Cost of Data Breach study, which involved 419 companies in 13 countries (Ponemon Institute Report, 2017). Henceforth, while the costs associated with cybersecurity attacks and the possibility of loss of revenue from negative media coverage inform organizations' cybersecurity concerns, the lack of control of personal information informs online users' concerns. Meanwhile, the costs of data breaches increased by 6.4% in the 2017 and the cost of each stolen record rose to $148 (Ponemon Institute Report, 2018).

The issue, today, is that users have limited to no control of their personal information. This lack of control on the collection, use, and storage of personal information has exacerbated users' information privacy concerns. Additionally, recent news of reporting delays, reactionary nature of cybersecurity incidents and attacks, and a shift in website analytics demand, from metrics to descriptive, from descriptive to predictive, from predictive to prescriptive, and now from prescriptive to causation—combination of descriptive and prescriptive analytics (Bekavac & Pranicevic, 2015; Fitz-enz, 2009), have not helped in reducing users' concerns. In a privacy and security study, which involved 41,000 households by the U.S. Census Bureau in 2015, Goldberg (2016) indicated that American are ambivalent and concerned about data breaches, cybersecurity incidents, and the privacy of online services. The paper suggested, "Forty-five percent of online households reported that these concerns stopped them from conducting financial transactions, buying goods or services, posting on social networks, or expressing opinions on controversial or political issues via the Internet, and 30 percent refrained from at least two of these activities" (Goldberg, 2016).

Surprisingly, but understandably, users have continued to disclose their personal information online despite the constancy of cybersecurity threats and vulnerabilities. Therefore, the motivation for this study is to understand why online users disclose their personal information based on obligatory passage point (OPP). This is necessary because while online users' willful disclosure of personal information and organizations use of technology to collect personal information are well documented in the extant literature (Belanger & Crossler, 2011; Dinev et al., 2013; Hong & Thong, 2013; Offor, 2016), personal information disclosure through the obligatory passage point is not. Hence, this study explored the personal information disclosure from OPP perspective.

The rest of the paper is structured and organized chronologically as follows. The delineation of the benefits of personal information disclosure is followed by the classification of personal information disclosure as willful disclosure, technology assisted disclosure, and obligatory passage point induced disclosure. Subsequently the research problem, the research argument, and the importance of the study were presented, in addition to the review of the phenomenon in the extant literature. In the methodology section, the paper described the conceptual framework and data collection, followed by the data analysis, result, and the conclusion.

BENEFITS OF PERSONAL INFORMATION DISCLOSURE

On one hand, productivity, data analytics, and direct marketing are some of the reasons why the disclosure of personal information is good for organizations. On the other hand, economic benefit is one of the reasons why it is also good for users. Electronic commerce has transformed the global economy and the supply chain management in the United States due to the disclosure of personal information (Gunasekara, et al., 2002). Today, a buyer has the ability to compare prices online with ease and obtain goods and services from any Internet capable device regardless of his or her physical location. Hence, the benefits of disclosing personal information online by users cannot be overemphasized, and so is the illusion of control of information privacy the users feel and experience constantly that allow them to disclose personal information.

The illusion of control, in the context, is the misguided belief that individuals have control of their personal information in an online setting. Moghaddam and Studer (1998) described illusion of control as the "mistaken beliefs that future changes in personal, social, economic, political, and other domains are under the control of humankind" (p. 1). In reality, the promise of information privacy has not been realized because (1) the disclosure of personal information online is mostly because the information is designated as required with validity and completeness checks, and (2) once the information is disclosed, a user would not be made aware of the subsequent use of his or her information.

CLASSIFICATION OF PERSONAL INFORMATION DISCLOSURE

In this study, the disclosure of personal information is classified into three as (1) willful disclosure, (2) technology assisted collection, and (3) through OPP induced disclosure (see Figure 1). In addition, personal information itself is classified into two as (1) transaction relevant and (2) transaction irrelevant. What follows are detail information on both classifications.

Willful Disclosure

Willful disclosure refers to the act of disclosing personal information online freely (Greene et al., 2006). The four states of privacy are intimacy, reserve, solitude, and anonymity (Westin, 1970), and the three core privacy orientation index are privacy unconcerned, pragmatist, and fundamentalist (Kumaraguru

& Cranor, 2005). The two classifications were aligned in (Offor, 2016), where information privacy states of intimacy, reserve, and solitude were aligned to the privacy orientations of the unconcerned, pragmatist, and fundamentalist respectively. The fourth privacy state of anonymity was found to cut across the other states of privacy, as well as the three core privacy orientations (Offor, 2016). People in the state of intimacy are those who naturally like to transact online irrespective of the risk; the reserves are those that are very cautious and selective online; the solitude refers to individuals who naturally and rarely transact online; and the anonymity are those who conceal their identity while transacting online. Therefore, it is possible to be in the information privacy state of intimacy, reserve, or solitude and in the anonymity state at the same time.

Regardless of the state of privacy or privacy orientation, online users have continued to disclose their personal willingly at times; even when there are perceived or associated risks or costs. Evidence also showed there are some who rarely disclose their personal information, except when they have a high need signal (Offor, 2016). In addition, online users' willingness to disclose personal information online have shown to dampen by their information privacy concerns, and their fear and anxiety of losing control of their personal information upon disclosure. Also, empirical evidence has shown that perceived benefits of information disclosure, transparency, and sensitivity of the information (Dinev et al., 2013; Moothersbaugh et al., 2012) affect the perceived risk. The perceived Internet privacy risk, Internet trust, Internet privacy concerns, and personal Internet interest (Dinev & Hart, 2006), and online users' cognitive predisposition based on need signal (Offor, 2016) are some of reasons that affect willful disclosure of personal information online as well.

Technology Assisted Collection

This is related to personal information of online users collected over the Internet with the aid of technology. Users' personal information is collected online, with or without the users' knowledge, via weblogs (log user's IP address, date and time stamps, time spent and packet transfer sizes), JavaScript tagging (counts the number of visits to a website), web beacons (tracks click trough behaviors across websites), and packet sniffing—advanced software/hardware user's information collector (Waisberg & Kaushik, 2009). While some websites would allow users to opt in today, rather than opt out, in cookie collection, others would not. It is important to note that the idea of allowing users to opt in is a recent development, possibly influenced by the recent General Data Protection Regulation (GDPR), European Union (EU) Regulation 2016/679. The regulation stated,

Consent should be given by a clear affirmative act establishing a freely given, specific, informed and unambiguous indication of the data subject's agreement to the processing of personal data relating to him or her, such as by a written statement, including by electronic means, or an oral statement. This could include ticking a box when visiting an internet website, choosing technical settings for information society services or another statement or conduct which clearly indicates in this context the data subject's acceptance of the proposed processing of his or her personal data (EU Regulation 2016/679, para. 32).

Obligatory Passage Point or Cohesive Disclosure

Assuming, you have three actors A_1, A_2, A_3, where A_1 is the information systems, A_2 is the consumer, and A_3 is the online merchant. An OPP exists, if A_3 insists on the disclosure of certain information by

A_2 in A_1 before A_2 can purchase the goods or services A_2 wanted to obtain online from A_3. E-commerce, e-government, e-healthcare, e-marketplace, and other users are forced, knowingly and unknowingly, to disclose their personal information. A user is forced to disclose personal information, knowingly, when the disclosure of such information is deemed as required, even though it would not be relevant to completing a transaction, i.e., insisting on getting access to a user's phone camera, calendar, or photo/media/files prior to allowing her to download an apps (Offor, 2016). Furthermore, users may share or allow online organizations to have access to their personal information online unknowingly or unintentionally, i.e., authorizing Internet cookies or not reading the opt-in/opt-out pop ups, or answering yes too quickly to personal information request dialog box messages, and not anticipating potential vulnerability of Internet bot activities. Internet bots "are software agents which perform automated tasks" (Koike & Nishizaki, 2013, p. 242), and Internet cookies "are small text files used for keeping track of settings or data for the Web site" (Huang & Lee, 2008, p. 3).

Relevant and Irrelevant Personal Information

A relevant personal information is one, which is necessary for completing a transaction online and receiving the goods or services. For example, an online user would need his or her name, a valid mailing address, a valid phone number and/or email address, and a valid credit card information to obtain goods or services online. Here, the data points are relevant because the name identifies the person making the purchase, the mailing/physical address is used for the delivery of the goods/services, the phone number and/or email address is used for contact and status update, and the credit card information is used for payment. The relevancy of the information lies in the fact that not having the information may impede on the user's ability to complete the transaction and take delivery and on the organization ability to deliver the product or service.

Personal information would be deemed irrelevant if the data is not necessary for a transaction, i.e., asking for a facial picture of a driver in addition to his or her driver's license and credit card, where the driver's license and credit card information are the most generally accepted artifacts for rental agreement. Asking for access to a user's camera, photos, media, or files for an app is irrelevant, especially if the utility of the app is unrelated. It is hard to think of any medical or financial or support reason for asking for marital status of a patient on a medical form or survey if the insurance, medical decision maker or durable power of attorney, and next of kin information are available (Walker, M. (2012). Note that an irrelevant personal data would still be in the willful disclosure column if it is not designated as required on an organization's website, but would become an OPP induced disclosure if designated as required.

Form, Fit, and Function Conception

To illustrate the point on the need to explore the use of the obligatory passage point by organizations as a mechanism for personal information collection better, the study used the Form, Fit, and Function concept of the engineering Bill of Material (BOM), which helps in removing manufacturing redundancies, improving product quality and timely delivery, and in minimizing service costs. The Form, Fit, and Function is the "physical and functional characteristics of an item as an entity" (DA PAM 700-60, 2008, p. 20). The Business Dictionary described it as the "physical, functional, and performance characteristics or specifications that uniquely identify a component or device and determine its interchangeability in a system.

Here, the Form, Fit, and Function is a managerial/engineering construct for identifying, creating, and deploying material interchangeability or substitutability, and for standardization based on the item's physical, functional, and performance specification. In the manufacturing of repair parts and other items, organizations use the Form, Fit, and Function to ensure that the spares, repair parts, or other items are interchangeable even as they change the models of the end item, i.e., equipment, automobile, aircraft, and the like. The form represents the physical characteristics or attributes of the item, i.e., shape, size, dimensions, and the like; the fit refers to the ability of the item to physically interface or interconnect or be integral to an assembly; and the function is the capability that the item delivers (Dassault Systemes, 2012). The capacity of parts or items to be interchangeable is "mainly determined by the physical, functional, and performance of the component or device" (Dassault Systemes, 2012, p. 3). For example, in Hiller (2014), a rear-view mirror, backup camera, and sensor were demonstrated as available form to provide a motorist a rear-view vision capability (function).

Following the Form, Fit, and Function concept, as presented in Figure 1, organizations are interested in obtaining users' personal information (function); they use willful disclosure, technology assisted collection, and OPP induced disclosure (form) in achieving the function; and they assess and use the attributes (fit) of the form to make the function achievable and for re-useable. Figure 1 presents an illustration of the Form, Fit, and Function analogous pathways through which organizations get personal information from online users today. Quite frankly, the objective of organizations, in this regard, is to collect users' personal information relevant to their business objectives and analytics, as such they are inclined to use any one or combination of the forms that satisfy their critical personal information needs, that has minimal risks, and is obtainable at the lowest costs.

Figure 1. Form, fit, and function modeled personal information disclosure

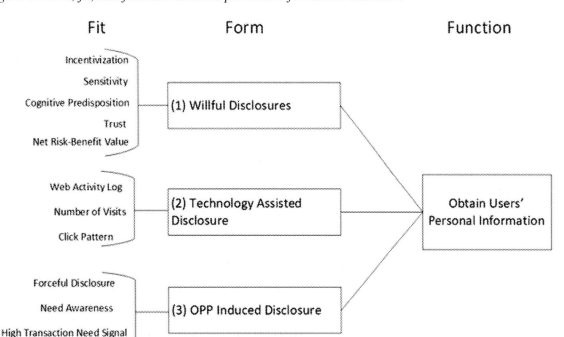

RESEARCH PROBLEM AND ARGUMENT

Managers in all facets of human endeavor are no longer contented with recording, relating, and comparing users' online transaction behaviors. They are more interested in predicting and prescribing them with high-level of probabilities or certainties. Some organizations are even more interesting in finding causations nowadays. Personal information not only support online transactions, it helps organizations in recording, relating, comparing, understanding, predicting, and prescribing their online users' behaviors based on all or a combination of the five business measurement variables, i.e., cost, time, quantity, quality, and human reaction (Fitz-enz, 2009). The finding in the extant literature is that the information privacy unconcerned would disclose their personal information willfully, most of the time, and the pragmatists use more cognitive judgements in disclosing personal information. Yet, the information privacy fundamentalists find it difficult to disclose their personal online without strong need signals (Offor, 2016). Consequently, organizations are constantly devising alternative ways to personal information collection online in order to support their business and data analytics objectives.

The obligatory passage point, in information privacy context, is the undoing or ruination of users' information privacy because users are forced to disclose personal information that are not necessarily relevant to the completion of a transaction in which they are engaged in. Information privacy is "the claim of individuals, groups, or institutions to determine for themselves when, how, and to what extent information about them is communicated to others" (Malhotra et al., 2004, p. 337). Offor (2016) defined it as "an assurance of good stewardship of the consumers' personal information, in terms of the collection, the use, and the security of the shared information, among individuals, groups, or organizations" (p. 10). Obviously, it is evident that online users have limited control of their personal information and the incessant occurrence of cybersecurity incidents have not helped matters. The first quarter of 2018 has seen about 458 breaches, exposing about 1.5 billion in 10 countries, including India, United States, Norway, Canada, France, Singapore, Israel, Malaysia, Japan, and Korea (Risk based Security Report, 2018). In addition, 8.5% of data breaches in the same period are from third-party organizations, representing a 3.5% increase from the same period in the previous year (Risk based Security Report, 2018). Henceforth, there is a need to understand the obligatory passage point induced personal information disclosure better.

This study argues that online users disclose their personal information online mostly because organizations use the obligatory passage point induced personal information collection mechanism. Note that the issue here is not whether organizations should set the field type of online forms as required or optional. The issue is whether those fields that are designated as required or mandatory are relevant to the completion of the transaction the user is engaged in. In the context, personal data or information is an obligatory passage point when the provision of such data or information is deemed as required by an online merchant, and enforced with validity and completeness checks or otherwise, even when the data is not relevant to the completion of the online transaction.

THE IMPORTANCE OF THE STUDY

This study advanced knowledge by classifying users' personal information requests online into two, transaction relevant and transaction irrelevant, and by showing that while acquisition of transaction relevant personal information is pertinent to an instance of an online transaction, transaction irrelevant personal information is not. Note that both classes of personal information could be requested simultaneously or in the same instance of a transaction. In addition, while online users are often willing to divulge the personal information they thought are relevant and would facilitate their transactions, they are ambivalent and hesitant in providing the information they thought are irrelevant.

In addition, this paper is innovative because it categorized the way in which organizations collect personal information, (1) willful disclosure, (2) technology assisted disclosure, and (3) obligatory passage point induced disclosure. At its core, the paper presented the degree to which obligatory passage point induced personal information disclosure has become one of the main reasons for personal information disclosure online. The paper used the analogous example of the European hotel manager (Latour, 1990, p. 104) to illuminate the concept better, which shows that organizations have better chance of collecting personal information online by making the provision of the information an obligatory passage point. Following the European hotel manager illustration, organizations force users hand in providing irrelevant personal data or information, rather than making the provision of such data optional.

The European hotel manager[1], ideation analogy is still pertinent today, especially with organizations who still engage in high volumes of customer traffic and whose business activities require the filling and/or signing of paperwork among other things, i.e., Walmart Customer Service Centers, Hospital Receptions, and the like. In these organizations, the clerks, sales associates, and nurses attach umbrella looking flowers and other artifacts to their pens to prevent customer from walking away with them. By attaching these objects to their pens, the clerks and the nurses would get most customers to drop off the pens once they filled their forms and/or signed the paper. As a result, the clerks or nurses would not have to rely on the customers' sense of remembrance or moral obligation. Therefore, this study shows that where willful disclosure of personal information, secure uniform resource locator (URL), privacy policy and statements, badge verifications (*Secure and Verified sign* and *SiteLock Trusted Seal*), and encryption detection lock icon (Taiji, 2015) have failed to encourage personal information disclosure to a certain degree, the use of innovative extraction mechanisms (technical and nontechnical), like the OPP induced disclosure, have succeeded.

Literature Review

The attitudes and views of individuals on information privacy risks and vulnerabilities today are relatively similar to the views of the general privacy, except that in the past, prior to the ubiquities of Internet enabled devices and the Internet of Things, the speed at which personal information is exchanged is not as massive as it is today. While general privacy is concerned with the right to be left alone (Warren & Brandeis, 1890), information privacy is concerned with the ability of individuals, groups, or institutions to determine how information about them are collected, stored, used, or shared (Malhotra et al., 2004; Offor, 2016).

In the review, this paper summarized the consensus in literature in the context of why people have continued to disclose their personal online notwithstanding known cybersecurity risk and vulnerabilities. In other words, the review concentrated on existing empirical explanations as to why online users are still disclosing their personal information daily, to complete whatever transactions they are engage in, even though cybercrime exploits or mischiefs by malicious and non-malicious attackers are well known and documented. What follows are evidence of cyberattacks, risks, and vulnerabilities, and the findings in the extant literature.

Unauthorized data collection, unauthorized primary and secondary use of data, unauthorized access to data, unauthorized modification of data, and cybersecurity data exposure due to operators' error are still some of the risks and vulnerabilities today (Belanger & Crossler, 2011). Risk Based Security Report (2018) noted that there were about 458 breaches already this year in 10 countries, which had exposed over 1.5 billion records. The impact of the 87 million users' information compromised at Facebook in 2016 is still subject of vigorous debate in the United States. In 2017, the Financial Services, Information and Communication Technology, Manufacturing, Retail, and the Professional Services were among organizations/industries most targeted (Alvarez et al., 2018). In addition, a major finding in the report was the near doubling of injection-type attack in 2017 to 79% when compared with the 2016's malicious attacks (Alvarez et al., 2018). The botnet-based command injection (CMDi) local file inclusion (LFI) attacks and the CMDi attacks containing embedded coin mining tools were instrumental to the malicious attacks. Injection-type attack is an input or command injection to an operating system (OS CMDi) or a SQL injection (SQLi) (Alvarez et al., 2018). Despite these attacks, online users had continued to disclose their personal information, and their attitudes toward the disclosure of personal information have not been consistent.

While many studies had argued that Internet users' attitudes toward the disclosure of personal information have not been consistent (Norberg et al., 2007), others argue that the inconsistency is due to users' cognitive risk-benefit calculations, otherwise called privacy calculus (Dinev & Hart, 2006; Laufer & Wolfe, 1977). Yet, some argue that latent variables or factors, such as Internet trust, risk, incentivization, information sensitivity, and users' information privacy predisposition are the reasons why online users have continued to disclose their personal information (D'Arcy et al., 2009; Keith et al., 2013; Norberg et at., 2007; Offor, 2016; Smith et al., 1996; Son & Kim, 2008). Interestingly, empirical evidence has also shown that consumers are also willing to pay a premium price for goods and services, from privacy protected websites, if privacy information is accessible and salient (Tsai et al., 2011).

METHODOLOGY

This section provides information on the conceptual framework, the research approach, the research model, the hypotheses, and the data collection. A quantitative research approach was used for this study, the data collection was with a survey instrument, and the study conducted a simple and multiple regression tests for data analysis because the input (predictor) and the outcome (response) variables are continuous variables. A continuous variable is one which can be measured on an interval scale or a ratio scale (Vogt & Johnson, 2016).

Conceptual Framework

The framework employed in this study is based on the concept of the obligatory passage point. Personal information or personal data would be considered as OPP if the information or data is deemed to be voluntary, but still designated as required in an online setting for completing a transaction (Offor, 2016). Just as the researchers in (Callon, 1986), who knew that their only path to a successful study that will preserve the Pecten Maximus scallop lies in identifying the actors (the fishermen of St. Brieuc, the three scientists, and the scallops of Brieuc) and in establishing an OPP in the network of their relationship, online merchants and organization know that the survival of e-commerce, e-government, or e-healthcare depends largely on their ability to collect personal information.

Note that in the scallop preservation inquiry, although the actors may have had varying reason for doing what they did, the outcome increased an understanding of that specie of scallops of St. Brieuc, increased the stock of the scallops, and sustained the fishermen. The same argument could be made today regarding the collection of personal information. Personal information disclosure allows organizations and businesses to do direct marketing and personalization (tailoring ads and discount opportunities based on an individual's purchase patterns and interests), and it supports overall productivity of the national and global economy. Individuals also benefit from the disclosure of personal information regardless of the means through which organization obtain it. Some of the benefits include the ability to obtain goods or services anytime anywhere, ability to receive or do price comparison, and the receipt of only advertisements of interest.

The proposition in Figure 2 is that an awareness of a need, either through knowledge, realization or perception, would cause or trigger an individual's need signal as shown in H_1. If an individual has the will and means to purchase the goods or services online, then he or she would have to abide by whatever data requirement or information the online merchant or organization needs, whether or not the data or information is relevant to the purchase or not, as shown in H_2 and H_3.

Summary of the hypotheses for this study is provided as follow:

H1: There is a causal relationship between an awareness of a need by an individual and his or her need signal.
H2: There is a casual relationship between the need signal and the personal information disclosure.
H3: The obligatory passage point moderates the casual relationship between the need signal and the personal information disclosure.

The notion is that once we know or realize that there is difference between what we need and what we have, our need signal would be triggered. Assuming we have the resources, financial and technology, to fill the gap online, we may choose to so. If we decide to purchase the goods or services online, the argument, in this study, is that we would provide the personal information required by the organization online to achieve our goal of completing the purchase, whether the personal information is relevant in

Figure 2. The cause-and-effect model of the OPP personal information disclosure

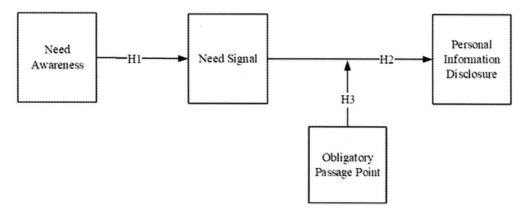

completing the transaction, from request to delivery, or not, especially when the irrelevant personal information is designated as required in a mandatory field.

Data Collection

This study used survey instrument for the data collection and a total of 155 responses were received. The respondents consist of 47.1% male and 52.9% female. About 67.1% of the sample subjects were between 18-60 years of age and 32.9% were above 60. In addition, 61% of them have a yearly income between $50,000 and $100,000.

The data was check for outlier and multicollinearity. An outlier is a data point or unit of analysis that is unusual or has extreme value, which could distort the interpretation of data or could be an indication of a sampling error (Vogt & Jonson, 2016). Multicollinearity ensures that the constructs or independent variables are not correlated because a data with multicollinearity could inflate the estimates of the coefficient or could create some difficulty in evaluating the direct and indirect effects of the constructs (George et al., 2005). The test for outlier was conducted using with the boxplot graphics and the test for multicollinearity was validated using the variance inflation factor (VIF). The VIF is used in measuring collinearity in the multiple regression analysis. The lowest value of collinearity is 1.0, which means no collinearity, nonetheless, VIF less than 10.0 is acceptable (Vogt & Jonson, 2016).

Figure 3 is the data comparison matrix. Although there are relationships among the variables, the relationship between the obligatory passage point and the personal information disclosure is more profound

Figure 3. Data comparison matrix for the independent and dependent variables

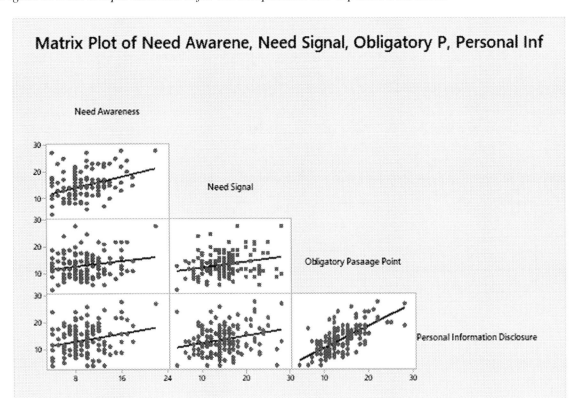

by visualization in the Minitab analytic software package. Further analysis and measure of statistical significance of the constructs are delineated in the data analysis and result section.

DATA ANALYSIS AND RESULT

In this section, the study expresses the result of the data analysis. In the analysis of the data, the study used the correlation coefficient and multiple regression tests. The use of these statistical tools was informed because although correlation measures the strength and direction of linear relationship between two constructs or variables, regression provide precision to the definition of the relationship. Regression "generates equation to describe the statistical relationship between one or more predictors and response variable and to predict new observations" (Minitab, 2017). In addition, the use of the multiple regression allowed the study to test for moderation in H3.

Reliability and Item Analysis

Item analysis is a measure of whether the items or observations in a latent variable are measuring the same characteristics. Cronbach's alpha was used to determine reliability of the items. Reliability is a measure of the measurement accuracy or internal consistency of the survey instrument (Offor, 2016). The reliability of the data for the constructs is adequate. The need awareness, the need signal, the obligatory passage point, and the personal information disclosure constructs have Cronbach's alpha of 0.60, 0.75, 0.55, and 0.73 respectively. Reliability coefficient of 0.70 or greater is generally acceptable (Awad & Krishnan, 2006; Offor, 2016) and reliability coefficient of 0.60 is appropriate for new items or for exploratory research (Straub et al., 2004).

Correlation and Regression

The inter-construct or predictor variable pairwise correlations were statistically significant. Although the correlation coefficient R in the correlation matrix in Table 1 is generally low, the coefficient R between the obligatory passage point and the personal information disclosure is high at 0.702. The VIF for the variables were very low and excellent, with Need Awareness = 1.18, Need Signal = 1.20, and Obligatory Passage Point = 1.08. The regression equation is Personal Information Disclosure = 0.62

Table 1. Latent variable correlation coefficient matrix

	Need Awareness	Need Signal	Obligatory Passage Point
Need Signal	0.371		
	0.000*		
Obligatory Passage Point	0.196	0.240	
	0.015*	0.003*	
Personal Information Disclosure	0.252	0.263	0.702
	0.002*	0.001*	0.000*

Sig. *p-value with 0.95 confidence interval

+ 0.1429 Need Awareness + 0.0704 Need Signal + 0.7915 Obligatory Passage Point. Therefore, with coefficient of 0.7915 in the Model Summary, the Obligatory Passage Point construct is significant in the presence of other independent or predictor variables because it has a *p-value* of 0.000. This means that a unit of change in the obligatory passage point induced disclosure will increase the disclosure of personal information by 0.7915.

The quantitative test for H1, H2, and H3 were statistically significant and hence supported. The need awareness has a rotated factor loading and communality with Varimax Rotation of 0.99 and direct effect of 0.371 to the need signal (see Figure 4). The need signal has a 1.00 of factor loading with direct effect of 0.263 and indirect effect of 0.240 to the personal information disclosure, and the obligatory passage point has 0.857 factor loading and 0.702 effect on the personal information disclosure. The personal information disclosure has 0.849 factor loading.

Best Subset Regression

The Best Subset Regression measurement was conducted to identify the model with the best fit, which is the model with minimum multicollinearity and most predictive accuracy (George et al., 2005). This is necessary in order not to rely only on p-value. To identify the model, the study assessed the candidate models and looked for the set of independent or input variables with the highest R^2, highest R^2 adjusted, and the smallest estimate of standard deviation. The R^2 adjusted is preferred for multiple regression (George et al., 2005). Upon the completion of the measure, the proposed model, with three (3) variables, remains the model with the best fit as presented in Table 2, with $R^2 = 51.0$, R^2 adjusted = 50.1, and standard deviation (S) = 3.6291.

Residual Analysis

Figure 5 is the result of the residual analysis. Residual analysis is "a standard part of assessing model adequacy any time a mathematical model is generated because residuals are the best estimate of error" (George et al., 2005, p.195). The normal probability plot indicates that the data used for this study is normally distributed because of its closeness to the diagonal line. There is equal variance because of the

Figure 4. The hypothesized obligation passage point model

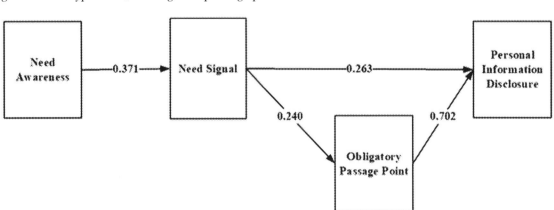

Table 2. Best subsets regression model

Vars	R-Sq	R-Sq (adj)	R-Sq (pred)	Mallows Cp	S	Need Awareness	Need Signal	OPP
1	49.3	49.0	47.9	5.3	3.6686			X
1	6.9	6.3	3.7	136.0	4.9707		X	
2	50.7	50.0	48.6	3.1	3.6309	X		X
2	50.2	49.6	47.9	4.4	3.6463		X	X
3	51.0	50.1	48.0	4.0	3.6291	X	X	X

Figure 5. The residual analysis quadrant for normality, equal variance, and independence

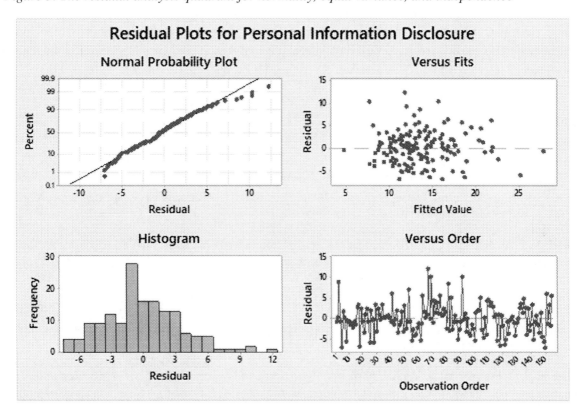

spread pattern of the data points as shown in the versus fits. The histogram was indicative of the normality of the data. Finally, there is independence in the data as shown in the versus order (George et al., 2005).

CONCLUSION

Based on the analysis of the data, 51% (50.1% with R^2 adjusted) of personal information disclosure online could be explained or be attributed to the disclosure of personal information due to the obligatory passage point because the results of the correlation analysis, where the correlation coefficient for the OPP and disclosure of personal information is $R = 0.702$, $R^2 = 51.0$, and the R^2 adjusted for the hypothesized model in the regression test $= 50.1$. The result of this study supports the research argument and the hypotheses, and shows that more than half of personal information disclosures online are due to the designation of the information or data as required by the organizations, even though some of the information would not be relevant in the completion of the transaction online.

This paper also categorized personal information disclosure into three major novel areas, (1) willful disclosure, (2) technology assisted disclosure, and (3) obligatory passage point induced disclosure' and it classified personal information as relevant or irrelevant. Although willful and technology assisted personal information disclosures are well documents in pure and applied researches, this study is part of the early work on the obligatory passage point induced disclosure. Hence, it presents an opportunity for future research.

Therefore, with the obligatory passage point induced personal information disclosure, the risk to online users' personal information is high, and users would have less not more control of their personal information. This means that the promise of information privacy is currently implausible, farfetched, and illusory.

REFERENCES

Alvarez, M., Bradley, N., Bryan, D., Craig, S., Kessem, L., Kravitz, J., . . . Usher, M. (2018). IBM X-Force threat intelligence index 2018: Notable security events of 2017 and a look ahead. *Microstrat*. Retrieved from https://microstrat.com/sites/default/files/security-ibm-security-solutions-wg-research-report-77014377usen-20180329.pdf

Awad, N. F., & Krishnan, M. (2006). The personalization privacy paradox: An empirical evaluation of information transparency and the willingness to be profiled online for personalization. *Management Information Systems Quarterly*, *30*(1), 13–28. doi:10.2307/25148715

Backhouse, J., Hsu, C. W., & Silva, L. (2006). Circuits of power in creating de jure standards: Shaping an international information systems security standard. *Management Information Systems Quarterly*, *30*(3), 413–438. doi:10.2307/25148767

Bekavac, I., & Pranicevic, D. G. (2015). Web analytics tools and web metrics tools: An overview and comparative analysis. *Croatian Operational Research Review*, *6*(2), 373–386. doi:10.17535/crorr.2015.0029

Bélanger, F., & Crossler, R. E. (2011). Privacy in the digital age: A review of information privacy research in information systems. *Management Information Systems Quarterly*, *35*(4), 1017–A1036. doi:10.2307/41409971

Callon, M. (1986). Some elements of a sociology of translation: Domestication of the scallops and the fishermen of St. Brieuc Bay. *Sociological Review. Mongraph*, *32*(1 Suppl.), 196–233. doi:10.1111/j.1467-954X.1984.tb00113.x

D'Arcy, J., Hovav, A., & Galletta, D. (2009). User awareness of security countermeasures and its impact on information systems misuse: A deterrence approach. *Information Systems Research*, *20*(1), 79–98. doi:10.1287/isre.1070.0160

DA PAM 700-60. (2008). Department of the Army sets, kits, outfits, and tools. Retrieved from https://armypubs.army.mil/epubs/DR_pubs/DR_a/pdf/web/p700_60.pdf

Dictionary, B. (2017). Form, fit, and function (F3). Retrieved from http://www.businessdictionary.com/definition/Form-Fit-and-Function-F3.html?utm_campaign=elearningindustry.com&utm_source=%2Flearning-design-form-fit-function-fff-applicable-elearning-industry&utm_medium=link

Dinev, T., & Hart, P. (2006). An extended privacy calculus model for e-commerce transactions. *Information Systems Research*, *17*(1), 61–80. doi:10.1287/isre.1060.0080

Dinev, T., Xu, H., Smith, J. H., & Hart, P. (2013). Information privacy and correlates: An empirical attempt to bridge and distinguish privacy-related concepts. *European Journal of Information Systems*, *22*(3), 295–316. doi:10.1057/ejis.2012.23

European Union (EU) Regulation. (2016). *Regulation EU 2016/679 of the European Parliament and of the Council*. Retrieved from https://publications.europa.eu/en/publication-detail/-/publication/3e485e15-11bd-11e6-ba9a-01aa75ed71a1/language-en

Fitz-enz, J. (2009). Predicting people: From metrics to analytics. *Employment Relations Today*, *36*(3), 1–11. doi:10.1002/ert.20255

George, M. L., Rowlands, D., Price, M., & Maxey, J. (2005). *The lean six sigma pocket toolbook: A quick references guide to nearly 100 tools for improving process quality, speed, and complexity*. New York, NY: McGraw-Hill.

Goldberg, R. (2016). Lack of trust in internet privacy and security may deter economic and other online activities. *NTIA*. Retrieved from https://www.ntia.doc.gov/blog/2016/lack-trust-internet-privacy-and-security-may-deter-economic-and-other-online-activities

Greene, K., Derlega, V. J., & Mathews, A. (2006). Self-disclosure in personal relationships. In The Cambridge Handbook of Personal Relationships (pp. 409-427).

Gunasekaran, A., Marri, H., McGaughey, R., & Nebhwani, M. (2002). E-commerce and its impact on operations management. *International Journal of Production Economics*, *75*(1), 185–197. doi:10.1016/S0925-5273(01)00191-8

Hiller, E. (2014). Form, fit, and function: A framework for your Bill of Material. *Engineering*. Retrieved from http://www.engineering.com/DesignerEdge/DesignerEdgeArticles/ArticleID/7004/Form-Fit-and-Function-A-Framework-for-your-Bill-of-Material.aspx

Hong, W., & Thong, L. (2013). Internet privacy concerns: An integrated conceptualization and four empirical studies. *Management Information Systems Quarterly*, *37*(1), 275–298. doi:10.25300/MISQ/2013/37.1.12

Huang, M.-J., & Lee, T.-L. (2008). An integrated software processor with autofilling out web forms. *Paper presented at the 13th Asia-Pacific Computer Systems Architecture Conference ACSAC 2008*.

Keith, M. J., Thompson, S. C., Hale, J., Lowry, P. B., & Greer, C. (2013). Information disclosure on mobile devices: Re-examining privacy calculus with actual user behavior. *International Journal of Human-Computer Studies*, *71*(12), 1163–1173. doi:10.1016/j.ijhcs.2013.08.016

Koike, E., & Nishizaki, S.-Y. (2013). Software analysis of internet bots using a model checker. *Paper presented at the 2013 International Conference on Information Science and Cloud Computing Companion (ISCC-C)*. 10.1109/ISCC-C.2013.124

Kumaraguru, P., & Cranor L. F. (2005). Privacy indexes: A survey of Westin's studies [Technical Report]. Carnegie Mellon University.

Latour, B. (1990). Technology is society made durable. *The Sociological Review*, *38*(S1), 103-131. doi:10.1111/j.1467-954X.1990.tb03350.x

Laufer, R. S., & Wolfe, M. (1977). Privacy as a concept and a social issue: A multidimensional developmental theory. *The Journal of Social Issues*, *33*(3), 22–42. doi:10.1111/j.1540-4560.1977.tb01880.x

Malhotra, N. K., Kim, S. S., & Agarwal, J. (2004). Internet users' information privacy concerns (IUIPC): The construct, the scale, and a causal model. *Information Systems Research*, *15*(4), 336–355. doi:10.1287/isre.1040.0032

Moghaddam, M., & Studer, C. (1998). *Illusion of control: Striving for control in our personal and professional lives*. Westport, CT: Praeger.

Moothersbaugh, D. L., Foxx, W. K., Beatty, S. E., & Wang, S. (2012). Disclosure antecedents in an online service context: The role of sensitivity of information. *Journal of Service Research*, *15*(1), 76–98. doi:10.1177/1094670511424924

Norberg, P. A., Horne, D. R., & Horne, D. A. (2007). The privacy paradox: Personal information disclosure intentions versus behaviors. *The Journal of Consumer Affairs*, *41*(1), 100–126. doi:10.1111/j.1745-6606.2006.00070.x

Offor, P. I. (2016). *Examining consumers' selective information privacy disclosure behaviors in an organization's secure e-commerce systems*. Nova Southeastern University, Ann Arbor. Retrieved from https://nsuworks.nova.edu/gscis_etd/981/

Pedersen, D. M. (1997). Psychological functions of privacy. *Journal of Environmental Psychology*, *17*(2), 147–156. doi:10.1006/jevp.1997.0049

Ponemon Institute. (2017). *2017 cost of data breach study*. Retrieved from https://info.resilientsystems.com/hubfs/IBM_Resilient_Branded_Content/White_Papers/2017_Global_CODB_Report_Final.pdf

Risk Based Security. (2018). *Data breach quickview report: Q1 2018 data breach trends*. Retrieved from https://pages.riskbasedsecurity.com/2018-Q1-breach-quickview-report

Smith, H. J., Milberg, S. J., & Burke, S. J. (1996). Information privacy: Measuring individuals' concerns about organizational practices. *Management Information Systems Quarterly*, *20*(2), 167–196. doi:10.2307/249477

Son, J.-Y., & Kim, S. S. (2008). Internet users' information privacy-protective responses: A taxonomy and a nomological model. *Management Information Systems Quarterly*, *32*(3), 503–529. doi:10.2307/25148854

Straub, D., Boudreau, M.-C., & Gefen, D. (2004). Validation guidelines for IS positivist research. *Communications of the Association for Information Systems*, *13*(24), 380–427.

Systemes, D. (2012). *Configuration: Enovia engineering configuration central*. Retrieved from https://www.3ds.com/uploads/tx_3dsportfolio/2012-05-24-enovia-ecc.pdf

Taiji, Z. (2015). How can I tell if a website is secure? Look for these 5 signs. *Sitelock*. Retrieved from https://blog.sitelock.com/2015/02/how-can-i-tell-if-a-website-is-secure-look-for-these-5-signs/

Tsai, J. Y., Egelman, S., Cranor, L., & Acquisti, A. (2011). The effect of online privacy information on purchasing behavior: An experimental study. *Information Systems Research, 22*(2), 254–268. doi:10.1287/isre.1090.0260

U.S. Department of Labor Statistics. (2015). *Monthly labor review: CES employment recovers in 2014*. Retrieved from https://www.bls.gov/opub/mlr/2015/article/ces-employment-recove rs-in-2014-3.htm

U.S. Government Accounting Office—GAO. (2013). *Information resellers: Consumer privacy framework needs to reflect changes in technology and the marketplace*. Retrieved from http://www.gao.gov/products/GAO-14-251T

Vogt, W. P., & Johnson, R. B. (2016). *Dictionary of statistics and methodology: A nontechnical guide for the social sciences* (5th ed.). Los Angeles, CA: Sage.

Waisberg, D., & Kaushik, A. (2009). Web analytics 2.0: Empowering customer centricity, *SEMJ. Org, 2*(1), 1–7.

Walker, M. (2012). Marital status is irrelevant. *Huffington Post*. Retrieved from http://www.huffingtonpost.com/mandy-walker/marital-status-is-irrevel_b_1346235.html

Warren, S. D., & Brandeis, L. D. (1890). The right to privacy. *Harvard Law Review, 4*(5), 193–220. doi:10.2307/1321160

Westin, A. (1970). *Privacy and freedom*. New York: Atheneum.

ENDNOTE

[1]   Consider a tiny innovation commonly found in European hotels: attaching large cumbersome weights to room keys in order to remind customers that they should leave their keys at the front desk every time they leave the hotel… an imperative statement inscribed on a sign - 'Please leave your room key at the front desk before you go out' - appears to be not enough to make customers behave according to the speakers wishes. Our fickle customers seemingly have other concerns, and room keys disappear into thin air. But if the innovator, called to the rescue, displaces the inscription by introducing a large metal weight, the hotel manager no longer has to rely on his customers' sense of moral obligation. Customers suddenly become only too happy to rid themselves of this annoying object which makes their pockets bulge and weigh down their handbags. Where the sign, the inscription, the imperative, discipline, or moral obligational failed, the hotel manager, the innovator and the metal weight succeeded (Latour, 1990, p. 104).

*This research was previously published in the International Journal of Smart Education and Urban Society (IJSEUS), 9(4);
edited by Miltiadis D. Lytras and Linda Daniela, pages 37-52, copyright year 2018 by IGI Publishing (an imprint of IGI Global).*

Chapter 75
Trust, Privacy, Issues in Cloud–Based Healthcare Services

Shweta Kaushik
JIIT Noida, India

Charu Gandhi
JIIT Noida, India

ABSTRACT

In recent era individuals and organizations are migrating towards the cloud computing services to store and retrieve the data or services. However, they have less confidence on cloud as all the task are handled by the service provider without any involvement of the data owner. Cloud system provides features to the owner, to store their data on some remote locations and allow only authorized users to access the data according to the role, access capability or attribute they possess. Storing the personal health records on cloud server (third party) is a promising model for healthcare services to exchange information with the help of cloud provider. In this chapter, we highlight the various security issues and concerns such as trust, privacy and access control in cloud based healthcare system that needs to be known while storing the patient's information over a cloud system.

INTRODUCTION

Utilization of most recent technology such as cloud computing in healthcare services provides a new direction for healthcare organizations to enhance the quality of service delivery, reduce the cost and make it efficient to be used by users belongs to different category. Popularity of healthcare services and cloud computing among users also make an increase in the demand of cloud based healthcare services. In addition, diseases are becoming more complex and new advancements in technology and research have facilitated the emergence of new and more effective diagnoses and treatment techniques (Singh, 2008). In the last few years, healthcare services have achieved many improvements from individual solutions to the organization level solution, and from a single individual system, which provides local and limited resolution to more interconnected ones, which provides incorporated and broad resolution for a particular diagnosis problem. Complexity of cloud based healthcare services also improve from

DOI: 10.4018/978-1-5225-8176-5.ch075

Copyright © 2019, IGI Global. Copying or distributing in print or electronic forms without written permission of IGI Global is prohibited.

passive and reactive system to active and interconnected systems, which mainly focuses on the quality of the system. Use of cloud in healthcare services also introduces the use of advance technology such as improved database system to provide a reliable solution. Cloud computing will also reduce the burden of healthcare services by introduction of service provider who is completely responsible for managing the complex data of different healthcare services and handling all the users queries which reduce the maintenance and operational cost of such a large system, as the same system is required by multiple healthcare organization so the service provider needs to setup one system which can be used by multiple organizations and so the cost can be divided among the organizations. Use of cloud computing also opened a new opportunity window for healthcare services to use and share their data with organizations and users such as researchers, doctors, hospitals, organizations like WHO etc. that will be helpful for introduction of new technique or improve the quality of existing techniques of any healthcare services. But this sharing of patient's data will not come alone, it also introduce the new security challenges that needs to be handled. Strict rules and regulations while sharing of patient's data is necessary to maintain its privacy such as who is going to use the data, what amount of critical information accessed by a particular user etc. Dealing with security and privacy of any confidential data which is shared over the network, introduces several threats such as exposure of patient's sensitive data, selling of the secret information of patient by a service provider to other service provider(s). Once an individual or organization stores the healthcare information over the cloud system they do not have any physical possession on it and cannot figure out that which information is sold or distributed to other users and what are the various securities needs to be concerned by that particular service provider. In this chapter, we understand the various privacy and security issues come into picture when integrate cloud computing with healthcare services and how to maintain trust between different communicating parties to develop an efficient and sound system. In addition, we also discuss the benefits and limitations of cloud based healthcare services with strategic recommendation for the adoption of cloud computing in healthcare services.

CLOUD BASED HEALTHCARE SERVICES CHALLENGES/ ISSUES

Although the cloud based healthcare service provide several benefits to various users such as healthcare industry, researchers, medical clinics and doctors, but also come with various challenges of cloud computing and e-healthcare services. These challenges require more attention as the system is storing, transferring and processing the very confidential and sensitive data of different patients. It increases the challenges for data storage and its maintenance because if the system is not secure than no user will store or retrieve the data. Various challenges specific to a cloud based health care system are broadly divided into two categories as (i) Technical (Momtahan, 2007) and (ii) Non- technical (Momtahan, 2007) challenges as shown in Figure 1, which are further summarized below as:

1. **Technical Challenges:** Introduction of new technique in existing technique will never come alone. It also comes with new challenges for its proper adoption and utilization in the existing techniques. Similarly, integration of cloud and healthcare services also come with new challenges, to be solved before adoption of cloud by any individual or organization. Some of the technical challenges as shown in Figure 1, in cloud based healthcare services are summarized as:
    a. **Availability:** Data and service availability is a crucial requirement for every healthcare service provider as without any data/service availability there is nothing to operate. Cloud based

healthcare service providers must ensure that data/ service required by the users is available for 24 x 7 without any interruption or degradation in service performance. Since, cloud data is stored at the remote server which may be lost due to software failure, hardware failure, network failure etc, it is necessary to take the data backup and replicate it at multiple locations. This ensures the continuity of services as per the user's requirements even after the loss of data. In addition to this, hardware and software upgrade, reconfiguration and installation should also not interrupt the healthcare services.

b. **Data Reliability:** In cloud based system, data will come from various remote locations which increase the chances of corrupt and incorrect data. To handle this problem, it is provider's responsibility to provide consistent and error-free data constantly without any disturbance due to hardware and software failure. Service provider always need to make sure that data replicated at different locations is consistent and follows the ACID (Atomicity, Consistency, Integrity, and Durability) property during any transaction.

c. **Data Management:** In cloud based healthcare services huge amount of patient's information is stored at server site which may include some confidential data as well. There is need for secure data storage and its maintenance against any security fault occurs in public cloud. Delivery and processing of confidential data also required some security concerns for its efficient and scalable delivery to the user according to the security measure defined.

d. **Scalability:** Cloud stores the medical data for millions of patient at different healthcare service providers which requires the scalability of cloud to handle increasing data in a skilled manner. In the cloud based system, this can be increased by increasing the capability of various service nodes such as network connections; efficient operational and management storage units. Scalability requires dynamic configuration and reconfiguration as well as an automatic resizing of used virtualized hardware resources (Vaquero, 2008).

e. **Interoperability:** Cloud based healthcare services are provided not from a single service provider instead different service providers are responsible for handling different types of data of a single patient. For example, one service provider may store highly resolution medical images of a patient while other one is responsible for storing its personal information, lab reports, prescription, and medical history. There is a requirement for interoperability which requires defining some open source API/ protocol or agreed framework between different service providers to achieve integrity and presence of different servers at the same time. A good interpolation system also facilitates an efficient migration between different service providers to access the required data. One of the prominent solutions for this is to utilize the concept of Service-oriented Architecture (SOA) (Al-Jaroodi, 2012) for cloud based healthcare services. SOA allows the services to be easily accessible and available as per users need using standardized protocol without considering the infrastructure, implementation, development or deployment model.

f. **Security:** Since, in cloud based healthcare services, the data is stored and retrieved from remote location without any physical access of the data owner and provided by number of service provider, requires the security concern regarding its storage, access control, integrity, confidentiality etc. It is a prime feature to provide secure and adequate access control and authentication management while transferring the data from service provider to users. In addition to this, there is also a requirement to store the data in encrypted format at the service provider's end to protect it from any malicious activity and vulnerability by any adversary or service provider to get the exact data. There are several mechanisms to impose high security, but requires high computation complexity and cost which make them inefficient for cloud based system.

2. **Non-Technical Challenges:** Apart from the technical challenges there are some non-technical challenges come in picture with the adoption of cloud in healthcare services which requires high concerns for its proper utilization and adaption by individual and organization. The various non-technical challenges as shown in Figure 1 are summarized as:

   a. **Organizational Change:** Use of cloud in healthcare services brings many important changes in the field of research, organization boundaries, medical treatments and business processes. Cloud based healthcare services introduce new workflow of business process as all the documentation and medical records are stored, retrieved, and processed at the cloud. It requires the businesses and organizations to be updated as per the cloud storage and deliverance for its confidential data storage and accessibility according to defined security policies without any physical introduction of owner for its maintainability.

   b. **Law & Standards:** There is no adequate definition for the law and standards to be followed for the cloud based healthcare services for any technical, clinical or business practices. It will bring new security requirements such as interoperability, data transmission, policies etc. Currently, some guidelines are defined for healthcare system which can be utilized by the cloud system to provide e-healthcare services. For example, the Systematized Nomenclature of Medicine (SNOMED) drafts a new layout for medicines for the purpose of storing and/ or retrieving records of any medical concern (Cote, 1986). Another example is World Health Organization (WHO) issued the International Classification of Diseases tenth revision (ICD-10) which specify the special coding for complaints, diseases, external reason for injury and sign of abnormal findings`.

Figure 1. Cloud based healthcare service issues

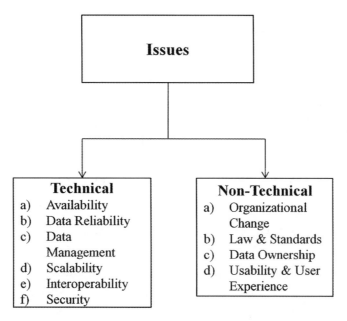

c. **Data Ownership:** There are no proper guidelines define for ownership of data in healthcare systems. As data of any patient can be claimed by patient itself, doctor who treat the patient and hospital or clinic which provide the medical treatment for that particular patient. This challenge needs to be highly concern to draw proper guidelines and policies when storing any patient record over cloud based services.

d. **Usability & End Users Experiences:** This challenge concerns for the data usage, access and storage at the cloud based healthcare services by the various users. There are different type of users exists who try to access their required data from the cloud, which requires the proper authentication and access control pre-implementation to provide the data to the users according to their usability and experiences.

LIMITATION FOR CLOUD BASED HEALTHCARE SERVICES

- **Implementation and Maintenance Cost:** Integration of healthcare services with cloud computing requires a lot of cost for its implementation and maintenance especially in small and medium sized organizations. The investment in hardware, software and technical infrastructure with healthcare services implementation is a time consuming process as it requires to maintain lots of data about many patients, doctors etc. In addition to this a well-qualified and dedicated team with proper funding is required for a regular day-to-day data management and maintenance activities.

- **Fragmentation and Insufficient Exchange:** In most healthcare systems separate administrative systems exist for the different departments of healthcare service provider. It stores the patient data in dispersed manner where certain part of information is associated with only restricted department, some associated with clinical purpose and some of the information available publically. All departments have their own way to store the data. This dispersal of patient data at several locations with their different storage brings a new challenge to combine the complete information about a particular patient and share it at different cloud based healthcare service providers.

- **Lack of Regulation:** There are no well-defined and established laws for the patient record communication between two communicating parties for its privacy maintenance. There is a high requirement to define the various rules and regulation for sharing of patient's personal health records at different level of user access, organizations and countries to maintain the security and privacy and protect the patient personal health record from any malicious activity.

- **Lack of Cloud Deployment Model:** There are no well-defined standards for cloud based healthcare service provider to build an effective and efficient system. It consists of data types for data storage, in which form data is stored, its usage, security protocols for its data access and storage, how to obtain data and at which time frequency a new data will be capture. Apart from these challenges a biggest challenge is to develop and maintain a multidimensional system.

TRUST IN CLOUD BASED HEALTHCARE SERVICES

Trust means a faith, confidence of doing a job as expected without introducing any vulnerability while performing any task. 'An entity A is considered to trust another entity B when entity A believes that entity B will behave exactly as expected and required'' (ITU, 2009). Trust can incorporate security by performing validity of its performance, loyalty, encoding data and user-friendliness to attract other towards it. In cloud based healthcare services, patient's data is stored at cloud provider and user will get the required data from cloud provider also. There is a need arise for a mutual trust between various communicating parties to ensure that data stored and retrieved from cloud is intact without any malicious activity done during data transformation. Data owner requires that the service provider should be trustworthy to store its confidential data without any exposure to unauthorized user and other service providers. On the other hand, users who will retrieve its data from the service provider also require that provider is trustworthy, who deliver the exact correct data without any loss of integrity and damage of data. Thus, trust plays a vital role in cloud based healthcare services as it stores the patient's sensitive data which is delivered to other users such as hospitals, researchers, medical clinics, pharmacies etc. in intact form. If there is no trust maintain between different communicating parties than patient will not store it's confidential and essential data for other users, over the cloud based healthcare services provider. One of the prominent solutions for trust maintenance between different communicating parties is Service Level Agreement (SLA) signed between them and another one is the inclusion of Trusted Third Party (TTP). This TTP is responsible for auditing the data stored at service provider either periodically or dynamically and report to data owner if any misbehavior found. Thus, the entire users and data owner relying on TTP for secure and efficient transactions as the malicious activities can be caught by TTP.

TRUST MECHANISMS IN CLOUD HEALTHCARE SERVICES

Broadly, trust can be classified based on trustor's anticipation as (Huang, 2013): 1) Trust in performance- is what the trustee performs and 2) Trust in belief - is what the trustee believes. Based upon these, various trust mechanisms are defined for defining the trust between different communicating parties, which are summarized as shown in Figure 2.

Figure 2. Trust mechanisms

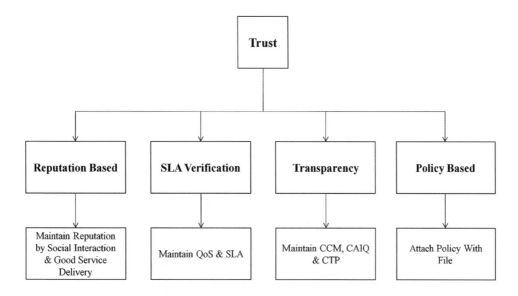

Reputation Based Trust

Reputation and trust are two different things but are related. Knowing the reputation of an entity, other entities can trust it but, having trust on an entity will not play any role to its reputation. Reputation based trust mechanism is broadly used in the area of P2P network and e-commerce. Reputation of any web service can be calculated by its collective analysis of feedback or opinions taken from different users on the basis of different aspect of service performance. The reputation of any cloud healthcare service or service provider will undoubtedly impact the choice of user for that particular service or service provider. Therefore, cloud based healthcare service provider needs to construct and maintain higher reputation. Usually, any web service which has high reputation is highly trusted by the most users. In cloud based healthcare services user first make a comparison of various service provider according to its reputation and then store and retrieve confidential data only on/from the service provider which has high rating given by the other entities without requiring any additional knowledge. At the initial stage, there is belief but afterward based on the performance of service delivered trust is maintain.

SLA Verification Based Trust

SLA (Service Level Agreement) is a legal contract signed between the different communicating parties in cloud based system. User (generally patient) stores the highly sensitive data on cloud, only if there is a proper contract signed for security and QoS maintenance assurance. On the other hand, different users (doctors, researchers, medical clinic, pharmacy etc.) will retrieve the data from service provider after establishing an initial trust and verifying the agreement signed between users and service provider regularly. Many SLA based trust models have been proposed (Haq, 2013,Pawar, 2012). Trust with verification is a best option for the fine relationship between the different communicating parties. Major issue with SLA is that user focuses only on visible components (such as GUI) of service provider while invisible components such as security and privacy issues are generally missed. Also user can not monitor QoS and SLA verification at their end because of less capability and require lots of computation and time requirements. Due to this a need for TTP arises to handle these entire tasks for data owner and user.

Transparency Based Trust

Transparency in the service user by the user creates a high trust and belief between the various parties for accessing the correct service without any discrepancy. To sustain and enhance the transparency of service provided by the service provider to the users Cloud Security Alliance (CSA) introduces the "Security, Trust and Assurance Registry (STAR)" program (CSA 2011). This program allows the service providers to circulate their self-impression of security control measures, in either "Cloud Control Matrix (CCM)" or "Consensus Assessments Initiatives Questionnaire (CAIQ)" form. Here, CCM is a cloud model which outlines the alignment of service provider with CSA security guide. CAIQ contains several questions which cloud users or auditor may ask to verify the transparency of service. Apart from this CSA also adopts Cloud Trust Protocol (CTP). This is a request-response mechanism used by the users for the confirmation of cloud provider transparency. The main aim of CTP with transparency is to generate an evidence- based assurance to check that everything is done in the same way as required without any vulnerability. Therefore, in cloud based healthcare services, data owner or user first check the transparency of the services provided by the service provider using one of the mechanisms i.e. CCM, CAIQ or CTP to establish trust and on the basis of that store or retrieve data.

Policy Based Trust

In earlier approaches a formal mechanism was defined for trust between different communicating parties in cloud system. In addition to this, Public Key Infrastructure (PKI) is also widely used to maintain trust by employing the digital signatures, key/ attribute certification and validation. To ensure that data retrieved / stored from/on service provider's end is intact a policy is defined which contains the access criteria associated with the data and its corresponding key / attribute. Only the user who has the valid set of key/attribute can access the data. Similarly, in cloud based healthcare services only the user who meets certain aspect or policy as mentioned by the owner can only store the data. To simplify this, consider the example as shown in figure 3. Suppose a doctor associated with hospital A retrieve some data from healthcare service provider supposedly after satisfying the policy P1="(profession=doctor)^(specialty = cancer treatment)^(organization = hospital A)", which is signed by a patient using his private key K_p and also attach a certificate with some policy assigned to the data. Since doctor has all the attributes required to access the data, he can only decrypt the received data using patient's public key and attribute the doctor possess and verify the integrity of data using the digital signature.

Attribute Based Trust

Like, policy based trust approach attribute based trust is also an informal approach for establishing the trust between different communicating parties. Here, only the users who have required set of attributes with satisfying values can retrieve the data. In general form, we can formalize the attribute based trust

Figure 3. Attribute hierarchy for data access

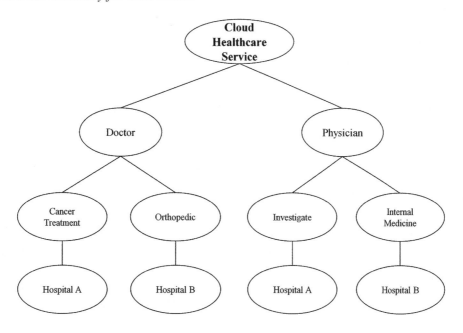

as follows: believe(A, attr$_1$(x,v$_1$)) &....&(believe(A,att$_n$(x,v$_n$)) = trust(A,x,c) [Huang, 2013], which states that, if a user A believes subjects s has attribute att$_1$,att$_2$...att$_n$ with values v$_1$,v$_2$........v$_n$ respectively. Than A can trust x performance and or data created/ delivered under specific situation c. Different cloud data owner may have their own different trust policies which involve different attributes for trust building. A common model sustains different attribute based trust using different policies for different users. The interrelation between policies based and attributes based relation is that, belief of a user to confirm a policy has a set of attribute with specified values for that particular policy.

As seen in Figure 4, trust of any entity in a cloud based system depends on several resources and other entities. A data owner can trust cloud provider for secure data storage using SLA based trust. A data owner can trust user by providing policy for trust. A data owner can trust auditor for its correct auditing by transparency based trust mechanism. Similarly, a user can trust cloud provider and cloud broker for correct delivery of required data/ service according to its reputation and SLA signed between them. Cloud broker, plays an important role in cloud system as the cloud broker is responsible for the conciliation between cloud users and service providers for the use of different services. The judgment of trust of various cloud entities depends on several attributes, as described in (Huang, 2013), which are shown in Figure 5.

Figure 4. Trust relation chain in healthcare services

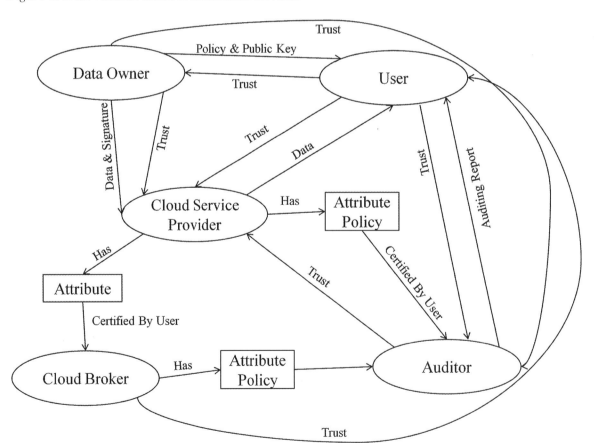

Figure 5. Judgment of cloud entities

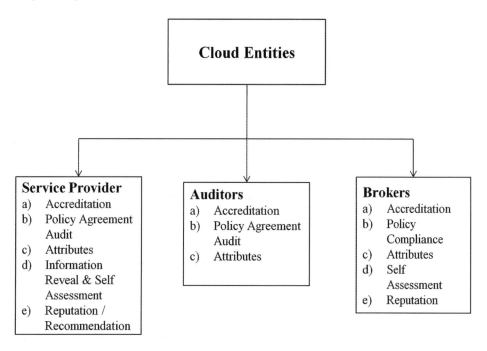

SECURITY AND PRIVACY REQUIREMENTS IN CLOUD BASED HEALTHCARE SERVICES

Privacy

Privacy means to keep the data secret and hide from unauthorized access. Privacy of data can be obtained by encoding, encryption, translations of data, which transforms the confidential data into some other form. It generally includes protection of data from any malicious activity by the adversary. In cloud based healthcare service, patient's information is stored which may include some sensitive information also. Users can access the data according to defined role, access criteria or attribute assigned to them. Data owner requires that service provider will deliver its data according to the access criteria defined by him in order to protect the data from unauthorized access. Since data owner can not completely trust service provider for its data privacy so he can encrypt the data before outsource.

Security Issues

Apart from privacy and trust maintenance between different parties there are another security issues need to be considered i.e. authorization and access control, integrity, non- repudiation, network security, confidentiality. To provide the authorization and access control data owner can decide one of three mechanisms i.e., role based access control, user based access control or attribute based access control to allow the users to get required data. Owner also needs to notify service provider about access control for verification purpose before transferring the data to users according to their request. To prove that data integrity is maintained without any vulnerabilities owner can encrypt the data with digital signature.

Only the authorized users have verification key to check the integrity of received data from the service provider to ensure that retrieved data is intact. As the data owner shares the verification key with user only. Some of the security requirements with their description and possible solutions are shown below in Table 1. In addition to this, security issues in cloud based system also encompasses the threats and risks, as summarized below, which may come because of external or internal users. Adoption of healthcare services in cloud based system requires having knowledge of these security risks and threats and a defined way to handle these.

Cloud Attacks

In a cloud system attacks can be divided into four types i.e. random, weak, strong and sustain attack. Each of these attacks depends on whether the attack is successfully activated and not on the threats they may introduce.

- **Random Attack:** In this attack, attacker will use simple tools and techniques to find any vulnerable work by scanning the internet randomly. Their main concern here is to find valuable information by deploying some tools/ technique and without any authentication.
- **Weak Attack:** In this attack, the target is service provider, to breach its security wall. These types of attackers are semi-skilled but more advanced and try to get the confidential information from the service provider with the help of customize tools.
- **Strong Attack:** In this attack, attackers are highly skilled with well-financed condition. Their target is a particular user or application in cloud which will be entirely exploit by them. Generally, this group is specialized to target any specific service.

Table 1. Security requirements

Security Requirement	Description With Solutions
Authentication and access control	To provide the patient's data to authorized users according to their access criteria, there is a need of identification system. This system will be able to differentiate between the authorized and unauthorized users and allow only authorized users to access the required data according to their access criteria such as role, capability, identification etc. defined by the owner for its data accessibility.
Confidentiality & Privacy	To guarantee the confidentiality and privacy the data needs to be encrypted first and digitally signed by data owner before transfer over cloud system. Only the authorized user having the decryption key can decrypt it to original data and use the verification key to check its consistency. Service provider is unaware of this decryption key and verification key.
Integrity	Data owner need to sign its data and only the authorized users has its verification key to check whether they got the exact or malicious data. It will help to preserve the consistency and accuracy of delivered data.
Auditing	It helps to maintain the interoperability feature in cloud based system. The malicious activity is monitored by auditor and auditing reports are sent to owner to alert him. Owner takes necessary action as required. Auditing can be done by the data owner itself or he can hire a trusted third party for this task.
Trust	This is required to belief that data is stored at right place and also retrieved correctly without introducing any vulnerability. It can be achieved by a contract signed between the different communicating parties such as service level agreement.
Non-repudiation	This is required to ensure that communicating party will not deny from accessing, storing or receiving the data. This can be implementing by using a timestamp, encryption or digital signature between the different communications done between different parties.

- **Substantial Attack:** In this attack, attackers are highly advanced and motivated to spoil any target service or organization even without any detection of targeted organization or investigative organizations who are specialized in internet security. They possess a very good knowledge of the resources and great intelligence to respond upon detection of their attacks.

Cloud Risks

In cloud, with each delivery model risks are associated which depends on several factors such as security requirements, development model, information confidentiality and resource availability. In general, various security risks in cloud without any concern for delivery model are summarized in Table 2.

Since last few years' research on cloud based healthcare service is growing fast and many researchers have presented their different framework which try to handle all the security issues as stated above. The security in healthcare services involves lot of challenges, as described earlier, that need to be addressed while delivering the patient confidential and sensitive data over cloud. It is like a multipart maze which requires lot of attention and hurdles to be solved before reaching to an optimal solution. The comparative analysis for the work of various researchers according to their approach, advantages and disadvantages is summarized in Table 3.

BENEFIT OF CLOUD BASED HEALTHCARE SERVICE

With the involvement of cloud computing in healthcare services many problems of patients, researchers, medical clinic, pharmacy and doctors can be resolved. As doctor can get its patient details from anywhere at any time and patient can get sufficient treatment without any delay. Researchers can get data easily

Table 2. Security risks

Risks	Description	Approach
Privileged user access	Cloud providers have all the data of owner, which may include sensitive information and has complete access to this. Provider is not trusted party, therefore, confidentiality and access control for privileged user access is required to secure the data from any malicious activity.	Encryption before outsource the data and enforce laws and regulations.
Data location and segregation	Owner of the data does not have information regarding its data storage. They have only contractual or regulatory obligation which increase the risk concern for its data leakage to other user or organization without its knowledge.	Virtualization and SLA management.
Data disposal	Deletion and disposal of owner data is a risk, especially where resources are dynamically issued to users based on their access criteria. The risk of data not being deleted from data stores, data replication storage and physical media as required may increase the risk within the cloud.	Ensure ACID property during transmission and use of media sanitization techniques as per agreement between owner and provider.
Regulatory compliance	Owner stores its confidential data over cloud which requires to be protected from unauthorized access of users and service providers. Owner requires maintaining the integrity of data by attaching a certification with this.	Auditing and certification
Assuring cloud security	User gets the data from service provider which is not trusted. Thus, there is a security requirement for data verification and auditing to confirm the correct delivery of data from provider.	Auditing and SLA management

Table 3. Comparative study of cloud based healthcare system

Scheme	Objective/Purpose	Approach/Technique	Advantages	Disadvantages
Ambulatory electrocardiographic monitoring in clinical and domestic environments (Saldarriaga, 2013)	An android and iOS based mobile application is developed for ambulatory electrocardiographic monitoring. It is utilized by the medical personnel to use their smart phones to guide diagnose procedures efficiently and manage the daily activities interconnecting several zones.	To get the ECG information of a patient kardia Board is utilized and for transmission Bluetooth 4.0 interface OS smart phones are utilized. Android and Apple iOS bases phones are used.	Patients can upload and view their ECG data as per requirements. Doctors are able to receive ECG waveform data about any patient from their smart phones compare it with previous ECGs and provide the diagnosis to patient's problems.	This application can be used only on Android based or apple iOS smart phones.
Securing Personal Health Records in Cloud Computing: Patient-centric and Fine-grained Data Access Control in Multi-owner Settings (Li, 2010)	Securing the personal health records of multiple owners.	Patient-centric and Fine-grained data access control to secure the health record of patients in cloud computing.	Provide the features as user revocation, break-glass access and fine grained data accessibility policies.	It increases the computation time for data owner and also there is a risk of patient's private data exposure by owner.
Managing Wearable Sensor Data through Cloud Computing (Doukas, 2011).	A wearable – textile platform is developed which collects the patient's heartbeat and motion data and send this detail to cloud system and store. This cloud system is responsible for monitoring, processing and send the alert for health to patients.	Use the Google cloud service for data storage and processing and HTTP/HTTPS protocol for data exchange. Google Chart for data visualization. Java for developing cloud application. Bluetooth interface to send data to Android Smartphone. Arduino board as a wearable part	This developed platform helps the doctors to monitor their patient's health and patients to get Health alert.	Did not consider patient's data privacy and use of Bluetooth interface, which is easy to handle and control by adversary.
Achieving secure, scalable and fine-grained data access control in cloud computing (Yu, 2010)	Secure personal health records of patient's, reduce the computation time for data owner for user administration and key distribution to various users.	Data owner the cloud provider to done all the computation tasks and user access control for him without disclosing data using some advanced techniques as Proxy Re-Encryption (PRE),Key-Policy Attribute- Based Encryption (KP-ABE), and lazy re-encryption.	Cloud service provider is not able to know the exact data and perform all the computation tasks for uses and owner which reduce their computation overhead and improver the scalability.	There is no mechanism is defined for emergency situations and also data access policy is limited.
Tackling cloud security issues and forensics model (Ahmed, 2010)	To ensure confidentially and privacy of electronic health records and track activities of cloud service provider for healthcare services in cloud environment.	This model supports the various mechanisms for data authentication, its access control, authorization and security against any nonvolatile information. To get any volatile information this model installs the forensic system on cloud systems.	To provide security against cyber crimes Computer Forensic Tools (CFT) provides digital evidence. Patient's medical data is kept safe from cloud service providers.	Use of CFT promises to track volatile actions; but it cannot physically stop volatile action by itself.
DACAR Platform for eHealth Services Cloud (Fan, 2011)	Develop a platform for secure services in e-Health Cloud.	Digital signature, access control, hashing, Single Point of Contact (SPoC), identity mapping, integrity check-sum, encryption and audit trial etc.	A complete secure platform which takes care of all the security aspects for a patient heath record management in cloud based system.	Comprehensive assessment in a real healthcare environment;
Privacy Engineering: Personal Health Records in Cloud Computing Environments (Kaletsch, 2011)	Whenever a referral is made a secure electronic health record (EHR) exchange is made possible.	Patient's confidential data is stored at only trusted environment such as the physicians' practices and all the data is encrypted and signed before any transmission done. This encrypted data can only be decrypted by specialist receiver.	For all documents to be transferred, suggested and provides secure encryption and signatures scheme for patient data security.	In this model no integration is defined for patient and patient-centric functions.
Co-Designing an Intelligent Doctors-Colleagues-Patients Social Network (Pirahandeh, 2012)	Develop a platform for Communication between specialists, clinics and patients.	Windows 7and 3 GHZ Core workstations and P2P Tester simulator.	Information sharing. Better Communication among doctors and patients. Better security as DCP is a private cloud system. Users can access their data using Internet, mobile phones.	No security algorithm is proposed and also no consideration for health alert system for patients.
Securing the E-Health Cloud (Lohr, 2010)	Provide secure platform for users when they will access e-Health Cloud.	Develop Trusted privacy domains (TVD) systems which are able to divide the execution environment in the end-user platform into separated domains that are isolated from each other.	Overcome limitations of security features within end user platforms; reduce security risks; Automatic management (transparent TVD establishment, key management and policy enforcement).	No scalability is defined and complex Hardware requirements

from a single place without moving everywhere and struggling for collecting the different types of data. It can reduce the time for their research work and the outcome of the research such as medicine of any disease, new solutions can be implemented in time. With electronic health record management patient can also get the prescription detail for the same type of problems easily and get the information about the various hospitals, doctors etc. to be consult from a single end without facing any problems. Collaboration solution can also be made easily with cloud system which helps in the improvement of research and medical world. Cloud based healthcare system also maintain the healthcare exchange information to deal with any serious problems during natural phenomena.

- **Better Patient Care:** Using cloud based healthcare services a doctor can acquire the complete information about its patient history and treatment previously given to him at anywhere, anytime and provide the suitable treatment accordingly.
- **Reduced Cost:** This feature is best suitable for small and medium healthcare service providers. As they can easily obtain the advanced technology and treatment for any diagnosis without investment in initial setup and operational cost. In addition to this, using cloud computing it becomes easy to get any patient medical record globally without investing any money in exchanging this information.
- **Resource Scarcity Resolved:** Use of cloud computing resolve the IT resources shortage issues. It will help the healthcare services providers to use the remote medical services to provide primary services for patient treatments. It also helps the diagnosis specialist to provide their services remotely which can be used by the user to save time and reduce the need of specialist in case of emergency.
- **Better Quality:** As the patient's data is stored on the cloud and the doctor, researcher, hospital and healthcare organization acts as a user so the data can be utilized by them to improve the facilities and increase the patient's safety. Thus provides a better quality of services to the patient.
- **Research Support:** Cloud based healthcare services stores a huge amount of data regarding many patients, diseases and diagnosis which can be globally accessible. Using this information a researcher can get the complete knowledge and can develop a new and improved version with less investment and time.
- **National Security:** The cloud based healthcare service enhances the capability to observe the increase of communicable diseases and/or other disease. So it helps in identifying growing disease, the region which is infected by the disease, the blueprint of the disease and the cause of its occurrence. The Cloud based healthcare service acts as a system that can be used to notify hospitals and organizations worldwide about any growing disease thus helps in national security.
- **Strategic Planning Support:** The cloud based healthcare service can be utilized by System architects in development, arrangement, scheduling and financial plan for healthcare services. The cloud based healthcare service can interact with each other to determine the requirement of doctors, nurse, helping staff, labs, equipment, operating rooms, patient beds, medicines etc. to optimize the existing healthcare services, setup new facilities in existing healthcare services and setup new the healthcare services.
- **Financial Operation Support:** Provides the ability to support all the financial operations between healthcare service providers and patients as cloud acts as a negotiator between them. Cloud is responsible for the entire task related to billing, approval and agreement process in between the communicating parties.

- **Facilitate Clinical Trials:** Data stored at service provider allows the researchers, pharmaceutical companies and medical institutions to get required information for the trials of new medicines. Cloud stored a huge amount of data in interconnected fashion which make it easy to get the patient's data related to specific case and try new clinical cases on them to provide a new solution.
- **Forming Registries**: The data which need to be stored and shared should follow a special registry specified for specific patient, diseases and diagnosis etc. For example a patient is targeted as either heart patient or cancer patient to store or retrieve data.

STRATEGIC APPROVAL FOR CLOUD BASED HEALTHCARE SERVICE

Use of cloud computing requires a coordinated and integrated approach. This approach is a fundamental description of how to utilize the cloud computing advantages in healthcare services by any healthcare service providers. These strategic approvals include the following tasks as stated below:

- Understand the patient's information sensitivity and its importance before moving towards cloud computing.
- Decision about which information required more security and what should be the access criteria.
- Explore different cloud models according to the information storage and find out the best one among them for workload.
- Develop a performance indicator for each strategy to determine the benefit of the strategy for any healthcare industry.
- Develop a complete patient record file and store it over the cloud system in encrypted form as cloud is not trusted. With this update the service provider about the access criteria as well.
- Users will acquire their requisite data from cloud system and also verify it to ensure its correctness.
- Scalability of data is prime concern as more patients' data can be feed into the system according to its popularity.
- Auditing of data is required to ensure the data is intact and deliver to the users as specified in access criteria without any modification or alteration.
- Portability of data is required to allow various users (patients, researchers, pharmacy and doctors) to retrieve the data and service at anywhere, anytime without any struggle.

Whenever, any health organization tries to move its services over the cloud system, it requires to make a strategic planning before actually moving towards building a new model. This planning requires determining the benefits, risks, capability of the new system and drawing a complete strategic plan for its sound implementation to make it more efficient than existing one. Many researchers have provided several guidelines and requirements that need to be considered for the strategic planning for the introduction of cloud computing in new work. Marks & Lozano (Marks, 2010) defines 9 stages for the adoption of cloud computing life cycle by users to build any cloud project. These 9 stages are proof of concept, strategy & roadmap, architecture & modeling, implementation planning, implementing the plan model, expansion, collaboration, maturity and integration of different activities.

The US Federal Health IT strategic plan (UDHHS, 2008), also introduce some strategic planning for the adoption of cloud computing which can be utilize by the government to implement a cloud based healthcare services project. This plan gives a leadership role to office of National Coordinator for Health

Information Technology, for the development and national level implementation of a healthcare system using the IT services to improve the efficiency and quality of healthcare services. This plan is mainly concern with 2 goals: population health and patient focused healthcare system with the objectives of adoption, privacy and security, interoperability and collaborative governance. Each strategy is also further associated with an objective to implement and assessed it.

Beside above guidelines, (Kuo, 2011) propose a Healthcare Cloud Computing Strategic Planning (HC2SP) model which can be used by any healthcare industry to gain the knowledge regarding the strategy, resources allocation and direction before migrate to cloud based healthcare services. This model includes the 4 stages as (see Figure 6): identification, evaluation, action and follow up.

Stage 1: Identification. In this stage first we need to analyze the current position and significance of healthcare organization's services and determine the basic objective of improvements in these systems after receiving the request of patient's. To get this root cause, analysis method can be used to find the exact problems in existing healthcare services.

The identification of correct objective with its scope is a prime concern to present an effective and efficient system to the patient (user). In addition, these teams also need to define the quality indicators for their defined services with its use and purpose. This stage is basically provides the strategic planning team with well defined problems and services required by the patients at his end.

Figure 6. HC²SP model

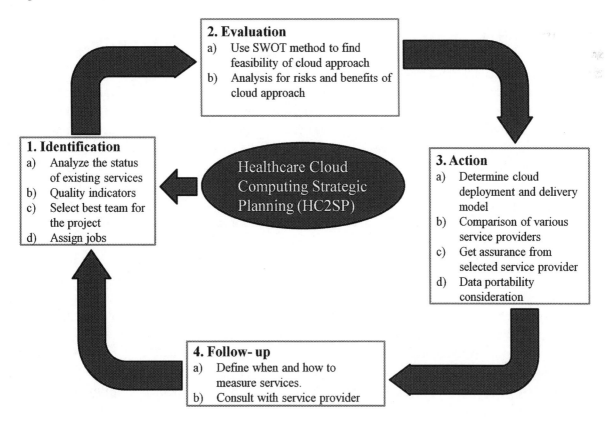

Stage 2: Evaluation. This stage deals with the evaluation of challenges and opportunities to be handle while adopting the cloud computing in healthcare services. To evaluate the risks and benefit for the adoption of cloud computing various evaluation strategies are defined in Cloud Security Alliance(Brunette, 2009), ENISA (ENISA, 2009) and NIST (Jansen, 2011)/ a patient/ user can also utilize the Strength, Weaknesses, opportunities and threats (SWOT) model to examine any cloud approach feasibility.

Stage 3: Action. After the evaluation of the new model, organization gets an idea whether it is feasible to go with the new model or not. If it is feasible than only organization moves towards the implementation step as stated below:

   ◦ Draw an idea about which type of cloud deployment and delivery model will be going to use.
   ◦ Make a comparison among various cloud provider according to their performance and reputation in the society.
   ◦ Select a best cloud provider among all after assuring the chosen one provides the security, privacy, quality of service as per the legal regulation and practices.
   ◦ Data portability, if required in future is easy to handle without any loss of data.

Stage 4: Follow- Up. After completing all the previous stages, the last task is to deploy the system and make a follow-up plan. This plan deals with measurement of the various services against specified indicators. If any discrepancy found, either from the user or provider prospective than resolve it at top priority. If the cloud service provider is not satisfying the service condition, than organization needs to either discuss the problems with service provider or migrate the data to another service provider for further processing.

DISCUSSION

It is clear that the cloud based healthcare service provides new promising direction for healthcare industry to move and succeed in this competitive world by introducing new advancement and experiments in existing one. It encompass the patient's data safety, reducing the operational cost, increase the popularity of healthcare services among the users, high computation and easy to access facility, maximum resources utilization, sharing of records, research support etc. In addition to this, sharing of knowledge and collaborate to introduce new medical services for all kind of diseases and provides diagnosis for them globally. As a result, cloud based healthcare services can be seen as potential solution for deliverance of high quality medical services at lower costs by healthcare providers. This integration of healthcare services and cloud computing provides many new IT solutions and advantages which may include:

• Allow multiple users such as doctors, patients, researchers to take benefit from this repository. Cloud store a huge amount of data which support medical research, enhance diagnosis, streamline process, administrative operation, financial support, resource abundance etc.
• It makes easy to exchange any medical information globally to enhance the medical activity and patient treatment using advance tools and techniques.
• Reducing the operation and maintenance cost of this integration results in all the related tasks are performed by the cloud providers.
• Increase the scalability, availability, flexibility and accessibility of healthcare information system.

However, these benefit not come alone. This integration also comes with the several security issues and challenges which need to be identified and resolved first before actually moving towards this new technology. The major concerns here are trust, privacy and security issues related to the patient's data which needs to be stored on cloud. The existing privacy and security measures introduce confidentiality, availability, authentication, access control etc. but it requires high computation with many loopholes. Since, patients store their sensitive/ confidential data over the cloud system. It reduces the high consideration for its data security regarding its accessibility, confidentiality, authenticity, auditing in order to provide a complete secure framework. In addition, there is proper care for various participants access criteria i.e, who can access the data and what amount of data it can access according to some predefined access criteria defined by the owner.

This collaboration of cloud and healthcare services also provides many feasible solutions for the distribution of responsibility and control among different users using trust maintenance between the communicating parties Trust is the prime concern that needs to be maintain between different community parties. Apart from these security concerns, some others challenges are also arise which require proper guidelines and standards need to be follow for the implementation and usage of cloud based healthcare services. These guidelines will handle the ability of data owners, user and service providers over the cloud system to maximize the cloud utilization with less investment cost. Many of these issues have been resolved and some needs to be resolved to obtain a sound system. To achieve this, there should be proper guidelines in this regards with suitable environment for development is required.

The cloud based healthcare services provides several benefit to small and medium healthcare industry and proves as a brilliant approach for them to utilize the latest technology with less operational cost. But, to make this possible in reality, there is a need of strong collaboration between the IT industry and research community to start their work in order to come up with an efficient and improve system. The system that handles all the issues and challenges that are faced by present cloud based healthcare services.

CONCLUSION

With the introduction of cloud computing in the field of healthcare service, a new direction is given to various users to communicate and share their required data from anywhere at any time and improve their practices and work. But, it also faces the various security concerns which need to deal carefully. In this chapter, we are dealing with the trust, privacy and various security issues in cloud based healthcare services and also provide the solutions to deal with any of these problems. In addition to this, we are also provides a brief description related to the benefit and strategic approval of cloud based healthcare services. Since patient's sensitive data is stored on cloud based healthcare services which require high level of security and care. In future, a complete secure framework can be designed which handles all the security issues wisely and we have a mature system with every implementation and new version.

REFERENCES

Ahmed, S., & Raja, M. (2010, December). Tackling cloud security issues and forensics model. In High-Capacity Optical Networks and Enabling Technologies (HONET), 2010 (pp. 190-195). IEEE. doi:10.1109/HONET.2010.5715771

Al-Jaroodi, J., & Mohamed, N. (2012). Service-oriented middleware: A survey. *Journal of Network and Computer Applications*, *35*(1), 211–220. doi:10.1016/j.jnca.2011.07.013

Brunette, G., & Mogull, R. (2009). Security guidance for critical areas of focus in cloud computing v2. 1. *Cloud Security Alliance*, 1-76..

Cloud Security Alliance. (2011). *STAR (security, trust and assurance registry) program*. doi:10.1007/978-3-642-29852-3_7

Cote, R. A. (1986, October). Architecture of SNOMED: its contribution to medical language processing. In *Proceedings of the Annual Symposium on Computer Application in Medical Care* (p. 74). American Medical Informatics Association.

Doukas, C., & Maglogiannis, I. (2011, November). Managing wearable sensor data through cloud computing. In *Cloud Computing Technology and Science (CloudCom), 2011 IEEE Third International Conference on* (pp. 440-445). IEEE. 10.1109/CloudCom.2011.65

European Network and Information Security Agency. (2009). *Cloud Computing: Benefits, risks and recommendations for information security*. ENISA.

Fan, L., Buchanan, W., Thuemmler, C., Lo, O., Khedim, A., Uthmani, O., . . . Bell, D. (2011, July). DACAR platform for eHealth services cloud. In *Cloud Computing (CLOUD), 2011 IEEE International Conference on* (pp. 219-226). IEEE. 10.1109/CLOUD.2011.31

Haq, I. U., Alnemr, R., Paschke, A., Schikuta, E., Boley, H., & Meinel, C. (2010). Distributed trust management for validating sla choreographies. In Grids and service-oriented architectures for service level agreements (pp. 45-55). Springer US. doi:10.1007/978-1-4419-7320-7_5

Huang, J., & Nicol, D. M. (2013). Trust mechanisms for cloud computing. *Journal of Cloud Computing*, *2*(1), 1–14.

Jansen, W., & Grance, T. (2011). Guidelines on security and privacy in public cloud computing. *NIST Special Publication*, *800*(144), 10-11.

Kaletsch, A., & Sunyaev, A. (2011). *Privacy engineering: personal health records in cloud computing environments*. Academic Press.

Kuo, A. M. H., Borycki, E., Kushniruk, A., & Lee, T. S. (2011). A healthcare Lean Six Sigma System for postanesthesia care unit workflow improvement. *Quality Management in Health Care*, *20*(1), 4–14. doi:10.1097/QMH.0b013e3182033791 PMID:21192203

Li, M., Yu, S., Ren, K., & Lou, W. (2010). Securing personal health records in cloud computing: Patient-centric and fine-grained data access control in multi-owner settings. In *Security and Privacy in Communication Networks* (pp. 89–106). Springer Berlin Heidelberg. doi:10.1007/978-3-642-16161-2_6

Löhr, H., Sadeghi, A. R., & Winandy, M. (2010, November). Securing the e-health cloud. In *Proceedings of the 1st ACM International Health Informatics Symposium* (pp. 220-229). ACM.

Löhr, H., Sadeghi, A.-R., & Winandy, M. (2010). Securing the e-health cloud. In *Proceedings of the 1st ACM International Health Informatics Symposium*. ACM.

Marks, E. A., & Lozano, B. (2010). *Executive's guide to cloud computing*. John Wiley and Sons.

Momtahan, L., Lloyd, S., & Simpson, A. (2007, June). Switched lightpaths for e-health applications: issues and challenges. In *Computer-Based Medical Systems, 2007. CBMS'07. Twentieth IEEE International Symposium on* (pp. 459-464). IEEE. 10.1109/CBMS.2007.104

Pawar, P. S., Rajarajan, M., Nair, S. K., & Zisman, A. (2012). *Trust model for optimized cloud services* (pp. 97–112). Trust Management, VI: Springer Berlin Heidelberg.

Pirahandeh, M., & Kim, D. H. (2012, April). Co-designing an intelligent doctors-colleagues-patients social network. In *Cloud Computing and Social Networking (ICCCSN), 2012 International Conference on* (pp. 1-4). IEEE. 10.1109/ICCCSN.2012.6215739

Recommendation, X. (2000). *509-The Directory: Public-key and attribute certificate frameworks*. International Telecommunication Union.

Saldarriaga, A. J., Pérez, J. J., Restrepo, J., & Bustamante, J. (2013, April). A mobile application for ambulatory electrocardiographic monitoring in clinical and domestic environments. In Health Care Exchanges (PAHCE), 2013 Pan American (pp. 1-4). IEEE. doi:10.1109/PAHCE.2013.6568306

Singh, H., Naik, A. D., Rao, R., & Petersen, L. A. (2008). Reducing diagnostic errors through effective communication: Harnessing the power of information technology. *Journal of General Internal Medicine*, *23*(4), 489–494. doi:10.100711606-007-0393-z PMID:18373151

US Department of Health and Human Services. (2008). *The ONC-Coordinated Federal Health IT Strategic Plan: 2008-2012*. US Department of Health and Human Services.

Vaquero, L. M., Rodero-Merino, L., Caceres, J., & Lindner, M. (2008). A break in the clouds: Towards a cloud definition. *Computer Communication Review*, *39*(1), 50–55. doi:10.1145/1496091.1496100

World Health Organization. (2012). *International classification of diseases*. ICD.

Yu, S., Wang, C., Ren, K., & Lou, W. (2010, March). Achieving secure, scalable, and fine-grained data access control in cloud computing. In Infocom, 2010 proceedings IEEE (pp. 1-9). IEEE. doi:10.1109/INFCOM.2010.5462174

This research was previously published in Cloud Computing Systems and Applications in Healthcare edited by Chintan M. Bhatt and S. K. Peddoju, pages 163-188, copyright year 2017 by Medical Information Science Reference (an imprint of IGI Global).

Chapter 76
The Role of Service Recovery in Online Privacy Violation

Bidyut B Hazarika
Western Michigan University, USA

James Gerlach
University of Colorado Denver, USA

Lawrence Cunningham
University of Colorado Denver, USA

ABSTRACT

In this study, the authors address the question of whether firms may successfully pursue service recovery strategies after severe online privacy violations. The study treats online privacy violations as a service failure and uses justice theory to measure repurchasing intention after consumer complaints in three different scenarios. The three scenarios differ in the sense that the accountability and the outcome of the service failure are different. The results indicate that despite the different instances of online privacy violation in each scenario, the service recovery efforts consistently created satisfaction with service recovery, significantly increased consumer trust, decreased perceived risk and increased repurchase intentions. The study finds that that both distributive and procedural justice plays an important role in online service recovery while interactional justice did not have any impact. Finally, even in cases of severe online privacy violation service recovery plays an important role generating repurchase intentions.

INTRODUCTION

The notion of privacy is a very old concept. The French philosopher Jean Jacques Rousseau proposed that people possess rights that they are born with (Rousseau, 1762). In the U.S. and Europe, one of the basic rights is the "right to privacy" (Kemp and Moore, 2007; Richardson, 2017). However, the ascendance of Big Data and fusion centers, the tsunami of data security breaches, the rise of Web 2.0, the growth of behavioral marketing, and the proliferation of tracking technologies have made it difficult for consumers to protect their information privacy from organizations. A study by "Privacy.org" over a period of six

DOI: 10.4018/978-1-5225-8176-5.ch076

Copyright © 2019, IGI Global. Copying or distributing in print or electronic forms without written permission of IGI Global is prohibited.

months found that the leading type of privacy abuse is the "unauthorized secondary use of information or data" (Cockcroft, 2002). Only 17 percentage of internet users believe that their personal information was secure online (Statista, 2017).

In this research, we treat online privacy violation as an instance of service failure. Service expectations are a normal part of every transaction involving services. Service expectations have been widely studied in the marketing literature (e.g. Kotler and Keller, 2009; Roy, Lassar, Ganguli, Nguyen and Yu, 2015). Service expectations are a set of attributes and conditions that buyers expect when they purchase a service. If those expectations are not met, there is service failure which may lead to service discontinuance or switching behavior. When consumers use various online services and share their personal information with online providers, there is an expectation from the buyers' side that the personal information will be safe and secure, and it would not be shared with third parties or other business partners. When the expectation of having your personal information secure is not met, there is service failure.

A service failure is defined as "a real or perceived service-related problem or where something has gone wrong when receiving a service" (Maxham, 2001, p. 12). It has been found that service failure leads to unfulfilled customer expectations (Chan and Wan, 2008; Jung and Seock, 2017), which cause a negative impact on customer trust and satisfaction, resulting in lower customer loyalty, lower repeat purchase and a higher chance of customer churn (Eshghi, Haughton, Teebay and Topi, 2006; Castro and Pitta, 2012). When a customer provides their personal information to a service provider, it is expected that the service provider will maintain customers' privacy and use that information appropriately in providing the service. This expectation of privacy is a severe problem because conflicts can arise between the customer who has an expectation of privacy and the service provider who wants to use their customers' personal information for profit or other organizational objectives. When a service provider violates the customer's expectations of privacy, it becomes a service failure in the opinion of the customer.

Firms may attempt to counteract the effects of service failure on customer satisfaction, loyalty, word of mouth and profitability through service recovery strategies (Zeithaml et al., 2006; Mikolon, Quaiser and Wieseke, 2015). Researchers have shown that customers who experience service failure may display higher levels of satisfaction with the service if they receive effective service recovery. In some cases under certain circumstances, customers may have higher levels of satisfaction than they exhibited prior to service failure (Zeithaml et al., 2006); this phenomenon is often referred to as the service recovery paradox and underscores the importance of effective service recovery. While a service recovery paradox is the optimal response from service recovery, a service recovery process may positively address customer satisfaction, mitigate word of mouth, maintain high loyalty levels and favorably influence profitability while at the same time contributing to service improvement in the short and long run.

Service recovery is a widely researched topic in the marketing literature, but the research has focused on formulating and evaluating the various service recovery strategies in brick and mortar settings (Blodgett, Hill and Tax, 1997; Kuo and Wu, 2012). Similar studies on service recovery strategies in the context of online services have also been undertaken by several researchers. Fan, Wu and Wu (2010) investigated the impacts of service failure recovery and perceived justice on consumer loyalty for online retailing service; Wang, Wu, Lin and Wang (2011) studied the service recovery and customer loyalty in case of e-tailing; Chang, Lai and Hsu (2012) looked at perceived justice and transaction frequency;

Chen and Chou (2012) explored customers' intentions to continue online shopping after a problem with online transactions; and Kuo and Wu (2012) studied post-recovery satisfaction and post-purchase intentions with service recovery of online shopping customers with five service failures and four recoveries.

Lin, Wang and Chang (2011) specifically established the importance of the role of perceived justice in service recovery process. They found that distributive justice, procedural justice, and interactional justice have a significant and positive impact on satisfaction. However, the subsequent effect of post-recovery satisfaction on customer retention is left relatively unexplored; specifically, the constructs of trust and perceived risk after service recovery effort, and their main effects on repurchase intention have not received much attention. Maxham (2001) studied the relationship between recovery efforts, satisfaction, and repurchase intention but did not examine the other constructs of trust and perceived risk. Sousa and Voss (2009) studied post-recovery satisfaction and repurchase intention, but none of the other constructs. Another study by Chen and Barnes (2007) examined the impact of perceived security, perceived privacy, perceived good reputation and willingness to customize on customer trust, but not in the post-recovery scenario.

In the context of online service recovery in privacy violation, Bansal and Zahedi (2015) examined the moderating effects of two types of privacy violation—hacking and unauthorized sharing on the trust violation and repair process. They investigated three response types – apology, denial and no response. Similarly, Goode, Hoehle, Venkatesh and Brown (2017) examined user compensation in the data breach recovery using the expectancy confirmation theory. We differentiate our research from the above two studies in two distinct ways. First, our research focuses on three different cases of privacy violation - firm's failure to uphold privacy policy, the presence of a liberal privacy policy that allows for privacy violation by the firm and because of the existence of web vulnerabilities associated with online users. Second, we consider three response types based on the justice theory- apology and compensation, apology but no admission of fault and vulnerabilities with the web from the user side. Additionally, a comprehensive examination of these constructs is necessary to gain full knowledge of the service recovery process.

With almost all of the business being conducted online starting from banking, loans, education etc. it has become imperative to safeguard personal information from intentional and unintentional data breaches. In addition, there has been an influx of companies competing in the same sphere. Because of the increase of competition, customers have the option of choosing a competitor after a service failure such as a privacy violation. Nevertheless, there has been a dearth of research that addresses the underlying issue as to how a company can retain their customer after such a breach. This paper addresses this gap by presenting a research model of service recovery for privacy violation that measures the effects of post-recovery satisfaction on customer trust and perceived risk and subsequent effects on repurchase intention through the justice framework. Furthermore, we strive to learn if firms using service recovery strategies can alleviate the effects of serious online privacy violations.

The paper is organized as follows. It first presents an overview of the literature pertaining to service failure and recovery and online privacy violation. Next, the model of the service recovery process is reviewed, and the hypotheses are posited. The research methods, data collection, and results are then presented. The paper concludes with a discussion of the research results, implications for managers and suggestions for future research.

LITERATURE REVIEW

Service Failure and Recovery

The impact of service failure and subsequent service recovery strategies on customer satisfaction and repurchase intention has been a topic of wide interest mainly due to the importance of the issue for organizations. Service recovery is generally defined as "actions taken by an organization in response to a service failure" (Zeitham et al., 2006). Miller, Craighead and Karwan (2000) specifically define service recovery as "the actions taken by an organization to correct service failures by reinstating customers' level of satisfaction and loyalty to ultimately retain these customers." Service recovery is also defined as the proactive and reactive actions of a service provider in response to customer complaints (Grönroos, 1994; Constantinides, 2006) or as a specific set of actions to resolve customer problems, alter negative attitudes of dissatisfied customers and ultimately restore customer loyalty (Miller et al., 2000). Researchers have suggested several actions for service recovery, such as employing active listening and being apologetic (e.g. Hess and Ganesan, 2003; Andreassen, 2000), providing quick solutions (e.g. Sirdeshmukh, Singh and Sabol, 2002), fulfilling promises (e.g. Sparks and McColl-Kennedy, 2001), engaging in proactive follow-up (e.g. Zeithaml, 2000) and explaining the issue (e.g. Mattila and Patterson, 2004). Poor service recovery could cause negative word of mouth (Lewis and McCann, 2004) and loss of confidence in the organization and could affect customer retention and churn (Ahmad, 2002). Customer loss leads to significant loss of profits, making service recovery a critical facet of an organization (Storbacka, Strandvik and Gronroos, 1994).

Much of the research in service failure and service recovery has been carried out in traditional brick and mortar settings. E-service failure and recovery is a relatively new area, because the Internet and e-commerce only gained momentum in the late 1990s and early 2000s. Online services and customer expectations are different from traditional expectations. Holloway and Beatty (2003) have extensively studied the various types of e-service failure and classified the failures into seven groups: delivery problem, website design problem, customer service problem, payment problem, security problem, miscellaneous and others. Another study by Holloway, Wang and Parish (2005) found that the perceived fairness by the consumer after has a greater impact on post-recovery satisfaction. Chang and Yao (2008) studied online service recovery and concluded that successful service recovery leads to greater customer satisfaction. They stated that service recovery mainly consists of five dimensions: explanation, communication, policy, feedback, and compensation. Of these five dimensions, the three dimensions of compensation, policy, and feedback have a greater influence on customer satisfaction and customer loyalty than the other dimensions.

Other researchers have studied the relationship between perceived justice and post-recovery satisfaction. When investigating the risks associated with consumers' information privacy concerns, Culnan and Bies (2003) suggested the use of the justice perspective. According to them, the fairness of privacy handling practices provides a level playing field for both involved parties. Justice theory was first proposed by Adams (1963) and has been extensively used by researchers to study and evaluate customer satisfaction, mainly after service failure and attempts at service recovery. Justice theory evaluates the basis for individual perceptions of the equity or fairness of a transaction and explains and seeks to understand how these perceptions affect satisfaction (Colquitt, 2001). It was originally used in an organizational setting to understand employees' feelings of being treated unfairly but has since become a widely researched topic in the service recovery context (Smith, Bolton and Wagner, 1999; Tax, Brown and Chandrasekharan,

1998) and has evolved into a three-dimensional concept that involves distributive justice, procedural justice and interactional justice (Patterson, Cowley and Prasongsuakarn, 2006; Schoefer, 2010).

One of the most important variables in a customer's evaluation of service recovery efforts is fairness (Schoefer and Ennew, 2005; Tax et al., 1998). According to justice theory, every exchange between a service provider and the customer is weighed according to the perceived inputs and perceived outputs. The inputs, in the case of service recovery, are costs and damages faced due to service failure, including monetary loss, time spent, energy expended and other physical costs. The outcomes include the ultimate result of the complaint, such as an apology or refund, along with the specific recovery processes used. The evaluation of the fairness of service recovery outcomes involves perceptions of justice at each of the three aforementioned dimensions (Blodgett et al., 1997; Maxham and Netemeyer, 2002; Smith et al., 1999; Tax et al., 1998). Distributive justice is the extent to which the final outcome of the service recovery is perceived as fair. Procedural justice deals with the extent to which the service recovery process and policies used are perceived as fair. Interactional justice is the extent to which the interactions with the service provider's employees are perceived as fair.

Smith et al. (1999) studied service recovery in restaurants and hotels and concluded that positive perceptions of distributive, procedural and interactional justice have a significant positive correlation with post-recovery customer satisfaction. Blodgett et al. (1997) also came to a similar conclusion and stated that overall perceived justice is the main determinant of post-recovery satisfaction and re-patronage intention. Recent studies in service recovery (e.g. Ha and Jang, 2009; Kim, Kim and Kim, 2009; Komunda and Osarenkhoe, 2012) all concluded that a positive perception of justice after service recovery leads to greater post-recovery customer satisfaction and positive word of mouth.

Online Privacy Violation

From the insights achieved so far on service failure and recovery, a number of issues may be noted related to the current focus on online privacy violation and service recovery. The most important issue is the privacy concerns of Internet users (Rainie and Duggan, 2016). About seven out of ten respondents to an online survey about privacy issues said that they worry many users of the Internet regarding it as a threat to their privacy generally (Irving, 1996). This is further validated by Turow, Hennessy and Draper (2015) found that consumers are more worried about how organizations would collect and use their personal information online then consider it as a tradeoff for the benefits they receive. Some of the dynamics of privacy also have been established. Not all privacy violations are equally odious (Buchanan, Paine, Joinson and Reips, 2007). Smith, Mailberg and Burke (1996) identified four dimensions of privacy violations: collection, error, unauthorized secondary use and improper access. In this study, we focus on unauthorized secondary use and improper access.

But, beyond demonstrating the importance of information privacy to Internet users and including information privacy as a component of e-service quality, researchers have not addressed privacy violation as service failure. That is not to say that researchers have not begun to address online service quality. To the contrary, research has emphasized the benefits of technology for improving service encounters (Bitner, Brown and Meuter, 2000; Meuter, Ostrom, Roundtree and Bitner, 2000; Parasuraman and Grewal,, 2000), including greater ability to manage consumer complaint management (Harrison-Walker, 2001; Strauss and Hill, 2001) and unparalleled opportunities for transaction value enhancement (Sarkar, Butler and Steinfield, 1995). Similarly, research has begun to address the nature of consumer response to e-service (Rust and Lemon, 2001), appropriate measures for the online consumer experience (Novak, Hoffman and

Yung, 2000) and the development of successful e-service strategy (Voss, 2000). Furthermore, research has begun to examine the enhanced means by which companies may engage in relationship building online (e.g. Baur, Grether and Leach, 2002;) and the various relationship orientations manifested by online consumers (Mathwick, 2002). However, the central problem of privacy violation has been largely ignored. Because the consumer can exit a relationship and switch to an alternative service provider with the click of a button, service recovery is as important as online service quality.

Based on the previous discussion, it is clear that we have advanced considerably our understanding of service failure and recovery, as well as a range of issues unique to the online service experience. However, research has yet to examine service failure and recovery in the context of online privacy violation where the circumstances surrounding the failure are likely to be quite different from the traditional online service context.

When customers are using an online service, they are facing a computer, not a human. It is, therefore, impossible for the customer to have a real-time, face-to-face communication with service personnel. Lacking the private atmosphere of a traditional setting, in which people communicate directly, greatly reduces the effect of communication and explanation (Chang and Wang, 2008). Despite these limitations, the service provider must attempt to recover the failure in order to gain the trust of their customers. Although poor service delivery (in this case privacy violation) may initially appear to be a disaster, service companies have opportunities to resolve problems and retain the customer. Therefore, this research aims to build from the service failure and recovery literature and to extend our knowledge of what is unique in the online environment relative to this topic, based on the research questions previously identified.

HYPOTHESES DEVELOPMENT

Based on a review of the literature, we developed a theoretical model for privacy violation as an instance of service failure and its impact on repurchase intention. The research model is depicted in Figure 1. The independent variables are the dimensions of justice theory: distributive justice, procedural justice, and interactional justice. We measure an individual's repurchase intention after his privacy has been violated and the individual has contacted the service provider expecting a recovery. We also consider various factors that have an impact on repurchase intention, such as satisfaction with service recovery, trust, and perceived risk. The following section elaborates on the theory base and derives the hypotheses.

Figure 1. Conceptual model

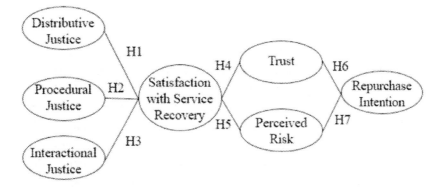

Smith et al. (1999) have defined distributive justice as "the distribution of costs and benefits in gaining unbiased exchange in relationships." In the context of service recovery, distributive justice refers to the perceived fairness of the service failure and recovery outcome (Holloway and Beatty, 2003). From the customer's point of view, distributive justice consists of the physical outcome of the service recovery efforts, such as product replacement, monetary refund, discounts or coupons (Mattila and Patterson, 2004; Santos and Fernandes, 2008; Sparks and McColl-Kennedy, 2001). However, compensation is not the only dimension of distributive justice. It has been found that an apology from the service provider also helps increase the perception of distributive justice (Tax et al., 1998). Several researchers have studied the relationship between distributive justice and customer satisfaction and have concluded that a positive perception of distributive justice leads to higher post-recovery satisfaction with the service recovery process (Boshoff, 1997; Goodwin and Ross, 1992; Smith et al. 1999). In fact, Maxham and Netemeyer (2002) found that a positive perception of distributive justice effects customer satisfaction with recovery along with the overall firm satisfaction. So, when a customer feels that they are being treated fairly, through either monetary compensation, or discount or coupons, during the service recovery process, they are more satisfied with the recovery process. Hence:

Hypothesis 1: In case of online privacy violation, perceived distributive justice during service recovery has a positive relationship with post-recovery satisfaction with service recovery.

Procedural justice refers to the "perceived fairness of the policies, procedures, and criteria used by decision makers in arriving at the outcome of a dispute or negotiation" (Blodgett, Wakefield and Barnes, 1995, pp. 31-42). In the context of service recovery, procedural justice refers to customer perception of the fairness of a service provider's recovery procedures and processes (Mattila and Patterson, 2004). Studies have found that a positive perception of procedural justice helps maintain the provider-customer relationship, even if the ultimate outcome is not in the customer's favor (Tax et al., 1998). Several studies have found that there is a positive perception of procedural justice and post-recovery satisfaction with service recovery (e.g. Blodgett et al., 1995; Goodwin and Ross, 1992; Mattila and Patterson, 2004; Smith et al., 1999). A recent study by Komunda and Osarenkhoe (2012) has also found similar results, which showed that perceived procedural justice has a positive impact on post-recovery customer satisfaction. Therefore, perceived procedural justice will help in improving satisfaction after service recovery among customers. Thus, we hypothesize:

Hypothesis 2: In case of online privacy violation, perceived procedural justice during service recovery has a positive relationship with post-recovery satisfaction with service recovery.

Interactional justice is defined as "the perceived fairness of interpersonal treatment that customers receive during the enactment of procedures" (Tax et al., 1998, pp. 60-76). In the context of service recovery, interactional justice refers to the evaluation of human interaction between the customer and the service provider (Sparks and McColl-Kennedy, 2001). There are seven main sub-dimensions of interactional justice. Blodgett et al. (1997) study three of the seven sub-dimensions: courtesy, respect, and apology. Sparks and McColl-Kennedy (2001) have studied the other four: honesty, explanation, empathy, and endeavor. Positive interactional justice leads to an increase in post-recovery satisfaction (Mattila and Patterson, 2004; Blodgett et al., 1997). Therefore, we anticipate that perceived interactional justice would improve post-recovery satisfaction. The following hypothesis is proposed:

Hypothesis 3: In case of online privacy violation, perceived interactional justice during service recovery has a positive relationship with post-recovery satisfaction with service recovery.

Every organization, online or offline, aims to create a customer base of highly satisfied and loyal customers. Research has found that a high level of trust is crucial if a company wishes to maintain long-term relationships with its customers (Garbarino and Slonim, 2003; Johnson, Sivadas and Garbarino, 2008; Krause and Ellram, 1997; Sirdeshmukh et al., 2002). Several researchers have confirmed the importance of trust in establishing long-lasting customer relationships in the online environment (Hoffman and Novak, 1999; Milne and Boza, 1999). In fact, in the online world, where the buyer and seller are physically separated and cannot see each other, trust is even more important than in the offline setting (Warrington, Abgrab and Caldwell, 2000). Due to the limited Web interface, consumers are not able to judge the trustworthiness of an online retailer as they would in a typical face-to-face transaction (Reichheld and Schefter, 2000).

With the rise of e-commerce companies, online service failure, service recovery, post-recovery satisfaction and post-recovery trust have become areas of significant interest (Pavlou, 2003; Ribbink, Van Riel, Liljander and Streukens, 2004). Santos and Fernandes (2008) found that post-recovery satisfaction had a significant positive influence on consumer trust. Further building upon their own findings and studied the impact of post-recovery satisfaction on consumer trust in the company's website and consumer trust in Internet shopping and surfing in general. They found that post-complaint satisfaction has a positive impact on consumer trust in the company's site but does not affect the trust in Internet shopping and surfing. In the case when a customer's privacy in violated online, a successful recovery will lead to increased satisfaction. Thus, we hypothesize:

Hypothesis 4: In case of online privacy violation, post-recovery satisfaction leads to increased customer trust.

Perceived risk is defined as "the degree to which a person expresses uncertainty about a service or good and, particularly, the consequence" (Bauer et al., 2002, pp. 39-55). In the online environment, customers do not have physical access to the store and do not meet the seller face to face, making it more difficult to judge the risk involved, increasing their uncertainty and, therefore, rendering perceived risk critical (Forsythe and Shi, 2003; Park and Stoel, 2005), all of which can affect purchase intention (Garbarino and Johnson, 1999).

Research suggests that the main concern of online customers is the relative inability to control their personal information (Phelps, D'Souza and Nowak, 2001). Service failure causes discomfort to the customer while effective service recovery gives the service provider an opportunity to understand the concerns of the customer and attempt to solve the issues, thereby restoring customer satisfaction levels. The effect of such post-recovery satisfaction on perceived risk is an important relationship, as it plays a critical role in determining future customer behavior. However, there is a lack of research in this field, with only one research study by Chang and Hsiao (2008) that studied the relationships among perceived justice, post-recovery satisfaction and perceived risk in the hospitality industry. They found that perceived justice has a positive influence on post-recovery satisfaction, which in turn has a negative influence on perceived risk. Few other studies, such as that by Ranaweera, McDougall and Bansal (2005), have confirmed the high satisfaction with service recovery leads to lower perceived risk. Therefore, if the customer is satisfied with the recovery effort, their level of perceived risk associated with the privacy violation decreases. Thus, we hypothesize:

Hypothesis 5: In case of online privacy violation, post-recovery satisfaction leads to decreased perceived risk.

Chen and Barnes (2007) examined customer trust and repurchase intention and found that high levels of trust lead to high levels of repurchase intention, but their research was not specific to a post-recovery scenario. Fang, Chiu and Wang (2011) studied 219 online shoppers and found that trust, along with net benefits and satisfaction, is a key determinant of customer repurchase intent but did not specifically examine the post-recovery behavior.

Goles, Rao, Lee and Warren (2009) studied the impact of violation of privacy rights by an online service provider and the subsequent effect of recovery efforts by examining data collected from 508 online users. This was one of the first studies that evaluated post-recovery trust and its relation to customer repurchases. Thereafter, another study by Santos and Fernandes (2008) found that post-recovery trust had a significant positive influence on customer repurchase intention. So, when a customer is satisfied with the recovery process, their level of trust towards the service provider increases, resulting in their decision to re-purchase/re-use the same service in the future. Thus, the following hypothesis is proposed:

Hypothesis 6: In case of online privacy violation, high levels of post-recovery trust lead to higher re-purchase intention.

There is no research on the effect of post-recovery perceived risk on repurchase intention of customers. However, there are many studies that confirm the existence of a relationship between perceived risk and future customer behavior, including repurchase intention. Bhatnagar and Ghose (2004), Eggert (2006) and Lu, Hsu and Hsu (2005) found that, in online services, the major risks were privacy risk, product risk, and financial risk, all of which have an impact on a customer's purchase intention. Researchers have studied the effect of perceived risk on e-commerce usage and shopping and found that higher levels of perceived risk lead to a decrease in shopping transactions and website usage (Doolin, Dillon, Thompson and Corner, 2007; Forsythe and Shi, 2003; Kuhlmeier and Knight, 2005; O'cass and Fenech, 2003; Park, Lee and Ahn, 2004; Shih, 2004; Van der Heijden, Verhagen and Creemers, 2003). Therefore, when a customer is satisfied with the service recovery effort, it results in low level of perceived risk resulting in re-purchase/re-use the same service in the future. Hence, we hypothesize that:

Hypothesis 7: In case of online privacy violation, low levels of post-recovery perceived risk leads to higher repurchase intention.

METHODOLOGY

To test our hypotheses, we created three hypothetical scenarios. The scenarios place the subject in the position of a subscriber to an online health forum offering quick access to medical advice on bipolar disorder. The subscribers pay a monthly subscription to be a member of the forum. With the membership, the subscriber can chat with medical experts who keep them informed about the latest treatments and drugs and provide them support and information on their ailment. The online health forum is world-renowned for its expertise on medical advice. After using the service effectively for an extended period of time, the subscriber began to suspect that his activity in the forum had been tracked, because he started to receive unsolicited ads for prescription drugs for his ailment, both mailed to his home and emailed to his personal and work email accounts.

This loss of privacy is what we consider a service failure in this research. The subscriber, as a result of the privacy violation, contacts the service provider complaining about the breach of privacy and expecting recovery. The three scenarios differ in the sense that each scenario describes a unique situation as to how an individual's privacy might be violated and the outcome of such a service failure. When service failure happens, customers take the time and effort to contact the service provider with expectations not only of getting a response, fixing the problem and receiving compensation but also of the service provider taking responsibility for the failure. We incorporate these factors in our scenarios but with different outcomes.

In the first scenario, which we call "Firm's failure to uphold privacy policy," the service provider demonstrates accepts responsibility for the service failure. The provider explains to the subscriber that one of its business partners misused the customer's information for direct marketing in violation of the provider's own information privacy policy. The provider also empathizes, apologizes and compensates the customer for the failure, assuring them that such failure will not happen in the future. The provider followed the prescribed steps for service recovery and was successful in satisfying the customer and retaining the customer using incentives.

The second scenario is called the "Presence of a liberal privacy policy that allows violation." In this scenario, the provider empathizes with the subscriber and apologizes for the inconvenience. The provider does not take any responsibility for the service failure and points out to the subscriber that their privacy policy allows them to share the subscriber's information with their business partners. They do not offer any compensation or corrective action.

The Internet is vulnerable because it is virtually open to anyone. User devices are not always adequately secured, which makes it relatively easy for others on the network to intercept messages or eavesdrop on communications. Exposures originate from users not practicing sound password management, being oblivious to the dangers of indiscriminate internet browsing, not restricting physical access to their own devices and carelessly emailing sensitive information to unauthorized or otherwise inappropriate parties. Based on such vulnerabilities, we developed our third scenario, which we call the "Web 2.0 vulnerabilities" (Scenario 3). The service provider does not take responsibility for the service failure. They do apologize for the inconvenience and empathize with the subscriber's privacy concerns. They assure the subscriber that no privacy violation has occurred on their side. Later, the subscriber realizes that he left his computer signed on to the provider's website and one of his colleagues was able to view the session. The Appendix gives the full scenarios used in the survey. Descriptions of the scenarios can be found in Table 1. For ease of usage, we refer to the scenarios as Scenario 1, Scenario 2 and Scenario 3, respectively, throughout the article.

Data Collection

We used snowball sampling for data collection. We gave our survey to 100 students, who in turn handed out the survey to five more individuals who may be their friends or family members. The survey takers were asked to read the survey and answer the questions that followed. Each subject completed the survey

Table 1. Scenarios

Service	Online medical advice forum		
Failure	Subscriber's online activities were tracked and unsolicited ads mailed to residence and emailed to personal and work accounts.		
	Scenario 1	**Scenario 2**	**Scenario 3**
Explanation	Provider's privacy policy permits sharing consumer data with business partners but not for direct marketing.	Provider's privacy policy permits sharing consumer data with business partners.	Assurance that the provider followed its privacy policy and did not send the ads.
Empathy	Yes	Yes	Yes
Apology	Breach of privacy	Inconvenience	Inconvenience
Responsibility	Provider accepted responsibility.	Provider explained away responsibility.	Provider denies responsibility.
Compensation	6 months of free service	None	None
Corrective Action	Future assurances that the privacy violations would not be repeated.	None	None

for one of the three scenarios. We received 150 responses for Scenario 1, 165 for scenario 2 and 170 for Scenario 3. We also collected information on education level, gender, age, marital status and ethnicity of the respondents. They were used as controls in the model. Table 2 provides details about the controls used in the model. We assessed non-response bias between respondents and non-respondents for each consumer characteristic, and no significant difference was observed for any of the variables (p>0.005 for all t-tests). All the respondents thought that all the scenarios were good representations of violation of privacy and that the severity of the violation was high for each one of them.

Table 2. Demographics

Control Variables	Scenario 1	Scenario 2	Scenario 3
Gender	Male- 61.3% Female- 38.7%	Male- 66.7% Female- 33.3%	Male- 71.4% Female- 28.6%
Age	18 to 25 – 54.3% 25 to 35 – 40.1% 35 to 45 – 3.6% 45 to 55 – 2%	18 to 25 – 61.7% 25 to 35 – 42.3% 35 to 45 - 3.8% 45 to 55 – 0.2%	18 to 25 – 59.6% 25 to 35 – 23.8% 35 to 45 – 7.8% 45 to 55 – 8.8%
Ethnicity	White- 81.3% Black/African American- 10.4% Hispanic- 4.8% Asian- 3.1% Other- 0.4%	White- 76.8% Black/African American- 12.8% Hispanic- 6.3% Asian- 2.8% Other- 1.3%	White- 85.6% Black/African American- 9.8% Hispanic- 3.3% Asian-0.8% Other- 0.5%
Marital Status	Single- 70% Married- 25.7% Widowed- 3.6% Divorced- 0.7%	Single- 82.7% Married- 14.1% Widowed- 0.5% Divorced- 2.7	Single- 78.6% Married- 19.8% Widowed- 0.6% Divorced- 1%
Education Level	Undergraduate- 75% Graduate- 20.8% High School- 4.2%	Undergraduate- 82.8% Graduate- 10.3% High School- 6.9%	Undergraduate- 69.8% Graduate- 25.7% High School- 4.5%

Measurement of Constructs

Measurement items were adapted from the literature wherever possible. Some new measures were developed to fit our study. The scales to measure the constructs are shown in Table 3. All the construct items were measured on seven-point "strongly disagree–strongly agree" scales. The scales for all three components of justice have been taken from Maxham and Netemeyer (2002), who adopted some of the items for procedural and interactional justice from Folger and Konovsky's (1989) scale and from the perceived justice framework developed by Blodgett et al. (1997). The items for satisfaction with service recovery were adopted from Del Rio-Lanza, Vazquez-Casielles and Diaz-Martin (2009), who adapted the items from Bitner (1990), Brown and Leigh (1996) and Davidow (2000) and modified them to fit his study. The constructs for trust and perceived risk were adopted from Pavlou and Gefen (2004). For perceived risk, Pavlou and Gefen (2004) followed Jarvenpaa, Tractinsky and Vitale (2000). These items measured the user's perception of risk involved with continuing with the online medical service provider once their privacy is violated. For the Repurchase Intention construct, we took the items from Chiu, Chang, Cheng and Fang (2009) and modified them to fit our scenario. Chiu et al. (2009) adopted the scales from Parasuraman, Zeithaml and Malhotra (2005) and Pavlou and Fygenson (2006). To determine

Table 3. Survey items

Constructs	Measurement Items	Reference
Interactional Justice	1. In dealing with the problem, (FIRM NAME's) personnel treated the person involved in a courteous manner. 2. During their effort to fix my problem, (FIRM NAME's) employee(s) showed a real interest in trying to be fair. 3. (FIRM NAME's) employee(s) got input from the person involved before handling the problem.	Maxham and Netemeyer (2002); Folger and Konovsky's (1989
Procedural Justice	1. Despite the hassle caused by the problem, (FIRM NAME) responded fairly and quickly. 2. I feel (FIRM NAME) responded in a timely fashion to the problem. 3. I believe (FIRM NAME) has fair policies and practices to handle problems.	Maxham and Netemeyer (2002); Folger and Konovsky's (1989
Distributive Justice	1. Although this event caused problems, (FIRM NAME) effort to fix it resulted in a very positive outcome. 2. The final outcome from (FIRM NAME) was fair, given the time and hassle. 3. Given the inconvenience caused by privacy violation, the outcome received from the (FIRM NAME) was fair.	Maxham and Netemeyer (2002); Folger and Konovsky's (1989
Satisfaction with Service Recovery	1. I am satisfied with the way the problem was dealt with and resolved. 2. I am satisfied with the treatment from the employees involved in resolving the problem 3. I am satisfied with the compensation offered by the firm (restore service. refund money and similar)	Del Rio-Lanza et al. (2009); Bitner (1990), Brown and Leigh (1996)
Trust	1. As a host/intermediary, (FIRM NAME) can be trusted at all times. 2. As a host/intermediary, (FIRM NAME) can be counted on to do what is right. 3. As a host/intermediary, (FIRM NAME) has high integrity.	Pavlou and Gefen (2004)
Perceived Risk	1. There is a considerable risk involved in participating in (FIRM NAME). 2. There is a high potential for loss involved in participating in (FIRM NAME). 3. My decision to participate in (FIRM NAME) is risky.	Pavlou and Gefen (2004); Jarvenpaa et al. (2000)
Repurchase Intention	1. Intend to revisit (FIRM NAME) when necessary. 2. Spend more time in (FIRM NAME) than other similar sites. 3. Interact with other (FIRM NAME) while looking for health advice.	Chiu et al. (2009); Pavlou and Fygenson (2006)

the choice of reflective and formative constructs, we assessed direction of causality. We operationalized distributive, procedural and interactional justice as formative constructs while satisfaction with service recovery, trust, perceived risk and repurchase intention as reflective constructs.

Data Analysis and Results

A single seven-point item was used to assess the subject's perception of the severity of the privacy violation. The severity means were 5.05, 5.18 and 5.34 for Scenarios 1, 2 and 3, respectively. The values indicate that the hypothetical scenarios used in this study reflect realistic privacy violation situations and are not so severe as to make service recovery extremely difficult.

Partial least squares (PLS) using SmartPLS software was used to test the hypothesized relationships shown in the model of Figure 1. PLS is appropriate for studies that have reflective and formative constructs, a relatively small sample size and an emphasis on theory development (Chin, Marcolin and Newsted, 2003). In our case, the sample size of each of the three scenarios were less than two hundred. In addition, distributive justice, interactive justice and procedural justice were measured as formative constructs, while satisfaction with service recovery, trust, perceived risk, and repurchase intention were measured as reflective constructs. The PLS model is evaluated in two steps: (1) assessment of the reliability and validity of the measurement model and (2) assessment of the structural model (Barclay, Higgins and Thompson, 1995).

Measurement Model Analysis

In order to focus on the psychometric properties of the measurement model, the study examined the composite reliability, convergent validity and discriminant validity of the constructs. Convergent validity can be assessed by an examination of the measurement model loadings. The loadings once deemed consistent with the underlying construct, were used to assess internal consistency and average variance extracted (AVE). Convergent and discriminant validity is adequate for constructs modeled using two or more reflective indicators when (1) all the constructs' AVE values are above 0.5 and (2) item loadings exceed 0.7 and load more highly on the constructs they are intended to measure (Chin, 1998). Table 5 shows composite reliability, AVE and latent variable correlation. The composite reliability of the constructs ranged from 0.85 to 0.93, which is above the recommended benchmark of 0.7 (Barclay et al., 1995; Chin, 1998). All of the constructs' AVE values were above the recommended level of 0.5 (Chin, 1998). Therefore, we found the measurement model's convergent validity to be satisfactory. The cross-loadings of measurement items of latent variables in Table 5 provide evidence of discriminant validity. Table 6 shows item loadings exceeded 0.7 and loaded more highly on the focal constructs than they were supposed to measure, demonstrating that the discriminant validity of the measurement model was satisfactory. Table 4 shows the internal consistency and mean.

Structural Model Analysis

Unlike covariance based Structural Equation Modelling (SEM), PLS does not provide summary statistics to assess the overall "fit" of the model. But the variance explained by the path model (r-squared) of the constructs (intention to repurchase) and the sign and significance of path coefficients are typically used to assess model fit. A bootstrapping approach was used to produce 500 random samples of the original

Table 4. Internal consistency and mean

Variables	Cronbach's Alpha	Mean	Cronbach's Alpha	Mean	Cronbach's Alpha	Mean
	Scenario 1		Scenario 2		Scenario 3	
Distributive Justice (DJ)	0.95	5.43	0.90	5.37	0.89	5.54
Procedural Justice (PJ)	0.89	5.05	0.88	5.18	0.85	5.34
Interactional Justice (IJ)	0.89	4.60	0.82	4.89	0.82	4.58
Satisfaction (SAT)	0.94	5.60	0.80	4.95	0.85	4.52
Trust (T)	0.90	5.78	0.89	5.05	0.92	3.79
Perceived Risk (PR)	0.90	4.65	0.88	4.52	0.89	4.46
Repurchase Intention (RI)	0.82	4.83	0.85	4.63	0.82	4.88

Table 5. Correlation tables

Variables		1	2	3	4	5	6	7
		Scenario 1						
1	DJ	**0.90**						
2	IJ	0.65	**0.90**					
3	RI	0.61	0.47	**0.88**				
4	PJ	0.74	0.73	0.58	**0.88**			
5	PR	-0.35	-0.11	-0.36	-0.31	**0.94**		
6	SAT	0.83	0.57	0.62	0.71	-0.30	**0.92**	
7	T	0.72	0.53	0.60	0.63	-0.30	0.67	**0.93**
		Scenario 2						
1	DJ	**0.91**						
2	IJ	0.68	**0.91**					
3	RI	0.60	0.53	**0.89**				
4	PJ	0.76	0.69	0.62	**0.89**			
5	PR	-0.29	-0.24	-0.34	-0.35	**0.94**		
6	SAT	0.78	0.54	0.57	0.72	-0.36	**0.93**	
7	T	0.70	0.55	0.59	0.62	-0.26	0.73	**0.91**
		Scenario 3						
1	DJ	**0.91**						
2	IJ	0.71	**0.91**					
3	RI	0.46	0.50	**0.91**				
4	PJ	0.62	0.75	0.52	**0.89**			
5	PR	-0.34	-0.25	-0.18	-0.33	**0.96**		
6	SAT	0.79	0.68	0.48	0.62	-0.38	**0.93**	
7	T	0.64	0.60	0.47	0.59	-0.31	0.67	**0.92**

Table 6. Cross loadings of measurement items of latent variables

Item	Distributive Justice	Procedural Justice	Interactional Justice	Satisfaction With Service Recovery	Trust	Perceived Risk	Repurchase Intention
DJ1	**0.822**	0.151	-0.091	-0.171	0.06	0.153	0.066
DJ2	**0.835**	0.177	-0.222	-0.12	0.001	0.262	0.018
DJ3	**0.845**	0.119	-0.065	-0.1	0.057	0.187	0.031
PJ1	0.358	**0.761**	0.076	-0.094	-0.059	0.09	-0.061
PJ 2	0.302	**0.807**	-0.11	-0.087	0.044	0.1	0.005
PJ 3	-0.095	**0.71**	-0.374	0.02	-0.019	0.244	0.188
IJ1	-0.115	-0.021	**0.883**	0.195	-0.054	-0.115	-0.005
IJ2	-0.238	-0.053	**0.813**	0.142	-0.027	-0.213	0.042
IJ3	-0.189	-0.146	**0.827**	0.098	0.049	-0.203	0.057
SR1	-0.144	-0.113	-0.039	**0.756**	0.243	0.059	0.131
SR2	-0.064	0.008	0.038	**0.723**	0.32	0.018	0.165
SR3	-0.088	-0.036	0.2	**0.814**	0.303	0.001	0.038
T1	-0.03	0.038	-0.112	0.264	**0.74**	-0.009	0.055
T2	-0.046	-0.078	-0.112	0.235	**0.862**	-0.062	0.022
T3	-0.051	-0.02	-0.022	0.276	**0.883**	-0.045	0.035
PR1	0.144	0.077	-0.064	-0.055	-0.053	**0.847**	0.031
PR2	0.135	0.031	-0.251	-0.032	-0.082	**0.76**	0.128
PR3	0.134	0.123	-0.115	0.05	-0.039	**0.88**	0.187
RI1	0.188	-0.12	-0.025	0.158	-0.038	0.115	**0.826**
RI2	-0.08	0.019	-0.062	-0.088	-0.017	0.031	**0.736**

sample size from the data set by sampling through replacement. This was necessary to obtain estimates of standard errors to test the statistical significance of the path coefficients. Such an approach provides valid estimates of the significance of the path coefficients in the PLS models (Mooney, Duval and Duval, 1993). Table 7 shows the r-squared values for the explained variables across the three scenarios. The values are all greater than 0.35, which signifies a good model fit.

We also tested the overall fit of the structural model. The overall fit of the model is assessed by chi-square statistic, normed fit index (NFI), and standard root mean square residuals (SRMSR). A good

Table 7. R-squares

Explained Variable	Scenario 1	Scenario 2	Scenario 3
Satisfaction with service recovery	0.49	0.46	0.48
Trust	0.53	0.41	0.51
Perceived Risk	0.49	0.50	0.46
Repurchase Intention	0.58	0.47	0.42

model fit is when NFI is close to 1, SRMR is close to 0 and chi-square is not significant. According to Kenny and McCoach (2003), if the sample size is small, the chi-square statistic lacks the power to distinguish poor fitting and good fitting models. To minimize the impact of the sample size on the model fit, Wheaton, Muthen, Alwin and Summers (1977) suggested using relative/normed chi-square (χ^2/df). As suggested by Hayduk (1987), a ratio less than three suggests a good model fit. As seen in Table 8, the ranges of the goodness of fit are within the acceptable range.

We also used the Chow test to check whether the independent variables had a different impact on the student population versus the respondents who responded to the questionnaire as a result of the snowball technique. The Chow test is used to check if the coefficient estimated over one group of the data equal to the coefficients estimated over another. If the Chow test is insignificant, it indicates that the two groups of respondent data can be combined. We found that in all three scenarios, the Chow test was insignificant at 0.05 level and therefore the datasets were combined.

RESULTS

The summary of empirical testing and validation of the theorized casual links are shown in Table 9. The three scenarios discussed in the paper are: firm failure to uphold privacy policy (Scenario 1); presence of a liberal privacy policy that allows violation (Scenario 2) and web 2.0 vulnerability (Scenario 3). Hypothesis 1 is supported across all three scenarios. The results offer confirmation of previous research studies, such as by the study by Chen and Chou (2012), which showed that perceived distributive justice has a positive impact on post-recovery satisfaction in online service failures. Hypothesis 2, procedural justice is partially supported. It is supported in Scenarios 1 and 2 but not 3. Hypothesis 3, interactional justice is not supported across all three scenarios. This is contrary to Mattila and Patterson (2004), who found that interactional justice does have a positive impact on post-recovery satisfaction.

Hypotheses 4, post recovery satisfaction and consumer trust and hypothesis 6, consumer trust and repurchase intention are also supported across all three scenarios. The constructs of perceived risk and trust have not been explored in detail by researchers in online privacy studies in scenario types of studies. This research found that high levels of satisfaction lead to higher levels of post-recovery trust and, consequently, higher repurchase intention. This is in line with the findings of Fang et al. (2011), who stated that trust is a key determinant of customer repurchase intent, but contrary to the findings by Chen and Chou (2012), who stated that the relationship between consumer trust and repurchase intention is negligible.

Hypothesis 5, post recovery satisfaction leads to decreased perceived risk, is supported across all three scenarios. The results offer confirmation of previous research studies such as by Kuhlmeier and

Table 8. Measures of goodness-of-fit

	Scenario 1	Scenario 2	Scenario 3
Normed fit index (NFI)	0.964	0.919	0.922
Standardized root mean square residuals (SRMR)	0.064	0.046	0.049
Ratio of χ^2 to degrees of freedom	1.505	1.38	1.96

Table 9. Path model

Hypotheses	Beta Coefficient (Scenario 1)	Beta Coefficient (Scenario 2)	Beta Coefficient (Scenario 3)
H1: In case of online privacy violation, perceived distributive justice during service recovery has a positive relationship with post-recovery satisfaction with service recovery.	0.59***	0.61***	0.57***
H2: In case of online privacy violation, perceived procedural justice during service recovery has a positive relationship with post-recovery satisfaction with service recovery.	0.19**	0.28**	0.16
H3: In case of online privacy violation, perceived interactional justice during service recovery has a positive relationship with post-recovery satisfaction with service recovery.	-0.07	-0.11	0.18
H4: In case of online privacy violation, post-recovery satisfaction leads to increased customer trust.	0.61***	0.69***	0.71***
H5: In case of online privacy violation, post-recovery satisfaction leads to decreased perceived risk.	-0.29**	-0.31**	-0.33**
H6: In case of online privacy violation, higher levels of post-recovery trust leads to higher levels of repurchase intention.	0.48**	0.41**	0.39**
H7: In case of online privacy violation, lower levels of perceived risk leads to higher levels of repurchase intention.	-0.24**	-0.19**	-0.17*

Significance levels: *** $p < 0.01$, ** $p < 0.05$, * $p < 0.1$

Knight (2005), which showed that post-recovery satisfaction after a service recovery process leads to decreased perceived risk.

Hypothesis 7 is supported across all three scenarios. The result suggests that lower levels of perceived risk lead to higher levels of repurchase intention, as suggested by other studies in service recovery (e.g. Doolin et al., 2007; Forsythe and Shi, 2003; Kuhlmeier and Knight, 2005).

DISCUSSION

In Scenario 1, the firm's failure to uphold its privacy policy, the consumer suspects that his medical information has been comprised because he has received unsolicited ads related to his medical condition. These ads were mailed to his home and emailed to his personal and work email accounts. In response to the consumer complaint, the provider acknowledges that one of their partner organizations has improperly utilized this information. As a consequence, the provider expresses concern, apologizes for the breach of policy and provides compensation and assurances that such violations will not be repeated in the future.

The empirical results for Scenario 1 indicate distributive justice and procedural justice have a significant positive relationship with post-recovery satisfaction. Interactive justice is non-significant. Post-recovery satisfaction has a significant positive relationship with increased customer trust and higher levels of post-recovery trust impact higher repurchase intentions. Higher levels of post-recovery satisfaction significantly decrease perceived risk, and lower levels of post-recovery perceived risk lead to higher repurchase intention. These results are consistent with the older literature on brick and mortar service failures and more recent studies on online services but represents a contribution in the context of online privacy. The fundamental difference is that this service failure is online and in a very sensitive service area; privacy.

The empirical results for scenario 1 suggest two primary issues. The first issue is that service recovery works when the firm fails to protect customer's data privacy. Such online violations have the potential to create substantial and permanent financial, social, psychological and continuous damage to a consumer. However, the study suggests providers have the opportunity to create satisfaction with service recovery with the resulting benefit of rebuilding consumer trust, reducing perceived risk and strengthening repurchase intention.

The other issue concerns interactional justice. Interactional justice does not seem to positively impact post-recovery satisfaction. While interactive justice may have proved important in physical service encounter, it has seemed to play a lesser role in satisfaction with service recovery in recent years. Is this just a function of the online space or does it also play a lesser role in physical settings? Has interactive justice outlived its usefulness in justice theory or just in circumstances with justice theory and service recovery? Perhaps, interactive justice is just ineffective in contributing to satisfaction in questionnaire based scenarios.

Interactional justice is also a social exchange between the consumer and the service provider focused on influencing the consumer's sense of fairness with the service recovery effort. Service provider sentimentalities such as empathy, courtesy, and concern are known positive influences. These are difficult to simulate in a survey research environment, which may provide some clarification for our research result. Another aspect, which is less understood by researchers, is the power of explanation to influence customers' post recovery experiences (Mattila and Patterson, 2004). Matilla and Patterson have shown that explanation can increase the consumers' sense of interactional justice. In each of our scenarios, a detailed explanation of the cause of the service failure was emphasized. However, other researchers (Tax et al., 1998) caution that the positive effects of explanation are realized if the explanations help the consumer understand the service failure and to obtain a quick and fair outcome (distributive justice). They posit that when the explanation is used to deny responsibility, the positive effect is nullified. Since the circumstances of a data privacy violation are often central to the service recovery effort, additional work on the power of explanation in service recovery is needed. It might be the case that consumers' expectations of data privacy make it difficult for service providers to explain away its responsibility.

In the presence of a liberal privacy policy that allows customer privacy violation (Scenario 2), the consumer has again received unsolicited ads for his medical issue. The consumer complains to the provider because the consumer suspects that his privacy has been compromised. While the provider empathizes and apologizes for the inconvenience, the firm explains that their information privacy policy allows the firm or the firm's partners to use consumer information for marketing purposes. The empirical results for Scenario 2 match the results for Scenario 1, again demonstrating that service recovery is possible. These empirical results suggest that the consumer is willing to accept privacy violation for continued access to the website. Thus, the consumer may be willing to accept an unfavorable privacy policy to gain access to a wanted online service.

Likewise, in the Web 2.0 vulnerability scenario (Scenario 3), the consumer complains to the provider about receiving unsolicited ads by mail and email. The company responds that it did not release any information about the consumer. The provider empathizes with the consumer, tells the consumer that they understand their concern and apologizes for the inconvenience. After the response, the consumer realizes that he had left his office computer signed on to the provider's website and a colleague was able to view the session. The source of the problem is not definitely revealed in the scenario, so the subject is left with some doubt as to the cause of the privacy violation. However, the company claims it had no knowledge or explanation of the reported privacy violation.

In this last scenario, the empirical results closely match those of scenarios 1 and 2 except for the lack of statistical significance for procedural justice. Since procedural justice deals with the fairness of company policies, criteria, and processes, it is logical that procedural justice is insignificant in post-recovery satisfaction for Scenario 3. The provider contends that it adhered to its privacy policy and is not responsible for the privacy violation, leaving the subject to discern the source and nature of the privacy violation. Company policies, criteria, and processes play no role in determining the outcome of the dispute or negotiation. Hence, the consumer does not experience procedural justice. However, the responsiveness of the firm, its expression of empathy and concern have the impact of increasing service recovery satisfaction and trust and decreasing perceived risk. The firm cannot solve the problem but might be perceived as a trusted agent for attempting service recovery and affirming that they have adhered to their information privacy policy that protects consumers. As in the previous scenarios, the resulting higher levels of consumer trust and lower levels of perceived risk led to significantly higher levels of repurchase intention.

By reviewing the study results across all three scenarios, the authors suggest several important observations. Foremost, service recovery worked in all three cases of online privacy violation. Consumers responded to service recovery despite a range of different types of causation for online privacy violation and severity of privacy violation. Consumers responded in a positive fashion with increases in satisfaction with recovery efforts, increases in trust, decreases in perceived risk and ultimately increases in intention to repurchase. Service recovery appears to be an effective tool in the online world and particularly applicable to privacy violation. If service recovery works on these circumstances, service recovery may be possible under many different and difficult online service failures. Second, distributive justice proved important in all three of our scenarios. Procedural justice was important in the first two scenarios but was a non-issue in the third scenario. Interactional justice, consistent with previous studies, may prove unimportant in online service recovery because there is no interactional quality to the recovery. The role of justice in relation to satisfaction with service recovery is most dependent on distributive justice. In scenarios where fault is difficult to identify, procedural justice has little usefulness. However, it clearly has usefulness in those circumstances where fault can be clearly ascertained by the provider.

Based on this study, future research should address the limits of service recovery for data privacy violation. There is a need to separately examine consumer perspectives of responsibility for the violation as well the impact of the severity of the violation. Researchers need to address whether consumer trust and perceived risk vary with consumer assessment of blame for the privacy violation. This issue is complicated in the online world where it may be more difficult for consumers in online privacy violation cases to assess blame.

Also, there is a need to determine the circumstances in which online service recovery is difficult or impossible. From a research perspective, it is important for future studies to consider the prospect of service recovery when the online service failure is considered very severe, or the consumer has experienced the failure more than once or on a regular basis. It is also important to carefully think about the type of service in terms of substitutability. For example, the market for providers of online air ticket sales is very competitive with many available substitutes. Other online services may have very limited competition. Researchers should focus on the consumer's willingness to tolerate privacy violation when there are no close substitutes. If switching costs are high or substitutability is low, consumers may be willing to tolerate high levels of privacy violation if provided with focused service recovery efforts.

CONCLUSION

Consumers seem willing to share their information with companies if that information is used in ways that add value to the relationship. Consumers benefit from discounts, personalized service, convenience, social networks and other free consumer applications, such as email and cloud storage. At the same time, consumers are also exposing themselves to potentially large privacy risk and potential damage. Privacy violations do and will happen as a usual course of direct marketing campaigns, viruses and security breaches. Even diligent firms with the highest standards of safeguards can experience events that violate consumer privacy. These privacy violations can have tremendous financial, social and psychological consequences for consumers.

The fundamental research and managerial question are whether there is anything that firms can do to recover from privacy violations. Are privacy violations events that forever compromise consumer trust and the intentions of consumers to patronize the firm? More importantly, is there anything that firms can do to restore consumer trust, lower perceived risk and stimulate intention to repurchase in an online scenario.

This study suggests that it is possible to reestablish consumer trust and perceived risk, along with repurchase intention, under the scenarios outlined in this study. In circumstances where the firm has disclosed the private information, the firm can, through service recovery, initiate a process that leads to a higher level of trust and decreased perceived risk, both of which are shown to generate higher repurchase intention. This is an important finding because even if the firm is at fault and violates its own information privacy policy, there is still the possibility of repairing and maintaining that customer relationship.

Further, this study indicates that firms that have very firm friendly privacy policies that are invasive to the consumer can still conduct effective service recovery. Evidently, the effort of the firm to undertake service recovery is enough to increase trust and decrease perceived risk in this case. The bottom line is that service recovery is an effective tool in stimulating higher levels of trust and patronization under different scenarios. Perhaps, in the consumer's mind, the effort of the firm to respond to customers in varying circumstances counts almost as much as the actual result.

LIMITATIONS

Like all research studies, this study has limitations. Each scenario in the study represents a different type of service failure. The study examines satisfaction with service recovery in each privacy violation scenario and the subsequent effects of a host of other variables, including trust, perceived risk and, most importantly, repurchase intention. While satisfaction with service recovery is an effective construct for understanding the impact on trust, perceived risk, and repurchase intention, it limits the ability of the researchers to determine whether there is a service recovery paradox produced in these scenarios. There is an opportunity in subsequent studies to examine the effects of the service recovery paradox through the use of an apriori and post hoc global satisfaction measure. While the study suggests that it is possible for service recovery (satisfaction with service recovery) to occur in these particular scenarios, it seems important in future studies to reach some conclusions regarding whether a service paradox exists (post-recovery satisfaction rising above apriori satisfaction) in the case of privacy violations. While such studies are taxing in terms of sample sizes, they may prove important in terms of theoretical contribution to the service recovery paradox literature and also to practitioners.

This paper utilizes a snowball sampling technique. Some researchers have argued that this technique is a perfect approach for examining sensitive issues in natural interacting units, e.g. privacy violation (Biernacki and Waldorf, 1981). While snowballing techniques have advantages, such as facilitating the collection of data in an economical, efficient and effective way, there are also clear and important disadvantages (Handcock and Gile, 2011). The problems include the lack of representativeness and the prejudice introduced by the inclusion of individuals with interrelationships. Researchers have also suggested that it is often difficult to initiate the chain referral process and fully monitor its execution (Dragan and Isaie-Maniu, 2012). A snowball sampling technique seemed particularly well suited for a classroom environment in which the students had fairly high maturity levels and often were already engaged in professional careers. However, in future studies, there is a need for random samples, which solve the problem of representativeness.

This study is a scenario-based field study in which respondents review scenarios that describe the experiences of users of a medical website. Scenarios are commonly used in morals and deterrence research (e.g. Harrington, 1996). Scenarios have the advantages of providing a less-intimidating way to respond to sensitive issues by offering realistic scenarios that place the subject in a decision-making role (Harrington, 1996) and offering an expanded range of research questions that can be addressed (Handcock and Gile, 2011). However, scenarios do pose the challenge of how to incorporate experiential factors, such as trust.

REFERENCES

Adams, J. S. (1963). Towards an understanding of inequity. *Journal of Abnormal and Social Psychology*, *67*(5), 422–436. doi:10.1037/h0040968 PMID:14081885

Ahmad, S. (2002). Service failures and customer defection: A closer look at online shopping experiences. *Managing Service Quality: An International Journal*, *12*(1), 19–29. doi:10.1108/09604520210415362

Andreassen, W. T. (2000). Antecedents to satisfaction with service recovery. *European Journal of Marketing*, *34*(1/2), 156–175. doi:10.1108/03090560010306269

Bansal, G., & Zahedi, F. M. (2015). Trust violation and repair:The information privacy perspective. *Decision Support Systems*, *71*, 62–77. doi:10.1016/j.dss.2015.01.009

Barclay, D., Higgins, C., & Thompson, R. (1995). The partial least squares (PLS) approach to causal modeling: Personal computer adoption and use as an illustration. *Technology Studies*, *2*, 285–309.

Bauer, H. H., Grether, M., & Leach, M. (2002). Customer relations through the Internet. *Journal of Relationship Marketing*, *1*(2), 39–55. doi:10.1300/J366v01n02_03

Bhatnagar, A., & Ghose, S. (2004). Segmenting consumers based on the benefits and risks of Internet shopping. *Journal of Business Research*, *57*(12), 1352–1360. doi:10.1016/S0148-2963(03)00067-5

Biernacki, P., & Waldorf, D. (1981). Snowball sampling: Problems and techniques of chain referral sampling. *Sociological Methods & Research*, *10*(2), 141–163. doi:10.1177/004912418101000205

Bitner, M. J. (1990). Evaluating service encounters: The effects of physical surroundings and employee responses. *Journal of Marketing*, *54*(2), 69–82. doi:10.2307/1251871

Bitner, M. J., Brown, S. W., & Meuter, M. L. (2000). Technology infusion in service encounters. *Journal of the Academy of Marketing Science*, *28*(1), 138–149. doi:10.1177/0092070300281013

Blodgett, J. G., Hill, D. J., & Tax, S. S. (1997). The effects of distributive, procedural, and interactional justice on postcomplaint behavior. *Journal of Retailing*, *73*(2), 185–210. doi:10.1016/S0022-4359(97)90003-8

Blodgett, J. G., Wakefield, K. L., & Barnes, J. H. (1995). The effects of customer service on consumer complaining behavior. *Journal of Services Marketing*, *9*(4), 31–42. doi:10.1108/08876049510094487

Boshoff, C. (1997). An experimental study of service recovery options. *International Journal of Service Industry Management*, *8*(2), 110–130. doi:10.1108/09564239710166245

Brown, S. P., & Leigh, T. W. (1996). A new look at psychological climate and its relationship to job involvement, effort, and performance. *The Journal of Applied Psychology*, *81*(4), 358–368. doi:10.1037/0021-9010.81.4.358 PMID:8751453

Buchanan, T., Paine, C., Joinson, A. N., & Reips, U. D. (2007). Development of measures of online privacy concern and protection for use on the Internet. *Journal of the Association for Information Science and Technology*, *58*(2), 157–165.

Castro, K., & Pitta, D. A. (2012). Relationship development for services: An empirical test. *Journal of Product and Brand Management*, *21*(2), 126–131. doi:10.1108/10610421211215580

Chan, H., & Wan, L. C. (2008). Consumer responses to service failures: A resource preference model of cultural influences. *Journal of International Marketing*, *16*(1), 72–97. doi:10.1509/jimk.16.1.72

Chang, H. H., Lai, M. K., & Hsu, C. H. (2012). Recovery of online service: Perceived justice and transaction frequency. *Computers in Human Behavior*, *28*(6), 2199–2208. doi:10.1016/j.chb.2012.06.027

Chang, H. H., & Wang, I. C. (2008). An investigation of user communication behavior in computer mediated environments. *Computers in Human Behavior*, *24*(5), 2336–2356. doi:10.1016/j.chb.2008.01.001

Chang, H. S., & Hsiao, H. L. (2008). Examining the casual relationship among service recovery, perceived justice, perceived risk, and customer value in the hotel industry. *Service Industries Journal*, *28*(4), 513–528. doi:10.1080/02642060801917646

Chang, Y., & Yao, H. (2008). Impact of service recovery on customer loyalty to Online B2C. In Proceedings of Wireless Communications, Networking and Mobile Computing. doi:10.1109/WiCom.2008.2173

Chen, Y. H., & Barnes, S. (2007). Initial trust and online buyer behaviour. *Industrial Management & Data Systems*, *107*(1), 21–36. doi:10.1108/02635570710719034

Chen, Y. T., & Chou, T. Y. (2012). Exploring the continuance intentions of consumers for B2C online shopping: Perspectives of fairness and trust. *Online Information Review*, *36*(1), 104–125. doi:10.1108/14684521211209572

Chin, W. W. (1998). The partial least squares approach to structural equation modeling. *Modern Methods for Business Research*, *295*, 295–336.

Chin, W. W., Marcolin, B. L., & Newsted, P. R. (2003). A partial least squares latent variable modeling approach for measuring interaction effects: Results from a Monte Carlo simulation study and an electronic-mail emotion/adoption study. *Information Systems Research*, *14*(2), 189–217. doi:10.1287/isre.14.2.189.16018

Chiu, C. M., Chang, C. C., Cheng, H. L., & Fang, Y. H. (2009). Determinants of customer repurchase intention in online shopping. Online Information Review, 33(4), 761–784.

Cockcroft, S. (2002). Gaps between policy and practice in the protection of data privacy. *Journal of Information Technology Theory and Application*, 4, 1–14.

Colquitt, J. A. (2001). On the dimensionality of organizational justice: A construct validation of a measure. *The Journal of Applied Psychology*, *86*(3), 386–400. doi:10.1037/0021-9010.86.3.386 PMID:11419799

Constantinides, E. (2006). The marketing mix revisited: Towards the 21st century marketing. *Journal of Marketing Management*, *22*(3-4), 407–438. doi:10.1362/026725706776861190

Culnan, M. J., & Bies, R. J. (2003). Consumer privacy: Balancing economic and justice considerations. *The Journal of Social Issues*, *59*(2), 323–342. doi:10.1111/1540-4560.00067

Davidow, M. (2000). The bottom line impact of organizational responses to customer complaints. *Journal of Hospitality & Tourism Research (Washington, D.C.)*, *24*(4), 473–490. doi:10.1177/109634800002400404

Del Río-Lanza, A. B., Vázquez-Casielles, R., & Díaz-Martín, A. M. (2009). Satisfaction with service recovery: Perceived justice and emotional responses. *Journal of Business Research*, *62*(8), 775–781. doi:10.1016/j.jbusres.2008.09.015

Doolin, B., Dillon, S., Thompson, F., & Corner, J. L. (2007). Perceived risk, the Internet shopping experience and online purchasing behavior: A New Zealand perspective. In *Electronic Commerce* (pp. 324–345). Concepts, Methodologies, Tools, and Applications.

Dragan, M., & Isaie-Maniu, A. (2012). Snowball sampling developments used in Marketing Research. *International Journal of Art and Commerce*, *1*, 214–223.

Eggert, A. (2006). Intangibility and perceived risk in online environments. *Journal of Marketing Management*, *22*(5-6), 553–572. doi:10.1362/026725706777978668

Eshghi, A., Haughton, D., Teebagy, N., & Topi, H. (2006). Determinants of customer churn behavior: The case of local telephone service. *Marketing Management Journal*, *16*, 179–187.

Fan, Y. W., Wu, C. C., & Wu, W. T. (2010). The impacts of online retailing service recovery and perceived justice on consumer loyalty. *International Journal of Electronic Business Management*, *8*, 239–249.

Fang, Y. H., Chiu, C. M., & Wang, E. T. (2011). Understanding customers' satisfaction and repurchase intentions: An integration of IS success model, trust, and justice. *Internet Research*, *21*(4), 479–503. doi:10.1108/10662241111158335

Folger, R., & Konovsky, M. A. (1989). Effects of procedural and distributive justice on reactions to pay raise decisions. *Academy of Management Journal*, *32*(1), 115–130.

Forsythe, S. M., & Shi, B. (2003). Consumer patronage and risk perceptions in Internet shopping. *Journal of Business Research*, *56*(11), 867–875. doi:10.1016/S0148-2963(01)00273-9

Garbarino, E., & Johnson, M. S. (1999). The different roles of satisfaction, trust, and commitment in customer relationships. *Journal of Marketing*, *63*(2), 70–87. doi:10.2307/1251946

Garbarino, E., & Slonim, R. (2003). Interrelationships and distinct effects of internal reference prices on perceived expensiveness and demand. *Psychology and Marketing*, *20*(3), 227–248. doi:10.1002/mar.10069

Goles, T., Rao, S. V., Lee, S., & Warren, J. (2009). Trust violation in electronic commerce: Customer concerns and reactions. *Journal of Computer Information Systems*, *49*, 1–9.

Goode, S., Höehle, H., Venkatesh, V., & Brown, S. A. (2017). User compensation as a data breach recovery action: An investigation of the Sony PlayStation Network breach. *Management Information Systems Quarterly*, *41*(3), 703–727. doi:10.25300/MISQ/2017/41.3.03

Goodwin, C., & Ross, I. (1992). Consumer responses to service failures: Influence of procedural and interactional fairness perceptions. *Journal of Business Research*, *25*(2), 149–163. doi:10.1016/0148-2963(92)90014-3

Grönroos, C. (1994). From marketing mix to relationship marketing: Towards a paradigm shift in marketing. *Management Decision*, *32*(2), 4–20. doi:10.1108/00251749410054774

Ha, J., & Jang, S. S. (2009). Perceived justice in service recovery and behavioral intentions: The role of relationship quality. *International Journal of Hospitality Management*, *28*(3), 319–327. doi:10.1016/j.ijhm.2008.12.001

Handcock, M. S., & Gile, K. J. (2011). Comment: On the concept of snowball sampling. *Sociological Methodology*, *41*(1), 367–371. doi:10.1111/j.1467-9531.2011.01243.x

Harrington, S. J. (1996). The effect of codes of ethics and personal denial of responsibility on computer abuse judgments and intentions. *Management Information Systems Quarterly*, *20*(3), 257–278. doi:10.2307/249656

Harrison-Walker, L. J. (2001). The measurement of word-of-mouth communication and an investigation of service quality and customer commitment as potential antecedents. *Journal of Service Research*, *4*(1), 60–75. doi:10.1177/109467050141006

Hayduk, L. (1987). *Structural equation modeling with LISREL- Essentials and advances*. Baltimore, MD: Johns Hopkins University Press.

Hess, R. L. Jr, Ganesan, S., & Klein, N. M. (2003). Service failure and recovery: The impact of relationship factors on customer satisfaction. *Journal of the Academy of Marketing Science*, *31*(2), 127–145. doi:10.1177/0092070302250898

Hoffman, D. L., Novak, T. P., & Peralta, M. (1999). Peralta M. Building consumer trust online. *Communications of the ACM*, *42*(4), 80–85. doi:10.1145/299157.299175

Holloway, B. B., & Beatty, S. E. (2003). Service failure in online retailing a recovery opportunity. *Journal of Service Research*, *6*(1), 92–105. doi:10.1177/1094670503254288

Holloway, B. B., Wang, S., & Parish, J. T. (2005). The role of cumulative online purchasing experience in service recovery management. *Journal of Interactive Marketing*, *19*(3), 54–66. doi:10.1002/dir.20043

Irving, L. (1996). Progress report on the information superhighway. *Macworld,* 260.

Jarvenpaa, S. L., Tractinsky, N., & Vitale, M. (2000). Consumer trust in an Internet Store. *Information Technology Management*, *1*(1/2), 45–71. doi:10.1023/A:1019104520776

Johnson, M. S., Sivadas, E., & Garbarino, E. (2008). Customer satisfaction, perceived risk and affective commitment: An investigation of directions of influence. *Journal of Services Marketing*, *22*(5), 353–362. doi:10.1108/08876040810889120

Jung, N. Y., & Seock, Y. K. (2017). Effect of service recovery on customers' perceived justice, satisfaction, and word-of-mouth intentions on online shopping websites. *Journal of Retailing and Consumer Services*, *37*, 23–30. doi:10.1016/j.jretconser.2017.01.012

Kemp, R., & Moore, A. (2007). Privacy. *Library Hi Tech*, *25*(1), 58–78. doi:10.1108/07378830710735867

Kenny, D. A., & McCoach, D. B. (2003). Effect of the number of variables on measures of fit in structural equation modeling. *Structural Equation Modeling*, *10*(3), 333–351. doi:10.1207/S15328007SEM1003_1

Kim, T. T., Kim, W. G., & Kim, H. B. (2009). The effects of perceived justice on recovery satisfaction, trust, word-of-mouth, and revisit intention in upscale hotels. *Tourism Management*, *30*(1), 51–62. doi:10.1016/j.tourman.2008.04.003

Komunda, M., & Osarenkhoe, A. (2012). Remedy or cure for service failure? Effects of service recovery on customer satisfaction and loyalty. *Business Process Management Journal*, *18*(1), 82–103. doi:10.1108/14637151211215028

Kotler, P., & Keller, K. L. (2009). *Dirección de marketing*. Madrid, Spain: Pearson Educación.

Krause, D. R., & Ellram, L. M. (1997). Critical elements of supplier development The buying-firm perspective. *European Journal of Purchasing & Supply Management*, *3*(1), 21–31. doi:10.1016/S0969-7012(96)00003-2

Kuhlmeier, D., & Knight, G. (2005). Antecedents to internet-based purchasing: A multinational study. *International Marketing Review*, *22*(4), 460–473. doi:10.1108/02651330510608460

Kuo, Y. F., & Wu, C. M. (2012). Satisfaction and post-purchase intentions with service recovery of online shopping websites: Perspectives on perceived justice and emotions. *International Journal of Information Management*, *32*(2), 127–138. doi:10.1016/j.ijinfomgt.2011.09.001

Lewis, B. R., & McCann, P. (2004). Service failure and recovery: Evidence from the hotel industry. *International Journal of Contemporary Hospitality Management*, *16*(1), 6–17. doi:10.1108/09596110410516516

Lin, H. H., Wang, Y. S., & Chang, L. K. (2011). Consumer responses to online retailer's service recovery after a service failure: A perspective of justice theory. *Managing Service Quality: An International Journal*, *21*(5), 511–534. doi:10.1108/09604521111159807

Lu, H. P., Hsu, C. L., & Hsu, H. Y. (2005). An empirical study of the effect of perceived risk upon intention to use online applications. *Information Management & Computer Security, 13*(2), 106–120. doi:10.1108/09685220510589299

Mathwick, C. (2002). Understanding the online consumer: A typology of online relational norms and behavior. *Journal of Interactive Marketing, 16*(1), 40–55. doi:10.1002/dir.10003

Mattila, A. S., & Patterson, P. G. (2004). Service recovery and fairness perceptions in collectivist and individualist contexts. *Journal of Service Research, 6*(4), 336–346. doi:10.1177/1094670503262947

Maxham, J. G. III. (2001). Service recovery's influence on consumer satisfaction, positive word-of-mouth, and purchase intentions. *Journal of Business Research, 54*(1), 11–24. doi:10.1016/S0148-2963(00)00114-4

Maxham, J. G. III, & Netemeyer, R. G. (2002). Modeling customer perceptions of complaint handling over time: The effects of perceived justice on satisfaction and intent. *Journal of Retailing, 78*(4), 239–252. doi:10.1016/S0022-4359(02)00100-8

Maxham, J. G. III, & Netemeyer, R. G. (2002). A longitudinal study of complaining customers' evaluations of multiple service failures and recovery efforts. *Journal of Marketing, 66*(4), 57–71. doi:10.1509/jmkg.66.4.57.18512

Meuter, M. L., Ostrom, A. L., Roundtree, R. I., & Bitner, M. J. (2000). Self-service technologies: Understanding customer satisfaction with technology-based service encounters. *Journal of Marketing, 64*(3), 50–64. doi:10.1509/jmkg.64.3.50.18024

Mikolon, S., Quaiser, B., & Wieseke, J. (2015). Don't try harder: Using customer inoculation to build resistance against service failures. *Journal of the Academy of Marketing Science, 43*(4), 512–527. doi:10.100711747-014-0398-1

Miller, J. L., Craighead, C. W., & Karwan, K. R. (2000). Service recovery: A framework and empirical investigation. *Journal of Operations Management, 18*(4), 387–400. doi:10.1016/S0272-6963(00)00032-2

Milne, G. R., & Boza, M. E. (1999). Trust and concern in consumers' perceptions of marketing information management practices. *Journal of Interactive Marketing, 13*(1), 5–24. doi:10.1002/(SICI)1520-6653(199924)13:1<5::AID-DIR2>3.0.CO;2-9

Mooney, C. Z., Duval, R. D., & Duval, R. (1993). *Bootstrapping: A nonparametric approach to statistical inference*. Thousand Oaks, CA: Sage Publications. doi:10.4135/9781412983532

Novak, T. P., Hoffman, D. L., & Yung, Y. F. (2000). Measuring the customer experience in online environments: A structural modeling approach. *Marketing Science, 19*(1), 22–42. doi:10.1287/mksc.19.1.22.15184

O'cass, A., & Fenech, T. (2003). Web retailing adoption: Exploring the nature of internet users Web retailing behaviour. *Journal of Retailing and Consumer Services, 10*(2), 81–94. doi:10.1016/S0969-6989(02)00004-8

Parasuraman, A., & Grewal, D. (2000). The impact of technology on the quality-value-loyalty chain: A research agenda. *Journal of the Academy of Marketing Science, 28*(1), 168–174. doi:10.1177/0092070300281015

Parasuraman, A., Zeithaml, V. A., & Malhotra, A. (2005). ES-QUAL a multiple-item scale for assessing electronic service quality. *Journal of Service Research, 7*, 213–233. doi:10.1177/1094670504271156

Park, J., Lee, D., & Ahn, J. (2004). Risk-focused e-commerce adoption model: A cross-country study. *Journal of Global Information Technology Management, 7*(2), 6–30. doi:10.1080/1097198X.2004.10856370

Park, J., & Stoel, L. (2005). Effect of brand familiarity, experience and information on online apparel purchase. *International Journal of Retail & Distribution Management, 33*(2), 148–160. doi:10.1108/09590550510581476

Patterson, P. G., Cowley, E., & Prasongsukarn, K. (2006). Service failure recovery: The moderating impact of individual-level cultural value orientation on perceptions of justice. *International Journal of Research in Marketing, 23*(3), 263–277. doi:10.1016/j.ijresmar.2006.02.004

Pavlou, P. A. (2003). Consumer acceptance of electronic commerce: Integrating trust and risk with the technology acceptance model. *International Journal of Electronic Commerce, 7*(3), 101–134. doi:10.1080/10864415.2003.11044275

Pavlou, P. A., & Fygenson, M. (2006). Understanding and predicting electronic commerce adoption: An extension of the theory of planned behavior. *Management Information Systems Quarterly, 30*(1), 115–143. doi:10.2307/25148720

Pavlou, P. A., & Gefen, D. (2004). Building effective online marketplaces with institution-based trust. *Information Systems Research, 15*(1), 37–59. doi:10.1287/isre.1040.0015

Phelps, J. E., D'Souza, G., & Nowak, G. J. (2001). Antecedents and consequences of consumer privacy concerns: An empirical investigation. *Journal of Interactive Marketing, 15*(4), 2–17. doi:10.1002/dir.1019

Rainie, L., & Duggan, M. (2016). Privacy and Information Sharing. *Pew Research Center*. Retrieved March 6, 2018, from http://www.pewinternet.org/2016/01/14/privacy-and-information-sharing/

Ranaweera, C., McDougall, G., & Bansal, H. (2005). A model of online customer behavior during the initial transaction: Moderating effects of customer characteristics. *Marketing Theory, 5*(1), 51–74. doi:10.1177/1470593105049601

Reichheld, F. F., & Schefter, P. (2000). E-loyalty. *Harvard Business Review, 78*, 105–113.

Ribbink, D., Van Riel, A. C., Liljander, V., & Streukens, S. (2004). Comfort your online customer: Quality, trust and loyalty on the internet. *Managing Service Quality: An International Journal, 14*(6), 446–456. doi:10.1108/09604520410569784

Richardson, M. (2017). *The Right to Privacy: Origins and Influence of a Nineteenth-century Idea, (40)*. Cambridge: Cambridge University Press. doi:10.1017/9781108303972

Rousseau, J. J. (1762). *The Social Contract.* Cranston: Harmonds.

Roy, S. K., Lassar, W. M., Ganguli, S., Nguyen, B., & Yu, X. (2015). Measuring service quality: A systematic review of literature. *International Journal of Services. Economics and Management, 7*(1), 24–52.

Rust, R. T., & Lemon, K. N. (2001). E-service and the consumer. *International Journal of Electronic Commerce, 5*(3), 85–101. doi:10.1080/10864415.2001.11044216

Santos, C. P. D., & Fernandes, D. V. D. H. (2008). Antecedents and consequences of consumer trust in the context of service recovery. *BAR - Brazilian Administration Review*, *5*(3), 225–244. doi:10.1590/S1807-76922008000300005

Sarkar, M. B., Butler, B., & Steinfield, C. (1995). Intermediaries and cybermediaries: A continuing role for mediating players in the electronic marketplace. *Journal of Computer-Mediated Communication*, *1*(3), 1–14.

Schoefer, K. (2010). Cultural moderation in the formation of recovery satisfaction judgments: A cognitive-affective perspective. *Journal of Service Research*, *13*(1), 52–66. doi:10.1177/1094670509346728

Schoefer, K., & Ennew, C. (2005). The impact of perceived justice on consumers' emotional responses to service complaint experiences. *Journal of Services Marketing*, *19*(5), 261–270. doi:10.1108/08876040510609880

Shih, H. P. (2004). An empirical study on predicting user acceptance of e-shopping on the Web. *Information & Management*, *41*(3), 351–368. doi:10.1016/S0378-7206(03)00079-X

Sirdeshmukh, D., Singh, J., & Sabol, B. (2002). Consumer trust, value, and loyalty in relational exchanges. *Journal of Marketing*, *66*(1), 15–37. doi:10.1509/jmkg.66.1.15.18449

Smith, A. K., Bolton, R. N., & Wagner, A. J. (1999). A model of customer satisfaction with service encounters involving failure and recovery. *JMR, Journal of Marketing Research*, *36*(3), 356–372. doi:10.2307/3152082

Smith, H. J., Milberg, S. J., & Burke, S. J. (1996). Information privacy: Measuring individuals' concerns about organizational practices. *Management Information Systems Quarterly*, *20*(2), 167–196. doi:10.2307/249477

Sousa, R., & Voss, C. A. (2009). The effects of service failures and recovery on customer loyalty in e-services: An empirical investigation. *International Journal of Operations & Production Management*, *29*(8), 834–864. doi:10.1108/01443570910977715

Sparks, B. A., & McColl-Kennedy, J. R. (2001). Justice strategy options for increased customer satisfaction in a services recovery setting. *Journal of Business Research*, *54*(3), 209–218. doi:10.1016/S0148-2963(00)00120-X

Statista. (2017). Online Privacy- Statistics & Facts. Retrieved March 6, 2018, from https://www.statista.com/topics/2476/online-privacy/

Storbacka, K., Strandvik, T., & Grönroos, C. (1994). Managing customer relationships for profit: The dynamics of relationship quality. *International Journal of Service Industry Management*, *5*(5), 21–38. doi:10.1108/09564239410074358

Strauss, J., & Hill, D. J. (2001). Consumer complaints by e-mail: An exploratory investigation of corporate responses and customer reactions. *Journal of Interactive Marketing*, *15*(1), 63–73. doi:10.1002/1520-6653(200124)15:1<63::AID-DIR1004>3.0.CO;2-C

Tax, S. S., Brown, S. W., & Chandrashekaran, M. (1998). Customer evaluations of service complaint experiences: Implications for relationship marketing. *Journal of Marketing*, *62*(2), 60–76. doi:10.2307/1252161

Turow, J., Hennessy, M., & Draper, N. (2015). *The tradeoff fallacy: How marketers are misrepresenting American consumers and opening them up to exploitation*. The Annenberg School for Communication: University of Pennsylvania.

Van der Heijden, H., Verhagen, T., & Creemers, M. (2003). Understanding online purchase intentions: Contributions from technology and trust perspectives. *European Journal of Information Systems*, *12*(1), 41–48. doi:10.1057/palgrave.ejis.3000445

Voss, C. (2000). Developing an eService strategy. *Business Strategy Review*, *11*(1), 21–34. doi:10.1111/1467-8616.00126

Wang, Y. S., Wu, S. C., Lin, H. H., & Wang, Y. Y. (2011). The relationship of service failure severity, service recovery justice and perceived switching costs with customer loyalty in the context of e-tailing. *International Journal of Information Management*, *31*(4), 350–359. doi:10.1016/j.ijinfomgt.2010.09.001

Warrington, T. B., Abgrab, N. J., & Caldwell, H. M. (2000). Building trust to develop competitive advantage in e-business relationships. *Competitiveness Review*, *10*(2), 160–168. doi:10.1108/eb046409

Wheaton, B., Muthen, B., Alwin, D. F., & Summers, G. F. (1977). Assessing reliability and stability in panel models. *Sociological Methodology*, *8*, 84–136. doi:10.2307/270754

Zeithaml, V. A. (2000). Service quality, profitability, and the economic worth of customers: What we know and what we need to learn. *Journal of the Academy of Marketing Science*, *28*(1), 67–85. doi:10.1177/0092070300281007

Zeithaml, V. A., Bolton, R. N., Deighton, J., Keiningham, T. L., Lemon, K. N., & Petersen, J. A. (2006). Forward-Looking Focus Can Firms Have Adaptive Foresight? *Journal of Service Research*, *9*(2), 168–183. doi:10.1177/1094670506293731

This research was previously published in the International Journal of E-Business Research (IJEBR), 14(4); edited by Payam Hanafizadeh and Jeffrey Hsu, pages 1-27, copyright year 2018 by IGI Publishing (an imprint of IGI Global).

APPENDIX: DETAILED SCENARIOS

Table 10. Detailed scenarios

Common Across Scenarios	You live in a rural area and your primary physician is 50 miles away. You suffer from bipolar disorder and require regular medical assistance between visits to his primary physician. You subscribe to an online health forum called MedAdvice for quick access to medical advice on bipolar disorder. You pay a monthly subscription fee of $30/month to be a member of the forum. With the membership, you can chat with medical expert who keep you informed about the latest treatments and drugs, and provide you support and information on how to cope with your ailment. MedAdvice is world renowned for its expertise on bipolar disorder. You have been using the forum for quite a while and you have continued to use their service because you found the medical advice you received from the doctors in the forum very beneficial. Recently, you began to suspect that your activity in the forum has been tracked because you started to receive unsolicited ads for prescription drugs for bipolar disorder, both mailed to your home and emailed to your personal and work email accounts. You were concerned about the ads and you decided to contact MedAdvice to address your concern. You spoke with their customer service department regarding your suspicion. Customer service assured you that they would look into the matter and get back to you within 5-6 business days.		
	Scenario 1	**Scenario 2**	**Scenario 3**
Difference Across Scenarios	You were concerned about the ads and you decided to contact MedAdvice to address your concern. You spoke with their customer service department regarding your suspicion. Customer service assured you that they would look into the matter and get back to you within 5-6 business days. After a few days of waiting, you get a call back from the customer service department and they informed you that in fact your private data was accessed by their business partner, which is a pharmaceutical company called CanPharma. The MedAdvice representative told you that their information privacy policy permitted sharing data with CanPharma, but that CanPharma was not authorized to use that information for marketing pharmaceuticals directly to MedAdvice members. The MedAdvice customer service provider empathized with you and told you that he understood your concern and apologized for the breach of privacy. He assured you that MedAdvice would take all necessary precautions to prevent CanPharma from misusing customer data in the future. MedAdvice also offered to give you 6 months of free membership to the forum.	You were concerned about the ads and you decided to contact MedAdvice to address his concern. You spoke with their customer service department regarding your suspicion. Customer service assured you that they would look into the matter and get back to you within 5-6 business days. After a few days of waiting, you get a call back from the customer service department and they informed you that in fact their business partner accessed your private data, which is a pharmaceutical company called CanPharma. The MedAdvice representative told you that their information privacy policy permitted sharing data with CanPharma. The MedAdvice customer service provider empathized with you and told you that he understood your concern and apologized for the inconvenience. The customer service representative reiterated that when you signed up for their service, you accepted their information privacy policy that permits sharing the customers' data with CanPharma.	You were concerned about the ads and you decided to contact MedAdvice. You spoke with their customer service department regarding your suspicion. Customer service assured you that they would look into the matter and get back to you within 5-6 business days. After a few days of waiting, you gets a call back from the customer service department and they informed you that they have completely adhered to their policy and they can assure you that the ads are not a result of the information they collected on you. Later you realized that you left your office computer signed on to the MedAdvice website and a colleague was able to view your session.

Chapter 77
A Cloud Based Solution for Collaborative and Secure Sharing of Medical Data

Mbarek Marwan
Chouaib Doukkali University, Morocco

Ali Kartit
Chouaib Doukkali University, Morocco

Hassan Ouahmane
Chouaib Doukkali University, El Jadida, Morocco

ABSTRACT

Healthcare sector is under pressure to reduce costs while delivering high quality of care services. This situation requires that clinical staff, equipment and IT tools to be used more equitably, judiciously and efficiently. In this sense, collaborative systems have the ability to provide opportunities for healthcare organizations to share resources and create a collaborative working environment. The lack of interoperability between dissimilar systems and operating costs are the major obstacle to the implementation of this concept. Fortunately, cloud computing has great potential for addressing interoperability issues and significantly reducing operating costs. Since the laws and regulations prohibit the disclosure of health information, it is necessary to carry out a comprehensive study on security and privacy issues in cloud computing. Based on their analysis of these constraints, the authors propose a simple and efficient method that enables secure collaboration between healthcare institutions. For this reason, they propose Secure Multi-party Computation (SMC) protocols to ensure compliance with data protection legislation. Specifically, the authors use Paillier scheme to protect medical data against unauthorized usage when outsourcing computations to a public cloud. Another useful feature of this algorithm is the possibility to perform arithmetic operations over encrypted data without access to the original data. In fact, the Paillier algorithm is an efficient homomorphic encryption that supports addition operations on ciphertexts. Based on the simulation results, the proposed framework helps healthcare organizations to successfully evaluate a public function directly on encrypted data without revealing their private inputs. Consequently, the proposed collaborative application ensures privacy of medical data while completing a task.

DOI: 10.4018/978-1-5225-8176-5.ch077

Copyright © 2019, IGI Global. Copying or distributing in print or electronic forms without written permission of IGI Global is prohibited.

1. INTRODUCTION

The adoption of collaborative software or groupware in healthcare domain would inevitably improve patient services (Lee & Leu, 2016). Indeed, it allows healthcare ecosystem to share data and tools efficiently. The ability of this model to easily build a collaborative environment has significantly attracted the attention of healthcare institutions. Despite its remarkable ability to facilitate coordination and data exchange, this concept requires massive investment in hardware and software. In this respect, we propose a highly efficient approach and framework to encourage communication and effective teamwork among healthcare professionals. This can be achieved by using cloud technology which ensures cost reduction, greater flexibility, elasticity and optimal resource utilization (Mell & Grance, 2009; Shameem, Johnson, Shaji, & Arun, 2017). Additionally, customers take advantage of a flexible usage-based pricing system for an optimal use of cloud resources (Arinze & Anandarajan, 2010). More precisely, metering and reporting tools are generally based on real-time usage and the quality-of-service requirements of cloud services. The features and characteristics of cloud are summarized in the Figure 1.

Although cloud services offer significant potential and advantages, the utilization of off-site solutions raise numerous security issues (Marwan et al., 2018). In order to use cloud services safely, it is of paramount importance to explore and seriously address cloud security risks. The next step is to design and develop a cloud platform that enables secure collaboration among medical professionals. The primary contribution of this research consists in using Secure Multi-party Computation (SMC) protocol in conjunction with Pallier cryptosystem to protect patient privacy against unauthorized users. Concretely, this technique enables various parties to conduct operations over distributed data without revealing confidential information. In reality, SMC protocol is widely used to guarantee data privacy in various

Figure 1. Definition of cloud computing according to NIST

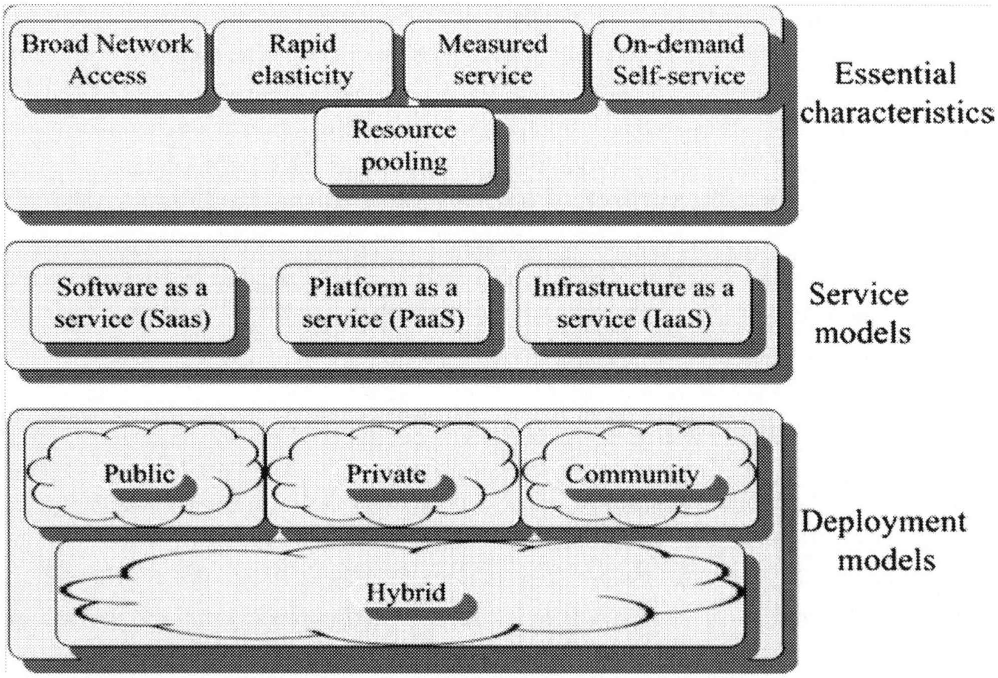

IT domain areas, such as price negotiations in electronic auction (Li et al., 2016), privacy-preserving computational geometry (Shundong et al., 2014) and privacy preserving data mining (Yi et al., 2015). In this study, this approach permits healthcare administrators to make the correct global decisions by using different homogeneous distributed databases. Simultaneously, this solution is perfectly suitable to use in heterogeneous systems to achieve interoperability.

The organization of this paper is as follows. In Section 2 and 3, we present and discusss security problems in cloud computing as well as the privacy requirements in the healthcare domain. We essentially provide some previous works and discuss their limitations in Section 4. Section 5 illustrates our proposed framework to meet security needs. We provide background information of Secure Multiparty Computation (SMC) protocol and its basic principles in Section 6. In Section 7, we implement our solution and discuss the results. We end this work in Section 8 by remarks and future research directions.

2. SECURITY ISSUES IN CLOUD COMPUTING

Cloud computing relies on the sustainable development of recent computing technologies, especially distributed systems, storage systems and applications. Essentially, it aims to drastically reduce costs by using the shared storage pool and the multi-tenancy architecture. Additionally, this model is an appropriate solution to improve collaboration between healthcare organizations. Nevertheless, the security and privacy risks are the primary barriers hindering the implementation of cloud computing (Radwan, Azer, & Abdelbaki, 2017; Jouini & Rabai, 2016). In this section, we explore the potential vulnerabilities and risks facing cloud computing and identify the main cause of these problems.

2.1. Virtualization

This solution allows many clients to share the same physical resources by creating virtual ones. This seeks to achieve higher levels of flexibility and optimization in resources management. The goal of this technique is to drastically reduce infrastructure costs while simultaneously ensuring availability and reliability. In addition, this technology helps cloud providers to mainly meet many quality-of-service (QoS) constraints, especially scalability, flexibility, resilience, elasticity, fault-tolerance, online backup and storage migration. Essentially, it offers the possibility to deploy and run multiple operating systems and applications using virtual resources. Although this new trend is considered a promising concept, a number of issues, such as VM image sharing, VM isolation, VM escape, hypervisor problems and VM migration issues (Mazhar, Samee, & Athanasios, 2015; Birje et al., 2017), need to be addressed to implement VM successfully.

2.2. Data Location

Cloud computing uses distributed systems to achieve its full potential and satisfy the growing needs of organizations. The cloud model also offers the possibility to save clients' data on various remote servers and different hosting data centers. In general, two major challenges arise in this new paradigm (Khan & Al-Yasiri, 2016; Iqbal et al., 2016). First, data are saved and spread out in offsite storage systems at unknown locations, which could lead to legal problems. Second, clients delegate storage management and computations to cloud providers; and hence, they lost control over their data. Furthermore, the management of a distributed system brings additional issues, especially with relation to availability, job scheduling, load balancing and resources provisioning. Beside data location, the use of cloud computing causes serious security threats due to cloud technology. Threats having to do with multi-tenant environment, data recovery vulnerability, improper media sanitization and data backup (Fernandes et al., 2013).

2.3. Web Services

In more general terms, cloud computing is a solution to properly facilitate access to remote data and resources and efficiently manage interoperability and complexity in health systems (Bajwa, Singh, & De, 2017). This is usually achieved by using web-based applications for providing ubiquitous connectivity to cloud services. In this scenario, clients use Application Programming Interface (API) to enable consumers to easily access cloud resources. Additionally, this technique helps users set up a connection between a locally-based application and a remote one in order to properly benefit from cloud resources. In spite of the multiple benefits of this key component, the use of web technology may jeopardize the privacy of clients' data and expose them to several security problems. The most common threats facing web-based application include but are not limited to SQL injection, broken authentication and session management, and Cross-Site Scripting (XSS), Cross-Site Request Forgery (CSRF) (Marwan, Kartit, & Ouahmane, 2016).

3. PRIVACY REQUIREMENTS IN HEALTHCARE DOMAIN

Typically, protecting patients' medical records requires strong security measures. In the context of public cloud, when using imaging tools, maintaining privacy and security becomes a priority. Since medical images are an efficient means to support diagnosis, they should remain unchanged and safe. In this regard, we carefully analyze different parameters involved in data protection, when adopting cloud computing. So, we provide a comprehensive taxonomy based on a broad range of existing literature sources (Shirazi et al., 2017; Ravi Kumar at al., 2017; Yüksel et al. 2017; Ramachandra et al., 2017; Krishna et al., 2016).

3.1. Confidentiality

In practice, imaging software and tools provide tremendous benefits to healthcare professionals. However, strong security measures are required in order to prevent the disclosure of sensitive data when using these applications to process medical images. Outsourcing image processing is yet another benefit being offered by the cloud computing because it does not require the clients to deploy local applications. This implies that consumers need to protect their digital records against cloud providers and other malicious clients. For the aforementioned reasons, it is mandatory to take preventive actions for safeguarding data confidentiality before using cloud services. To this objective, many approaches such as Shamir's Secret Share (SSS) scheme, homomorphic encryption and Secure Multi-Party Computation (SMC) are used to maintain data confidentiality. This work intends to explore SMC encryption and its application to mitigate cloud computing security pitfalls and risks.

3.2. Integrity

Considering the importance of images in healthcare field, data integrity is essential to make correct clinical decisions. In this regard, it is of the utmost importance to guarantee the accuracy and consistency of the data during transmission, storage and processing. For this reason, it is equally important to use necessary the mechanisms to maintain data unchanged during the utilization of cloud solutions. In order to properly ensure confidentiality, both encryption techniques and data processing operations must be performed without affecting the quality of medical information. Obviously, methods used for integrity protection need to be both lossless and reversible. Since data are outsourced to an external party, the integrity check becomes particularly confusing as clients do not possess the original data files. Practically, a new concept is suggested in which a third-party auditor (TPA) verifies the integrity of the data on behalf of cloud consumers.

3.3. Availability

Globally, digital technology has a great impact on the quality of medical services. In parallel, cloud computing is an efficient way to ensure timely availability of required imaging tools. In this case, the used techniques allow tradeoffs between data usability and data privacy. More precisely, it is important to ensure that suggested security measures enable healthcare to rapidly access medical records. Meanwhile, clients must use efficient algorithms to improve performance. Unfortunately, wide range of factors can influence the availability of cloud services, namely Distributed Denial of Service (DDoS), network failure, etc.

3.4. Data Ownership

In the Digital Imaging and Communications in Medicine (DICOM) standard, each electronic health record encompasses both digital records and patients' identifying information. The latter often refers to various common identifiers, such as name, address, birth date and Social Security Number (SSN). Accordingly, data ownership is typically the process that establishes a connection between medical records and their owner. In this case, the owners should have legal rights, complete control and unrestricted access to their medical data. In this regard, watermarking methods are widely used in cloud-based services to determine the legitimate owner of a medical record.

3.5. Authentication

Since a public cloud is meant to serve a multitude of clients and organizations, it is necessary to implement authentication mechanisms in order to identify the end user of a cloud service. In such a scenario, the authentication server is used to check and validate a user's identity by using a wide range of authentication methods, including username and secret password, certified digital signature, biometric authentication systems Zero-Knowledge Authentication Protocol (ZKAP), Single Sign-On (SSO), etc.

3.6. Access Control

In cloud model, a third party delivers imaging tools at any time and from any location through the Internet. Hence, access control mechanisms are necessary to deny, restrict or allow client access to cloud applications. In an access control decision, various attributes come into play. They are mainly related to access control policies and attributes of subjects and objects (Babrahem & Monowar, 2017). The primary goal of this mechanism is to guarantee that only consumers having the right privilege can gain access to specific cloud resources. In the same line, it is necessary to monitor all login attempts to enforce security measures during cloud utilization. To accomplish this, multiple access control schemes such as role-based models, attribute-based encryption models and multi-tenancy models are developed to protect patients' data. For instance, Attribute-Based Access Control (ABAC) is widely used and largely effective in cloud environment (Sifou, Hammouch, & Kartit, 2018). In fact, it provides a flexible and dynamic access control mechanisms to support dynamic nature of cloud and data sharing.

3.7. Anonymization

Privacy protection appears as a fundamental concern when adopting cloud computing in the healthcare domain. In fact, unauthorized users or entities should not reveal any information about patients. This is achieved by using data anonymization techniques to comply with data protection laws. In particular, the identity of a patient is considered as sensitive data that should be confidential and secret. Amongst several existing solutions, the k-anonymity algorithms allow clients to maintain privacy when using cloud services (Anjum et al., 2018).

3.8. Unlinkability

Deploying medical data in the cloud requires strong security measures to ensure data protection. Besides, it is important to implement strong methods to prevent unauthorized internal or external users to evaluate and establish relationship between outsourced data and their owner. In other words, this mechanism seeks not only to secure sensitivity but also to prevent unauthorized entities to link with any items. In this regard, for example, a collision-resistant hash function is used to achieve high unlinkability between inputs and outputs.

3.9. Auditing Capability

Beside the security mechanisms outlined above, healthcare professionals and the nominated third party must record all occurred events (Abouelmehdi, Beni-Hessane, & Khalouf, 2018). More precisely, it is mandatory to formally keep a log for all actions and activities executed by cloud consumers. The key objective of this concept is to guarantee that users' requests comply with a predefined security policy. In high-security environments, this technique is the core element of digital forensic tools as it determines the potential causes of the security breach and collects some relevant evidence. In general, this process is outsourced to an external entity called Third Party Auditor (TPA).

4. RELATED WORK

Developing a secure collaborative system has become necessary to improve health outcomes. However, to date, there has been little work done on data protection using Secure Multiparty Computation (SMC) in conjunction with homomorphic encryption. This protocol is the most powerful way to prevent corruption because it has the ability to allow many organizations to securely compute some joint functions of their private inputs. We stress that in our definition the result is correctly calculated even though some of the participants are corrupted. In spite of the ambiguity of the term, this concept has gained wide popularity in the collaborative system. However, there may still exist security risks when applying this protocol on medical data due to their highly sensitive nature. Accordingly, relatively few studies have been done in this area; only few qualitative frameworks have been developed even if there have been numerous attempts and research efforts over the past years. In (Harsha Sandaruwan & Ran Oppgave, 2013), the authors develop an efficient Framework that enables statistical analysis on encrypted data. Basically, the authors use fully homomorphic encryption for statistical data analysis of encrypted data. In this study, the ElGamal algorithm is used for the aggregation of data that are distributed across multiple repositories. The primary purpose of this protocol is to prevent accidental disclosure during data manipulation, including arithmetic and logic operations. Consequently, the proposed solution is an efficient approach to promote and encourage the collaborative system in the healthcare system. The work in (Molina, Salajegheh, & Fu, 2009) aims to collect the medical information generated by each healthcare organization to efficiently help combat healthcare frauds and abuses. In practice, this often takes the form of a collaborative system in which medical data are shared among healthcare organizations safely. This scheme uses the arithmetic cryptographic protocol using polynomial functions, which is more suitable for implementing a secure multiparty computation protocol. Therefore, the proposal offers the possibilty to perform joint computations without revealing private data in an organized and efficient way. In the same line, the authors in (Hu, Cheung, & Nguyen, 2006) propose a scalable collaborative filtering framework based on secure multiparty computation techniques. Essentially, a combination of rank reduction and random permutation is used in this approach to process digital data and minimize their exposure to a potential disclosure. In parallel with this, securing an inner product is developed to maintain privacy in linear filtering.

5. PROPOSED FRAMEWORK

Clearly, the collaborative working environment (CWE) is a simple and cost effective method for performing distributed computation tasks. Thus, using this concept in healthcare will not only improve the overall quality of care, but it will also increase coordination among healthcare professionals (Abomhara & Ben Lazrag, 2016). Although there are many benefits of adopting collaborative systems and digital platforms (Masuda et al., 2018), there are also some significant barriers that prevent the effective utilization of these solutions. First, security is a primary concern in the healthcare domain due to the sensitivity and the confidentiality of medical data. This actually restricts the successful implementation of the CWE. Second, ensuring the interoperability between heterogeneous healthcare information still faces serious challenges despite the improvements made in recent years. In this respect, we propose a secure cloud framework to promote collaboration between healthcare organizations in order to facilitate data exchange. More importantly, we rely on cloud technology to ensure the reliability and availability of cloud services. In this paper, we use the secure multiparty computation technique to prevent unauthorized modification or disclosure of data. We typically use homomorphic encryption based on the Paillier algorithm to achieve this goal. In this sense, every hospital in the country is ordered to start sending its private data after having successfully encrypted them. Accordingly, a third party (TP), which is a cloud provider of the software as a service (SaaS) model, uses sophisticated tools to compute arbitrary functions on encrypted data. Next, the TP module sends encrypted results to all parties involved in statistical data analysis. Lastly, each participating hospital decrypts the encrypted data using its private key to get the final result. This is illustrated in Figure 2.

As a result, this method allows multiple healthcare institutions to jointly compute a function over their private inputs without revealing patients' information to other parties. So, patients' data are encrypted and sent to the TP using Algorithm 1.

In the same order of ideas, each hospital decrypts the data sent by the third party to obtain the final result, using the Algorithm 2.

Figure 2. The proposed architecture for securing healthcare collaboration

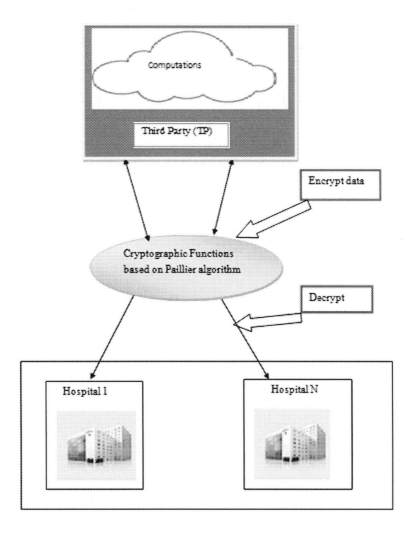

Algorithm 1. Data_Encryption

```
Input: D₁, D₂, Dₙ are data from n parties and F is Paillier algorithm.
Output: REn is the encrypted result
procedure 1: Data_Compute ()
1.  begin
2.    for i=1 to n do
3.      begin
4.        // encrypt the data using Paillier.//
5.            Compute Deni ←F (Dᵢ)
6.            Forward DEnᵢ to the TP
7.      end
8.  end
procedure 2: TP_Compute ()
9.  begin
10.   for i=1 to n do
11.     begin
12.         TP receives the encrypted data DEnᵢ
13.     end
// TP makes computation on the encrypted data received from all the parties. //
      for i=1 to n do
14.   begin
              Ren ← Compute (DEnᵢ,..., DEnₙ)     // calculate encrypted result using Paillier//
15.   end
16.         return < REn >
17. end
```

Algorithm 2. Data_Decrypt ()

```
Input: REn, Pk, where REn is the encrypted result sent by TP and Pk is the Paillier private key
Output: R is the final result

1. begin
2. // each party decrypts the encrypted results obtained from TP to get the final computation
   result by using Paillier algorithm. //
3.    R←Paillier (REn, Pk)
4.    return < R >
5.  end
```

Based on these measures, the proposed method ensures security and privacy in cloud computing during data collection and computations. Therefore, it is an appropriate solution to encourage collaboration among healthcare professionals, thereby helping to reduce medical errors and increase quality.

6. SECURE MULTIPARTY COMPUTATION

One essential aspect of a SMC protocol is that different organizations can compute data upon their sensitive information without any fear that the information will be disclosed (Grigoriev, Kish, & Shpilrain, 2017). For this reason, this technique is being increasingly and widely used as a solution to ensure privacy-preserving in the data sharing system. Generally speaking, the principle and basic background on secure multiparty computation protocol was first introduced by Yao (Yao, 1982; Yao, 1986). Basically, this protocol offers the possibility to evaluate a function based on distributed inputs in a secure manner. In other words, the participants' inputs should remain secret even though they are used in the computations, while the results should simultaneously be correct. Frequently, the SMC technique is used in a situation where n parties who are having private data x_1, x_2, x_3,...,x_n are interested in cooperating to evaluate a given public function f (x_1, x_2, x_3,..., x_n) in such a way that each entity u_i is not able to reveal any information about x_j in case i ≠ j (Liu, Li, Chen, Xu, Zhang, & Zhou, 2017). Accordingly, this approach allows multiple organizations to securely outsource the evaluation of a joint function that uses secret inputs. In this context, there are two models that facilitate a successful presentation of this protocol namely real and ideal model (Tawfik, Sabbeh, & EL-Shishtawy, 2018). In an ideal world, participants can interact directly with a central authority, which is often a trusted third party (TTP). In this case, all parties encrypt their private data, and then send them to the TTP via the Internet. The latter offers the necessary resources to ease computations of the function f and delivers the result in an effective way. Finally, users decrypt the encrypted value to obtain the final result. The fundamental principles and basic functionality of SMC is presented in Figure 3.

Unlike the model above, no trusted third party exists in the real concept. Hence, clients implement and run a real protocol through the exchange of a series of messages, as shown in Figure 4.

Usually, the ideal world specifications are used to evaluate the privacy level in the SMC protocol. In this approach, each entity u_i transmits its input x_1, x_2, x_3,..., x_m to a central entity, thereby replacing the trusted party. Next, this component calculates the value of a public function f(x_1, x_2, x_3,..., x_m) and returns the result to all users, as shown in Figure 5.

Figure 3. Architecture of SMP in an ideal model

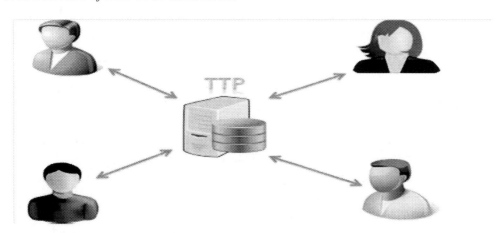

Figure 4. Architecture of SMP in a real model

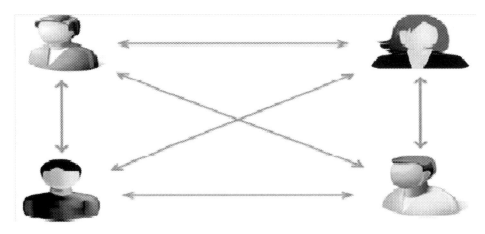

Figure 5. Principle of the SMC protocols

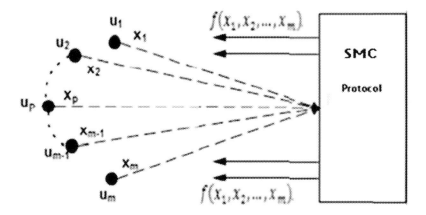

6.1. Security Models

This section discusses a situation in which an adversarial entity can control some subsets of the involved parties in order to attack the protocol execution. To this end, many aspects must be taken into account when designing a multiparty computation protocol (Lindell & Pinkasy, 2009; Canetti, 2000; Jarecki & Shmatikov, 2007). Concretely, any secure algorithm need to meet the following requirements, i.e., privacy, correctness, independence of inputs, guaranteed output delivery and fairness. This implies that all parties should receive their outputs with a high level of accuracy. More specifically, we study the power of the adversary that attacks participated entities during the protocol execution. In general, three major parameters are used to determine the influence of an adversary in the security of SMC protocols, namely corruption strategy, adversarial behavior and complexity (Goldreich, 2009; Aumann, 2010).

- **Corruption Strategy:** This technique seeks to determine when and how clients are corrupted. The corruption takes place when a malicious adversary has control over clients. Basically, two main models are proposed to simulate the corruption strategy, i.e., static and adaptive models. Ideally, corrupted parties are set in advance in the first model. In contrast, the adversary may be allowed to corrupt participating entities during the protocol execution in the adaptive corruption model.

- **Adversarial Behavior:** This parameter is meant to describe properly the behavior of the corrupted parties during the running SMC algorithm. More precisely, all parties even the corrupted ones correctly follow the protocol specifications in the presence of static semi-honest adversaries. It is interesting to note that corrupted parties can arbitrarily make the protocol execution deviate from its normal course. In this case, honest parties follow all instructions, while others may behave arbitrarily according to the adversary's instructions.

- **Computational Complexity:** Many factors might seriously impact system performance during the protocol execution. More formally, polynomial-time and computationally unbounded model are the most widely used parameters for evaluating the time complexity of an SMC algorithm. Subsequently, there are two parameters that an adversary is allowed to take. The first case is typically represented using probabilistic polynomial-time algorithms. In the second option, the malicious adversary has no computational limits during the execution of an SMC protocol.

6.2. Basic Computation Primitives

Practically, to implement a SMC protocol for securing computation tasks, we can use various approaches to satisfy the requirements of each situation. For all these methods, we need to execute the appropriate protocol for secure function evaluation. This paper explores the most common methods of implementing the SMC protocols.

- **Boolean Circuits (Malkhi, Nisan, Pinkas, & Sella, 2004; Yao, 1986):** The basic principle of this method was introduced by Yao in order to address the millionaire problem more efficiently. The proposed solution is typically based on Oblivious Transfer (OT) called Garbled Circuit (Feng, Ma, & Chen, 2015). More precisely, a boolean circuit is used to model a function that ensures privacy-preserving during the execution of the SMC algorithm. Mainly, this concept uses scrambled circuit evaluation to achieve an efficient fair and secure protocol. Technically speaking, the first party permuts and encodes the inputs by means of a scrambled circuit, while the second one evaluates this created scrambled circuit.

- **Secret Share Scheme (Shamir, 1979; Deepthi, Lakshmi, & Deepthi, 2017):** In this model, the secret data M are broken up into n shares $(S_1, S_2, ..., S_n)$ to support a distributed storage system. In reality, we need to define a threshold to determine the number of shares. For example, the threshold A (t, n) creates n small parts and at least t portions are required to recover the secret data. Therefore, (t-1) or fewer shares cannot reconstruct the secret M. Formally, the secret data M is represented as a polynomial function. To this aim, we choose a large prime p and randomly select coefficients $(a_1, a_2, ..., a_{t-1})$, defining the follwing function f. Equation (1) shows a representation of the function f.

$$f(x) = M + a_1x + a_2x^2 + \dots + a_{t-1}x^{t-1} \pmod p) \; 1 \le t \le n \tag{1}$$

In this concept, each portion is represented by (x_i, y_i), where $x_i = 1\dots n$ and $y_i = f(x_i)$. Similarly, to reconstruct the secret data M, we combine t pairs of (xi, yi) by using the Lagrange interpolation polynomial, as presented in Equation (2).

$$M \equiv \sum_{k=1}^{t} y_k \left[\prod_{i=1, i \ne k}^{t} \frac{-x_i}{x_k - x_i} \right] \bmod p \tag{2}$$

Accordingly, this technique A (t, n) is used to share data among n parties, and ensure that private data cannot be disclosed.

- **Homomorphic Encryption:** The novelty of these methods consists in their ability to perform mathematical operations on encrypted data without compromising the encryption (Marwan, Kartit, & Ouahmane, 2018). Interestingly, cloud providers rely on these techniques to secure basic arithmetic operations, such as addition, multiplication and division, without knowledge of the private key. Clients subsequently obtain the final result using the corresponding private key. To preserve the client's privacy, data are encrypted automatically on a local machine before being uploaded to an off-site application. To this aim, various schemes have been developed to secure processing of sensitive data within untrusted clouds. Among them, the cryptosystems based on Paillier or RSA is showing particular promise as a safe and simple option to process encrypted data.

In reality, the Paillier scheme (Paillier, 1999) is a probabilistic asymmetric algorithm designed to support homomorphic addition. Essentially, this public-key cryptography relies on composite degree residousity classes to perform certain mathematical operations safely. In this respect, Paillier cryptosystem is composed of three main modules, namely key generation, encryption and decryption. We first consider two numbers (p and q) that are large primes to calculate the composite n = p·q. Second, we randomly select g, and then check whether n and $L\left(g^\lambda \bmod n2\right)$ are coprime. In this case, L refers to the function L (u) = (u-1)/n. Note that λ is the Carmichael function $\lambda\left(p.q\right)$ = lcm (p-1, q-1), and lcm is the least common multiple. Section 7 provides more information about the Paillier algorithm and its main functions involved in this cryptosystem.

Alternatively, the RSA algorithm (Rivest, Shamir, & Adleman, 1978) is used as an encryption technique that typically satisfies multiplicative homomorphic property. In this cryptosystem, we use two large primes p and q to compute the value n = p·q. Further, we choose e that satisfies the following equation gcd (e, φ (p.q)) = 1, where φ (the Euler's Totient function) is calculated as φ (n) = (p - 1)(q - 1). We consider both C_1 and C_2 as the ciphertexts of two secret data m_1 and m_2 using RSA algorithm with public key pk.

$$C_1 \cdot C_2 = E(m_1, pk) \cdot E(m_2, pk) \tag{3}$$

$$= m_1^e \times m_2^e \pmod n \tag{4}$$

$$= (m_1 \cdot m_2)^e \pmod n \tag{5}$$

$$= E(m_1 \cdot m_2, pk) \tag{6}$$

Based on the Equation (6), the RSA cryptosystem allows a user to perform multiplication operations on encrypted data.

7. SIMULATION RESULTS

The proposed framework is particularly helpful for situations that require statistical analysis functions for medical research. In the healthcare domain, this implies collecting clinical information that is stored in distributed databases. To better understand this concept more simply, the medical authority decides to calculate the disease rate. In such cases, we use different databases of all participating institutions to determine the number of affected persons. At the same time, developing effective security mechanisms is necessary to protect confidential data. The basic idea is to encrypt the hospital's data with homomorphic encryption to avoid any disclosure, and send them to a trusted authority. The latter performs the requested operations on encrypted medical information and returns an encrypted result to all clients in a secure manner. To realize such an approach, we use the Paillier encryption since it supports algebraic operations over encrypted inputs. Basically, Paillier cryptosystem is composed of three main functions, as illustrated in the Algorithm 3 (Ganesan, Balasubramanian, & Muthusamy, 2018).

Algorithm 3. Paillier_Cryptosystem

Input: m is data, where $m \in \mathbb{Z}_n$

Output: c is encrypted data, where ($c \in \mathbb{Z}_n$)

function KeyGeneration ($p, q \in \mathbb{P}$)

    Step 1: Compute $n = p \cdot q$

    Step2: Choose $g \in \mathbb{Z}_n^*$ such that gcd (L (L g mod n^2)), n) = 1, with $L(u) = \frac{u-1}{n}$

return < Public key: pk =(n, g), Secret key: sk = (p, q) >

function Encryption ($m \in \mathbb{Z}_n$

    Step 1: Choose $r \in \mathbb{Z}_n$

    Step2: Compute $c = g^m r^n \bmod n^2$

return $< c \in \mathbb{Z}_n >$

function Decryption ($c \in \mathbb{Z}_n$)

    Compute $\quad m = \dfrac{L(c^\lambda \bmod n^2)}{L(g^\lambda \bmod n^2)} \bmod n$

return < m >

Concretely, the hospital 1 and hospital 2 use Paillier public key pk to encrypt their patients' data, i.g., m_1 and m_2. Thus, we obtain two ciphertexts c_1 and c_2 respectively.

So,

$$c_1 = E(m1, pk); c_2 = E(m_2, pk) \tag{7}$$

$$c_1 = g^{m_1} r_1^n \left(\bmod\ n^2\right); c_2 = g^{m_2} r_2^n \left(\bmod\ n^2\right) \tag{8}$$

In this scheme, the third party (TP) performs the multiplication of the encrypted inputs.

$$c_1 \cdot c_2 = E(m_1, pk).\ E(m_2, pk); c_1 \cdot c_2 = (g^{m_1} r_1^n)\left(g^{m_2} r_2^n\right) \left(\bmod\ n^2\right) \tag{9}$$

$$c_1 \cdot c_2 = (g^{m_1} r_1^n)\left(g^{m_2} r_2^n\right) \left(\bmod\ n^2\right) \tag{10}$$

$$c_1 \cdot c_2 = g^{m_1 + m_2} (r_1 r_2)^n \left(\bmod\ n^2\right) \tag{11}$$

$$c_1 \cdot c_2 = E(m_1 + m_2, pk) \tag{12}$$

Therefore

$$D\ (E(m_1, pk) \cdot E(m_2, pk)\ (\bmod\ n^2)) = m_1 + m_2\ (\bmod\ n) \tag{13}$$

Accordingly, each hospital uses its secret key to calculate the final result. Only after we decrypted this result we get the sum of two numbers m_1 and m_2, as shown in Equation (13).

The main objective of this section is to show that Pailler algorithm can perform additional operation on encrypted numeric data. Practically, we implement this algorithm to prove its homomorphic properties and to show its main benefits. To this end, we use JAVA 8 with Eclipse as a programming tool. In this study, we calculate the sum of two values: 200 and 80 using Paillier cryptosystem, as summurized in Table 1.

Based on the simulation results, the proposed solution is designed to provide a collaborative approach for computing a desired function with secret inputs. More precisely, this method enables various hospitals to perform addition on encrypted values. Interestingly, our solution prevents the unauthorized use of the confidential information by using encryption techniques. Consequently, the proposal is a simple and efficient method to boost collaboration systems in the healthcare domain.

Table 1. Secure addition using Paillier algorithm

Value 1	200
Value 2	80
Value of public key n	37424179519538756688517435737142680069377272034874446428301468124453148511384258934538298337907409178702574975675483345959323
Value of public key g	100
Value of private key p	5885646212560664696538203598671798456067702226458074557279599
Value of private key q	6358550644731437320185681182946097312923842830147133451353587
Encrypted value 1	534541499488116765527247784976850093946536340695284125389328275334286635737225571834181024968695427584957684696077386955574319429404519903493384403027493465040098582799837305995127645164014365472900647545610686060750475455839753895950873184203607
Encrypted value 2	79786514957875374524051292949249474309682166826220037843779721131616359008524915754790581691005525068126094801134579556637459159729193115079203728182701677856251139694036187449278765102196773180288751215356685896511242540162873353496035347317717739
Encrypted product	41641128933543118515236142300200397369070310302894344972402663773309845133132440146838835278840198831551862905474258979350289108416042330912981815998726144266224983282614941564834017578895383073509588676670506808959964133897719250390173312556603
Traditional addition	280
Homomorphic addition	280
Execution time	15 ms

8. CONCLUSION AND FUTURE WORK

From an economic perspective, cloud computing aims at reducing operating costs because its resources are served in a pay-per-use model. Ideally, this technology is designed to ensure interoperability among different Electronic Health Record (EHR) systems, thereby improving collaboration. To this end, we propose a cloud application to help health professionals to communicate and collaborate more effectively. Despite its remarkable advantages, the use of cloud computing may jeopardize data confidentiality and expose them to serious security concerns. In this respect, we use secure multiparty computation (SMC) algorithms to prevent the potential disclosure of confidential information. Technically, there are various approaches for implementing a SMC protocol, namely arithmetic circuit, secret share scheme and homomorphic encryption. In this work, we typically use the Paillier algorithm. It is a homomorphic encryption scheme that supports the addition of encrypted data. Based on this concept, the proposed framework can be used to allow different hospitals to jointly calculate the total number of patients suffering from a disease. We therefore propose a homomorphic encryption to improve the safety and operate encrypted data. Consequently, SMC protocol is a promising approach in the context of privacy preservation in collaborative systems. In future work, we intend to implement Fully Homomorphic (FH) schemes in order to improve computation on encrypted data since they perform both addition and multiplication over the ciphertext. Moreover, we will address issues related to Cryptographic Key Management (CKM) for an effective data exchange between healthcare providers.

REFERENCES

Abomhara, M., & Ben Lazrag, M. (2016). UML/OCL-based modeling of work-based access control policies for collaborative healthcare systems. In *International Conference on e-Health Networking, Applications and Services (Healthcom)* (pp. 1–6). 10.1109/HealthCom.2016.7749461

Abouelmehdi, K., Beni-Hessane, A., & Khalouf, H. (2018). Big healthcare data: preserving security and privacy. *Journal of Big Data,* vol. 5, no. 1.

Anjum, A., Malik, S. R., Choo, K. R., Khan, A., Haroon, A., Khan, S., ... Raza, B. (2018). An efficient privacy mechanism for electronic health records. *Computers & Security, Elsevier, 72,* 196–211. doi:10.1016/j.cose.2017.09.014

Arinze, B., & Anandarajan, M. (2010). Factors that determine the adoption of cloud computing: A global perspective. *International Journal of Enterprise Information Systems, 6*(4), 55–68. doi:10.4018/jeis.2010100104

Aumann, Y., & Lindell, Y. (2010). Security against covert adversaries: Efficient protocols for realistic adversaries. *Journal of Cryptology, 23*(2), 281–343. doi:10.100700145-009-9040-7

Babrahem, A. S., & Monowar, M. M. (2017). Maintaining security and privacy of the patient's EHR using cryptographic organization based access control h cloud environment. In *International Conference on Intelligent Communication and Computational Techniques (ICCT)*, Jaipur, India (pp. 182-188). 10.1109/INTELCCT.2017.8324042

Bajwa, N. K., Singh, H., & De, K. K. (2017). Critical success factors in electronic health records (EHR) implementation: An exploratory study in north India. *International Journal of Healthcare Information Systems and Informatics, 12*(2), 1–17. doi:10.4018/IJHISI.2017040101

Birje, M. N., Challagidad, P. S., Goudar, R. H., & Tapale, M. T. (2017). Cloud computing review: Concepts, technology, challenges and security. *International Journal of Cloud Computing, 6*(1), 32–57. doi:10.1504/IJCC.2017.083905

Canetti, R. (2000). Security and composition of multiparty cryptographic protocols. *Journal of Cryptology, 3*(1), 143–202. doi:10.1007001459910006

Deepthi, S., Lakshmi, V. S., & Deepthi, P. P. (2017) Image processing in encrypted domain for distributed storage in cloud. In *International Conference on Wireless Communications, Signal Processing and Networking (WiSPNET)* (pp. 1478-1482). 10.1109/WiSPNET.2017.8300008

Feng, Y., Ma, H., & Chen, X. (2015). Efficient and verifiable outsourcing scheme of sequence comparisons. *Intell. Autom. Soft Comput., 21*(1), 51–63. doi:10.1080/10798587.2014.915109

Fernandes, D. A. B., Soares, L. F. B., Gomes, J. V., Freire, M. M., & Inácio, P. R. M. (2013). Security issues in cloud environments: A survey. *International Journal of Information Security, 13*(2), 113–170. doi:10.100710207-013-0208-7

Ganesan, I., Balasubramanian, A. A. A., & Muthusamy, R. (2018). An efficient implementation of novel Paillier encryption with polar encoder for 5G systems in VLSI. *Computers and Electrical Engineering*, *65*, 153–164. doi:10.1016/j.compeleceng.2017.04.026

Goldreich, O. (2009). Foundations of cryptography (Vol. 2). Cambridge University Press.

Grigoriev, D., Kish, L. B., & Shpilrain, V. (2017). Yao's millionaires' problem and public-key encryption without computational assumptions. *International Journal of Foundations of Computer Science*, *28*(04), 379–389. doi:10.1142/S012905411750023X

Harsha Sandaruwan, G. P., & Ran Oppgave, P. S. (2013). *Secure multi-party based cloud computing framework for statistical data analysis of encrypted* [Master's Thesis]. University of Agder.

Hu, N., Cheung, S., & Nguyen, T. (2006). Secure image filtering. In *Proceeding of the IEEE International Conference on Image Processing (ICIP)* (pp. 1553–1556).

Iqbal, S., Kiah, M. L. M., Anuar, N. B., Daghighi, B., Wahab, A. W. A., & Khan, S. (2016). Service delivery models of cloud computing: Security issues and open challenges. *Security and Communication Networks*, *9*(17), 4726–4750. doi:10.1002ec.1585

Jarecki, S., & Shmatikov, V. (2007). Efficient two-party secure computation on committed inputs. In M. Naor (Ed.), *Advances in Cryptology - EUROCRYPT 2007, LNCS* (Vol. 4515, pp. 97–114). Springer. doi:10.1007/978-3-540-72540-4_6

Jouini, M., & Rabai, L. B. A. (2016). A security framework for secure cloud computing environments. [IJCAC]. *International Journal of Cloud Applications and Computing*, *6*(3), 32–44. doi:10.4018/IJCAC.2016070103

Khan, N., & Al-Yasiri, A. (2016). Cloud security threats and techniques to strengthen cloud computing adoption framework. *International Journal of Information Technology and Web Engineering*, *11*(3), 50–64. doi:10.4018/IJITWE.2016070104

Krishna, B. H., Kiran Dr, S., Murali, G., & Reddy, R. P. K. (2016). Security issues in service model of cloud computing environment. *Procedia Computer Science*, *87*, 246–251. doi:10.1016/j.procs.2016.05.156

Lee, L. J. H., & Leu, J. D. (2016). Exploring the effectiveness of IT application and value method in the innovation performance of enterprise. *International Journal of Enterprise Information Systems*, *12*(2), 47–65. doi:10.4018/IJEIS.2016040104

Li, W., Larson, M., Hu, C., Li, R., Cheng, X., & Bie, R. (2016). Secure multi-unit sealed first-price auction mechanisms. *Security and Communication Networks*, *9*(16), 3833–3843. doi:10.1002ec.1522

Lindell, Y. & Pinkasy, B. (2009). Secure multiparty computation for privacy-preserving data mining. *Journal of Privacy and Confidentiality*, 59-98.

Liu, X., Li, S., Chen, X., Xu, G., Zhang, X., & Zhou, Y. (2017) Efficient Solutions to two-party and multiparty millionaires' problem. In Security and Communication Networks.

Malkhi, D., Nisan, N., Pinkas, B., & Sella, Y. (2004) Fairplay: a secure two-party computation system. In *Proc. 13th USENIX Security Symposium* (pp. 287-302).

Marwan, M., Kartit, A., & Ouahmane, H. (2016). Cloud-based medical image issues. *International Journal of Applied Engineering Research, 11*(5), 3713–3719.

Marwan, M., Kartit, A., & Ouahmane, H. (2018). A Framework to secure medical image storage in cloud computing environment. *Journal of Electronic Commerce in Organizations, 16*(1), 1–16. doi:10.4018/JECO.2018010101

Marwan, M., Kartit, A., & Ouahmane, H. (2018). Using homomorphic encryption in cloud-based medical image processing: Opportunities and challenges. *Lecture Notes in Networks and Systems, 37*, 824–835. doi:10.1007/978-3-319-74500-8_75

Masuda, Y., Shirasak, S., Yamamoto, S., & Hardjono, T. (2018). Architecture board practices in adaptive enterprise architecture with digital platform: A case of global healthcare enterprise. *International Journal of Enterprise Information Systems, 14*(1), 1–20. doi:10.4018/ijeis.2018010101

Mazhar, A., Samee, U. K., & Athanasios, V. (2015). Security in cloud computing: Opportunities and challenges. *Information Science, Elsevier, 305*, 357–383. doi:10.1016/j.ins.2015.01.025

Mell, P., & Grance, T. (2009). The NIST definition of cloud computing. National Institute of Standards and Technology. *Technical Report, 15*, 1–3.

Molina, A. D., Salajegheh, M., & Fu, K. (2009). HICCUPS: health information collaborative collection using privacy and security. In *Proceedings of the 1st ACM Workshop on Security and Privacy in Medical and Home-Care Systems (SPIMACS '09)* (pp. 21–30). 10.1145/1655084.1655089

Paillier, P. (1999) Public-key cryptosystems based on composite degree residuosity classes. In *Proceedings of the 17th International Conference on Theory and Application of Cryptographic Techniques, EUROCRYPT'99* (pp. 223–238). Springer. 10.1007/3-540-48910-X_16

Radwan, T., Azer, M. A., & Abdelbaki, N. (2017). Cloud computing security: Challenges and future trends. *International Journal of Computer Applications in Technology, 55*(2), 158–172. doi:10.1504/IJCAT.2017.082865

Ramachandra, G., Iftikhar, M., & Khan, F. A. (2017). A comprehensive survey on security in cloud computing. *Procedia Computer Science, Elsevier, 110*, 465–472. doi:10.1016/j.procs.2017.06.124

Ravi Kumar, P., Herbert Raj, P., & Jelciana, P. (2017). Exploring security issues and solutions in cloud computing services – a survey. *Cybernetics and Information Technologies, 17*(4), 3–31.

Rivest, R., Shamir, A., & Adleman, L. (1978). A method for obtaining digital signatures and public key cryptosystems. *Communications of the ACM, 21*(2), 120-126.

Shameem, P. M., Johnson, N., Shaji, R. S., & Arun, E. (2017). An effective resource management in cloud computing. *International Journal of Communication Networks and Distributed Systems, 19*(4), 448–464. doi:10.1504/IJCNDS.2017.087388

Shamir, A. (1979). How to share a secret. *Communications of the ACM, 22*(11), 612–613. doi:10.1145/359168.359176

Shirazi, F., Seddighi, A., & Iqbal, A. (2017). Cloud computing security and privacy: an empirical study. In Human-Computer Interaction (pp. 534–549). Springer.

Shundong, L., Chunying, W., Daoshun, W., & Yiqi, D. (2014). Secure multiparty computation of solid geometric problems and their applications. *Information Sciences, 282*, 401–413. doi:10.1016/j.ins.2014.04.004

Sifou, F., Hammouch, A., & Kartit, A. (2018). Ensuring security in cloud computing using access control: A survey. *Lecture Notes in Networks and Systems, Springer, 37*, 255–264. doi:10.1007/978-3-319-74500-8_23

Tawfik, A.M., & Sabbeh, S.F. & El-Shishtawy, T. (2018). Privacy-preserving secure multiparty computation on electronic medical records for star exchange topology. *Arabian Journal for Science and Engineering*, 1–10.

Yao, A. C. (1982). Protocols for secure computations. In *Proceedings of the 23rd Annual Symposium on Foundations of Computer Science, SFCS '82* (pp. 160-164). IEEE Computer Society, Washington DC, USA.

Yao, A. C. (1986). How to generate and exchange secrets. In *27th IEEE Symposium on Foundations of Computer Science* (pp. 162-167).

Yi, X., Rao, F. Y., Bertino, E., & Bouguettaya, A. (2015) Privacy-preserving association rule mining in cloud computing. *In Proceedings of the 10th ACM Symposium on Information, Computer and Communications Security* (pp. 439-450). ACM. 10.1145/2714576.2714603

Yüksel, B., Küpçü, A., & Özkasap, Ö. (2017). Research issues for privacy and security of electronic health services. *Future Generation Computer Systems, 68*, 1–13. doi:10.1016/j.future.2016.08.011

This research was previously published in the International Journal of Enterprise Information Systems (IJEIS), 14(3); edited by Madjid Tavana, pages 128-145, copyright year 2018 by IGI Publishing (an imprint of IGI Global).

Chapter 78
Trust Relationship Establishment Among Multiple Cloud Service Provider

Abhishek Majumder
Tripura University, India

Samir Nath
Tripura University, India

Arpita Bhattacharjee
Tripura University, India

Ranjita Choudhury
Tripura University, India

ABSTRACT

Trust relationships among multiple Cloud Service Providers is a concept in which multiple cloud service providers from multiple distributed Identity Provider can access resources of each other, only if they are trusted with their Identity Provider. In this chapter a scheme has been proposed to enhance the security of data in a multi-cloud environment by improving trust relationships among multiple clouds. The scheme is also designed to overcome interoperability problem between different clouds. In the proposed scheme concept of proxy is used. Client organization tries to communicate with multiple cloud service providers through proxy. Client organization send resource request to cloud service providers. On receiving the resource request the cloud service provider collect the authentication confirmation from proxy. Then it sends the reply and data to requested client organization. Numerical analysis and comparative study of the proposed scheme with some of the existing scheme has been carried out.

DOI: 10.4018/978-1-5225-8176-5.ch078

Copyright © 2019, IGI Global. Copying or distributing in print or electronic forms without written permission of IGI Global is prohibited.

INTRODUCTION

Cloud computing (Armbrust et. al., 2010) is known as a distributing computing, which is used to store client data and application in scattered data centre around the world, so that, client can access their data or grant applications from anywhere just with an internet connection. User's data and information is stored in the cloud data centre. Cloud service provider allows access to applications, operating systems and hardware.

For example, e-mail service like Gmail and Hotmail are type of cloud computing services. In the cloud, users can easily access their email from different browsers and computers just with the help of an internet connection. The emails are hosted in servers, but not stored locally on the client computer.

The cloud service provided to the user may be provided by a single cloud service provider. But the problem with single cloud service provider is the problem of availability. For overcoming this problem, the concept of multiple CSP (AlZain et al., 2012) has come into picture. Though multi cloud computing environment overcomes some of the security problems encountered in single cloud computing environment, but introduction of multi-cloud environment creates some new problems. One of these important issues is lack of trust relationships in Interoperability among multiple cloud service providers. Trust relationship among multiple Cloud Service Providers (CSPs) is a concept in which multiple CSPs from multiple distributed Identity Provider's (IdP) can access resources of each other, only if they are trusted with the Identity Provider's (IdP).

Figure 1. Cloud computing

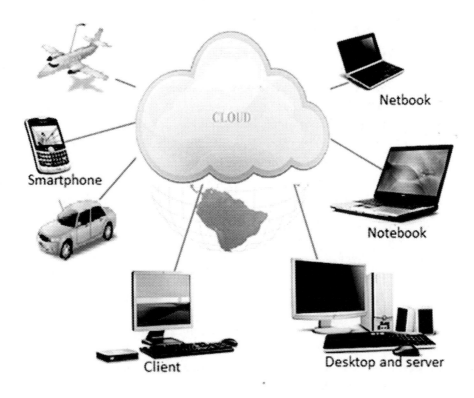

In this chapter, some of the existing schemes that had been designed to provide services to the client in multi clod environment have been discussed. A proxy based scheme has been proposed for multi-cloud environment with the following objectives:

- To enhance the security of data by improving trust relationship between multiple clouds.
- To overcome interoperability problem between different clouds.
- To reduce time consumption by introducing proxy.

MULTI-CLOUD COMPUTING

Popularity of single cloud providers are decreasing days by day, because of unavailable of service and malicious insider. Now-a-days multi-cloud computing have becoming in place of a single cloud computing.

Multi cloud strategy is a combination of two or more cloud services, which is used to avoid the risk of data loss, malicious insider etc. specially, user's data and information are stored in multiple cloud in multi-cloud computing environment.

Switching from single cloud to multi-cloud computing is most essential. Multi-cloud computing controls multiple clouds. Multi-cloud is not only reasonable but also important many reasons given here under.

- **Data Integrity:** Integrity is prevention of improper modification of information (Celesti et al., 2010; AlZain et al., 2011). Since in multi-cloud computing system copy of user data is stored in multiple CSPs, if one CSP get infected, the result from other CSP will contradict with that affected one. Therefore, it is not possible in multi-cloud environment to violet the integrity of the stored data.
- **Service Unavailability:** No compensation will be given by the company if system becomes failure (AlZain et al., 2011; AlZain et al., 2011) in single cloud provider. On the contrary, data is stored in multiple CSPs. So, even with failure of one system there is hardly chance of data loss in multi-cloud computing.
- **Data Intrusion:** In case of a single cloud provider data intrusion (AlZain et al., 2011) may take place. It is not possible to hack, access and modify the accounts password, information and resources in the case of multi-cloud computing environment. As multiple copies of same data are stored in multiple clouds, and retrieval of all of the copies is almost impossible.
- **Data Leakage:** Unauthorized transmission among two-user organization is known as data leakage (Ristenpart et al., 2009). Data leakage may occur in single cloud provider as because the service providers are not trusted to each other. Whereas in the case of multi-cloud trust relationship is the root to avoid any leakage.
- **Authenticity:** Data authentication assures that the returned data is the same as the stored data. Only the authorize users can access any information stored in multi-clouds.
- **Data Confidentiality:** Data Confidentiality (Yau et al., 2010) may be followed up only by the authenticated users of multi-cloud because multiple copies of the same data are stored in multiple distinct clouds with different types of encryption techniques.
- **Trust Relationship Between CSP:** Due to lack of trust relationships among user and cloud service provider no one can put faith on each other, which is a major problem. Trust relationship between multiple CSPs can build up only in multi-cloud computing.

LITERATURE REVIEW

In this section the existing schemes designed for providing cloud services in Multi cloud environment have been discussed.

Interoperability of Identity Management System

Le et al. (2008) introduces Identity Management Model. The theme of interoperability of Identity Management system is identified as follows:

- Cardspace from Microsoft
- Liberty from Liberty Alliance Project.

Windows Cardspace (Chappell et. al., 2006) is designed based on the law of identities and idea of identity meta-system. User-centric approach for digital identity management is windows Cardspace. It provides users secure way to manage their online identities. Windows Cardspace provides user two types of cards, namely:

- Self-issued cards, can be issued by the user himself.
- Managed cards, are accepted by the user but issued by other IdPs.

These cards are also known as information cards. Information card contains meta data which is useful to retrieve the users information at the identity provider side, and thus it establishes trust relationships among the user and identity provider.

Figure 2. Cardspace interaction and standards

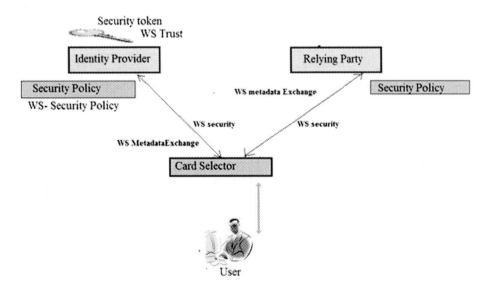

Liberty Project is founded in 2001 (Alliance, 2002) and is based on the idea of federated network identity and circle of trust in which service providers and identity providers establish a business relationship among them so that a principal (internet user in Liberty terminology) can perform business transaction in secure environment.

Liberty architecture is based on three frame work:

- ID-FF stands for Liberty Identity-Federation Framework. As its name indicates, this framework provides the specification for identity federation and simplified sign-on. It also supplies mechanisms for the termination of Federation and for single logout.
- ID-WSF stands for Identity-Web Service framework. It provides identity-based web services specification. It also defines a framework for creating, discovering and consuming identity services
- ID-SIS stands for Identity-Services Interface Specification. It is a collection of specifications. It enables network identity services by using ID-FF and ID-WSF.

If a user want to access service provider's resources, the service provider will ask the user to choose an identity provider and the user is redirected to the selected identity provider. This identity provider will require to the user to authenticate him with his account and to give him a security token. His security token will be forwarded to the service provider. The service provider will verify the token with the identity provider through a secured channel. As soon as the verification is terminated with a positive result, the user will be granted to access service provider's resources. With the belief of identity federation, after authentication, the user can access to any service provider's resource without asking for log-in again within a same circle of trust.

Drawback

It is not easy to find circles of trust due to complicated relationships among actors residing in different circles of trust. It brings out a problem of interoperability at two different levels:

1. Interoperability at the level of web simplified sign-on(SSO) of intraperimeter and of inter-perimeter.
2. Interoperability at the level of attributes sharing.

Proxy Based Model

Mukesh Singhal et al. (2013) proposed proxy based model. It is like firewalls, that carryout operation on the behalf of CSP's and/or client. The main purpose of using proxy is, it does not require prior agreement. The prior agreement means pre-established business.

Agreement between CSP's Proxy based model consists of five strategies:

- Cloud hosted proxy
- Proxy as a service
- Peer to peer proxy
- On premises proxy
- Hybrid proxy infrastructure

Figure 3. Cloud hosted proxy

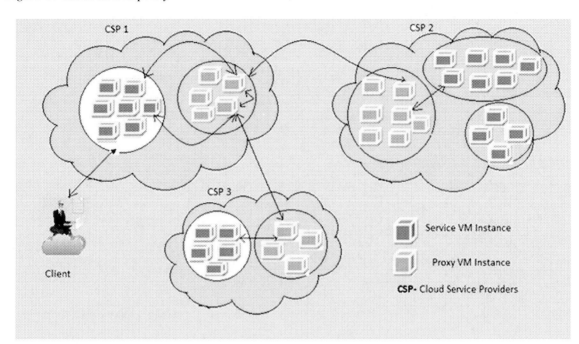

In the cloud hosted proxy, proxies are hosted by each and every CSP. As soon as any service request is received by one CSP, the same is forwarded to others through proxy. Proxy is used here for collaboration. Here, the user sends a request to cloud C1. Cloud C1 authentically sends the request to cloud C2 and C3.

Here proxy is considered to be an autonomous cloud itself. Proxy provides services to the clients and CSPs. Whenever a set of CSPs wants to collaborate, it can be managed by PSP (Proxy Service Provider).

In a peer-to-peer network interaction among the proxies can be done by a group of collaborating CSPs or a PSP. Alternatively, every proxy in the peer-to-peer network can be independent for its management. In proxy is capable of handling the service requests.

In case of on-premises proxy, a client can host and manages proxies those are within the client's organization's infrastructure. Here, a client uses on-premises proxy whenever wants to collaborate. For collaborating with other CSPs, the CSP needs to employ proxies which are within the domain of the service requestor client.

Hybrid proxy infrastructure is a combination of peer to peer proxy, on premises proxy, PSP maintained and cloud hosted proxy. It selects proxies depending on the type of the requested services and the cloud that starts collaboration with other cloud.

Drawback

The security issues founded in multi-cloud computing environment during the collaboration among multiple clouds are isolation management, data exposure and confidentiality and lack of trust relationships among multiple clouds, etc.

Figure 4. Proxy as a service. (a) Two proxies are employed to interact with CSPs C1 and C2 by the client. (b) C1 requires to discover services from C2 after a client requests a service to C1

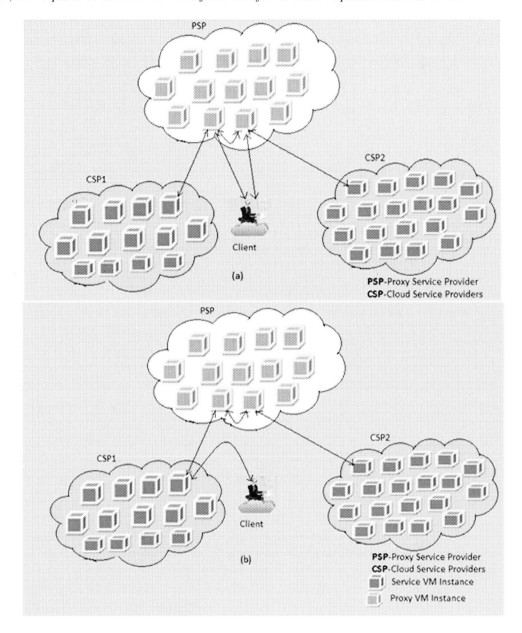

Security and Privacy Model

Jensen Meiko et al. (2013) presented a security and privacy model which provides different security solutions for multi-cloud adoption environment. Security and privacy model meditate on public clouds. It provides four distinct models for multi-cloud architectures.

In this model, different architectural models are introduced for distributing resources to multiple cloud service providers. Four architectural patterns are used:

Figure 5. On-premises proxy. Clients deploy proxies within the infrastructure of their organization. (a) Two proxies are employed by the client for interaction with CSPs C1 and C2. (b) Service request is initiated with C1, and it discovers that service from C2 is needed

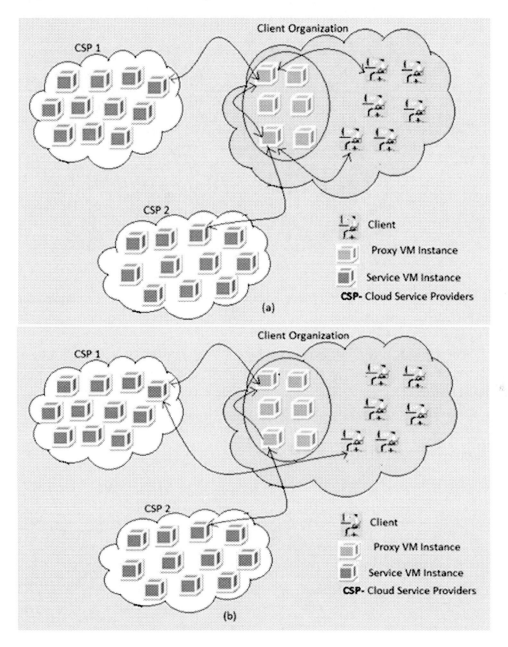

- Republication of application.
- Partition of application System into tries.
- Partition of Application logic into fragments.
- Partition of application data into fragment.

Figure 6. Republication of application system

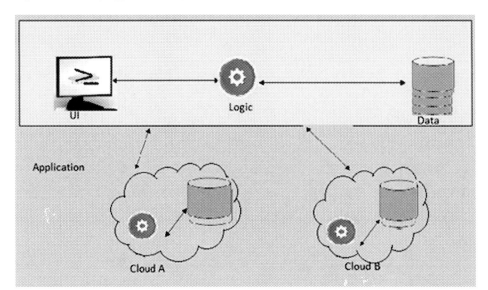

In the republication of application system, same operation is performed in multiple clouds and a comparison is made between the respective results, which allow users to have the evidence. In this way data integrity is preserve here.

In partition of application system tries data and logic are separated and stored in two different clouds. If the execution of logic and data are performed within the user's system, it will not be possible for the application provider to know about the outcome of the execution. In this model, data and logic are separated, so there may not be any risk of data leakage.

Figure 7. Partition of application system into tries

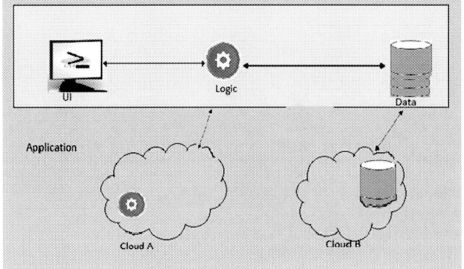

Figure 8. Partition of application logic into fragments

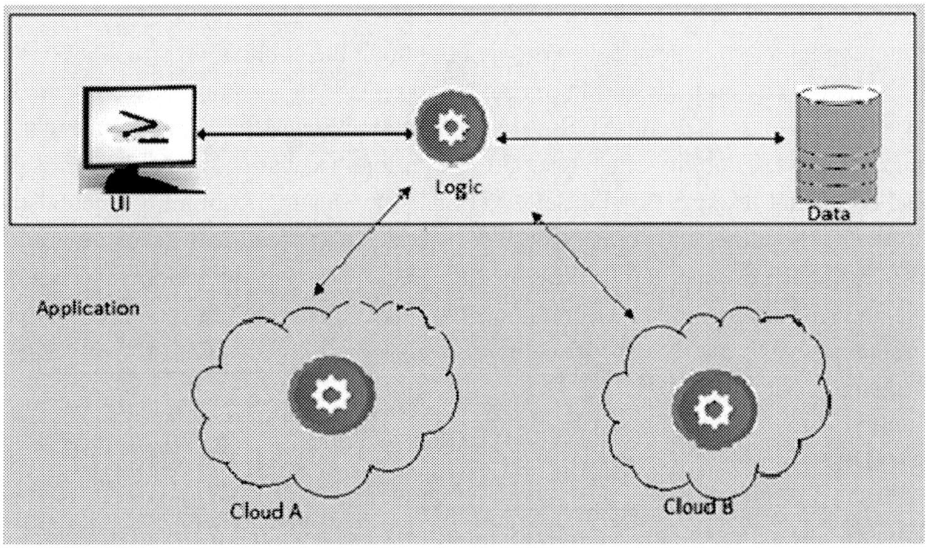

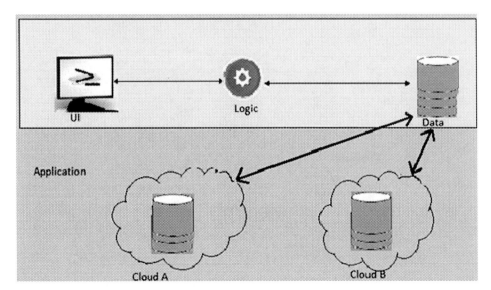

Data confidentiality is preserved in partition of application logic into fragments because the application logic is distributed among two clouds. The sharing of the computational load is lying with entrusted cloud, that is, public cloud and the part of critical share is laying with trusted cloud, that is private cloud.

Data confidentiality is also preserved by partitioning of application data into fragments. Since the application data is divided into two parts, they are stored in two different clouds. Therefore, the clouds will not able to access full data.

Figure 9. Partition of application data into fragments

Drawback

The complaint reoperation of logic and data is only possible if the application provider does not receive the customer's data in any case. Processing needs to take place in a secure environment. This can be present in the customer's own premises. But this almost annihilates the benefits of outsourcing, cost reduction, and seamless scalability of using cloud computing, because the customer needs to provision sufficient and complaint resources by himself. Alternatively, the application logic can also take place in a different tier of the complaint storage cloud, or on a different cloud with similar compliance level.

The drawback is the customer has to fully trust those cloud service providers that receive all information, logic and data. This somewhat contradicts the initial motivation of this multi-cloud approach. The disadvantageous in terms of confidentiality is every cloud provider learns everything about the application logic and data.

Depsky Model

Bassani et al. (2013) presented a simple model for multi-cloud system. It is a virtual storage cloud system. It consists of different clouds to build a cloud-of-clouds. By using multi-cloud provider the availability and confidentiality of data is preserved in the storage.

This system model is based on four clouds. All of these are storage clouds and being used independently. As this model uses the concept of secret sharing algorithm, therefore data can be encrypted before storing in the cloud.

Figure 10. Depsky model

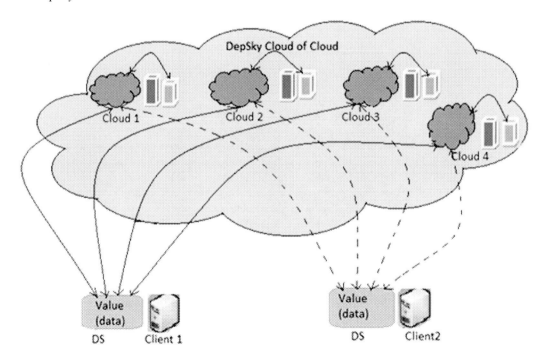

Drawback

Data need to be manipulated in virtual machine of cloud providers, which will not happen if the data has been encrypted.

Multi Cloud Database Model

Mohammed A. AlZain et al. (2011) proposed multi cloud database model (MCDB), which stated the data security and privacy issues of cloud computing, such as data intrusion, data integrity, service availability etc. MCDB model uses the concept of multi cloud service provider and secret sharing algorithm (Shamir, 1979). Some security risk like malicious insider and failing of cloud services can be overcome by this model.

MCDB model uses the concept of multi share technique (AlZain et al., 2011), in which multiple copies of the user's data are stored into multiple distinct clouds. Therefore, it avoids the drawbacks of single cloud, and minimizes the security risk from malicious insider. Database management system manages and controls the operations between the clients and the CSP. The components of different layers of MCDB are shown in Table 1. Overview of MCDB components are shown in Table 2.

INTER-CLOUD IDENTITY MANAGEMENT INFRASTRUCTURE MODEL

Celesti et. al. (2010) proposed Inter-cloud Identity Management Infrastructure (ICIMI) Model. This model is useful to overcome the Identity Management (IdM) and authentication issues in a cloud federation scenario. Here cloud is distinguished into two types: home cloud and foreign cloud. Home cloud

Table 1. MCDB layer

Layer Name	Component
Presentation Layer	User, HTTP Server
Application Layer	Servlet Engine
Management Layer	DBMS, CSP and data storage

Table 2. Overview of MCDB component

Component	Description
User	End user's web browser is accountable for displaying user interface.
HTTP Server	HTTP server manages the communication between the application and the browser. Execution of the application from the server side generates user interface
Servlet Engine	Servlet engine uses JDBC protocol to communicate with the data source
DBMS (Data source)	DBMS is responsible for rewriting the user's query, generating polynomial values, handling the user's query to each CSP and then receiving the result from CSP.
CSP and Dara Storage	CSP is responsible for storing the data in its cloud storage, that is divided into n shares and then returning the relevant shares to the DBMS that consists of the user's query result

Figure 11. MCDB model

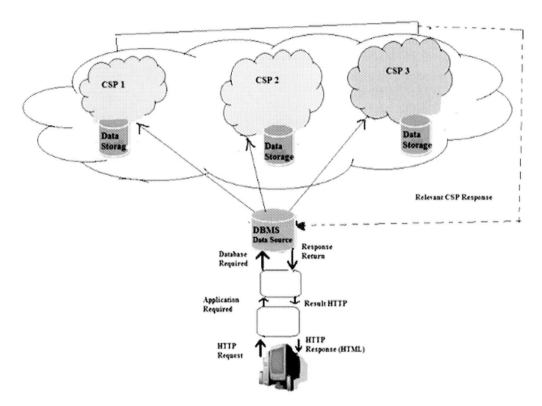

is a cloud service provider which forwards service request to the foreign cloud. The foreign cloud in turn accepts the request from the home cloud and provides the corresponding response to the requested services. The concept of single sign-on (SSO) authentication (Hursti, 1997) and digital identities are used in this model.

The following logical components are used in this model:

1. **End-User:** It is a person or a software/hardware which deserves a particular digital identity and who interacts with an on-line application.
2. **User Agent:** In the common case of the human interaction, it can be a browser or another software application.
3. **Service Provider (SP):** It is a system, or administrative domain. Identity provider provides information to the service provider and the service provider shall have to rely on the information of identity provider.
4. **Identity Provider (IdP) or Asserting Party:** It is a system or administrative domain, who provides information about the user's authentication.

In Figure 12, cloud A is considered to be home cloud and cloud B, C, and D as foreign cloud. Cloud A sends resource request to the cloud B, C, and D and an authentication task is performed in the IdPs of the respective foreign clouds.

Figure 12. Inter-cloud identity management infrastructure

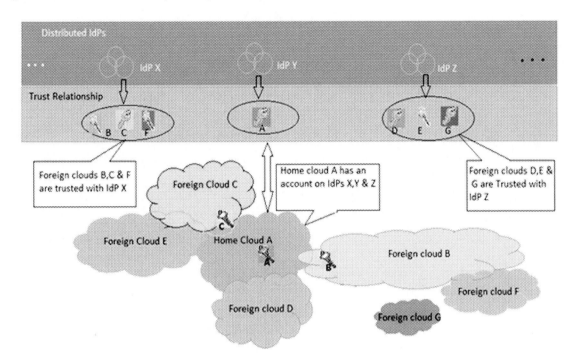

To access the resources from foreign cloud B, C and D, home cloud A requires creating an account on IdP X and IdP Z respectively. When home cloud A wants to access resources from cloud B and cloud C, clouds B and C forwards the same request to their IdP X. IdP X then verify the identity of home cloud A. If home cloud A is authenticated, only the requested resource is delivered to the home cloud A. The same is also applicable in case of foreign cloud C.

Proposed Scheme

It is already known that to establish a trust relationship among multiple CSPs a prior agreement is required. Therefore, use of proxy enables user to make a trust relationship without any prior agreements. In the proposed scheme, Pearson's correlation algorithm is used to select the foreign cloud which will be providing services.

In Figure 13, it is assumed that client Organization is trusted with IdP X and CSP 1 CSP 2 is trusted with IdP Y. Here, client organization is considered to be Home cloud and CSP1 & CSP 2 is considered to be foreign cloud.

Steps of the proposed scheme are given as follows

1. The authentication module of client starts the authentication toward the corresponding peer of CSP1 providing its identity. Also, clients in client organization send resource request to CSPl through proxy, to access the resources in CSP1
2. The authentication module of CSP 1 forwards the authentication request to the IdP Y.

Figure 13. Communication between home cloud and foreign cloud

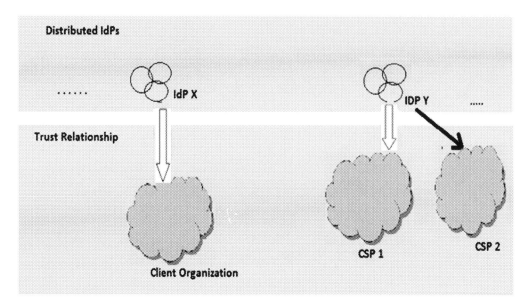

3. An authentication interaction between the authentication module of CSP1 & the IdP Y is initiated, and it will lead to the generation of a security context for the client in the client organization.
4. IdP Y sends the attributes (i.e., the credentials needed for executing local authentication) associated to the authenticated client in the client organization back to the authentication module of CSP1.
5. Finally, the requested resource is sent to the client organization from CSP1.

Figure 14. Trust relationship establishment

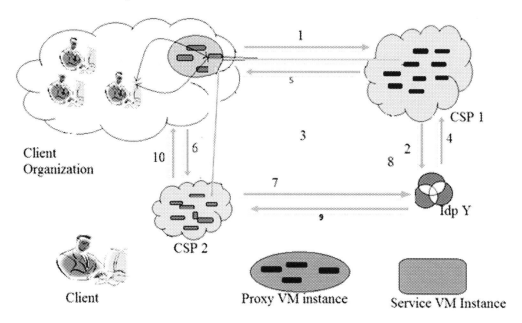

6. The authentication module of client starts the authentication toward the corresponding peer of CSP2, providing its identity. Also, clients in client organization send resource request to CSP2 through proxy, to access the resources in CSP2.
7. The authentication module of CSP2 forwards the authentication request to the IdP Y.
8. Since a security context already exists for client organization, so generation of security context will not be performed.
9. The attributes for authenticating client with CSP2 will be directly sent to the authentication module of CSP2.
10. Finally, the requested resource is sent to the proxy of the client organization from CSP2.

NUMERICAL ANALYSIS

In this scheme the concept of proxy is used because, proxy provides the facility for collaboration between the cloud service providers without the need of any prior agreement. The proposed scheme uses Pearson's Correlation to select the foreign cloud.

Pearson's Correlation is denoted by r. Correlation between two variables say X and Y are represented by

$$r_i = \frac{\sum XY_i}{\sqrt{\sum X^2 \sum Y_i^2}}$$

$$= \frac{\text{covarience of } (x,y)}{\sqrt{\text{covarience of } x}\sqrt{\text{covarience of } y}}$$

where, $X = x - \bar{x}, Y = y - \bar{y}$ i.e., X and Y are the deviations measured from their respective means.

Let, HC and F (F_1, F_2, F_3, F_4 and F_5) are the quantifiable parameters of home cloud and foreign cloud.

In this analysis one home cloud and five foreign clouds is considered. Let both of them are trusted. Suppose parameters of home cloud and foreign clouds are as follows:

	CPU Speed (GHz)		Working Time (AM / PM)	
HC =	[2.8	2	12	3]
F1 =	[1.4	1	12	2.5]
F2 =	[1.9	1.5	10	2.4]
F3 =	[2.5	3	8	4]
F4 =	[3.0	4	8	4]
F5 =	[2.7	2.8	6	3.2]
	RAM (GB)		Transmission rate (B / sec)	

Relation (r_1) between Home cloud (HC) and Foreign cloud (F_1) can be calculated in the following way:

The mean of quantifiable parameters of HC, $\bar{x} = \dfrac{\sum HC}{n} = \dfrac{(2.8+2+12+3)}{4} = 4.95$

The mean of quantifiable parameters of F_1, $\bar{y} = \dfrac{\sum F1}{n} = \dfrac{(1.4+1+12+2.5)}{4} = 4.225$

where, n = the total number of quantifiable parameters of Home cloud and Foreign cloud.
Now,

$$r_1 = \frac{\sum XY}{\sqrt{\sum X^2 Y^2}} = \frac{73.765}{\sqrt{66.83*81.8075}} = 0.997626681$$

Relation (r_2) between Home cloud (HC) and Foreign cloud (F_2) can be calculated in the following way:

The mean of quantifiable parameters of HC, $\bar{x} = \dfrac{\sum HC}{n} = \dfrac{(2.8+2+12+3)}{4} = 4.95$

The mean of quantifiable parameters of F_2, $\bar{y} = \dfrac{\sum F2}{n} = \dfrac{(1.9+1.5+10+2.4)}{4} = 3.95$

Now,

$$r_2 = \frac{\sum X Y}{\sqrt{\sum X^2 Y^2}} = \frac{31.93}{\sqrt{66.83*18.861}} = 0.905398981$$

Table 3.

HC	F_1	X = HC - 4.95	Y= F_1 - 4.225	X^2	Y^2	X*Y
2.8	1.4	-2.15	-2.825	4.6225	7.980625	6.07375
2	1	-2.95	-3.225	8.7025	10.400625	9.51375
12	12	7.05	7.775	49.7025	60.450625	54.81375
3	2.5	-1.95	-1.725	3.8025	2.975625	3.36375
19.8	16.9	0	0	66.83	81.8075	73.765

Table 4.

HC	F2	X= HC - 4.95	Y= F_2 - 3.95	X^2	Y^2	X*Y
2.8	1.9	-2.15	-2.05	4.6225	4.2025	4.4075
2	1.5	-2.95	-2.45	8.7025	6.0025	7.2275
12	10	7.05	6.05	49.7025	6.0025	17.2725
3	2.4	-1.95	-1.55	3.8025	2.4025	3.0225
19.8	15.8	0	0	66.83	18.61	31.93

Relation (r_3) between Home cloud (HC) and Foreign cloud (F_3) can be calculated in the following way:

The mean of quantifiable parameters of HC, $\bar{x} = \dfrac{\sum HC}{n} = \dfrac{(2.8+2+12+3)}{4} = 4.95$

The mean of quantifiable parameters of F_3, $\bar{y} = \dfrac{\sum F3}{n} = \dfrac{(2.5+3+8+4)}{4} = 4.375$

Now,

$$r_3 = \frac{\sum X\ Y}{\sqrt{\sum X^2\ Y^2}} = \frac{34.375}{\sqrt{66.83 * 18.6875}} = 0.972705504$$

Relation (r_4) between Home cloud (HC) and Foreign cloud (F_3) can be calculated in the following way:

The mean of quantifiable parameters of HC, $\bar{x} = \dfrac{\sum HC}{n} = \dfrac{(2.8+2+12+3)}{4} = 4.95$

The mean of quantifiable parameters of F_4, $\bar{y} = \dfrac{\sum F4}{n} = \dfrac{(3.0+4+8+4)}{4} = 4.75$

Now,

$$r_4 = \frac{\sum X\ Y}{\sqrt{\sum X^2\ Y^2}} = \frac{30.35}{\sqrt{66.83 * 14.75}} = 0.966667137$$

Relation (r_5) between Home cloud (HC) and Foreign cloud (F_5) can be calculated in the following way:

Table 5.

HC	F_3	X= HC - 4.95	Y= F_3- 4.375	X^2	Y^2	X*Y
2.8	2.5	-2.15	-1.875	4.6225	3.515625	4.03125
2	3	-2.95	-1.375	8.7025	1.890625	4.05625
12	8	7.05	3.625	49.7025	13.140625	25.55625
3	4	-1.95	-0.375	3.8025	0.140625	0.73125
19.8	17.5	0	0	66.83	18.6875	34.375

Table 6.

HC	F_4	X= HC - 4.95	Y=F_4- 4.75	X^2	Y^2	X*Y
2.8	3.0	-2.15	-1.75	4.6225	3.0625	3.7625
2	4	-2.95	-0.75	8.7025	0.5625	2.2125
12	8	7.05	3.25	49.7025	10.5625	22.9125
3	4	-1.95	-0.75	3.8025	0.5625	1.4625
19.8	19	0	0	66.83	14.75	30.35

The mean of quantifiable parameters of HC, $\bar{x} = \dfrac{\sum HC}{n} = \dfrac{(2.8+2+12+3)}{4} = 4.95$

The mean of quantifiable parameters of F_5 $\bar{y} = \dfrac{\sum F5}{n} = \dfrac{(2.7+2.8+6+3.2)}{4} = 3.675$

Now,

$$r_5 = \frac{\sum XY}{\sqrt{\sum X^2 Y^2}} = \frac{21.995}{\sqrt{66.83 * 7.3475}} = 0.99258667$$

There must need to arrange the values of relation(r) in descending order, like as given under:

$r_1 = 0.997626681$, $r_2 = 0.905398981$, $r_3 = 0.972705504$, $r_4 = 0.966667137$, $r_5 = 0.99258667$

Antonio Celesti et al. (2010) propose one mathematical analysis process, in which they use Weighted Euclidean Distance formula for analysis. According to their analysis, only those foreign clouds whose SLA matches with the SLA of home cloud are able to share or access resources from each other. But the problem is that, those foreign clouds whose SLA does not match with the home cloud SLA will not be able to share resources. They may have the requested resource that a particular home cloud is looking for.
Let,

$$F = (4) = \begin{bmatrix} 14 & 1 & 12 & 2.5 \\ 1.9 & 1.5 & 10 & 2.4 \\ 2.5 & 3 & 8 & 4 \\ 3.0 & 4 & 8 & 4 \\ 2.7 & 2.8 & 6 & 3.2 \end{bmatrix}$$

where, F is the K X N matrix in which only the matched foreign clouds are present.

The entries shown in the given matrix are supposed to be the quantifiable parameters of those foreign clouds. The formula for calculating the distance between the home cloud and a particular foreign cloud is,

$$d_i = \sqrt{\sum_{j=0}^{N} W_j \left(p^i_j - h_j\right)^2}$$

Table 7.

HC	F_5	X= HC - 4.95	Y.= F5- 3.675	X^2	Y^2	X*Y
2.8	2.7	-2.15	-0.975	4.6225	0.950625	2.09625
2	2.8	-2.95	-0.875	8.7025	0.765625	2.58125
12	6	7.05	2.325	49.7025	5.405625	16.39125
3	3.2	-1.95	-0.475	3.8025	0.225625	0.92625
19.8	14.7	0	0	66.83	7.3475	21.995

where,

P_j^i = i-th row and j-th column of matrix F and is considered as a vector.
d_i = Distance between home cloud and i-th foreign cloud.
h_j= Vector of N quantifiable parameters of home cloud.
W_j= The vector whose N elements w_j represent the weight associated to the j-th term of Euclidean distance. It is related to SLA.

They uses the concept of Kronecker delta (Δ_i) and calculates i-th row of matrix F by $p^i = \Delta_i \bullet F$. According to Kronecker delta,

$\Delta_i = 0$, *if* $i \neq j$

$= 1$, if $i = j$

Therefore,

$\Delta_1 = \begin{bmatrix} 1 & 0 & 0 & 0 & 0 \end{bmatrix}$

$\Delta_1 = \begin{bmatrix} 0 & 1 & 0 & 0 & 0 \end{bmatrix}$

$\Delta_1 = \begin{bmatrix} 0 & 0 & 1 & 0 & 0 \end{bmatrix}$

$\Delta_1 = \begin{bmatrix} 0 & 0 & 0 & 1 & 0 \end{bmatrix}$

$\Delta_1 = \begin{bmatrix} 0 & 1 & 0 & 0 & 1 \end{bmatrix}$

let,

$H = \begin{bmatrix} 2.8 & 2 & 12 & 3 \end{bmatrix}$

and

$W = \begin{bmatrix} 5 & 10 & 15 & 20 \end{bmatrix}$

now,

$$p^1 = \begin{bmatrix} 1.4 & 1 & 12 & 2.5 \end{bmatrix}$$

$$p^2 = \begin{bmatrix} 1.9 & 1.5 & 10 & 2.4 \end{bmatrix}$$

$$p^3 = \begin{bmatrix} 2.5 & 3 & 8 & 4 \end{bmatrix}$$

$$p4 = \begin{bmatrix} 3.0 & 4 & 8 & 4 \end{bmatrix}$$

$$p^5 = \begin{bmatrix} 2.7 & 2.8 & 6 & 3.2 \end{bmatrix}$$

According to the Weighted Euclidean distance formula, distance between home cloud and foreign cloud is calculated as,

$$d_i = \sqrt{\sum_{j=0}^{N} W_j \left(p_j^i - h_j \right)^2}$$

$$
\begin{aligned}
d_1 &= \sqrt{W_1 \left(p_1^1 - h_1 \right)^2 + W_2 \left(p_2^1 - h_2 \right)^2 + W_3 \left(p_3^1 - h_3 \right)^2 + W_4 \left(p_4^1 - h_4 \right)^2} \\
&= \sqrt{5\left(1.4 - 2.8\right)^2 + 10\left(1 - 2\right)^2 + 15\left(12 - 12\right)^2 + 20\left(2.5 - 3\right)^2} \\
&= \sqrt{24.8}
\end{aligned}
$$

$d_1 = 4.979959839$

$$
\begin{aligned}
d_2 &= \sqrt{W_1 \left(p_1^2 - h_1 \right)^2 + W_2 \left(p_2^2 - h_2 \right)^2 + W_3 \left(p_3^2 - h_3 \right)^2 + W_4 \left(p_4^2 - h_4 \right)^2} \\
&= \sqrt{5\left(1.9 - 2.8\right)^2 + 10\left(1.5 - 2\right)^2 + 15\left(10 - 12\right)^2 + 20\left(2.4 - 3\right)^2}
\end{aligned}
$$

$d_2 = 8.587782019$

$$
\begin{aligned}
d_3 &= \sqrt{W_1 \left(p_1^3 + h_1 \right)^2 + W_2 \left(p_2^3 + h_2 \right)^2 + W_3 \left(p_3^3 + h_3 \right)^2 + W_4 \left(p_4^3 + h_4 \right)^2} \\
&= \sqrt{5\left(2.5 - 2.8\right)^2 + 10\left(3 - 2\right)^2 + 15\left(8 - 12\right)^2 + 20\left(4 - 3\right)^2}
\end{aligned}
$$

$d_3 = 16.44536409$

$$d_4 = \sqrt{W_1\left(p_1^4 + h_1\right)^2 + W_2\left(p_2^4 + h_2\right)^2 + W_3\left(p_3^4 + h_3\right)^2 + W_4\left(p_4^4 + h_4\right)^2}$$
$$= \sqrt{5\left(3.0 - 2.8\right)^2 + 10\left(4 - 2\right)^2 + 15\left(8 - 12\right)^2 + 20\left(4 - 3\right)^2}$$

$d_4 = 17.32628062$

$$d_5 = \sqrt{W_1\left(p_1^5 + h_1\right)^2 + W_2\left(p_2^5 + h_2\right)^2 + W_3\left(p_3^5 + h_3\right)^2 + W_4\left(p_4^5 + h_4\right)^2}$$
$$= \sqrt{5\left(2.7 - 2.8\right)^2 + 10\left(2.8 - 2\right)^2 + 15\left(6 - 12\right)^2 + 20\left(3.2 - 3\right)^2}$$

$d_5 = 23.39337513$

Now, all the results of the distance are needed to be arranged in ascending order, like, $d_1 = 4.979959839$, $d_2 = 8.587782019$, $d_3 = 16.44536409$, $d_4 = 17.32628062$, $d_5 = 23.39337513$.

According to Euclidean distance the values of the vector di are sorted in ascending order, like d_1, d_2, d_3, d_4 and d_5. Minimum distanced home cloud and foreign cloud will share resources with each other. Here, value of d_1 is the minimum. Therefore, the resource transmission will take place between the home cloud and first foreign cloud. And the rest of the transmission will follow the same procedure.

According to Pearson's correlation the values of relation (r) are sorted in descending order, like r_1, r_2, r_3, r_4, r_5. This means that, maximum correlation between home cloud and foreign cloud will share resources with each other. Here, value of r_1 is the maximum. Therefore, the resource transmission will take place between the home cloud and first foreign cloud. Next will occur between home cloud and fifth foreign cloud, home cloud and third foreign cloud, home cloud and fourth foreign cloud, and lastly between home cloud and second foreign cloud.

ADVANTAGES OF USING CORRELATION

By using Pearson's correlation, it became possible to give chance to every trusted cloud to share their resources with each other without checking their policies. Since the concept of proxy is used, there is no need to create any prior agreements (SLA) among multiple cloud service providers. The numerical analysis is completely based on the quantifiable parameters of every trusted cloud. Quantifiable parameter means RAM (total memory needed), CPU speed, working time, transmission rate, etc. Correlation will reduce the time needed to check the agreements between two or more different clouds.

CONCLUSION AND FUTURE SCOPE

There are some security risks and issues in single cloud computing environment which can be overcome by introducing the concept of multi-cloud computing environment. But multi-cloud computing environment also have some security problems, some of those are interoperability, trust relationship among multiple CSPs, malicious insider etc. To establish trust relationship among multiple CSPs prior legal agreement is required, but this legal agreement varies CSP to CSP.

In this chapter a proxy based trust relationship establishment technique has been proposed to overcome the problem of pre-agreement in federated cloud environment. The proposed scheme uses Pearson's correlation mechanism to select the foreign cloud. The proposed scheme does not consider the scalability of the system. Therefore, scalability of the proposed scheme remains as future work.

REFERENCES

AlZain, M. A., & Pardede, E. (2011, January). Using multi shares for ensuring privacy in database-as-a-service. In *Proceedings of 44th Hawaii International Conference on System Sciences* (pp. 1-9). 10.1109/HICSS.2011.478

AlZain, M. A., & Pardede, E. (2011, December). Using Multi Shares for Ensuring Privacy in Database-as-a-Service. In *Proceedings of 44th Hawaii International Conference on System Sciences* (pp. 1-9). 10.1109/HICSS.2011.478

AlZain, M. A., Pardede, E., Soh, B., & Thom, J. A. (2012, January). Cloud computing security: from single to multi-clouds. In *Proceedings of 45th Hawaii International Conference on System Science (HICSS)* (pp. 5490-5499). 10.1109/HICSS.2012.153

AlZain, M. A., Soh, B., & Pardede, E. (2011, December). Mcdb: using multi-clouds to ensure security in cloud computing. In *Proceedings of Ninth International Conference on Dependable, autonomic and secure computing (DASC)* (pp. 784-791). 10.1109/DASC.2011.133

Armbrust, M., Stoica, I., Zaharia, M., Fox, A., Griffith, R., Joseph, A. D., ... Rabkin, A. (2010). A view of cloud computing. *Communications of the ACM, 53*(4), 50–58. doi:10.1145/1721654.1721672

Bessani, A., Correia, M., Quaresma, B., André, F., & Sousa, P. (2013). DepSky: dependable and secure storage in a cloud-of-clouds. *ACM Transactions on Storage, 9*(4), 12:1-12:33.

Bohli, J. M., Gruschka, N., Jensen, M., Iacono, L. L., & Marnau, N. (2013). Security and privacy-enhancing multicloud architectures. *IEEE Transactions on Dependable and Secure Computing, 10*(4), 212–224. doi:10.1109/TDSC.2013.6

Celesti, A., Tusa, F., Villari, M., & Puliafito, A. (2010, July). How to enhance cloud architectures to enable cross-federation. In *Proceedings of 3rd International Conference on Cloud Computing* (pp. 337-345). 10.1109/CLOUD.2010.46

Celesti, A., Tusa, F., Villari, M., & Puliafito, A. (2010, June). Security and cloud computing: Intercloud identity management infrastructure. In *Proceedings of 19th IEEE International Workshop on Enabling Technologies: Infrastructures for Collaborative Enterprises* (pp. 263-265).

Chappell, D., ... (2006). Introducing Windows CardSpace. Retrieved 15.02.17 from https://msdn.microsoft.com/en-us/library/aa480189.aspx

Hursti, J. (1997, November). Single sign-on. In *Proc. Helsinki University of Technology Seminar on Network Security*.

Le, H. B., & Bouzefrane, S. (2008, October). Identity management systems and interoperability in a heterogeneous environment. In *Proceedings of the International Conference on of Advanced Technologies for Communications* (pp. 239-242). 10.1109/ATC.2008.4760564

Liberty Alliance. (2002). Liberty alliance project. Retrieved from http://www.project liberty.org

Ristenpart, T., Tromer, E., Shacham, H., & Savage, S. (2009, November). Hey, you, get off of my cloud: exploring information leakage in third-party compute clouds. In *Proceedings of the 16th ACM Conference on Computer and Communications Security* (pp. 199-212). 10.1145/1653662.1653687

Shamir, A. (1979). How to share a secret. *Communications of the ACM, 22*(11), 612–613. doi:10.1145/359168.359176

Singhal, M., Chandrasekhar, S., Ge, T., Sandhu, R., Krishnan, R., Ahn, G. J., & Bertino, E. (2013). Collaboration in multicloud computing environments: Framework and security issues. *Computer, 46*(2), 76–84. doi:10.1109/MC.2013.46

Yau, S. S., & An, H. G. (2010). Confidentiality Protection in Cloud Computing Systems. *International Journal of Software Informatics, 4*(4), 351–365.

ADDITIONAL READING

Abadi, D., Madden, S., & Ferreira, M. (2006, June). Integrating compression and execution in column-oriented database systems. *In Proceedings of the International Conference on Management of Data* (pp. 671-682). 10.1145/1142473.1142548

Abraham, I., Chockler, G., Keidar, I., & Malkhi, D. (2006). Byzantine disk paxos: Optimal resilience with Byzantine shared memory. *Distributed Computing, 18*(5), 387–408. doi:10.100700446-005-0151-6

Abu-Libdeh, H., Princehouse, L., & Weatherspoon, H. (2010, June). RACS: a case for cloud storage diversity. In *Proceedings of the 1st ACM Symposium on Cloud Computing* (pp. 229-240). 10.1145/1807128.1807165

Adam, N. R., & Worthmann, J. C. (1989). Security-control methods for statistical databases: A comparative study. *ACM Computing Surveys, 21*(4), 515–556. doi:10.1145/76894.76895

Agrawal, D., El Abbadi, A., Emekci, F., & Metwally, A. (2009, March). Database management as a service: Challenges and opportunities. In *Proceedings of IEEE 25th International Conference on Data Engineering* (pp. 1709-1716).

Alrodhan, W. A., & Mitchell, C. J. (2008, March). A client-side CardSpace-Liberty integration architecture. In *Proceedings of the 7th symposium on Identity and trust on the Internet* (pp. 1-7).

Amazon. (2006, October). Amazon Web Services. Web services licensing agreement.

Anthes, G. (2010). Security in the cloud. *Communications of the ACM, 53*(11), 16–18. doi:10.1145/1839676.1839683

Ateniese, G., Burns, R., Curtmola, R., Herring, J., Kissner, L., Peterson, Z., & Song, D. (2007, October). Provable data possession at untrusted stores. In *Proceedings of the 14th ACM Conference on Computer and Communications Security* (pp. 598-609).

Bernstein, D., & Vij, D. (2010, November). Intercloud security considerations. In *Proceedings of the Second International Conference on Cloud Computing Technology and Science (CloudCom).* (pp. 537-544).

Birman, K., Chockler, G., & van Renesse, R. (2009). Toward a cloud computing research agenda. *ACM SIGACT News, 40*(2), 68–80. doi:10.1145/1556154.1556172

Bowers, K. D., Juels, A., & Oprea, A. (2009, November). HAIL: A high-availability and integrity layer for cloud storage. In *Proceedings of the 16th ACM Conference on Computer and Communications Security* (pp. 187-198). 10.1145/1653662.1653686

Brunette, G., & Mogull, R. (2009). Security guidance for critical areas of focus in cloud computing. *Cloud Security Alliance*.

Buyya, R., Yeo, C. S., & Venugopal, S. (2008, September). Market-oriented cloud computing: Vision, hype, and reality for delivering it services as computing utilities. In *Proceedings of the 10th IEEE International Conference on High Performance Computing and Communications* (pp. 5-13).

Cachin, C., Haas, R., & Vukolic, M. (2010). Dependable storage in the Intercloud (Research Report RZ, 3783).

Cachin, C., Keidar, I., & Shraer, A. (2009). Trusting the cloud. *ACM SIGACT News, 40*(2), 81–86. doi:10.1145/1556154.1556173

Cachin, C., & Tessaro, S. (2006, June). Optimal resilience for erasure-coded Byzantine distributed storage. In *Proceedings of the International Conference on Dependable Systems and Networks* (pp. 115-124). 10.1109/DSN.2006.56

Castro, M., & Liskov, B. (1999, February). Practical Byzantine fault tolerance. *Operating Systems Review, 99*, 173–186.

Chandrasekhar, S., Chakrabarti, S., Singhal, M., & Calvert, K. L. (2010). Efficient proxy signatures based on trapdoor hash functions. *IET Information Security, 4*(4), 322–332. doi:10.1049/iet-ifs.2009.0204

Chockler, G., Guerraoui, R., Keidar, I., & Vukolic, M. (2009). Reliable distributed storage. *Computer, 42*(4), 1–7. doi:10.1109/MC.2009.126

Concordia project. (n. d.). Retrieved from http://projectconcordia.org/index.php/Main_Page

Feldman, A. J., Zeller, W. P., Freedman, M. J., & Felten, E. W. (2010, October). SPORC: Group Collaboration using Untrusted Cloud Resources. In OSDI (Vol. 10, pp. 337-350).

Garfinkel, S. (2007). An evaluation of amazon's grid computing services: EC2, S3, and SQS (Technical Report TR-08-07). *Harvard University*.

Garfinkel, S. L. (2003). Email-based identification and authentication: An alternative to PKI? *IEEE Security and Privacy, 99*(6), 20–26. doi:10.1109/MSECP.2003.1253564

Goh, E. J., Shacham, H., Modadugu, N., & Boneh, D. (2003, February). SiRiUS: Securing Remote Untrusted Storage. In *Proceedings of Network and Distributed System Security Symposium* (Vol. 3, pp. 131-145).

Goodson, G. R., Wylie, J. J., Ganger, G. R., & Reiter, M. K. (2004, June). Efficient Byzantine-tolerant erasure-coded storage. In *Proceedings of International Conference on Dependable Systems and Networks* (pp. 135-144).

Grosse, E., Howie, J., Ransome, J., Reavis, J., & Schmidt, S. (2010). Cloud computing roundtable. *IEEE Security and Privacy, 8*(6), 17–23. doi:10.1109/MSP.2010.173

Hammer-Lahav, E. (2010). The OAuth 1.0 protocol.

Hendricks, J., Ganger, G. R., & Reiter, M. K. (2007, October). Low-overhead byzantine fault-tolerant storage. In *Proceedings of 21st ACM SIGOPS symposium on Operating systems principles.* (pp. 73-86). 10.1145/1294261.1294269

Higgins Project. (n. d.). Retrieved from http://www.eclipse.org/higgins/

Hui, M., Jiang, D., Li, G., & Zhou, Y. (2009, March). Supporting database applications as a service. In *Proceedings of 25th International Conference on Data Engineering* (pp. 832-843).

Jin, J., Ahn, G. J., Hu, H., Covington, M. J., & Zhang, X. (2011). Patient-centric authorization framework for electronic healthcare services. *Computers & Security, 30*(2), 116–127. doi:10.1016/j.cose.2010.09.001

Juels, A., & Kaliski, B. S. Jr. (2007, October). PORs: Proofs of retrievability for large files. In *Proceedings of the 14th ACM conference on Computer and Communications Security* (pp. 584-597). 10.1145/1315245.1315317

Kamara, S., & Lauter, K. (2010, January). Cryptographic cloud storage. In *Proceedings of the International Conference on Financial Cryptography and Data Security* (pp. 136-149). 10.1007/978-3-642-14992-4_13

Krawczyk, H., Canetti, R., & Bellare, M. (1997). HMAC: Keyed-hashing for message authentication.

Kuznetsov, P., & Rodrigues, R. (2010). BFTW 3: Why? when? where? workshop on the theory and practice of byzantine fault tolerance. *ACM SIGACT News, 40*(4), 82–86. doi:10.1145/1711475.1711494

Lamport, L., Shostak, R., & Pease, M. (1982). The Byzantine generals problem. *ACM Transactions on Programming Languages and Systems, 4*(3), 382–401. doi:10.1145/357172.357176

Loscocco, P. A., Smalley, S. D., Muckelbauer, P. A., Taylor, R. C., Turner, S. J., & Farrell, J. F. (1998, October). The inevitability of failure: The flawed assumption of security in modern computing environments. In *Proceedings of the 21st National Information Systems Security Conference* (Vol. 10, pp. 303-314).

Mahajan, P., Setty, S., Lee, S., Clement, A., Alvisi, L., Dahlin, M., & Walfish, M. (2011). Depot: Cloud storage with minimal trust. *ACM Transactions on Computer Systems, 29*(4), 1–16. doi:10.1145/2063509.2063512

Maheshwari, U., Vingralek, R., & Shapiro, W. (2000, October). How to build a trusted database system on untrusted storage. In *Proceedings of the 4th conference on Symposium on Operating System Design & Implementation.*

Maler, E., & Reed, D. (2008). The venn of identity: Options and issues in federated identity management. *IEEE Security and Privacy, 6*(2), 16–23. doi:10.1109/MSP.2008.50

Malinen, J. (2006, Autumn). Windows Cardspace. In *Proceedings of the Seminar on Network Security, Helsiki University of Technology*.

Malkhi, D., & Reiter, M. (1998). Byzantine quorum systems. *Distributed Computing, 11*(4), 203–213. doi:10.1007004460050050

Martin, J. P., Alvisi, L., & Dahlin, M. (2002, October). Minimal byzantine storage. In *Proceedings of the International Symposium on Distributed Computing* (pp. 311-325).

Mell, P., & Grance, T. (2009). *Perspectives on cloud computing and standards*. NIST.

Merkle, R. C. (1980, April). Protocols for public key cryptosystems. In *Proceedings of the IEEE Symposium on Security and Privacy* (pp. 122-122).

Microsoft Windows Cardspace. (n. d.). Retrieved from http://netfx3.com/content/WindowsCardspace-Home.aspx

Mykletun, E., Narasimha, M., & Tsudik, G. (2006). Authentication and integrity in outsourced databases. *ACM Transactions on Storage, 2*(2), 107–138. doi:10.1145/1149976.1149977

Ortiz, S. (2011). The Problem with Cloud Computing Standardization. *Computer, 44*(7), 13–16. doi:10.1109/MC.2011.220

Papamanthou, C., Tamassia, R., & Triandopoulos, N. (2008, October). Authenticated hash tables. In *Proceedings of the 15th ACM conference on Computer and Communications Security* (pp. 437-448).

Papazoglou, M. P., & van den Heuvel, W. J. (2011). Blueprinting the cloud. *IEEE Internet Computing, 15*(6), 74–79. doi:10.1109/MIC.2011.147

Pease, M., Shostak, R., & Lamport, L. (1980). Reaching agreement in the presence of faults. *Journal of the ACM, 27*(2), 228–234. doi:10.1145/322186.322188

Perez, R., Sailer, R., & van Doorn, L. (2006, July). vTPM: virtualizing the trusted platform module. In *Proceedings of 15th Conference on USENIX Security Symposium* (pp. 305-320).

RedHat. (n. d.). Critical: openssh security update. Retrieved from https://rhn.redhat.com/errata/RHSA-2008-0855.html

Rocha, F., & Correia, M. (2011, June). Lucy in the sky without diamonds: Stealing confidential data in the cloud. In *Proceedings of IEEE/IFIP 41ˢᵗ International Conference on Dependable Systems and Networks Workshops* (pp. 129-134).

Rochwerger, B., Breitgand, D., Epstein, A., Hadas, D., Loy, I., Nagin, K., ... Tofetti, G. (2011). Reservoir-when one cloud is not enough. *Computer, 44*(3), 44–51. doi:10.1109/MC.2011.64

Santos, N., Gummadi, K. P., & Rodrigues, R. (2009). Towards Trusted Cloud Computing. *HotCloud, 9*(9), 1–5.

Sarno, D. (2009). Microsoft says lost sidekick data will be restored to users. *Los Angeles Times*.

Schneider, F. B., & Zhou, L. (2005). Implementing trustworthy services using replicated state machines. In Replication (pp. 151-167). Springer Berlin Heidelberg. doi:10.1109/MSP.2005.125

Shraer, A., Cachin, C., Cidon, A., Keidar, I., Michalevsky, Y., & Shaket, D. (2010, October). Venus: Verification for untrusted cloud storage. In *Proceedings of the ACM Workshop on Cloud Computing Security Workshop* (pp. 19-30).

Subashini, S., & Kavitha, V. (2011). A survey on security issues in service delivery models of cloud computing. *Journal of Network and Computer Applications*, *34*(1), 1–11. doi:10.1016/j.jnca.2010.07.006

Sun. (n. d.). Amazon S3 silent data corruption. Retrieved from http://blogs.sun.com/gbrunett/entry/amazon_s3_silent_data_corruption

Takabi, H., Joshi, J. B., & Ahn, G. J. (2010). Security and privacy challenges in cloud computing environments. *IEEE Security and Privacy*, *8*(6), 24–31. doi:10.1109/MSP.2010.186

Van Dijk, M., & Juels, A. (2010). On the impossibility of cryptography alone for privacy-preserving cloud computing. In *Proceedings of HotSec* (pp. 1–8). .

Viega, J. (2009). Cloud computing and the common man. *Computer*, *42*(8), 106–108. doi:10.1109/MC.2009.252

Vukolić, M. (2010). The Byzantine empire in the intercloud. *ACM SIGACT News*, *41*(3), 105–111. doi:10.1145/1855118.1855137

Wu, R., Ahn, G. J., & Hu, H. (2012, January). Towards HIPAA-compliant healthcare systems. In *Proceedings of the 2nd International Health Informatics Symposium* (pp. 593-602).

Xiong, L., Chitti, S., & Liu, L. (2007). Preserving data privacy in outsourcing data aggregation services. *ACM Transactions on Internet Technology*, *7*(3), 17, es. doi:10.1145/1275505.1275510

Zhang, Y., & Joshi, J. (2009). Access control and trust management for emerging multidomain environments. In Handbooks in Information Systems (Vol. 4, pp. 421–452). Emerald Group Publishing.

KEY TERMS AND DEFINITIONS

Cloud Client: A cloud client contains software and/or hardware that rely on the cloud for providing services. It is designed to provide cloud services only. Without the connectivity with the cloud the cloud client is totally useless.

Cloud Computing Security: The collection of policies and control technologies used to comply with the rules of regulatory authorities and to protect infrastructure, data, information and application associated with the cloud computing environment is known as cloud computing security.

Cloud Service Provider: A Cloud service provider (CSP) is a company which provides infrastructure, network services, business applications or platform through the cloud. A data center hosts the services of the cloud. Users access cloud services through network connectivity. Major advantages of using CSP are its low cost and scalability. The individuals or the companies need not setup and maintain their own infrastructure for supporting the internal applications and services. They can purchase the required resources from a CSP in a very less price. CSP shares the infrastructure for providing services to the clients. CSP mainly provides three categories of services: Software as a Service (SaaS), Platform as a Service (PaaS) and Infrastructure as a Service (IaaS). In SaaS CSP provides access to the application software. In case of PaaS, a platform for hosting or developing application is provided by CSP. In IaaS CSP provides a computing infrastructure or entire network to the client. The differentiation between them is not distinct because many CSPs provide multiple types of services to their clients. For instance, one can go to a CSP, such as Rackspace, for hosting a website and purchase either IaaS or PaaS.

Identity Provider: An Identity provider (IdP), is an entity having the following functionalities: For interaction with the system, the IdP provides identifiers to the users. If the identifier produced by the user is known to the IdP, it recognizes and asserts the system. It also provides all the information that it knows about the user.

Multiple Cloud Computing: Multiple cloud computing is an environment where services from two or more clouds are used to reduce the risk of data loss or down time because of component failure in any of the cloud computing environment.

Proxy: It is a dedicated server or a software system which is running within a computer. It works as an intermediate device between the client and another server to which the clients wants to send a request for some service. In this mechanism, the client requests for the required services to the proxy. The proxy now acts as a client and sends that request to the server for the service. The server sends reply to the proxy which in turn will be returned to the client. The primary advantage of using proxy is that it enhances the security of the communication and can use cache for faster response.

Trust Relationship: Let D be the truster and E be the trustee. X represent successful performance in context K claimed by E. The trust relationship means that if E believes X in context K, then D also believes X in that in the same context.

This research was previously published in Cloud Computing Technologies for Green Enterprises edited by Kashif Munir, pages 351-384, copyright year 2018 by Business Science Reference (an imprint of IGI Global).

Chapter 79
The Attitudes of Chinese Organizations Towards Cloud Computing:
An Exploratory Study

Tomayess Issa
Curtin University, Australia

Yuchao Duan
Curtin University, Australia

Theodora Issa
Curtin University, Australia

Vanessa Chang
Curtin University, Australia

ABSTRACT

Cloud Computing become a significant factor in E-commerce and E-business processes and will reduce negative IT impacts on the environment without compromising the needs of future generations. This chapter aim to examine the attitudes of Chinese Organizations towards Cloud Computing adoption. This chapter provides an answer to the question: "What are the advantages and disadvantages of Cloud Computing adoption in Chinese organizations?" The answer was sought by means of an online survey of (N=121) respondents. The survey results revealed the Chinese position regarding the cloud movement, its strengths and weaknesses, the threats posed by Cloud Computing in China, and the specific advantages and disadvantages of this new technology that Chinese organizations and research communities should embrace for the realization of future cloud systems.

DOI: 10.4018/978-1-5225-8176-5.ch079

Copyright © 2019, IGI Global. Copying or distributing in print or electronic forms without written permission of IGI Global is prohibited.

INTRODUCTION

Information Communication Technology products and services are used via several organizations and individuals to enhance their performance and productivity. However, this technology brings several negative impacts to the environment from e-waste, energy consumption and carbon emissions. To reduce this impact, organizations and various stakeholders should tackle this problem and impact by using a smart technology such as cloud computing. Cloud Computing is an Internet-based computing service that provides on-demand computing power, in addition to being cheaper, and requiring low maintenance and fewer Information Technology (IT) staff. However, this technology can pose several risks in terms of security, privacy and legality. The study presented in this chapter was intended to assess, via an online survey, the strengths and weaknesses of Cloud Computing performance in Chinese organizations.

The preliminary analyses of collected data indicated that, for the majority of those surveyed, Cloud Computing technology is simply recognized and known, but 78% of the survey participants were unaware of whether or not their organizations are using cloud computing. From the responses to the final question in section one of the surveys it became evident that those who already know about 'cloud computing', albeit to a limited extent, regard such technology as being scalable, flexible, sustainable, green and decreases operating expenses, however, cloud computing adoption by Chinese organizations still is risky and vulnerable. A factor analysis tool was adopted to examine the survey outcomes, and the Cronbach's Alpha was .953, indicating excellent internal consistency of the scale items. Also, the survey outcomes confirmed that cloud computing usage in China increased various benefits, although some of the participants in the Chinese organizations voiced their concern regarding the level of risk and security associated with cloud computing

Finally, this chapter examines the level of awareness of Chinese organizations' – public and private – about cloud computing. This chapter is organized as follows: 1) Introduction; 2) Cloud Computing; 3) Advantages and Disadvantages of Cloud Computing; 4)Cloud Computing in Chinese Organizations; 5) Research Method and Question; 6) Participants 7) Results; 8) Discussion; 9) Limitation; 10) Conclusion.

CLOUD COMPUTING

Cloud Computing is reviewed from different aspects and this research focuses particularly on the attitude of Chinese organizations towards cloud computing. Thus, in the real world, cloud service providers can use the results to identify the requirements and concerns of potential Cloud Computing users in China in order to provide better cloud service. An actual example of the use of Cloud Computing is the cloud-based navigation service. Cloud Computing can be used to identify the state of traffic in urban road networks (Liu, Ma, Sun, & Dan, 2010). Traffic jams are now becoming a serious problem in China, according to China Daily (2012), with the number of registered cars in Beijing – the capital city of China – having passed five million in 2012. With the help of cloud computing, the dynamic traffic data can be received, analysed in the cloud-based server and sent to the GPS terminal or the end users. According to Ye (2011), the total output value of satellite navigation industry in China was 50 billion Yuan in 2010 (approximately equal to $7.7 billion Australian Dollar), and it will reach 265 billion Yuan (roughly $40.8 billion AUD) by the year of 2015; there will be 130 million satellite navigation terminals and 350 million end users at that time. The Cloud Computing industry will grow more quickly with the support of the theory; research articles like this one will help the service provider to have a better understanding of the cloud users' attitudes.

Cloud Computing is an Internet-based computing model whereby numerous servers and computers are connected to the Internet, resources, software or operating systems and can be shared by the users based on the requirements (Chi & Gao, 2011). As Armbrust et al. (2010) point out, Cloud Computing can be provided by the applications which are running as services via the Internet. Vouk (2008) holds the same opinion: Cloud Computing is about to move the software, hardware, data and other different devices from the local data centres to the cloud-based servers, in which case, end users can connect to those resources which are located in the cloud anywhere anytime via the client software. Minimizing the cost of computing and maximizing the profit are the main purposes of cloud computing.

There are different models of cloud services, namely SaaS (Software as a Service), PaaS (Platform as a Service) and IaaS (Infrastructure as a Service) (see Figure 1). Software as a service means that an application or software is running on a virtual server which can be accessed anywhere any time as long as there is an Internet connection (Cusumano, 2010). Google Calendar and Google Mail are based on the SaaS.

An advantage of SaaS is that it is timesaving. The implementation of the applications is quite time-consuming and is always accompanied by a failure rate. SaaS will make this process faster and the productivity can be improved (Liao & Tao, 2008). Moreover, software licenses are cheaper. Liao and Tao (2008) claim that as the software are offered by the cloud server provider and run in the cloud-based servers, it is not necessary for users to buy those software or to upgrade them; the provider will deal with those things. Several studies indicate (Cubitt, Hassan, & Volkmer, 2011; Marks, 2010 ; Schulz, 2009) by using the SaaS, there is no need for enterprises to install and maintain hardware, monitor devices, or maintain the software. High-level security can be provided by the SaaS as a result of the resource integration, and providers understand that the customers are concerned about the security of data. Providers of SaaS will regularly upgrade the software to the current version, which means that users are able to focus on their own work rather than have to pay much attention to the software compatibility.

Figure 1. SaaS, PaaS, IaaS (Prepared by the authors)

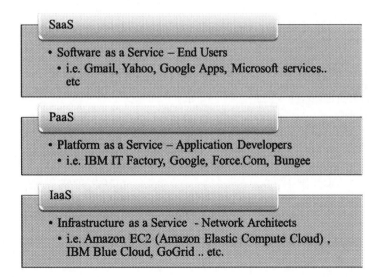

The main disadvantage of SaaS (Liao and Tao 2008) is single point failure. The Internet connection is almost everything; the company can come to a standstill if the connection to the Internet has been cut. The functionalities of the software, which is running in the cloud, might not be as good as the ones running on a local server. Response time cannot be controlled as it depends on the traffic of the Internet and the stability of cloud servers.

The PaaS is another cloud server model which can provide required resources to users in order to create applications and services in the cloud; in other words, users no longer need to download or install applications (Qayyum et al., 2011). For instance, the App Engine of Google is a type of PaaS.

IaaS is a storage space; hardware, servers and other devices can be offered by the IaaS platform provider; this equipment can be used directly and the platform provider is responsible for the maintenance tasks (Bhardwaj, Jain, & Jain, 2010). Amazon EC2 (Amazon Electric Cloud Computing) is a good example of IaaS. It was established 2006. Web interface and virtual machine instances are available for clients to manage the virtual machine which is provided by the Amazon EC2 (Juve et al., 2010). Amazon EC2 is a virtual computing environment from which users can launch instances via the interfaces of a web service. According to Juve et al. (2010), Amazon EC2 can be easily adopted using four steps: choose a pre-configured template image; configure the access level and security details of the network; choose the operating system and the type of instance; confirm whether the Amazon EC2 will run in different locations.

Just as cloud services have different models such as SaaS, PaaS and IaaS; there are different deployment models of Cloud Computing as well, namely: private, public, hybrid, and community (see Figure 2). According to Wyld (2010), in the private cloud method, the cloud infrastructure is owned solely by a company and it may be managed by the organization or a third party and may exist on the premises or off-premises. Schubert (2010) points out those private clouds are normally operated by the respective organization; the functionalities are not exposed to the customers directly and it is similar to Software as a Service from the customer's perspective. An example is eBay.

The cloud infrastructure can be accessed by the public cloud users or a large-scale industry group and is owned by the cloud provider (Wyld 2010). According to Rouse (2009), public cloud is based on the standard Cloud Computing model and the cloud service provider will make resources such as storage space or applications available to the general public Cloud Computing users through the Internet. The

Figure 2. Private, community, public and hybrid clouds (Prepared by the authors)

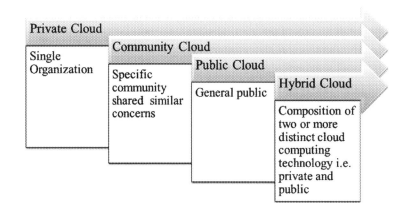

subscription models of public cloud services include a pay-per-usage model or may even be free while both internal and external providers maintain the hybrid cloud.

According to VMware (2010), hybrid cloud is a cloud infrastructure consisting of two or more clouds; private and public cloud can be combined under standardized technology and specific rules that enable application and data portability. The community cloud is shared by several organizations and supports a specific community that has shared concerns (e.g., mission, security requirements, policy, and compliance considerations); this cloud can be managed by the organizations or a third party and may exist on-premise or off-premise (Cisco, 2012). Schubert (2010) points out that, generally, cloud systems are restricted to the local infrastructure; for instance, public cloud service providers offer their own computing infrastructure to users. However, community clouds can either aggregate public clouds or be dedicated resource infrastructures. In other words, small or medium sized organizations can contribute their infrastructures and resources to build a community cloud from which all the organizations can benefit.

ADVANTAGES AND DISADVANTAGES OF CLOUD COMPUTING

Cloud Computing technology offers organizations many advantages in terms of cost, storage, access to information from, anywhere, anytime and any device. However, issues of security, technical glitches and privacy are major concerns for any organization (Avram, 2014; Berl et al., 2010; Issa, Chang, & Issa, 2010; Johnson, 2013; Lee & Zomaya, 2012; Marston, Li, Bandyopadhyay, Zhang, & Ghalsasi, 2011; Oliveira, Thomas, & Espadanal, 2014; Singh & Malhotra, 2012; Son, Lee, Lee, & Chang, 2014; Zissis & Lekkas, 2011; Zissis & Lekkas, 2012) (see Figure 3). Compared with traditional desktop software, Cloud Computing is considered as a cost-efficient method to use, maintain and upgrade. For instance, the licensing fees for traditional desktop software for different departments' terminals will require a lot in terms of investment (Viswanathan, 2012). On the other hand, several studies indicate (Cubitt et al., 2011; Marks, 2010 ; Singh & Malhotra, 2012; Velte, Velte, & Elsenpeter, 2010) that Cloud Computing provides cheaper IT services which can reduce the amount of investment that an organization makes in IT. What's more, there are different scalable options available such as pay-as-you-go and one-time-payment, which makes Cloud Computing a very reasonable choice for companies. All the data can be stored in

Figure 3. Advantages and disadvantages of cloud computing (Prepared by the authors)

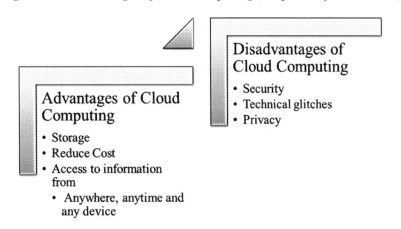

the cloud, which provides companies with almost unlimited memory capacity. Therefore, companies do not need to be anxious about running out of memory space or increasing the current memory capacity. The process of backing up or restoring data and information from the cloud is much easier than doing these things on physical devices. Besides, majority of cloud service providers offer recovery services for customers in order to sharpen the competitive edge. Thus, it will be simpler for companies to back up or recover data compared with traditional methods of data storage.

By using Cloud Computing technology, the data stored in the cloud can be accessed anywhere any time as long as there is an Internet connection available. Users just need to register, and data can be reviewed or modified easily. Users will not be perplexed or inconvenienced by geographic locations and time zones because of this convenient feature of cloud computing.

Cloud Computing can also provide the advantage of speedy deployment. The entire cloud-based system can be fully functional in a short time after all the settings have been finalised. Companies need only to select the appropriate system configuration based on their requirements; the cloud service providers will handle other issues. In spite of the overwhelming benefits mentioned above, Cloud Computing also has several drawbacks. Organizations, especially small or medium sized ones, should be aware of the following disadvantages before moving to the cloud.

Several studies (Brender & Markov, 2013; Johnson, 2013; Zissis & Lekkas, 2011; Zissis & Lekkas, 2012) indicate that security is always a major issue of cloud computing. Before adopting cloud-computing technology, companies should be aware that all the data including sensitive information will be handed over to a third-party cloud service provider, and therefore there is a potential risk to the organization. Data may be stored anywhere as the cloud servers may be in different locations or even different countries. Hence, organizations need to make sure that the cloud service provider has the ability to keep all the data absolutely secure. Although it is true that data stored on the cloud servers can be obtained anytime from anywhere with an Internet connection, some unpredictable system dysfunctions can occur without timely warning. Companies have to face the fact that all technologies are always prone to outages and other technical issues. Moreover, a stable and reliable Internet connection is required in order to avoid network and connectivity problems as all the services are web-based. As a result of the data being stored in the cloud servers, organizations will face potential risks, which make them vulnerable to external hack attacks and threats.

CLOUD COMPUTING IN CHINESE ORGANIZATIONS

Recently, China has started to show more interest in the ICT (Information and Communications Technology) development and innovation area, especially the Cloud Computing technology. However, as a result of poor enforcement of intellectual property rights and the strict policy which discriminates against overseas-funded enterprises or foreign-owned enterprises in government procurement, the development of Cloud Computing in China still has a long way to go (BSA World Wide Headquarters, 2012).

According to the research report from BSA Global Cloud Computing Scorecard-A blueprint for Economic Opportunity (2012), strict laws on cybercrime and intellectual property laws have been promulgated by the Chinese government, although enforcement deficiencies are evident. If China can impose and implement effective and relevant Cloud Computing laws, then the digital economy, confidence and trust will be boosted (Zhang, 2010). On the other hand, there is an additional risk as a result of administration rules of Internet content in China including the mandatory rules of censorship and filtering of

Internet content(BSA World Wide Headquarters, 2012). Overall, significant progress regarding Cloud Computing has been made and this new technology is quickly expanding in China.

Firstly, in the new period, national policy is promoting the development of cloud computing. There are seven emerging industries in China's current development strategy: energy saving, a new generation of information technology, biological sciences, alternative energy, advanced material and hybrid vehicle. Information technology, being in second position among all those sectors, indicates that the government attaches great importance to IT area. Cloud Computing is considered as a revolution of IT and it plays a significant role in communication and information technology and has therefore captured the government's attention. International Data Corporation (IDG) believes that by the end of 2012, the global market of Cloud Computing services will bring in an income of $420 billion U.S. (Chi & Gao, 2011). This great opportunity should not be ignored. Beijing, Shanghai, Wuxi and other major cities in China already have a Cloud Computing development plan. For instance, Shanghai is implementing a 3-year plan with 3.1 billion RMB invested; Beijing is trying to build a Cloud Computing base of world-class scale (Zhang, 2010).

Secondly, the industrial chain of Cloud Computing is taking shape: the ability to build Cloud-Computing infrastructure has improved and the overall strength of the software industry has increased equably. The network servers, storage and other relevant technologies or devices have vastly improved due to the great efforts made by the government (Chi & Gao, 2011). In addition, in recent years, the capacity to build Cloud Computing has continued to improve. Internet-based enterprises are growing rapidly in China. Meanwhile, large-scale network companies such as Tencent, Alibaba and Baidu have already accumulated rich experience and technology resources from cloud computing. Thus, Chinese corporations enrich the content of Cloud Computing constantly and the industrial chain of Cloud Computing in China is based on the contributions made by Chinese enterprises. The Cloud Computing industrial chain in China is gradually taking shape. The industrial chain is expected to provide benefits to all relevant sectors, and different corporations as shown below can represent each sector of the industrial chain: On-demand software, platform of hardware, automatic balance loading and virtualization. In this field, IBM, Cisco and the traditional leaders in the hardware and software manufacturing area play significant roles. Inspur, HuaSheng, ZTE and Lenovo are domestic enterprises also doing well in this area. Systems integrators are demanded for helping cloud users build the platform for software and hardware. Amazon and Google are international leaders in this area. The largest companies in this field in China include Inspur and Neusoft Group. Service providers are also included in the industry chain of Cloud Computing since they provide storage, personal and business computing or other resources. Tasks like computing or development of applications are based on these services. Pengboshi and SUJING Tech are doing well in the domestic service market.

The development of Cloud Computing provides good opportunities for Chinese industry and economy. For one thing, by using the cloud infrastructure services, small or medium size enterprises are able to redirect their resources easily to adopt a long-term strategy for their future development (Li, Tang, Guo, & Hu, 2010). In the traditional IT model, pre-investment is required in order to acquire the software and hardware. What is more, during the life cycle of a project, servers and software need to be maintained regularly which will require more investment. However, by shifting to the cloud, the new payment method, which is the pay-as-you-go model, will provide numerous benefits to companies. For instance, the Microsoft-hosted Exchange Online services allow customers to access their calendars or emails anywhere anytime at a cost of $10 U.S. monthly. For another, it is a good chance for domestic IT companies to catch up with the advanced international level of Cloud Computing field (Chen, Xu,

Wang, Li, & Jin, 2011). At present, Cloud Computing is still in the exploratory phase and technologies associated with this new concept are still immature; hence, if Chinese IT enterprises can seize this opportunity, a qualitative change may occur in the IT industry in China.

In addition, it is noted that Chinese IT companies have begun to change their strategy from simply adopting current technology from overseas top level corporations by creating their own new principles and technologies (Wei, Zhang, & Zeng, 2009). For instance, a company named 360 provides a free cloud-based antivirus program to the end users; the Baidu Company creates a frame computing system based on the cloud. It is a good signal for the domestic IT industry and it can be seen that these companies are becoming more creative and competitive than before (Li et al., 2010).

Besides the benefits that Cloud Computing can provide such as ease of development and management and scalability, several challenges of Cloud Computing should be taken into consideration as well, such as the ownership and control of data, privacy issues and trust (Erdogmus, 2009). Before implementing cloud computing, numerous aspects of security issues should be resolved by the service providers in order to increase the adoption of Cloud Computing (Christodorescu, Sailer, & Schales, 2009). On the other hand, some of the cloud service providers claim that the security processes and measures they provide are better than most of those offered by IT organizations; hence, their security status will be improved if their cloud solution can be adopted. Cellary and Strykowski (2009) claim that at the cloud service provider end, security of hardware and software can be ensured as a result of maintenance provided by professional security technicians. For the purpose of ensuring widespread adoption of cloud computing, relieving the security concerns of customers is a key issue which should be taken into consideration (Chebrolu, 2010). As the techniques of encryption become more mature, the security of Cloud Computing can be enhanced in the future. The complex integration of Cloud Computing presents significant challenges for Chinese organizations, including, malware detection and immediate intrusion response. In order to decrease the impact, problem analysis and solving should be done promptly (Li et al., 2010; Ye, 2011; Zaheer, 2012). During the entire life cycle of the service management in the cloud, incidence management should always be considered.

Chinese IT companies have discovered many potential advantages of cloud computing. They believe that by adopting this new technology, IT investment costs will be decreased and the capabilities of the corporations can be enhanced. Basically, Chinese IT companies prefer to use cloud servers offered by overseas providers. However, they may be concerned about the risks of sending sensitive data out of the country, so if the cloud service provider has a data centre located in China, the provider will be more popular (Zhou, Zhang, Xie, & Qian, 2010). Chinese Cloud Computing explorers prefer to adopt virtualization and outsource their IT infrastructure, as they do not really care about the ownership of IT infrastructure. In order to build cloud services internally, virtualization development attracts much attention nowadays (Wei et al., 2009). Overall, Chinese cloud explorers consider Cloud Computing to be a valuable technology with great potential which will play a significant role in improving China's economic competitiveness in the near future (Alter, Peng, Lin, & Harris, 2010).

RESEARCH METHOD AND QUESTION

The study presented in this chapter intended to answer: "What are the advantages and disadvantages of Cloud Computing adoption in Chinese organizations?" to answer this study, quantitative online survey is used by using the positivism research philosophy. In the beginning, a critical review of literature is organized to develop the research strategy and questions, and then an online survey is invented based on the findings of the literature review. Employing an online survey in any study will allow the researcher to answer the research questions; confirm and to endorse the findings of the literature review in line to develop new theoretical significance, and to answer the research questions. Using online survey can offer greater anonymity, less expensive and more accessibility (Gordon & McNew, 2008; Issa, 2013; Porter, 2004); on the other hand, online survey disadvantages are technical failure, computer viruses, internet crimes, hacking, and privacy, and these can lead to decrease in the response rate (Fan & Yan, 2010)

The online survey consisting of two sections namely the first section contains demographic questions, the responses to which will allow the generation of the profile of those surveyed. This first section concludes with an open question for respondents, inviting them to provide their opinion concerning the issue of 'cloud computing'. The second section contains fourteen statements seeking respondents' opinions using a seven-point Likert scale ranging from 'Strongly disagree' to 'Strongly agree' with an additional option 'Do not know'. The fourteen statements were intended to investigate and examine the attitudes in Chinese Organizations and their personnel towards this relatively new development in the ICT industry, i.e. 'Cloud computing'. The population of interest was managers in the Information Technology Organisations in China. This chapter derives from data gathered through this survey of 121 respondents, which was collected by using various techniques from social media i.e. Facebook, Linkedin, twitter and word of mouth. The survey data was collected within one month.

PARTICIPANTS

This study was conducted in China in order to examine the main concerns that Chinese organizations have with moving to the cloud. The survey was distributed to organizations in China and the survey response rate was 88.9%. Table 1 provides a summary of the respondents' details including gender, industry sector type and qualifications.

Table 2 shows the number of survey respondents in public and private organizations in China. It was noted that the majority of respondents work in small, medium and large organizations. Furthermore, the majority of respondents worked in communication services, education, and finance and insurance (24%, 21%, and 12% respectively) (see Table 3).

Finally, results presented in Table 4 confirm that 40% of personnel in Chinese organizations are still unaware of Cloud Computing applications, although 21% are currently using various applications such as Opera, Google Doc and MongoDB.

RESULTS

A total of 136 participants from China responded to the online survey. With 15 responses not accepted because of missing data, this resulted in 121 valid cases of responses for China for the following Factor Analysis. Based on the Mean and STD Deviation results, it was confirmed that the majority of the personnel in Chinese organizations have neutral agreement behind cloud-computing services; but in scalable services, efficient, green and sustainability factors the mean was higher compared to the other factors (see Table 5).

Table 1. Summary of the respondents' details: China

Number and Percentage of Questionnaires	
Questionnaires Distributed	136
Questionnaires Returned	121
Response Rate	88.9%
Gender	
Male Respondents	84
Female Respondents	53
Sector Type	
Public Sector Organization	70
Private Sector Organization	65
Qualifications	
Bachelor Degree	59
Master Degree	56
Doctorate (PhD)	10
Other, Please specify	13

Table 2. Number of employees in public and private organizations in China

0-50	18
51 to 200	10
201 to 500	10
501 to 2000	9
2001 to 8000	7
8001- 100000	9
Total	63

To assess the survey results, further research carried out by the researchers using SPSS version 21, adopted principal axis factoring for factor extraction, and oblique rotation was applied using the direct oblimin method to correlate the variables (Costello & Osborne, 2005; Hair, Black, Babin, & Anderson, 2009).

To measure the sampling adequacy, researchers carried out specific testing using Cronbach's Alpha, Kaiser-Meyer-Olkin and Bartlett's test. Firstly, the Cronbach's Alpha for all 14 variables was .953, indicating an excellent internal consistency of the items in the scale (Gliem & Gliem, 2003). Secondly, the Kaiser-Meyer-Olkin measure of sampling adequacy was .922 above the recommended value of .6, indicating that a good sample size has been obtained from the analysis (Hill, 2012). Thirdly, the Bartlett's test of sphericity is highly significant, $\chi^2 = 1474.258$, df = 91, p < .000, indicating that the items of the scale are sufficiently correlated to factors to be found (Burns & Burns, 2008). Finally, the communalities were all over .05 (see Table 6) except for statement 9, as Chinese organizations still have some concerns that Cloud Computing will increase operating expenses.

Table 3. Organization types in China

Organizations	Number	Percentage
Accommodation, Cafes and Restaurants	3	2%
Agriculture, Forestry and Fishing	2	1%
Communication Services	32	24%
Construction	5	4%
Cultural and Recreational Services	11	8%
Education	29	21%
Electricity, Gas and Water Supply	12	9%
Finance and Insurance	16	12%
Government Administration and Defence	8	6%
Health and Community Services	7	5%
Manufacturing	5	4%
Mining	4	3%
Personal and Other Services	13	10%
Property and Business Services	1	1%
Retail Trade	2	1%
Transport and Storage	2	1%
Wholesale Trade	2	1%

Table 4. Cloud computing usage in private and public organizations in China

Answer	Response
Don't Know	53
No	54
Yes If you answered 'yes' to this question, please provide details in the space below of applications you access via cloud computing.	29

Furthermore, the researchers used principle components analysis to estimate the factor-loading matrix for the factor analysis model as well the standard correlation matrix. The Eigen values are assessed to determine the number of factors accounting for the correlations amongst the variables. As demonstrated in Table 7, this model of eight factors explains a total of 57.279% of the variation. The Eigen values and the amount of variances explained by each of these factors are presented in Table 7 (after rotation).

Furthermore, to measure the regression coefficients (i.e. slopes), the researchers carried out the factor loadings. The factor loadings are based on most of the items that have a high loading value and the one with the cleanest factor structure is considered as important; items Q8_13 and Q8_10 are shared factor loadings between the two factors (Costello & Osborne, 2005). The Q8_13 and Q8_10 under Factor 2 had a factor loading below .5 based on the rule of thumb of Stevens (1992) for a sample size above 100. Variables excluded are highlighted in light blue (see Table 8).

Table 5. Descriptive statistics: Mean and STD deviation

	Mean	Std. Deviation
Cloud Computing is more flexible than traditional computing.	3.64	1.063
Cloud Computing is more efficient than traditional computing.	3.77	1.047
Cloud Computing helps organisations become 'greener'.	3.64	1.024
Cloud Computing helps provide scalable services.	3.81	1.075
Cloud Computing helps provides reliable services.	3.56	1.064
Cloud Computing helps provides ease of maintenance.	3.39	1.113
Cloud Computing makes staffing easier.	3.44	1.072
Cloud Computing decreases operating expenses.	3.50	1.111
Cloud Computing increases operating expenses.	3.03	1.110
Cloud Computing reduces capital costs.	3.40	1.029
Cloud Computing introduces security problems.	3.40	1.012
Cloud Computing is more risky than traditional computing.	3.31	1.017
Cloud Computing reduces organisations' carbon footprint.	3.55	1.017
Cloud Computing contributes to organisations' sustainability.	3.66	1.092

Table 6. Cloud computing – communalities

Communalities	Initial	Extraction
Cloud Computing is more flexible than traditional computing	.755	.751
Cloud Computing is more efficient than traditional computing	.796	.733
Cloud Computing helps organisations become 'greener'	.764	.733
Cloud Computing helps provide scalable services	.770	.747
Cloud Computing helps provide reliable services	.718	.703
Cloud Computing helps provide ease of maintenance	.712	.597
Cloud Computing makes staffing easier	.765	.700
Cloud Computing decreases operating expenses	.631	.561
Cloud Computing increases operating expenses	.489	.307
Cloud Computing reduces capital costs	.662	.602
Cloud Computing introduces security problems	.777	.726
Cloud Computing is more risky than traditional computing	.744	.977
Cloud Computing reduces organisations' carbon footprint	.698	.620
Cloud Computing contributes to organisations' sustainability	.691	.655

Extraction Method: Principal Axis Factoring.

The Pattern Matrix revealed two factors: Factor 1: Operational benefits and Factor 2: Risk and security. The mean and standard deviation of the factor average is presented in Table 9.

Overall, it became evident that the organizations in China believed that using Cloud Computing tools is more efficient than traditional computing, scalable, easier, reliable, and flexible; moreover, the sur-

Table 7. Cloud computing: Total variance explained

Factor	Initial Eigenvalues			Extraction Sums of Squared Loadings			Rotation Sums of Squared Loadings[a]
	Total	% of Variance	Cumulative %	Total	% of Variance	Cumulative %	Total
1	8.473	65.177	65.177	8.168	62.831	62.831	8.028
2	1.092	8.401	73.578	.898	6.907	69.738	4.704
3	.670	5.157	78.735				
4	.565	4.345	83.079				
5	.449	3.453	86.532				
6	.342	2.632	89.164				
7	.308	2.366	91.531				
8	.274	2.108	93.638				
9	.212	1.628	95.266				
10	.198	1.523	96.788				
11	.158	1.219	98.007				
12	.141	1.083	99.090				
13	.118	.910	100.000				

Extraction Method: Principal Axis Factoring.
a. When factors are correlated, sums of squared loadings cannot be added to obtain a total variance.

Table 8. Cloud computing: Pattern matrix

	Factor	
	1	2
Cloud Computing is more efficient than traditional computing	.905	
Cloud Computing helps provide scalable services	.902	
Cloud Computing makes staffing easier	.875	
Cloud Computing helps provide reliable services	.871	
Cloud Computing is more flexible than traditional computing	.865	
Cloud Computing helps organisations become 'greener'	.821	
Cloud Computing contributes to organisations' sustainability	.794	
Cloud Computing decreases operating expenses	.758	
Cloud Computing helps provide ease of maintenance	.705	
Cloud Computing reduces organisations' carbon footprint	.638	.214
Cloud Computing reduces capital costs	.631	.216
Cloud Computing is more risky than traditional computing		.943
Cloud Computing introduces security problems	.107	.821

Extraction Method: Principal Axis Factoring.
Rotation Method: Oblimin with Kaiser Normalization.[a]
a. Rotation converged in 4 iterations.

Table 9. Cloud computing: Descriptive statistics (N=121)

	Mean	Std. Deviation
Factor 1: Operational benefits	3.60	1.073
Factor 2: Risk and Security	3.36	1.01

vey indicated that the use of Cloud Computing technology in China will assist organizations to become greener and more sustainable. However, the survey outcomes confirmed that although cloud-computing usage in China is believed to have various advantages, there is nevertheless some concern regarding the issue of risk and security.

DISCUSSION

The main aim of this chapter was to analyze the attitude of Chinese organizations towards Cloud Computing technology. Currently, the number of Internet users worldwide is increasing rapidly as a result of the development of the Internet infrastructure construction. Because of the increase in the number of Internet users and companies' inability to efficiently handle the task load of network access, more and more corporations have started to adopt cloud technology in order to provide more flexible, efficient and reliable services to users. Cloud Computing is based on the Internet and all the data, software or even the operating system can be moved into the cloud, as long as there is an Internet connection. Data can be accessed anywhere at any time by the end users. Cloud Computing is becoming a significant factor in E-commerce and E-business processes. The literature review (Avram, 2014; Chang, Issa, & Issa, 2011; Marston et al., 2011; Oliveira et al., 2014; Son et al., 2014; Zissis & Lekkas, 2012) indicates that the most well-known Cloud Computing providers in China are Google, Microsoft and IBM. However, some companies with excellent reputations in the global Cloud Computing market like Amazon, Salesforce. com and EMC are not expanding in the Chinese cloud market.

Most organizations are aware that Cloud Computing can reduce capital costs, is easy to implement, and decreases operating expenses. Companies are greatly concerned about reducing capital costs, including reducing the initial IT equipment expenses and decreasing maintenance costs. However, a number of companies, especially small or medium-sized ones, doubt that Cloud Computing can really reduce costs. The most important advantage of Cloud Computing is that it decreases total capital costs; however, the lack of successful cases means that this has not been satisfactorily proven. The advantages of Cloud Computing includes cost efficiency, availability of almost unlimited storage, easy backup and recovery, easy access to information, and quick deployment, to name a few. Disadvantages of Cloud Computing include security in the cloud, technical issues, proneness to attack, etc. Organizations believe that the obstacles to the development of Cloud Computing in China include the following: lack of successful cases of cloud computing; lack of professional knowledge of cloud technology; network bandwidth and limited budget; security; lack of cloud industry standards and policies. The study confirmed the research question, as Chinese organizations still have some concerns about adopting Cloud Computing in their organizations; they perceive its weaknesses to be issues of security and risk. However, Cloud Computing does provide advantages in that it is scalable, efficient, easy to maintain, reliable, flexible, sustainable, green and reduce cost, nevertheless. Moreover, it was confirmed that the adoption of Cloud

Computing in China would allow organizations to become more sustainable, especially in the Information Technology departments.

Figure 4 shows the new advantages and disadvantages factor (*New factors with red font color and italic*) by the Chinese organizations. This chapter added new theoretical significance about the attitudes of Chinese Organizations towards Cloud Computing, as the survey results confirmed that Cloud Computing adoption is scalable, efficient, easy to maintain, reliable, flexible, sustainable, green and decreases operating expenses, nevertheless, Cloud Computing adoption by the Chinese organizations is risky and vulnerable which confirmed the literature.

As security and risk are the most important concerns for organizations, future research could include an in-depth review of the security and privacy issues and possible solutions. Furthermore, it can be seen that security is the most important concern to Chinese organizations. For security purposes, both organizations and cloud providers should have a backup solution; the business sensitive information should be encrypted. In addition, it is important to avoid cloud outages; the cloud provider should check the entire infrastructure regularly; main servers and backup servers should be in different locations in order to avoid power failure or any other unpredictable accident, so that if anything happens to the main servers, the backup servers will not be affected. For organizations, moving to the cloud is about balancing risks and benefits. They should not make the decision just because all other companies have the cloud plan; the cloud strategy should be based on the realities of each organization's circumstances and position.

LIMITATIONS

The study presented in this chapter was limited to a survey of 121 participants from both public and private organizations in China. The rationale for this study was to assess Chinese organizations' attitudes

Figure 4. Advantages and disadvantages of cloud computing adoption in China (Prepared by the authors)

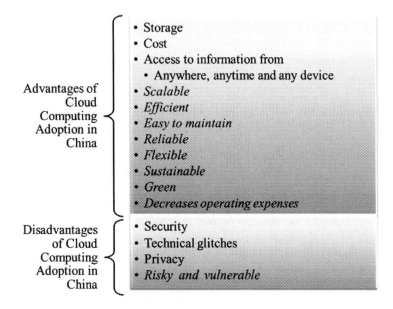

to Cloud Computing adoption. The online survey responses strongly indicated that Chinese organizations are aware of these concepts, although the level of awareness is low. Therefore, further research with larger and more diverse groups of organizations is required in the future to strengthen the research findings.

CONCLUSION

This chapter examined the strengths and weaknesses of Cloud Computing performance in Chinese organizations. As can be seen from the analysis, respondents from the public sector are more aware of cloud computing. Based on the survey result, the Chinese Organizations consider Cloud Computing is flexible and efficient than traditional computing. It can help Chinese Organizations to become greener and provides scalable, reliable services; it makes the maintenance and staffing easier, thereby decreasing operating expenses. Security and risks are the major concerns of Chinese organizations when considering a move to the cloud. Therefore, to address these concerns, further research should be carried out to examine the security aspects. Moreover, standards and guidelines tailored specifically to address the security and privacy issues of Cloud Computing should be established and implemented, not only in China, but also worldwide. Finally, to increase the awareness of cloud computing, sustainability and green IT concepts in China and worldwide, universities should develop and present courses and units related to these concepts. Since today's students will be tomorrow's leaders, universities and academics have the responsibility of raising students' awareness and make, their decisions part of the Information Technology solution, not a problem in the future.

REFERENCES

Alter, A. E., Peng, Y., Lin, R., & Harris, J. G. (2010). China's Pragmatic Path to Cloud Computing. Accenture Institute for High Performance.

Armbrust, M., Fox, A., Griffith, R., Joseph, A. D., Katz, R., Knowinski, A., ... Zaharia, M. (2010). A View of Cloud Computing. *Communications of the ACM, 53*(4), 50–58. doi:10.1145/1721654.1721672

Avram, M. G. (2014). Advantages and Challenges of Adopting Cloud Computing from an Enterprise Perspective. *Procedia Technology, 12*(0), 529-534.

Berl, A., Gelenbe, E., Di Girolamo, M., Giuliani, G., Meer, H., Dang, M., & Pentikousis, K. (2010). Energy-Efficient Cloud Computing. *The Computer Journal, 53*(7), 1046–1051. doi:10.1093/comjnl/bxp080

Bhardwaj, S., Jain, L., & Jain, S. (2010). Cloud Computing: A Study of Infrastructure as a Service (IAAS). *International Journal of Engineering and Information Technology, 2*(1), 60–63.

Brender, N., & Markov, I. (2013). Risk perception and risk management in cloud computing: Results from a case study of Swiss companies. *International Journal of Information Management, 33*(5), 726–733. doi:10.1016/j.ijinfomgt.2013.05.004

World Wide Headquarters, B. S. A. (2012). *BSA Global Cloud Computing Scorecard*. Washington, DC.

Burns, R. P., & Burns, R. (2008). *Business Research Methods and Statistics Using SPSS*. Atlanta, GA, USA: Sage.

Cellary, W., & Strykowski, S. (2009). e-government based on cloud computing and service-oriented architecture. *Proceedings of the 3rd International Conference on Theory and Practice of Electronic Governance* (pp. 5-10).

Chang, V., Issa, T., & Issa, T. (2011). Cloud computing and sustainability: an Australian public sector perspective. *Proceedings of the International Society for Professional Innovation Management (ISPIM) Conference*, Hamburg, Germany.

Chebrolu, S. B. (2010). Assessing the relationships among cloud adoption, strategic alignment and information technology effectiveness. *ProQuest Dissertations & Theses database,*

Chen, S., Xu, Y., Wang, P., Li, D., & Jin, D. (2011). The usage of cloud computing in China Regional Healthcare. *Proceedings of the 2011 IEEE International Conference on Cloud Computing and Intelligence Systems* (pp. 1-5).

Chi, C., & Gao, F. (2011). The Trend of Cloud Computing in China. *Journal of Software*, *6*(7), 1230–1235. doi:10.4304/jsw.6.7.1230-1234

Beijing Car Ownership Exceeds 5 Million. (2012, September 19). China Daily. Retrieved from http://www.chinadaily.com.cn/china/2012-02/17/content_14628019.htm

Christodorescu, M., Sailer, R., & Schales, D. L. (2009). Cloud security is not (just) virtualization security: A short paper. *Proceedings of the 2009 ACM Workshop on Cloud Computing Security* (pp. 97-102).

Cisco. (2012, September 19). Cloud Computing in Higher Education: A Guide to Evaluation and Adoption. Retrieved from http://www.cisco.com/web/offer/email/43468/5/Cloud_Computing_in_Higher_Education.pdf

Costello, A., & Osborne, J. (2005). Best Practices in Exploratory Factor Analysis: Four Recommendations for Getting the Most from Your Analysis. *Practical Assessment, Research & Evaluation*, *10*(7), 1–9.

Cubitt, S., Hassan, R., & Volkmer, I. (2011). Does Cloud Computing have a Silver Lining. *Media Culture & Society*, *33*(1), 149–158. doi:10.1177/0163443710382974

Cusumano, M. (2010). Cloud computing and SaaS as new computing platforms. *Communications of the ACM*, *53*(4), 27–29. doi:10.1145/1721654.1721667

Erdogmus, H. (2009). Cloud computing: Does Nirvana hide behind the Nebula. *IEEE Software*, *26*(11), 4–6.

Fan, W., & Yan, Z. (2010). Factors affecting response rates of the web survey: A systematic review. *Computers in Human Behavior*, *26*(2), 132–139. doi:10.1016/j.chb.2009.10.015

Gliem, J., & Gliem, R. (2003). Calculating, Interpreting, and Reporting Cronbach's Alpha Reliability Coefficient for Likert-Type Scales. Proceedings of the Midwest Research to Practice Conference in Adult, Continuing and Community Education (pp. 82 - 88).

Gordon, D., Wirz, M., Roggen, D., & Tröster, G., & Beigl, M. (2014). Group affiliation detection using model divergence for wearable devices. *Proceedings of the 2014 ACM International Symposium on Wearable Computers*, Seattle, Washington (pp. 19-26). ACM. doi:10.1145/2634317.2634319

Gordon, J., & McNew, R. (2008). Developing the Online Survey. *Nurs Clin N Am, 43*(4), 605 – 619..

Hair, J., Black, W., Babin, B., & Anderson, R. (2009). *Multivariate data analysis.* Upper Saddle River, NJ: Prentice Hall.

Hill, B. D. (2012). *The Sequential Kaiser-Meyer-Olkin Procedure As An Alternative For Determining The Number Of Factors In Common-Factor Analysis: A Monte Carlo Simulation* [Dissertation].

Issa, T. (2013). Online Survey: Best Practice. In P. Isaias, M.B. Nunes (Eds.), Information Systems Research and Exploring Social Artifacts: Approaches and Methodologies (pp. 1–19). Hershey, PA, USA: IGI Global. doi:10.4018/978-1-4666-2491-7.ch001

Issa, T., Chang, V., & Issa, T. (2010). The Impact of Cloud Computing and Organizational Sustainability. *Cloud Computing and Virtualization 2010*, Singapore.

Johnson, P. E. (2013). A Review of "Cloud Computing for Libraries". *Journal of Access Services, 10*(1), 71–73. doi:10.1080/15367967.2013.738572

Juve, G., Deelman, E., Vahi, K., Mehta, G., Berriman, B., Maechling, P., & Berman, B. P. (2010). Data Sharing Options for Scientific Workflows on Amazon EC2. *High Performance Computing, Networking, Storage and Analysis*, 1-9.

Lee, Y. C., & Zomaya, A. Y. (2012). Energy efficient utilization of resources in cloud computing systems. *The Journal of Supercomputing, 60*(2), 268–280. doi:10.100711227-010-0421-3

Li, R., Tang, S., Guo, C., & Hu, X. (2010). Thinking the cloud computing in China. *Information Management and Engineering* (pp. 669-672).

Liao, H., & Tao, C. (2008). An Anatomy to SaaS Business Mode Based on Internet. *Paper presented at the 2008 International Conference on Management of e-Commerce and e-Government*. http://dx.doi.org: doi:10.1109/ICMECG.2008.16

Liu, W. N., Ma, Q. L., Sun, D. H., & Dan, Y. F. (2010). Traffic State Identification Methods Based on Cloud computing Model. Retrieved from http://202.164.55.108/CSE/CSE/traffic%20state.pdf

Marks, E. A. (2010). *Executive's Guide to Cloud Computing.* USA: John Wiley and Sons.

Marston, S., Li, Z., Bandyopadhyay, S., Zhang, J., & Ghalsasi, A. (2011). Cloud computing — The business perspective. *Decision Support Systems, 51*(1), 176–189. doi:10.1016/j.dss.2010.12.006

Oliveira, T., Thomas, M., & Espadanal, M. (2014). Assessing the determinants of cloud computing adoption: An analysis of the manufacturing and services sectors. *Information & Management, 51*(5), 497–510. doi:10.1016/j.im.2014.03.006

Porter, S. (2004). Pros and Cons of Paper and Electronic Surveys. In *New Directions for Institutional Resaerch* (Vol. 2004, pp. 23–38). Wiley Periodicals, Inc. doi:10.1002/ir.103

Qayyum, J., Khan, F., Lal, M., Gul, F., Sohaib, M., & Masood, F. (2011). Implementing and Managing framework for PaaS in Cloud Computing. *International Journal of Computer Science Issues, 8*(5), 474–479.

Rouse, M. (2009). Traffic State Identification Methods Based on Cloud computing Model). Public Cloud. Retrieved from http://searchcloudcomputing.techtarget.com/definition/public-cloud

Schubert, L. (2010). Traffic State Identification Methods Based on Cloud computing Model). The Future of Cloud Computing-Opportunities for European Cloud Computing Beyond 2010. Retrieved from http://cordis.europa.eu/fp7/ict/ssai/docs/cloud-report-final.pdf

Schulz, W. (2009). What is SaaS, Cloud Computing, PaaS and IaaS? Retrieved from http://www.s-consult.com/2009/08/04/what-is-saas-cloud-computing-paas-and-iaas/

Singh, A., & Malhotra, M. (2012). Agent Based Framework for Scalability in Cloud Computing *International Journal of Computer Science & Engineering Technology,* April, 41-45.

Son, I., Lee, D., Lee, J.-N., & Chang, Y. B. (2014). Market perception on cloud computing initiatives in organizations: An extended resource-based view. *Information & Management, 51*(6), 653–669. doi:10.1016/j.im.2014.05.006

Stevens, J. (1992). *Applied multivariate statistics for the social sciences. NJ.* Hillsdale: Erlbaum.

Velte, A. T., Velte, T. J., & Elsenpeter, R. (2010). *Cloud Computing - A Practical Approach.* USA: McGraw Hill.

Viswanathan, P. (2012). Cloud Computing – Is It Really All That Beneficial? Retrieved from http://mobiledevices.about.com/od/additionalresources/a/Cloud-Computing-Is-It-Really-All-That-Beneficial.htm

VMware. (2010). Public Cloud Service Definition (Technical White Paper). Retrieved from http://www.vmware.com/files/pdf/VMware-Public-Cloud-Service-Definition.pdf

Vouk, M. A. (2008). Cloud Computing – Issues, Research and Implementations. *Journal of Computing and Information Technology, 16*(4), 235–246. doi:10.2498/cit.1001391

Wei, X., Zhang, J., & Zeng, S. (2009). Study of the Potential SaaS Platform Provider in China. *Proceedings of the 2009 WRI World Congress on Software Engineering, 4,* 78-80.

Wyld, D. (2010). The Cloudy Future of Government It: Cloud Computing and the Public Sector around the World. *International Journal of Web & Semantic Technology, 1*(1).

Ye, X. (2011). Cloud Computing Era Dawns for China's Navigation Industry Retrieved from http://english.peopledaily.com.cn/90882/7455078.html

Zaheer. (2012). China has the largest number of internet users with more than 500 million people. Retrieved from http://www.americanlivewire.com/china-has-the-largest-number-of-internet-users-with-more-than-500-million-people/

Zhang, Y. (2010). Cloud Computing Assisted Instructions in China. *Education and Information Technologies, 2,* 438–440.

Zhou, M., Zhang, R., Xie, W., & Qian, W. (2010). Security and Privacy in Cloud Computing: A Survey. *Proceedings of the 2010 Sixth International Conference on Semantics, Knowledge and Grids* (pp. 105-112).

Zissis, D., & Lekkas, D. (2011). Securing e-Government and e-Voting with an open cloud computing architecture. *Government Information Quarterly*, 2–13.

Zissis, D., & Lekkas, D. (2012). Addressing Cloud Computing Security Issues. *Future Generation Computer Systems*, 28(3), 583–592. doi:10.1016/j.future.2010.12.006

ADDITIONAL READING

Anderson, A., & Strecker, M. (2012). Sustainable Development: A Case for Education. *Environment: Science and Policy for Sustainable Development*, 54(6), 3-16.

Berl, A., Gelenbe, E., Di Girolamo, M., Giuliani, G., Meer, H., Dang, M., & Pentikousis, K. (2010). Energy-Efficient Cloud Computing. *The Computer Journal*, 53(7), 1046–1051. doi:10.1093/comjnl/bxp080

Buyya, R., Yeo, C. S., Venugopal, S., Broberg, J., & Brandic, I. (2009). Cloud Computing and emerging IT Platforms: Vision, hype, and reality for delivering computing as the 5th utility. *Future Generation Computer Systems*, 25(6), 599–616. doi:10.1016/j.future.2008.12.001

Goldsmith, S., & Samson, D. (2006). *Sustainable Development and Business Success*. Melbourne: Thomson.

Groot, M. (2008). *Metrics and Criteria for Success in Infrastructure Managing Financial Information in The Trade Lifecycle* (pp. 217–251). Burlington: Academic Press.

Grossman, R. L. (2009). The Case for Cloud Computing. Retrieved from Computer.org/ITPro

Hamm, S. (2008). Cloud Computing: Eyes on the Skies. Retrieved from http://www.businessweek.com/magazine/content/08_18/b4082059989191.htm

Hayward, B. (2012). Sustainable ICT. *Telecommunications Journal of Australia*, 62(5), 1–10. doi:10.7790/tja.v62i5.373

Issa, T., Chang, V., & Issa, T. (2010). The Impact of Cloud Computing and Organizational Sustainability. *Proceedings of the Cloud Computing and Virtualization 2010*, Singapore.

Issa, T., Chang, V., & Issa, T. (2010). Sustainable Business Strategies and PESTEL Framework. *GSTF International Journal on Computing*, 1(1), 73–80.

Issa, T., Issa, T., & Chang, V. (2011). Would teaching sustainable development business strategies shift students' mindsets? An Australian experience. *The International Journal of Environmental, Cultural. Economic & Social Sustainability*, 7(5), 257–272.

Jagers, N. (2009). Bringing Corporate Social Responsibility to the World Trade Organisation. In D. McBarnet, A. Voiculescu, & T. Campbell (Eds.), *The New Corporate Accountability - Corporate Social Responsibility and the Law* (pp. 177–206). Cambridge.

Lee, Y. C., & Zomaya, A. Y. (2012). Energy efficient utilization of resources in Cloud Computing systems. *The Journal of Supercomputing 60*(2), 268–280.

Mayo, R., & Perng, C. (2009). Cloud Computing Payback: An explanation of where the ROI comes from.

Mell, P., & Grance, T. (2011). *The NIST Definition of Cloud Computing.*

O'Neill, R. (2006). The advantages and disadvantages of qualitative and quantitative research methods. Retrieved from http://www.roboneill.co.uk/papers/research_methods.htm

O'Toole, W. (2011). *Event metrics and checklists Events Feasibility and Development* (pp. 231–250). Oxford: Butterworth-Heinemann. doi:10.1016/B978-0-7506-6640-4.10011-1

Poston, L. (2008). Computers Without Borders: Cloud Computing and Political Manipulation. Retrieved from http://profy.com/2008/05/25/cloudcomputingpolitics/

Prasad, A., Saha, S., Mishra, P., Hooli, B., & Murakami, M. (2010). Back to Green. *Journal of Green Engineering, 1*(1), 89-110.

Preston, R. (2008). Will Cloud Computing Rain On IT's Parade? *Information Week, 1173*, 52.

Rainey, D. (2006). *Sustainable Business Development.* UK: Cambridge University Press. doi:10.1017/CBO9780511617607

ScottJ.StahelW.LovinsH.GraysonD. (2010). *The Sustainable Business.*

Wakkary, R. (2009). *A Sustainable Identity: Creativity of Everyday Design.* Paper presented at the CHI2009. 10.1145/1518701.1518761

Weybrecht, G. (2010). *The Sustainable MBA - The Manager's Guide to Green Business.* UK: John Wiley & Sons.

Wirtenberg, J. (2009). *Beyond Green: Going Green and Sustainable Environments Transitioning to Green.* Retrieved from http://www.greenbaumlaw.com/Wirtenberg.ppt

KEY TERMS AND DEFINITIONS

Cloud Computing and Green IT: Smart Technology used to reduce energy and e-waste.

Cloud Computing Services: Services made available to users via the Internet, i.e. SaaS (Software as a Service), PaaS (Platform as a Service) and IaaS (Infrastructure as a Service).

Cloud Computing Strategy: Approach used by organizations to reduce energy, carbon emission and e-waste.

Cloud Computing Strengths: Flexible, efficient, scalable, reliable, reduce cost and maintenance.

Cloud Computing Weakness: Security, legal and law, privacy, physical location of data and unavailability of service due to crashes or bugs in the providers' storage.

This research was previously published in Managing Big Data in Cloud Computing Environments edited by Zongmin Ma, pages 231-251, copyright year 2016 by Information Science Reference (an imprint of IGI Global).

Chapter 80
Security and Privacy Issues of Big Data

José Moura
Instituto Universitário de Lisboa, Portugal & Instituto de Telecomunicações, Portugal

Carlos Serrão
Instituto Universitário de Lisboa, Portugal & Information Sciences, Technologies and Architecture Research Center, Portugal

ABSTRACT

This chapter revises the most important aspects in how computing infrastructures should be configured and intelligently managed to fulfill the most notably security aspects required by Big Data applications. One of them is privacy. It is a pertinent aspect to be addressed because users share more and more personal data and content through their devices and computers to social networks and public clouds. So, a secure framework to social networks is a very hot topic research. This last topic is addressed in one of the two sections of the current chapter with case studies. In addition, the traditional mechanisms to support security such as firewalls and demilitarized zones are not suitable to be applied in computing systems to support Big Data. SDN is an emergent management solution that could become a convenient mechanism to implement security in Big Data systems, as we show through a second case study at the end of the chapter. This also discusses current relevant work and identifies open issues.

INTRODUCTION

The Big Data is an emerging area applied to manage datasets whose size is beyond the ability of commonly used software tools to capture, manage, and timely analyze that amount of data. The quantity of data to be analyzed is expected to double every two years (IDC, 2012). All these data are very often unstructured and from various sources such as social media, sensors, scientific applications, surveillance, video and image archives, Internet search indexing, medical records, business transactions and system logs. Big data is gaining more and more attention since the number of devices connected to the so-called "Internet of Things" (IoT) is still increasing to unforeseen levels, producing large amounts of data which needs to be transformed into valuable information. Additionally, it is very popular to buy on-demand

DOI: 10.4018/978-1-5225-8176-5.ch080

Copyright © 2019, IGI Global. Copying or distributing in print or electronic forms without written permission of IGI Global is prohibited.

additional computing power and storage from public cloud providers to perform intensive data-parallel processing. In this way, security and privacy issues can be potentially boosted by the volume, variety, and wide area deployment of the system infrastructure to support Big Data applications.

As Big Data expands with the help of public clouds, traditional security solutions tailored to private computing infrastructures, confined to a well-defined security perimeter, such as firewalls and demilitarized zones (DMZs) are no more effective. Using Big Data, security functions are required to work over the heterogeneous composition of diverse hardware, operating systems, and network domains. In this puzzle-type computing environment, the abstraction capability of Software-Defined Networking (SDN) seems a very important characteristic that can enable the efficient deployment of Big Data secure services on-top of the heterogeneous infrastructure. SDN introduces abstraction because it separates the control (higher) plane from the underlying system infrastructure being supervised and controlled. Separating a network's control logic from the underlying physical routers and switches that forward traffic allows system administrators to write high-level control programs that specify the behavior of an entire network, in contrast to conventional networks, whereby administrators (if allowed to do it by the device manufacturers) must codify functionality in terms of low-level device configuration. Using SDN, the intelligent management of secure functions can be implemented in a logically centralized controller, simplifying the following aspects: enforcement of security policies; system (re)configuration; and system evolution. The robustness drawback of a centralized SDN solution can be mitigated using a hierarchy of controllers and/or through the usage of redundant controllers at least for the most important system functions to be controlled.

The National Institute of Standards and Technology (NIST) launched very recently a framework with a set of voluntary guidelines to help organizations make their communications and computing operations safer (NIST, 2014). This could be achieved through a systematic verification of the system infrastructure in terms of risk assessment, protection against threats, and capabilities to respond and recover from attacks. Following the last verification principles, Defense Advanced Research Projects Agency (DARPA) is creating a program called Mining and Understanding Software Enclaves (MUSE) to enhance the quality of the US military's software. This program is designed to produce more robust software that can work with big datasets without causing errors or crashing under the sheer volume of information (DARPA, 2014). In addition, security and privacy are becoming very urgent Big Data aspects that need to be tackled (Agrawal, Das, & El Abbadi, 2011). To illustrate this, the social networks have enabled people to share and distribute valuable copyrighted digital contents in a very easy way. Consequently, the copyright infringement behaviors, such as illicit copying, malicious distribution, unauthorized access and usage, and free sharing of copyright-protected digital contents, will become a much more common phenomenon. To mitigate these problems, Big Data should have solid solutions to support author's privacy and author's copyrights (Marques & Serrão, 2013a). Also, users share more and more personal data and user generated content through their mobile devices and computers to social networks and cloud services, loosing data and content control with a serious impact on their own privacy. Finally, one potentially promising approach is to create additional uncertainty for attackers by dynamically changing system properties in what is called a cyber moving target (MT) (Okhravi, Hobson, Bigelow, & Streilein, 2014). They present a summary of several types of MT techniques, consider the advantages and weaknesses of each, and make recommendations for future research in this area.

The current chapter endorses the most important aspects of Big Data security and privacy and is structured as follows. The first section discusses the most important challenges to the aspects of information security and privacy imposed by the novel requirements of Big Data applications. The second section presents and explains some interesting solutions to the problems found in the previous section. The third and fourth sections are related with two case studies in this exciting emergent area.

BIG DATA CHALLENGES TO INFORMATION SECURITY AND PRIVACY

With the proliferation of devices connected to the Internet and connected to each other, the volume of data collected, stored, and processed is increasing everyday, which also brings new challenges in terms of privacy and security. In fact, the currently used security mechanisms such as firewalls and DMZs cannot be used in the Big Data infrastructure because the security mechanisms should be stretched out of the perimeter of the organization's network to fulfill the user/data mobility requirements and the policies of BYOD (Bring Your Own Device). Considering these new scenarios, the pertinent question is what security and privacy policies and technologies are more adequate to fulfill the current top Big Data security and privacy challenges (Cloud Security Alliance, 2013). These challenges may be organized into four Big Data aspects such as infrastructure security (e.g. secure distributed computations using MapReduce), data privacy (e.g. data mining that preserves privacy/granular access), data management (e.g. secure data provenance and storage) and, integrity and reactive security (e.g. real time monitoring of anomalies and attacks).

Considering Big Data there is a set of risk areas that need to be considered. These include the information lifecycle (provenance, ownership and classification of data), the data creation and collection process, and the lack of security procedures. Ultimately, the Big Data security objectives are no different from any other data types – to preserve its confidentiality, integrity and availability.

Being Big Data such an important and complex topic, it is almost natural that immense security and privacy challenges will arise (Michael & Miller, 2013; Tankard, 2012). Big Data has specific characteristics that affect security and privacy: variety, volume, velocity, value, variability, and veracity (Figure 1). These challenges have a direct impact on the design of security solutions that are required to tackle all these characteristics and requirements (Demchenko, Ngo, Laat, Membrey, & Gordijenko, 2014). Currently, such out of the box security solution does not exist.

Cloud Secure Alliance (CSA), a non-profit organization with a mission to promote the use of best practices for providing security assurance within Cloud Computing, has created a Big Data Working Group that has focused on the Big Data security and privacy challenges (Cloud Security Alliance, 2013). CSA has categorized the different security and privacy challenges into four different aspects of the Big Data ecosystem. These aspects are Infrastructure Security, Data Privacy, Data Management and, Integrity and Reactive Security. Each of these aspects faces the following security challenges, according to CSA:

- Infrastructure Security
  - Secure Computations in Distributed Programming Frameworks
  - Security Best Practices for Non-Relational Data Stores
- Data Privacy
  - Privacy Preserving Data Mining and Analytics
  - Cryptographically Enforced Data Centric Security
  - Granular Access Control

Figure 1. The five V's of Big Data
(Adapted from ("IBM big data platform - Bringing big data to the Enterprise," 2014))

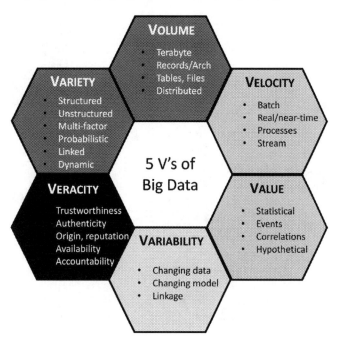

- Data Management and Integrity
  - Secure Data Storage and Transaction Logs
  - Granular Audits
  - Data Provenance
- Reactive Security
  - End-point Validation and Filtering
  - Real Time Security Monitoring.

These security and privacy challenges cover the entire spectrum of the Big Data lifecycle (Figure 2): sources of data production (devices), the data itself, data processing, data storage, data transport and data usage on different devices.

A particular aspect of Big Data security and privacy has to be related with the rise of the Internet of Things (IoT). IoT, defined by Oxford[1] as "a proposed development of the Internet in which everyday objects have network connectivity, allowing them to send and receive data", is already a reality – Gartner estimates that 26 billion of IoT devices will be installed by 2020, generating an incremental revenue of $300 billion (Rivera & van der Meulen, 2014). The immense increase in the number of connected devices (cars, lighting systems, refrigerators, telephones, glasses, traffic control systems, health monitoring devices, SCADA systems, TVs, home security systems, home automation systems, and many more) has led to manufacturers to push to the market, in a short period of time, a large set of devices, cloud systems and mobile applications to exploit this opportunity. While it presents tremendous benefits and opportunities for end-users it also is responsible for security challenges.

Figure 2. Security and Privacy challenges in Big Data ecosystem
(Adapted from (Cloud Security Alliance, 2013))

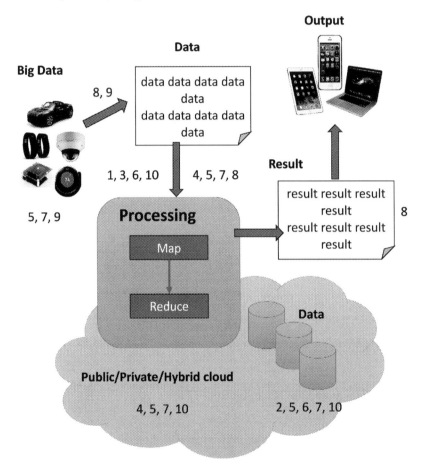

HP recently conducted a study on market-available IoT solutions and concluded that 70% of those contain security problems. These security problems were related with privacy issues, insufficient authorization, lack of transport encryption, insecure web interface and inadequate software protection (HP, 2014). Based on some of these findings, HP has started a project at OWASP (Open Web Application Security Project) that is entitled "OWASP Internet of Things Top Ten" (OWASP, 2014) whose objective is to help IoT suppliers to identify the top ten security IoT device problems and how to avoid them. This project, similar to the OWASP Top 10, identified the following security problems:

- **Insecure Web Interface:** Which can allow an attacker to exploit an administration web interface (through cross-site scripting, cross-site request forgery and SQL injection) and obtain unauthorized access to control the IoT device.
- **Insufficient Authentication/Authorization:** Can allow an attacker to exploit a bad password policy, break weak passwords and access to privileged modes on the IoT device.
- **Insecure Network Services:** Which can lead to an attacker exploiting unnecessary or weak services running on the device, or use those services as a jumping point to attack other devices on the IoT network.

- **Lack of Transport Encryption:** Allowing an attacker to eavesdrop data in transit between IoT devices and support systems.
- **Privacy Concerns:** Raised from the fact the most IoT devices and support systems collect personal data from users and fail to protect that data.
- **Insecure Cloud Interface:** Without proper security controls an attacker can use multiple attack vectors (insufficient authentication, lack of transport encryption, account enumeration) to access data or controls via the cloud website.
- **Insecure Mobile Interface:** Without proper security controls an attacker can use multiple attack vectors (insufficient authentication, lack of transport encryption, account enumeration) to access data or controls via the mobile interface.
- **Insufficient Security Configurability:** Due to the lack or poor configuration mechanisms an attacker can access data or controls on the device.
- **Insecure Software/Firmware:** Attackers can take advantage of unencrypted and unauthenticated connections to hijack IoT devices updates, and perform malicious update that can compromise the device, a network of devices and the data they hold.
- **Poor Physical Security:** If the IoT device is physically accessible than an attacker can use USB ports, SD cards or other storage means to access the device OS and potentially any data stored on the device.

It is clear that Big Data present interesting opportunities for users and businesses, however these opportunities are countered by enormous challenges in terms of privacy and security (Cloud Security Alliance, 2013). Traditional security mechanisms are insufficient to provide a capable answer to those challenges. In the next section, some of these solutions/proposals are going to be addressed.

SOLUTIONS/PROPOSALS TO ADDRESS BIG DATA SECURITY AND PRIVACY CHALLENGES

There is no single magical solution to solve the identified Big Data security and privacy challenges and traditional security mechanisms, which are tailored to securing small-scale static data, often fall short (Cloud Security Alliance, 2013). There is the need to understand how the collection of large amounts of complex structured and unstructured data can be protected. Non-authorized access to that data to create new relations, combine different data sources and make it available to malicious users is a serious risk for Big Data. The basic and more common solution for this includes encrypting everything to make data secure regardless where the data resides (data center, computer, mobile device, or any other). As Big Data grows and its processing gets faster, then encryption, masking and tokenization are critical elements for protecting sensitive data.

Due to its characteristics, Big Data projects need to take an holistic vision at security (Tankard, 2012). Big Data projects need to take into consideration the identification of the different data sources, the origin and creators of data, as well as who is allowed to access the data. It is also necessary to conduct a correct classification to identify critical data, and align with the organization information security policy in terms of enforcing access control and data handling policies. As a recommendation, different security mechanisms should be closer to the data sources and data itself, in order to provide security right at the origin of data, and mechanisms of control and prevention on archiving, data leakage prevention and access control should work together (Kindervag, Balaouras, Hill, & Mak, 2012).

The new Big Data security solutions should extend the secure perimeter from the enterprise to the public cloud (Juels & Oprea, 2013). In this way, a trustful data provenance mechanism should be also created across domains. In addition, similar mechanisms to the ones used in (Luo, Lin, Zhang, & Zukerman, 2013) can be used to mitigate distributed denial-of-service (DDoS) attacks launched against Big Data infrastructures. Also, a Big Data security and privacy is necessary to ensure data trustworthiness throughout the entire data lifecycle – from data collection to usage.

The personalization feature of some Big Data services and its impact on the user privacy is discussed in (Hasan, Habegger, Brunie, Bennani, & Damiani, 2013). They discuss these issues in the backdrop of EEXCESS, a concrete project aimed to both provide high level recommendations and to respect user privacy. A recent work describes proposed privacy extensions to UML to help software engineers to quickly visualize privacy requirements, and design them into Big Data applications (Jutla, Bodorik, & Ali, 2013).

While trying to take the most of Big Data, in terms of security and privacy, it becomes mandatory that mechanisms that address legal requirements about data handling, need to be met. Secure encryption technology must be employed to protect all the confidential data (Personally Identifiable Information (PII), Protected Health Information (PHI) and Intellectual Property (IP) and careful cryptographic material (keys) access management policies, need to be put in place, to ensure the correct locking and unlocking of data – this is particularly important for data stored. In order to be successful these mechanisms need to be transparent to the end-user and have low impact of the performance and scalability of data (software and hardware-based encryptions mechanisms are to be considered) (Advantech, 2013).

As previously referred, traditional encryption and anonymization of data are not adequate to solve Big Data problems. They are adequate to protect static information, but are not adequate when data computation is involved (MIT, 2014). Therefore, other techniques, allowing specific and targeted data computation while keeping the data secret, need to be used. Secure Function Evaluation (SFE) (Lindell & Pinkas, 2002), Fully Homomorphic Encryption (FHE) (Gentry, 2009) and Functional Encryption (FE) (Goldwasser et al., 2014), and partition of data on non-communicating data centers, can help solving the limitations of traditional security techniques.

Homomorphic encryption is a form of encryption which allows specific types of computations (e.g. RSA public key encryption algorithm) to be carried out on ciphertext and generate an encrypted result which, when decrypted, matches the result of operations performed on the plaintext (Gentry, 2010). Fully homomorphic encryption has numerous applications, as referred in (Van Dijk, Gentry, Halevi, & Vaikuntanathan, 2010). This allows encrypted queries on databases, which keeps secret private user information where that data is normally stored (somewhere in the cloud – in the limit an user can store its data on any untrusted server, but in encrypted form, without being worried with the data secrecy) (Ra Popa & Redfield, 2011). It also enables private queries to a search engine - the user submits an encrypted query and the search engine computes a succinct encrypted answer without ever looking at the query in the clear which could contain private user information such as the number of the national healthcare service. The homomorphic encryption also enables searching on encrypted data - a user stores encrypted files on a remote file server and can later have the server retrieve only files that (when decrypted) satisfy some boolean constraint, even though the server cannot decrypt the files on its own. More broadly, the fully homomorphic encryption improves the efficiency of secure multiparty computation.

An important security and privacy challenge for Big Data is related with the storage and processing of encrypted data. Running queries against an encrypted database is a basic security requirement for secure Big Data however it is a challenging one. This raises questions such as a) is the database encrypted with a single or multiple keys; b) does the database needs to be decrypted prior to running the query; c) do the queries need to be also encrypted; d) who as the permissions to decrypt the database; and many more. Recently a system that was developed at MIT, provides answers to some of these questions. CryptDB allows researchers to run database queries over encrypted data (Ra Popa & Redfield, 2011). Trustworthy applications that intent to query encrypted data will pass those queries to a CryptDB proxy (that sits between the application and the database) that rewrites those queries in a specific way so that they can be run against the encrypted database. The database returns the encrypted results back to the proxy, which holds a master key and will decrypt the results, sending the final answer back to the application. CryptDB supports numerous forms of encryption schemes that allow different types of operations on the data (RA Popa & Redfield, 2012). Based on CryptDB, Google has developed the Encrypted Big Query Client that will allow encrypted big queries against their BigQuery service that enables super, SQL-like queries against append-only tables, using the processing power of Google's infrastructure (Google, 2014).

Apart from more specific security recommendations, it is also important to consider the security of the IT infrastructure itself. One of the common security practices is to place security controls at the edge of the networks however, if an attacker violates this security perimeter it will have access to all the data within it. Therefore, a new approach is necessary to move those security controls near to the data (or add additional ones). Monitoring, analyzing and learning from data usage and access is also an important aspect to continuously improve security of the data holding infrastructure and leverage the already existing security solutions (Kindervag et al., 2012; Kindervag, Wang, Balaouras, & Coit, 2011).

A CASE STUDY IN A SECURE SOCIAL APPLICATION

Social networks are one of the key-applications for a large number of users. Millions and millions of persons are connected to some kind of social network – e.g. Facebook according to its own accounting has more than 829 million daily active users on average (654 million with mobile access). Social networks are quite attractive to users because they allow communication with new persons and concede users the ability to expose their own network of friends to others, creating new relations and pairings among users and between users and content (McKenzie et al., 2012). Users take advantage of this functionality to share all kinds of digital content within the social network, with other users (either they are their direct contacts or they are in other one's connections). These social network-sharing functionalities are extremely powerful and engaging of further social interaction. However, they are at the same time, the cause of serious privacy and security problems because sharing control is not on the end-user side. This represents a serious threat to the user privacy since content shared in these platforms can easily be exposed to a wider audience in just a few seconds. It is difficult, for an ordinary user, to select specific sharing properties for the content placed in social network and ensure that it stays under its control.

With the emergence of Web 2.0, users have changed from being simply information consumers to become important content producers. User generated content is content that is voluntarily developed by an individual or a consortium, and distributed through an online platform. The volume of user generated content currently produced and made available through several platforms is already immense and continues to grow in size (Kim, Jin, Kim, & Shin, 2012). For instance, Facebook stores, accesses, and analyzes more than 30 Petabytes of user generated data (100 terabytes of data are uploaded daily to Facebook) and YouTube users upload 48 hours of new video every minute of the day (McKenzie et al., 2012).

Currently, social network platforms already present a set of pre-defined but limited content privacy and security sharing controls (X. Chen & Shi, 2009). Major social network platforms offer the possibility for users to share content under specific privacy rules, which are defined by the social platform and not by the end-user. Most of the times, these rules are extremely permissive and differ from platform to platform. Also, on social networks, content is shared in a non-protected manner, making it easier for unauthorized usage and sharing. Users are also bound by subsequent privacy policies changes that threaten more and more the user right to protect its personal information and personal content.

The other problem that is most of the times associated with the security and privacy of content shared on social networks, is related to the security of the social network platform itself (Gross & Acquisti, 2005). The exploitation of the social network infrastructure can lead to security and privacy threats. On the other hand, recently on the media there have been some allegations about the cooperation of some of the most important IT suppliers (including some major social platforms) with governmental agencies to allow the unauthorized access to user's information and content. This latter fact is quite relevant, because, in theory, the social network service supplier has unlimited access to the information and content of all its customers.

This is an increasing serious problem, not only for end-users but also for organizations. More and more, organizations rely on social network services as a mean to disseminate information, create relations with and between employees and customers, knowledge capture and dissemination. The privacy and security challenges presented by these new ways of communication and interaction are very pertinent topics for both end users and organizations.

The continuous growing proliferation of mobile devices (mostly smartphones and tablets, but soon more devices will enter this scenario) with capabilities of producing content (mainly audio recordings, videos and pictures) at the palm of every user's hand, following them everywhere and anytime is also a serious threat to their content privacy and security (De Cristofaro, Soriente, Tsudik, & Williams, 2012). This user generated content creates cultural, symbolic, and affective benefit including personal satisfaction, enhanced skill or reputation, improved functionality for existing games or devices, community building or civic engagement. In more simplistic terms, user generated content creates value, economic or not.

Having all of this into consideration, it seems clear that it is necessary to have a clear separation among the social network platform providers, their social functionalities, and the user generated content that they hold. It is important to create mechanisms that transfer part of the security and sharing control to the end-user side. Having this into consideration, in this section, it is proposed and presented a paradigm shift that implies a change from the current social networks security and privacy scenario based on a social network platform centric, to another paradigm that empowers social networks users' on the control and safeguard of its privacy, passing the user generated content sharing control to the end-user side, using rights management systems (Marques & Serrão, 2013b). Also, the entity that is responsible for the storage and protection of the user generated content is independent of the social network platform itself.

This new approach creates a mechanism that protects the shared user generated content on the social network platform while it provides the content sharing and access control to the end-user.

Overall System Architecture

As referred on the previous section, the novel approach that is followed is based on open rights management systems – in particular, and for this sake, it is based on OpenSDRM (Carlos Serrão, Neves, Trevor Barker, & Massimo Balestri, 2003; Serrão, 2008). OpenSDRM is an open and distributed rights management architecture that allows the implementation of different content business models. Moreover, OpenSDRM was created having into consideration interoperability aspects (Serrão, Rodriguez, & Delgado, 2011) that permit that the different modules that compose the system to be decoupled and re-integrated to allow interoperability (Serrão, Dias, & Kudumakis, 2005; Serrão et al., 2011) with other non-OpenSDRM components, using an open and well-defined API (Figure 3). Additionally there may exist also more than one instance of each of the services on the platform, allowing the scalability and growth of the set of all possible configuration options (Serrão, Dias, & Delgado, 2005).

For the proposed scenario, the social network platform can be integrated with the rights management system, using different methods. If the social network implements a development API or if it is open-source, a much tighter integration scenario can be achieved. If not, it is possible to use other publicly available mechanisms on the platform (or out of the platform) to enable a lesser integrated scenario, but that maintains the privacy and security characteristics sought. Using mechanisms on the platform is the most common scenario and therefore is the approach that will be reflected here.

In this architecture there are some elements that cooperate in order to provide the necessary functionalities to both the end-users and the social network platform, in order to implement the necessary mechanisms to provide security and privacy to user generated content.

OpenSDRM, as an open rights management framework is composed by different services (Figure 4). Some of the services are deployed on the server-side while other are implemented on the user-side. On the user-side, the authorization service handles the requests to render some type of content on the user device, processing the requests and matching them to existing credentials, licenses and permissions to

Figure 3. Overview of the architecture integrated with the rights management system

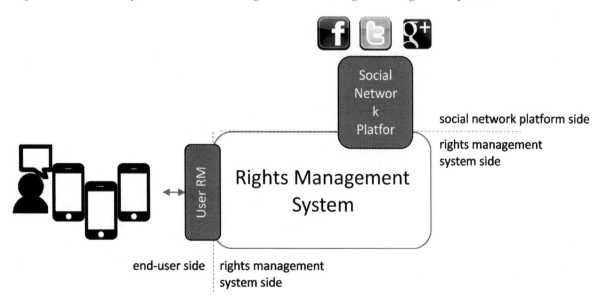

Figure 4. Overview of the architecture integrated with the rights management system

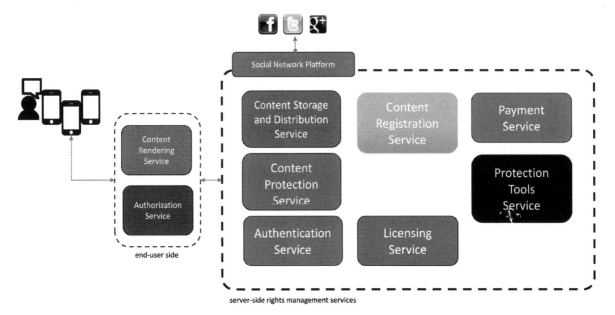

render the content. Also, on the end-user side the content rendering service is responsible for verifying the necessary requirements to render the content (encryption, scrambling, and others) and effectively renders the content for the end user.

On the server-side, is where a large part of the rights management responsibility lies. A set of decoupled components with a well-defined API that allows an integration between the necessary ones to implement the specific content business model. These services are the following:

- **Content Storage and Distribution Service:** This service is responsible for the storage and distribution of user generated content in a protected manner;
- **Content Protection Service:** The service is responsible for the protection of the content. The content is protected by specific protection tools and specific protection mechanisms that may change according to the content and the business model that is going to be implemented;
- **Content Registration Service:** This service is responsible for registering the content on the platform that will be used to uniquely identify the content on the system. This unique identifier is used to identify the user generated content throughout the entire content lifecycle;
- **Payment Service:** If the business model includes the possibility to trade content, this payment service is responsible to communicate with a payment gateway that implements the necessary mechanisms to process payments;
- **Protection Tools Service:** This service is responsible for the registration of content protection tools on the system and for making those tools available for the content protection service to use when implementing the content protection schemas (such as encryption, scrambling, watermarking and others);
- **Authentication Service:** Handles the registration of users and services on the system as well as the requests for authenticate users on behalf of other services;

- **Licensing Service:** This is one of the most important services of the rights management framework, responsible for creating license templates, define and produce new content licenses (that represent the type of rights, permissions and/or restrictions of a given user, or group of users, over the content) and provide licenses, upon request, to specific users.

The following sections of this document will provide a description on how the user can utilize this platform to share user generated content on the social network, and how a user can access content shared by other users.

Registration on the Platform

This novel platform presupposes that all the system services are initially registered on that platform. This means that each one of the different services, either server-side or client-side have to be individually registered at the platform. This registration process assigns unique credentials to each one of the services, ensuring that they are uniquely registered and that these credentials will be used to identify and differentiate the services in future interactions (Figure 5). This registration process is conducted by the authentication service that on its turn issues credentials to all the other services and acts as a central trustworthy mechanism. Moreover, all the communication between the different services is conducted over a secure and authenticated channel, using Secure Sockets Layer/Transport Layer Security(SSL/TLS) – this ensures the authentication and security of the servers where the services are deployed and allowing the establishment of secure communication channels (Stephen A Thomas, 2000).

1. The authentication service (AS) has cryptographic material (K_{pub}^{AS}, K_{priv}^{AS}) and credentials that were self-issued (C^{AS}_{AS}) or issued by other trustworthy entity (C^{CA}_{AS});

Figure 5. Handling the registration of new services on the platform

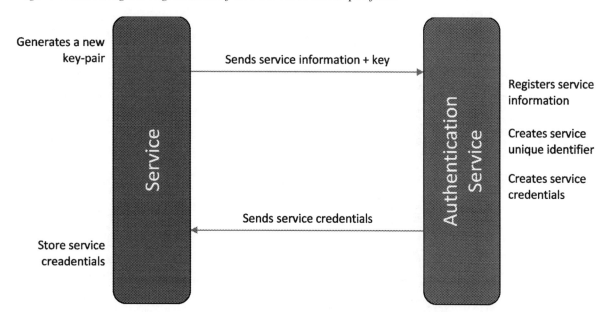

2.   The service that needs to be registered generates a key pair (K_{pub}^{S}, K_{priv}^{S}) and sends a registration request to the AS, passing some information about the service (S_{info}) and the public key (K_{pub}^{S}) of the service: $S_{info} + K_{pub}^{S}$;

3.   AS receives this information, verifies it and then creates a unique service identifier (S_{UUID}). After this verification the AS creates the service credentials that will identify this service globally and uniquely on the platform: $C^{AS}_{S[UUID]} = K_{priv}^{AS}\{S_{UUID}, K_{pub}^{S[UUID]}, C^{AS}_{AS}\}^2$. These credentials, which are signed by AS, are then returned to the requesting service;

4.   The requesting service, stores the credentials. This credential contains also the public key of the authentication service (K_{pub}^{AS}). This is used to prove this credentials to other entities that also rely on the same AS – services that trust AS, also trust on credentials issued by AS, presented by other services.

The service registration process, as described above needs to be repeated according to the number of services available within the social network platform. This enables the entire ecosystem of services to be trusted on that platform.

Another important aspect of the registration process concerns the registration of the users on the rights management platform. The registration of the user on the rights management platform can be dependent or independent of the social network platform. In the example that is presented here, it is assumed that this registration process is performed fully integrated with the social network platform.

This process performs in the following manner (Figure 6):

1.   Assuming that the user still has no account on a social network platform, the user starts the registration process on the social network. In order to do that the user needs to supply its email address (as username) and a password;

Figure 6. Overview of the user registration process

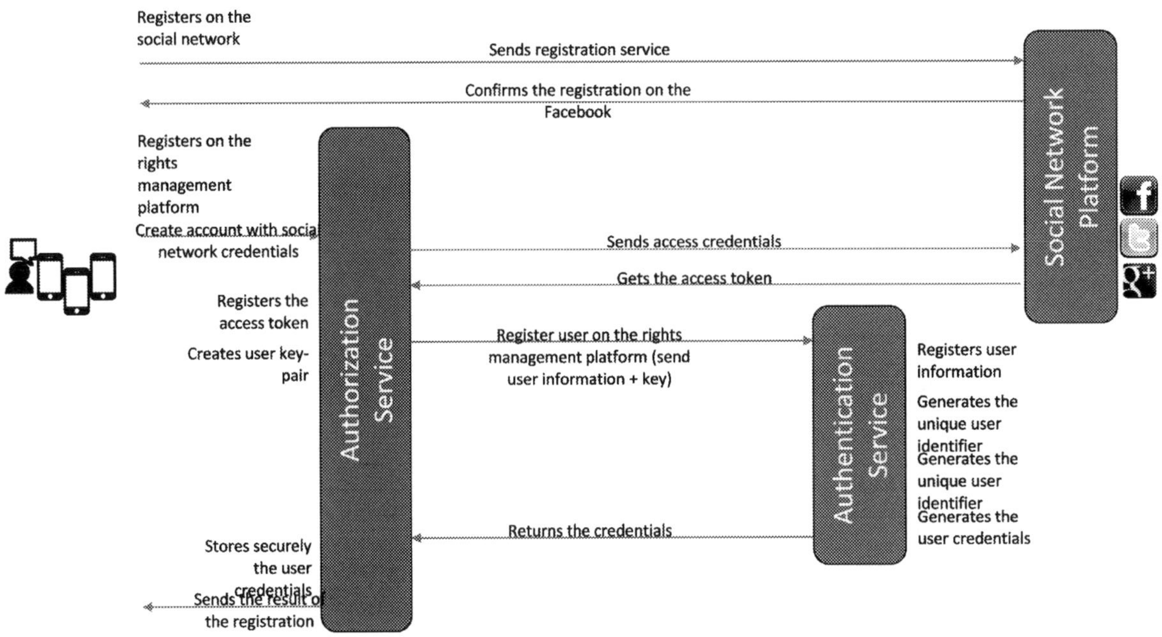

2. The registration process on the social network platform finishes and a confirmation message is sent to the end-user;

3. Next, the user, using the client-side rights management authorization service (AUTS), initiates the registration process in the rights management platform. The AUTS presents several registration options to the end-user (integrated with some social network platforms -using either Oauth- or an independent mode). For this case, the user will use registration options by using the mode of integrated authentication;

4. The user introduces the social account credentials (email, password) on the AUTS that starts the authentication process on the social network platform. If successful, the social network returns an access token that has a specific validity and a set of permissions to conduct different operations on the social network on behalf of the user;

5. AUTS, using the user credentials (email, password) creates a secret key that is used to initialize a secure storage on the authorization service: $S_k^{SStorage} = SHA1[email+password]$;

6. The AUTS securely stores the user information, and the social network access token. Additionally, the AUTS creates a key-pair for the user (K_{pub}^U, K_{priv}^U) also storing it in a secure manner: $S_k^{SStorage}(K_{pub}^U$, K_{priv}^U, user_info, token);

7. AUTS contacts the AS to register the user on the platform. This is performed using the $C^{AS}_{S[AUTS]}$ that contains the K_{pub}^{AS}. $C^{AS}_{S[AUTS]}$ is also sent to ensure that the AUTS has been previously registered: K_{pub}^{AS} (email, K_{pub}^U, $C^{AS}_{S[AUTS]}$);

8. The AUTS receives all this information and after deciphering it, and validating the AUTS credential, registers the user information, generates a unique identifier for the user and creates credentials for the user: $C^{AS}_{UUID} = K_{priv}^{AS} \{UUID, K_{pub}^U\}$;

9. The credentials are returned to the AUTS and are securely stored: $S_k^{SStorage}(C^{AS}_{UUID})$. The user is notified about the result of the registration operation.

This is the concluding step of the service and user registration on the rights management platform. The user is now prepared to use both the rights management service and the social network platform.

Sharing Content on the Platform

The other important functionality on the system is the sharing of user generated content (UGC) on the social network. This sharing mechanism is performed through the rights management platform, and the content is stored securely on a configured location (it can be on a specific storage location, on the social platform or on the rights management platform). When the user uploads user generated content, the content is protected and the rights, permissions and restrictions about the content can be defined by the user.

This process assumes that both user that generates the content and the users willing to access the content are properly registered and authenticated on the social network platform and on the rights management platform (Figure 7).

In a brief discussing way, the user generated content is uploaded to the rights management platform, the access rights and permissions are defined by the user, the content is protected, and a URI is returned to be shared on the social network platform.

The novel content sharing process, using the mechanisms described in this chapter, can be now defined in the following steps:

Figure 7. Overview of the user generated content secure sharing on the social network platform

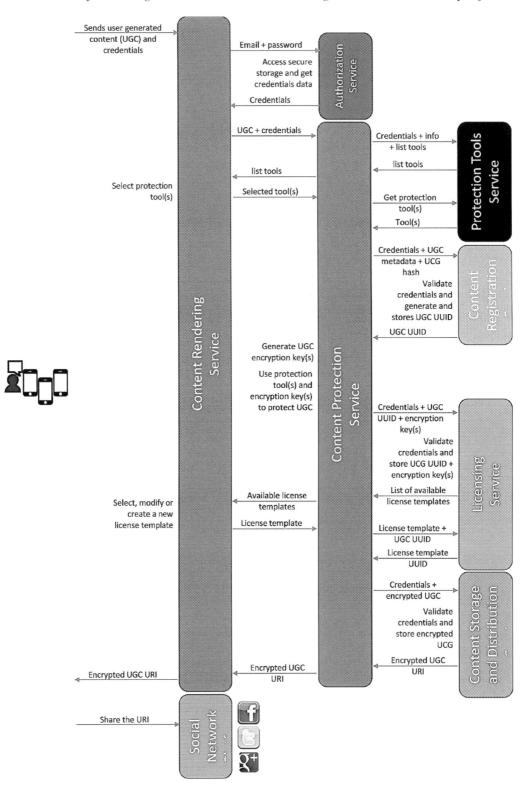

1. The user sends the user generated content (UGC) that it expects to share on the social network. This UGC is uploaded through the content rendering service (CRS). This service requires the user to enter its credentials (email and password), if the user is not yet authenticated. These credentials are used to access the secure storage: $S_k^{SStorage} = SHA1[email+password]$;

2. The CRS contacts the AUTS, which reads from the secure storage the user rights management system credentials: C^{AS}_{UUID};

3. The CRS uploads to the content protection service (CPS) the UGC and sends the user credentials, obtained in the previous step: UGC_{UUID}, C^{AS}_{UUID};

4. The CPS, after retrieving some metadata information about the UGC (such as the type, the format, the encoding, among others), contacts the protection tools service (PTS), requesting a list of available protection tools, that can be suitable to protect the UGC. The PTS sends its credentials and some information about the content: C^{AS}_{CPS}, UGC_info;

5. The PTS also returns a list of protection tools that match the request made by the CPS. This information is signed by PTS: $K_{priv}^{PTS}\{protection\_tools\_list\}$;

6. The CPS returns the list of protection tools to the CRS, and presents it to the user. The user selects the most appropriate protection tools, adjusting the parameters of applicability of the tools to the UGC and submits its request about the necessary protection tools;

7. The CPS requests the selected protection tools from the protection tools service. The PTS returns the requested tools to the CPS;

8. Next, the CPS requests to the content registration service for the UGC to be registered. For this, the CPS send its credentials, the UCG metadata and the content hash: C^{AS}_{CPS}, UGC_info, SHA1[UGC];

9. The content registration service (CRGS), stores the received information, and generates a unique content identifier that is returned to the content protection service: $K_{priv}^{CRS}\{UGC_{UUID}\}$;

10. The CPS generates one or more content encryption keys (CEK[1], CEK[2] … CEK[n]) that are applied over the UGC, using the selected protection tools, in order to ensure the appropriate content protection;

11. Following this protection process, the CPS sends the content encryption keys for registration at the licensing service. Each of the content encryption keys is protected with the user key, and the entire message is protected by the CPS key: C^{AS}_{CPS}, $K_{pub}^{CPS}(K_{pub}^{U}(CEK[1], CEK[2] … CEK[n])$, $UGC_{UUID})$;

12. The licensing service (LS) after validating all the received information, returns a list of licensing templates to the content protection service. The CPS returns the list of licensing templates to CRS, and the user can select the most appropriate license template, modify it and adapt it, or simply create a new one;

13. The license template (LIC_{TPL}) is sent to the CPS that after sends it to the licensing service and associates it with the identifier of the UGC: LIC_{TPL}, UGC_{UUID}. The licensing service returns the license template identifier (LIC_{TPL} [UUID]);

14. In the next stage, the CPS sends the protected UGC to the content storage and distribution service that stores the encrypted content: C^{AS}_{CPS}, $K_{priv}^{CPS}\{CEK[n](UGC), UGC_{UUID}\}$;

15. The content storage and distribution service returns a URI for the location of the stored encrypted UGC. This URI is returned to the user that can share it on the social network platform afterwards.

After this process is completed, the UGC shared by the user is shared on the social network platform. The user can also use the social network sharing mechanisms as a way to control how the UGC is propagated on the social network. But, in order to have a fine grained control over the UGC, the user needs to use the rights management system to produce specific licenses with the conditions under which the UGC can be used. These licenses are produced in multiple formats (either in ODRL or MPEG-21 REL). In addition, these licenses are used to support the expression of rights over the UGC. Therefore, when the user uploads user generated content to the rights management system, and after the process that was described previously, the subsequent steps are the following:

1. The CPS contacts licensing service to obtain the appropriate license template for the specific UGC, which was previously created: LIC_{TPL} [UUID]. The license template is an XML-formatted document that contains parameterized fields that can be adapted to specific rights situations;
2. A typical license template for user generated content would be composed by following elements:
    a. User unique identifier (UUID), multiple users ($UUID_1$, $UUID_2$,..., $UUID_n$) or a group identifier (G_{UUID}): these fields represent the unique identifiers of the users or groups to whom the user generated content is going to be shared;
    b. The unique identifier of the content: UGC_{UUID};
    c. List of permissions ($Permission_1$...$Permission_n$);
    d. List of restrictions ($Restriction_1$...$Restriction_n$);
    e. Validity date (validity);
    f. The different content encryption keys (CEK[1], CEK[2] ... CEK[n]). The content encryption keys are protected with user public key: K_{pub}^U(CEK[1], CEK[2] ... CEK[n]);
    g. The license signature, where the license contents are signed by the licensing service: License = K_{priv}^{LIS} {$UUID_1$.. $UUID_n$, $G_{UUID}1$, $G_{UUID}n$, UGC_{UUID}, $Permission_1$ ..$Permission_n$, $Restriction_1$ ..$Restriction_n$, Validity, K_{pub}^U (CEK[1] ... CEK[n])}.
3. The license is stored on the licensing service, where it can be accessed by legitimate users.

Accessing Content on the Platform

Finally the last process in this case-study is to present how the users can access user generated content that was shared by other users on the social network platform. In order to do that, the user needs to be registered on the social network platform and on the rights management system.

When navigating through the timeline of the social network platform, user generated content that was shared over the social network platform, is presented in the form of a special URI, that, when clicked, is intercepted by the rights management platform, and the access process is started.

The referred process is described in the following steps:

1. The CRS, while trying to render the content that is shared on the social network platform, detects that it is protected content, and contacts the authorization service to access the appropriate information to try rendering the content;
2. The user authenticates to the system using the authorization service, supplying its credentials (email and password) to unlock the secure storage and retrieve the user information;
3. The authorization service, using the UGC_{UUID} embedded on the URI, checks if a license for this UGC already exists on the secure storage. If a license already exists:
    a. The authorization service checks the license contents, validating the license digital signature and verifying the UGC_{UUID};

b. If the UGC_{UUID} is the right one, the Validity is checked and the list of permissions and restrictions are evaluated;

c. If the conditions are met, the content can be deciphered and rendered by the content rendering service. The content encryption keys can be retrieved from the license, and used to decipher the content: $K_{priv}^{U}(K_{pub}^{U}(CEK[1] \dots CEK[n]))= CEK[1] \dots CEK[n]$;

d. Content is rendered by the CRS while the license conditions are fulfilled;

4. If the authorization still does not possess a valid license for the UGC_{UUID} that the content rendering service is trying to render to view, the following process should occur:

a. The user authenticates to the system using the authorization service, supplying its credentials (email and password) to unlock the secure storage and retrieve the user information;

b. The authorization service, after getting the appropriated user information, including the credentials, from the secure storage, allows the CRS to contact the licensing service, passing its credentials (C^{AS}_{CRS}), the user credentials (C^{AS}_{UUID}) and the user generated content identifier (UGC_{UUID}) the user is trying to render;

c. The licensing service receives and validates the data that was sent by the CRS, and uses the user generated content unique identifier (UGC_{UUID}) and the user unique identifier (UUID) to verify the existence of a valid license. If the license exists on the system, that license is returned to the CRS, that passes it, for validation and storage, to the authorization service: License = K_{priv}^{LIS} {$UUID_1 \dots UUID_n$, $G_{UUID}1$, $G_{UUID}n$, UGC_{UUID}, $Permission_1 \dots Permission_n$, $Restriction_1 \dots Restriction_n$, Validity, $K_{pub}^{U}(CEK[1] \dots CEK[n])$};

d. The authorization service validates the license signature, verifying its contents and validity and asserting the correct UGC_{UUID};

e. If the UGC_{UUID} is the right one, the Validity is checked and the list of permissions and restrictions are evaluated;

f. If the conditions are met, the content can be deciphered and rendered by the CRS. The content encryption keys can be retrieved from the license, and used to decipher the content: $K_{priv}^{U}(K_{pub}^{U}(CEK[1] \dots CEK[n]))= CEK[1] \dots CEK[n]$;

g. Content is rendered by the CRS while the license conditions are satisfied.

After this process is executed, the access to the CRS can be granted or not, depending on the conditions expressed on the license. For simplicity sake, there are several other processes that were not included in this description, such as, for instance, the verification of the protection mechanisms that were applied to the content, and the download of the appropriated mechanisms to allow the local temporarily unprotected version of the user generated content to be rendered.

The usage of rights management systems to offer security and privacy to shared user generated content, offers additional privacy and security mechanisms that are out of the control of the social network platform itself (Rodríguez, Rodríguez, Carreras, & Delgado, 2009). The users can take advantage of both (the rights management system and the social network platform) to offer a finer control on the content sharing privacy and security properties. This is a novel approach (Marques & Serrão, 2013b) that clearly puts the security and privacy control on the end-user side.

A CASE STUDY FOR AN INTELLIGENT INTRUSION DETECTION/ PREVENTION SYSTEM ON A SOFTWARE-DEFINED NETWORK

This section presents and discusses a case study about an intelligent Intrusion Detection/Prevention System (IDS/IPS) belonging to a software-defined network. In this case study, the IDS/IPS behavior is controlled by a Kinetic module (Feamster, 2014). The Kinetic language (Monsanto, Reich, Foster, Rexford, & Walker, 2013) is an SDN control framework where operators can define a network policy as a Finite State Machine (FSM). The transitions between states of a FSM can be triggered by different types of dynamic events in the network, (e.g. intrusion detection, host state). Based on different network events, operators can enforce different policies to the network using an intuitive FSM model. Kinetic is implemented as a Pyretic controller module written in Python. For more information about Pyretic and Python, consult respectively (Pyretic, 2014) and (Python, 2014).

"A Kinetic control program permits programmer-defined events to dynamically change forwarding behavior for an arbitrary set of flows. Such events can range from topology changes (generated by the Pyretic runtime) to security incidents (generated by an intrusion detection system). The programmer specifies an FSM description that contains set of states, each of which maps to some network behavior that are encoded using Pyretic's policy language; and a set of transitions between those states, each of which may be triggered by events that the operator defines" (Feamster, 2014). For more details on Kinetic, see (Monsanto et al., 2013).

In this case study, an implementation of an IDS/IPS security module will be developed, which should behave as follows:

- If a host is infected and is not a privileged host then it is dropped;
- If a host is infected and is a privileged (exempt) host then the traffic from that host is automatically redirected to a garden wall host, where some corrective security actions could be issued over that infected host (e.g. clean and install security patches for trying to recover it);
- If a host is not infected then the traffic from that host is forwarded towards its final destination.

Code Explanation

In Table 1, it is displayed a partial view of the Python code that implements the Kinetic control program that will be used in this section to evaluate the intelligent IDS/IPS. To become clearer, this code functionality is explained in the following paragraph.

Each time a new packet arrives to the system, the IDS/IPS initially processes that packet and defines the policy to be applied to that packet (i.e. drop | redirect | forward). This policy is then delivered to a second module that implements further MAC functionality, namely the learning algorithm of MAC addresses to enhance the L2 packet forwarding. This second module is the one that effectively forwards or redirects the packet (otherwise if the packet is to be drooped, this second module will not receive any packet at all because it was already discarded by the first IDS/IPS module).

The code shown in Table 1 corresponds to the IDS/IPS module and has its code encapsulated inside a class designated by "gardenwall", which was instantiated from class "DynamicPolicy" (to support the processing of JSON events, as it will be explained below). The function "lpec" is like a packet input filter because it only selects the packets whose source IP address is specified by variable *srcip*. This aims to process the first packet of a flow exactly in the same way as all the following packets of that flow. In

Table 1. Partial view of the code for the module IDS/IPS.

```
class gardenwall(DynamicPolicy):
def __init__(self):
# Garden Wall
def redirectToGardenWall():
client_ips = [IP('10.0.0.1'), IP('10.0.0.2')]
rewrite_policy = rewriteDstIPAndMAC(client_ips, '10.0.0.3')
return rewrite_policy
### DEFINE THE LPEC FUNCTION
def lpec(f):
return match(srcip=f['srcip'])
## SET UP TRANSITION FUNCTIONS
@transition
def exempt(self):
self.case(occurred(self.event),self.event)
@transition
def infected(self):
self.case(occurred(self.event),self.event)
@transition
def policy(self):
# If exempt, redirect pkt to gardenwall;rewrite dstip to 10.0.0.3
self.case(test_and_true(V('exempt'),V('infected')), C(redirectToGardenWall()))
# If infected, drop pkt
self.case(is_true(V('infected')),C(drop))
# Else, identity -> forward pkt
self.default(C(identity))
### SET UP THE FSM DESCRIPTION
self.fsm_def = FSMDef(
infected=FSMVar(type=BoolType(),
init=False,
trans=infected),
exempt=FSMVar(type=BoolType(),
init=False,
trans=exempt),
policy=FSMVar(type=Type(Policy,
{drop,identity,redirectToGardenWall()}),
init=identity,
trans=policy))
### SET UP POLICY AND EVENT STREAMS
fsm_pol = FSMPolicy(lpec,self.fsm_def)
json_event = JSONEvent()
json_event.register_callback(fsm_pol.event_handler)
super(gardenwall,self).__init__(fsm_pol)
```

this example, a transition function encodes logic that indicates the new value a state variable should take when a particular event arrives at the controller. For example, the *infected* transition function encodes a single case: when an *infected* event occurs, the new value taken by the state variable *infected* is the value of that event (i.e. FALSE or TRUE). This is an example of an exogenous transition (i.e. the state variable *infected* is changed by an external event); other exogenous transition in this scenario is the one associated with the state variable *exempt*. In opposition, the transition associated to the state variable *policy* is endogenous because its state is triggered by both internal state variables of the current FSM: *infected* and *exempt*.

The Finite State Machine (FSM) (see Figure 8) used in the current scenario associates the transition functions previously defined with the appropriate state variables. The FSM definition consists of a set of state variable definitions. Each variable definition simply specifies the variable's type (i.e., set of allow-

Figure 8. Finite State Machine (FSM)
(Feamster, 2014)

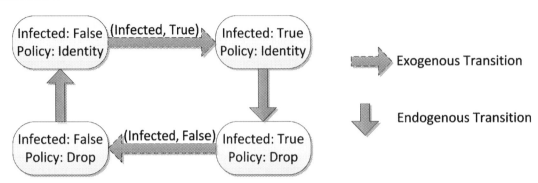

able values), initial value, and associated transition functions. The infected variable is a boolean whose initial value is FALSE (representing the assumption that hosts are initially not infected), and transitions based on the infected function defined previously. Likewise, the policy variable can take the values *drop* or *identity*, initially starts in the *identity* state, and transitions based on the policy function defined previously. The FSMPolicy that Kinetic provides automatically directs each incoming external event to the appropriate *Ipec* FSM, where it will be handled by the exogenous transition function specified in the FSM description (i.e. the function *self.fsm_def*). In this way, it is ensured that the FSM works as expected.

Evaluation

The network topology used in the current evaluation made with a network emulator is shown in Figure 9. All the evaluation was performed in a single Linux virtual machine (Ubuntu).

Figure 9. Network Topology under test
(Feamster, 2014)

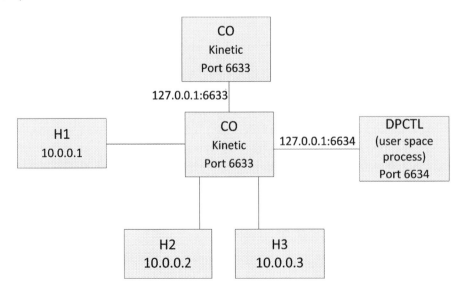

We now initiate the evaluation, opening a Linux shell, and run our Kinetic controller application with the following commands:

```
$ cd ~/pyretic
$ pyretic.py pyretic.kinetic.examples.gardenwall
```

As shown in Figure 10, the kinetic controller prints out some results from a verification of network policies using the NuSMV symbolic model checker (NuSMV, 2014). Kinetic automatically generates a NuSMV input from the program written by the programmer/operator, and verifies logic statements written in CTL (Computation Tree Logic) (CTL, 2014).

In a second shell, we start the network emulator "mininet", performing the following command:

```
$ sudo mn --controller=remote --topo=single,3 --mac -arp
```

The obtained output result is visualized in Figure 11. In addition, the bottom line of Figure 12 shows that the Kinetic controller discovered the emulated switch.

Imagine now the situation that host "h1" become compromised (infected). This situation originates the transmission of an event to change the state of the FSM in a way that any traffic originated in that host should be discarded in the switch. In this network status, the traffic ICMP between hosts "h1" and "h2" becomes blocked. We issue the transmission of the "infected" event to the controller executing in a third terminal the following command:

Figure 10. Kinetic controller terminal

```
*** Please report bugs to <numsv-users@fbk.eu>
*** Copyright (c) 2010, Fondazione Bruno Kessler
*** This version of NuMSV is linked to the CUDD library version 2.4.1
*** Copyright (c) 1995-2004, Regents of the University of Colorado
*** This version of NuMSV is linked to the MiniSat SAT solver.
*** See http://www.cs.chalmers.se/Cs/Research/FormalMethods/MiniSat
*** Copyright (c) 2003-2005, Niklas Een, Niklas Sorensson

-- specification AG ((infected & !exempt) -> AX policy = policy_1)  is true
-- specification AG (!infected -> AX policy = policy_2) is true
-- specification AG ((infected & exempt) -> AX policy = policy_3)  is true
-- specification A [ policy = policy_2  U infected ]  is true
system diameter: 3
reachable states: 12 (2^3.58496) out of 12 (2^3.58496)
========================= NuSMV Output End =========================

POX 0.1.0 (betta) / Copyright 2011-2013 James McCauley, et al.
Connected to pyretic frontend.
INFO:core:POX 0.1.0 (betta) is up.
```

Figure 11. Mininet terminal

```
mininet@mininet-vm:~$ sudo mn --controller=remote --topo=single, 3 --mac --arp
*** Creating network
*** Adding controller
*** Adding hosts:
h1 h2 h3
*** Adding switches:
s1
*** Adding links:
(h1, s1) (h2, s1) (h3, s1)
*** Configuring hosts
h1 h2 h3
*** Startting controller
*** Startting 1 switches
s1
*** Startting CLI:
mininet>
```

Figure 12. Switch contacts the controller

```
*** Copyright (c) 2010, Fondazione Bruno Kessler
*** This version of NuMSV is linked to the CUDD library version 2.4.1
*** Copyright (c) 1995-2004, Regents of the University of Colorado
*** This version of NuMSV is linked to the MiniSat SAT solver.
*** See http://www.cs.chalmers.se/Cs/Research/FormalMethods/MiniSat
*** Copyright (c) 2003-2005, Niklas Een, Niklas Sorensson

-- specification AG ((infected & !exempt) -> AX policy = policy_1)   is true
-- specification AG (!infected -> AX policy = policy_2) is true
-- specification AG ((infected & exempt) -> AX policy = policy_3)   is true
-- specification A [ policy = policy_2  U infected ]   is true
system diameter: 3
reachable states: 12 (2^3.58496) out of 12 (2^3.58496)
========================= NuSMV Output  End =========================

POX 0.1.0 (betta)  / Copyright 2011-2013 James McCauley, et al.
Connected to pyretic frontend.
INFO:core:POX 0.1.0 (betta) is up.
INFO: openflow.of_01: [None 1] closed
INFO: openflow.of_01: [00-00-00-00-00-01 2] connected
```

```
$ python json_sender.py -n infected -l True --flow="{srcip=10.0.0.1}" -a
127.0.0.1 -p 50001
```

The "infected" event was sent to the controller as it is possible to be visualized in Figure 13.

After some milliseconds, the Kinetic controller received the event informing that host h1 is infected (see Figure 14). As a consequence of this, the controller changed the policy to drop the packets originated by host "h1".

Figure 13. JSON event transmitted to the controller

```
mininet@mininet-vm:~/pyretic/pyretic/kinetic$ python json_sender.py -n infected -l
True --flow ="{srcip=10.0.0.1}" -a 127.0.0.1 -p 50001

Flow_Str = {srcip=10.0.0.1}

Data Payload = {'dstip': None, 'protocol': None, 'srcmac': None, 'tos': None,
'vlan_pcp': None, 'dstmac': None, 'inport': None, 'switch': None, 'ethtype': None,
'srcip': '10.0.0.1', 'dstport': None, 'srcport': None, 'vlan_id': None}

Ok
mininet@mininet-vm:~/pyretic/pyretic/kinetic$
```

Figure 14. Controller changes the policy to drop

```
-- specification A [ policy = policy_2  U infected ]    is true
system diameter: 3
reachable states: 12 (2^3.58496) out of 12 (2^3.58496)
========================= NuSMV Output  End =========================


POX 0.1.0 (betta)  / Copyright 2011-2013 James McCauley, et al.
Connected to pyretic frontend.
INFO:core:POX 0.1.0 (betta) is up.
INFO: openflow.of_01: [None 1] closed
INFO: openflow.of_01: [00-00-00-00-00-01 2] connected
Received connection from ('127.0.0.1', 42143)
Received event infected is True related with flow {'srcip': 10.0.0.1}
fsm_policy:event_name= infected
fsm_policy:event_value= True
fsm_policy:event_state= {'policy': drop, 'infected': True, 'exempt': False}
fsm_policy:self.policy = if
   match:  ('srcip', 10.0.0.1)
then
   [DynamicPolicy]
   drop
else
   identity
```

After this, we have tried to send two ping messages from host "h1" to host "h2" but as it is shown in Figure 15 without any success. This occurs because the IDS/IPS installed in the switch between "h1" and "h2" a policy to drop the packets originated by host "h1".

Next, assuming that host "h1" was classified as a privileged (exempt) terminal, then the controller will be notified from this through the following event:

```
$ python json_sender.py -n exempt -l True --flow="{srcip=10.0.0.1}" -a
127.0.0.1 -p 50001
```

Almost immediately, the Kinetic controller received the event informing that host "h1" is infected (see Figure 16). As a consequence of this, the controller changed the policy to redirect the packets originated by host "h1" to host "h3" (policy modify) for further analysis. This policy is installed in the switch.

The redirection of traffic from host "h1", it is perfectly visible in Figure 17, after we repeat the ping command. One can note that the host replying to the ping is host "h3" instead of "h2". As already explained, host "h3" is responsible to recover in terms of security any privileged hosts that by some reason become compromised.

After, some corrective actions performed in host "h1" by "h3", one can assume that host "h1" has recovered. In this way, a new event is sent to the controller notifying host "h1" changed to the state of "not infected", as follows:

```
$ python json_sender.py -n infected -l False --flow="{srcip=10.0.0.1}" -a
127.0.0.1 -p 50001
```

Figure 18 illustrates some controller´s output informing that the last event was received and the forwarding policy changed to forward the traffic towards host "h2" (policy identity).

Figure 15. ICMP traffic is dropped

```
s1
*** Adding links:
(h1, s1) (h2, s1) (h3, s1)
*** Configuring hosts
h1 h2 h3
*** Startting controller
*** Startting 1 switches
s1
*** Startting CLI:
mininet> h1 ping -c 2 h2
PING 10.0.0.2 (10.0.0.2) 56(84) bytes of data.


--- 10.0.0.2 ping statistics ---
2 packets transmitted, 0 received, 100% packet loss, time 1008ms

mininet>
```

Figure 16. Policy is changed to redirect the traffic

```
fsm_policy:event_name= infected
fsm_policy:event_value= True
fsm_policy:event_state= {'policy': drop, 'infected': True, 'exempt': False}
fsm_policy:self.policy = if
    match: ('srcip', 10.0.0.1)
then
    [DynamicPolicy]
    drop
else
    identity
Received connection from ('127.0.0.1', 42144)
Received event exempt is True related with flow {'srcip': 10.0.0.1}
fsm_policy:event_name= exempt
fsm_policy:event_value= True
fsm_policy:event_state= {'policy': modify: ('dstip', 10.0.0.3) ('dstmac',
00:00:00:00:00:03), 'infected':True, 'exempt': True}
fsm_policy:self.policy = if
    match: ('srcip', 10.0.0.1)
then
    [DynamicPolicy]
    modify: ('dstip', 10.0.0.3) ('dstmac', 00:00:00:00:00:03)
else
    identity
```

Figure 17. ICMP traffic is redirected

```
mininet> h1 ping -c 2 h2
PING 10.0.0.2 (10.0.0.2) 56(84) bytes of data.
64 bytes from 10.0.0.3 icmp_req=1 ttl=64 time=115 ms
64 bytes from 10.0.0.3 icmp_req=2 ttl=64 time=112 ms

--- 10.0.0.2 ping statistics ---
2 packets transmitted, 2 received, 0% packet loss, time 1002ms
rtt min/avg/mdev = 112.492/114.106/115.720/1.614 ms
mininet>
```

From Figure 19 is possible to conclude that host "h1" is now receiving response from host "h2" itself.

At this point, we finish our current evaluation of the intelligent IDS/IPS system. In the context of Big Data this is an important contribution once it facilitates the identification and solving of some attacks that a distributed Big Data architecture (in different phases of the Big Data lifecycle – from data capture to data processing and consumption) can suffer.

Figure 18. Policy returns back to traffic pass through (identity)

```
match:  ('switch', 1) ('dstmac', 00:00:00:00:00:01)
then
   [DynamicPolicy]
   fwd 1
else
   flood on:

   -----------------------------------------------------------------------------------
   switch  |  switch edges  |  egress ports                                    |
   -----------------------------------------------------------------------------------
   1       |                |  1[2]---, 1[3]---, 1[1]---                        |
Received connection from ('127.0.0.1', 42145)
Received event infect is False related with flow {'srcip': 10.0.0.1}
fsm_policy:event_name= infected
fsm_policy:event_value= False
fsm_policy:event_state= {'policy': identity, 'infected': False, 'exempt': True}
fsm_policy:self.policy = if
   match:  ('srcip', 10.0.0.1)
then
   [DynamicPolicy]
   identity
else
   identity
```

Figure 19. ICMP traffic is reaching again host h2

```
64 bytes from 10.0.0.3 icmp_req=1 ttl=64 time=115 ms
64 bytes from 10.0.0.3 icmp_req=2 ttl=64 time=112 ms

--- 10.0.0.2 ping statistics ---
2 packets transmitted, 2 received, 0% packet loss, time 1002ms
rtt min/avg/mdev = 112.492/114.106/115.720/1.614 ms
mininet> h1 ping -c 2 h2
PING 10.0.0.2 (10.0.0.2) 56(84) bytes of data.
64 bytes from 10.0.0.2 icmp_req=1 ttl=64 time=113 ms
64 bytes from 10.0.0.2 icmp_req=2 ttl=64 time=59.5 ms

--- 10.0.0.2 ping statistics ---
2 packets transmitted, 2 received, 0% packet loss, time 1001ms
rtt min/avg/mdev = 59.529/86.713/113.897/27.184 ms
mininet>
```

BIG DATA SECURITY: FUTURE DIRECTIONS

Throughout this chapter it was possible to present some of the most important security and privacy challenges that affect Big Data projects and their specificities. Although the information security practices, methodologies and tools to ensure the security and privacy of the Big Data ecosystem already exist, the particular characteristics of Big Data make them ineffective if they are not used in an integrated manner. This chapter also presents some solutions for these challenges, but it does not provide a definitive solution for the problem. It rather points to some directions and technologies that might contribute to solve some of the most relevant and challenging Big Data security and privacy issues.

Next, two different use cases were presented. Both of the use-cases present some directions that contribute to solving part of the large Big Data security and privacy puzzle. In the first use-case it was presented an approach that tries solving security and privacy issues on social network user generated content. In this approach, an open an interoperable rights management system was proposed as a way to improve the privacy of users that share content over social networks. The processes described show how the rights management system puts the end-users on the control of their own user-generated content, and how they prevent abuses from either other users or the social network platform itself. The second use-case presented the capabilities offered by SDN in increasing the ability to collect statistics data from the network and of allowing controller applications to actively program the forwarding devices, are powerful for proactive and smart security policy enforcement techniques such as active security (Hand, Ton, & Keller, 2013). This novel security methodology proposes a novel feedback loop to improve the control of defense mechanisms of a networked infrastructure, and is centered around five core capabilities: protect, sense, adjust, collect, counter (Kreutz et al., 2014). In this perspective, active security provides a centralized programming interface that simplifies the integration of mechanisms for detecting attacks, by i) collecting data from diverse sources (to identify attacks with more assertiveness), ii) converging to a consistent policy configuration for the security appliances, and iii) enforcing countermeasures to block or minimize the effect of such attacks. Previous aspects were partially covered by our IDS/IPS case study but notably need to be further developed and are an important contribution to the security and privacy of Big Data ecosystem.

As noted throughout this chapter, although some important steps are being given towards solving Big Data security and privacy issues, there is still a long road ahead. In the conclusion of this chapter, the authors would like to refer some interesting topics where the research community could work actively to develop new Big Data security and privacy solutions.

Research challenges in this Big Data ecosystem range from the data creation (and the Big Data sources - devices), data storage and transportation, data transformation and processing, and finally data usage. To support this lifecycle, a high capacity and highly distributed architecture will be necessary, exposed to an hostile environment subject to all kinds of attacks. The SDN approach as proposed on this chapter is a possible solution to counter these threats, however further research needs to be conducted, in particular on what concerns to automatic adaptation of switching and behavior-based security policies (P. Chen, Jorgen, & Yuan, 2011; Dohi & Uemura, 2012).

There are also important research challenges on maintaining end to end data security and privacy. Ensuring that data is never revealed in clear, in particular to non-authorized parties, on any point of the Big Data lifecycle. Moving from data to programs, there are techniques for protecting privacy in browsing, searching, social interactions, and general usage through obfuscation methods. However, there is more research to be conducted on the processing of encrypted data and privacy protection in the context of both computer programs and web-based systems.

More research challenges in the Big Data area include developing techniques to perform a transparent computations over encrypted data with multiple keys, from multiple sources and multiple users. In terms of research it would be challenging to study and develop ways to delegate limited functions over encrypted data, so that third parties can analyze it. All the aspects related with key management, authorization delegation, management of rights, are topics that require further research in this field.

When considering secure and private-aware system, trust is everything. In particular, in the case of Big Data, a trustworthy environment should be established for most of the scenarios (healthcare, assisted living, SCADA systems and many others). It is particularly challenging in terms of research directions how this environment can be attained. Trusting applications that are capable of querying and processing Big Data and extract knowledge from it and, trusting devices that collect all the data from multiple sources, constitute a basic security requirement. Understand how trust can be established among the end-users, the devices (IoT) and the applications is a hot research topic for the coming years.

On what concerns Big Data, these research challenges represent only the tip of the iceberg about the problems that still need to be studied and solved on the development of secure and privacy-aware Big Data ecosystem.

REFERENCES

Advantech. (2013). *Enhancing Big Data Security*. Retrieved from http://www.advantech.com.tw/nc/newsletter/whitepaper/big_data/big_data.pdf

Agrawal, D., Das, S., & El Abbadi, A. (2011). Big data and cloud computing. In *Proceedings of the 14th International Conference on Extending Database Technology - EDBT/ICDT '11* (p. 530). New York: ACM Press. 10.1145/1951365.1951432

Chen, P., Jorgen, B., & Yuan, Y. (2011). Software behavior based trusted attestation. In *Proceedings - 3rd International Conference on Measuring Technology and Mechatronics Automation, ICMTMA 2011* (Vol. 3, pp. 298–301). doi:10.1109/ICMTMA.2011.645

Chen, X., & Shi, S. (2009). A literature review of privacy research on social network sites. In *Multimedia Information Networking and Security, 2009. MINES'09. International Conference on* (Vol. 1, pp. 93–97). 10.1109/MINES.2009.268

Cloud Security Alliance. (2013). *Expanded Top Ten Security and Privacy Challenges*. Retrieved from https://downloads.cloudsecurityalliance.org/initiatives/bdwg/Expanded_Top_Ten_Big_Data_Security_and_Privacy_Challenges.pdf

CTL. (2014). *Computation tree logic*. Retrieved July 17, 2014, from http://en.wikipedia.org/wiki/Computation_tree_logic

DARPA. (2014). *Mining and understanding software enclaves (MUSE)*. Retrieved August 03, 2014, from http://www.darpa.mil/Our_Work/I2O/Programs/Mining_and_Understanding_Software_Enclaves_(MUSE).aspx

De Cristofaro, E., Soriente, C., Tsudik, G., & Williams, A. (2012). Hummingbird: Privacy at the time of twitter. In *Security and Privacy (SP), 2012 IEEE Symposium on* (pp. 285–299). IEEE.

Demchenko, Y., Ngo, C., de Laat, C., Membrey, P., & Gordijenko, D. (2014). Big Security for Big Data: Addressing Security Challenges for the Big Data Infrastructure. In W. Jonker & M. Petković (Eds.), *Secure Data Management* (pp. 76–94). Springer International Publishing. doi:10.1007/978-3-319-06811-4_13

Dohi, T., & Uemura, T. (2012). An adaptive mode control algorithm of a scalable intrusion tolerant architecture. Journal of Computer and System Sciences, 78, 1751–1754. doi:10.1016/j.jcss.2011.10.022

Feamster, N. (2014). *Software Defined Networking*. Retrieved August 02, 2014, from https://www.coursera.org/course/sdn

Gentry, C. (2009). *A fully homomorphic encryption scheme*. Stanford University. Retrieved from http://cs.au.dk/~stm/local-cache/gentry-thesis.pdf

Gentry, C. (2010). Computing arbitrary functions of encrypted data. *Communications of the ACM, 53*(3), 97. doi:10.1145/1666420.1666444

Goldwasser, S., Gordon, S. D., Goyal, V., Jain, A., Katz, J., Liu, F.-H. … Zhou, H.-S. (2014). Multi-input functional encryption. In Advances in Cryptology--EUROCRYPT 2014 (pp. 578–602). Springer.

Google. (2014). *Encrypted Big Query Client*. Retrieved August 03, 2014, from https://code.google.com/p/encrypted-bigquery-client/

Gross, R., & Acquisti, A. (2005). Information revelation and privacy in online social networks. In *Proceedings of the 2005 ACM workshop on Privacy in the electronic society* (pp. 71–80). 10.1145/1102199.1102214

Hand, R., Ton, M., & Keller, E. (2013). Active security. In *Proceedings of the Twelfth ACM Workshop on Hot Topics in Networks - HotNets-XII* (pp. 1–7). New York: ACM Press. 10.1145/2535771.2535794

Hasan, O., Habegger, B., Brunie, L., Bennani, N., & Damiani, E. (2013). A Discussion of Privacy Challenges in User Profiling with Big Data Techniques: The EEXCESS Use Case. In *2013 IEEE International Congress on Big Data* (pp. 25–30). IEEE. 10.1109/BigData.Congress.2013.13

HP. (2014). *Internet of Things Research Study*. Retrieved from http://fortifyprotect.com/HP_IoT_Research_Study.pdf

IBM big data platform - Bringing big data to the Enterprise. (2014, July). CT000.

IDC. (2012). *Big Data in 2020*. Retrieved from http://www.emc.com/leadership/digital-universe/2012iview/big-data-2020.htm

Juels, A., & Oprea, A. (2013). New approaches to security and availability for cloud data. *Communications of the ACM, 56*(2), 64. doi:10.1145/2408776.2408793

Jutla, D. N., Bodorik, P., & Ali, S. (2013). Engineering Privacy for Big Data Apps with the Unified Modeling Language. In *2013 IEEE International Congress on Big Data* (pp. 38–45). IEEE. 10.1109/BigData.Congress.2013.15

Kim, C., Jin, M.-H., Kim, J., & Shin, N. (2012). User perception of the quality, value, and utility of user-generated content. *Journal of Electronic Commerce Research*, *13*(4), 305–319.

Kindervag, J., Balaouras, S., Hill, B., & Mak, K. (2012). *Control And Protect Sensitive Information In the Era of Big Data*. Academic Press.

Kindervag, J., Wang, C., Balaouras, S., & Coit, L. (2011). *Applying Zero Trust To The Extending Enterprise*. Academic Press.

Kreutz, D., Ramos, F. M. V., Verissimo, P., Rothenberg, C. E., Azodolmolky, S., & Uhlig, S. (2014). *Software-Defined Networking: A Comprehensive Survey, 49. Networking and Internet Architecture*. Retrieved from http://arxiv.org/abs/1406.0440

Lindell, Y., & Pinkas, B. (2002). Privacy Preserving Data Mining. *Journal of Cryptology*, *15*(3), 177–206. doi:10.100700145-001-0019-2

Luo, H., Lin, Y., Zhang, H., & Zukerman, M. (2013). Preventing DDoS attacks by identifier/locator separation. *IEEE Network*, *27*(6), 60–65. doi:10.1109/MNET.2013.6678928

Marques, J., & Serrão, C. (2013a). Improving Content Privacy on Social Networks Using Open Digital Rights Management Solutions. *Procedia Technology*, *9*, 405–410. doi:10.1016/j.protcy.2013.12.045

Marques, J., & Serrão, C. (2013b). Improving user content privacy on social networks using rights management systems. *Annals of Telecommunications -. Annales des Télécommunications*, *69*(1-2), 37–45. doi:10.100712243-013-0388-1

McKenzie, P. J., Burkell, J., Wong, L., Whippey, C., Trosow, S. E., & McNally, M. B. (2012, June 6). User-generated online content: overview, current state and context. *First Monday*. Retrieved from http://firstmonday.org/ojs/index.php/fm/article/view/3912/3266

Michael, K., & Miller, K. W. (2013). Big Data: New Opportunities and New Challenges. *Computer*, *46*(6), 22–24. doi:10.1109/MC.2013.196

MIT. (2014). *Big Data Privacy Workshop, Advancing the state of the art in Technology and Practice - Workshop summary report*. Retrieved from http://web.mit.edu/bigdata-priv/images/MITBigDataPrivacyWorkshop2014_final05142014.pdf

Monsanto, C., Reich, J., Foster, N., Rexford, J., & Walker, D. (2013). Composing software-defined networks. *Proceedings of the 10th USENIX Conference on Networked Systems Design and Implementation*, 1–14. Retrieved from http://dl.acm.org/citation.cfm?id=2482626.2482629\nhttp://www.frenetic-lang.org/pyretic/

NIST. (2014). *Framework for Improving Critical Infrastructure Cybersecurity*. Retrieved from http://www.nist.gov/cyberframework/upload/cybersecurity-framework-021214-final.pdf

NuSMV. (2014). *An overview of NuSMV*. Retrieved July 23, 2014, from http://nusmv.fbk.eu/NuSMV/

Okhravi, H., Hobson, T., Bigelow, D., & Streilein, W. (2014). Finding Focus in the Blur of Moving-Target Techniques. *IEEE Security and Privacy*, *12*(2), 16–26. doi:10.1109/MSP.2013.137

OWASP. (2014). *OWASP Internet of Things Top Ten Project*. Retrieved August 05, 2014, from https://www.owasp.org/index.php/OWASP_Internet_of_Things_Top_Ten_Project

Popa, R., & Redfield, C. (2011). Cryptdb: protecting confidentiality with encrypted query processing. *Proceedings of the ...*, 85–100. 10.1145/2043556.2043566

Popa, R., & Redfield, C. (2012). CryptDB: Processing queries on an encrypted database. *Communications*, *55*, 103. doi:10.1145/2330667.2330691

Pyretic. (2014). *Pyretic Language*. Retrieved August 05, 2014, from https://github.com/frenetic-lang/pyretic/wiki/Language-Basics

Python. (2014). *Python Language*. Retrieved August 03, 2014, from https://www.python.org/

Rivera, J., & van der Meulen, R. (2014). *Gartner Says the Internet of Things Will Transform the Data Center*. Retrieved August 05, 2014, from http://www.gartner.com/newsroom/id/2684915

Rodríguez, E., Rodríguez, V., Carreras, A., & Delgado, J. (2009). A Digital Rights Management approach to privacy in online social networks. In *Workshop on Privacy and Protection in Web-based Social Networks (within ICAIL'09), Barcelona*.

Serrão, C., Neves, D., Barker, T., & Balestri, M. (2003). OpenSDRM -- An Open and Secure Digital Rights Management Solution. In *Proceedings of the IADIS International Conference e-Society*.

Serrão, C. (2008). *IDRM - Interoperable Digital Rights Management: Interoperability Mechanisms for Open Rights Management Platforms*. Universitat Politècnica de Catalunya. Retrieved from http://repositorio-iul.iscte.pt/handle/10071/1156

Serrão, C., Dias, J. M. S., & Kudumakis, P. (2005). From OPIMA to MPEG IPMP-X: A standard's history across R&D projects. *Signal Processing Image Communication*, *20*(9), 972–994. doi:10.1016/j.image.2005.04.005

Serrão, C., Dias, M., & Delgado, J. (2005). *Using Web-Services to Manage and Control Access to Multimedia Content*. ISWS05-The 2005 International Symposium on Web Services and Applications, Las Vegas, NV.

Serrão, C., Rodriguez, E., & Delgado, J. (2011). Approaching the rights management interoperability problem using intelligent brokerage mechanisms. *Computer Communications*, *34*(2), 129–139. doi:10.1016/j.comcom.2010.04.001

Tankard, C. (2012). Big data security. *Network Security*, (7), 5–8. doi:10.1016/S1353-4858(12)70063-6

Thomas, S. A. (2000). SSL & TLS Essentials: Securing the Web (Pap/Cdr., p. 224). Wiley.

Van Dijk, M., Gentry, C., Halevi, S., & Vaikuntanathan, V. (2010). Fully homomorphic encryption over the integers. In Advances in Cryptology–EUROCRYPT '10 (pp. 24–43). doi:10.1007/978-3-642-13190-5_2

KEY TERMS AND DEFINITIONS

Big Data: The term that represents data sets that are extremely large to handle through traditional methods. Big data represents information that has such a high volume, velocity, variety, variability, veracity and complexity that require specific mechanisms in order to produce value from it.

BYOD: Abbreviation of the term for Bring Your Own Device representing the policy that allows employees to bring their own personal mobile devices to their workplace, and make use of the company information and applications.

DMZ: A Demilitarized Zone, also known as perimeter network, used to create a physical or logical separation between the organization internal and external-facing services to a public network, for instance, the Internet. An outside network device can only get access to the services on the organization DMZ.

IDS: Intrusion Detection System is a system that actively monitors networks or other systems for security policy violations or unusual activities.

IoT: The term refers to the Internet of Things, representing a network of devices that are integrated and operate with the surrounding environment, enabling the communication with other systems or with each other to improve the offered value to customers.

IPS: Intrusion Prevention Systems are a subset of IDS that besides the detection of malicious activity can also block that activity from occurring.

JSON: Although originated from Javascript, the Javascript Object Notation is a language-independent and open data format that can be used to transmit human-readable text-based object information, across domains, using an attribute-value pair's notation.

SCADA: Supervisory Control and Data Acquisition refers to systems that are used to control infrastructure processes (for instance, electrical power supply), facility-based processes (for instance, airports) or industrial processes (for instance, production).

SDN: Software Defined Networking allows network administrators to manage network services through the decoupling of the traffic sending decisions (control) system from the underlying (data) traffic forwarding systems. Some advantages of using SDN are decreasing the maintenance cost and fostering innovation on the networking infrastructure.

ENDNOTES

[1]   http://www.oxforddictionaries.com/definition/english/Internet-of-things

[2]   Some notes about the notation used: key(content) means the "content" is encrypted using "key"; key{content} represents "content" is signed using "key"; algo[content] means that "content" is hashed with the "algo" algorithm.

This research was previously published in the Handbook of Research on Trends and Future Directions in Big Data and Web Intelligence edited by Noor Zaman, Mohamed Elhassan Seliaman, Mohd Fadzil Hassan, and Fausto Pedro Garcia Marquez, pages 20-52, copyright year 2015 by Information Science Reference (an imprint of IGI Global).

Chapter 81
SOHO Users' Perceptions of Reliability and Continuity of Cloud–Based Services

Cornel L. Levy
Western Governors University, USA

Nilsa I. Elias
Western Governors University, USA

ABSTRACT

The adaptation of cloud computing services is continually growing because of its popularity, its ubiquitous, ease-of-use, and inexpensive nature. Small office/home office (SOHO) businesses are joining large organizations and purchasing cloud services to help with the continuity of their business services. However, cloud computing and its effect in business continuity and information security by SOHO users is not well understood. A qualitative case study was conducted to examine the perspectives of SOHO users of cloud services during Hurricane Sandy in the states of New York and New Jersey. SOHO cloud users were questioned about their understanding of cloud services for business continuity, the services provided by cloud vendors, and their perceptions about cloud data management and security services. The results of this study demonstrated that SOHO users gravitate to the cloud because it of its ubiquitous nature, however, they lack understanding of the business continuity and disaster recovery features and their impact in data security and, their business endurance.

INTRODUCTION

Since 1980, one of the strengths associated with information technology (IT) management is the ability to collect and store information or data electronically through digital means. After data are collected and stored, they must be protected. Security of data involves the protection of their confidentiality, integrity, and availability (Gelbstein, 2011). Traditionally, data in electronic form have been protected by physical means (e.g., hard-drives, tapes, and compact discs) and are stored, physically, in hot-sites (production site) or warm-sites (a redundant site that will take hours to get up to production level).

DOI: 10.4018/978-1-5225-8176-5.ch081

Copyright © 2019, IGI Global. Copying or distributing in print or electronic forms without written permission of IGI Global is prohibited.

Because of its reported low cost and ease of use, cloud computing is reportedly becoming the de facto standard by which information is backed up, stored, and retrieved (Choudhary & Vithayathil, 2013). However, concerns surround cloud computing regarding whether it can effectively provide the necessary protection of confidentiality, integrity, and availability that traditional backup and retrieval systems have been providing with data in motion or data at rest (Ahmed, Chowdhury, Ahmed, & Rafee, 2012; Anthes, 2010; Bedi, Marwaha, Singh, Singh, & Singh, 2012; Choubey, Dubey, & Bhattacharjee, 2011; Mohamed, AlSudiari, & Vasista, 2012). One of the major concerns is whether the cloud will work well under duress such as a manmade or natural disaster.

An IT organization's business continuity/disaster recovery plan provides a structured approach for responding to unplanned incidents, which threaten an IT infrastructure (Speight, 2011; Takazawa & Williams, 2011; Tammineedi, 2010). The business continuity planning process is the assessment of the potential risks to the business and business data that could be caused through critical incidents, catastrophes, or emergencies. Experts must consider all the possible incidences and the impact each may have on the organization's capability to continue to provide its normal business services.

Arora and Gupta (2012) explained cloud computing as business continuity while Speight (2011), Takazawa and Williams (2011), and Tammineedi (2010) defined disaster recovery as a contemporary disaster plan, and Lawler (2010) explained the tolerant cloud model. However, few studies exist on how the cloud can be used as a tool for the backup and retrieval of business critical data, or how it can be used as a disaster recovery tool.

In this study, the researchers used Hurricane Sandy, a natural disaster, to identify the resilience of the cloud and business continuity services when small office/home office (SOHO) cloud users were under duress. In October 2012, Hurricane Sandy emaciated the Atlantic coast with record winds and flooding. The storm's devastation left approximately eight million people without power; businesses shut down for days, and more than $800 billion accrued in damages. In the United States, among the 12 states affected, 19 counties in New York and New Jersey were predominantly hit the hardest (Abramson & Redlener, 2012; Force, 2013; Kwasinski, 2013). The researchers investigated SOHO users' understanding of cloud computing, as well as their knowledge about business continuity/disaster recovery management and the effect of these services during a real disaster.

This qualitative study contributes to the body of scientific knowledge because it facilitates an understanding of how cloud services, as well as business continuity and disaster recovery plans, perform in the face of a natural disaster. In addition, this study adds knowledge to the field of IT, specifically cloud computing, providing an understanding of how well cloud-computing vendors' services performed under duress as well as which as-a-service option from vendors worked best during a disaster. Furthermore, the overall importance of the study is based on the details it provides regarding how users can significantly reduce their cost by having an effective data recovery system that is cloud-based as well as to help users decide if the cloud is a good option for data security and business continuity and disaster recovery.

SOHO BUSINESSES

Since the events of 9/11, companies have made a concerted effort to prolong their businesses after a disaster, be it manmade or natural. In October 2012, Hurricane Sandy emaciated the Atlantic shore of the United States with record winds and flooding. Hurricane Sandy's devastation left more than eight million people without power, thousands of small as well as large businesses shut down for days, and billions of dollars lost in damages. This natural disaster was one of the most devastating disasters experienced in the northeastern section of the United States, second to the atrocities of the manmade events of 9/11. In the United States, 12 states were affected including 19 counties in the New York, New Jersey areas, which were predominantly hit hard (Dun & Bradstreet, 2012).

According to Dun and Bradstreet (2012), the potential business impact by the state, for New York's total businesses affected more than 800,000 businesses as shown in Figure 1. For small businesses (SOHO), more than 600,000 businesses were affected. In New Jersey, the total businesses affected were more than 200,000.

Regarding Hurricane Sandy's potential impact on jobs in New York State, Dun and Bradstreet (2012) reported that over five million employees were affected. Additionally, more than two million SOHO employees were also affected. In the New York metropolitan area, 97 people died in the wake of the hurricane and thousands of citizens, including SOHO citizens, were displaced from their homes. Furthermore, two of New York City's major hospitals required perilous evacuations (Abramson & Redlener, 2012). Thibodeau (2012) provided an in-depth analysis of the effects of Hurricane Sandy on small as well as large businesses. Figure 2 shows a comparison of Hurricane Sandy's effects on employees in New York and New Jersey. The total employees affected included approximately two million and approximately one million small business employees.

Data recovery experts in New York and New Jersey were busy in the wake of Hurricane Sandy because it left a large number of data centers underwater, damaged equipment, which posed a major threat to business-critical data. According to Thibodeau (2012), data centers apparently disregarded weather forecasters' extensive warnings and underestimated the power of the storm. As a result, many businesses did not attempt to move computer equipment and IT communications equipment to safety until it was too late. Additionally, many data centers were victims of violent winds that damaged the infrastructure of major New York-based businesses and interrupted Internet service across the country. Furthermore, the storm-damaged equipment ranged from desktop computers to high-end servers, which included stand-alone RAID systems that ran primary office systems at small, midsize, to large businesses located in affected areas of New York and New Jersey. This included a prominent data recovery firm was still hard at work two weeks after Sandy in an attempt to restore customers' waterlogged drives (Thibodeau, 2012).

Figure 1. Potential business impact by state
(Dun & Bradstreet, 2012)

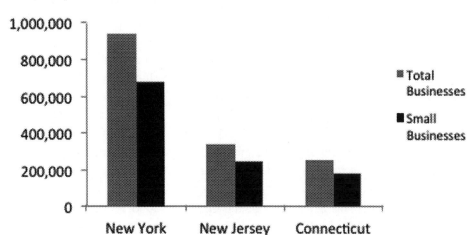

Figure 2. Potential impact on jobs
(Dun & Bradstreet, 2012)

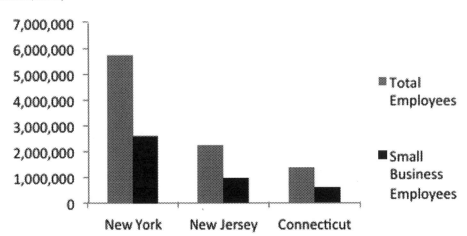

BACKGROUND

Since 2005, business or individuals who have used the Internet for pleasure and business purposes have found it necessary to shift from a traditional means of backing up and retrieving business critical information to a more contemporary way of doing business in the cloud. Since 1985, one of IT management's strengths was the ability to collect and store information data electronically through digital means. After data are collected and stored, they must be protected.

Protection of data involves the protection of their confidentiality, integrity, and availability. Traditionally, data were moved, physically, from one location to the next for storage and protection using the popular redundant array of independent disks, originally RAID, SAN, or NAS. This form of physical storage has become dated. Companies are finding innovative ways to store, backup, and retrieve data in a global IT management system using virtual means.

The paradigm for data storage and retrieval has shifted from a physical realm to a virtual realm that is now considered computing in the cloud or cloud computing. Because of its reported low cost and ease of use, cloud computing is becoming the de facto standard by which information is backed up, stored, and retrieved. However, concerns surround cloud-computing regarding whether it can effectively provide the necessary protection of confidentiality, integrity, and availability that traditional backup and retrieval systems have been providing.

Historically, during a natural or manmade disaster, companies have depended on RAID (P. Chen, Lee, Gibson, Katz & Patterson, 1994); SANs (Abhang & Chowdhay, 2007); NAS (Gibson & Meter, 2000; Hunter, 2006); and cold, warm, and hot sites (Rohde, Haskett & Ledgard, 1990) for continuity of business (Rodger, Bhatt, Chaudhary, Kline, & McCloy, 2015) and recovery of business (Takazawa & Williams, 2011; Speight, 2011; Tammineedi, 2010). These strategies returned an organization to a pre-disaster state. Prior to businesses making elaborate business continuity and disaster recovery plans, the concept of using the cloud as a collaborative tool was in development longer than what cloud vendors or users seemed to acknowledge.

Jadeja and Modi (2012) explained that although the characteristics of cloud computing were explored for the first time in 1966 by Douglas Parkhill in his book, The Challenge of the Computer Utility, the history of the term cloud computing originated in the telecommunications world. The telecommunications world was where telecom corporations started offering Virtual Private Network (VPN) services to large and small users with equal quality of service at a much cheaper rate. Before the advent of VPN, corporations provided devoted point-to-point data circuits, which caused some redundancies or wastage of bandwidth. However, by using VPN services, these corporations gained the ability to switch network traffic quickly to balance utilization of the overall network.

Cloud computing now extends this to cover servers and network infrastructure. Jadeja and Modi (2012) posited that many companies in the computer industry embraced cloud computing and began implementing it. Jadeja and Modi believed that Amazon played a pivotal role with the launch of the Amazon Web Service in 2006. Consequently, Google and IBM started research projects in cloud computing that set the stage for the industry today.

Jadeja and Modi's (2012) ideas were supported by Hailu's (2012) chronicle. According to Hailu, the roots of cloud computing technology can be traced to the grid computing period of the 1990s. Hailu claimed this development allowed the networking of many computing devices to work together mainly in scientific research where advanced level parallel computation was required. The progression was from grid computing, which grew into utility computing in the late 1990s.

Utility computing then tried to provide metered computing services similar to public utility services (e.g., gas, electricity, and water). The early 2000s saw the birth of software as a service (SaaS) that allowed cloud users to access commercial off-the-shelf software offered online for a stipend instead of purchasing licensed applications. Figure 3 illustrates the paradigm shift from grid computing to cloud computing. This shift transformed computing operations, which once required major fiscal investment into an available and affordable service.

CONTINUITY OF BUSINESS SERVICES USING THE CLOUD

Cloud computing is considered the contemporary solution for business continuity and disaster recovery in a small business. Using the cloud as a vehicle for disaster preparedness implies a service-oriented architecture through the offering of software and platforms as services. This will help reduce IT overhead for the end-user, increase their flexibility in what tools they use, reduce total cost of ownership, and offer on-demand services. SaaS, PaaS, and IaaS are rapidly becoming the standard software and infrastructure platform for many organizations seeking to reduce their IT costs and take advantage of the inherent flexibility, quick deployment, ready access, and scalability of these *as a* service concepts.

Figure 3. The advancement of cloud computing
(A. Hailu, 2012)

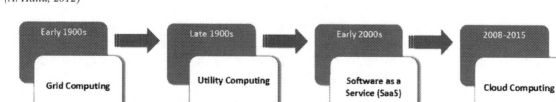

Barlas, Queen, Radowitz, Shillam, and Williams (2007) identified the top 10 technology concerns of 2007. The first concern included information security management, which is an organized approach to incorporating people, methods, and IT systems to protect critical systems and data, protecting them from internal and external threats. The second concern was identity and access management, which is where hardware, software, and processes are used together to authenticate users' identity and then provide users with appropriate access to systems and data based on pre-established rights and privileges.

The third concern was conforming to assurance and compliance standards, which is actually the creation of formal strategies and systems to address organizational objectives and statutory requirements. The fourth concern was the management of privacy. This was related to the rights and obligations of individuals and organizations with respect to the gathering, use, disclosure, and preservation of personal information.

The fifth concern was disaster recovery planning (DRP) and business continuity management (BCM). These two technological concerns complement each other and become a holistic managerial course of action that categorizes possible threats to a business and the impact those threats may have on business processes. The sixth concern was IT governance, which is a gathering of relationships and processes that direct and control an organization and help it achieve its goals by adding value while balancing risk versus return over IT and its processes. The seventh concern was securing and controlling information distribution, which involves the protection and control of the dissemination of digital data.

The eighth concern was mobile and remote computing, regarding technologies that enabled users to connect to key resources securely anywhere, anytime, regardless of physical location. The ninth concern was electronic archiving and data retention, which involve technologies that enable appropriate archiving and recovery of key information over a given period of time, while improving productivity and access to the information. The tenth and final concern was: document, content, and knowledge administration, which is the actual process of capturing, indexing, storing, retrieving, searching, and managing information electronically, including database management of PDFs and other file formats (Barlas et al., 2007).

Today, all 10 concerns are still credible and should be addressed by security professionals who seek to increase information and technology security. One of the most important ideas expressed by Barlas et al. (2007) was that disaster recovery planning and business continuity management were all-inclusive management processes that identify likely threats to a business and the impact those threats may have on business processes. This specific concern was critical for this research.

Business Continuity, Data Security and Disaster Recovery

Jrad, Morawski, and Spergel (2004) and Jones (2011) posited that since 1999, the world has experienced significant manmade as well as natural disasters such as the 9/11 attacks in New York, Hurricane Katrina in Louisiana, the earthquake in Japan, and Hurricane Sandy in the Northeastern United States. Considering the impact of these disasters, it is safe to conclude that companies are truly at risk of losing important data if adequate disaster recovery planning and business community management are not included as a part of a company's risk management plans. Managers or chief information officers (CIOs) of large and small business should make sure that as a part of their organization's security posture, they use disaster recovery planning and business continuity management as integral factors in their security plans.

Business continuity planning is part of a business continuity management process that identifies potential risks and vulnerabilities and their impacts on an organization. Business continuity management provides processes and procedures for mitigating risks and effectively responding to a disruptive event in a way that safeguards the interests of the organization's key stakeholders, reputation, brand, and value-creating activities (Lawler, 2010). To be successful, business continuity management must be fully integrated across the entire organization as a required management process.

Business continuity management includes business continuity planning, which focuses mainly on incident response and, depending on the organization, can include records and information security and risk management processes (Jones, 2011). Company's risk management planners who are forward thinking will make sure that their business continuity management is in place. Business continuity management is the plan that occurs prior to a disaster; disaster recovery planning generally occurs immediately after a disaster. The need for disaster recovery has always existed; however, the emphasis is shifting from reactive (recovery) to proactive (preparedness) to minimize damage from disasters and limit disaster impact through proper planning (Jrad et al., 2004).

Small Office/Home Office Users and Hurricane Sandy: Natural Disaster That Tests Continuity of Service Plans

Small businesses or SOHO users of the cloud are eager to adopt cloud-based technologies for their business without understanding the technology or the services offered by cloud vendors (Y. Chen et al., 2010; Gupta et al., 2013; Low et al., 2011). However, cloud technology is gradually shifting from a corporate to a consumer market. There is an increasing trend of small business (SOHO) users who rely on cloud-based technology without truly understanding the technologies or inherent risks in the technologies (Leimeister et al., 2010; Low et al., 2011).

Since the events of 9/11, companies have made a concerted effort to prolong their businesses after a disaster, be it manmade or natural. In October 2012, Hurricane Sandy emaciated the Atlantic shore of the United States with record winds and flooding. Hurricane Sandy's devastation left more than eight million people without power, thousands of small as well as large businesses shut down for days, and billions of dollars lost in damages.

This natural disaster was one of the most devastating disasters experienced in the northeastern section of the United States, second to the atrocities of the manmade events of 9/11. In the United States, 12 states were affected including 19 counties in the New York, New Jersey areas, which were predominantly hit hard (Dun & Bradstreet, 2012). Dun and Bradstreet (2012) explained the potential business impact by state, for New York's total businesses affected more than 800,000 businesses, including small businesses (SOHO) where more than 600,000 businesses were affected. In New Jersey, the total businesses affected were more than 200,000. However, just fewer than 200,000 New Jersey SOHO businesses were affected. Figure 1 illustrates statistics for businesses affected by Hurricane Sandy.

Dun and Bradstreet (2012) reported that over five million employees were affected in the New York area. Additionally, more than two million SOHO employees were also disrupted. Additionally, in the New York metropolitan area, 97 people died in the wake of the hurricane and thousands of citizens, including SOHO citizens, were displaced from their homes. Furthermore, two of New York City's major hospitals required perilous evacuations due to disrupted services (Abramson & Redlener, 201F2).

Thibodeau (2012) provided an in-depth analysis of the effects of Hurricane Sandy on small as well as large businesses. Figure 2 shows a comparison of Hurricane Sandy's effects on employees in New York and New Jersey. The total employees affected included approximately two million and approximately one million small business employees.

Data recovery experts in New York and New Jersey were busy in the wake of Hurricane Sandy due to a large number of data centers underwater, damaged equipment, which posed a major threat to business-critical data. According to Thibodeau (2012), data centers apparently disregarded weather forecasters' extensive warnings and underestimated the power of the storm. As a result, many businesses did not attempt to move computer equipment and IT communications equipment to safety until it was too late.

Additionally, many data centers were victims of violent winds that damaged the infrastructure of major New York-based businesses and interrupted Internet service across the country. Moreover, the storm-damaged equipment ranged from desktop computers to high-end servers, which included stand-alone RAID systems that ran primary office systems at small, midsize, to large businesses located in affected areas of New York and New Jersey. This included a prominent data recovery firm was still hard at work two weeks after Sandy in an attempt to restore customers' waterlogged drives (Thibodeau, 2012).

MAIN FOCUS OF THE CHAPTER

Purpose of the Study

In 2011, Mell and Grance reported that cloud computing could be too new a technology to be considered the new secured and efficient tool for backup and recovery. Other researchers also believed that the cloud could have inherent security flaws (Ahmed et al., 2012; Anthes, 2010; Bedi et al., 2012; Choubey et al., 2011; Mohamed et al., 2012). Because of the infancy of the technologies, concerns exist in the IT industry regarding the effectiveness of cloud computing.

The purpose of this qualitative case study was to investigate the perceptions of SOHO users of cloud computing technologies in the New York City and New Jersey areas that were impacted by Hurricane Sandy. The focus of this study to ascertain if the cloud was effective for business continuity and as a disaster recovery tool by small business users. SOHO were considered small business owners or consumers who used cloud technologies for business purposes.

In this research, cloud computing and its reaction to a disaster are defined as the continuity of services in the cloud during a disaster. The study identified if SOHO users were able to retrieve their data and maintain security after Hurricane Sandy. The intent of this qualitative case study was to determine the effectiveness of using cloud-computing services as a continuity of operations and data security as a solution during a disaster.

This study was based on Yin (2009) methodology for data richness and saturation and used several data collection methods. Data collection methods included structured and unstructured interviewing of cloud computing users. Additionally, Yin's (2014) recommendations were followed in regards to seeking out the six primary collection sources:

1. Documentation.
2. Archival records.
3. Interviews.
4. Direct observations.
5. Participant observation.
6. Artifacts.

These collection methods enhanced the richness of the study's data. Records pertaining to cloud usage during Hurricane Sandy were identified from various sources including the Bureau of Statistics, News articles, Peer Reviewed Articles, Association of Contingency Planners (ACP), Information System Security Association (ISSA), FEMA, New York City's Chamber of Commerce, and other disaster preparedness websites. In essence, common themes were identified among cloud-computing SOHO users who were impacted by Hurricane Sandy and had previously purchased cloud services.

By studying what happened to the cloud and its artifacts in a disaster, such as Hurricane Sandy, the findings from this study will serve as a valuable source on how cloud-computing services performed in the face of a disaster.

Technology Acceptance Model

Davis et al. (1989) conducted one of the first quantitative studies to investigate why computer users were reluctant to use IT to enhance job performance. Technology Acceptance Model (TAM) was designed to answer the question about peoples' reluctance to use, more effectively, the computer systems. The external variables that make up TAM are attitude, behavioral intention, perceived ease of use, and perceived usefulness.

Alternatively, in today's terms, perceived ease of use implies the computer system is user-friendly, or anyone could use this system without expending much time learning about the system. In addition, perceived ease of use also had significant effects on the objectives to end users when deciding to use the computer system (Davis, 1989, 1993; Davis et al., 1989). Perceived ease of use is the degree of ease connected with the use of the computer or information system.

Perceived usefulness strongly influence peoples' intentions. Perceived usefulness is the point in which end users believe that using a computer system will help him or her increase job performance. Behavioral intention is the point to which an end user has made conscious plans to use or not to use the computer system Venkatesh (2009). Other important external factors are computer anxiety, where end users are fearful about the possibility of using the computer, and computer self-efficacy, where the end user believes that he or she has the ability to use any computer system without any formal training (Bandura, 1977).

Unified Theory of Acceptance and Use of Technology

Over the years, significant adjustments have been made to the TAM Models (Amirkhani, Salehahmadi, Kheiri, & Hajialiasgari, 2011). According to Amirkhani et al., one of the most noteworthy upgrades to TAM was the Unified Theory of Acceptance and Use of Technology (UTAUT) model, which is a model that leveraged eight technology acceptance theories. The theories are combined TAM and TPB, the theory of planned behavior (TPB), innovation diffusion theory, social cognitive theory, and theory of reasoned action (Thomas, Singh, & Gaffar, 2013).

According to Thomas et al. (2013), the TAM assumed that whenever an individual desires to act on a task that action can be done without hindrance or limitation. Despite that philosophy, many other researchers believed that this assumption may not be realistic because there will be numerous factors of limitations to an individual's desire to act (Amirkhani et al., 2011). Venkatesh, Thong, and Xu (2012) reviewed and synthesized eight theories of models of technology use to define the latest technology acceptance model, UTAUT.

UTAUT technology acceptance model is a completely different model from any of the earlier TAMs. The perceived usefulness and perceived ease of use were major tenants evident in all the prior models but were not evident in the UTAUT model. The constructs were replaced with behavioral intention and user behavior as the determining factors that change a user's attitude toward using a computer system. The external variables that connect, directly or indirectly, to the two major tenants (behavioral intention and user behavior) were effort expectancy, performance expectancy, social influence, and facilitating conditions.

The most relevant strengths of UTAUT rests in its ability to cross cultures. However, Alshare, Mesak, Grandon, and Badri (2011) argued that most TAMs did not represent all cultures. Yet, because UTAUT had a focus on a user's age, gender, experience and voluntariness, many studies were conducted outside of the United States in countries, such as China and India (Venkatesh et al., 2012). Conclusively, it appears that UTAUT is a more universally accepted model for user acceptance of IT.

Best Fit Technology Acceptance Model for the Cloud

The National Institute of Standards and Technology (NIST) defined cloud computing as a model for allowing widespread, appropriate, and on-demand network access to a joint pool of configurable computing resources (e.g., networks, servers, storage, applications, and services) that can be quickly provisioned and released with minor management effort or service provider interaction (Jansen & Grance, 2011; Mell & Grance, 2011). Mell and Grance explained that the cloud ideal is a model of enabling ubiquitous, useful, on-demand network access to a common pool of configurable resources and is made up of five crucial elements (networks, servers, storage, applications, and services).

It is extremely expensive to run a computer business. However, the contemporary cloud computing technology was seen as a means to cut cost as well as add security to transporting information over the Internet (Han et al., 2011; S. Ristov et al., 2012). If the users of information systems are reluctant to use the computer systems, despite how hard a company tries to save money by using various innovative ways to access data, there will still be a loss because the technology will not be used or used incorrectly. For cloud computing vendors as well as small companies that purchase services from vendors, the TAM may not be the same because they do have different expectations for their employees. Vendors expect to sell as much service to users as possible while users expect to get the most service from vendors at the least possible cost.

S. Ristov et al. (2012) defined control objective metrics and their importance to cloud computing vendors and users. They questioned how important backup services of the cloud are to users as well as vendors. They believed that in a measurable analysis for each cloud computing service, the number of control objectives with depreciated importance for each Cloud service layer (SaaS, IaaS, and PaaS) is significantly greater than the number of the control objectives with increased importance when migrating to the cloud. This study appealed to many features of the UTAUT model such as effort expectancy, social influence, performance expectancy, facilitating condition, voluntariness of use, and experience in an effort to help understand cloud computing use and acceptance.

Conversely, Alshare and Alkhateeb (2008) studied data gathered from pupils from Chile and United Arab Emirates in an attempt to provide a different perspective from the studies regularly conducted in the United States. The result of their study showed that perceived usefulness was a noteworthy predictor of Internet usage for pupils of these countries. Alshare and Alkhateeb (2008) further stated that while gender expressively affected the Emirates students' use of the Internet, voluntary-reported knowledge about computers dramatically affected Chilean students' usage of the cloud. This study is, therefore, a complement of TAM.

Behrend, Wiebe, London, and Johnson (2011) studied students' Internet usage in community colleges in the United States and appeared to be proponents of TAM3 regarding community college managers who sought to integrate cloud computing into the higher education settings. However, Wu, Lan, and Lee (2011) argued against all technology acceptance models including TAM and UTAUT models and refuted that they were a good fit for any of the artifacts of the cloud such as SaaS.

Despite the findings regarding using TAMs for Internet and cloud usage, the UTAUT appears to be the best fit for the cloud. Mathur and Dhulla (2014) studied UTAUT and concluded that users' performance expectancy have greatly influenced the new paradigm of cloud computing. The authors believed that ease of use brings ability in the work performance of the user (Mathur & Dhulla, 2014).

Gashami, Chang, and Park (2013) were proponents of UTAUT. They posited that one of the major benefits of the cloud was that it allowed organizations to save time and money on computer technology. Gashami et al. analyzed factors of cloud adoption in the public sector where they did some verification on the association between performance expectancy, effort expectancy, and behavioral intention as they related to cloud users. Based on their finding, UTAUT was a good user acceptance model for cloud computing implementation, not only the United States but also worldwide (Dachyar & Prasetya, 2012).

In conclusion, implementing technological changes are sometimes the most expensive venture that a small business can undertake. However, it becomes even more expensive when the prospective users of that system refuse to use the system because of fear or other psychological factors. Companies intend to invest in IT, must be cognizant of the fact that although they might purchase state-of-the-art systems, users may refuse to accept or use them because they are not considered beneficial to their own personal growth.

Methodology

The purpose of this qualitative case study was to understand the perceptions of small business users of cloud computing technologies in the New York City and New Jersey areas who survived Hurricane Sandy. Small users were considered small business owners or small office/home office (SO/HO) consumers who used cloud technologies for business purposes. Cloud technologies business purpose can be viewed as a means of storing data in a remote or centralized location that can be accessed by users through the Internet.

The study aimed to investigate important factors that influence SOHO users in selecting the best cloud-computing service for the continuance of their organization if faced with a manmade or natural disaster. For this research study, semi-structured, open-ended questions were used to collect data about cloud computing knowledge by stating the importance of using the cloud as a business continuity and disaster recovery, and security tool in SOHO businesses. In addition, data triangulation methods were used to enhance validity and reliability of the research study.

Research Questions

The research questions formulated to guide this study are:

1. How did using cloud computing services protect users' critical data during Hurricane Sandy?
2. What level of service and support did small users receive from vendors that guaranteed 24/7/365 confidentiality, integrity, and availability of their business-critical or personal data when faced with a natural disaster such as Hurricane Sandy?

Sample Frame, Population and Sample Size

Data was collected from a subset or sample of SOHO users who purchased and used cloud services during Hurricane Sandy. The definition of SOHO business is businesses with 1–10 employees or 11–99 employees (Gupta et al., 2013). To avoid shallow, one-sided, and data lacking in proof as well as to get feasible data from the general population, purposive sampling was used for this case study.

Purposive sampling involves choosing specific people within the population to use for a research project (Luborsky and Rubinstein, 1995). Luborsky and Rubinstein further posited that the concentration should be on people with particular characteristics who would be better able to assist with providing relevancy to research. The sample frame of SOHO users were recruited by word-of-mouth and other social media tools. These contemporary tools were frequently used by people who were likely to use the cloud as a service. Therefore, these tools were used as one of the primary methods to identify participants.

Sample Size

According to Patton (1990, 2002), there are no set rules for sample size in qualitative investigations. Sample size depends on what is to be known, the purpose of the investigation, what is at stake, what will be useful, what will have credibility, and what can be done with available time and resources. Yin (2009) and Brod, Tester & Christensen (2009) stated that a good sample size for a qualitative case study should be from 5-10 or 6-10, respectively, the researchers decided on a sample of 13 participants.

The participants were identified as SOHO users of cloud services who were purposively selected from small companies that were located in the New York and New Jersey areas and were severely affected by Hurricane Sandy. From small businesses, the participants who were interviewed, used the following cloud-based applications and services:

- Microsoft's Office 365.
- Hotmail.
- Gmail, Google App Engine, and Google Docs.
- WebEx.
- Drop Box.
- Sales Force.
- iCloud.

A recruitment communication containing pertinent information about the study was sent to each participant. This letter contained consent forms to participate in the study as well as the technological tools needed for the research, and the screening and selection process (Salmons, 2010). Participants who agreed to take part in the research were set up for interview at their convenience.

The interviews were conducted through video conference and an additional screening was conducted ensure eligibility. For the first five minutes of the call the participants were screened for age and geographic location as a participant had to be over 18 and have lived in the New York or New Jersey areas during Hurricane Sandy. Questionnaires included indirect questions, related to the experience of back up and recovering users' data during Hurricane Sandy. Participants who met the requirements of the study were asked 17 semi-structured, open-ended questions in order to examine their perceptions regarding business continuity and security of data through cloud services during a disaster.

Setting

This research was conducted in a natural setting that included the home and business offices of the SOHO users. According to Creswell (2009), a research in a natural setting is where the researcher is an instrument of data collection that gathers words or pictures from the participants. The researchers then analyzed the data inductively, focused on the story of participants, and used information gathered to describe a process that is expressive and persuasive in language (Creswell, 2009).

Instrumentation

The main instrument for this research study was the researchers as they were investigators who had access to participants and to describe their personal experiences. A field test was conducted to develop an interview guide to optimize data gathering and to ensure that the content of the questionnaire had validity. The field test was administered to three cloud computing experts and helped to optimize questionnaire design for the ultimate purpose of gathering high- quality data about cloud computing, business continuity and data security during a disaster.

In-depth interviews were conducted, taking the form of a conversation in which the researchers probed deeply to uncover new clues, to open up new dimensions of cloud computing and to secure vivid, accurate and detailed accounts that are based on the personal experience of SOHO users of the cloud during a disaster. The researchers examined current literature (2010-2015), conducted video conferencing and telephone interviews with the purposively selected participants, and used them as the sources from which information was gathered for this research.

Data Collection

For this study, telephone and video-conference interviews were used as the primary methods of collecting data. All of the interviews were conducted using Microsoft Lync 2013. The participants of this research were asked to respond to semi-structured (open-ended) questions during the interview process.

To increase research effectiveness, the researchers remained alert and eager to provide follow-up or additional questions that were not a part of the initial 17 questions to document participants' perceptions and descriptions of their experiences with cloud services during Hurricane Sandy more accurately. Optimal listening skills were applied during the interview process to allow the researchers to take notes as well as making it easier for to ask more appropriate follow-up questions (Kvale & Brinkmann, 2009).

Between April 2015 and July 2015, a number of hours were spent identifying and interviewing participants to gather information. The interview sessions with participants lasted between 30 and 40 minutes. However, this time frame was sometimes extended based on how extensive a participant was with his or her answers to the 17 questions posed.

Data Analysis

Data collected from interviews was analyzed to discern themes and patterns among participants. Marshall and Rossman (2011) believed that researchers must understand how to apply analytic procedures in order to get the best results from gathered data and categorically stated that typical analytic procedures fall into seven phases, which follow in order:

1. Organizing the data.
2. Immersion in the data.
3. Generating categories and themes.
4. Coding the data.
5. Offering interpretations through analytic memos.
6. Searching for alternative understandings.
7. Writing the report or other format for presenting the study (p. 209).

Following the directions of Welsh (2002), the information collected using Microsoft Word was entered into NVivo® 10 for analysis. Node analysis was used for the data analysis process. Node analysis represents a code, theme, or idea about the data in a research project (Wong, 2008). Subjective responses to the interview questions were categorized and then grouped into patterns of similarity, otherwise known as nodes and themes (Lewis, 2009). The data from the interviews were coded using NVivo software and analyzed to identify themes or patterns (Medley, 2001).

The researcher examined the responses and separated them into categories using NVivo 10 software. The constant comparative method, which involved comparing data-to-data, data-to-code, code-to-code, code-to-category, category-to-category, and relationships among categories, was followed from the beginning of the first interview. Establishing patterns from collected data was critical to identifying the perspectives of SOHO cloud users.

Validity and Reliability

The accuracy, dependability and credibility of a research study depend on the validity and reliability of the data. In qualitative research, rigor and trustworthiness are confirmed by safeguarding the study's credibility, transferability, dependability, and confirmability (Creswell, 2009). The researchers used triangulation of information between different sources of data, member checking (comments from contributors) and, expert review to add validity to the interpretation of qualitative observations.

For this study, a pilot test was conducted with cloud technologies expert to help determine the questions to be included in the interview and to ensure the data collected was relevant to the phenomenon being researched. The panel included subject matter experts (SMEs) who were familiar with Business Continuity/Disaster Recovery as well as cloud computing. The panel reviewed the potential questions and suggested changes to some questions that would help to elicit more information from the participants. These suggested changes help to form what became the list of 17 questions.

Credibility is synonymous with validity and trustworthiness in qualitative research. Memoing, the act of recording reflective notes about what the researcher is learning from the data, was simultaneously done during data collection. After transcribing data gathered from the interviews, the data was made available to participants in order to verify information provided by the targeted group to allow the participant the opportunity to correct any errors or misinterpretation of their responses to the interview questions.

Checks and verifications were applied throughout the research process to guarantee that the research is rigorous in its entirety. For this research, one of the methods used to address credibility was the purposive selection of participants, and the collection and thorough analysis of the interview transcripts. Data saturation was achieved after interviewing 13 participants and using node analysis to obtain themes, ideas and concepts about cloud computing use and business continuity among SOHO users of the cloud.

SOLUTIONS AND RECOMMENDATIONS

Summary of Key Findings

This study used a qualitative methodology with a case study approach to explore the perceptions as well as the experiences of SOHO users of the cloud, based on two research questions:

1. How did using cloud computing services protect users' critical data during Hurricane Sandy?
2. What level of service and support did small users receive from vendors that guarantee 24/7/365 confidentiality, integrity, and availability of their business-critical or personal data when faced with a natural disaster such as Hurricane Sandy?

From the textual data gathered and analyzed by NVivo, six themes developed. The developed themes were:

1. Small user perceptions.
2. Service levels.
3. Perceived role of the cloud.
4. Small user knowledge.
5. Data criticality.
6. Use of the cloud.

The six themes were then used to conduct an in-depth analysis of the perception and experiences of the SOHO users regarding the cloud, its services as well as continuity of services strategies.

The categorization of the participants' perceptions was done and, the categories of perceptions were segregated (grouped) into nodes or patterns. The analytic functions of NVivo (Create and Analyze) used 13 Nodes (participants) in order to identify the themes. Additionally, for the in-depth analysis of data, an NVivo10 expert (Dr. Ahmad Khan) was used. The data collected from these 13 participants produced the following major findings:

Table 1. Summary of demographical characteristics of participants

Participants/Pseudonum	Gender	Age	Profession/Business
P01	Male	36	Attorney
P02	Male	50	Consultant
P03	Female	55	Travel
P04	Male	45	Engineering
P05	Male	35	Small Business Continuity Business
P06	Male	36	Small Disaster Recovery Business
P07	Male	40	Small Direct Mail Business
P08	Female	50	Small Home Office Business
P09	Female	54	Home Office Energy Business
P10	Male	51	Small Self-Storage Business
P11	Male	67	Small Insurance Business
P12	Male	40	Home Office Business Continuity Business
P13	Male	32	Small Computer Service Business

1. Sixty-nine percent of SOHO users perceived the cloud as insecure, yet they purchase and use cloud services.
2. Fifty-four percent of participants had no measured service levels.
3. All participants (100%) were severely hindered by the lack of power during the hurricane.
4. Only eight percent of the participants had any form of security plans even though they all believed that data is critical to their businesses.
5. Most participants (77%) did not use the cloud as a business continuity or disaster recovery tool but used the small applications that this service affords (SaaS).

To maintain confidentiality, pseudonyms were used for each participant. The pseudonyms were only identifiable by the researcher. The nicknames were made up of the initials of the participants plus a two-digit number. The pseudonyms for the 13 participants follow: P01, P02, P03, P04, P05, P06, P07, P08, P09, P10, P11, P12, and P13. The participants' ages ranged from 25 to 67 years old. Table 1 displays the ages, gender, and profession or business of the 13 participants, and Table 2 summarizes the main themes generated from the 13 participants.

P01 was a 36-year-old attorney who coordinated the volunteer efforts of a church in the New York area. He considered himself a volunteer coordinator during the Hurricane Sandy disaster. He coordinated some 30,000 volunteers and used Cloud Based SW with Crisis Cleanup to aid in the disaster recovery process for this church as well as other entities in the New York areas. P01 was well versed in business continuity and disaster recovery management and had an in-depth understanding of the cloud.

P02 was a 25-year-old male who was a part owner of a small business in the New York City area. The small business was a consulting group with sub-businesses. P02 consulted emerging markets from Wall Street regarding Catch Funds and Governmental Business. P02's understanding of the cloud was shallow. Same was true for his understanding of business continuity and disaster recovery planning.

P03 was a 55-year-old female who owned a travel service that operated out of New York. P03 had a small travel agency, which was hit hard by Hurricane Sandy. However, this participant had little understanding of the cloud and its use as a business continuity or disaster recovery tool.

P04 was a 45-year-old male who owned an engineering company in the New York City area, which specializes in the design and building of solar energy systems. P04 had a broad understanding of the cloud as well as business continuity and disaster recovery planning.

P05 was a 35-year-old male who was a manager of a small Business Continuity as a Service business. P05 lived outside of the New York and New Jersey areas but operated a business in those areas during Hurricane Sandy. He showed an in-depth knowledge of the cloud and its capabilities as a business continuity and disaster recovery tool.

P06 was a 36-year-old male who worked for a small nonprofit disaster recovery property staffing organization, which was headquartered in Florida but operated in New York. This small business operated as a source of aid to other businesses and individuals in times of a disaster. P06 demonstrated a broad knowledge of the cloud and an in-depth knowledge of business continuity and disaster recovery planning.

P07 was a 40-year-old male who was the chief information officer (CIO) of a small nonprofit, direct mail, fundraising business. As the CIO of the business, P07 had an extensive understanding of both cloud and its usage as a business continuity and disaster recovery tool.

P08 was a 50-year-old female who operated a small home office in New York City. Her home office business used the cloud for banking and document storage. P08 had a broad knowledge of the cloud and its services and a cursory knowledge of business continuity and disaster recovery planning.

P09 was a 54-year-old female who had a home office and worked for an energy (gas) company operating out of the New York City area. MG09 showed a broad understanding of the cloud and its artifacts and a cursory understanding of business continuity and disaster recovery planning.

P10 was a 51-year-old male who operated a small self-storage business in various New York City areas. P10 had a cursory understanding of the cloud and its artifacts as well as business continuity and disaster recovery planning.

P11 was a 67-year-old male who lived in and conducted business out of New York City. P11 was one of the owners of a small insurance company operating out of New Your City. He had a broad understanding of both the cloud and its services as well as business continuity and disaster recovery planning.

P12 was a 40-year-old male who lived in New York during Hurricane Sandy. He operated a home office business, which provided business continuity service to customers in the New York City area. P12 had an in-depth knowledge of both the cloud as well as business continuity and disaster recovery planning.

P13 was a 32-year-old male who lived on the border of New Jersey. He operated a small computer support business with customers in New Jersey. P13 worked in the IT industry as a system engineer and Web developer for many years and, as such, had an extensive knowledge about the cloud and its services as well as business continuity and disaster recovery planning.

Theme 1: Small User Perception

The user perceptions explained what the participants were actually thinking when they heard about the cloud and its artifacts. According to Gupta et al. (2013), cloud computing has become the buzzword in the IT industry today because of its ubiquitous nature because of the proliferation of Internet, broadband, mobile devices, better bandwidth, and mobility requirements for end-users. From the main theme, Small User Perceptions, four subthemes were derived: availability, ease-of-use, not secure, and secure.

Table 2. Summary of the main themes generated from the 13 participants

Theme	Sub-Themes	Tally
Small User Perceptions	Availability	38%
	Ease of Use	46%
	Not Secure	69%
	Secure	31%
Small User Knowledge	Specific	62%
	Vague	15%
	No Knowledge	23%
Service Levels	Measured & Reported	0%
	Not Measured	54%
	No Knowledge	46%
Data Criticality	DR Plan (Cloud + Backup)	54%
	No DR Plan	38%
	Security Plan	8%
Perceived Role of Cloud	Help (availability continuity)	46%
	Hinder (dependency on connectivity)	54%
	Power Interrupted	100%
Use of Cloud	System	23%
	Small Application	77%

Based on the ubiquitous nature of cloud technologies, SOHO users' perceptions are an offering of elasticity, transparency, scalability, high availability, and affordable price-per-usage factors, which will exist (Arora & Gupta, 2012). Further, Ahmed et al. (2012) believed that SOHO users buy cloud-computing services because they perceived that the cloud would offer:

- Lower initial investment.
- Manageability.
- Scalability.
- Faster deployment.
- Location independence.
- Device independence.
- Reliability.
- Security.

Based on NVivo node analysis, 38% of the participants believed the cloud offered availability to their data or the availability of the cloud services to their businesses. Forty-eight percent of the participants' noted the cloud was actually easy to use over traditional backup and recovery services. Ease-of-use includes everything to do with accessibility of data, the affordable of the data, onboarding the services, so the users do not have to make significant investment, pay any excessive monthly fee to obtain cloud services, and they can actually get on to the cloud at their convenience.

Thirty-one percent of the participants, on the other hand, believed that the cloud offered security so they have no compunction using the cloud to store sensitive information. However, 69% of the participants noted that although the cloud was readily available and was easy to use, it did not offer them the degree of security that traditional backup and recovery services offered. Participants' perception is that they are aware that the cloud may not be entirely secure as a tool for housing their critical data but they were still comfortable using it because of its ubiquitous nature. Participants' perceptions are depicted in Figure 4.

Theme 2: Service Level Agreements

Boampong and Wahsheh (2012), Gelbstein (2011), and Nepal Rastra Bank Information Technology Guidelines (2012) defined service level agreement (SLA) as a legal binding or contractual obligation between two entities (cloud vendor and their users) regarding the protection of the confidentiality, integrity, and availability of business critical data. Figure 5 demonstrates how participants responded to the questions regarding service level agreements.

None of the participants reported having any measured and reported service level.

For example, PS11 reported that, "When we first started, yes, we went over the services they were going to provide. But we took the default or all the services they were offering." Forty-six percent of the participants, on the other hand, have no knowledge of SLAs. When asked if he knew if he and his vendor had a service level agreement in place, BR02 stated: "I don't know. Not that I can recall. No, I am not sure about that. No!"

On the other hand, 54% of the participants stated that when they signed up for their cloud service they just clicked or signed on the dotted line to accept service without knowing the specific details of the agreement including the type of disaster or events would be covered, and the vendor's responsibili-

Figure 4. Small user perceptions

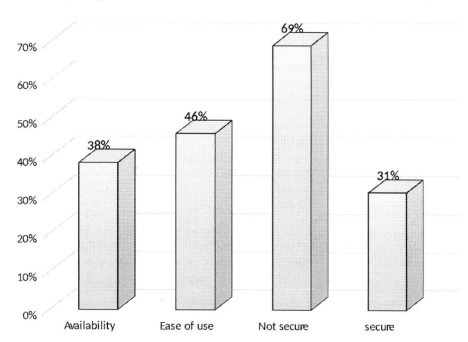

Figure 5. Service level agreement

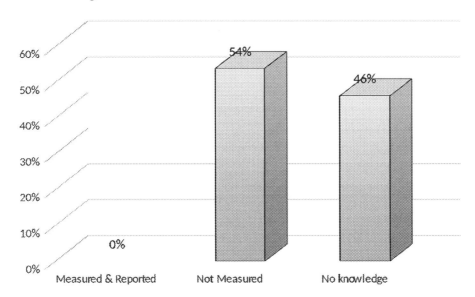

ties in the event of a disaster. These findings imply that the participants assumed that there is a service level agreement but that they were not sure what the service agreement entails or how it was measured.

Theme 3: Perceived Role of Cloud

Ahmed et al. (2012) posited that SOHO customers buy cloud-computing services because of:

- Lower initial investment.
- Ease to manage.
- Scalability.
- Faster deployment.
- Location independence.
- Device independence.
- Reliability.
- Security.

In this section of the study, participants related their perception of whether the above assumptions of cloud technologies were helpful to them or were they hindrances. Figure 6 illustrates participants' responses regarding cloud availability and business continuity.

Forty-six percent of the participants perceived the cloud as helpful. These participants believed that their data was always available and their service was continuous and, equated data security to data availability. That is, even though the data is available and they can get to it whenever and wherever they want, this does not mean that it is secure, however, participants believed that because data were stored in the cloud it was secure. Conclusively, participants could not differentiate between security and continuity.

In regards to the cloud ability to prevent or hinder SOHO users' ability to continue business during a disaster, 54% of the participants perceived it as a hindrance based on the cloud's dependency on

Figure 6. Perceived role of the cloud

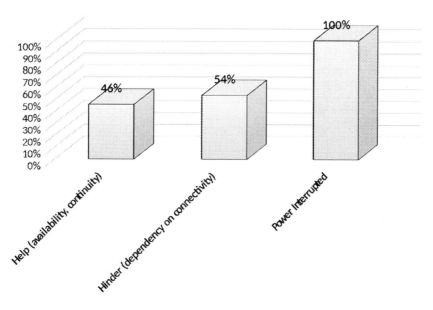

connectivity. All the participants (100%) expressed that they experienced power loss from a few hours up to 2.5 weeks. Twenty-seven percent of the participants had a backup of their critical data on thumb or local hard drives. However, after the battery pack of those computers ran out, access to critical data was no longer available. In conclusion, although all participants had data stored in the cloud, the loss of power during Hurricane Sandy caused participants to also lose connectivity to the Internet, therefore rendering them unable to access their data.

Theme 4: Small User Knowledge

Small Office and Home Office (SOHO) users refer to the category of business that involves from 1 to 200 workers (Gupta et al., 2013). The Small User Knowledge theme included three subthemes: specific knowledge, vague knowledge, and no knowledge. The small user knowledge theme did not have an equal spread regarding users who had specific knowledge or no knowledge at all about the cloud and its artifacts. This theme investigated about the use of the cloud and its service as a continuity of business tool. Figure 7 is a graphical representation of the split regarding small business users' knowledge of the cloud.

Sixty percent of the participants interviewed had very specific or in-depth knowledge about the existence the cloud and what it can offer a small business; fifteen percent had a vague knowledge, and 23% had no knowledge at all about the cloud and its artifacts. Even though the participants who had specific knowledge was 62%, some of the participants had more knowledge than others in this percentile.

Sixty-two percent of the participants were specific about how they are using the cloud and what applications they were using. For example, some were using Drop-Box, Lotus Notes, Google Docs and what other cloud application or services they were using. Fifteen percent of the participants had a vague idea of what cloud tools they were using for their businesses' standard daily operations. They knew that something was shared in the cloud but their idea of what is being shared was very vague.

Figure 7. Small user knowledge of the cloud

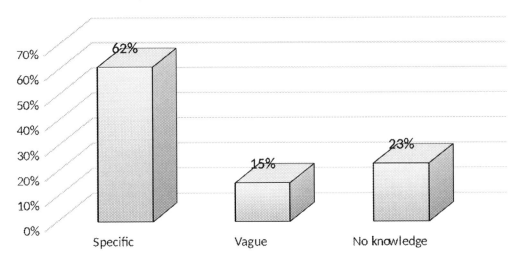

While seventy-seven percent of the participants had specific to vague understanding of the cloud, there was another twenty-three percent that had no knowledge about the artifacts or services of the cloud. The users just take or adopt the services as they are, without knowing that the service being used is a service being offered by a cloud vendor.

Theme 5: Data Criticality

Mell and Grance (2011) asserted that the cloud is a potential solution for disaster recovery planning. However, some researchers believed inadequacies exist in cloud computing regarding how it can be a more effective tool for continuity of services (Lawler, 2010; Tammineedi, 2010). Wood, Cecchet, Ramakrishnan, Shenoy, Van Der Merwe & Venkataramani (2010) explained that cloud computing can facilitate disaster recovery by significantly lowering costs:

- The cloud's pay-as-you go pricing model significantly lowers costs due to the different level of resources required before and during a disaster.
- Cloud resources can quickly be added with fine granularity and have costs that scale smoothly without requiring large upfront investments.
- The cloud platform manages and maintains the DR servers and storage devices, lowering IT costs and reducing the impact of failures at the disaster site. (p. 6).

Figure 8 summarized the criticality of data regarding disaster recovery (DR) planning as well as security planning.

The participants were worried about their data and wanted continuity and availability one hundred percent of the time and that is the reason why the data is stored in the cloud. However, only fifty-four percent of the participants had disaster recovery plans that they understood as either moving their data

Figure 8. Data criticality

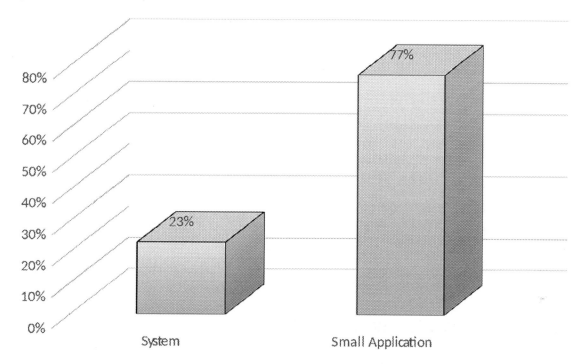

to the cloud or having a local backup. Conversely, thirty-eight percent of the participants did not have a disaster recovery plan at all. Eight percent of participants talked about a secured systems and a security plan and standards that needed to be met regarding the security of critical data.

These results imply that around 92% of SOHO users did not think about security when they purchased cloud service. Furthermore, the lack of disaster recovery plans and lack of knowledge about security standards among SOHO cloud users, pointed toward serious gaps in understanding the relationship between data criticality, information security and business continuity.

Theme 6: Use of Cloud

The Use of Cloud theme gave details on the perception of how the users think about the cloud as a business continuity and disaster recovery tool. About 73% participants used small applications such as email, notes sharing, and Google Docs for everyday business application. Twenty-three percent of the participants actually reported that they used a system that is actually cloud-based. Of the 23% percent who used cloud-based systems, one was a cloud service provider and retailer, and the other one used Lotus notes that were hosted in the cloud. Figure 9 is a graphical representation of how the participants used the cloud during the time of the hurricane.

The findings for theme 6 demonstrated that 77% of the participants were not heavily dependent on the cloud. Again, the findings corroborate claims that cloud technology is not used to its fullest potential and therefore neither is understood.

Figure 9. Use of the cloud

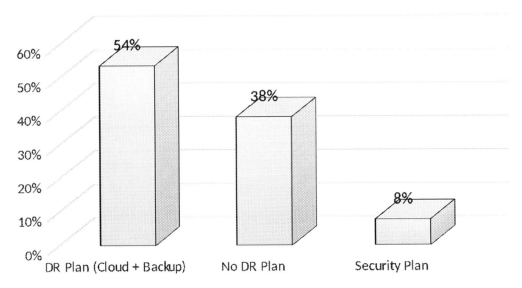

THEORETICAL AND PRACTICAL IMPLICATIONS

The basic premise of this study was the examination of how cloud artifacts performed, how well SOHO users understood cloud services, and what part did privacy play in their successes or failures (Y. Chen et al., 2010; Gupta et al., 2013; and Low et al., 2011). This study found that SOHO users do not clearly understand the artifacts of the technology as well as the differences between data backup, data security and their relationship to business continuity, therefore, they are not able to realize the full potential of the technology. The data collected from the 13 participants produced the following major findings:

1. Sixty-nine percent of SOHO users perceived the cloud as insecure, yet the purchase and use cloud services;
2. Fifty-four percent of participants had no measured service levels;
3. All participants (100%) were severely hindered by the lack of power during the hurricane;
4. Only eight percent of the participants had any form of security plans even though they all believed that data is critical to their businesses; and
5. Most participants (77%) did not use the cloud as a business continuity or disaster recovery tool but used the small applications that this service affords (SaaS).

The results of this study demonstrated that SOHO cloud users in the New York and New Jersey areas during Hurricane Sandy did not have structured plans for their critical data and as such did not implement any form of disaster recovery or security plans for their organizations. SOHO cloud users lack the understanding of how disaster recovery planning relates to backing up or migrating data using cloud services. Furthermore, SOHO users assume that cloud data is available and may test data recovery, but do not test their ability to actively restore dependent applications or to synchronize disparate systems.

SOHO users need to be aware that although a disaster such as Hurricane Sandy may not have a sizeable impact in their organizations, it may have a greater impact on third parties on whom they rely for business. This was evident in the study by a 100% of participants unable to conduct business due to power outages to their area and their cloud provider located on the hurricane landing area. Furthermore, SOHO users were not aware that data backup and disaster recovery were not interchangeable terms, regardless of how many vendors assuredly switch around the two.

Additionally, the study confirms that there is a significant amount of trust placed on the vendors to deliver the services promised. None of the participants confirmed having any measured reporting or knowledge about service level agreements between their organizations and their vendors. This study highlighted the importance of SOHO users to clearly understand disaster recovery planning in order to maintain business continuity during a disaster. The process of developing and implementing a business continuity plan starts with identifying and prioritizing applications, services, and data, and determining for each one the amount of downtime that is acceptable to minimize business disruption and negative impact (Castagna, 2012).

FUTURE RESEARCH DIRECTIONS AND LIMITATIONS

This study used a qualitative approach to answering the research questions. Qualitative methodology is not as precise as quantitative approaches and may not provide the accuracy in numbers that a quantitative approach would permit. However, a quantitative cross-sectional study would provide an opportunity to add reliability to research by exploring the causal mechanisms and identifying variables and the underlying statistical association between business continuity and disaster recovery. Future longitudinal studies may add value to the qualitative themes revealed in this study.

Another limitation of the study was the small sample size used. Participants from the hurricane ravished areas of New York and New Jersey, identified as the geographical regions for the study, may have moved away, which made them unavailable. Future studies should use larger sample sizes to increase data richness and precision of themes derived from the study.

CONCLUSION

The paradigm is shifting from traditional physical backup and recovery system to a cloud services system for the continuance of IT related services. Research has demonstrated that the use of the cloud is still maturing and cannot yet be considered the de facto standard for business continuity and disaster recovery. This study revealed that for a small group of cloud users (SOHO) the cloud is not yet fully understood and as such more emphasis should be placed on educating these users about how best to use the cloud to enhance their continuity of operations.

The Data Cloud analysis showed that the participants were less concerned with data integrity, security, and service level agreements, than they were about the vendors they choose and the type of cloud services offered. Sixty-nine percent of the participants agreed that cloud is not 100% secured, but they were still buying cloud-based services without being mindful of security. From a small user perspective, they used online every-day applications and they were somewhat worried about security although they trusted that their vendors prevented the hacking of their information.

SOHO users believed that the applications they used are stored in their provider's data center and available to users provided they have power, thus they thought that the data was theoretically recoverable and protected. Furthermore, the results of this study demonstrated that backing up the information on the cloud was never a problem; however, the lack of alternate data recovery sites was evidenced by power loss that affected businesses and cloud provider who were in the same power grid.

The approach of data duplication and synchronization has come a long way from the traditional backup and recovery systems. The cloud significantly extends disaster recovery options, can produce significant cost savings, and enable disaster retrieval approaches for small and medium-sized businesses that were previously available to large organizations only. However, the cloud itself cannot change the importance of solidifying business continuity plans, testing them periodically and properly training cloud users.

This study highlighted the importance of SOHO users to clearly understand disaster recovery planning in order to maintain business continuity during a disaster. The process of developing and implementing a business continuity plan starts with identifying and prioritizing applications, services and data, and determining for each one the amount of downtime that is acceptable to minimize business disruption and negative impact (Castagna, 2012). Finally, although cloud services are moving from niche applications into mainstream use, especially in the SOHO business sector, users must exercise due diligence when evaluating cloud services including understanding and implementing business continuity plans and, data security measures.

REFERENCES

Abbadi, I. M., & Martin, A. (2011). Trust in the cloud. *Information Security Technical Report, 16*(3-4), 108–114. doi:10.1016/j.istr.2011.08.006

Abhang, S. P., & Chowdhay, G. V. (2007). WDM-based storage area network (SAN) for disaster recovery operations. *International Journal of Computer Information & Systems Science & Engineering, 1*, 248–251.

Abramson, D. M., & Redlener, I. (2012). Hurricane Sandy: Lessons learned, again. *Disaster Medicine and Public Health Preparedness, 6*(04), 328–329. doi:10.1001/dmp.2012.76 PMID:23241461

Addis, B., Ardagna, D., Panicucci, B., & Zhang, L. (2010). Autonomic management of cloud service centers with availability guarantees. In *Cloud Computing (CLOUD), 2010 IEEE 3rd International Conference* (pp. 220–227). Miami, FL: IEEE. doi:10.1109/CLOUD.2010.19

Ahmed, M., Chowdhury, A. S., Ahmed, M., & Rafee, M. M. H. (2012). An advanced survey on cloud computing and state-of-the-art research issues. *International Journal of Computing Science Issues, 9*, 201–207.

Alshare, K. A., & Alkhateeb, F. B. (2008). Predicting students usage of internet in two emerging economies using an extended technology acceptance model (TAM). *Academy of Educational Leadership Journal, 12*, 109–128.

Alshare, K. A., Mesak, H. I., Grandon, E. E., & Badri, M. A. (2011). Examining the moderating role of national culture on an extended technology acceptance model. *Journal of Global Information Technology Management, 14*(3), 27–53. doi:10.1080/1097198X.2011.10856542

Amirkhani, A., Salehahmadi, Z., Kheiri, E., & Hajialiasgari, F. (2011). The TAM models applications in technology transition. *Interdisciplinary Journal of Contemporary Research in Business, 3*, 867–879.

Anthes, G. (2010). Security in the cloud. *Communications of the Association for Computer Machinery, 53*(11), 16–18. doi:10.1145/1839676.1839683

Armstrong, D., & Djemame, K. (2011). Performance issues in clouds: An evaluation of virtual image propagation and I/O paravirtualization. *The Computer Journal, 54*(6), 836–849. doi:10.1093/comjnl/bxr011

Arora, I., & Gupta, A. (2012). Cloud databases: A paradigm shift in databases. *International Journal of Computer Science Issues, 9*(4), 77–83.

Bandura, A. (1977). Self-efficacy: Toward a unifying theory of behavioral change. *Psychological Review, 84*(2), 191–194. doi:10.1037/0033-295X.84.2.191 PMID:847061

Barlas, S., Queen, R., Radowitz, J., Shillam, P., & Williams, K. (2007). Top 10 technology concerns. *Strategic Finance, 88*(10), 21–23.

Bedi, R., Marwaha, M., Singh, T., Singh, H., & Singh, A. (2012). *Analysis of different privacy preserving cloud storage frameworks.* Retrieved from http://arxiv.org/abs/1205.2738

Behrend, T. S., Wiebe, E. N., London, J. E., & Johnson, E. C. (2011). Cloud computing adoption and usage in community colleges. *Behaviour & Information Technology, 30*(2), 231–240. doi:10.1080/0144929X.2010.489118

Bernard, H. R., & Ryan, G. W. (2010). *Analyzing qualitative data: Systematic approaches.* Thousand Oaks, CA: Sage.

Bernard, L. (2011). *A risk assessment framework for evaluating software-as-a-service (SaaS) cloud services before adoption* (Doctoral dissertation). Retrieved from ProQuest Dissertations and Theses. (910888491)

Boampong, P. A., & Wahsheh, L. A. (2012). Different facets of security in the cloud. In *Proceedings of the 15th Communications and Networking Simulation Symposium* (p. 5). Society for Computer Simulation International. Retrieved from http://dl.acm.org/citation.cfm?id=2331767

Brod, M., Tesler, L. E., & Christensen, T. L. (2009). Qualitative research and content validity: Developing best practices based on science and experience. *Quality of Life Research: An International Journal of Quality of Life Aspects of Treatment, Care and Rehabilitation, 18*(9), 1263–1278. doi:10.100711136-009-9540-9 PMID:19784865

Castagna, R. (2012). *Cloud Backup and Cloud Disaster Recovery.* Retrieved October 4, 2015, from http://docs.media.bitpipe.com/io_10x/io_105179/item_544278/EssentialGuide_CloudBackup_final.pdf

Chen, P. M., Lee, E. K., Gibson, G. A., Katz, R. H., & Patterson, D. A. (1994). RAID: High-performance, reliable secondary storage. *ACM Computing Surveys, 26*(2), 145–185. doi:10.1145/176979.176981

Chen, Y., Paxson, V., & Katz, R. H. (2010). *What's new about cloud computing security.* University of California, Berkeley Report No. UCB/EECS-2010-5 January, 20(2010), 2010-2015.

Choubey, R., Dubey, R., & Bhattacharjee, J. (2011). A survey on cloud computing security, challenges and threats. *International Journal on Computer Science and Engineering, 3,* 1227–1231.

Choudhary, V., & Vithayathil, J. (2013). The impact of cloud computing: Should the IT department be organized as a cost center or a profit center? *Journal of Management Information Systems, 30*(2), 67–100. doi:10.2753/MIS0742-1222300203

Creswell, J. (2009). *Research design: Qualitative, quantitative, and mixed methods approaches* (3rd ed.). London: Sage.

Dachyar, M., & Prasetya, M. D. (2012). Cloud computing implementation in Indonesia. *International Journal of Applied, 2,* 138–142.

Davis, F. D. (1989). Perceived usefulness, perceived ease of use, and user acceptance of information technology. *Management Information Systems Quarterly, 13*(3), 319–340. doi:10.2307/249008

Davis, F. D. (1993). User acceptance of information technology: System characteristics, user perceptions and behavioral impacts. *International Journal of Man-Machine Studies, 38*(3), 475–487. doi:10.1006/imms.1993.1022

Davis, F. D., Bagozzi, R. P., & Warshaw, P. R. (1989). User acceptance of computer technology: A comparison of two theoretical models. *Management Science, 35*(8), 982–1003. doi:10.1287/mnsc.35.8.982

Deloitte. (Ed.). (2012). *Disaster Recovery: 10 Lessons from Hurricane Sandy.* Retrieved from The Wall Street Journal: http://deloitte.wsj.com/cio/2012/11/29/disaster-recovery-planning-10-lessons-learned-from-hurricane-sandy/

Dun & Bradstreet. (2012). *Hurricane Sandy disaster impact report.* Retrieved from http://www.dnb.com/lc/credit-education/after-hurricane-sandy-hurricane-impact-report-on-business.html

Force, H. S. (2013). *Hurricane Sandy rebuilding strategy.* US Department of Housing and Urban Development. Retrieved from http://co.monmouth.nj.us/documents/24%5CSandy_Hurricane%20Sandy%20Rebuilding%20Strategy_081913.pdf

Gashami, J. P., Chang, Y., & Park, M. C. (2013). *Cross-national study on factors affecting cloud computing adoption in the public sector: Focus on perceived risk.* doi:. Retrieved from http://www.researchgate.net/publication/273452399_Cross-national_study_on_factors_affecting_cloud_computing_adoption_in_the_public_sector_Focus_on_perceived_risk doi:10.13140/2.1.4178.2564

Gelbstein, E. (2011). Data integrity—information security's poor relation. *Information Systems Audit and Control Association Journal, 6,* 20–25.

Gibson, G. A., & Meter, R. V. (2000). Network attached storage architecture. *Communications of the ACM, 43*(11), 37–45. doi:10.1145/353360.353362

Gittlen, S. (2005). *SOHO business continuity tips.* Retrieved October 06, 2016, from http://www.networkworld.com/article/2321579/router/soho-business-continuity-tips.html

Gupta, P., Seetharaman, A., & Raj, J. R. (2013). The usage and adoption of cloud computing by small and medium businesses. *International Journal of Information Management, 33*(5), 861–874. doi:10.1016/j.ijinfomgt.2013.07.001

Hailu, A. (2012). *Factors influencing cloud-computing technology adoption in developing countries* (Doctoral dissertation). Retrieved from ProQuest Dissertations and Theses. (3549131)

Han, B., Hui, P., & Srinivasan, A. (2011). Mobile data offloading in metropolitan area networks. *Mobile Computing and Communications Review, 14*(4), 28–30. doi:10.1145/1942268.1942279

Hunter, P. (2006). Network attached storage: No longer on the edge. *Information Professional, 3*(5), 35–38. doi:10.1049/inp:20060504

ISE. (2013, April 8). *SoHo Routers Hacked*. Retrieved October 06, 2016, from https://securityevaluators. com/knowledge/case_studies/routers/soho_router_hacks.php

Jadeja, Y., & Modi, K. (2012). Cloud computing-concepts, architecture and challenges. In *Computing, electronics and electrical technologies (ICCEET), 2012 International Conference on IEEE* (pp. 877-880). Retrieved from ftp://213.176.96.142/ieee4e57ed3e-fd29-20140701102130.pdf

Jansen, W., & Grance, T. (2011). Guidelines on security and privacy in public cloud computing. *National Institute of Standards and Technology's Special Publication, 800*, 144–150.

Jones, V. A. (2011). How to avoid disaster: RIM's crucial role in business continuity planning. *Information Management Journal, 45*(6), 36–40.

Jrad, A., Morawski, T., & Spergel, L. (2004). A model for quantifying business continuity preparedness risks for telecommunications networks. *Bell Labs Technical Journal, 9*(2), 107–123. doi:10.1002/bltj.20029

Kvale, S., & Brinkmann, S. (2009). *Interviews: Learning the craft of qualitative research interviewing*. Thousand Oaks, CA: Sage.

Kwasinski, A. (2013). Lessons from field damage assessments about communication networks power supply and infrastructure performance during natural disasters with a focus on Hurricane Sandy. Brooklyn, NY: *FCC Workshop Network Resiliency*.

Lawler, C. M. (2010). *A disaster tolerant cloud computing model as a disaster survival methodology* (Doctoral dissertation). Retrieved from ProQuest Dissertations and Theses. (868186191)

Leimeister, S., Böhm, M., Riedl, C., & Krcmar, H. (2010). *The business perspective of cloud computing: Actors, roles and value networks*. Retrieved from http://home.in.tum.de/~riedlc/res/LeimeisterEtAl2010-preprint.pdf

Lewis, N. (2009). *Identifying critical dimensions that shape the business and information technology alignment process: A case study of a university* (Doctoral dissertation). Retrieved from Dissertations & Theses, Capella University. (305164668)

Low, C., Chen, Y., & Wu, M. (2011). Understanding the determinants of cloud computing adoption. *Industrial Management & Data Systems, 111*(7), 1006–1023. doi:10.1108/02635571111161262

Luborsky, M. R., & Rubinstein, R. L. (1995). Sampling in qualitative research: Rationale, issues, and methods. *Research on Aging, 17*(1), 89–113. doi:10.1177/0164027595171005 PMID:22058580

Marshall, C., & Rossman, G. B. (2011). *Designing qualitative research* (5th ed.). Thousand Oaks, CA: Sage.

Mathur, S. K., & Dhulla, T. V. (2014). Factors influencing professionals' decision for cloud computing adoption. *International Journal of Research in Advent Technology*, 2, 2321–9637.

Medley, M. D. (2001). Using qualitative research software for CS education research. Proceeding of the 16th annual conference on innovation and technology in computer science education. *Association for Computing Machinery, 6*(1), 141-144. Retrieved from http://dl.acm.org/citation.cfm?id=507758.377668

Mell, P., & Grance, T. (2011). The NIST definition of cloud computing. *National Institute of Standards and Technology Special Publication, 800*(145), 1–8.

Nepal Rastra Bank Information Technology Guidelines. (2012). *Bank Supervision Department Nepal Rastra Bank*. Retrieved from http://bfr.nrb.org.np/circular/2069-70/2069_70--Circular_02- Attachment-IT Guideline 2012.pdf

Parkhill, D. F. (1966). *Challenge of the computer utility*. Reading, MA: Addison-Wesley.

Patton, M. Q. (1990). *Qualitative research and evaluation methods* (2nd ed.). Thousand Oaks, CA: Sage.

Patton, M. Q. (2002). *Qualitative research and evaluation methods* (3rd ed.). Newbury Park, CA: Sage.

Ristov, P., Mrvica, A., & Miskovic, T. (2014). Secure data storage. In *Information and communication technology, electronics and microelectronics (MIPRO), 2014 37th International Convention* (pp. 1586–1591). Miami, FL: IEEE. Retrieved from http://ieeexplore.ieee.org/xpl/login.jsp?tp=&arnumber=6859818&url=http%3A%2F%2Fieeexplore.ieee.org%2Fxpls%2Fabs_all.jsp%3Farnumber%3D6859818

Ristov, S., Gusev, M., & Kostoska, M. (2012). Cloud computing security in business information systems. *International Journal of Network Security & Its Applications, 4*(2), 75–93. doi:10.5121/ijnsa.2012.4206

Rodger, J. A., Bhatt, G., Chaudhary, P., Kline, G., & McCloy, W. (2015). The impact of business expertise on information system data and analytics resilience (ISDAR) for disaster recovery and business continuity: An exploratory study. *Intelligent Information Management, 7*(04), 223–239. doi:10.4236/iim.2015.74017

Rohde, R., Haskett, J., & Ledgard, H. (1990). Disaster recovery planning for academic computing centers. *Communications of the ACM, 33*(6), 652–657. doi:10.1145/78973.78975

Salmons, J. (2010). *Online interviews in real time*. Los Angeles, CA: Sage.

Speight, P. (2011). Business continuity. *Journal of Applied Security Research, 6*(4), 529–554. doi:10.1080/19361610.2011.604021

Suo, S. (2013). *Cloud implementation in organizations: Critical success factors, challenges, and impacts on the it function* (Doctoral dissertation). Retrieved from ProQuest Dissertations & Theses Global. (3576584)

Takazawa, A., & Williams, K. (2011). Communities in disasters: Helpless or helping? *Perspectives on Global Development and Technology, 10*(3-4), 429–440. doi:10.1163/156914911X610394

Tammineedi, R. L. (2010). Business continuity management: A standards-based approach. *Information Security Journal: A Global Perspective, 19*(1), 36-50. doi:10.1080/19393550903551843

Thibodeau, P. (2012). *Hurricane Sandy leaves wounded servers in its wake.* Retrieved from http://www.computerworld.com/article/2493139/data-center/hurricane-sandy-leaves-wounded-servers-in-its-wake.html

Thomas, T., Singh, L., & Gaffar, K. (2013). The utility of the UTAUT model in explaining mobile learning adoption in higher education in Guyana. *International Journal of Education & Development Using Information & Communication Technology, 9*(3), 71-76.

Venkatesh, V. (2000). Determinants of perceived ease of use: Integrating control, intrinsic motivation, and emotion into the technology acceptance model. *Information Systems Research, 11*(4), 342–365. doi:10.1287/isre.11.4.342.11872

Venkatesh, V. (2009). *Technology acceptance.* Retrieved from http://www.vvenkatesh.com/it/organizations/theoretical_models.asp

Venkatesh, V., Thong, J. Y., & Xu, X. (2012). Consumer acceptance and use of information technology: Extending the unified theory of acceptance and use of technology. *Management Information Systems Quarterly, 36,* 157–178.

Welsh, E. (2002, May). Dealing with data: Using NVivo in the qualitative data analysis process. In *Forum Qualitative Sozialforschung/Forum: Qualitative. Social Research, 3*(2).

Wong, L. P. (2008). Data analysis in qualitative research: A brief guide to using NVivo. *Malaysian Family Physician: The Official Journal of the Academy of Family Physicians of Malaysia, 3*(1), 14. PMID:25606106

Wood, T., Cecchet, E., Ramakrishnan, K. K., Shenoy, P., Van Der Merwe, J., & Venkataramani, A. (2010). Disaster recovery as a cloud service: Economic benefits & deployment challenges. In *Proceedings of the 2nd USENIX conference on hot topics in cloud computing* (pp. 8–8). USENIX Association. Retrieved from https://www.usenix.org/legacy/events/hotcloud10/tech/full_papers/Wood.pdf

Wu, W. W., Lan, L. W., & Lee, Y. T. (2011). Exploring decisive factors affecting an organizations SaaS adoption: A case study. *International Journal of Information Management, 31*(6), 556–563. doi:10.1016/j.ijinfomgt.2011.02.007

Yang, Q., Xiao, W., & Ren, J. (2006). Trap-array: A disk array architecture providing timely recovery to any point-in-time. *ACM SIGARCH Computer Architecture News, 34*(2), 289–301. doi:10.1145/1150019.1136511

Yin, R. K. (1981). The case study crisis: Some answers. *Administrative Science Quarterly, 26*(1), 58–65. doi:10.2307/2392599

Yin, R. K. (2009). *Case study research: Design and methods* (4th ed.). Thousand Oaks, CA: Sage.

Yin, R. K. (2014). *Case study research: Design and methods* (5th ed.). Thousand Oaks, CA: Sage.

KEY TERMS AND DEFINITIONS

Business Continuity/Disaster Recovery: Business functions designed to prolong the life of individuals as well as the survival of an organization before and after a disaster (Lawler, 2010; Mell & Grance, 2011; Tammineedi, 2010).

Cloud Computing Users: Corporations that purchase services, such as infrastructure or software, or purchase computer-sharing space or platform services, or individuals who purchase one of the as-a-service artifacts of cloud computing (Addis, Ardagna, Panicucci, & Zhang, 2010).

Cloud Computing Vendors: Service providers, such as Google and Microsoft Azure, that charge a fee for (a) housing business critical data, (b) providing software services, or (c) providing infrastructure services to customers (Addis et al., 2010).

Medium Businesses: Small businesses with 100–200 employees (Gupta et al., 2013).

Recovery Point Objective (RPO): When the customer expects that should a disaster or incident occur, their information will be backed up to a certain point in time (Yang, Xiao, & Ren, 2006).

Recovery Time Objective (RTO): May occur when the customer expects the service to be up and running in a specific timeframe (Yang et al., 2006).

Service Level Agreements (SLA): Legal bindings between users and the vendors regarding the protection of the confidentiality, integrity, and availability of business critical data (Boampong, & Wahsheh, 2012).

Small Office/Home Office (SOHO): Users are small businesses with 1–10 employees or 11–99 employees (Gupta et al., 2013).

This research was previously published in Cybersecurity Breaches and Issues Surrounding Online Threat Protection edited by Michelle Moore, pages 248-287, copyright year 2017 by Information Science Reference (an imprint of IGI Global).

Index

S

Purchase Print, E-Book, or Print + E-Book

IGI Global books are available in three unique pricing formats:
Print Only, E-Book Only, or Print + E-Book. Shipping fees apply.

www.igi-global.com

Recommended Reference Books

ISBN: 978-1-6831-8016-6
© 2017; 197 pp.
List Price: $180

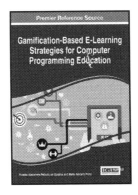

ISBN: 978-1-5225-1034-5
© 2017; 350 pp.
List Price: $200

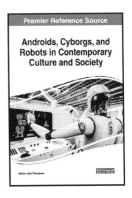

ISBN: 978-1-5225-2973-6
© 2018 ; 286 pp.
List Price: $205

ISBN: 978-1-5225-2589-9
© 2017; 602 pp.
List Price: $345

ISBN: 978-1-5225-2229-4
© 2016; 1,093 pp.
List Price: $465

ISBN: 978-1-5225-2857-9
© 2018; 538 pp.
List Price: $265

Do you want to stay current on the latest research trends, product announcements, news and special offers?
Join IGI Global's mailing list today and start enjoying exclusive perks sent only to IGI Global members.
Add your name to the list at **www.igi-global.com/newsletters.**

Publisher of Peer-Reviewed, Timely, and Innovative Academic Research

www.igi-global.com Sign up at www.igi-global.com/newsletters facebook.com/igiglobal twitter.com/igiglobal linkedin.com/igiglobal

Ensure Quality Research is Introduced to the Academic Community

Become an IGI Global Reviewer for Authored Book Projects

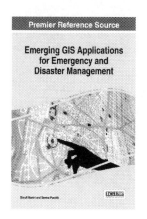

The overall success of an authored book project is dependent on quality and timely reviews.

In this competitive age of scholarly publishing, constructive and timely feedback significantly expedites the turnaround time of manuscripts from submission to acceptance, allowing the publication and discovery of forward-thinking research at a much more expeditious rate. Several IGI Global authored book projects are currently seeking highly qualified experts in the field to fill vacancies on their respective editorial review boards:

Applications may be sent to:
development@igi-global.com

Applicants must have a doctorate (or an equivalent degree) as well as publishing and reviewing experience. Reviewers are asked to write reviews in a timely, collegial, and constructive manner. All reviewers will begin their role on an ad-hoc basis for a period of one year, and upon successful completion of this term can be considered for full editorial review board status, with the potential for a subsequent promotion to Associate Editor.

If you have a colleague that may be interested in this opportunity,
we encourage you to share this information with them.

www.igi-global.com

Celebrating 30 Years of Scholarly
Knowledge Creation & Dissemination

InfoSci®-Books

A Collection of 4,000+ Reference Books Containing Over 87,000 Full-Text Chapters Focusing on Emerging Research

This database is a collection of over 4,000+ IGI Global single and multi-volume reference books, handbooks of research, and encyclopedias, encompassing groundbreaking research from prominent experts worldwide. These books are highly cited and currently recognized in prestigious indices such as: Web of Science™ and Scopus®.

Librarian Features:
- No Set-Up or Maintenance Fees
- Guarantee of No More Than A 5% Annual Price Increase
- COUNTER 4 Usage Reports
- Complimentary Archival Access
- Free MARC Records

Researcher Features:
- Unlimited Simultaneous Users
- No Embargo of Content
- Full Book Download
- Full-Text Search Engine
- No DRM

To Find Out More or To Purchase This Database:
www.igi-global.com/infosci-books

eresources@igi-global.com • Toll Free: 1-866-342-6657 ext. 100 • Phone: 717-533-8845 x100

IGI Global
DISSEMINATOR OF KNOWLEDGE
www.igi-global.com

IGI Global Proudly Partners with

eContent Pro
International

Enhance Your Manuscript with
eContent Pro International's Professional
Copy Editing Service

Expert Copy Editing

eContent Pro International copy editors, with over 70 years of combined experience, will provide complete and comprehensive care for your document by resolving all issues with spelling, punctuation, grammar, terminology, jargon, semantics, syntax, consistency, flow, and more. In addition, they will format your document to the style you specify (APA, Chicago, etc.). All edits will be performed using Microsoft Word's Track Changes feature, which allows for fast and simple review and management of edits.

Additional Services

eContent Pro International also offers fast and affordable proofreading to enhance the readability of your document, professional translation in over 100 languages, and market localization services to help businesses and organizations localize their content and grow into new markets around the globe.

IGI Global Authors Save 25% on eContent Pro International's Services!

Scan the QR Code to Receive Your 25% Discount

The 25% discount is applied directly to your eContent Pro International shopping cart when placing an order through IGI Global's referral link. Use the QR code to access this referral link. eContent Pro International has the right to end or modify any promotion at any time.

Email: customerservice@econtentpro.com

econtentpro.com

Information Resources Management Association

Advancing the Concepts & Practices of Information Resources
Management in Modern Organizations

Become an IRMA Member

Members of the **Information Resources Management Association (IRMA)** understand the importance of community within their field of study. The Information Resources Management Association is an ideal venue through which professionals, students, and academicians can convene and share the latest industry innovations and scholarly research that is changing the field of information science and technology. Become a member today and enjoy the benefits of membership as well as the opportunity to collaborate and network with fellow experts in the field.

IRMA Membership Benefits:

- **One FREE Journal Subscription**

- **30% Off Additional Journal Subscriptions**

- **20% Off Book Purchases**

- Updates on the latest events and research on Information Resources Management through the IRMA-L listserv.

- Updates on new open access and downloadable content added to Research IRM.

- A copy of the Information Technology Management Newsletter twice a year.

- A certificate of membership.

IRMA Membership $195

Scan code or visit **irma-international.org** and begin by selecting your free journal subscription.

Membership is good for one full year.

www.irma-international.org

Available to Order Now

Order through www.igi-global.com with **Free Standard Shipping**.

www.igi-global.com

The Premier Reference for Information Science & Information Technology

50% Off

100% Original Content
Contains 705 new, peer-reviewed articles with color figures covering over 80 categories in 11 subject areas

Diverse Contributions
More than 1,100 experts from 74 unique countries contributed their specialized knowledge

Easy Navigation
Includes two tables of content and a comprehensive index in each volume for the user's convenience

Highly-Cited
Embraces a complete list of references and additional reading sections to allow for further research

Included in:
InfoSci-Books

Encyclopedia of Information Science and Technology Fourth Edition
A Comprehensive 10-Volume Set

Mehdi Khosrow-Pour, D.B.A. (Information Resources Management Association, USA)
ISBN: 978-1-5225-2255-3; © 2018; Pg: 8,104; Release Date: July 2017

For a limited time, receive the complimentary e-books for the First, Second, and Third editions with the purchase of the *Encyclopedia of Information Science and Technology, Fourth Edition* e-book.**

The **Encyclopedia of Information Science and Technology, Fourth Edition** is a 10-volume set which includes 705 original and previously unpublished research articles covering a full range of perspectives, applications, and techniques contributed by thousands of experts and researchers from around the globe. This authoritative encyclopedia is an all-encompassing, well-established reference source that is ideally designed to disseminate the most forward-thinking and diverse research findings. With critical perspectives on the impact of information science management and new technologies in modern settings, including but not limited to computer science, education, healthcare, government, engineering, business, and natural and physical sciences, it is a pivotal and relevant source of knowledge that will benefit every professional within the field of information science and technology and is an invaluable addition to every academic and corporate library.

Scan for Online Bookstore

New Low Pricing!

Hardcover: **$2,848****
~~List Price: $5,695~~

E-Book: **$2,848****
~~List Price: $5,695~~

Hardcover + E-Book: **$3,448****
~~List Price: $6,895~~

Both E-Book Prices Include:
- *Encyclopedia of Information Science and Technology, First Edition E-Book*
- *Encyclopedia of Information Science and Technology, Second Edition E-Book*
- *Encyclopedia of Information Science and Technology, Third Edition E-Book*

*Purchase the Encyclopedia of Information Science and Technology, Fourth Edition e-book and receive the first, second, and third e-book editions for free. Offer is only valid with purchase of the fourth edition's e-book.

**50% discount cannot be combined with any other offer except the free first, second, and third editions e-book offer. Discount is valid on the Encyclopedia of Information Science and Technology, Fourth Edition when purchased directly through the IGI Global Online Bookstore and may not be used by distributors or book sellers.

Recommend this Title to Your Institution's Library: www.igi-global.com/books

Printed in the United States
By Bookmasters